Lecture Notes in Computer Science   8954

Commenced Publication in 1973
Founding and Former Series Editors:
Gerhard Goos, Juris Hartmanis, and Jan van Leeuwen

Services Science

Subline of Lectures Notes in Computer Science

More information about this series at http://www.springer.com/series/7408

Farouk Toumani · Barbara Pernici
Daniela Grigori · Djamal Benslimane
Jan Mendling · Nejib Ben Hadj-Alouane
Brian Blake · Olivier Perrin
Iman Saleh · Sami Bhiri (Eds.)

Service-Oriented Computing – ICSOC 2014 Workshops

WESOA; SeMaPS, RMSOC, KASA, ISC, FOR-MOVES, CCSA and Satellite Events
Paris, France, November 3–6, 2014
Revised Selected Papers

 Springer

Editors

Farouk Toumani
Blaise Pascal University
Aubiere
France

Nejib Ben Hadj-Alouane
National Engineering School of Tunis
Tunis
Tunisia

Barbara Pernici
Politecnico di Milano
Milano
Italy

Brian Blake
University of Miami
Coral Gables, FL
USA

Daniela Grigori
Université Paris Dauphine
Paris
France

Olivier Perrin
University Lorraine
Nancy
France

Djamal Benslimane
Université Claude Bernard Lyon 1
Villeurbanne
France

Iman Saleh
University of Miami
Coral Gables, FL
USA

Jan Mendling
Vienna University of Economics
Vienna
Austria

Sami Bhiri
Telecom SudParis
Evry
France

ISSN 0302-9743   ISSN 1611-3349   (electronic)
Lecture Notes in Computer Science
ISBN 978-3-319-22884-6   ISBN 978-3-319-22885-3   (eBook)
DOI 10.1007/978-3-319-22885-3

Library of Congress Control Number: 2015947417

Springer Cham Heidelberg New York Dordrecht London

Printed on acid-free paper

Springer International Publishing AG Switzerland is part of Springer Science+Business Media
(www.springer.com)

Preface

This volume presents the proceedings of the scientific satellite events that were held in conjunction with the 2014 International Conference on Service-Oriented Computing, which took place in Paris, France, November 3–6, 2014.

The satellite events provide venues for specialist groups to meet, to generate focused discussions on specific sub-areas within service-oriented computing, and to engage in community-building activities. These events helped significantly enrich the main conference by both expanding the scope of research topics and attracting participants from a wider community.

The selected scientific satellite events were organized around three main tracks, including a workshop track, a PhD symposium track, and a demonstration track.

The ICSOC 2014 workshop track consisted of seven workshops on a wide range of topics that fall into the general area of service computing:

- WESOA 2014: The 10th International Workshop on Engineering Service-Oriented Applications
- RMSOC 2014: The First Workshop on Resource Management in Service-Oriented Computing
- KASA 2014: The First International Workshop on Knowledge-Aware Service-Oriented Applications Performance Assessment and Auditing in Service Computing 2012
- ISC 2014: Workshop on Intelligent Service Clouds
- SeMaPS 2014: The Third International Workshop on Self-Managing Pervasive Service Systems
- FOR-MOVES 2014: The First International Workshop on Formal Modeling and Verification of Service-Based Systems
- CCSA 2014: The 4th International Workshop on Cloud Computing and Scientific Applications

The workshops were held on November 3, 2014. Each workshop had its own chairs and Program Committee who were responsible for the selection of papers. The overall organization for the workshop program, including the selection of the workshop proposals, was carried out by Farouk Toumani, Barbara Pernici, and Daniela Grigori.

The ICSOC PhD Symposium is an international forum for PhD students to present, share, and discuss their research in a constructive and critical atmosphere. It also provides students with fruitful feedback and advice on their research approach and thesis. The PhD symposium Track was chaired by Djamal Benslimane, Jan Mendling, and Nejib Ben Hadj-Alouane.

The ICSOC Demonstration Track offers an exciting and highly interactive way to show research prototypes/work in service-oriented computing (SOC) and related areas. The Demonstration Track was chaired by Brian Blake, Olivier Perrin, and Iman Saleh.

We would like to thank the workshop, PhD symposium, and demonstration authors, as well as keynote speakers and workshop Organizing Committees, who together contributed to this important aspect of the conference.

We hope that these proceedings will serve as a valuable reference for researchers and practitioners working in the service-oriented computing domain and its emerging applications.

February 2015

Farouk Toumani
Barbara Pernici
Daniela Grigori
Djamal Benslimane
Jan Mendling
Nejib Ben Hadj-Alouane
Brian Blake
Olivier Perrin
Iman Saleh
Sami Bhiri

Organization

General Chair

Samir Tata   Télécom SudParis, France

Advisory Board

Paco Curbera   IBM Research, USA
Paolo Traverso   ITC-IRST, Italy

Program Chairs

Xavier Franch   Universitat Politècnica de Catalunya, Spain
Aditya K. Ghose   University of Wollongong, Australia
Grace A. Lewis   Carnegie Mellon Software Engineering Institute, USA

Steering Committee Liaison

Boualem Benatallah   University of New South Wales, Australia

Workshop Chairs

Daniela Grigori   University of Paris Dauphine, France
Barbara Pernici   Politecnico di Milano, Italy
Farouk Toumani   Blaise Pascal University, France

Demonstration Chairs

Brian Blake   University of Miami, USA
Olivier Perrin   University de Lorraine, France
Iman Saleh   University of Miami, USA

Panel Chairs

Marlon Dumas   University of Tartu, Estonia
Henderik A. Proper   Henri Tudor Center, Luxembourg
Hong-Linh Truong   Vienna University of Technology, Austria

PhD Symposium Chairs

Djamal Benslimane	Claude Bernard University of Lyon 1, France
Jan Mendling	WU Vienna, Austria
Nejib Ben Hadj-Alouane	ENIT, Tunisia

Publicity Chairs

Kais Klai	University of Paris 13, France
Hanan Lutfiyya	University of Western Ontario, Canada
ZhangBing Zhou	China University of Geosciences, China

Local Organization Chairs

Walid Gaaloul	Télécom SudParis, France
Daniela Grigori	University of Paris Dauphine, France

Publication Chair

Sami Bhiri	Télécom SudParis, France

Web Chairs

Chan Nguyen Ngoc	LORIA, France
Mohamed Sellami	Ecole des Mines de Nantes, France

Engineering Service-Oriented Applications (WESOA 2014)

George Feuerlicht	HCTD University of Technology, Sydney, Australia
Winfried Lamersdorf	University of Hamburg, Germany
Guadalupe Ortiz	University of Cádiz, Spain
Christian Zirpins	Seeburger AG, Germany

Self-Managing Pervasive Service Systems (SeMaPS 2014)

Weishan Zhang	Department of Software Engineering, China University of Petroleum, China
Klaus Marius Hansen	Department of Computer Science, University of Copenhagen, Denmark
Paolo Bellavista	DEIS, Università di Bologna, Italy
JieHan Zhou	University of Oulu, Finland

Resource Management in Service-Oriented Computing (RMSOC 2014)

Cristina Cabanillas   Vienna University of Economics and Business, Austria
Alex Norta   Tallinn University of Technology, Estonia
Nanjangud C.   Cognizant Technology Solutions, Bangalore, India
  Narendra
Manuel Resinas   University of Seville, Spain

Knowledge-Aware Service-Oriented Applications (KASA 2014)

Sami Bhiri   Télécom SudParis, France
Walid Gaaloul   Télécom SudParis, France
Nizar Messai   University François Rabelais Tours, France

Intelligent Service Clouds (ISC 2014)

Roman Vaculin   IBM T.J. Watson Research Center, USA
Alexander Norta   Tallinn University of Technology, Estonia
Rik Eshuis   Eindhoven University of Technology, The Netherlands

Formal Modeling and Verification of Service-Based Systems (FOR-MOVES 2014)

Kais Klai   LIPN, University Paris 13, France
Amel Mammar   Samovar, Télécom SudParis, France

Cloud Computing and Scientific Applications (CCSA 2014)

Surya Nepal   CSIRO, Australia
Suraj Pandey   IBM Research, Australia
Shiping Chen   CSIRO, Australia

Introduction

Introduction to the 10th International Workshop on Engineering Service-Oriented Applications (WESOA 2014)

George Feuerlicht[1,2,3], Winfried Lamersdorf[4], Guadalupe Ortiz[5], Christian Zirpins[6]

[1]Unicorn College
[2]Prague University of Economics
[3]University of Technology, Sydney
george.feuerlicht@uts.edu.au
[4]University of Hamburg
lamersdorf@informatik.unihamburg.de
[5]University of Cádiz
guadalupe.ortiz@uca.es
[6]SEEBURGER AG
c.zirpins@seeburger.de

The Workshop on Engineering Service Oriented Applications (WESOA) focuses on core service software engineering issues keeping pace with new developments such as methods for engineering of cloud services. Our aim is to facilitate evolution of ideas in service engineering research across multiple disciplines and to encourage participation of researchers from academia and industry, providing a common platform for exchange of ideas between these groups. Over the past ten years WESOA has been able to attract high-quality contributions across a range of service engineering topics. The 10th Workshop on Engineering Service Oriented Applications (WESOA 2014) was held in Paris, France on 3 November 2014. The workshop included a keynote presentation by Michal Kökörčený titled *Building Enterprise Applications using Unicorn Universe Services*, followed by five research papers. Each paper submission was reviewed by at least three reviewers with the following papers accepted for presentation at the workshop and publication in the ICSOC 2014 Workshop Proceedings: *Cloud Migration Patterns: A Multi-Cloud Service Architecture Perspective,* by Pooyan Jamshidi, Claus Pahl, Chinenyeze Samuel, and Xiaodong Liu, *Service Interface Synthesis in Business Networks*, by Fuguo Wei, Alistair Barros and Chun Ouyang, *Virtualizing Communication for Hybrid and Diversity-Aware Collective Adaptive Systems,* by Philipp Zeppezauer, Ognjen Scekic, Hong-Linh Truong, and Schahram Dustdar, *GovOps: The Missing Link for Governance in Software-defined IoT Cloud Systems* by Stefan Nastic, Christian Inzinger, Hong-Linh Truong and Schahram Dustdar, and *MoDAS: Methodology and Tool for Model-Driven Adaptable Services by* Guadalupe Ortiz, Sonia Peinado, Alfonso Garcia de Prado and Juan Boubeta-Puig.

Workshop Organizers

George Feuerlicht, UTS, Sydney, Australia, Unicorn College, PUE, Czech Republic
Winfried Lamersdorf, University of Hamburg, Germany
Guadalupe Ortiz, University of Cádiz, Spain
Christian Zirpins, SEEBURGER AG, Germany

Program Committee

Marco Aiello, University of Groningen, Netherlands
Vasilios Andrikopoulos, University of Stuttgart, Germany
Muneera Bano, University of Technology, Sydney, Australia
Alena Buchalcevova, Prague University of Economics, Czech Republic
Anis Charfi, SAP Research CEC Darmstadt, Germany
Javier Cubo, University of Malaga, Spain
Andrea Delgado, Universidad de la República, Uruguay
Schahram Dustdar, Technical University of Vienna, Austria
Daniel Florian, University of Trento, Italy
Valeria de Castro, Universidad Rey Juan Carlos, Spain
Laura Gonzalez, Universidad de la República, Uruguay
Paul Greenfield, CSIRO, Australia
Agnes Koschmieder, Karlsruhe Institute of Technology, Germany
Mark Little, Red Hat, United States
Leszek Maciaszek, Wroclaw University of Economics, Poland
Michael Maximilien, IBM Almaden Research, United States
Marcelo Medeiros, PUC-Rio, Brasil
Massimo Mecella, Univ. Roma LA SAPIENZA, Italy
Daniel Moldt, University of Hamburg, Germany
Rebecca Parsons, ThoughtWorks, United States
Andreas Petter, SEEBURGER AG, Germany
Pierluigi Plebani, Politecnico di Milano, Italy
Franco Raimondi, Middlesex University, United Kingdom
Wolfgang Reisig, Humboldt-University Berlin, Germany
Norbert Ritter, University of Hamburg, Germany
Nelly Schuster, FZI Forschungszentrum Informatik, Germany
Thai Tran, University of Technology, Sydney, Australia
Yi Wei, University of Notre Dame, United States of America
Eric Wilde, UC Berkeley School of Information, United States of America
Erik Wittern, FZI Research Center for Information Technology, Germany
Olaf Zimmermann, HSR FHO, Switzerland

Acknowledgements

The organizers of the WESOA 2014 workshop would like to thank all authors for their contributions to this workshop, and members of the program committee whose expert input made this workshop possible. Finally, we thank ICSOC 2014 workshop chairs Farouk Toumani, Barbara Pernici, and Daniela Grigori, for their direction and guidance.

Introduction to the 1st Workshop on Resource Management in Service-Oriented Computing (RMSOC) 2014

Cristina Cabanillas[1], Alex Norta[2], Nanjangud C. Narendra[3],
and Manuel Resinas[4]

[1]Vienna University of Economics and Business, Austria
cristina.cabanillas@wu.ac.at
[2]Tallinn University of Technology, Estonia
alex.norta@gmail.com
[3]Cognizant Technology Solutions, Bangalore, India
ncnaren@gmail.com
[4]University of Seville, Spain
resinas@us.es

1 Preface

The First Workshop on Resource Management in Service-Oriented Computing (RMSOC)[1] was held in conjunction with the ICSOC 2014 conference in Paris, France. The workshop focused on exploring how human as well as non-human resources are involved and can be managed in intra- and inter-organizational processes. In particular, contributions related to resource management in the design, modeling and analysis of processes that are executed within a single organization or distributed among several organizations, were relevant for the workshop. Therefore, it covered topics such as resource assignment, allocation, prioritization, planning, analysis, resource-aware process discovery and matching, work-as-a-service, and social computing and crowdsourcing for distributed work. The aforementioned research can be tackled from different perspectives and is attractive to several research communities, such as the agents, the service-oriented or the BPM communities. The idea of the workshop was also to combine these different fields towards common goals.

The RMSOC 2014 had two keynote speakers. The keynote of Prof. Paul Grefen from the Eindhoven University of Technology, The Netherlands, presented results in the investigation of the role of resources in a contemporary framework for service-dominant business design (BASE/X), which was developed in close cooperation between research and industry. The keynote of Prof. Schahram Dustdar from the Vienna University of Technology, Austria, presented ways to integrate the Internet of Things with people and processes into one composite system that can be modeled,

---

[1] https://ai.wu.ac.at/rmsoc2014/

programmed, and deployed on a large scale in an elastic way, considering modern Cloud Computing and Elasticity principles.

The five RMSOC-workshop papers were selected after a thorough peer-review by the Workshop Program Committee Members and fell into two categories of related topics. Following is a brief overview of the contributions.

The first paper category focuses on discovering and modeling resources in processes, and it comprises three full papers. The paper "Supporting Rule-based Process Mining by User-Guided Discovery of Resource-Aware Frequent Patterns" by Stefan Schoenig, Florian Gillitzer, Michael Zeising and Stefan Jablonski, proposes an approach to automatically discover resource-aware rules for a given domain from an event log by using frequent pattern mining techniques. The paper "BPM supported Privacy by Design for cross-organization Business Processes" by Jovan Stevovic, Paolo Sottovia, Maurizio Marchese and Giampaolo Armellin, introduces an approach on privacy by design to show that it is possible to develop tools to support analysts, designers, project managers and privacy experts to satisfy both privacy and technical requirements, by modeling inter-organizational processes and by focusing on involved actors and managed resources. The third paper in this category, titled "Resource-Aware Process Model Similarity Matching" and authored by Michaela Baumann, Michael Heinrich Baumann, Stefan Schoenig and Stefan Jablonski, also investigates inter-organizational processes, specifically how to use human and non-human resource information to match process models that may have different granularity levels.

The second paper category focuses on the optimization of the use of resources in processes, and it comprises one full paper and one short paper. The former, titled "Learning 'Good Quality' Resource Allocations from Historical Data" and authored by Renuka Sindhgatta, Aditya Ghose and Gaargi Banerjee Dasgupta, uses data from event logs to identify resource allocations that have resulted in an expected service quality to improve service quality and utilization of service workers in subsequent executions, by developing a learning model that predicts the quality of service for specific allocations of tasks to workers. The latter, titled "Optimizing Resource Utilization by Combining Running Business Process Instances" and authored by Christine Natschlaeger, Andreas Boegl and Verena Geist, presents a novel approach for combining activity instances and sharing resources across running process instances to optimize resource utilization.

We sincerely thank the Program Committee Members of the RMSOC 2014 workshop for their time and support throughout the reviewing process.

Cristina Cabanillas, Alex Norta, Nanjangud C. Narendra and Manuel Resinas
RMSOC 2014 Workshop Chairs

2   Organization Details

2.1   Workshop Chairs

Dr. Cristina Cabanillas Vienna University of Economics and Business, Austria.
E-mail: cristina.cabanillas@wu.ac.at

Dr. Alex Norta. Tallinn University of Technology, Estonia.
E-mail: alex.norta@gmail.com

Dr. Nanjangud C. Narendra. Cognizant Technology Solutions, Bangalore, India.
E-mail: ncnaren@gmail.com

Dr. Manuel Resinas. University of Seville, Spain. E-mail: resinas@us.es

2.2   Program Committee Members

Claudio Bartolini, HP Labs Palo Alto, USA
Anne Baumgrass, Hasso Plattner Institute at the University of Potsdam, Germany
Alessandro Bozzon, Delft University of Technology, The Netherlands
Fabio Casati, University of Trento, Italy
Florian Daniel, University of Trento, Italy
Joseph Davis, University of Sydney, Australia
Claudio Di Ciccio, Vienna University of Economics and Business, Austria
Schahram Dustdar, Vienna University of Technology, Austria
Félix García, University of Castilla-La Mancha, Spain
Christian Huemer, Vienna University of Technology, Austria
Jan Mendling, Vienna University of Economics and Business, Austria
Manfred Reichert, University of Ulm, Germany
Stefanie Rinderle-Ma, University of Vienna, Austria
Antonio Ruiz-Cortés, University of Seville, Spain
Anderson Santana de Oliveira, SAP Labs, France
Sigrid Schefer-Wenzl, FH Campus Vienna, Austria
Mark Strembeck, Vienna University of Economics and Business, Austria

Introduction to the 1st International Workshop on Knowledge Aware Service Oriented Applications (KASA 2014)

Sami Bhiri[1], Walid Gaaloul[1] and Nizar Messai[2]

[1]Samovar, Télécom SudParis, France
sami.bhiri@gmail.com,
walid.gaaloul@telecom-sudparis.eu
[2]University François Rabelais Tours, France
nizar.messai@univ-tours.fr

The workshop on Knowledge Aware Service Oriented Applications (KASA) focuses on exploring advanced techniques for managing service oriented applications from a business and semantic level. Indeed, in spite of the tremendous advances and adoption of service oriented computing, a considerable manual work is still required to align the implementation of service-based systems with business and end-users requirements.

This first edition was held in conjunction with the ICSOC 2014 conference in Paris, France. It was an opportunity to discuss new approaches aiming at bridging the gap between business and end-users level on one hand and the implementation and technical layer on the other hand. The workshop succeeded to bring together researchers and practitioners working in semantically enabled and knowledge aware service oriented systems in order to present, discuss and share original research works and practical experience.

Each paper submission was reviewed by at least three reviewers. Six papers were accepted after a thorough peer-review by the workshop program committee members. The selected papers fell into two categories of related topics.

The first category focuses on knowledge-aware management of business processes and includes two regular and one short papers: (1) Discovering and Categorizing Goal Alignments from Mined Process Variants, by Karthikeyan Ponnalagu, Aditya Ghose, Nanjangud C. Narendra, and Hoa Khanh Dam; (2) Supporting Enterprise Changes Using Actor Performance Assessment, by Marwen Jabloun, Yemna Sayeb, Henda Ben Ghezala, and Khaled Gaaloul; and (3) Reasoning on Incomplete Execution Traces using Action Languages, by Chiara Di Francescomarino, Chiara Ghidini, Sergio Tessaris, and Itzel Vázquez Sandoval.

The second category deals with knowledge-aware management of services. It also includes two regular and one short papers: (1) Towards a Framework for Semantically-enabled Compliance Management in Financial Services, by Amal Elgammal, Elie Abi-Lahoud, and Tom Butler; (2) A Planning-Based Service Composition Approach for Data-Centric Workflows, by Carlos-Manuel López-Enríquez, Víctor Cuevas-Vicenttín, Genoveva Vargas-Solar, Christine Collet, and José-Luis Zechinelli-Martini; and (3) Semantic Web Services Approach For Collaboration In E-Gov Context, by Amal Latrache, El habib Nfaoui, and Jaouad Boumhidi.

Finally we would like to thank ICSOC 2014 workshop chairs as well as all members of our program committee.

Workshop Organizers

Sami Bhiri, Télécom SudParis, France
Walid Gaaloul, Télécom SudParis, France
Nizar Messai, University François Rabelais Tours, France

Program Committee

Nour Assy, Télécom SudParis, France
Jorge Cardoso, University of Coimbra, Portugal
Edward Curry, DERI, University of Ireland, Galway, Ireland
Wassim Derguech, DERI, University of Ireland, Galway, Ireland
Khaled Gaaloul, Public Research Centre Henri Tudor, Luxembourg
Feng Gao, DERI, University of Ireland, Galway, Ireland
Claude Godart, LORIA, Nancy, France
Mohamed Graiet, ISIMA, University of Monastir, Tunisia
Imen Grida Ben Yahia, Orange, France
Marianne Huchard, LIRMM, CNRS, University Montpellier 2, France
Kais Klai, University Paris 13, France
Mourad Kmimech, ISIMA, University of Monastir, Tunisia
Massimo Mecella, SAPIENZA, University of Rome, Italy
Amedeo Napoli, LORIA, Nancy, France
Olivier Perrin, LORIA, Nancy, France
Pierluigi Plebani, Politecnico di Milano, Italy
Yacine Sam, LI, University François Rabelais Tours, France
Brahmananda Sapkota, University of Twente, Netherlands
Mohamed Sellami, RDI Group, LISITE LAB, ISEP Paris, France
Samir Tata, Institut Mines-Telecom, Telecom SudParis, France
Tomas Vitvar, Czech Technical University, Czech Republic
Zhangbing Zhou, CUG Beijing, China

Introduction to the Proceedings of the Workshop on Intelligent Service Clouds (ISC) 2014

Alexander Norta[1], Roman Vaculin[2], Rik Eshuis[3]

[1]Department of Informatics, Tallinn University of Technology,
12618 Tallinn, Estonia
`alex.norta.phd@ieee.org`
[2]IBM Research, Yorktown Heights, NY USA
`vaculin@us.ibm.com`
[3]TU-Eindhoven, PAV D11, POBox 513, 5600 MB Eindhoven,
The Netherlands
`h.eshuis@tue.nl`

1 Introduction

The First Workshop on Intelligent Service Clouds (ISC) 2014 was held in conjunction with the ICSOC 2014 conference in Paris, France. The workshop followed the increasing interest in big data, cloud, analytics services and rich combinations with human driven services. The goal of the workshop was to provide a platform for exploring this exciting landscape and new challenges in the context of intelligent service clouds. It aimed at bringing together researchers from various communities interested in the challenges. We solicited contributions that study fundamental as well as practical aspects. At the fundamental, solution side we sought approaches that study adequate service models addressing above characteristics, mechanism for specification, discovery, composition, delivery and scaling of intelligent cloud services, data, computational, security and privacy aspects of analytics services, and cloud environments for analytics services, and address specific technical intelligent service-oriented cloud solutions, e.g., analytics; mining, visualization; self-management; security; trust mechanisms; collaboration mechanisms. At the practical problem side, we were interested in case studies in which intelligent service-oriented cloud computing technologies are applied in socio-technical systems/processes like smart logistics, smart manufacturing, healthcare, commerce, public administration, etc. The ISC 2014 workshop was a direct successor of the successful, full day first Workshop on Pervasive Analytical Service Clouds for the Enterprise and Beyond which we organized in conjunction with ICSOC 2013.

The ISC 2014 keynote of Prof. Michael Papazoglou who holds the chair of Computer Science and is director of the INFOLAB at Tilburg University, focused on smart clouds for manufacturing towards Smart Manufacturing-as-a-Service (SMaaS). Important elements of this trend are the analytics of manufacturing bid data and the ad-hoc establishment of smart manufacturing networks. These factors address key challenges of the status-quo such as the need to track and trace products along their lifecycles, bridging the disconnect between the enterprise and shopfloor applications, establishing a point-to-point connectedness between business IT and factory automation, identifying the work order performance related to on-time completions and quality adherence, and so on.

Furthermore, the four full- and one short ISC-workshop papers were selected after a thorough peer-review by the Workshop Program Committee Members. Following is a brief overview of the contributions. The full research paper with the title 'Using COBIT 5 for Risk to Develop Cloud Computing SLA Evaluation Templates' by authors Onyeka Illoh, Shaun Aghili and Sergey Butakov focuses on the use of cloud services as a business solution that keeps growing. However, there are significant associated risks that must be addressed. Despite the advantages and disadvantages of cloud computing, service integration and alignment with existing enterprise architecture remains an ongoing priority. The authors emphasize the implementation of a proposed SLA evaluation template aimed at cloud services, based on the COBIT 5 for Risk framework.

The full research paper with the title 'Contextualised security operation deployment through MDS@run.time architecture' by authors Wendpanga Francis Ouedraogo, Frédérique Biennier and Philippe Merlov focuses on the fast development of Cloud-based services and applications that have a significant impact on Service Oriented Computing as it provides an efficient support to share data and processes. However, new security challenges emerge such as providing a consistent protection depending on the business environment conditions and on the deployment platform specific threats and vulnerabilities. The authors propose a MDS@run.time architecture, coupling Model Driven Security (MDS) and Models@run.time approaches.

The full research paper with the title 'Domain Specific Monitoring of Business Processes Using Concept Probes' by author Adrian Mos proposes a monitoring framework that has business concepts at its core. Rather than relying on generic mechanisms to provide monitoring data, it proposes the notion of concept probes that fully match the business concepts used in the definition of business processes. These concept probes combine monitoring information from business process execution as well as service execution into aggregate information that makes sense from a business concept point of view. The solution can lead to faster reaction time in fixing problems, changes in business partners (that provide better services), or improvements in the underlying infrastructure or application parameters.

The full research paper with the title 'Towards a Model for Resource Allocation in API Value Networks' by authors James Houghton, Michael Siegel and Maja Vukovic states that an effective API strategy must consider not just how the API will be built, but how it will be sold and offered in the Cloud environments. The authors extend traditional software marketing models to include this multi-party complexity, and contrasts optimal strategies over a variety of possible model parameters.

The short paper with the title 'A Non-Parametric Data Envelopment Analysis Approach for Cloud Services Evaluation' by authors Chunxiang Xu, Yupeng Ma and Xiaobo Wang discusses the challenge to choose proper services in a Cloud. Besides QoS requirements, customers expect more efficient services which provide better performance but with minimum cost. The authors propose a non-parametric method for evaluating relative efficiency of cloud services based on Data Envelopment Analysis.

We sincerely thank the Program Committee Members of the ISC 2014 workshop for their time and support throughout the reviewing period.

Alex Norta, Roman Vaculin, Rik Eshuis
ISC 2014 Workshop Chairs

2   Organization Details

2.1 Workshop Chairs

Roman Vaculin, IBM T.J. Watson Research, USA
Alexander Norta, Tallinn University of Technology, Estonia
Rik Eshuis, Eindhoven University of Technology, The Netherlands

2.2 Program Committee Members

Stefan Schulte, Vienna University of Technology
Alexander Wöhrer, Vienna Science and Technology Fund, Austria
George Feuerlicht, Prague University of Economics
Claus Pahl, Dublin City University
Smita Ghaisas, Tata Research Design and Development Center
Akhil Kumar, Penn State University
Yuqing Tang, Carnegie Mellon University
Antonio Brogi, University of Pisa
Shiping Chen, Networking Technologies Laboratory, CSIRO Australia
Adrian Mos, Xerox Research, France
Cesare Pautasso, University of Lugano, Switzerland

Introduction to the 3rd International Workshop on Self-Managing Pervasive Service Systems (SeMaPS 2014)

Weishan Zhang[1], Klaus Marius Hansen[2], Paolo Bellavista[3] and JieHan Zhou [4]

[1]China University of Petroleum, China
zhangws@upc.edu.cn
[2]University of Copenhagen, Denmark
klausmh@diku.dk
[3]Università di Bologna, Italy
paolo.bellavista@unibo.it
[4]University of Oulu, Finland
jiehan.zhou@ee.oulu.fi

The vision of self-managing systems is an important step to the realization of smart life and smart cities. To realizing the self-management capabilities, retrieving context information is of utmost importance before self-management actions can be taken. On the other hand, supporting infrastructure is one of the key technologies for enabling self-management. Papers in SeMaPS 2014 are focusing on these two issues. 'Retrieving Sensors data in Smart Buildings through Services: a similarity algorithm' and 'A Lightweight User State Monitoring System on Android Smartphones' addresses how to retrieve data in a reasonable manner and how to obtain user contexts through a smart phone. 'Developing Service Platform for Web Context-Aware Services Towards Self-Managing Ecosystem' presents a service platform working as PaaS for self-managing Web Context-Aware Services where clients can rapidly create, update, delete and execute custom contexts and services.

Workshop Organizers

Weishan Zhang, China University of Petroleum, China.
Klaus Marius Hansen, University of Copenhagen, Denmark.
Paolo Bellavista, Università di Bologna, Italy.
JieHan Zhou, University of Oulu, Finland

Program Committee

Klaus Marius Hansen, University of Copenhagen, Denmark
Paolo Bellavista, Università di Bologna, Italy
Julian Schütte, Fraunhofer AISEC, Germany
Su Yang, Fudan University, China

Zhipeng Xie, Fudan University, China
Weishan Zhang, China University of Petroleum, China
Yan Liu, Tongji University, China
Yue Lv, Eastern China Normal University, China
Bin Guo, Northwestern Polytechnical University, China
Hongyu Zhang, Tsinghua University, China
Qinghua Lu, NICTA, Australia
Yuan Rao, Xi'an Jiao Tong University, China
JieHan Zhou, University of Oulu, Finland
Yangfan Zhou, Chinese University of Hongkang, China

Introduction to the 1st International Workshop on Formal Modelling and Verification of Service-based Systems (FOR-MOVES 2014)

Kais Klai[1], Amel Mammar[2]

[1]LIPN, University Paris 13, France
kais.klai@lipn.univ-paris13.fr
[2]Samovar, Télécom SudParis, France
amel.mammar@telecom-sudparis.eu

During the few last years the use of formal approaches for the modelling and the verification of service-based processes is increasingly widespread. On the one hand, formal modelling allows one to define unambiguous semantics for the languages and protocols used for the specification of service oriented systems. On the other hand, formal verification approaches are popular means of checking the correctness properties of these applications, such as safety, liveness, QoS requirements and security. Such properties can be considered as a behavioural criteria for compatibility between different local services/processes. The aim of FOR-MOVES workshop was to provide a venue for the presentation and discussion of new ideas and work in progress in formal modeling and verification methods, in the field of Service Oriented Computing (SOC).

For this workshop, we have received 10 submissions from different countries (France, Germany, China, India and Australia) and accepted 2 long papers:

Paper "Parameterized Automata Simulation and Application to Service Composition" introduces parametrized automata ("PAs"), i.e., an extension of finite state automata with infinite domain variables. This allows answering the service composition problem by showing that the simulation preorder of PAs is decidable. The service composition problem is stated as follows: given a client and a community of available services, is there an agent (called the mediator) that suitably delegates the actions requested by the client to the available community of services?

Paper "Optimal Virtual Machine Placement in Multi-Tenant Cloud" addresses the problem of virtual machines (VMs) placement in geographically distributed data centers, where tenants may require a set of networking VMs. The aim of the work is to plan and optimize the placement of tenant's VMs requests in a geographically distributed Cloud environment while considering location and system performance constraints.

Finally we would like to thank all members of our program committee.

Workshop Organizers

Kais Klai LIPN, University Paris 13, France
Amel Mammar Samovar, Télécom SudParis, France

Program Committee

Etienne André (LIPN, University Paris 13, France)
Boualem Benatallah (University of New South Wales, Sydney)
Nejib Ben Hadj-Alouane (ENIT, Tunisia)
Jörg Desel (University of Hagen)
Michael Dierkes (Rockwell Collins)
Marc Frappier (University of Sherbrooke)
Mohamed Graiet (ISIM, Monastir, Tunisia)
Serge Haddad (ENS Cachan, France)
Sun Jun (Singapore University of Technology and Design)
Pierre Kelsen (University of Luxembourg)
Michael Leuschel (University of Düsseldorf)
Meriem Ouederni (ENSEEIHT, France)
Denis Poitrenaud (University Paris Descartes, France)
Mohammad Reza Mousavi (Halmstad University, Sweden)
Liu Yang (Nanyang Technological University, Singapore)

Introduction to the 4th International Workshop on Cloud Computing and Scientific Applications (CCSA 2014)

Shiping Chen[1], Surya Nepal[1] and Suraj Pandey[2]

[1]CSIRO Digital Productivity Flagship
{shiping.chen, surya.nepal}@csiro.au
[2]IBM Research Australia
suraj.pandey@au.ibm.com

CCSA workshop has been formed to share and exchange new ideas and experiences of enabling and scaling scientific applications using distributed computing paradigms, such as cluster, Grid, and Cloud Computing. With the exponentially growing size and complicity of big data, there are strong demands for new technologies and approaches to storing, transferring and processing the big data to meet the requirements of various applications. On the other hand, cloud trends to become next-generation data centres to store and process big data with its scalable resources and reliable services. In context of eReseaerch, scientists will be able to deploy various algorithms and scientific applications to process big scientific data from a Cloud anywhere in the world on demand. To address the growing needs of both scientific applications and Cloud computing paradigm, CCSA brings together researchers and practitioners from both industry and research community to share their experiences with focus on modelling, executing, and monitoring scientific applications on Clouds. This year, CCSA accept three regular research papers to be presented on this workshop.

Summary of Papers Presented in the Workshop

The paper titled "Exploiting the Parallel Execution of Homology Workflow Alternatives in HPC Compute Clouds" explores a drug discover technology - Homology modelling (HM), using cloud. The main contributions of this paper are: (i) to provide a specification of an HM workflow that represents several variations for each activity with associated validation rules and (ii) to assist scientists in analysing their HM workflows by exploring and querying the provenance database, obtaining information about each HM workflow variation from the same database. This is a very compelling application of deploying and executing scientific workflows in Cloud.

The paper titled "A Validation Method of Configurable Business Processes Based on Data-flow" proposes an approach to modelling configurable business to be deployed and executed on cloud. The authors use the Colored Petri Net (CPN) as a formalism model to express the business process model and extends the business process model by adding the data-flow, which enables it to deal with the data semantic in the business process mode. As a result, they can transform the business process model with the data-flow into the configurable business process model. They also developed the approach to evaluating the business process in their proposed model.

The paper titled "Vertical Scaling Capability of OpenStack Survey of Guest Operating Systems, Hypervisors and the Cloud Management Platform" addresses a scalability issue of cloud. The paper evaluates the feasibility of vertical scaling for OpenStack. In particular, this paper examines what extent common guest operating systems, popular hypervisors, and OpenStack itself support vertical scaling. We would like to thank all PC members to help review the submitted papers.

Workshop Organizers

Surya Nepal CSIRO, Australia
Suraj Pandey IBM Research, Australia
Shiping Chen CSIRO, Australia

Program Committee

Dr. Chi-Hung Chi, CSIRO, Australia
Dr. Keman Huang, Tianjin University, China
Dr. Julian Jang-Jaccard, CSIRO, Australia
Dr. Jun Shen, University of Wollongong, Australia
Dr. Zhongjie Wang, Harbin Institute of Technology (HIT), China
Dr. Xuyun (Sean) Zhang, The University of Melbourne, Australia

PhD Symposium Preface

This volume is the proceeding of the International PhD Symposium on Service Computing that was held in conjunction with the 12th International Conference on Service oriented Computing (ICSOC 2014). ICSOC 2014 took place on November 3, 2014 in Paris, France.

The ICSOC PhD Symposium 2014 is an international forum for PhD students working in all the areas related to the service computing. Its goals are: (1) to bring together PhD students and established researchers in the field of service oriented computing, (2) to enable PhD students to interact with other PhD students and to stimulate an exchange of ideas, suggestions, and experiences among participants, (3) to give PhD students the opportunity to present, share and discuss their research in a constructive and critical atmosphere, and (4) to provide students with fruitful feedback and advice on their research approach.

After a thorough review process of each submission by the Program Committee members, seven papers out of eleven were accepted to constitute the program of the PhD symposium. A keynote presentation on "Three research perspectives on service-oriented computing", also, featured the program.

We gratefully acknowledge the support of the contributors to this PhD symposium. We express specially our great esteem first, to the PhD Symposium program committee members for the time and effort they have put in reviewing papers, and second to the organizing committee of ICSOC 2014 for assisting us throughout the running of the PhD symposium.

November 2014

Nejib Ben Hadj-Alouane
Djamal Benslimane
Jan Mendling

PhD Symposium Chairs

Djamal Benslimane	Claude Bernard University of Lyon 1, France
Jan Mendling	WU Vienna, Austria
Nejib Ben Hadj-Alouane	ENIT, Tunisia

Program Committee Members

Djamel Belaid	Telecom Sud Paris, France
Moez Ben Haj Hmida	National School of Engineers of Tunis, Tunisia
Frederique Biennier	INSA of Lyon, France
Ivona Brandic	Vienna University of Technology, Austria
Cristina Cabanillas	Institute for Information Business, Vienna, Austria
Bruno Defude	Telecom Sud Paris, France
Massimo Mecella	SAPIENZA University of Roma, Italy
Brahim Medjahed	University of Michigan, Dearborn
Michael Sheng	The University of Adelaide, Australia
Matthias Weidlich	Imperial College, UK
Moez Yeddes	National School of Applied Sciences, Tunisia

Demonstration Track

The ICSOC 2014 Demonstration Track was held in conjunction with the 12th International Conference on Service Oriented Computing (ICSOC 2014) on 3rd-6th November 2014 in Paris, France. This track allowed researchers and practitioners to demonstrate innovative SOC systems, providing them an opportunity to present and discuss their approaches and ideas.

We received 8 submissions, of which 4 were accepted. These demos clearly showed interesting improvments and significance from existing systems, and offered the ability to fruitful discussions:

– TL-VIEWS: A Tool for Temporal Logic Verification of Transactional Behavior of Web Service Compositions
– SmartPM: Automated Adaptation of Dynamic Processes
– WS-Portal: An Enriched Web Services Search Engine
– SUPER: Social-based Business Process Management Framework

We would like to thank the authors for their submissions, our Reviewing Committee for their work and for submitting their reviews on time, and the organizers of the ICSOC 2014 conference for their support which made this demo track possible.

November 2014

Brian Blake
Iman Saleh
Olivier Perrin

Demonstration Chairs

Brian Blake   University of Miami, USA
Olivier Perrin   University de Lorraine, France
Iman Saleh   University of Miami, USA

Program Committee Members

Sonia Ben Mokhtar   LIRIS, CNRS, France
Djamal Benslimane   University of Lyon, France
Athman Bouguettaya   RMIT University, Australia
Ivona Brandic   Vienna University of Technology, Austria
Florian Daniel   University of Trento, Italy
Onyeka Ezenwoye   Georgia Regents University, USA
Adnene Guabtni   NICTA, Australia
Armin Haller   CSIRO, Australia
Raman Kazhamiakin   SOA Research Unit, Fondazione Bruno Kessler, Trento
Philippe Lalanda   Joseph Fourier University, France
Philipp Leitner   University of Zurich, Switzerland
Xumin Liu   Rochester Institute of Technology, USA
Helen Paik   University of New South Wales, Australia
Pierluigi Plebani   Politecnico di Milano, Italy
Mohammad Sadoghi   IBM Research, USA
Wei Tan   IBM Research, USA
David Wei   Microsoft, USA
Yuhong Yan   Concordia University, Canada
Uwe Zdun   University of Vienna, Austria

Contents

Knowledge Aware Service Oriented Applications

Intelligent Service Clouds

Self-Managing Pervasive Service Systems

Formal Modeling and Verification of Service-Based Systems

Cloud Computing and Scientific Applications

PhD Symposium Track

Demo Track

Engineering Service-Oriented Applications

Building Enterprise Applications Using Unicorn Universe Services

Michal Kökörčený[✉] and Vladimír Kovář

Department of Information Technologies, Unicorn College, V Kapslovně 2767/2,
130 00 Prague 3, Czech Republic
michal.kokorceny@unicorncollege.cz,
vladimir.kovar@unicornuniverse.eu

Abstract. Service Oriented Architecture has become the architecture of choice providing a flexible and responsive enterprise computing architecture that addresses the business needs of modern organizations. However, developing SOA applications involves many challenges, in particular for large-scale projects that require highly skilled practitioners. In this paper we discuss the challenges associated with developing SOA applications and describe how such challenges are addressed using the uuApp framework.

Keywords: SOA · Application development frameworks

1 Introduction

The main challenge that developers SOA (Service Oriented Architecture) applications face today is the complexity of the environment requiring high level of skills in a range of technologies and methods that constitute SOA environment. This makes SOA projects difficult to manage, in particular for SMEs (Small and Medium Size Enterprises) that lack the required technical and financial recourses. Large-scale SOA projects often result in excessive costs and time overruns. To address these issues we have been focusing our research and development efforts on simplification of SOA development environment with the objective to reduce development costs, making the SOA development platform accessible to smaller organizations. In this paper we briefly describe the Unicorn Universe Application platform (uuApp) that simplifies the development of SOA applications and increases the efficiency of the development process.

2 uuApp Architecture

uuApp (Unicorn Universe Application) platform is a framework for building SOA enterprise applications that facilitates the composition of SOA applications from individual services. In designing the uuApp framework we have avoided the use of established technologies such as WS-BPEL [1] and Service Component Architecture (SCA) [2], and instead based our platform on the Ruby programming platform [3]. This reduces the complexity of the uuApp framework and improves its functionality.

© Springer International Publishing Switzerland 2015
F. Toumani et al. (Eds.): ICSOC 2014, LNCS 8954, pp. 3–5, 2015.
DOI: 10.1007/978-3-319-22885-3_1

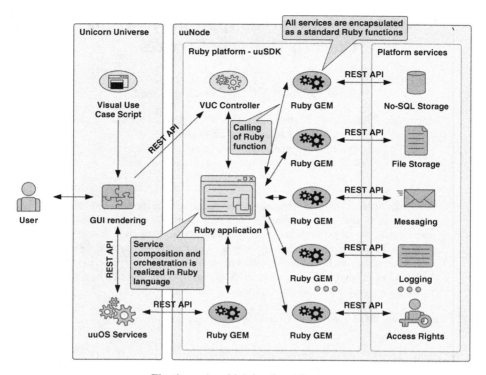

Fig. 1. uuApp high-level architecture

uuApp framework illustrated in Fig. 1 supports a range of standard reusable Platform Services, including JSON data storage, binary file storage, Inter-Process Messaging, Application Logging, User Access Management, and other services not shown in the figure. All services have standard REST APIs and use JSON as the serialization data format. In order to simplify the use of these APIs all services are encapsulated by GEM - the standard Ruby packaging mechanism, making it possible to invoke any service as a single Ruby function call. Service orchestration is implemented using scripts written in the Ruby programming language. The uuApp user interface is implemented using Visual Use Cases (VUC). A Visual Use Case typically represents a form that contains visual components (e.g. buttons, labels, edit lines, combo boxes etc.) and a graphical layout stored in a script file using a special source format. Form layout is created using a design editor or can be dynamically generated at runtime using an API. The VUC controller is a Ruby macro, which is responsible for runtime processing of events generated by VUC. At execution time VUC layout definition script is loaded into the runtime engine, which is responsible for rendering the form in HTML, and sending runtime events to VUC controlling service via the REST API. VUC controlling service translates REST calls into Ruby class method calls. Processing of events is implemented using a Ruby controller script, which can call other uuApp services. The VUC architecture allows incorporation of external HTML or XML content, including JavaScript code. uuApp applications can have GUI interface (in the form of a

VUC) or can be packaged as a service and externalized via an API, making applications reusable as building blocks for other applications.

3   Conclusion

The success of SOA projects depends on a number of factors that include correctness of the analysis, stability and functionality of the development platform, and not least on the level of expertise and skills of IT (Information Technology) architects, application designers and developers. The principal aim of the uuApp platform is to hide the complexity of the SOA development environment and to give developers a comprehensive set of tools and services that lead to a reduction of the cost and a faster implementation of SOA projects.

References

1. OASIS: OASIS Web Services Business Process Execution Language (WSBPEL) TC (2007). http://www.oasis-open.org/committees/tc_home.php?wg_abbrev=wsbpel
2. IBM: Service Component Architecture (2007). http://www.ibm.com/developerworks/library/specification/ws-sca/
3. Flanagan, D., Matsumoto, Y.: The Ruby Programming Language. O'Reilly Media Inc., Sebastopol (2008)

Cloud Migration Patterns: A Multi-cloud Service Architecture Perspective

Pooyan Jamshidi[1], Claus Pahl[1(✉)], Samuel Chinenyeze[2],
and Xiaodong Liu[2]

[1] IC4 – the Irish Centre for Cloud Computing and Commerce,
Dublin City University, Dublin, Ireland
{pooyan.jamshidi,claus.pahl}@computing.dcu.ie
[2] Centre for Information and Software Systems, School of Computing,
Edinburgh Napier University, Edinburgh, UK
{S.Chinenyeze,X.Liu}@napier.ac.uk

Abstract. Many organizations migrate their on-premise software systems to the cloud. However, current coarse-grained cloud migration solutions have made a transparent migration of on-premise applications to the cloud a difficult, sometimes trial-and-error based endeavor. This paper suggests a catalogue of fine-grained service-based cloud architecture migration patterns that target multi-cloud settings and are specified with architectural notations. The proposed migration patterns are based on empirical evidence from a number of migration projects, best practices for cloud architectures and a systematic literature review of existing research. The pattern catalogue allows an organization to (1) select appropriate architecture migration patterns based on their objectives, (2) compose them to define a migration plan, and (3) extend them based on the identification of new patterns in new contexts.

Keywords: Cloud architecture · Cloud migration · Migration pattern · Multi-cloud

1 Introduction

Cloud migration [1] benefits from the cloud promise of converting capital expenditure to operational cost [2]. Mixing cloud architecture with private data centers adds operational efficiency for workload bursts while legacy systems [3] on-premise still support core business services. Instead of re-architecting applications, they can be re-hosted from on-premise to possibly multiple cloud architectures, either private or public ones. We are concerned with the migration of legacy *on-premise* software to *multi-cloud* architectures. Multi-cloud deployment [4] is particularly effective in dealing with the following challenges:

- Users are widely distributed where they are located around multiple data centers.
- Country regulations limit options for storing data in specific data centers, e.g., EU.
- Circumstances where public clouds are used jointly with on-premises resources.
- Cloud-based application must be resilient to the loss of a single data center.

© Springer International Publishing Switzerland 2015
F. Toumani et al. (Eds.): ICSOC 2014, LNCS 8954, pp. 6–19, 2015.
DOI: 10.1007/978-3-319-22885-3_2

Current migration solutions are coarse-grained, making detailed planning difficult. For these cloud migration processes [1], a migration plan as a verifiable artefact is not considered. The plan is prepared at either a very broad strategic level with no technical value or very thorough and technical not suitable for non-technical stakeholders. Thus, the repeatability of migration processes decreases. Architecture migration patterns can make this repeatable and transparent.

We address (i) how to reorganize multi-tier applications into disjoint groups of service components, such that (ii) each such group can be deployed separately in different platforms (i.e., cloud platforms, on-premise platform) while preserving and in most cases enhancing the desired properties of the application. We report on 9 fined-grained core and 6 variant cloud-specific architecture migration patterns, extracted based on empirical evidence from a number of migration projects [5], best practice for cloud architectures [4, 6] and a systematic literature review [1]. Our main contribution is a set of fine-grained service-oriented migration fragments that allows application developers and architects to plan the migration and communicate the plan and the decision with non-technical stakeholders.

The patterns define architectural change in the application re-engineering and deployment setting, through which an application is gradually modernized and deployed in a multi-cloud. A migration plan is defined as a composition of selected patterns for specific situations.

Cloud migration methods define activities to plan, execute and evaluate migration [7]. To account for the situational context of applications, e.g., security, performance, availability needs, existing approaches [1] suggest a trade-off between flexibility and ease of migration using a fixed set of migration strategies. We propose an assembly-based approach based on our experience in situational method engineering [8] where a method is constructed from reusable method *fragments* and *chunks* [9]. This allows creating a migration plan from scratch by combining existing migration building blocks in the form of migration patterns. The usability of the approach is evaluated through a cloud migration case study at the end.

2 Background

We first introduce architecture migration patterns and the multi-cloud deployment setting.

Migration Patterns. For each *migration pattern*, an architectural migration schema has to be defined. A migration pattern is represented by an architecture diagram of the service architecture deployment before and after migration, i.e. a migration pattern is a *transformation triple* consisting of source and target architecture together with the applied pattern as the transformation specification. Each architecture is represented by well-defined architectural elements including services and connectors, deployment platforms (on-premise and cloud-based) and cloud services. The notation here is loosely aligned with UML component diagrams, with specific component types

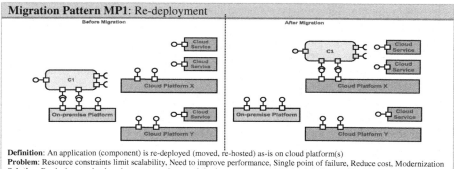

Migration Pattern MP1: Re-deployment

Definition: An application (component) is re-deployed (moved, re-hosted) as-is on cloud platform(s)
Problem: Resource constraints limit scalability, Need to improve performance, Single point of failure, Reduce cost, Modernization
Solution: Re-deploy on cloud environments, make use of elastic resources, multiple cloud deployment for failover and scalability.
Benefits: Improved Backup and Failover, Coarse-grained scalability at application level, Simple coarse-grained re-deployment.
Challenges: Existing architecture constrains portability, deployment time/cost, scalability, integration may introduce complexity.

color-coded. A service component can either be atomic or contain internal components allowing for hierarchical decomposition. For example, the migration pattern MP1 consists of a coarse-grained component that consumes services of an on-premise deployment platform. These can be coordination services that orchestrate different components in larger compartments or simply configurable IaaS resources providing required operating system or storage features. After migration, this component, instead of using on-premise platforms, uses public cloud platform services offered. Thus, the application component is re-deployed as-is on a cloud platform. The current architecture is mirrored in the cloud, but can take advantage of virtualization to not only reduce operational expenditure, but also to create multiple instances of the application to improve scalability and failover without increasing capital expenditure. The key risk is that underlying architecture issues are not addressed. A monolithic legacy application in the cloud is still monolithic with limitations such as lack of scalability. Scalability is coarse-grained and cannot easily be achieved if, e.g., the architecture does not allow the database to be updated by multiple instances.

Multi-cloud. In order to build highly scalable and reliable applications, a *multi-cloud deployment* is appropriate. Our objective is to provide architectural guidance for migrating cloud-based systems that run on multiple independent clouds. Multi-cloud denotes the usage of multiple, independent clouds by a client or a service. A multi-cloud environment is capable of distributing work to resources deployed across multiple clouds [10]. A multi-cloud is different from *federation* where, a set of cloud providers voluntarily interconnect their infrastructures to allow sharing of resources [10]. *Hybrid deployment* can be considered as a special case of multi-cloud where an application is deployed in both on-premise as well as cloud platforms. This deployment model is essential in cases where critical data needs to be kept in house in corporate data centers. We reviewed different application types and their requirements that necessitate multi-cloud deployment – see the supplementary materials here [11].

Note that we primarily target Platform-as-a-Service (PaaS) clouds that provide middleware services to host and manage application services. PaaS clouds like Microsoft Azure or Cloud Foundry generally provide mechanisms to support the re-architecting activities here.

3   Research Methodology

The first step to identify migration patterns was to identify the concerns of organizations moving on-premise applications to the cloud. We have identified four categories based on feedback from industry partners in our IC4 research centre [5]:

- **Availability.** Cloud environments typically guarantee a minimum availability.
- **Management.** Use runtime information to monitor and support on-the-fly changes.
- **Scalability.** Scale out to meet bursts in demand and scale in when demand decreases.
- **Resiliency.** Provide ability for systems to gracefully handle and recover from failure.

Focus Groups/Expert Interviews. We used focus groups to identify migration process concerns. The organizations involved were consultants for SME migration and larger multi-nationals – technology providers and systems integrators [5]. Through migration expert interviews, we looked at common processes for migration towards cloud as a framework for more fine-grained patterns. These covered IaaS, PaaS and SaaS migration projects.

Systematic Literature Review (SLR). We recorded existing cloud design and architecture patterns [4, 6]. A major role in this process played a SLR on cloud migration [1]. We detected shortcomings associated with these design patterns when we applied them in migration planning. The patterns were either limited to specific platforms [4] or fine-grained at a very technical level [6]. To redesign an on-premise application with these patterns, it requires deep knowledge of vendor-specific services as well as fair understanding of detailed design documents. Thus, a migration plan based on these patterns cannot be communicated with non-technical stakeholders. Thus, we generalize the architectural elements of these cloud architectures with general concepts of software architecture, i.e., components, connector, on-premise/cloud platform, cloud service, cloud broker.

Empirical Analysis and Pattern Synthesis. We analyzed migration projects for a range of CRM and retail systems as well as PaaS platform services. We generalized emerging patterns, considering patterns retrieved from the SLR based on different architecture scenarios that satisfy the migration concerns. Coarse-grained on-premise applications are not agile enough to respond to variations in workload. In the cloud, the deployment of high-usage components can be optimized independently of low-usage ones. Re-architecting into independent components reduces dependencies and enables optimization for scalability and performance. However, challenges remain: (1) on-premise application modernized in isolation, not part of a consistent architecture,

(2) modernization performed primarily for technical reasons resulting in sub-optimal response to business change, (3) architectures determined bottom-up from existing APIs and transactions may need re-evaluation for multi-clouds.

4 Cloud Architecture Migration Patterns

Some applications are integrated and support core business processes and services, but many of them support utility needs, are certainly non-core applications and are independent. The latter category may be obvious candidates for direct re-deployment. For the former integrated core ones, refactoring (re-architecting or redesigning) is more appropriate. Our migration patterns are sequences of architectural changes in the application deployment setting, through which the current application is gradually modernized.

To obtain unambiguous pattern descriptions and to ground pattern-based migration planning, we provide a template-based definition of migration patterns. This definition is based on the semantics of architectural schemas before and after migration. In some migration patterns, it may only be possible to deploy application components in a public cloud. However, for those patterns that consider re-architecting, the application can be deployed in hybrid public/private platforms. Due to space limitations, we do not describe all patterns fully, for more details refer to [11]. We use a template-based description of patterns. The usability of the patterns in migration planning will be shown through a method engineering process in Sect. 5 and through a case study in Sect. 6.

For space reasons, only the core patterns are presented. The patterns missing from this list are variants of some core patterns (which will be summarized afterwards). The core patterns highlight the different construction principles for the cloud architecture: re-deployment, cloudification, relocation, refactoring, rebinding, replacement and modernization.

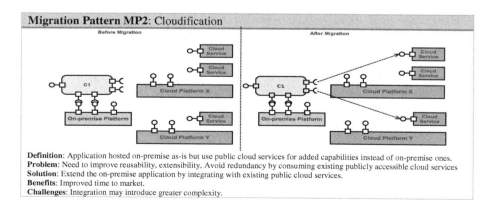

Migration Pattern MP2: Cloudification

Definition: Application hosted on-premise as-is but use public cloud services for added capabilities instead of on-premise ones.
Problem: Need to improve reusability, extensibility, Avoid redundancy by consuming existing publicly accessible cloud services
Solution: Extend the on-premise application by integrating with existing public cloud services.
Benefits: Improved time to market.
Challenges: Integration may introduce greater complexity.

Migration Pattern MP3: Relocation [see variant MP4]

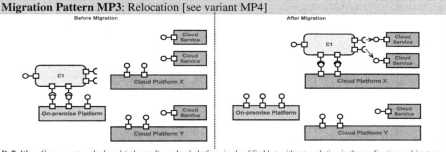

Definition: Component re-deployed (relocated) on cloud platform is cloudified but without evolution in the application architecture.
Problem: Enhance performance without significant architecture change, without capital expenditure for on-premise hardware.
Solution: Use cloud services to improve throughput by leveraging Queues, Database partitioning/sharding, NoSQL, Cache
Benefits: As component re-hosting in cloud and optimized performance.
Challenges: The type of application requests changes over time for example proportion of read only calls reduces, Cloud provider does not provide the necessary services to wrap the optimizations around the application without re-architecting.

Migration Pattern MP5: Multi-Cloud Refactoring [see variants MP6, MP7, MP8, MP9]

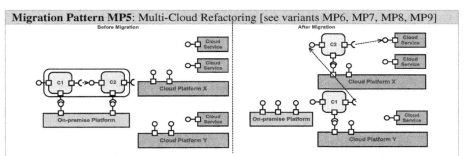

Definition: An on-premise application is re-architected for deployment on cloud platform to provide better QoS.
Problem: Coarse-grained applications are not agile enough to respond to requirement changes or variations in workload, and cannot take full advantage of the performance improvements that can be offered by cloud platforms.
Solution: Application re-architected into fine-grained components; deployment of high-usage comp. optimized independently of low-usage ones; parallel design for better throughput to multi-cloud platforms; components as independent integrity units.
Benefits: Optimal scalability/performance, range of multi-cloud deployment options, agility to respond to business/IT change.
Challenges: On-premise application is modernized in isolation; Modernization is performed primarily for technical reasons, Component architecture is only determined bottom-up may need to be re-evaluated because of multi-cloud environment.

Migration Pattern MP10: Multi-Cloud Rebinding [see variant MP11]

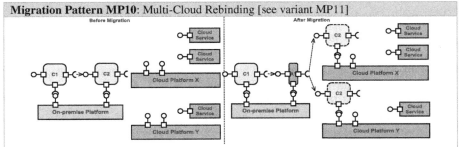

Definition: A re-architected application is deployed partially on multiple cloud environments and enables the application to continue to function using secondary deployment when there is a failure with the primary platform.
Problem: Failure such as a bug or configuration error that impacts cloud services may cause a failure to a cloud platform.
Solution: Architecture for resilient systems (routes users to closest data center) used for failover: monitor services, if unavailable, traffic is routed to healthy instances. On-premise adapter (bus or load balancer) provides integration of components
Benefits: As unhealthy services become healthy again, traffic can be delivered, returning system responsiveness to maximum.

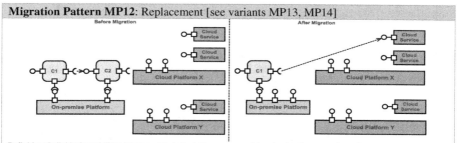

Migration Pattern MP12: Replacement [see variants MP13, MP14]

Definition: Individual capabilities in a re-architected solution are re-provisioned rather than re-engineered.
Problem: Some existing components provided by current application are not the best alternative to meet business requirements.
Solution: Analyze and identify capabilities to be replaced by cloud services (capabilities that can be supported by re-architected system), identify alternative cloud services with benefit over re-engineering of current capability to replace components
Benefits: The solution is improved though best-in-class cloud services, Re-engineering costs and effort are saved.
Challenges: Cloud services presume specific communication protocol that make the replacement a challenging tasks.

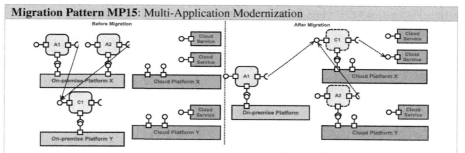

Migration Pattern MP15: Multi-Application Modernization

Definition: Different on-premise applications A1/A2, C1 are re-architected as a portfolio and deployed on cloud environment.
Problem: The re-architecting of on-premise applications in isolation does not remove inconsistencies in data or duplicated functionalities, nor reduce the cost of their combined operation or maintenance.
Solution: Current applications are analyzed jointly to identify opportunities for consolidation/sharing. Separation of service and solution architecture enables the identification of components (capabilities) that are shared by more than one solution.
Benefits: Consistent information / rules in shared components, Reduced operation / maintenance costs for shared components,
Challenges: Lack of business commitment to shared capabilities.

Variants for the following core patterns can be identified [11]:

- MP3 **Relocation:** MP4 (relocation for multi-clouds)
- MP5 **Multi-Cloud Refactoring:** MP6 (hybrid refactoring), MP7 (hybrid refactoring with on-premise adaptation), MP8 (hybrid refactoring with cloud adaptation), MP9 (hybrid refactoring with hybrid adaptation)
- MP10 **Multi-Cloud Rebinding:** MP11 (rebinding with cloud brokerage)
- MP12 **Replacement:** MP13 (replacement with on-premise adaptation), MP14 (replacement with cloud adaptation)

Further variants can be added, but we will show the sufficient completeness of the given set to model common PaaS migration scenarios in the use case evaluation.

5   Assembly-Based Situational Architecture Migration

To enable migration planning as a tractable process, appropriate building blocks have to be selected and combined. Migration patterns embed desirable principles for the target architectural deployment. Migration patterns represent fine-grained migration activities to be combined into a migration plan, ensuring that combined patterns do not violate pattern properties. For example, a pattern for the replacement of an on-premise component can be combined with a pattern for refactoring. This ensures that an architecture migration plan can be created incrementally. Figure 1 shows this pattern composition process. The patterns form a sequence of activities by which an application is gradually migrated and refined.

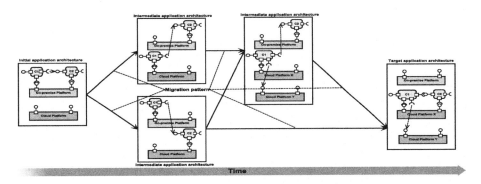

Fig. 1. Migration transition graph.

A migration transition graph provides a generic migration plan based on situations and possible migration patterns. The graph nodes are current architectural configurations and edges are migration patterns. The directed nature of the graph shows sequencing of patterns. Since multiple edges can enter a node, the model is able to represent many candidate plans. There are initial and target architectures, but also intermediate application architectures. Migration plans are triples <*source config, pattern, target config*> that correspond to a migration step to achieve the target configuration from a specific configuration following a particular pattern. Note that one path from the source configuration (current on-premise application architecture) to the target (multi-cloud application architecture) will be chosen.

Table 1 shows the patterns base as a mapping of migration patterns and concerns for which they are suitable. These patterns can be used to form a plan (see Fig. 1). This mapping is used to narrow down the related patterns and we can select the final pattern by comparing the situation through the "benefit" part in the pattern template. The selected patterns can be integrated based on the presence/absence of overlaps between patterns. The flexibility of this approach is restricted only by the set of available migration patterns. The patterns can be extended over time, e.g., by integrating a new

Table 1. Cloud migration pattern selection.

Objective	MP1	MP2	MP3	MP4	MP5	MP6	MP7	MP8	MP9	MP10	MP11	MP12	MP13	MP14	MP15
Time to market	☺	--	✗	✗	✗	--	--	--	--	✗	✗	☺	☺	☺	☺
New capabilities	✗	☺	☺	☺	☺	☺	☺	☺	☺	☺	☺	--	--	--	--
Reduce operational cost	☺	☺	--	--	✗	--	--	--	--	✗	✗	☺	☺	☺	☺
Leverage investments	☺	☺	--	--	--	☺	☺	☺	☺	☺	☺	✗	✗	✗	☺
Free up on premise resources	☺	☺	☺	☺	☺	☺	☺	☺	☺	☺	☺	☺	☺	☺	☺
Scalability	✗	--	--	--	☺	☺	☺	☺	☺	☺	☺	--	--	--	--
Operational efficiency	☺	--	--	--	☺	--	--	--	--	☺	☺	☺	☺	☺	--

solution to new problems. For a more detailed description of the assembly-based approach, see the supplementary material [11].

6   Case Study and Validation

The *usability* of the migration patterns shall be evaluated through a case study. We use a sample migration project based on our work with Microsoft Azure as a PaaS cloud for illustration and validation. This project acts as a representative for a range of migrations we examined (and for the latter two categories also implemented). These include several CRM systems (e.g., larger configurations based on commercial products), online retail solutions and services utilizing cloud storage solutions. Usability refers to the suitability of the pattern set to provide options and facilitate staged migration plans. Thus, we need to demonstrate the utility of all patterns, but also that the set is sufficiently complete to model a range of cases.

Context. A financial services company decides to migrate in-house applications to the cloud. It uses Microsoft technologies, but it also has legacy systems deployed on UNIX. Some applications have external ports, while others are exclusively for internal use. The importance of the applications ranges from marginal to critical. A significant portion of the IT budget is spent on maintaining applications with marginal importance.

Challenges. New applications take long for deployment, causing problems with adapting to changes. For any application, requirements must be analyzed, procurement processes must be initiated and networks must be configured. The infrastructure is used inefficiently. The majority of servers are underutilized. It is difficult to deploy new applications with the required SLA to the existing hardware. Applications in a public cloud platform can take advantage of economies of scale and have automated processes for managing.

Concerns. An objective is to improve the user experience. Some applications vary in usage (e.g., used once every two weeks, like salary-wages, but rarely at other times). They would benefit from the cloud-based increased responsiveness during peak times. A second objective is to expand ways to access applications. Applications located in the public cloud are available over the Internet, but authentication concerns exist. A third goal is portability, i.e., it can be moved between a cloud and a private data center without modification to application code or operations. Furthermore, a tractable migration plan is essential.

Application. The migration starts with the *Expense* application. This allows employees to submit and process expenses and request reimbursements. Employees can tolerate occasional hours of downtime, but prolonged unavailability is not acceptable. Most employees submit expenses within the last days before the end of each month, causing high demand peaks. The infrastructure for the application is scaled for average use only. The application is deployed on-premise. It requires high volume storage because most stored receipts are scanned.

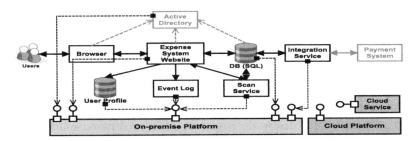

Fig. 2. Application architecture before migration to the cloud.

Expense is an ASP.NET application. It uses Windows authentication for security. To store user preferences, it relies on ASP.NET profile providers. Exceptions and logs are implemented with Enterprise Library's Exception Handling Application Block and Logging Application Block. It uses Directory Service APIs to query data. It stores information on SQL Server. Receipts are stored in a file system. The architecture is illustrated in Fig. 2.

The Migration Plan. The existing servers, networks, and associated systems such as power supply and cooling are managed by the company. We present a set of migration steps and decisions made to reach a tractable migration plan by adopting the presented patterns.

Step 1. Move the application to a cloud platform unchanged providing infrastructure reliability and availability. Management costs for running the hosted operating system and OS licenses must be considered, but development costs can be reduced as applications do not need to be refactored. Migration patterns **MP1, MP3, MP4** suit, of which **MP1** was selected, because only copy-as-is to the cloud without need for environmental services required.

Step 2. An alternative is to adapt Expense to run as hosted on a platform by an external partner. This would avoid costs of porting the application to a different system and reduces management cost. There is work involved in refactoring the application to run in cloud-hosted roles. **MP5-MP11** can be selected. Since the user profiles were to be kept on-premise. Pattern **MP6** was selected because there was no need for any interface adaptation (as in MP7-MP9) or multi-cloud deployment (as in MP10 and MP11).

Step 3. Abandon the own payment application and rent a typically more generic cloud service, which needs to be evaluated regarding security, performance, and usability. **MP12, MP13, MP14** suit, but a need to integrate Expense with a Payment service, favors **MP13**.

Step 4. For an external hosting decision, data storage facilities offered by cloud platforms are required. Expense requires a relational database system and NoSQL storage to store receipt images. **MP12** was selected as Azure SQL and Storage offerings meet requirements.

Step 5. Remote applications need to be integrated with other cloud services and on-premise for data access and monitoring. A systems operation or authentication tool could be used for monitoring, requiring remote services to be integrated. **MP7, MP8, MP9, MP12, MP13, MP14** can be selected. Due to a need for some adaptations, **MP14** was selected.

Step 6. Although only employees use Expense, the payment sub-system also used by other applications must always be available. **MP10, MP11** can be selected, but if the development of failover rebinding is to be avoided, a broker as in **MP11** is utilized (e.g., to deploy the payment system on Amazon and keep a mirror on Azure to route requests in case of failure).

Step 7. Value-added services from the cloud such as caching can maximize performance when retrieving data or can cache output, session state and profile information **MP3** was selected to accommodate these environmental services of the cloud provider.

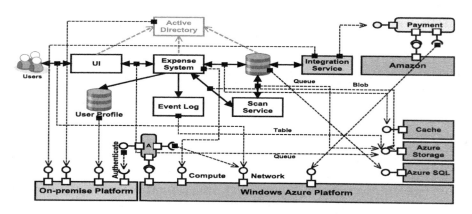

Fig. 3. Application architecture after migration to the cloud.

Migration Path. A possible migration path is presented below. The result is the architecture in Fig. 3. The migration steps are illustratively represented in [11]. Depending on the concerns of an organization, different combinations of hosting, data store and cloud services are possible. For example, MP1 step 1 follows a gradual migration by adopting the hosting approach, but uses SQL Server hosted in a VM before moving to an Azure SQL Database. Using MP3 instead would take advantage of storage capabilities (table/blob storage) and caching instead of relational databases to improve performance early rather than late.

Migration step	Requirement	Chosen patterns
1	Minimal code changes to application and familiarity with platform	**MP1**
2	Granular control of resource usage and opportunity for auto-scaling	**MP6**
3	Lower cost although some limitations on feature availability	**MP13**
4	Replacing on-premise storage with cloud offerings	**MP12**
5	Integration with cloud utility services	**MP14**
6	Highly available service replacement	**MP11**
7	Better user experience, improved efficiency, and load leveling	**MP3**

Discussion. For the migration plan we had different requirements, but were able to find a satisfactory patterns solution. Thus, the requirement satisfaction in this case is achieved and met by the proposed patterns [8]. Technically, we can only conclude that the migration patterns are complete and useful for all situations arising from the use case. However, we have analyzed and considered other migration, e.g., different IaaS/PaaS/SaaS migration processes [5]. The storage refactoring options relating to relational, table and blob storage, particularly addressed by patterns MP1 and MP3, are specifically addressed in [12]. This paper highlights the re-architecting options that advanced PaaS clouds offer, but also shows that while in this paper quality concerns such as scalability or availability are covered, their quantification and a trade-off analysis with cost aspects is not covered. Often, which specific paths are chosen is driven by more in-depth quality concerns. Our solution focuses on functional architecture aspects and only includes quality and cost concerns qualitatively.

7   Related Work

We conducted a review [1] aiming to identify, taxonomically classify, and systematically compare the existing research focused on planning, executing, and validating migration of legacy systems towards cloud-based software based on earlier architecture evolution work [13]. We found a lack of repeatable and verifiable practices as one of the key reasons that cloud migration is not a fully mature domain. In the context of the Cloud-RMM migration framework [1], our work here can be categorized as a contribution to migration planning.

Cloud migration approaches range from *decision making* to *enabling legacy software migration* with approaches reporting *best practice, experience and lessons learned* in between. Decision making for cloud adoption (e.g., [14]) is inherently complex and influenced by multiple factors such as cost and benefits through migration [15]. In contrast, some approaches enable the actual migration of legacy software in terms of procedures and model transformation (e.g., [16]). Some other work reports on lessons learned and best practices [17] – providing empirical evidence for migration research.

A number of migration strategies and best practices have been suggested in terms of patterns in [18–20]. These are rather informal and do not consider a multi-cloud setting. The objective there was mainly classification of existing best practice into migration strategies. The key advantage and novelty of our work, more than a set of patterns, is the notion of assembly-based situational migration at the architecture level, specifically towards pattern-based migration planning for multi-cloud deployment. It enhances the state-of-the-art by a tractable planning approach based on composable patterns.

8 Conclusion and Outlook

We identified cloud migration patterns, which in combination allow planning the migration of applications for multiple cloud platform deployment. The introduction of migration patterns complements existing migration practices and allows for an engineering approach towards constructing and evaluating the migration plan. The migration patterns are reusable and composable architectural change patterns that we see as building blocks of an overall migration process, reflected through a migration plan as a sequence of pattern applications.

Future work will include the development of a migration pattern repository as a tool that facilitates migration planning as well as application of the patterns to new domains and migration cases. To demonstrate the usability and completeness of the patterns beyond business-oriented SaaS and standard PaaS-level services such as storage, currently we are in the process of evaluating others for migration planning in three cases with our industry partners. We also plan to formally represent the relations between migration patterns in order to form a pattern map and work toward a pattern language for migration practices.

Acknowledgments. The research work described in this paper was supported by the Irish Centre for Cloud Computing and Commerce (an Irish national Technology Centre funded by Enterprise Ireland and the Irish Industrial Development Authority) and the Royal Irish Academy/Royal Society International Cost Share Grant IE131105.

References

1. Jamshidi, P., Ahmad, A., Pahl, C.: Cloud migration research: a systematic review. IEEE Trans. Cloud Comput. **1**(2), 142–157 (2013)
2. Armbrust, M.: Above the clouds: a Berkeley view of cloud computing (2009)
3. Khadka, R., Saeidi, A., Idu, A.: Legacy to SOA evolution: a systematic literature review. In: Migrating Legacy Applications (2012)

4. Wilder, B.: Cloud Architecture Patterns. Oreilly, San Antonio (2012)
5. Pahl, C., Xiong, H., Walshe, R.: A comparison of on-premise to cloud migration approaches. In: Lau, K.-K., Lamersdorf, W., Pimentel, E. (eds.) ESOCC 2013. LNCS, vol. 8135, pp. 212–226. Springer, Heidelberg (2013)
6. Fehling, C., et al.: Cloud Computing Patterns. Springer, Berlin (2014)
7. Tran, V., Keung, J., Liu, A. Fekete, A.: Application migration to cloud. In: SECLOUD 2011 (2011)
8. Gholami, F., Sharifi, M., Jamshidi, P.: Enhancing the OPEN process framework with service-oriented method fragments. Soft. Syst. Model. 13, 361–390 (2011)
9. Mirbel, I., Ralyté, J.: Situational method engineering: combining assembly-based and roadmap-driven approaches. Requir. Eng. 11, 58–78 (2006)
10. Grozev, N., Buyya, R.: Inter-cloud architectures and application brokering: taxonomy and survey. Softw. Pract. Exp. 44(3), 369–390 (2014)
11. Jamshidi, P., Pahl, C.: Cloud migration patterns - supplementary materials (2014). http://www.computing.dcu.ie/~pjamshidi/Materials/CMP.html
12. Gamma, E., et al.: Design Patterns: Elements of Reusable Object-Oriented Software. Pearson, New York (1994)
13. Jamshidi, P., Ghafari, M., Ahmad, A., Pahl, C.: A framework for classifying and comparing architecture-centric software evolution research. In: 17th European Conference on Software Maintenance and Reengineering CSMR 2013, pp. 305–314. IEEE (2013)
14. Frey, S., Hasselbring, W., Schnoor, B.: Automatic conformance checking for migrating software systems to cloud infrastructures and platforms. J. Softw. Evol. Process 25, 1089–1115 (2013)
15. Misra, S.C.: Identification of a company's suitability for the adoption of cloud computing and modelling its corresponding return on investment. Math. Comput. Model 53, 504–521 (2011)
16. Frey, S., Hasselbring, W.: The cloudmig approach: model-based migration of software systems to cloud-optimized applications. Int. J. Adv. Softw. 4, 342–353 (2011)
17. Andrikopoulos, V., Binz, T., Leymann, F., Strauch, S.: How to adapt applications for the cloud environment. Computing 95(6), 493–535 (2012)
18. Wilkes, L.: Application migration patterns for the service oriented cloud (2011). http://everware-cbdi.com/ampsoc
19. Mendonca, N.C.: Architectural options for cloud migration. Computer 8, 62–66 (2014)
20. Fehling, C., et al.: Service migration patterns - decision support and best practices for the migration of existing service-based applications to cloud environments. In: ICSOC (2013)

GovOps: The Missing Link for Governance in Software-Defined IoT Cloud Systems

Stefan Nastic[✉], Christian Inzinger, Hong-Linh Truong,
and Schahram Dustdar

Distributed Systems Group, Vienna University of Technology, Vienna, Austria
{nastic,inzinger,truong,dustdar}@dsg.tuwien.ac.at

Abstract. Cloud computing and the IoT are converging ever stronger, enabling the proliferation of diverse large-scale IoT cloud systems. Such novel IoT cloud systems offer numerous advantages for the variety of involved stakeholders. However, due to scale, complexity, and inherent geographical distribution of IoT cloud systems, governing new IoT cloud resources and capabilities poses numerous challenges. In this paper, we introduce GovOps – a novel approach and a conceptual model for cloud-based, dynamic governance of software-defined IoT cloud systems. By introducing a suitable *GovOps reference model* and a dedicated *GovOps manager*, it simplifies realizing governance processes and enables performing custom governance tasks more efficiently in practice. We introduce real-world case studies in the building automation and vehicle management domains, to illustrate the main aspects and principles of our approach to governance of large-scale software-defined IoT cloud systems.

1 Introduction

To date, cloud computing models and techniques, such as infrastructure virtualization and management, Compute-, Storage- and Network-as-a-Service, etc., have been intensively exploited for large-scale Internet of Things (IoT) systems [7,14,18]. Recently, software-defined IoT cloud systems have been introduced [10] in order to enable easier provisioning and management of IoT cloud resources and capabilities. Generally, software-defined denotes a principle of abstracting low-level components (e.g., hardware) and enabling their management, programmatically through well-defined APIs [8]. This enables refactoring the underlying infrastructure into finer-grained resource components whose functionality can be (re)defined after they have been deployed. While IoT cloud systems introduce numerous possibilities, a plethora of challenges to govern and operate these new IoT cloud resources and capabilities emerge.

Various domains, such as smart building and vehicle management, increasingly rely on IoT cloud resources and capabilities. Consequently, governance issues such as security, safety, legal boundaries, compliance, and data privacy concerns are ever stronger being addressed [4,5,17], mainly due to their potential impact on the variety of involved stakeholders. However, existing approaches are mostly

© Springer International Publishing Switzerland 2015
F. Toumani et al. (Eds.): ICSOC 2014, LNCS 8954, pp. 20–31, 2015.
DOI: 10.1007/978-3-319-22885-3_3

intended for high-level business stakeholders, neglecting support, e.g., tools and frameworks, to realize governance strategies in large-scale, geographically distributed IoT cloud systems. Approaching IoT cloud from the operations management perspective, different approaches have been presented, e.g. [2,14,15,18]. Such approaches deal with IoT cloud infrastructure virtualization and its management, enabling utilization of cloud computation resources and operating cloud storage resources for big IoT data. However, most of these approaches do not consider high-level governance objectives such as legal issues and compliance. This increases the risk of lost requirements or causes over-regulated systems, potentially increasing costs and limiting business opportunities.

Currently, IoT governance mostly addresses the *Internet* part of the IoT, e.g., in the context of the Future Internet services[1], while IoT operations processes mostly deal with *Things* (e.g., in [3]) as additional resources that need to be operated. Therefore, governance objectives (law, compliance, etc.) are not easily mapped to operations processes (e.g., querying sensory data streams or adding/removing devices). Contemporary models, which assume that business stakeholders define governance objectives, and operations managers implement and enforce them, are hardly feasible in IoT cloud systems. In practice, bridging the gap between governance and operations management of IoT cloud systems poses significant challenges, because traditional management and governance approaches are hardly applicable for IoT cloud systems, mainly due to the large number of involved stakeholders, novel requirements for shared resources and capabilities, dynamicity, geographical distribution, and the sheer scale of IoT cloud systems.

This calls for a systematic approach to govern and operate IoT cloud resources and capabilities. Extending the previously developed concepts [10], in this paper we introduce GovOps – a novel approach for cloud-based dynamic governance and operations management in software-defined IoT cloud systems. The main objectives of GovOps are twofold. On the one side, it aims to enable seamless integration of high-level governance objectives with concrete operations processes. On the other side, it enables performing operational governance processes for IoT cloud systems in such manner that they are feasible in practice. We present a GovOps reference model that defines required roles, concepts, and techniques to reduce the complexity of realizing IoT cloud governance processes. GovOps enables performing custom governance tasks more efficiently, thus reduces time, costs, and potential consequences of insufficient or ineffective governance.

The remainder of this paper is structured as follows: Sect. 2 presents motivating scenarios that will be used throughout the paper. In Sect. 3, we present the GovOps approach to governance and operations management in software-defined IoT cloud systems; Sect. 4 outlines the GovOps reference model; Sect. 5 discusses the related work; Finally, Sect. 6 concludes the paper and gives an outlook of our future work.

---

[1] http://ec.europa.eu/digital-agenda/en/internet-things.

2   Scenarios: Governing Software-Defined IoT Systems

Consider the following scenarios in the Building Automation and Vehicle Management domains that we will refer to throughout the rest of this paper. The scenarios are derived from our work conducted in the P3CL lab[2].

2.1   Scenario 1 – Fleet Management System

General Description. Fleet Management System (FMS) is responsible for managing electric vehicles deployed worldwide, e.g., on different golf courses. We have identified three stakeholders who rely on the FMS to optimize their business tasks: vehicle manufacturer, distributors and golf course managers. The stakeholders have different business models. For example, as the manufacturer only leases the vehicles, he is interested in the complete fleet, e.g., regular maintenance, crash reports and battery health. On the other side, golf course managers are mostly interested in vehicles security (e.g., geofencing features), preventing misuse, and safety on the golf course.

Infrastructure Setup. The FMS is an IoT cloud system comprising vehicles' proprietary on-board gateways, network and cloud infrastructure. The on-board gateway is capable to host lightweight applications for: vehicle maintenance, tracking, monitoring and club set-up. Vehicles communicate with the cloud via 3G, GPRS or Wi-Fi network to exchange telematic and diagnostic data. On the cloud we host different FMS subsystems and services to manage and analyze this data, e.g., determine vehicle status, perform remote diagnostics, batch configuration and software updates. Legacy vehicles that are not capable to host applications are integrated using a CAN-IP bridge, and any custom business logic needs to be executed in the cloud.

2.2   Scenario 2 – Building Automation System

General Description. Building Automation System (BAS) is responsible to monitor and control various building assets, such as HVAC, lighting, elevators and humidity control systems, as well as to handle fault events and alarms (e.g., fire or gas leakage). For safety-critical services (e.g., alarm handling), timely processing of the events and the availability of the BAS play a crucial role and need to be ascertained.

Infrastructure Setup. Generally, BAS comprises a set of cloud-based services, gateways and various sensors and actuators integrated with the building's assets. Gateways which support typical BAS device protocols (ModBus, BACnet, LonWorks and Fox), e.g., Niagra or Sedona[3], are used to communicate with sensors

---

[2] http://pcccl.infosys.tuwien.ac.at/.
[3] http://www.tridium.com/.

and actuators. For local processing, the gateways usually allow executing custom triggers, rules and some form of complex event processing (CEP) queries. For permanent storage and more resource-demanding processing, the gateways send streams of data to the remote cloud services.

2.3 System Characteristics

We notice that both the FMS and the BAS have large-scale, geographically distributed infrastructure. Additionally, the FMS utilizes virtualized IoT cloud infrastructure, such as virtual gateways (VGW), to support integrating legacy vehicles. Depending on stakeholder and task-at-hand our systems have different customization requirements and non-functional requirements (e.g., regarding fault-tolerance and availability). For example in BAS, while for safety-critical services, real-time delivery and processing is essential, for services such as HVAC controller, cost reduction is more important. Due to the multiplicity of the involved stakeholders, the FMS needs to allow for flexible runtime customizations in order to exactly meet the stakeholder's functional requirements, depending on the problem-at-hand and availability or accessibility of the vehicles, as well as desired system's non-functional properties.

3   GovOps – A Novel Approach to Governance and Operations Management in IoT Cloud

The main objective of our GovOps approach (Governance and Operations) is twofold. On the one side it aims to enable seamless integration of high-level governance objectives and strategies with concrete operations processes. On the other side, it enables performing operational governance processes for IoT cloud systems in such manner that they are feasible in practice.

Figure 1 illustrates how GovOps relates to IoT cloud governance and operations. It depicts the main idea of GovOps to bring governance and operations closer together and bridge the gap between governance objectives and operations processes, by incorporating the main aspects of both IoT cloud governance and operations management. To this end, we define *GovOps principles and design process* of GovOps strategies (Sect. 4) that support determining what can and needs to be governed, based on the current functionality and features of an IoT cloud system, and that allow for aligning system's capabilities with regulations and standards. Additionally, we introduce a novel role, *GovOps manager* (Sect. 3.3) responsible to guide and manage designing GovOps strategies,

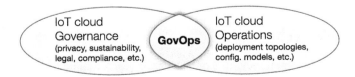

Fig. 1. GovOps in relation to IoT cloud governance and operations.

because in practice it is very difficult, risky, and ultimately very costly to adhere to traditional organizational silos, separating business stakeholders from operations managers. Therefore, GovOps integrates business rules and compliance constraints with operations capacities and best-practices, from early stages of designing governance strategies in order to counteract system over-regulation and lost governance requirements.

It is worth noting that GovOps does not attempt to define a general methodology for IoT cloud governance. There are many approaches (Sect. 5), which define governance models and accountability frameworks for managing governance objectives and coordinating decision making processes. Most of these approaches can be applied within GovOps without substantial modifications.

3.1 Governance Aspects

From our case studies, we have identified various business stakeholders such as building residents, building managers, governments, vehicle manufacturers and golf course managers. Typically, they are interested in energy efficient and greener buildings, sustainability of building assets, legal and privacy issues regarding sensory data, compliance (e.g., regulatory or social), health of the fleet, as well as security and safety issues related to the environments under their jurisdiction.

Depending on the concrete (sub)system and the involved stakeholders, governance objectives are realized via different governance strategies. Generally, we identify the following governance aspects: (i) *environment-centric*, (ii) *data-centric* and (iii) *infrastructure-centric governance*.

Environment-centric governance deals with issues of overlapping jurisdictions in IoT cloud managed environments. For example, in our BAS, we have residents, building managers and the government that can provide governance objectives, which directly or indirectly affect an environment, e.g., a residential apartment. In this context, we need to simultaneously articulate multiple governance objectives related to comfort of living, energy efficiency, safety, health and sustainability.

Data-centric governance mostly deals with implementing the governance strategies related to the privacy, quality, and provenance of sensory data. Examples include addressing legal issues, compliance, and user preferences regarding the sensory data.

Infrastructure-centric governance addresses issues about designing, installing, and deploying IoT cloud infrastructure. This mostly affects the early stages of introducing an IoT cloud system and involves feasibility studies, cost analysis, and risk management. For example, it supports deciding between introducing new hardware or virtualizing the IoT cloud infrastructure.

3.2 Operations Management Aspects

Operations managers implement various processes to manage BAS and FMS at runtime. Generally, we distinguish following operational governance aspects: (i) *configuration-centric*, (ii) *topology-centric*, and (iii) *stream-centric governance*.

Configuration-centric governance includes dynamic changes to the configuration models of deployed software-defined IoT cloud systems at runtime. Example processes include (a) enabling/disabling an IoT resource or capability (e.g., start/stop a unit), (b) changing an IoT capability at runtime (e.g., communication protocol), and (c) configuring an IoT resource (e.g., setting sensor poll rate).

Topology-centric governance addresses structural changes that can be performed on software-defined IoT systems at runtime. For example, (a) Pushing processing logic from the application space towards the edge of the infrastructure; (b) Introducing a second gateway and an elastic load balancer to optimize resource utilization; (c) Replicating a gateway, e.g., for fault-tolerance or datasource history preservation.

Stream-centric governance addresses runtime operation of sensor data streams and continuous queries, e.g., to perform custom filtering, aggregation, and querying of the available data streams. For example, to perform local filtering the processing logic is executed on physical gateways, while complex queries, spanning multiple data streams are usually executed on VGWs. Therefore, operations managers perform processes like: (a) Placement of custom filters (e.g., near the data source to reduce network traffic); (b) Allocation of queries to VGWs; and (c) Stream splitting, i.e., sending events to multiple VGWs.

3.3   Integrating Governance Objectives with Operations Processes

The examples presented in Sects. 3.1 and 3.2 are by no means a comprehensive list of IoT cloud governance processes. However, due to dynamicity, heterogeneity, geographical distribution and the sheer scale of IoT cloud, traditional approaches to realize these processes are hardly feasible in practice. This is mostly because such approaches implicitly make assumptions such as physical on-site presence, manually logging into gateways, understanding device specifics, etc., which are difficult, if not impossible, to meet in IoT cloud systems. Therefore, due to a lack of a systematic approach for operational governance in IoT systems, currently operations managers have to rely on ad hoc solutions to deal with the characteristics and complexity of IoT cloud systems when performing governance processes.

Further, Table 1 lists examples of governance objectives and according operations management processes to enforce these objectives. The first example comes from the FMS, since many of the golf courses are situated in countries with specific data regulations, e.g., the US or Australia. In order to enable monitoring of the whole fleet (as required by the manufacturer) the operations managers need to understand the legal boundaries regarding data privacy. For example, in Australia, the Office of the Australian Information Commissioner (OAIC) has issued an extensive guidance[4] as to what reasonable steps to protect personal information might include, that in practice need to be interpreted by operations managers. The second example contains potentially conflicting objectives supplied by stakeholders, e.g., building manager, end user, and the government,

---

[4] http://www.oaic.gov.au/privacy/applying-privacy-law/app-guidelines/.

Table 1. Example governance objectives and operations processes.

	Governance objectives	Operations processes
1	Fulfill legal requirements w.r.t. sensory data in country X. Guarantee history preservation	Spin-up an aggregator gateway. Replicate VGW, e.g., across different availability zones.
2	Reduce GHG emission. User preferences regarding living comfort. Consider health regulations	Provide configuration directives for an IoT cloud resource (e.g., HVAC).
3	Data quality compliance regarding location tracking services	Choose among available services, e.g., GPS vs. GNSS (Global Navigation Satellite System) platform.

leaving it to the operations team to solve the conflicts at runtime. The third example hints that GNSS is usually better-suited to simultaneously work in both northern and southern high latitudes. Therefore, even for these basic processes, an operations team faces numerous difficulties, since in practice there is no one-size-fits-all solution to map governance objectives to operations processes.

To address these issues, GovOps proposes a novel role, *GovOps manager*, as a dedicated stakeholder responsible to bridge the gap between governance strategies and operations processes in IoT cloud systems. The main rationale behind introducing a GovOps manager is that in practice designing governance strategies needs to involve operations knowledge about the technical features of the system, e.g., physical location of devices, configuration models, placement of queries and component replication strategies. Reciprocally, defining systems configurations and deployment topologies should incorporate standards, compliance, and legal boundaries at early stages of designing operations processes. To achieve this, the GovOps manager is positioned in the middle, in the sense that he/she continuously interacts with both business stakeholders (to identify high-level governance issues) and operations team (to determine operations capacities).

The main task of a GovOps manager is to determine suitable tradeoffs between satisfying the governance objectives and the system's capabilities, as well as to continuously analyze and refine how high-level objectives are articulated through operations processes. In this context, a key success factor is to ensure effective and continuous communication among the involved parties during the decision making process, facilitating (i) openness, (ii) collaboration, (iii) establishment of a dedicated GovOps communication channel, along with (iv) early adoption of standards and regulations. This ensures that no critical governance requirements are lost and counteracts over-regulation of IoT cloud systems. On the other side, in order to support performing runtime operations processes in IoT cloud systems, while considering system characteristics (e.g., large-scale, geographical distribution and dynamicity), GovOps proposes a set of concepts that includes: (i) central point of operation, (ii) automation, (iii) fine-grained control, (iv) late-bound policies, and (v) resource autonomy.

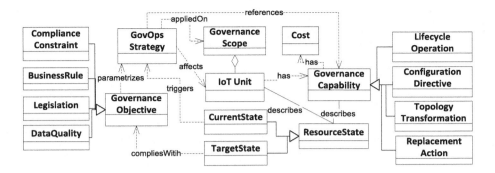

Fig. 2. Simplified UML diagram of GovOps model for IoT cloud governance.

4   A Reference Model for GovOps in IoT Cloud

4.1   Overview of GovOps Model for Software-Defined IoT Cloud Systems

To realize the GovOps approach we need suitable abstractions to describe IoT cloud resources that allow IoT cloud infrastructure to be (re)defined after it has been deployed. We show in [10] how this can be done with *software-defined IoT units*. The GovOps model (Fig. 2) builds on this premise and extends our previous work with fundamental aspects of operational governance processes: (i) describing states of deployed IoT resources, (ii) providing capabilities to manipulate these states at runtime, and (iii) defining governance scopes.

Within our model, the main building blocks of GovOpsStrategies are *GovernanceCapabilities*. They represent operations which can be applied on IoT cloud resources, e.g., query current version of a software, change communication protocol, and spin-up a virtual gateway. These operations manipulate IoT cloud resources in order to put an IoT cloud system into a specific (target) state. Governance capabilities are described via software-defined APIs and they can be dynamically added to the system, e.g., to a software-defined gateway. From a technical perspective, they behave like add-ons, in the sense that they extend resources with additional operational functionality. Generally, by adopting the notion of governance capabilities, we allow for processes to be automated to a great extent, and also give a degree of autonomy to IoT cloud resources.

Since the meaning of a resource state is highly task specific, we do not impose many constraints to define it. Generally, any useful information about an IoT cloud resource is considered to describe the *ResourceState*, e.g., a configuration model or monitoring data such as CPU load. Technically, there are many frameworks (e.g., Ganglia or Nagios) that can be used to (partly) describe resource states. Also configuration management solutions, such as OpsCode Chef, can be used to maintain and inspect configuration states. Finally, design best practices and reference architectures (e.g., AWS Reference Architectures[5]) provide a higher-level description of the desired target states of an IoT cloud system.

---

[5] http://aws.amazon.com/architecture/.

The *GovernanceScope* is an abstract resource, which represents a group of
IoT cloud resources (e.g., gateways) that share some common properties. Therefore, our governance scopes are used to dynamically delimit IoT cloud resources
on which a *GovernanceCapability* will have an effect. This enables writing the
governance strategies in a scalable manner, since the IoT cloud resources do
not have to be individually addressed. It also allows for backwards compatible
GovOps strategies, which do not directly depend on the current resource capabilities. This means that we can move a part of the problem, e.g., fault and
exception handling, inside the governance scope. For example, if a gateway loses
a capability the scope simply will not invoke it i.e., the strategy will not fail.

4.2   Design Process of GovOps Strategies

As described in Sect. 3, the GovOps manager is responsible to oversee and guide
the GovOps design process and to design concrete GovOps strategies. The design
process is structured along three main phases: (i) identifying governance objectives and capabilities, (ii) formalizing strategy, and (iii) executing strategy.

Generally, the initial phase of the design process involves eliciting and formalizing governance objectives and constraints, as well as identifying required
fine-grained governance capabilities to realize the governance strategy in the
underlying IoT cloud system. GovOps does not make any assumptions or impose
constraints on formalizing governance objectives. To support specifying governance objectives the GovOps manager can utilize various governance models and
frameworks, such as 3P [13] or COBIT [6]. However, it requires tight integration
of the GovOps manager into the design process and encourages collaboration
among the involved stakeholders to clearly determine risks and tradeoffs, in
terms of what should and can be governed in the IoT cloud system, e.g., which
capabilities are required to balance building emission regulations and residents
temperature preferences. To this end, the GovOps manager gathers available governance capabilities in collaboration with the operations team, identifies missing
capabilities, and determines if further action is necessary. Generally, governance
capabilities are exposed via well-defined APIs. They can be built-in capabilities
exposed by IoT units (e.g., start/stop), obtained from third-parties (e.g., from
public repositories or in a market-like fashion), or developed in-house to exactly
reflect custom governance objectives. By promoting collaboration and early integration of governance objectives with operations capabilities, GovOps reduces
the risks of lost requirements and over-regulated systems.

After the required governance capabilities and relevant governance objectives have been identified, the GovOps manager relies on the aforementioned
concepts and abstractions (Sect. 4.1) to formally define the GovOps strategy
and articulate the artifacts defined in the first phase of the design process. Governance capabilities are the main building blocks of the GovOps strategies. They
are directly referenced in GovOps strategies to specify the concrete steps which
need to be enforced on the underlying IoT cloud resources, e.g., defining a desired
communication protocol or disabling a data stream for a specific region. Also in
this context, the GovOps reference model does not make assumptions about

the implementation of governance strategies, e.g., they can be realized as business processes, policies, applications, or domain specific languages. Individual steps, defined in the generic strategy, invoke governance capabilities that put the IoT cloud resources into desired target state, e.g., which satisfies a set of properties. Subsequently, the generic GovOps strategy needs to be parameterized, based on the concrete constraints and rules defined by the governance objectives. Depending on the strategy implementation these can be realized as process parameters, language constraints (e.g., Object Constraint Language), or application configuration directives. By formalizing the governance strategy, GovOps enables reusability of strategies, promotes consistent implementation of established standards and best practices, and ensures operation within the system's regulatory framework.

The last phase involves identifying the system resources, i.e. the governance scopes that will be affected by the GovOps strategy and executing the strategy in the IoT cloud system. It is worth mentioning that the scopes are not directly referenced in the GovOps strategies, rather the GovOps manager applies the strategies on the resource scopes. Introducing scopes at the strategy-level shields the operations team from directly referencing IoT cloud resources, thus enables designing declarative, late-bound strategies in a scalable manner. Furthermore, at this point additional capabilities identified in the previous phase will be acquired and/or provisioned, whereas unused capabilities will be decommissioned in order to optimize resource consumption.

5   Related Work

The IoT governance has been receiving a lot of attention recently. For example, in [17] the author evaluates various aspects of the IoT governance, such as privacy, security and safety, ethics, etc., and defines main principles of IoT governance, e.g., legitimacy and representation, transparency and openness, and accountability. In [16], the authors deal with issues of data quality management and governance. They define a responsibility assignment matrix that comprises roles, decision areas and responsibilities and can be used to define custom governance models and strategies. Traditional IT governance approaches, such as SOA governance [1,12] and governance frameworks like CMMI [9], the 3P model [13], and COBIT [6], provide a valuable insights and models which can be applied in GovOps processes, usually without substantial modifications. Compared to these approaches, GovOps does not attempt to define a general methodology for IoT cloud governance. Therefore, such approaches conceptually do not conflict with GovOps and can rather be seen as complementary to our approach.

Also approaches addressing operations management in IoT cloud system have recently emerged. For example, in [14,18] the authors deal with IoT infrastructure virtualization and its management on cloud, whereas [2] utilizes the cloud for additional computation resources. In [15] the authors focus on operating cloud storage resources for IoT data, and [11] present approaches for monitoring IoT systems and enforcing QoS aspects. Such approaches provide useful concepts and techniques, which can be used to support the GovOps processes in

IoT cloud systems. In [7] the authors develop an infrastructure virtualization framework, based on a content-based pub/sub model for asynchronous event exchange. In [18] the authors propose virtualizing physical sensors on the cloud and provide management and monitoring mechanisms for the virtual sensors. Such approaches provide various governance capabilities, e.g., template-based controlling of sensor groups, registering and decommissioning sensors and monitoring the QoS that can seamlessly be integrated with our GovOps approach.

The GovOps model builds on these approaches and addresses the issue of bridging the gap between governance objectives and operations processes, by introducing the GovOps manager as a dedicated stakeholder, as well as defining the suitable GovOps reference model to support early integration of governance objectives and operations processes.

6   Conclusion and Future Work

In this paper, we introduced the GovOps approach to governance of software-defined IoT cloud systems. We presented the GovOps reference model that defines suitable concepts and a flexible process to design IoT cloud governance strategies. We introduced the GovOps manager, a dedicated stakeholder responsible to determine tradeoffs between satisfying governance objectives and IoT cloud system capabilities, and ensure early integration of these objectives with operations processes, by continuously refining how the high-level objectives are articulated through operations processes. We showed how GovOps enables systematically approaching IoT cloud governance to counteract system over-regulation and lost requirements. Further, it allows for IoT cloud governance processes to be easily and flexibly realized in practice, without worrying about the complexity and scale of the underlying IoT cloud and diversities of various legal and compliance issues. In the future, in order to support GovOps managers, we will develop a comprehensive framework for GovOps that implements the presented concepts and required toolset.

Acknowledgments. This work is sponsored by Pacific Controls Cloud Computing Lab (PC3L), as well as the Austrian Science Fund under grant P23313-N23 (Audit 4 SOAs).

References

1. Charfi, A., Mezini, M.: Hybrid web service composition: business processes meet business rules. In: Second International Conference on Service-Oriented Computing - ICSOC 2004 Proceedings, pp. 30–38, New York, 15–19 November 2004
2. Chun, B., Ihm, S., Maniatis, P., Naik, M., Patti, A.: Clonecloud: elastic execution between mobile device and cloud. In: Proceedings of the Sixth European Conference on Computer systems (EuroSys 2011), pp. 301–314, Salzburg, 10–13 April 2011

3. Copie, A., Fortis, T., Munteanu, V.I., Negru, V.: From cloud governance to iot governance. In: 27th International Conference on Advanced Information Networking and Applications Workshops (WAINA 2013), pp. 1229–1234, Barcelona, 25–28 March 2013

4. DeLoach, D.: Internet of Things: Critical issues around governance for the Internet of Things. http://tinyurl.com/mxnq3ma. Accessed on July 2014

5. European Commission: Report on the public consultation on IoT governance. http://tinyurl.com/mx24d9o. Accessed on August 2014

6. Hardy, G.: Using IT governance and COBIT to deliver value with IT and respond to legal, regulatory and compliance challenges. Inf. Sec. Techn. Report **11**(1), 55–61 (2006)

7. Hassan, M.M., Song, B., Huh, E.: A framework of sensor-cloud integration opportunities and challenges. In: Proceedings of the 3rd International Conference on Ubiquitous Information Management and Communication (ICUIMC 2009), pp. 618–626, Suwon, 15–16 January 2009

8. Lantz, B., Heller, B., McKeown, N.: A network in a laptop: rapid prototyping for software-defined networks. In: Proceedings of the 9th ACM Workshop on Hot Topics in Networks. HotNets 2010, p. 19, Monterey, 20–21 October 2010

9. Lawler, B.: Review of cmmi distilled: a practical introduction to integrated process improvement. ACM SIGSOFT Softw. Eng. Notes **30**(1), 37–38 (2005). Addison Wesley, 2004, paperback. ISBN 0-321-18613-3

10. Nastic, S., Sehic, S., Le, D., Truong, H.L., Dustdar, S.: Provisioning software-defined iot cloud systems. In: 2014 International Conference on Future Internet of Things and Cloud, FiCloud 2014, pp. 288–295, Barcelona, 27–29 August 2014

11. Nef, M.A., Perlepes, L., Karagiorgou, S., Stamoulis, G.I., Kikiras, P.K.: Enabling qos in the internet of things. In: CTRQ 2012, The Fifth International Conference on Communication Theory, Reliability, and Quality of Service, pp. 33–38 (2012)

12. Niemann, M., Miede, A., Johannsen, W., Repp, N., Steinmetz, R.: Structuring SOA governance. IJITBAG **1**(1), 58–75 (2010)

13. Sandrino-Arndt, B.: People, portfolios and processes: the 3p model of it governance. Inf. Sys. Control J. **2**, 1–5 (2008)

14. Soldatos, J., Serrano, M., Hauswirth, M.: Convergence of utility computing with the internet-of-things. In: Sixth International Conference on Innovative Mobile and Internet Services in Ubiquitous Computing (IMIS 2012), pp. 874–879, Palermo, 4–6 July 2012

15. Stuedi, P., Mohomed, I., Terry, D.: Wherestore: Location-based data storage for mobile devices interacting with the cloud. In: Proceedings of the 1st ACM Workshop on Mobile Cloud Computing and Services: Social Networks and Beyond (MCS 2010), pp. 1:1–1:8. ACM, New York (2010)

16. Weber, K., Otto, B., Österle, H.: One size does not fit all-a contingency approach to data governance. J. Data Inf. Q. **1**(1), 4 (2009)

17. Weber, R.H.: Internet of things governance quo vadis? Comput. Law Secur. Rev. **29**(4), 341–347 (2013)

18. Yuriyama, M., Kushida, T.: Sensor-cloud infrastructure - physical sensor management with virtualized sensors on cloud computing. In: The 13th International Conference on Network-Based Information Systems (NBiS 2010), pp. 1–8, Takayama, September 14–16 2010

MoDAS: Methodology and Tool for Model-Driven Adaptable Services

Guadalupe Ortiz(✉), Sonia Peinado, Alfonso García de Prado,
and Juan Boubeta-Puig

School of Engineering, University of Cádiz,
Avda. de la Universidad de Cádiz nº 10, 11519 Puerto Real, Cádiz, Spain
{guadalupe.ortiz,sonia.peinado,alfonso.garciadeprado,
juan.boubeta}@uca.es

Abstract. Context-aware software for mobile and desktop users is an emerging field for software development. Due to the increasing market, most of the industry and scientific proposals in this field focus on solving context-aware adaptation issues for browser-based applications only. However, other applications, such as web services, also require context adaptation. This paper aims at providing a solution for context-aware web services and their desktop or mobile clients. In this regard, we provide a model-driven methodology for developing adaptable web services: from the initial system model, we will identify where context awareness is required and afterwards the main system skeleton code along with the context adaptation code will be automatically generated. Using this methodology, and also the provided tool, developers will be able to easily create well structured and modularized context-adaptable services, where final service code will be completely separate from context-related functionalities through an aspect-oriented implementation.

Keywords: Web service · Context awareness · Model-driven development

1 Introduction

In computing, context can be defined as any information that can be used to characterize the situation of an entity, this being a person, place, or object that is considered relevant to the interaction between a user and an application, including the user and applications themselves [1]. A system is considered context-aware if it uses context to provide relevant information and/or services to the user, where relevance depends on the user's task [2]. In this scope, context-aware software solutions have vastly increased in popularity and are highly demanded, especially by mobile users. We have to bear in mind that mobile devices have acquired big prominence over the last years, and the number of connections to the Internet is sometimes even higher than desktop ones in some countries. The large amount of devices and their continuous use clearly illustrate the importance of access both to desktop and to mobile services. Let us clarify at this point that for simplicity when talking about mobile devices we are referring to those which have less resources (such as mobile phones) and when talking about desktop devices we are referring to devices which have higher resources (as a laptop or

© Springer International Publishing Switzerland 2015
F. Toumani et al. (Eds.): ICSOC 2014, LNCS 8954, pp. 32–43, 2015.
DOI: 10.1007/978-3-319-22885-3_4

a high-quality tablet, even though they are mobile). It is important to mention that, even though context awareness seems to be strongly associated with mobile applications, many users start to demand desktop context-aware applications. Besides, there are also users who have the same application installed on several devices. Thus, both markets —desktop and mobile apps— are relevant when talking about context awareness. In any case, for mobile and desktop users, current approaches mostly focus on solving context-aware issues for browser-based applications only, such as [3] or [4]; web responsive design can be a suitable option for browser-based applications, but what about personalization out of user interfaces?

Concerning services development, developers have mainly focused on services which are designed to be accessible well from desktop computers, well from mobile devices; or they have designed two different services and applications for attending the necessities of these two types of devices. We firmly believe that the better practise would be designing one unique application which automatically adapts to any context requirement. On the other hand, most solutions focus on adaptation on the client-side [5, 6]; this means further computation, resources and larger bandwidth required, which might be a hindrance for mobile devices or mobile Internet users. It might be the case that the mobile device does not have enough resources for context adaptation or that we are slowing down and raising the price of the process due to doing it in the client, rather than in the service side, where resources are expected to be much higher.

In this paper, we provide a context-awareness solution specific for SOAP-based web services. Web services can be invoked from any type of applications, not only browser-based ones and, thanks to their usefulness for distributed systems [7], are popular for their use both from desktop and mobile applications. However, even though there are excellent tools and frameworks for service development, their adaptation to context has not been properly focused on to date (most approaches turned their focus on web adaptation, such as [3]), encountering the problems we mentioned before. Solving these problems is the main aim of this paper: profiting from our previous experience adapting services to mobile devices [8], we propose MoDAS: a methodology and tool[1] for Model-Driven Adaptable Services in which adaptation to context is fulfilled in the service side, no requiring additional applications depending on the device or other context aspects, and reducing the client computational and monetary costs. Concerning technological issues, our methodology allows the developer to easily define services and their adaptation to different context elements in UML. Afterwards a model-driven process is followed procuring the automatic generation of the services skeleton, as well as a set of separate aspect-oriented modules with the complete code for context awareness. This separation will allow us to maintain the main service code completely decoupled from context-related code [9], therefore facilitating context maintenance and evolution according to the web services philosophy. Developers are spared the need of learning an aspect-oriented language thanks to the automatic code generation. The provided tool —an Eclipse plugin—facilitates the methodology

---

[1] The plugin is available for public download at https://neptuno.uca.es/redmine/attachments/download/318/MoDAS.zip; we are working on a help document that will be available soon.

adoption to be used in conjunction with other widely used existing tools for UML-based software modelling and Java-based web services development.

The remainder of the paper is organized as follows: Sect. 2 provides background on technologies and related work. Then, Section 3 describes the context types and methodology proposed in this paper. Afterwards, Sect. 4 explains the tool main features. Evaluation and conclusions are presented in Sects. 5 and 6, respectively.

2   Background

As previously mentioned, in our methodology we will combine model-driven development and aspect-oriented techniques for web services implementation; for this reason, we are going to shortly introduce several concepts related to these technologies. We also discuss the more closely related work in this scope.

2.1   Model-Driven Development

Model-driven development (MDD) aims to promote the role of models, allowing the separation of the final implementation technology from the business logic adopted by the system. Transformations between models enable the automated development of the system from models, reducing implementation costs. Following OMG Model-Driven Architecture proposal, we might consider three main model categories: *Platform-Independent Models* (PIM) representing the system without coupling it to any specific platform or language, *Platform-Specific Models* (PSM) which expresses the system based on a specific platform, technology and programming languages, and finally, Code Layer provides the final application as code. Transformation rules may also be created in order to transform the system PIM into PSMs and PSMs into code automatically [10]. A fourth more abstract level could be considered —*Computation-Independent Model* (CIM)—; however, due to its independence from computation, it is generally not taken into account for computational systems; this is the case for us. In order to mark (stereotype) the models to facilitate the transformations profiles might be used [11].

2.2   Aspect-Oriented Programming

Aspect-Oriented Programming (AOP) arises due to well-known problems detected in Object-Oriented Programming (OOP). One of the early objectives of OOP was the encapsulation and modularity of related data and methods that address common goals. Nevertheless, experience has shown that sometimes it is impossible to model several concerns into a structured decomposition with OOP practices (see [12]). These are called *crosscutting concerns*. AOP allows us to modularize crosscutting concerns by encapsulating them into meaningful independent units called aspects. Afterwards, a method to weave the aspect code with the original one is applied [13].

2.3   Related Work

Due to the relevance of the topic, there is a lot of research focused on finding solutions to properly deal with context awareness. In this section we have conducted an in-depth study on approaches particularly related to our proposal. Context-aware user interface adaptation is very stablished area, but as previously mentioned in this paper we do not focus on the client-side adaptations but on the service side. For further information the reader can see the survey on context-related work published in [14].

Sheng and Benatallah [15] propose ContextUML: a modeling language for context-aware model-driven web services. Several years later they improved their proposal supplying a platform for developing context-aware web services [16]. This platform, named ContextServ and provides an integrated environment where developers can specify and deploy context-aware services as well as generating BPEL code. The main drawback of this proposal is that only BPEL code can be generated for services, and that the adaptation code is merged and tightly coupled to the service one. In our case, any Java-based service can be used in conjunction with the adaptation aspects, which, thanks to their decoupleness from main functionality code, can be reused even with already developed Java services. Follow-ups on the project are focused on BPEL compositions [17], or user personalization [18].

Vale and Hammoudi [19] focus their work on developing context-aware web services. They propose an architecture called CSOA (Context-aware Service Oriented Architecture), which provides business, context and composition views in a more abstract level, as well as platform-specific adaptation and service views; however they do not provide any code generation and their approach only focuses on the abstract models of the system. Monfort and Hammoudi propose [20] two approaches to facilitate service adaptation: the first one based on aspects implementation; the second one on model-driven context. For the first one, they propose ASW (Aspect Service Weaver), a utility to intercept SOAP messages between client and service, adding new behaviours using *Aspect-Oriented Programming* (AOP). In the second one they present a context metamodel to identify the most relevant context entities in mobile applications. Their latest work follows this research line by providing the way to make a parameterized adaptation for services and compositions [21]. For this purpose, they use ontologies and OCL for context description. There are two main differences with our proposal: firstly we only use UML in order to model services and their contexts, providing a more simplified, standardized and easier to understand way of modeling the system for development. Secondly, thanks to the Eclipse plugin provided, our methodology can be integrated de facto in the development process used by many software developers with commonly used development tools and without any learning curve; not obliging the user to change his usual development tools.

Prezerakos et al. [22] propose decoupling the service from context functionalities using a model-driven and aspect-oriented approach modifying ContextUML. There is one main drawback in this approach: the developer have to fully define any context every time he wants to implement it; we provide a set of predefined contexts which can be re-used or modified should it be necessary; therefore saving developing time for quite common context characteristics. Also the interesting work from Ayed et al., concerning a context profile and the initial steps of a model-driven approach for context-aware application was not followed up or validated [23].

Finally, Carton et al. depict a model-driven development and aspect-oriented implementation for generating context-aware mobile applications [24]. Their proposal, based on ThemeUML [25], does not seem to have evolved from their initial stages of development. Besides, this approach focuses on performing client-side adaptation, which we already argued is not a suitable solution for efficient context adaptation.

Please bear in mind that, as previously mentioned, a relevant difference between all these proposals and the one presented in this paper is the fact that we provide an Eclipse plugin which is perfectly compatible with other well-known and standard tools, not only for modeling the system but also for compiling the generated code. The learning curve for Eclipse users is almost null and there is no need at all for the developer to learn AOP, since all the AspectJ code is automatically generated by provided contexts in MoDAS; for new contexts the developer only has to replace a comment line in the aspect code by the adaptation functionality in Java.

3 MoDAS Context Types and Methodology

MoDAS uses different sets of transformation rules depending on the context type. This is why, previous to explaining the methodology (Sect. 3.2), we describe the defined context types (Sect. 3.1).

3.1 Context Types

The variety of contexts to which a web service can be adapted is enormous. Even though there are some very common ones (some of which are mentioned in this paper), of course they always depend on specific needs of the system in question. Our research in this scope led us to propose three different types of context since they carry different procedures to be followed in the model driven process. Many particular contexts can be included in one of these three categories. Hence, the classification we did was based on our lessons learned concerning the development process and consists of the following general contexts types:

- *Reduction Contexts:* contexts in which the information to be sent has to be reduced (for instance, device adaptation).
- *Transformation Contexts:* contexts in which the information has to be transformed (for instance, currency adaptation).
- *Filter Contexts:* contexts in which the information has to be filtered depending on several factors (for instance, location adaptation).

We will use one of these contexts to illustrate the methodology description; due to space limitations we have not included the explanation for the other two types, neither the complete profile defined in MoDAS for several common contexts.

3.2   Methodology Description

The methodology starts at the services' design phase and consists of three main steps:

PIM UML Modeling and Stereotyping. Firstly, the UML platform-independent model has to be designed: it will consist of a UML class diagram including the web services and the types required. In the named model, a web service will be represented by a class stereotyped with «webService». In these classes, the operations will represent the web service operations. Those operations for which the user wants to generate context-aware code will have to be stereotyped in the class model. For example, for transformation contexts, such as currency adaptation (see Fig. 1), the stereotypes to be used are the following:

- Stereotype «*currency*» has to be applied to all methods which are going to return a different value depending on the currency.
- Stereotype «*currency*» will also be used to mark the complex types which are returned by «*currency*» operations.

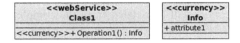

Fig. 1. Platform independent model with currency adaptation

As an alternative to creating the PIM from scratch, we can generate it by importing a WSDL file. This can be done automatically thanks to MoDAS tool (see Sect. 4); alternatively, this can also be done through the use of any other tool available in the market and start using MoDAS from the obtained service classes. Once the WSDL is imported we would proceed to stereotyping the class diagram as just described.

PSM Automatic Generation and Modification. The developed tool will allow us to automatically generate another UML class diagram from a PIM: the platform-specific model. MoDAS will run the transformations depending on the stereotypes applied to the elements in the PIM. Some elements will be automatically stereotyped with «genCode» in the PSM; «genCode» will provide a tagged value in order to identify the stereotyped element. The purpose of using this stereotype is for the user to be able to make changes in the PSM —when necessary— and still be able to recognize these stereotyped elements at code generation. At this point, the user can see the model ready for code generation and introduce additional modifications if necessary. The changes the tool automatically applies to the PIM to obtain the PSM in the case of currency context are (see Fig. 2):

- The class that represents a complex type stereotyped with «*currency*» will include a new method: *convertCurrency*; its input parameters will be the new currency we want to convert the amount to, and the exchange rate.

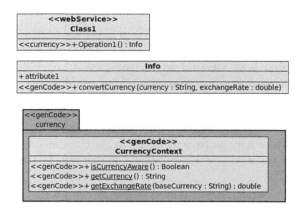

Fig. 2. Platform-specific model with currency adaptation

- The new method *convertCurrency* –automatically generated by MoDAS- will be stereotyped with «*genCode*» to be identified at the code generation stage.
- The «*currency*» stereotype will be deleted from the complex type since the transformation has already been done.

Code Automatic Generation and Completion. Finally, the context-aware code will be generated for the services represented in the PSM. The generated code consists of the Java code providing the service skeleton and the AspectJ aspect-oriented code which implements the context awareness. The developer should complete the generated code with the system service business logic.

Let us explain the aspect code that is generated for an operation with currency adaptation: the aspect declaration is found on line (1). Line (2) specifies the pointcut, that is, the point in the service execution which we are going to intercept. In this case, we are intercepting the execution of the service when Operation 1 in Class 1 is going to be executed. Lines (3–11) implement the advice: the code which we are executing in the point intercepted in the program's execution. As we can see in line (3), it is an around advice, which means that this code will be executed instead of the intercepted operation execution. The advice must return the same class with which the intercepted service operation has been defined and it will have the same parameters too (in this case Info type). Then, in line (4) we allow the intercepted operation's execution to run as usual (proceed) and the resulting information is recorded in a standard result type. In line (5) we check whether currency adaptation needs to take place. If *true*, the currency will be obtained (depending on the context) in line (6); in line (7) the developer has to include the necessary code to obtain the base currency, in line (9) we obtain the exchange rate and finally currency conversion is made in line (10). In line (11) the service operation result is returned after the execution of the context-aware code.

```
(1) public aspect Adapting_Operation1 {
(2)  pointcut PC_Operation1 (String parameter) :
execution (* Class1.Operation1(String)) && args (parameter);
(3)  Info around (Sting parameter) : PC_Operation1 (parameter) {
(4)    Info tmp = proceed(parameter);
(5)  if(CurrencyContext.isCurrencyAware()) {
(6)    String currencyCode = CurrencyContext.getCurrency();
(7)    // TODO: get base currency from tmp
(8)    String baseCurrencyCode = null;
(9)    double exchangeRate = CurrencyContext.getExchangeRate(baseCurrencyCode);
(10)   tmp.convertCurrency(currencyCode, exchangeRate); }
(11)   return tmp;  }  }
```

Let us clarify that whether the developer wants to adapt a web service to a context not defined in our methodology, they may use the stereotype «contextAware», applying it to the method that represents the service operation in the PIM. This way, the aspect skeleton will be generated with a comment replacing lines 5-to-10; later on, the developer will be able to include their own Java-based context-aware code in the mentioned comment. Besides, sometimes the client must send some context information to the service; please see our previous work [8] where we evaluated several alternatives and we decided to use an optional tag in the invocation SOAP message header.

4 MoDAS Tool

MoDAS is a plugin for Eclipse IDE which allows us to automate adaptation to context for the services represented in a UML class diagram. The tool implementation bears in mind future needs for extensions; its kernel is flexible enough so that new contexts can be added without modifying it. In the following paragraphs we will explain the procedures to follow from the initial class diagram to code.

1. **PIM UML Modeling and Stereotyping**
   (a) **Creating the Platform-Independent Model.** There are two alternatives for the creation of the platform-independent model:
      (i) The developer must create a UML class diagram using any Eclipse UML editor. To represent a web service implementation class we will use a UML class which will be later stereotyped —if necessary— in step 2.
      (ii) Using MoDAS or other existing tools, developers can automatically generate the class diagram from a WSDL file. When developers want to run this action with MoDAs they have to choose option *Generate UML class diagram from WSDL* on the contextual menu.
   (b) **Stereotyping the Platform-Independent Model.** MoDAS automatically generates context-aware code from the UML class diagram. Then, developers have to stereotype the UML diagram. In this regard, MoDAS provides the profiles needed for the adaptations explained in Sect. 3. Developers might use their preferred UML editor in Eclipse to stereotype their diagrams.

2. **PSM Automatic Generation and Modification.** Using MoDAS, it is possible to automatically obtain the PSM from the PIM. The advantage of generating this diagram is that the developer may make changes to it before code generation. Another benefit is that the developer has a graphical view of the code to be generated. The obtained PSM will depend on the PIM stereotypes, where transformations explained in Sect. 3 will be applied. For running this action option *Generate UML platform-specific model* has to be chosen on MoDAS contextual menu.

3. **Code Automatic Generation and Completion.** When developers want to run this action they choose *Generate UML context-aware Web Services* on MoDAS contextual menu; then code generation will be executed. The result is a project with the aspects containing context-aware and Java code of the elements in the PSM, as well as all necessary configuration files in the project created for the services.

5   Evaluation

The code generated for services and context was described in the previous sections. In order to evaluate the whole proposal in general and this code in particular we have followed the same procedure as in our previous proposal; please check [8] for details. The case study included a service with 3 operations where 4 adaptations were conducted (*reducing* and *transformation* to *Operation 1*, *filtering* to *Operation 2*, and *transformation* to *Operation 3*). We implemented the system with and without AOP and with adaptation in the client and in the service-side. Results are summarized in the following paragraphs:

- Aspect-Oriented Evaluation. The use of aspect-oriented techniques in the implementation provides better separation of concerns in systems, as well as less coupling and good crosscutting system modularization. Concerning the performance the results showed equivalent times for the aspect and object oriented implementations; in any case, differences between execution rates in the object-oriented implementation and the aspect-oriented one were below 10 percent, which in general can be regarded as insignificant [26].

- Service-Side versus Client-Side Evaluation. Results showed that the execution takes longer when performing the adaptation in the client side (see Table 1). We have also measured the amount of data sent in response to the client invocation. When the adaptation is pursued in the client side the amount of bytes to be sent rises up (see

Table 1. Average response time and message size with service-side and client-side adaptations

Operation	Execution time (ms)		Message size (bytes)	
	Client-side adaptation	Service-side adaptation	Client-side adaptation	Service-side adaptation
Operation 1	12840	12840	14646	1899
Operation 2	13310	877	15966	1529
Operation 3	8409	465	8427	463

Table 1). Therefore, we can conclude that we also save additional client resources, since we are sending less data thanks to developing the adaptation in the service side. This may imply not only saving time and device processing capacity, but also paying less for the data transmitted to the charging company.
- Code Generation Evaluation. Regarding the code generation process, we measured the percentage of context-related generated code, as shown in Table 2. In general, we can conclude that the percentages of code for context-adaptation automatically generated are quite satisfactory.

Table 2. System lines of code and MoDAS automatically generated lines of code

Operation	Total lines of code	Automatically generated lines of code
All	505	292 (57 %)
Operation 1	126	56 (44.4 %)
Operation 2	38	36 (94.7 %)
Operation 3	42	27 (64.28 %)

We also analyzed some additional characteristics of the model-driven process and model-driven generated models and code. The conclusions were, as expected, that (a) modularity and encapsulation increased thanks to the separation of context adaptation from service models; (b) as a consequence of the previous characteristic traceability of the systems is maintained along all the development process (c) simplicity in the transformations, thanks to good modularity and encapsulation and together with the traceability, improved the system maintainability. Finally, MDA provides us with faster and error-free development by generating code rather than handwriting each file, and having the system well structured and modelled since early stages of development.

6 Conclusions

In this paper, we have presented a tool and methodology for model-driven adaptable services: MoDAS. MoDAS allows us to define our context-aware services from initial system models and -through a set of automated transformations- easily obtain skeleton code for services and most code for their context-adaptation.

A set of predefined types of context has been provided with the tool and described in this paper. For these context types complete adaptation code is automatically generated by the tool. The limitation of MoDAS to a predefined set of contexts is alleviated by the readiness of the tool to be easily extended with new required contexts. The fact that the adaptation code and services skeleton are automatically generated from the model-driven process, provides the benefit of avoiding errors and supplying a solid structure for the system. Besides, the aspect-oriented implementation of the context-aware code avoids the coupling between the main system and the context-related code, thus facilitating system evolution and maintenance as well as plug and play of new contexts required by the system: contexts can be removed or added to the system without affecting its main business logic code. Let us remind the reader that MoDAS user does not need to learn anything about aspect-oriented programming or AspectJ. Even more, as already explained service-side adaptation avoids overloading the use of the device resources and communication lines as well as reduces computation time in the client side, with the corresponding benefits for the final user.

Currently, we are considering how to improve MoDAS raising its level of abstraction in regards to the types of context provided and facilitating different behaviour options for the diverse provided context types, as well as more facilities for customized contexts. In our future work, we plan to extend MoDAS also with services which might be dynamically invoked depending on context events as envisioned in [27].

Acknowledgements. G. Ortiz and J. Boubeta-Puig acknowledge the support from FEDER and the Spanish Ministry of Science and Innovation under the National Program for Research, Development and Innovation, project MoD-SOA (TIN2011-27242).

References

1. Dey, A.K.: Understanding and using context. Pers. Ubiquit. Comput. **5**, 4–7 (2001)
2. Abowd, G.D., Dey, A.K.: Towards a better understanding of context and context-awareness. In: Gellersen, H.-W. (ed.) HUC 1999. LNCS, vol. 1707, pp. 304–307. Springer, Heidelberg (1999)
3. Zhang, D.: Web content adaptation for mobile handheld devices. Commun. ACM **50**, 75–79 (2007)
4. Ceri, S., Daniel, F., Matera, M.: Extending WebML for modeling multi-channel context-aware web applications. In: WISE – MMIS 2003 Workshop (Mobile Multi-channel Information Systems), pp. 225–233. IEEE (2003)
5. Alves, V.: Identifying variations in mobile devices. J. Object Technol. **4**, 51–56 (2005)
6. Laakko, T., Hiltunen, T.: Adapting web content to mobile user agents. IEEE Internet Comput. **9**, 46–53 (2005)
7. Alonso, G., Casati, F., Kuno, H., Machiraju, V.: Web services: concepts, architectures, and applications. Springer, Berlin (2004)
8. Ortiz, G., De Prado, A.G.: Improving device-aware web services and their mobile clients through an aspect-oriented, model-driven approach. Inf. Softw. Technol. **52**, 1080–1093 (2010)
9. Bardram, J.E.: The java context awareness framework (JCAF) – a service infrastructure and programming framework for context-aware applications. In: Gellersen, H.-W., Want, R., Schmidt, A. (eds.) PERVASIVE 2005. LNCS, vol. 3468, pp. 98–115. Springer, Heidelberg (2005)
10. Stahl, T., Völter, M., Bettin, J., Haase, A., Helsen, S.: Model-Driven Software Development: Technology, Engineering, Management. Wiley, New York (2006)
11. Aquino, N., Vanderdonckt, J., Valverde, F., Pastor, O.: Using profiles to support model transformations in the model-driven development of user interfaces. In: Lopez Jaquero, V., Montero Simarro, F., Molina Masso, J.P., Vanderdonckt, J. (eds.) Computer-Aided Design of User Interfaces VI, pp. 35–46. Springer, London (2009)
12. Kiczales, G., Hilsdale, E.: Aspect-oriented programming. SIGSOFT Softw. Eng. Notes **26**, 313 (2001)

13. Elrad, T., Aksit, M., Kiczales, G., Lieberherr, K., Ossher, H.: Discussing aspects of AOP. Commun. ACM **44**, 33–38 (2001)
14. García de Prado, A., Ortiz, G.: Context-aware services: a survey on current proposals. In: The Third International Conferences on Advanced Service Computing, Rome, Italy, pp. 104–109 (2011)
15. Sheng, Q.Z., Benatallah, B.: ContextUML: a UML-based modeling language for model-driven development of context-aware web services. In: International Conference on Mobile Business, pp. 206–212 (2005)
16. Sheng, Q.Z., Pohlenz, S., Yu, J., Wong, H.S., Ngu, A.H.H., Maamar, Z.: ContextServ: a platform for rapid and flexible development of context-aware web services. In: International Conference on Software Engineering, pp. 619–622 (2009)
17. Yahyaoui, H., Mourad, A., Almulla, M., Yao, L., Sheng, Q.Z.: A synergy between context-aware policies and AOP to achieve highly adaptable Web services. Serv. Oriented Comput. Appl. **6**, 379–392 (2012)
18. Yu, J., Han, J., Sheng, Q.Z., Gunarso, S.O.: PerCAS: an approach to enabling dynamic and personalized adaptation for context-aware services. In: Liu, C., Ludwig, H., Toumani, F., Yu, Q. (eds.) Service Oriented Computing. LNCS, vol. 7636, pp. 173–190. Springer, Heidelberg (2012)
19. Vale, S., Hammoudi, S.: Model driven development of context-aware service oriented architecture. In: 2008 11th IEEE International Conference on Computational Science and Engineering – Workshops, San Paulo, Brazil, pp. 412–418 (2008)
20. Monfort, V., Hammoudi, S.: Towards adaptable SOA: model driven development, context and aspect. In: Baresi, L., Chi, C.-H., Suzuki, J. (eds.) ICSOC-ServiceWave 2009. LNCS, vol. 5900, pp. 175–189. Springer, Heidelberg (2009)
21. Monfort, V., Hammoudi, S.: When parameterized model driven development supports aspect based SOA. Int. J. E-Bus. Res. **7**, 44–62 (2011)
22. Prezerakos, G.N., Tselikas, N.D., Cortese, G.: Model-driven composition of context-aware web services using contextUML and aspects. In: IEEE International Conference on Web Services (ICWS 2007), Salt Lake City, UT, USA, pp. 320–329 (2007)
23. Ayed, D., Delanote, D., Berbers, Y.: MDD approach for the development of context-aware applications. In: Kokinov, B., Richardson, D.C., Roth-Berghofer, T.R., Vieu, L. (eds.) CONTEXT 2007. LNCS (LNAI), vol. 4635, pp. 15–28. Springer, Heidelberg (2007)
24. Carton, A., Clarke, S., Senart, A., Cahill, V.: Aspect-oriented model-driven development for mobile context-aware computing. Presented at the 1st international workshop on software engineering for pervasive computing applications, systems, and environments, Washington, DC, USA (2007)
25. Carton, A., Driver, C., Jackson, A., Clarke, S.: Model-driven theme/UML. In: Katz, S., Ossher, H., France, R., Jézéquel, J.-M. (eds.) Transactions on Aspect-Oriented Software Development VI. LNCS, vol. 5560, pp. 238–266. Springer, Heidelberg (2009)
26. Garcia, A., Sant'Anna, C., Figueiredo, E., Kulesza, U., Lucena, C., von Staa, A.: Modularizing design patterns with aspects: a quantitative study. Presented at the 4th international conference on aspect-oriented software development, New York, USA (2005)
27. Ortiz, G., Boubeta-Puig, J., García de Prado, A., Medina-Bulo, I.: Towards event-driven context-aware web services. In: Adaptive Web Services for Modular and reusable Software Development: Tactics and Solutions, pp. 148–159. IGI Global (2012). doi:10.4018/978–1–4666–2089–6.ch005

Service Interface Synthesis in Business Networks

Fuguo Wei[✉], Alistair Barros, and Chun Ouyang

Queensland University of Technology, Brisbane, Australia
{f.wei,alistair.barros,c.ouyang}@qut.edu.au

Abstract. We propose a framework to allow the analysis of service interfaces, useful for interoperability in heterogeneous settings such as business networks. The framework supports analysis of large and overloaded operational signatures to derive focal artefacts, namely the underlying business objects of services. A more simplified and comprehensive service interface layer is created based on these, and rendered into semantically normalised interfaces, given an ontology accrued through the framework from service analysis history. This opens up the prospect of supporting capability comparisons across services, and run-time request backtracking and adjustment, as consumers discover new features of a service's operations through corresponding features of similar services. This paper provides a first exposition of the service interface synthesis framework, describing algorithms for business object derivation and service behavioural interface generation. A prototypical implementation and analysis of web services drawn from commercial logistic systems are used to validate the algorithms and identify open challenges and future research directions.

Keywords: Service · Service interface synthesis · Business networks

1 Introduction

Services are becoming the established means of ensuring that companies lower the total cost of ownership of their business processes, focusing on core competencies, and leveraging capabilities through loosely coupled collaborations with partners. However, the degree of data heterogeneity and the rate of evolution of functional capabilities of services are outpacing the conventional means to adapt and interoperate services in diffuse network settings, scaled out to the Internet. Considering, for example, the e-commerce services provided by Amazon are in form of a WSDL interface along with exhaustive free-text usage documentation[1] [1], manual effort is generally needed to comprehend the data types of operations and operational invocation sequences, and to generate adaptors accordingly with invoking applications.

This work is sponsored by Smart Service CRC Australia and in part by ARC Discovery Grant DP140103788.

[1] http://aws.amazon.com/ecommerce-applications/.

F. Toumani et al. (Eds.): ICSOC 2014, LNCS 8954, pp. 44–55, 2015.
DOI: 10.1007/978-3-319-22885-3_5

One reason for the complexity of service interfaces is variants. For example, according to Stollberg and Muth [1], the input message of SAP goods movement Enterprise Service consists of 104 parameters of which only 12 are mandatory for the correct invocation of the service. The other 92 data types and properties support various usage options for different industries, and they can be used to form a large number of variants. This complexity makes it very difficult for consumers to understand and determine which sets of parameters are part of valid service interactions.

Existing adaptation techniques [2] often result in too much reliance on service providers to gain an understanding of the intricate details of service interfaces so that service consumers or third-parties can feasibly build or derive the necessary service adapters. In fact, most service providers, especially legacy ones, do not advertise structural and behavioural interfaces like the ones needed by service adapters but instead advertise simple interface signatures such as WSDL specification [3]. Thus, it incurs significant lead times and costly maintenance to yield service adapters, and their productivity in the context of dynamic service growth on the scale of the Internet remains uncertain.

This paper develops a new and *complementary* strategy to conventional service adaptation, whereby the details of service interfaces and knowledge required to interact with them can be unilaterally synthesised by service consumers. Existing interface synthesise techniques build on type elicitation and data dependencies by automatically analysing service interfaces [4]. We extend the analysis to derive business objects that are manipulated by service operations and relationships between business objects, containment in particular, in order to refactor service operations along modular operations of business objects (i.e., create, read, update, and delete operations). Our approach is to define a service interface synthesis framework, which helps consumers analyse service interfaces through service structural interface analysis and behavioural interface generation. The structural analysis derives business objects and entails a combination of type matching with prior ontological concepts and self-learning through trial/error interactions against exposed service interfaces. The behavioural interface generation generates protocols for each CRUD operation of a business object.

The paper firstly reviews related research work (in Sect. 2). This is followed by elaboration on the key steps of the interface synthesis framework and the detailed insights into its most novel features (in Sect. 3). Section 4 shows the implementation of the framework using FedEx web services and reveals some open issues. Finally, Sect. 5 concludes the paper and outlines the future work.

2   Related Work

Service analysis techniques have been proposed over many years to address challenges of service integration concerning structural and behavioural aspects of interfaces. Different approaches have been proposed including use of semantic ontologies to annotate interfaces to facilitate discovery, use, and composition of services [5]. As an example, Falk et al. [6] adapted automata learning to the problem of service interaction analysis. This proposal usefully combines automated

analysis with semantic ontologies in that it needs semantically annotated interface descriptions showing preconditions and effects as the prerequisite to learn
interaction protocols. These semantically annotated descriptions are usually not
provided by service providers in practice, and the development and maintenance
of semantic ontologies requires significant lead times and adoption. Complementary to semantic techniques, log mining algorithms [7] have been proposed for
matching data type of target services for service requests, which can also be used
at design-time to develop adapters. These incur overheads for aggregating logs
and can suffer from missing information for derivation of association dependencies. Our approach concerns static analysis of service interfaces in order to derive
the structure and behaviour of services, complementary to semantic and mining
approaches.

The first challenge of static service interface analysis is to identify business
entities in operations, noting that operations of especially larger systems can
have more than one entity, with potential overloading arising from bad service
interface design. Identification of business entities is a complex problem requiring an insight into the clustering of different attributes which imply structural
type cohesion of an entity. Proposals for static interface analysis proceed from
assumptions of attribute to entity type associations based on the use of prior
matching techniques (ontology or mining based). The approach of Kumaran
et al. [8] proposes heuristics for understanding basic business entity relationships based on the domination theory of business entities, however the derived
relationship type is strict containment, which leads to a limited understanding of
operation invocation dependencies across services. More advanced proposals for
behavioural interface synthesis has been proposed by [4] based on data dependencies between service operations's input and output parameters, but the study
has not been exposed to overloaded service interfaces such as the aforementioned
examples from enterprise and Internet players. Service composition approaches
have also been used in the context of service adaptation, the common problem
being addressed is "how to automatically generate a new target service protocol
by reusing some existing ones" [9]. However, this technique assumes that the
interfaces of individual services involved in a composition are available.

3   Service Interface Synthesis

3.1   Overview

The framework is comprised of two modules (Fig. 1). The first is the service
interface analysis, which analyses service structural interfaces and discovers the
order to invoke operations of a service. The second module is the service interface
normalisation and it normalises interfaces revealed from similar services.

The service interface analysis module has three components. The *BO data
model derivation* component analyses the input and output parameters of operations on a service and map them to a business object based service data model
(BO data model). Services, in essence, focus on how resource states are addressed
and transferred. This research argues that business objects are the primary

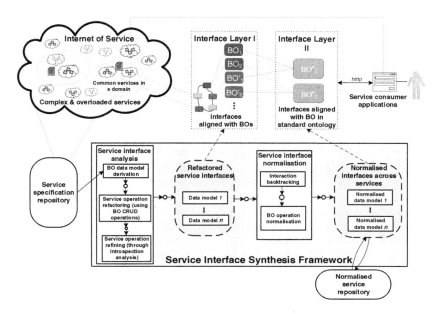

Fig. 1. An overview of the service interface synthesis framework.

resource manipulated by services in the context of global business networks. Therefore, the analysis is carried out based on the notion of business object. As a result of this component, complex interfaces of a service are mapped onto a BO data model, which presents business objects and the relations among them inherent in the service. The *Service operation refactoring* component categorises operations provided by a service according to what each operation does to a business object (i.e., to CREATE, READ, UPDATE or DELETE (CRUD) a business object). In addition, this component also generates the protocols for each CRUD operation of a business object. As an output, these service specific BO CRUD operations form the interface layer 1. In this way, complex and over-loaded service interfaces are encapsulated and simplified. Having these struc-tured interfaces, unique combinations of input parameter sets could be easily derived. The *Service operation refining* component then invokes services using these combinations with sample data values in order to determine the set of valid invocations.

The normalisation module consists of two components. The *Interaction backtracking* is proposed to apply knowledge learnt from other similar service providers and refine the requests from service consumers. The *BO operation normalisation* component normalises the BO data models and CRUD protocols of business objects inherent in services that offer a similar capability. As an output, it produces the second interface layer, where structural interfaces and CRUD protocols of business objects from heterogeneous services are normalised. The normalised interfaces are then stored as references in the *Normalised service repository* for service adaptation.

As the first step of this study, this paper focuses on the first two components of the service interface analysis module.

3.2   BO Data Model Derivation

Definition 1 (Operation and Parameter). Let OP be a set of operations and op any operation in OP. $\mathcal{N}(op)$ specifies the name of op, $\mathcal{I}(op)$ the set of input parameters, and $\mathcal{O}(op)$ the set of output parameters used by op.

Let P be a set of parameters, p any parameter in P, and $P' = P\backslash\{p\}$. $\mathcal{N}(p)$ specifies the name of p, $\gamma(p) \in \{primitive, complex\}$ whether p is of a primitive or a complex type (i.e., an user-defined type), $type(p)$ the type of data (e.g. string, LineItem) carried by p, and $nest(p) \in 2^{P'}$ the set of parameters nested in p where $nest(p) = \varnothing$ if and only if $\gamma(p) = primitive$.

Definition 2 (Business Object). Let BO be a set of business objects, bo any object in BO, and OP a set of operations. $\mathcal{N}(bo)$ specifies the name of bo, $key(bo)$ the unique identifier of bo, $oprt(bo) \in 2^{OP}$ the set of operations applied to bo, and $\mathcal{A}(bo)$ the set of attributes associated with bo. For each attribute $a \in \mathcal{A}(bo)$, $\mathcal{N}(a)$ is the name of a and $type(a)$ is the type of data carried by a. In this research, we propose an abstract business object with four modular operations and they are CREATE, READ, UPDATE, and DELETE (CRUD). The abstract business object is the parent of all business objects. $oprt(bo)$ is further categorised into four group: $C(bo)$, $R(bo)$, $U(bo)$, and $D(bo)$. They are used to represent the set of operations for creating, reading, updating, and deleting a business object respectively.

For each complex input and output parameter p (i.e., $\gamma(p) = complex$) of an operation op on a service s, we check if there is a corresponding business object. To semantically match a parameter with a business object, we assure the existence of an ontology to allow users to designate business objects for a particular context at design time. The business objects are stored in a business object repository $\mathcal{BO}$. At run-time, a complex parameter is checked against the ontology to determine if there is a business object in $\mathcal{BO}$ that semantically matches with the parameter.

In this study, we derive the *containment* relation according to the hierarchical relation between complex parameters. In other words, some objects are contained in others because their corresponding parameters are nested in other parameters. For example, in the FedEx shipping service, PackageLineItem is contained in ShippingOrder because its corresponding parameter is nested in the parameter that represents ShippingOrder. A business object that is contained in another business object is called a weak object. Conversely, one that is not contained in any other business objects is called a strong object.

Definition 3 (Containment). bo is p's corresponding business object, bo' is p''s business object, If $p' \in nest(p)$, bo contains bo'. That is to say, the relation between bo and bo' is containment. We use $\xi \subseteq BO \times BO$ to capture the containment relation between objects, i.e. for any two objects $(bo, bo') \in \xi$, bo contains bo'.

A business object that is contained in another business object is called a weak object. Conversely, one that is not contained in any other business objects is called a strong object. A service s maintains M, which contains a set of strong business objects inherent in s. We can easily get strong objects from ξ.

Definition 4 (Service Data Model). A service s is a tuple (OP, BO, ξ). OP consists of a number of operations provided by s. BO is the set of business objects inherent in s. $\xi \subseteq BO \times BO$ captures the containment relation between objects in BO. ξ is a transitive relation, and (BO, ξ) forms a directed graph.

Based on a given service specification such as a WSDL file, we firstly derive its BO data model. It is straightforward to populate OP, as operations are usually listed in a service WSDL specification. So, the key to derive a BO data model for a service is to extract the business objects and their relations inherent in the service interfaces. We can derive business objects and their relations through Algorithm 1. The algorithm takes an operation op ($op \in OP(s)$), a complex parameter p ($p \in I(op)$ or $p \in O(op)$), a business object bo that contains p's corresponding business object, the set BO that keeps all business objects involved in a service s, the containment relation ξ between these business objects, and the business repository $\mathcal{BO}$ as the inputs. There is actually an overview algorithm which loops through operations of a service and call Algorithm 1. However, due to space limit, the overview algorithm is not presented in this paper, and its details can be found in our report [10]. Algorithm 1 contains three main steps. The first mainly involves the function ONTOLOGYCHECK which takes name ($\mathcal{N}(p)$) and type ($type(p)$) of p, and the business object repository ($\mathcal{BO}$) as the inputs, and returns the matching business object in $\mathcal{BO}$ for p. It will return nothing if there is no match found. The second step records the business object and its containment relation. If there is a business object bo' matching with p, bo' is added to BO, the current operation op is added to $oprt(bo')$ that keeps all operations applied to bo', p's nested parameters $nest(p)$ are converted and added to bo''s attribute list $\mathcal{A}(bo')$. The conversion involves interpreting these nested parameters as attributes of bo' and skipping parameters that should not be attributes. If there is a business object bo containing bo', this relation is recorded. The final step takes every complex parameter p' in $nest(p)$ and calls the algorithm itself to process it. The current bo' is passed in to form containment relation with p''s corresponding business object.

As a result of the above algorithm, structural input and output interfaces of operations on a service are mapped to a BO data model. Figure 2 presents a generic BO data model. In this model, there are four concrete business objects (there could be more in a real example) and they are generated based on $\mathcal{I}(op_1)$ and $\mathcal{O}(op_1)$. p_1, a complex parameter ($type(p_1) = Complex1$), is mapped to BusinessObjectA. Each p in $nest(p_1)$ is then possibly mapped to an attribute of the business object. For instance, $p_2 \in nest(p_1)$ is mapped to a_1 ($a_1 \in \mathcal{A}(BusinessObjectA)$). As p_4 ($p_4 \in nest(p_1)$) is a complex parameter, it implies that its corresponding business object (i.e., BusinessObjectB) is contained in p_1's corresponding business object (i.e., BusinessObjectA). This kind of relation is kept in ξ and it is represented using dashed arrow line in

---

Algorithm 1. IDENTIFYBOANDRELATION

Input: operation op, (complex) parameter p, business object bo, set of objects BO, relations between objects ξ, business object repository $\mathcal{BO}$

   /∗ *Find a matching business object from the repository via ontology check* ∗/
   $bo' = \text{ONTOLOGYCHECK}(\mathcal{N}(p), type(p), \mathcal{BO})$

   /∗ *Record the business object and derive the relation with its parent object* ∗/
   if $bo' \neq \perp$ **then**
      ADDTOSET$(\{bo'\}, BO)$ /∗ *i.e.* $BO = BO \cup \{bo'\}$ ∗/
      ADDTOSET$(\{op\}, oprt(bo'))$
      CONVERTANDADDTOSET$(nest(p), \mathcal{A}(bo'))$
      if $bo \neq \perp$ **then**
         ADDTOSET$(\{(bo, bo')\}, \xi)$
      end if
      /∗ *Recursively call this algorithm for each complex parameter nested in* p ∗/
      for each $p' \in nest(p)$ and $\gamma(p') = complex$ **do**
         $(BO, \xi) = \text{IDENTIFYBOANDRELATION}(op, p', bo', BO, \xi, \mathcal{BO})$
      end for
   end if
   return (BO, ξ)

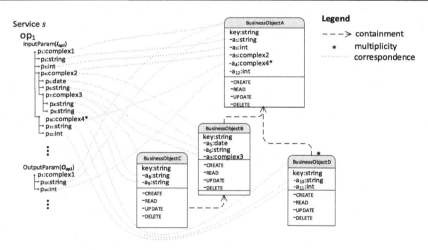

Fig. 2. A generic BO data model.

Fig. 2. Similarly, as $p_{10} \in nest(p_1)$ and it is an array of complex4, BusinessObjectA has a collection of BusinessObjectD and this indicates a one-to-many containment. In Fig. 2, BusinessObjectA is the only strong busines object, i.e., $M(s) = \{BusinessObjectA\}$.

3.3 Service Operation Refactoring

To categorise operations provided by a service into four modular operations of a business object, we propose a mapping mechanism. Based on our analysis, we identified the following mapping rules.

CREATE. If the invocation of an operation requires some input parameters which are actually attributes of *bo* and it returns a value of *key*(*bo*), the operation is for creating a *bo* instance. In other words, an operation that is designed to create a business object usually requires its users to pass in values for some parameters which are attributes of the business object. For instance, to create a shipment order, a create operation often needs to know details of shipper, recipient, and items to be shipped. As a result, the create operation should return a reference (i.e., id) of the shipment order created. There may be multiple operations designed for creating a business object, so we use the set *C*(*bo*) (as defined in Sect. 3.2) to keep them.

READ. If the invocation of an operation requires a reference to a business object (i.e., *key*(*bo*)) and it returns values of parameters that are attributes of the business object, the operation is for reading a *bo* instance. The set (i.e., *R*(*bo*)) to keep READ operations is singleton because there is usually only one operation to read a *bo* instance.

UPDATE. If the invocation of an operation requires some input parameters which are actually attributes of *bo* as well as a reference to a business object (i.e., *key*(*bo*)), the operation is for updating a *bo* instance.

DELETE. If the invocation of an operation requires a reference to a business object (i.e., *key*(*bo*)) and returns nothing related to *bo* but just a status, the operation is for deleting a *bo* instance.

We propose an algorithm that invokes each operation *op* that manipulates a business object *bo* (i.e., *op* ∈ *oprt*(*bo*)) and then analyses the input and output parameters according to the aforementioned mapping rules to determine the category of *op*, i.e. whether *op* is to create, read, update or delete *bo*. As a result, the algorithm groups each *op* and adds it into one of the following sets: *C*(*bo*), *R*(*bo*), *U*(*bo*), and *D*(*bo*). Due to space limit, this algorithm is not presented in this paper, and its details can be found in our report [10]. At this stage, there could be many operations in *C*(*bo*), *U*(*bo*), and *D*(*bo*). For example, to create a shipping order, there are a number of operations and a service consumer needs to follow certain sequence constraints, so the next step is to generate these sequences for each modular operation.

Service behavioural interfaces (some studies call them protocols) describe a set of sequencing constraints and they define legal order of messages. In this study, a service protocol is defined as follows.

Definition 5 (Service Protocol Specification). A service protocol specification is a Petri net (Q, T, F). T is a set of transitions that specify service operations, Q a set of places that specify the pre- and post-conditions of service operations, and $F \subseteq (Q \times T \cup T \times Q)$ a set of flow relations that connect a (pre-)condition to an operation or an operation to a (post-)condition.

As defined in containment in 3.2, a service *s* maintains a set *M* to keep strong objects. For each *bo* ∈ *M*(*s*), we generate protocols for its CRUD operations. For example, the protocol for CREATE operation defines the operations and their invocation order in order to create a business object. Due to page limit, this paper only presents the details of CREATE protocol generation. Algorithm 2 takes a service's BO data model (OP, BO, ξ), and a strong $bo \in M(s)$ as inputs and produces the protocol specification (Q, T, F) for bo's CREATE. This algorithm consists of two main steps. The first is to retrieve all weak objects that are contained in bo and this is achieved by invoking READ operations of these weak objects. Containment relation reveals that, in order to create a strong business object, we firstly need to get its contained objects in place. For example, to create a shipping order in the FedEx shipping service, we firstly need to know who the shipper is and who is going to receive the goods (i.e., recipient) and etc. To get these details, we can call the READ operation of these weak objects. A weak object may further contain other weak objects, and they are indirectly contained in bo. These indirect weak objects need to be read before direct weak objects. Each read operation is mapped to a Petri net module, which is then connected together in sequence as the first part of the CREATE protocol for bo. The second step is to retrieve all operations in $C(bo)$ and identify their sequence through trial/error invocation. Each op is called and the response is analysed. If it is positive, the invocation is in sequence. Otherwise, other operations in $C(bo)$ are called. This process proceeds until either all operations are in order or all operations have been checked. Figure 3 demonstrates an abstract case to depict Algorithm 2.

Figure 3(b) is the protocol specification of the model shown in Fig. 3(a). In this case, $M(s) = \{bo\}$, $C(bo) = \{op_1, op_2, op_3\}$. In Fig. 3(a), as x_8 is at the fourth level (the bottom level), and it is contained in x_3, rd_{x_8} (i.e., the read transition of x_8) should take place before rd_{x_3} as shown in Fig. 3(b). Similarly, other weak objects are read according to their hierarchical level. cr_{op1}, cr_{op2} and cr_{op3} are the transitions of op_1, op_3, op_3 respectively and Fig. 3(b) shows that op_1, op_2, and op_3 should be invoked sequentially to create bo.

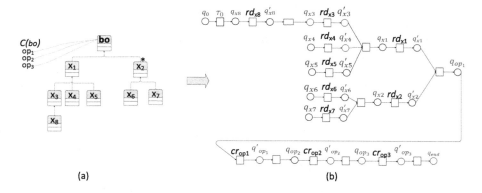

Fig. 3. An abstract demonstration for Algorithm 2.

Algorithm 2. GENERATEPROTOCOLFORCREATEBO

Input: (Service) BO data model (OP, BO, ξ) of s, a strong $bo \in M(s)$

/* Initialise the protocol specification (a Petri net) for creating bo */
$Q := \{q_0\}$
$T := \{\tau_0\}$
$F := \{(q_0, \tau_0)\}$
/* Find all the business objects that directly or indirectly depend on bo */
$X_{bo} = \{x \in BO\backslash\{bo\} \mid (bo, x) \in \xi^+\}$
/* Map each business object and its read operation to a Petri net module */
for each $x \in X_{bo}$ **do**
    $rd_x = $ MAPTOTRANSITION$(op \in R_x)$ /* we assume R_x is a singleton */
    ADDTOSET$(\{q_x, q'_x\}, Q)$
    ADDTOSET$(\{rd_x\}, T)$
    ADDTOSET$(\{(q_x, rd_x), (rd_x, q'_x)\}, F)$
end for
/* Connect the above Petri net modules based on the logic flow of read operations */

CONNECTREADOPERATIONSFORBOS$(bo, X_{bo}, \xi, Q, T, F)$

/* Map each create operation of bo to a transition */
for each $op \in C_{bo}$ **do**
    $cr_{op} = $ MAPTOTRANSITION(op)
    ADDTOSET$(\{cr_{op}\}, T)$
end for
/* Identify the sequence of create operations for bo via trial/error invocation */
$Y := C_{bo}$
while $Y \neq \varnothing$ **do**
    $Z := Y$
    repeat
        select $op \in Z$
        $rsp = $ INVOKEOPERATION$(op, I(op))$
        $Z = Z \setminus \{op\}$
    until $rsp \neq \perp$ /* i.e. until a positive response */
    /* Add this create operation and transition flow to the protocol specification */
    ADDTOSET$(\{q_{op}, q'_{op}\}, Q)$
    ADDTOSET$(\{(q_{op}, cr_{op}), (cr_{op}, q'_{op})\}, F)$
    $Y = C_{bo} \setminus \{op\}$
end while
ADDTOSET$(\{q_{end}\}, Q)$
return (Q, T, F)

4   Implementation and Validation

To validate the service interface synthesis framework, we have developed a prototype that analyses service interfaces and generates business object data models and protocols for CRUD of a business object. This prototype is called service integration accelerator and it implements the algorithms presented in the previous sections.

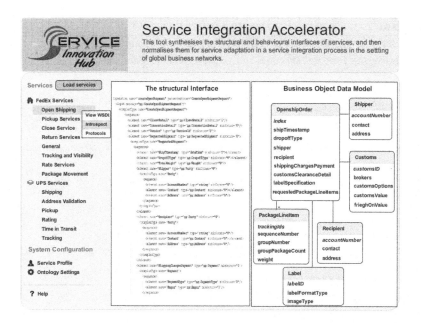

Fig. 4. Interface analysis on the FedEx Open shipping service.

We applied the prototype to the FedEx web services[2]. There were 5 basic services such as the Rate service and the Tracking service, and 7 advanced services such as the Open Shipping, the Pickup and the Return service. The results show that, on average, each service has 11 operations, and 17 business objects. The average number of input parameters and out parameters that an operation has is 123 and 98 respectively. Figure 4 shows a screenshot of the generated data model for the FedEx Open Shipping service[3] and this is the result of applying Algorithm 1 in Sect. 3.2. The business objects derived are OpenshipOrder, PackageLineItem, Payment, Shipper, Recipient, CustomsClearance, and Label. The details of the generated behavioural protocol model are presented in [10]. The validation shows that our approach can derive 70 % of the service behavioural interfaces. We found that, in addition to the containment relationship, there are also other types relationships such as association between service interfaces, and these relations will be studied in future.

5 Conclusion

This paper presented a service interface synthesis framework for addressing the service interoperability challenges in the context of open and diffuse setting of global business networks. Specifically, it described a few key components

---

[2] http://www.fedex.com/us/web-services/.

[3] https://github.com/jzempel/fedex/blob/master/fedex/wsdls/OpenShipService_v5.wsdl.

of the framework, detailing service interface synthesis. We also validated the framework using complex services drawn from the logistic domain. The study demonstrated that the business object based synthesis technique is an effective solution to determining valid invocations made against large, overloaded operations in interfaces inherent with multiple service variants. Future work will focus on improving the service structural interface analysis to include more detailed relations between business objects such as association, strong and weak containment, and we will also examine the relations between data models in the context of RESTful web services. The rules of categorising service operations need to be extended to consider operations that do not fit in CRUD-like operations. Finally, we will extend the framework to support behavioural interface derivation, backtracking and normalisation and the prototypical tool will be openly used and validated on the Internet.

References

1. Stollberg, M., Muth, M.: Efficient business service consumption by customization with variability modelling. J. Syst. Integr. **1**(3), 17–32 (2010)
2. Motahari Nezhad, H.R., Benatallah, B., Martens, A., Curbera, F., Casati, F.: Semi-automated adaptation of service interactions. In: Proceedings of the 16th International Conference on World Wide Web (WWW 2007), pp. 993–1002. ACM, New York, NY, USA (2007)
3. Issarny, V., Bennaceur, A., Bromberg, Y.-D.: Middleware-layer connector synthesis: beyond state of the art in middleware interoperability. In: Bernardo, M., Issarny, V. (eds.) SFM 2011. LNCS, vol. 6659, pp. 217–255. Springer, Heidelberg (2011)
4. Bertolino, A., Inverardi, P., Pelliccione, P., Tivoli, M.: Automatic synthesis of behavior protocols for composable web-services. In: Proceedings of the the 7th Joint Meeting of the European Software Engineering Conference and the ACM SIGSOFT Symposium on the Foundations of Software Engineering, ESEC/FSE 2009, pp. 141–150. ACM, New York, NY, USA (2009)
5. Oberle, D., Barros, A., Kylau, U., Heinzl, S.: A unified description language for human to automated services. Inf. Syst. **38**(1), 155–181 (2013)
6. Howar, F., Jonsson, B., Merten, M., Steffen, B., Cassel, S.: On handling data in automata learning. In: Margaria, T., Steffen, B. (eds.) ISoLA 2010, Part II. LNCS, vol. 6416, pp. 221–235. Springer, Heidelberg (2010)
7. Motahari-Nezhad, H., Saint-Paul, R., Benatallah, B., Casati, F.: Protocol discovery from imperfect service interaction logs. In: IEEE 23rd International Conference on Data Eng. 2007, pp. 1405–1409 (2007)
8. Kumaran, S., Liu, R., Wu, F.Y.: On the Duality of Information-Centric and Activity-Centric Models of Business Processes. In: Bellahsène, Z., Léonard, M. (eds.) CAiSE 2008. LNCS, vol. 5074, pp. 32–47. Springer, Heidelberg (2008)
9. Ragab Hassen, R., Nourine, L., Toumani, F.: Protocol-based web service composition. In: Bouguettaya, A., Krueger, I., Margaria, T. (eds.) ICSOC 2008. LNCS, vol. 5364, pp. 38–53. Springer, Heidelberg (2008)
10. Wei, F., Barros, A.P., Ouyang, C.: Introspective service interface synthesis in business networks. Technical report, Queensland University of Technology (2014)

Virtualizing Communication for Hybrid and Diversity-Aware Collective Adaptive Systems

Philipp Zeppezauer, Ognjen Scekic[✉], Hong-Linh Truong,
and Schahram Dustdar

Distributed Systems Group, Vienna University of Technology, Vienna, Austria
{zeppezauer,oscekic,truong,dustdar}@dsg.tuwien.ac.at

Abstract. Hybrid and Diversity-Aware Collective Adaptive Systems (HDA-CAS) form a broad class of highly distributed systems comprising a number of heterogeneous human-based and machine-based computing (service) units. These units collaborate in ad-hoc formed, dynamically-adaptive collectives. The flexibility of these collectives makes them suitable for processing elaborate tasks, but at the same time, building a system to support diverse communication types in such collectives is challenging. In this paper, we address the fundamental communication challenges for HDA-CAS. We present the design of a middleware for virtualizing communication within and among collectives of diverse types of service units. The middleware is able to handle numerous, intermittently available, human and software-based service units, and manages the notion of collectivity transparently to the programmer. A prototype implementation for validation purpose is also provided.

1 Introduction

Collective Adaptive System (*CAS*) [1] is an umbrella-term denoting distributed systems comprised of multiple autonomous computing/service units with different individual properties, but with the fundamental property of collectiveness. *Collectiveness* implies that the individual units need to communicate and collaborate in order to reach common decisions, or perform tasks jointly. *Adaptiveness* is another basic property of CASs, implying open systems where units may join and leave, and dynamically alter collective compositions or task execution goals. CASs come in a variety of forms. *Hybrid and Diversity-Aware CASs* (*HDA-CAS*s) [2] additionally add the *heterogeneity* to the founding principles. This means that they inherently support communication and collaboration among different types of units, such as software, people and sensors.

Motivation. Let us consider a smart-city *maintenance provider* (*MP*) – a company running a monitoring center covering thousands of sensors and equipment systems geographically dispersed in numerous smart buildings (e.g., Galaxy[1]).

---

[1] Pacific Controls Galaxy. http://www.pacific-galaxy.com/.

© Springer International Publishing Switzerland 2015
F. Toumani et al. (Eds.): ICSOC 2014, LNCS 8954, pp. 56–67, 2015.
DOI: 10.1007/978-3-319-22885-3_6

The MP provides the centralized service of both *predictive* and *corrective* maintenance to its customers (building/equipment owners/tenants). This means that MP control centers actively monitor events originating from various sensors and perform Complex Event Processing on these data flows. If a potential or actual malfunction is detected they dispatch collectives of experts to analyze the situation in detail, and, if necessary, perform the physical maintenance work on the ground. The (human) experts are contracted to work on-demand with the MP, subject to their availability. Since each equipment manufacturer defines different issue analysis and reparation procedures, when equipment from different manufacturers is interconnected in a smart building, detecting the cause of an anomaly event sequence cannot easily be done by following prescribed procedures. The complexity grows further when considered at the scale of a smart city, with thousands of building, each with a unique equipment mix, age, environment, and agreed service-level. Therefore, such a scenario does not lend itself well to a conventional workflow type of orchestration. Rather, collectives of human experts perform loosely-controlled collaboration patterns (Sect. 2) in order to detect and repair the problem in the most efficient way, considering the particular context, and making use of supporting software tools when needed (e.g., for data analysis, communication).

Contribution. In the described motivational scenario the MP needs a platform to communicate with, deploy and orchestrate ad-hoc assembled, dynamic teams of human-based and machine-based service units in order to execute, often unpredictable, complex collaboration patterns. A HDA-CAS, as the one being researched in *SmartSociety* project [3], can support these requirements. In this paper, we present the design of one of the SmartSociety's core components: the *virtualization and communication middleware* – SMARTCOM, providing the communication and virtualization primitives to support heterogeneity, collectivity and adaptiveness. SMARTCOM is actually an independent component usable with a wide number of HDA-CAS platforms. SMARTCOM fulfils the following characteristic of most service buses: (a) *Heterogeneity* – supporting various types of communications channels (protocols) between the platform and service units as well as among service units/collectives, transparently to the HDA-CAS platform user. (b) *Communication* – providing primitives for: message transformation, routing, delivery with configurable options (e.g., retries, expiry, delayed, acknowledged). (c) *Persistence* – message persistence and querying. (d) *Security* – Handling authentication and encryption, as well as preventing message flooding. (e) *Scalability* – ability to handle large number of intermittently available service units.

In addition to these features, the distinguishing novelty of SMARTCOM is its native support for virtualizing collectives: (i) SMARTCOM hides the complexity of communication with a dynamic collective as a whole and passing of instructions from the HDA-CAS execution engine to it, making it a first-class, programmable entity; (ii) Communication with the collective members is transparent to the HDA-CAS, regardless of whether they are human or machine-based, with SMARTCOM interpreting the messages for the human-based service units; (iii) A single human, sensor or software service endpoint can participate in different collectives concurrently, acting as a different service unit with different SLA, delivery and privacy policies. These novel properties make SMARTCOM especially suitable for supporting scenarios such as predictive maintenance. To the best of our knowledge, no other platforms or middleware systems offer the collective virtualization in a similar manner.

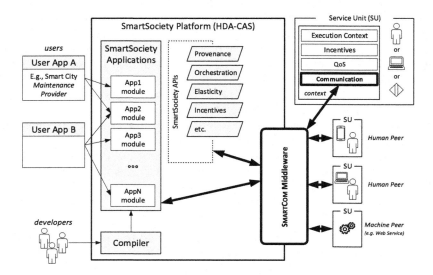

Fig. 1. Operational context for the SMARTCOM middleware. Middleware components are marked with thick lines.

Paper Organization. In the following section we present the operational context of the SMARTCOM middleware. In Sect. 3 we present SMARTCOM's architecture and design choices. In Sect. 4 we describe the implementation and illustrates a realistic use-case. Section 5 presents the related work. Section 6 concludes the paper.

2 Operational Context of Collective Communication

Figure 1 shows the high-level architecture of the SmartSociety platform and presents SMARTCOM's operational context. SmartSociety platform supports 'programming' and execution of hybrid human-computer 'computations'. These computations consist of different general-purpose tasks being submitted to the platform for execution. More precisely, the platform *users* (e.g., a smart-city maintenance provider) submit complex tasks to a *SmartSociety application* running on the platform. The application performs the task by assembling and engaging **collectives** of **service units** to execute the (sub-)tasks collaboratively.

The service unit (SU) is an entity provisioned and utilized through service models (e.g., on-demand and pay-per-use use), as described in [4]. An SU consists of: *(i) Peer* – a human, a machine, or a thing (e.g., a sensor) performing the computation or executing a task; *(ii) Context* – a set of parameters describing the execution context of the particular HDA-CAS application in which the SU is participating. The context parameters can include: execution ID, QoS requirements, performance metrics, associated incentives. To describe the communication with a SU, the context comprises the *Communication Context* part which defines the context-dependent communication and virtualization channels (e.g., using email, SMS). The SU can use different communication channels to interact with SMARTCOM, e.g., a human-based SU can communicate with the platform via email and Twitter interchangeably, receive task descriptions and track progress through a web application, and communicate with other SUs within the collective through a dedicated mobile app. Human-based SUs can make use of software-based SUs in the collective, serving as collaborative and utility tools. For example, a software service like Doodle can be used to agree upon participation times, Dropbox as a common repository for performed tasks, or Splunk for data analytics.

Both humans and machines can drive the task processing—e.g., a software may invoke workflow activities which are performed by human-based service units; or, conversely, human-based service units can orchestrate the execution independently, using software services as data analytics, collaboration and coordination tools. How exactly a task is processed is effectively controlled by the SmartSociety application. As an important design principle of the SmartSociety platform is to achieve 'smartness' by leveraging human intelligence and capabilities whenever possible, the applications try to minimize the use of conventional workflows to describe the task processing, and rely primarily on the use of *collaboration patterns*. A collaboration pattern governs the effort within a collective in a loose manner; rather than over-regulating humans, the collaboration patterns set the limits within which the service units are allowed to self-organize, using familiar collaboration tools and environments.

A collaboration pattern consists of the following elements: (1) *Relationship topology* – specifying different topologies (e.g., independent, tree, ring, sink, random) and relation types formalizing relationships among service units in a collective. The meaning of the relations is application specific, and can be used to express communication/data/command flow. (2) *Collaboration environment* – specifying access to familiar external tools that the service units can use to collaborate among themselves (e.g., Google Docs, Dropbox). When a collective is formed, service units are provided with instructions and appropriate access credentials for the previously set up collaboration environment. (3) *Communication channels* – analogously to the collaboration environment, the pattern should specify access to familiar external tools that the service units can use to communicate among themselves and with SmartSociety Platform. (4) *Elasticity policies* – definitions of metrics to be monitored and algorithms for collective composition and adaptation. (5) *Security and privacy policies* – policies to restrict communication to specific (sub-)collective or to predefined communication channels.

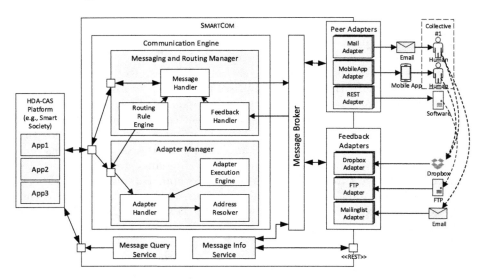

Fig. 2. Simplified architecture of the SMARTCOM middleware.

3   Middleware Design and Architecture

Figure 2 shows the conceptual architecture of the SMARTCOM middleware. The *HDA-CAS Platform* components (e.g., executing application modules) pass the messages intended for collectives to the *Communication Engine* through a public API. The task of the Communication Engine is to effectively virtualize the notions of 'collective' and 'service unit (SU)' for the HDA-CAS platform. This means that the communication with different service units and collectives has to be handled transparently to the HDA-CAS platform, independent of unit's actual type and availability. In the following sections, for brevity, when referring to the communicational aspect of SU's functionality we will use the short term "peer" denoting the computing human/machine element within the SU that is the sender or receiver of information/data; and the term "adapter" denoting the middleware component in charge of handling the communication.

Messaging and Routing. All communication between the peers and the platform is handled asynchronously using normalized messages. A queue-based *Message Broker* is used to decouple the execution of SMARTCOM's components and the communication with peers. SMARTCOM supports unicast as well as multicast messages. Therefore, multiple peers can also be addressed as collectives and the SMARTCOM will take care of sending the message to every single member of the collective.

The *Messaging and Routing Manager* (MRM) is SMARTCOM's principal entry point for HDA-CASs. It consists of the following components: 1. The *Message Handler* takes incoming messages from HDA-CAS and transforms them into an internal representation. If the receiver of the message is a collective, it resolves the current member peers, and their preferred communication channels;

2. The *Routing Rule Engine* then determines the proper route to the peers, invoking the Adapter Manager to instantiate appropriate adapters in order to complete the route, if needed (see below); 3. The *Feedback Handler* waits for feedback messages received through feedback adapters and passes them to the Message Handler. Afterwards they will be handled like normal messages again, and re-routed where needed, e.g., back to the HDA-CAS. A *route* may include different communication channels as delivery start-/endpoints. Figure 3 shows the conceptual overview of SMARTCOM's routing. For each message the route will be determined by the Routing Rule Engine using the pipes-and-filters pattern, determining the route based on the message properties: receiver ID, message type and message subtype, with decreasing priority. Note that there may be multiple routes per message (e.g., a single peer can be contacted using a mobile app, email and SMS concurrently).

Fig. 3. Messages are routed to Peer Adapters (P_a) which forward the messages to the corresponding Peers (P_1 to P_5). Feedback is sent back by human peers, software peers (e.g., Dropbox) and sensors using Feedback Adapters (F_a). The HDA-CAS Platform can also send and receive messages.

Adapters. In order to use a specific communication channel, an associated *adapter* needs to be instantiated. The communication between peers and the adapters is unidirectional — *peer adapters* are used to send messages to the peers; *feedback adapters* are used to receive messages from peers. SMARTCOM originally provides some common peer/feedback adapters (e.g., SMTP/POP, Dropbox, Twitter). In addition, being developed in the context of a research project, it also provides adapters for dedicated SmartSociety Android/Web peer apps. The role of adapters should be considered from the following two perspectives: *(1)* functional; and *(2)* technical.

Functionally, the adapters allow for: *(a)* Hybridity – by enabling different communication channels to and from peers; *(b)* Scalability – by enabling SMARTCOM to cater to the dynamically changing number of peers; *(c)* Extensibility – new types of communication and collaboration channels can easily be added at a later stage transparently to the rest of the HDA-CAS platform. *(d)* Usability – human peers are not forced to use dedicated applications for collaboration, but rather freely communicate and (self-)organize among themselves by relying on familiar third-party tools. *(e)* Load Reduction and Resilience – by requiring that all the feedback goes exclusively and unidirectionally through external tools first, only to be channelled/filtered later through a dedicated feedback adapter, the SMARTCOM is effectively shielded from unwanted traffic load, delegating the initial traffic impact to the infrastructure of the external tools. At the same time, failure of a single adapter will not affect the overall functioning of the middleware.

Technically, the primary role of adapters is to perform the message format transformation. Optional functionalities include: message filtering, aggregation, encryption, acknowledging and delayed delivery. Similarly, the adapters are used to interface SMARTCOM with external software services, allowing the virtualization on third party tools as common software peers. The *Adapter Manager* is the component responsible for managing the adapter lifecycle (i.e., creation, execution and deletion of instances), elastically adjusting the number of active instances from a pool of available adapters. This allows scaling the number of active adapter instances out as needed. This is especially important when dealing with human peers, due to their inherent periodicity, frequent instability and unavailability, as well as for managing a large number of connected devices, such as sensors. The Adapter Manager consists of following subcomponents:

- *Adapter Handler*: managing adapter instance lifecycle. It handles the following adapter types: *(i)* Stateful peer adapters – peer adapters that maintain conversation state (e.g., login information). For each peer a new instance of the adapter will be created; *(ii)* Stateless peer adapters – peer adapters that maintain no state. An instance of an adapter can send messages to multiple peers; *(iii)* Feedback pull adapters – adapters that actively poll software peers for feedback. They are created on demand by applications running on the HDA-CAS platform and will check regularly for feedback on a given communication channel (e.g., check if a file is present on an FTP server); *(iv)* Feedback push adapters – adapters that wait for feedback from peers.
- *Adapter Execution Engine*: executing the active adapters.
- *Address Resolver*: mapping adapter instances with peers' external identifiers (e.g., Skype/Twitter username) in order to initiate the communication.

Feedback messages from peers (e.g., subtask results) or external tools (e.g., Dropbox file added, email received on a mailing list) are consumed by the adapters either by a push notification or by pulling in regular intervals (more details in Sect. 4). Due to space constraints, a detailed description of the described architectural components and their implementation, as well as the full API specification is provided in the supplement materials[2].

Other Functionalities. All sent and received messages as well as internal messages are persisted in a NoSQL database. Stored messages can be queried and analyzed through the *MessageQuery* public API (e.g., to derive metrics or identify conditions for applying incentives). Since messages can be of arbitrary subtype and contain an arbitrary payload, human peers (and their local third-party applications) might not know how to interpret the message. The *MessageInfoService* provides: *(a)* The semantic meaning/description of message type and contents in a human-readable way; *(b)* Dependencies to other messages; *(c)* Timing constraints (e.g., expiry, priority). This is especially useful when supporting complex task acceptance negotiations, where human peers are required to fully understand the message meaning and send back valid answers. Currently, the

---

[2] https://github.com/tuwiendsg/SmartCom/wiki.

service annotates the message field types, provides a natural-language description of the expected fields contents and provides a state-machine description describing the allowed message exchange sequence with respect to dependency and timing constraints. The *MessageInfoService* can also be extended to provide an ontology of message types enabling machine-readable message descriptions, and use of personal software agents searching for tasks and participating in negotiations on behalf of human peers [5].

SMARTCOM supports specifying and observing delivery and privacy policies on message, peer and collective level: *Delivery policies* stipulate how to interpret and react to possible communication exceptions, such as: failed, timed out, unacknowledged or repeated delivery. *Privacy policies* restrict sending or receiving messages or private data to/from other peers, collectives or HDA-CAS applications under different circumstances. Apart from offering predefined policies, SMARTCOM also allows the users to import custom, application- or peer-specific policies. As noted, both types of policies can be specified at different levels. For example, a peer may specify that he can be reached only by peer 'manager' via communication channel 'email', from 9am to 5pm in collective 'Work'. The same person can set to be reachable via 'SMS' any time by all collective members except 'manager' in collective 'Bowling'. Similarly, a HDA-CAS platform application could specify the collective delivery policy stating that when sending instructions to a collective it suffices that the delivery to a single member succeeds to consider the overall delivery successful on the collective level. SMARTCOM takes care of combining and enforcing these policies transparently to the HDA-CAS user in different collective contexts.

Peer authentication is handled externally. Before instantiating the corresponding adapter, SMARTCOM requires the peers to authenticate with the external tool and obtains from the tool the token that is used to authenticate messages from/to the peer. More information is provided in the supplement materials.

4   Implementation and Illustrative Example

SMARTCOM prototype was implemented in the Java programming language and can be used directly by HDA-CAS platforms running on the Java Virtual Machine. Additionally, other platforms can interact with SMARTCOM using the set of provided APIs. The prototype comes with some implemented standard adapters (e.g., Email, Twitter, Dropbox) that can be used to test, evaluate and operate the system. Additional third-party adapters can be loaded as plug-ins and instantiated when needed. SMARTCOM uses MongoDB[3] as a database system for its various subsystems. Depending on the usage of the middleware, either an in-memory or dedicated database instances of MongoDB can be used. To decouple the execution of the HDA-CAS platform and the communication we use Apache ActiveMQ[4] as the message broker. The source code, as well as runnable integration tests showcasing the usage and functioning of the middleware can

---

[3] http://www.mongodb.org.
[4] http://activemq.apache.org.

be found in SMARTCOM's GitHub repository[5]. The various subsystems and the whole system can be built using Maven. The APIs are provided in the `api` module. Additional documentation regarding the design, implementation and usage is provided on the repository's Wiki page.

Based on the motivating scenario presented in Sect. 1 we formulate a concrete use-case to validate the presented design and its fulfilment of the stated requirements: *A predictive maintenance SmartSociety application receives sensor readings from a smart building and performs Complex Event Processing (CEP) on them. If an indication of a potential malfunction is detected, further investigation is required. A collective (COL1) of available human experts is formed[6] and a collaborative pattern imposed (Sect. 2). The application appoints an expert to lead the peer collaboration within the collective and sets up a Dropbox repository for sharing the findings and equipment logs between the SmartSociety application and the collective. Additionally, it provides to the COL1 manager the contact details of the manufacturer of the malfunctioning equipments in case additional consultations are required. Finally, SMARTCOM also provides COL1 peers with mediated access to a data analysis tool (e.g., Splunk[7]).*

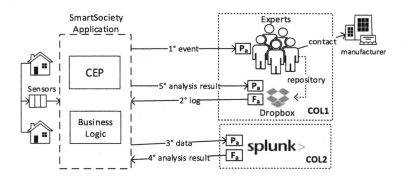

Fig. 4. Supporting predictive maintenance use-case. Collectives of human expert and software service units participate in a joint collaboration to identify the cause of a detected malfunction event.

Figure 4 shows the two collectives participating in this scenario. COL1 containing human expert service units (SUs) and a single software SU — the Dropbox service. Furthermore, each human SU is assigned a dedicated peer adapter (P_a) instance, while for the Dropbox service, both a P_a and a feedback adapter (F_a) instance are executed, in order to support two-way communication with the SmartSociety platform. COL2 contains a single SU that does data analysis. To support two-way communication we introduce again a P_a and a F_a.

The use-case starts by SmartSociety application notifying peers that their participation is needed (Fig. 4, 1°) by sending a message to `MessagingAnd`

---

[5] https://github.com/tuwiendsg/SmartCom.

[6] Selection of collective peers is out of scope of this paper.

[7] www.splunk.com.

RoutingManager which will initialize the routing. Some peers expressed in their profiles the preference for being notified by SMS, others by email. To send an SMS MessagingAndRoutingManager reads the phone number of a peer from its profile and hands it to AdapterManager which instantiates and executes the SMS adapter. PeerAdapter sends the message by using the most cost-efficient mobile operator. Those peers that prefer to be contacted through email will be sent an email using a stateless email adapter through an external mail service. This preference can be set using DeliveryPolicy. The contents of the message are provided by the SmartSociety application. In this case, the message contains the URL pointing to the description of the detected event, Dropbox repository URL and access tokens for sharing the results, the name and contact details of the selected collective manager as well as a natural language description of the required activities and contractual terms. Furthermore, the manager is sent the contact details of the equipment manufacturer's customer service, and the address of another collective – COL2, which in practice contains a single software peer, the Splunk service.

For the sake of simplicity, we assume that expert peers do accept the terms and participate in COL1. The manager freely organizes the collaboration in COL1. At a certain point, human peers need to run an additional data analysis on the log. The collaboration pattern foresees that if a file with predefined filename is deposited in the shared Dropbox repository, the dedicated feedback adapter would pick up that file (2°) and forward it to the COL2 for analysis. The middleware ensures that FeedbackPullAdapter for Dropbox (DropboxFeedbackAdapter) regularly checks if there are new files available (e.g., once a minute). The system will then create and send a message to the Splunk Peer Adapter which contains the location of the file and further information on the analysis (3°). Once Splunk has finished analyzing the data, Splunk will deposit the results file back to the Dropbox repository (4° + 5°) and its FeedbackPushAdapter will push a multicast notification message to the COL1 members (1° again). The COL1 can then continue their work.

5 Related Work

SMARTCOM encompasses different design choices that, taken individually, can be compared with existing solutions. However, to the best of our knowledge, no existing system incorporates a similar set of functionalities as the one SMART-COM offers to support an effective virtualization of communication for dynamic, hybrid human-machine collectives. Popular open-source and proprietary Enterprise Service Buses and Integration Technologies provide the same support and flexibility for custom adapters as SMARTCOM does. On the other hand, many ESBs lack the support of multi-tenancy (e.g., Apache ServiceMix[8] and JBoss-ESB[9]) or do have restrictions on implementing custom adapters (e.g., JBoss-ESB). Others do not support the dynamical enforcement of policies (e.g., WSO2

---

[8] http://servicemix.apache.org.

[9] http://jbossesb.jboss.org/.

ESB[10]) and there is in general no support of the addressing of collectives at all which is one of the key features of SMARTCOM. Furthermore the support of humans interacting with the system is generally not considered.

Service-oriented CASs usually involve addressing peers as Web Services, lacking the ability to communicate with peers using different communication channels, especially external tools. For example, the ALLOW Ensembles project [6] concentrates on the concept of cell ensembles, which consist of cells that have a defined behaviour. They use BPEL4Chor [7] for the communication between cells, which allows communication between web services. The ASCENS project focuses on the peer-to-peer approach where some peers of the system know at least some other peers in the system [8]. They use Pastry [9] and extend it with the SCRIBE protocol [10] to support any- and multi-casts. As previously shown, this behavior differs from ours, in that we do not support anycast, but multicast specifically within collective boundaries. In [11], authors propose a middleware that supports communication among agents on different platforms and programming languages. They use a different runtime for each platform and exchange messages between those runtimes to achieve a cross-platform communication of agents. Compared to our approach it focuses on the peer-to-peer interaction instead of the interaction of the system with peers. The intention of the middleware is to exchange the messages between the runtime systems compared to direct message exchange with peers in our approach. Social Computing platforms like Jabberwocky [12] or TurKit [13] utilize human capabilities to solve problems. However, they rely on existing crowdsourcing platforms and rely on their communication model that does not supporting collectives at all.

6   Conclusions and Future Work

In this paper we presented SMARTCOM – a middleware supporting hybridity in a variety of aspects, including: different computation types (human- vs. machine-based service units), different communication channels, and loose-coupling to promote use of familiar third-party services. This is of high importance in order to create a platform which is able to scale to a potentially high number of service units organized in multiple dynamic collectives. SMARTCOM allows addressing collectives of service units transparently to the HDA-CAS, relieving the HDA-CAS programmer the duty to keep track of current members of a collective, allowing the collective to scale up and down when needed seamlessly. The described design was validated through a prototype implementation.

The focus of our future research will be on modeling the primitives for integrated monitoring and execution of elasticity actions, such as imposing of optimal topologies, dynamical adjustment of collective members, and support for incentive application. Currently, these actions have to be fully specified on the HDA-CAS (SmartSociety) application level, presenting an unnecessary burden for the developers.

---

[10] http://wso2.com/.

Acknowledgment. This work is supported by the EU FP7 SmartSociety project under grant № 600854.

References

1. Anderson, S., Bredeche, N., Eiben, A.E., Kampis, G., van Steen, M.: Adaptive collective systems herding black sheep. In: BookSprints for ICT Research (2013)
2. Giunchiglia, F., Maltese, V., Anderson, S., Miorandi, D.: Towards hybrid and diversity-aware collective adaptive systems. Technical report, Univ. of Trento (2013). http://eprints.biblio.unitn.it/4214/
3. Miorandi, D., Maltese, V., Rovatsos, M., Nijholt, A., Stewart, J. (eds.): Social Collective Intelligence: Combining the Powers of Humans and Machines to Build a Smarter Society. Springer, New York (2014)
4. Truong, H.L., Dustdar, S., Bhattacharya, K.: Conceptualizing and programming hybrid services in the cloud. Int. J. Coop. Inf. Syst. **22**(04), 1341003 (2013)
5. Gal, Y., Kraus, S., Gelfand, M., Khashan, H., Salmon, E.: An adaptive agent for negotiating with people in different cultures. ACM Trans. Intell. Syst. Technol. **3**(1), 8:1–8:24 (2011)
6. Andrikopoulos, V., Bucchiarone, A., Gómez Sáez, S., Karastoyanova, D., Mezzina, C.A.: Towards modeling and execution of collective adaptive systems. In: Lomuscio, A.R., Nepal, S., Patrizi, F., Benatallah, B., Brandić, I. (eds.) ICSOC 2013. LNCS, vol. 8377, pp. 69–81. Springer, Heidelberg (2014)
7. Decker, G., Kopp, O., Leymann, F., Weske, M.: Bpel4chor: extending bpel for modeling choreographies. In: IEEE International Conference on Web Services, ICWS 2007, pp. 296–303 (2007)
8. Mayer, P., Klarl, A., Hennicker, R., Puviani, M., Tiezzi, F., Pugliese, R., Keznikl, J., Bures, T.: The autonomic cloud: a vision of voluntary, peer-2-peer cloud computing. In: 2013 IEEE 7th International Conference on Self-Adaptation and Self-Organizing Systems Workshops (SASOW), pp. 89–94 (2013)
9. Rowstron, A., Druschel, P.: Pastry: scalable, decentralized object location, and routing for large-scale peer-to-peer systems. In: Guerraoui, R. (ed.) Middleware 2001. LNCS, vol. 2218, pp. 329–350. Springer, Heidelberg (2001)
10. Castro, M., Druschel, P., Kermarrec, A.M., Rowstron, A.: Scribe: a large-scale and decentralized application-level multicast infrastructure. IEEE J. Sel. Areas Commun. (JSAC) **20**(8), 1489–1499 (2002)
11. Cabri, G., Domnori, E., Orlandini, D.: Implementing agent interoperability between language-heterogeneous platforms. In: 20th IEEE International Workshop on Enabling Technologies: Infrastructure for Collaborative Enterprises (WETICE), pp. 29–34 (2011)
12. Ahmad, S., Battle, A., Malkani, Z., Kamvar, S.: The jabberwocky programming environment for structured social computing. In: Proceedings of the 24th Annual ACM Symposium on User Interface Software and Technology, UIST 2011, pp. 53–64. ACM (2011)
13. Little, G.: Turkit: Tools for iterative tasks on mechanical turk. In: IEEE Symposium on Visual Languages and Human-Centric Computing, VL/HCC 2009, pp. 252–253 (2009)

Resource Management
in Service-Oriented Computing

BPM Supported Privacy by Design for Cross-Organization Business Processes

Jovan Stevovic[1]([⊠]), Paolo Sottovia[2], Maurizio Marchese[2],
and Giampaolo Armellin[1]

[1] Centro Ricerche GPI, Trento, Italy
{jovan.stevovic,giampaolo.armellin}@cr-gpi.it
[2] Department of Information Engineering and Computer Science,
University of Trento, Trento, Italy
{paolo.sottovia,maurizio.marchese}@unitn.it

Abstract. Satisfying privacy related obligations within IT systems that involve multiple organizations is one of the most important, yet challenging tasks in security engineering. When systems involve multiple actors, resources and computing devices, identifying data flows, actors' liabilities and accesses on data become fundamental requisites for taking appropriate design choices to preserve privacy. To facilitate these tasks, principles such as Privacy by Design have been proposed. However, applying such principles implies rethinking the whole project development lifecycle in order to fulfil at the same time privacy, technical and administrative requirements from early stages of systems design.

This paper reports our work on a project undertaken by the Province of Trento (Italy) on integrating social, health and other assistance services for elders. Within the project, we used business processes to support systems' design and development, from analysis to execution, while at the same time fulfilling privacy related objectives. Specifically, we show how by modelling cross-organization processes and by focusing on involved actors and managed resources, we can provide the necessary tools to involve analysts, designers, project managers and privacy experts during systems' design and support them to satisfy both privacy and technical requirements. The resulting process models are also used for partial automation and integration of involved services.

Keywords: BPM · Privacy by design · Process design · Resource lifecycle analysis

1 Introduction

Services that are offered jointly by multiple organizations typically involve different actors and computing devices that exchange data. Such data sharing can improve services quality and, for example in healthcare, it can enable caregivers to make better decisions. However, this opportunity brings also a higher responsibility for service providers regarding the management of users' data and requires the definition of precise organizations' liabilities and development of proper safeguards to preserve users' privacy.

In fact privacy represents a rising concern and a fundamental requirement in information systems (IS) development. Privacy related requirements are defined by

© Springer International Publishing Switzerland 2015
F. Toumani et al. (Eds.): ICSOC 2014, LNCS 8954, pp. 71–83, 2015.
DOI: 10.1007/978-3-319-22885-3_7

strict and frequently changing regulations [7, 8, 12, 13] and involve both technical (e.g. anonymisation techniques, access control policies) and bureaucratic obligations (e.g. privacy impact assessment definition, privacy guarantor approval). Satisfying such obligations within cross-organization IS that involve both human (administrators, users, operators) and IT resources (devices, databases, services) is extremely challenging.

To facilitate such task, approaches such as Privacy by Design (PbD) [5] provide guidelines on how to proactively consider privacy during the entire software development process: from analysis to execution. PbD deals mainly with suggestions about proper information lifecycle management including controlling who accesses, stores and manages data and for which purposes. Due to its importance, PbD has been also introduced in the proposal of the European General Data Protection Regulation [8] as the mandatory approach for projects that manage privacy sensitive data. However, PbD provides only a set of abstract guidelines and therefore appropriate practical actions need to be undertaken case-by-case within each project to consider its principles within design specifications of IS [10]. In other words PbD needs to be implemented for each project based on its specific setting.

To consider PbD in parallel with other functional and non-functional requirements during IS design and development brings up the need for a new approach that focuses on the overall representation and understanding of the cross-organization processes and the resources that are created and exchanged. Such new approach needs to be able to involve technical (service designers, analysts) and non-technical (privacy experts, lawyers) people in identifying requirements by providing detailed descriptions of business processes and information lifecycle.

This paper reports our work done within a research and development project called Suitcase [23] in which we used Business Process Model and Notation (BPMN 2.0) [17] during the analysis phase to model cross-organization processes and data flows and to tackle from the beginning privacy requirements. To model processes we analysed technical documentation, involved devices, actors and exchanged resources. By highlighting the information lifecycle we helped legal experts in the creation of the Privacy Impact Assessment (PIA) document [25], a fundamental step of PbD approach. The visual representation of BPMN provided to stakeholders the necessary tools to reason and share their understanding about privacy aspects extracted from Italian legislation [12], and enabled a multidisciplinary collaboration during the design and implementation of the IS.

The paper shows practical examples of diagrams and summarizes the content of reports used to describe processes and identified non-functional requirements including privacy issues. It reports also the results of evaluation with lawyers experts in privacy and data protection in healthcare domain. Together with them we validated the project compliance with the privacy laws and defined the Privacy Impact Assessment.

The rest of the paper is organised as follows. Section 2 gives an overview of research effort in related areas. Section 3 presents the use case scenario and a summary of requirements including privacy. The proposed methodology and its application on the use case study scenario are presented in Sect. 4. In Sect. 5 we analyse the validation of the methodology with privacy experts and other stakeholders while in Sect. 6 we provide some final comments on the proposed methodology.

2   Related Work

Privacy has become a crucial requirement in designing and developing IS that manage sensitive data. One of the currently most relevant approaches in considering privacy into IS design is Privacy by Design (PbD) [5]. PbD considers privacy as a first-class requirement during the whole development process of IS and represents an example of value sensitive design [9], which takes human values into account in a well-defined way throughout the design process. PbD has been explicitly included as the reference model into the General Data Protection Regulation proposal [8]. However, applying PbD requires identifying both methodological and technological design choices through IS development [10, 15].

Many researchers have studied the relation between non-functional requirements such as privacy and business processes [3]. For example many works propose techniques to design processes taking into account policies extracted from legislations. The work [16] provides a compliance-by-design methodology for cross-organization processes in the context of business contracts. In [14] the authors propose a technique that generates a compliant business process model starting from a set of given object lifecycle specifications. Works such as [11] annotates business processes with clauses, conditions and security policies that need to be satisfied at each process step. In [21, 22] authors have considered the use of BPM as a tool to achieve compliance at runtime by exploiting BPM understability for non-technical people [4]. They provide a framework for sharing privacy sensitive data that provides transparency about data management aspects.

Our current approach is inspired by the above state of the art work and by our previous experience in [21] and aims at proposing BPMN processes as a tool to support IS design by considering privacy related issues and PbD approach.

Such approach has been already studied with works such as [19] that presents differences between object-oriented and process-oriented modelling and shows how it is possible to transform a meta-model that is based on objects-oriented development approach into a business process based on process-oriented development approach. The work [6] claims that BPM can improve the purpose analysis of IS and understanding of functional requirements while in work [18] processes have been used to map non-functional requirements. In particular, authors propose an extension of BPMN to model operating conditions and constrains. Similarly, in [24] BPMN syntax is extended to model authorizations rules.

Instead we propose using processes as a tool to help involved users understanding privacy related requirements and applying holistically the Privacy by Design principles. We focus on the whole IS development lifecycle and on fulfilling requirements such as the definition of the Privacy Impact Assessment [25].

3   The Suitcase Project Case Study

Suitcase (SUstainable, Integrated and Territorial CAre SErvices) [23] is a project developed by various private and public bodies in Province of Trento (Italy) aiming at providing a set of services to support the ageing phenomena. More specifically, it aims at extending the welfare system by developing a framework in which new services can be provided by private institutions under the supervision of the public administration, which establishes service protocols and rules according to regulations.

The key enabling technology is an IT platform that offers a shared communication infrastructure to create a strong link among service providers, coordinators and elders. The platform enables different uses of data for both service delivery and related research, e.g. patient profiling, data and service interoperability, on-body and environmental sensor networks, usability studies, aesthetics and user centred design, social and ethnographic analysis, business process improvement, privacy [23].

Suitcase project is a perfect example of a complex scenario involving many stakeholders delivering jointly assistance services where privacy issues are relevant. Figure 1 shows the overall project scenario, involved actors and a high-level platform conceptual architecture.

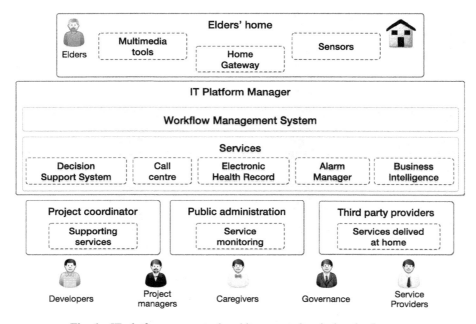

Fig. 1. IT platform conceptual architecture and main involved actors.

3.1   Motivation Scenario

One of the services offered by the platform that served as the motivating scenario of our work is the "gas leak" detection and emergency procedure, executed as follows:

"Sensors that are deployed at elders' homes detect alarms and notify them to the Alarm Manager component within the IT Platform. Each alarm is persisted and forwarded to the Decision Support System, which triggers an emergency procedure (based on the measured gas density). Alarm information is saved also on the Data Warehouse within the Business

Intelligence service for later analytics use. Workflow Manager governs the data exchange and automates both integration aspects and human tasks for alarm management procedure. The procedure is executed step by step by a call centre operator that interacts with the elder, its caregivers, emergency and fire fighters. To execute the procedure, the operator need access to elder's personal information. Generated data is saved on Data Warehouse and accessed later by public administration and project coordinator to monitor service delivery and outcomes. Also Decision Support System needs data to improve its knowledge and make better decisions. Sometimes the data is saved also on the Electronic Health Record system to update elder's health record."

The multiplicity of involved actors and platform components, as well as the specificity of health domain, make the scenario a challenging example in which the sensitivity of the managed data among different systems (and their internal components) is high and is accessed for disparate purposes.

3.2   Privacy and Design Requirements

Data protection regulations [7, 8, 12] and technical guidelines defined specifically for healthcare [13] represent the set of requirements that applies to the considered scenario. They define technical and bureaucratic obligations that need to be satisfied [22], which includes:

- Security requirements: strong identification of all actors accessing data, accountability, encryption of stored data, encryption on data transfers, backup strategy, etc.
- Privacy requirements: data minimization and proportionality of access, data owners' consent for data collection and management, data anonymisation for analytics purposes, Privacy Impact Assessment definition, etc.

To facilitate the application of such complex set of requirements, Privacy by Design principles have been defined giving a set of high-level guidelines on how to consider privacy within IS [5], namely:

1. Proactive not Reactive; Preventative not Remedial
2. Privacy as the Default Setting
3. Privacy Embedded into Design
4. Full Functionality – Positive-Sum, not Zero-Sum
5. End-to-End Security – Full Lifecycle Protection
6. Visibility and Transparency – Keep it Open
7. Respect for User Privacy – Keep it User-Centric.

In summary, these principles suggest considering privacy obligations as one of the fundamental requirements during the whole lifecycle of IS development.

However, in addition to privacy, we need to consider other non-functional requirements concerning service design and integration coming from different stakeholders. These requirements include for example the integration of existing IS and data sources, and compliance with national-wide guidelines for healthcare data management (protocols, representation standards, etc.). In addition, IS need to respect business interests of involved organizations that sometimes imply trade-offs and ad-hoc solutions to satisfy all interests simultaneously.

In summary, to consider all those challenges we need a methodology that goes from analysis to implementation, and that is focused on privacy and at the same time on other requirements related to service design. It needs to involve people having different backgrounds and expertise (which includes also non technical people), and support the sharing of knowledge and interaction among them. In addition, the methodology needs to be independent from software design approaches such as Waterfall, Agile, or others.

Next section describes the methodology we propose and how it has been applied within the "gas leak" scenario to identify privacy issues and complete design phase.

4 Business Process Modelling for a Holistic Requirements Analysis

To tackle the mix of requirements described in the previous section, we tried to identify a methodology (i.e. a set of tools and guidelines) that is pragmatic, simple and immediately applicable to the considered project.

4.1 The Proposed *BPMN 4 PbD* Methodology

The key intuition of our methodology relies on the usage of BPMN 2.0 [17] as the modelling notation for cross-organization processes and managed resources, from analysis to execution. As sketched in Fig. 2, process models serve as the mechanism to involve different stakeholders during project phases and enable them to collect, represent and share the maximum quantity of information. To improve the understanding of the BPMN formalism to a wider range of stakeholders, we complement standard diagrams with textual documentation providing additional detailed description of actors, interactions and exchanged resources.

As shown in Fig. 2, to model the processes and the managed resources we need to involve:

- *Project managers and stakeholders* involved in service design to define the overall business process, business goals and cross-organization interaction and exchanged resources (document, information, etc.). We need to identify all the actors, their roles within the project, the data owners and who have access to data and their needed data (whole or parts, anonymised, aggregated/reports).
- *Technical people* from all involved departments and organisations to identify which systems, and sometimes which components, are involved (depending on how much detailed the process needs to be). They provide also information about data within existing databases (formats and contents), and communication protocols.
- *Privacy experts and lawyers* to identify privacy issues and strategies for service/process design. For example to define what is the communication strategy with users (which papers need to be signed to provide access to data, or how they will interact with the system to do so). They define also the Privacy Impact Assessment document that incudes both technical and administrative considerations and suggestions. Sometimes there is also the need to involve national Privacy

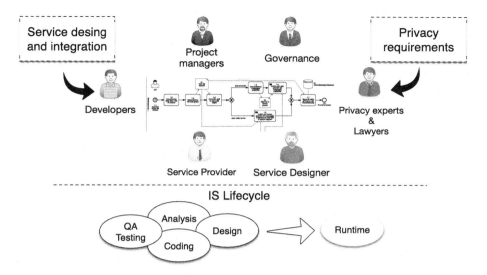

Fig. 2. Process based methodology to involve actors into the platform design and development.

Guarantors for IS validation, especially in case of big projects involving also public institutions.

The defined models describe the overall interactions among actors, technology components and resources involved in the considered scenarios (e.g. "gas leak"). In addition to the process models we provide also a detailed description of data that is exchanged by describing and analysing the content at each step.

4.2 "Gas Leak" Scenario Modelling

We applied the previously described methodology during the analysis of the "gas leak" scenario and produced the BPMN diagram represented in Fig. 3 by using the Signavio BPM editor [20]. Each lane corresponds to each involved system components. Due to large size of the overall diagram, we detail at the top of Fig. 3 a portion of it describing the Workflow Manager component as an example of the details of one process description. In every lane the following entities are analysed:

- **Actors:** all actors accessing the system component within a lane of the diagram are highlighted in the left hand side of the diagram.
- **Tasks:** describing how the system works and how the main steps are performed by components and involved actors.
- **Data:** represented by a document on the diagram, refer to the data managed (accessed, stored or produced) by tasks within a given component.

Before discussing the interactions among these entities, we summarize in the following the identified actors, their roles and related IT components.

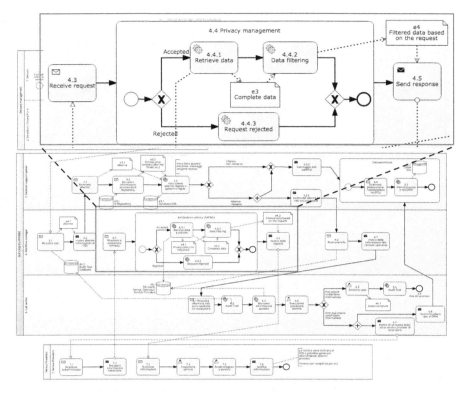

Fig. 3. BPMN diagram representing the "gas leak" management scenario

Identified Actors and Their Roles. The actors involved in the "gas leak" scenario were:

- **IT Platform Manager** is the leading company and co-owner of the information contained within the project. The company is developing and commercializing the platform.
- **Project coordinator** is the public funded body responsible for project management, test-bed definition for first 3 years of the project and co-owner of the information. The collaboration with the IT Platform Manager will end once the project is developed.
- **Public Administration** monitors, regulates and partially funds services delivered by IT Platform Manager and third party service providers.
- **Third party service providers** are cooperatives and other companies providing social assistance and services at elder's home.

Identified Platform Components and Their Roles. The IT Platform is composed of several components that collect and exchange data. In the following we describe briefly each of them.

- **Sensors** detect and forward alarms to the **Alarm Manager** (both within the blue lane) which checks abnormalities, assigns a unique identifier, and sends them to the Suitcase Platform.
- **Workflow Manager** within the Suitcase Platform (orange lane) is the orchestrator between the various systems and users. It executes procedures for managing alarms such as emergency procedures.
- **Decision Support System** is responsible for taking actions based on received alarms. It analyses and interprets alerts and provides an assessment about actions to perform to solve the detected problem.
- **Business Intelligence** stores all data relevant to the computation of performance indicators in anonymised form.
- **Call Centre** processes alarms with the help of trained operators that access to the elders' personal information, health records and other information to assist elders. Sometimes also external organizations are involved.
- **Third-party Service Providers** (yellow lane) deliver socio-health services to elders and have access to their medical records.
- **Audit Trail System** provides advanced logging accordingly to ATNA standard [2], which guarantees security, confidentiality and integrity.

Interaction and Exchanged Data. The highlighted portion shows steps performed within the Workflow Manager and is executed as follows:

4.3: The task receives data requests containing the elders' unique identifier. The request is then verified against access control policies for that requester.

4.4.1: If authorized, personal data is retrieved from the database using the elder unique identifier and generating the event *e3*.

4.4.2: Based on purpose of use of data, the *e3* is filtered eliminating unnecessary data [22]. The outcome is the event *e4*.

4.4.3: In case of access denied, an error is generated and sent to the requester.

4.5: Filtered data is sent to the requester.

The identified resources within the example are:

e3: Contains the requested record including elders personal data.

e4: Filtered *e3* by removing unnecessary data for specified purpose of use.

Both resources are retrieved from the database containing elders' personal information and health records.

Figure 4 summarizes the content of events *e3* and *e4* and shows how data anonymisation has been applied on event content. The anonymisation is based on the principle of purpose of use of data in order to select what is needed by the data requester [22]. In particular Fig. 4 shows an anonymisation for *business intelligence* purpose for which personal information is hashed in order to forbid the user identification.

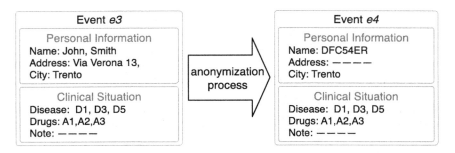

Fig. 4. Examples of events *e3* and *e4* and of the anonymisation process.

4.3   Diagram Description Documentation

In addition to BPMN diagrams we produced a document describing the processes and providing detailed information about identified components and resources. The document has been shared among involved stakeholders to help them understanding the diagrams and making design choices. The document describes:

- **Actors** accessing the system and their purposes of access.
- **Components** and their roles, liabilities and purpose within the entire system.
- **Tasks** and all actions that components execute. Every step is labelled with a unique code to identify the specific step inside the diagram.
- **Data content** managed by each task and each component. It includes also a detailed description of data repositories.

The document describes also already developed techniques and safeguards to protect privacy within the existing integrated systems and components. This description is fundamental to understand if the already developed techniques provide necessary guarantees or if they present bottlenecks or weaknesses.

5   Validation

The outcomes of the modelling activity have been successfully used during the project analysis phase to better identify privacy requirements and, later on, to take appropriate actions during the design phase. The resulting artefacts (i.e. business processes and document describing processes and resources) involved all stakeholders who had different backgrounds and expertise in requirements gathering. Furthermore, a portion of identified processes have been further detailed and translated into an executable process to govern the emergency procedure executed by call centre operators. Executable processes have been defined and executed within the Activiti BPM platform [1], a light-weight Java based engine and process designer.

The undertaken actions can be grouped in two categories: technical design choices and bureaucratic privacy related obligations (e.g. Privacy Impact Assessment).

From the technical point of view, diagrams have been used in the design phase to interact with all involved actors to highlight the privacy and other design issues.

By showing clearly the interactions among various systems, it allowed designers to define access control policies for each generated event and offered service. Access control is managed through credentials and an authorization system (LDAP) authorizes requests. The information exchange between the components is managed by filtering out unnecessary information depending on the purpose of use of information. This helped ensuring that information exchange is compliant with data minimization policy [15], i.e. ensuring that only the necessary information is shared among actors. Information filtering is achieved through application of purpose-based access control policies. This mechanism and policies have been already proved to be an efficient mechanism to preserve privacy and deliver only the necessary information to the right users [22]. Data transmission among independent systems is done over a secure channel and the information is encrypted. The information persisted on various databases within the different components is managed by different database instances which ensure data security. In addition, each database performs an appropriate backup of the information contained to prevent data loss.

In addition to technical design choices, a fundamental achievement is given by legal validation of proposed technology by legal experts in order to verify project compliance with privacy law. The documentation has been analysed by the involved legal experts and lawyers that needed a detailed description of the information flow and the involved actors and their liabilities. Privacy experts analysed the produced documentation and appreciated the ease of understanding of the enriched BPMN diagrams and related documents, which provided detailed descriptions of accesses to data and services. This led to a clearer understanding of the information processing through the system allowing them to give their judgment with respect to their specific competence in the field of law.

In conclusion the proposed *BPMN 4 PbD* methodology helped us applying the PbD principles in terms of prevention of privacy issues starting from the design phase, by considering the complete lifecycle of data, putting privacy in the centre of the business processes and emphasizing the process visibility and transparency. Furthermore, BPM technology enabled us to support the execution of parts of defined processes that is a fundamental aspect in PbD, which indeed focuses on the whole system lifecycle.

6   Conclusions

Privacy law compliance is a challenging and complex goal to achieve while developing IS that manage and share sensitive data. This paper presents our initial work on defining a methodology to consider privacy requirements while developing IS that involve business processes that cross multiple organizations. The key intuition of the proposed methodology is to exploit the advantages of visual representations of BPMN diagrams to provide a tool to involved stakeholders to reason about privacy and other requirements during IS design and development.

The methodology has been validated by modelling cross-organization processes within a project in Province of Trento (Italy) and by considering privacy requirements and policies from Italian legislations. It provided the tools to involve all stakeholders in completing the IS design phase and enabled them to define privacy related safeguards and bureaucratic obligations following Privacy by Design principles.

By interacting with privacy experts and lawyers emerged that the BPM technology can simplify the elicitation of privacy related requirements and IS validation processes. It can improve greatly the collaboration and the sharing of knowledge among stakeholders with different backgrounds. Furthermore the adoption of the same visual representations from the first stages of analysis up to the execution, can ensure that what is designed is also executed at runtime.

As future work we aim at pursuing further our vision toward a methodology that can support a more extensive execution of BPMN diagrams that are used during the first project stages. Although they are currently used for the management of emergency procedures, we are further trying to understand if we can execute them more extensively. Our vision is to reduce the gap between artefacts used during the analysis and execution, and BPMN sounds the most promising approach.

References

1. Activiti BPM Platform. http://www.activiti.org/
2. Audit Trail and Node Autentication (ATNA). http://wiki.ihe.net/index.php?title=Audit_Trail_and_Node_Authentication
3. Barth, A., Mitchell, J.C., Datta, A., Sundaram, S.: Privacy and utility in business processes. CSF **7**, 279–294 (2007)
4. Bellamy, R.K., Erickson, T., Fuller, B., Kellogg, W.A., Rosenbaum, R., Thomas, J.C., Vetting Wolf, T.: Seeing is believing: designing visualizations for managing risk and compliance. IBM Syst. J. **46**(2), 205–218 (2007)
5. Cavoukian, A.: Privacy by Design. Take the Challenge. Information and Privacy Commissioner of Ontario, Canada (2009)
6. de la Vara, J.L., Sánchez, J., Pastor, Ó.: Business process modelling and purpose analysis for requirements analysis of information systems. In: Bellahsène, Z., Léonard, M. (eds.) CAiSE 2008. LNCS, vol. 5074, pp. 213–227. Springer, Heidelberg (2008)
7. European Parliament and Council: Directive 95/46/EC: directive on protection of individuals with regard to the processing of personal data and on the free movement of such data (1995)
8. European Parliament and Council: Proposal for a regulation on the protection of individuals with regard to the processing of personal data and on the free movement of such data (General Data Protection Regulation) (2014)
9. Himma, K.E., Tavani, H.T.: The Handbook of Information and Computer Ethics. Wiley, Hoboken (2008)
10. Hoepman, J.-H.: Privacy design strategies. In: Cuppens-Boulahia, N., Cuppens, F., Jajodia, S., Abou El Kalam, A., Sans, T. (eds.) SEC 2014. IFIP AICT, vol. 428, pp. 446–459. Springer, Heidelberg (2014)
11. Hoffmann, J., Weber, I., Governatori, G.: On compliance checking for clausal constraints in annotated process models. Inf. Syst. Front. **14**(2), 155–177 (2012)
12. Italian Data Protection Authority: Personal Data Protection Code. Legislative Decree no. 196, 30 June 2003
13. Italian Ministry of Innovation and Technology: InFSE: Technical Infrastructure for Electronic Health Record Systems, v. 1.2 Legislative Decree no. 196/2003 (2012)

14. Küster, J.M., Ryndina, K., Gall, H.C.: Generation of business process models for object life cycle compliance. In: Alonso, G., Dadam, P., Rosemann, M. (eds.) BPM 2007. LNCS, vol. 4714, pp. 165–181. Springer, Heidelberg (2007)
15. Le Métayer, D.: Privacy by design: a matter of choice. In: Gutwirth, S., Poullet, Y., De Hert, P. (eds.) Data Protection in a Profiled World, pp. 323–334. Springer, Netherlands (2010)
16. Lu, R., Sadiq, S.K., Governatori, G.: Compliance aware business process design. In: ter Hofstede, A.H.M., Benatallah, B., Paik, H.-Y. (eds.) BPM Workshops 2007. LNCS, vol. 4928, pp. 120–131. Springer, Heidelberg (2008)
17. OMG: Business Process Model and Notation (BPMN) v2.0 specification (2011)
18. Pavlovski, C.J., Zou, J.: Non-functional requirements in business process modeling. In: Asia-Pacific conference on Conceptual Modelling, vol. 79, pp. 103–112. Australian Computer Society (2008)
19. Redding, G., Dumas, M., ter Hofstede, A.H.M., Iordachescu, A.: Reconciling object-oriented and process-oriented approaches to information systems engineering. In: Proceedings of the 3rd International Workshop on Business Process Design (2007)
20. Signavio BPM Editor. http://www.signavio.com/
21. Stevovic, J., Bassi, E., Giori, A., Casati, F., Armellin, G.: Enabling privacy by design in medical records sharing. In: Proceedings of Computers, Privacy and Data Protection (CPDP) Reforming Data Protection: The Global Perspective. Springer, Netherlands (2014)
22. Stevovic, J., Li, J., Motahari-Nezhad, H.R., Casati, F., Armellin, G.: Business process management enabled compliance–aware medical record sharing. Int. J. Bus. Proc. Integr. Manage. **6**(3), 201–223 (2013)
23. Suitcase project. http://www.suitcaseproject.it/
24. Wolter, C., Meinel, C.: An approach to capture authorisation requirements in business processes. Requirements Eng. **15**(4), 359–373 (2010)
25. Wright, D., de Hert, P.: Privacy Impact Assessment, vol. 6. Springer, Heidelberg (2012)

Learning 'Good Quality' Resource Allocations from Historical Data

Renuka Sindhgatta[1,2](✉), Aditya Ghose[2], and Gaargi Banerjee Dasgupta[1]

[1] IBM Research-India, Bangalore, India
{renuka.sr,gdasgupt}@in.ibm.com
[2] University of Wollongong, Wollongong, NSW, Australia
aditya.ghose@uow.edu.au

Abstract. Effective and efficient delivery of services requires tasks to be allocated to appropriate and available set of resources. Much of the research in task allocation, model a system of tasks and resources and determine which tasks should be executed by which resources. These techniques when applied to service systems with human resources, model parameters that can be explicitly identified, such as worker efficiency, worker capability based on skills and expertise, authority derived from organizational positions and so on. However, in real-life workers have complex behaviors with varying efficiencies that are either unknown or are increasingly complex to model. Hence, resource allocation models that equate human performance to device or machine performance could provide inaccurate results. In this paper we use data from process execution logs to identify resource allocations that have resulted in an expected service quality, to guide future resource allocations. We evaluate data for a service system with 40 human workers for a period of 8 months. We build a learning model using Support Vector Machine (SVM), that predicts the quality of service for specific allocation of tasks to workers. The SVM based classifier is able to predict service quality with 80 % accuracy. Further, a latent discriminant classifier, uses the number of tasks pending in a worker's queue as a key predictor, to predict the likelihood of allocating a new incoming request to the worker. A simulation model that incorporates the dispatching policy based on worker's pending tasks shows an improved service quality and utilization of service workers.

Keywords: Resource allocation · Classification · Simulation model

1 Introduction

Service System as defined by Sphorer [11] is an important unit of analysis in support of understanding operations of an organization. A Service System (SS) comprises of resources (that include people, organizations, shared information, technology) and their interactions that are driven by a process to create a suitable outcome to the customer. In SS, the participants have to collaborate together to provide right outcome(s) effectively to the customer. In [15], the authors

© Springer International Publishing Switzerland 2015
F. Toumani et al. (Eds.): ICSOC 2014, LNCS 8954, pp. 84–95, 2015.
DOI: 10.1007/978-3-319-22885-3_8

argue the need for optimal allocation of resources in SS. Resources in SS are predominantly human resources and referred to as Service Workers (SW). Unlike machines or equipment, behavior and efficiency of human resources varies. In [1], the authors identify common pitfalls associated with building simulation models that includes incorrect modeling of human resources. Incorrect representation or modeling of human resources and simulation of business processes causes models to provide misleading outcome measures. Outcome measures refer to the average utilization of resources, average throughput or number of requests completed periodically, service quality that includes completing work within a specified target time.

There are several complexities in modeling human resources. Resources in a team have different efficiencies although they may have similar skills and competencies. Efficiency of a single SW is not constant and varies with the work allocated to the SW [13,20]. In this paper, we use historical task allocation data, stored in process aware information systems (PAIS) as event logs or process execution logs. Allocations that yield 'good' and 'bad' quality are identified. We use this data to build a learning based model that is able to predict allocations of tasks to resources resulting in 'good' quality. Our objective is to use historical allocation that inherently considers SW behavior to guide future allocations. The categorization of an outcome as 'good' or 'bad' quality, is generic and can be applied in the context of any SS and outcome measure.

The outline of this paper is as follows: We motivate relevance of our work with observations from a real-life SS and state our contributions in Sect. 2. Next, we present key concepts and discuss our data collection i.e. the data we used for our analysis, in Sect. 3. Section 4, presents our learning models to predict outcome of allocating tasks to resources and predicting the resources to allocate new tasks. In Sect. 5, we build a simulation model to evaluate the improvements possible when allocation of tasks to resource considers their individual performance or behavior. We discuss validity of our results in Sect. 6 and related work in Sect. 7. Section 8 concludes the paper.

2   Motivation

We analyzed the data for a real-life service system (SS) that tracks critical IT system failures (incidents) of different customers. A team of 40 service workers (SW) belonging to the service provider organization, ensure that incidents or service requests from customers are immediately responded. Customers represent different organizations, the service provider supports. As shown in Fig. 1, the service requests from customers are placed in a queue. A human dispatcher monitors the queue and assigns requests to a suitable SW. A SW could be assigned multiple requests and the number of requests currently being handled by a worker represents worker queue. The key measure of service quality is the *time taken to respond to the customer*. The total time to respond - the time elapsed between the creation of the request and response from a service worker to the customer is a measure of service quality. As these are critical system failures, the time to respond should be lower than a set time or the *service target time* agreed by the customer and the provider. If the time to respond exceeds the service target time, the request is said to have missed or breached the service quality. After responding to the customer, the SW identifies the problem, identifies the team(s) that should work towards solving the issue and disengages from the request. While there are several other performance indicators indicating service quality, in the context of the SS under consideration, time to respond within the service target time is used as a measure of service quality. In this SS, all requests require the same skill (e.g. operating system maintenance) and expertise level (e.g. high expertise).

We make the following observations on the data analyzed for the SS.

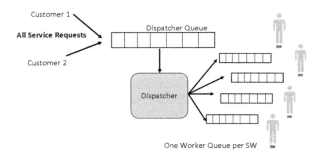

Fig. 1. Application maintenance process

Service Workers with Similar Measurable Skills or Capabilities Have Different Response Times. In the SS under study, all the SWs are of the same organizational role (e.g. Subject Matter Experts) and have same expertise and skill level (e.g. High). However, we observe different means of response time for the workers. Figure 2 shows the box plot with median, upper and lower quartile response times for different service workers (depicting the variance in their means). A one-way ANOVA test [8] for analysis of variance of response time means across different service workers yields a statistically significant difference ($p < 0.01$). Hence, we conclude that service workers with similar capabilities or skills have different efficiencies.

Queue of Pending Requests, Impacting Service Quality, Is Different for Each Service Worker. The worker queue length or the number of pending requests, of SW, impacts the time to respond to a new incoming service request and hence in meeting or breaching the service quality. Figure 2 shows the box plot of queue length of SW, measured for an incoming request that has met or breached service quality. The Work queue lengths have been shown for only 10 of the 40 service workers due to space constraints. A factorial ANOVA indicates a variance in the mean queue length across two factors - requests that meet or miss target response time and service workers ($p < 0.05$). i.e. the mean work queue length varies for each service worker and is lower when arriving requests meet target response time.

These observations suggest that allocation of tasks to resources considering them to have similar efficiency and behavior will result in inaccurate or misleading results. In this paper, we will investigate if a learning based model can be used to guide allocation of tasks to resources. Through this work, we aim to provide the following technical contributions:

- build a learning based classification model to predict the service quality when tasks are allocated to specific resources.
- build prediction model to guide allocation of tasks to a resource.
- build a simulation model to evaluate the performance of a service system that allocates tasks to resources taking into consideration efficiencies of individual resources.

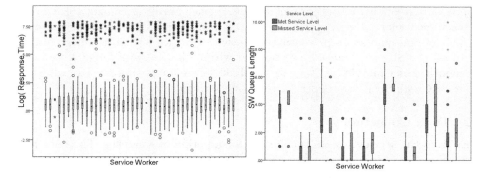

Fig. 2. Box plot indicating response time of workers and queue length at which requests meet of breach service levels

3   Background

In this section, we present concepts relevant to the service system and data collected for the system under consideration.

3.1   Service System Concepts

We define key concepts underpinning the service system below:

Service Request or Incident. Service requests (SR) or incident constitute inputs to the service system and are handled by service workers. Typically, an incident is characterized by priority. In the system we evaluate, all the request are of high priority.

Work Arrivals. The arrival pattern of service requests is captured for finite set of time intervals T (e.g. hours of a week). That is, the arrival rate distribution is estimated for each of the time intervals in T, where the arrival rate is assumed to follow a stationary Poisson arrival process within these time intervals (one hour time periods) [4,7].

Response Time. Response time refers to the time taken by a service worker to respond to a customer. This is the time interval between a customer creating request to the time a service worker responds to the customer of its receipt.

Service Time. Service time refers to the time a service worker spends on addressing the request. In the service system being studied, it is the time spent by SW in identifying suitable team(s) to handover the request. Hence, service time is the time interval, the request remains with the service worker.

Worker Queue Length. A service worker handles multiple service requests at a time, and the request remains in the worker queue till the SW hands it over to another person or team. The number of requests that remain with the worker, at any point in time, is the worker queue length.

Service Target Time and Service Level Agreement. Service levels are a measure of quality or outcome of service. Service Level Agreement (SLA), for each customer $\gamma_i = (\alpha_i, r_i), \alpha_i, r_i \subset \mathbb{R}$, is a map from each customer i to a pair of real numbers representing the service time target and the percentage of all the SRs that must be responded within this *service target time* in a month. For example, $\gamma_{Customer_1} = <1, 95>$, denotes that 95 % of all SRs from $Customer_1$ in a month be responded within 1 h.

3.2   Data Collection

Data from the service system is collected for a period of 8 months. The data for each request is obtained from a process aware ticketing system that contains the time a customer opened the SR, the worker allocated to the SR, the time taken to respond and the service time of the SR. Given the data, we collate following features for our prediction model measured at hourly time intervals (an example shown in Table 1):

- Hour of the day
- Number of requests arriving into the system
- Number of incoming requests assigned to each SW
- Work Queue Length of each SW (number of pending requests with SW)

Hence, for each hour, we have 82 features extracted for the model - 40 features represent the number of incoming requests assigned to SW, 40 features depict the work queue length of each SW. In addition, we have total number of requests arriving in the system (total number of incoming requests).

4   Experimental Analysis

In this section, we present the models that are built to validate our hypothesis on the suitability of using historical data to predict valid or suitable resource allocations. We use IBM SPSS Modeler 14.1 [10] to build our prediction models.

Table 1. Example set of features for learning model

Hour of day	Number of incoming requests	AgentA allocated	AgentA queue length	AgentB allocated	AgentB queue length	..	AgentC allocated	AgentC queue length
0	2	0	4	1	2	..	0	1
1	1	0	3	0	1	..	1	0

4.1 Predicting Service Quality Using Support Vector Machines (SVM)

The objective is to build a prediction model that is capable of identifying if allocation of requests to the chosen set service workers will result in meeting or missing the service quality. To train the prediction model, we use input features and define a boolean flag *Outcome*, valued 'GOOD' if all requests have met the target response time and valued 'BAD' if one or more request missed the target response time. Hence *Outcome* constitutes target feature of the prediction model, for the conditions of input volume of requests, worker queue lengths and worker assignment.

We use support vector machines (SVM) to classify and label the *Outcome* parameter. Logistic regression, Naive Bayes and SVM classifiers are very popular and widely used classification techniques. In [14], it is shown that prediction accuracy of classification techniques vary with the number of features defined in the model and the size of the training set. We carried out preliminary analysis using naive Bayes, logistic regression and SVM classifier. SVM was found to be more robust to the random samples of training and testing data sets and resulted in higher prediction accuracy.

The prediction accuracy of the model is measured by the percentage of unseen instances it correctly classifies. A good classifier must fit the training data well, in addition to accurately classifying the data it has never seen before (test data). We partition the data into training and test samples. The prediction accuracy of the training sample is 80.43 % and that of the testing sample is 78.9 %. Figure 3 shows the prediction accuracy and the confidence probability of the model for the test sample. The accuracy of prediction improves with increase in confidence probability, for the testing samples. It can be seen that, at higher confidence intervals (> 0.87), the accuracy of correct predictions is 90 %. The histogram shows the frequency distribution of confidence probability assigned by the model. A large number of predictions have higher confidence probability. Hence, historical samples can be used to learn and predict the quality outcome of requests assigned to service workers.

4.2 Predicting Allocation of Request to Service Worker

In the previous section, the objective was to categorize allocation of tasks to SWs as good or bad, considering their queue lengths and number of requests

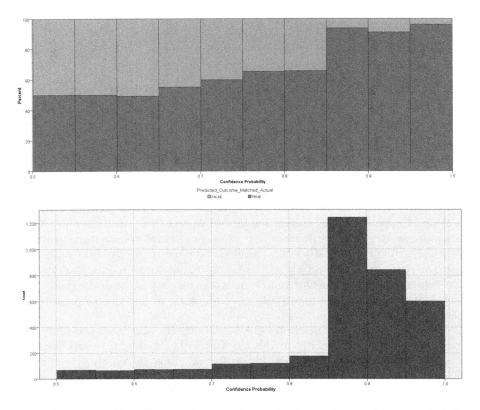

Fig. 3. Percentage of predictions that match actual outcome Vs. confidence probability and frequency distribution of confidence probability

arriving in the system. In a scenario, where a dispatcher allocates one task at a time to a SW, a model to assist the dispatcher in predicting if a request should be allocated to a SW or not, would be useful. Here, our training sample contains all allocations that have resulted in a good service quality. We build a classification model for each SW. The input to model is the number of requests and the queue length of all SW including the SW for which the model is built. A *SWAllocate* flag is the target feature which is set to 'TRUE' if a request can be allocated to the SW and 'FALSE' otherwise. In the data under consideration, for a large number of observations, a SW does not get a request allocated as the number of requests arriving in the system may be low and there are many SW. For most SW, *SWAllocate* is set to FALSE for 90 % of the observations. Hence, if we assign FALSE to all SWAllocate, it would still lead to 90 % prediction accuracy. Therefore, we evaluate a learning model that can predict TRUE allocations accurately. Logistic regression and SVM fail to make accurate predictions of SWAllocate. Linear Discriminant Analysis (LDA) based classifier [19], predicts resource allocations to a SW with 65 %–80 % accuracy. Figure 4 shows the accuracy of predictions for the SWAllocate with 'TRUE' values for one SW. As shown, logistic regression fails to predict them with 0 % accuracy at 99 % confidence probability. We also realize that the training data needs to contain more observations where allocation of request is made to a SW. However, with the lack of large training data, LDA can be used to guide allocations to a SW when the confidence probability is high, as indicated in Figure Percentageregression. This prediction model is build for each SW.

The dominant predictors or coefficients of LDA for predicting the allocation to a SW are the number of requests arriving into the system and the work queue length of SW for whom the allocation model is built. We have seen that SW work queue length, that impacts the service target time of an incoming request, varies for each SW (Sect. 3). In the next section we build a simulation model to compare results of a model that incorporates the SW work queue length during allocation of request to SW.

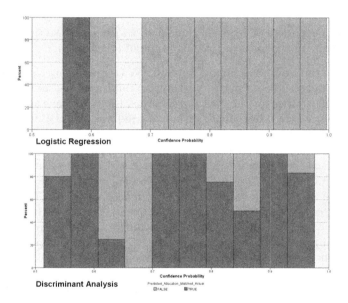

Fig. 4. Percentage of predictions that match actual allocation Vs. confidence probability for a single SW having resource allocation set to TRUE

5   Simulation Based Evaluation of SLA

In this section, we describe the simulation set up that mimics the service system being evaluated. The inputs to the model are the following:

- A finite set of time intervals for arriving work, denoted by T, containing one element for each hour of week. Hence, $|T| = 168$. Each time interval is one hour long. Work arrivals rates are defined for each time interval.

– Maximum Work Queue Length $Qmax_i$ for SW $i \in \{1, 2 \ldots n\}$: The work
queue length is derived from the data for worker i (SW_i). It is the queue
length of SW_i below which the worker meets target response time.
– Service Time: The mean service time for which a request remains with the
SW till it is handed over.
– Response Time : The response time for a request depends on the $Qmax_i$ for
SW_i. The response time is less than service target time when the worker queue
length is lower than $Qmax_i$ and greater than service target time otherwise.

We build the service system model using AnyLogic simulation software [5, 18]
which supports discrete event simulation technique. We simulate up to 40 weeks
of simulation runs. Measurements are taken at end of each week. No measurements are recorded during the warm up period of first four weeks. For our experiments, we consider request arrivals follow a Poisson model where the inter-arrival
times follow an exponential distribution. In steady state the parameters that are
measured include:

– SLA or the percentage of requests that meet target response time.
– Resource utilization (captures the busy-time of a resource)

We evaluate the simulation model with 10 SW (representing a single working
shift). We simulate three scenarios to compare and contrast our results. The
dispatching policy varies for these three scenarios. First, we have a model (Naive
Dispatch Model) where a dispatcher dispatches request to a SW with minimum
work queue length. This model is naive as it does not consider the $Qmax_i$ of
SW_i when allocating the request to worker.

Second, we have a model considers all service workers to behave in a similar
manner i.e. the $Qmax_i$ is set to an average value, for all service workers and
is derived from the data ($\forall i : Qmax_i = Qmax_{mean} = 3$). The dispatcher
dispatches the request to first SW with a work queue length less than $Qmax_{mean}$
(Common Behavior Model). The Common Behavior Model represents scenario
where workers having same experience of skill are consider similar.

Last, we run the simulation model considering each SW_i to behave different
i.e. $Qmax_i$ for each SW_i is set. The dispatcher dispatches the request to the
first SW_i with a work queue length less than $Qmax_i$ (Advanced Model). The
advanced model reflects our learning model where the dispatcher uses the worker
queue length derived from past allocations, to decide current allocation. Based on
the data, we observe and set the values as: $2 \leq Qmax_i \leq 4$ and $Qmax_{mean} = 3$.
In latter two models, if there is no SW_i with a work queue length lower than
the $Qmax_i$, then the request is routed to the SW with the minimum work queue
length.

Table 2 shows the results obtained for the three dispatch models. The results
indicate that the Advanced dispatch model outperforms the other two models
in meeting the service quality. It is interesting to note that the naive model
performs better than the common behavior model as the naive model tries to
dispatch the request to the SW with the minimum work queue while the common
behavior model assumes that workers with a work queue length lower than the

threshold will be efficient. This assumption leads to sub-optimal allocation of requests and hence the percentage SLA attained is much lower.

As discussed, our simulation model uses the parameter $Qmax_i$ to distinguish SW behavior and allocate request to compare and contrast the service quality with models that accommodate service worker behavior.

Table 2. Percent SLA and Percent Utilization for different dispatching models.

Dispatch Model	Percent SLA		Percent SW Utilization	
	Mean SLA	95 % Conf. Interval	Mean Utilization	95 % Conf. Interval
Naive Dispatch	86.84	(85.2,87.86)	64.4	(64.36,64.44)
Common Behavior	78.9	(78.08,79.72)	66.2	(66.15,66.24)
Advanced Dispatch	92.9	(91.78,94.02)	59.3	(57.71,60.89)

6   Threats to Validity

In this section, we identify the limitation of our study with respect of *construct validity, internal validity* and *external validity*.

Construct Validity. denotes that the variables are measured correctly. All the features or parameters used in the learning model been evaluated and used in earlier studies on dispatching, allocation and planning. Our study does not include additional parameters such as expertise, priority as they were not relevant to the system under study. We plan to extend our study to a service system where such parameters play a significant role.

Internal Validity. is established for a study if it is free from systematic errors and biases. During the measurement interval of 8 months, issues that can affect internal validity such as mortality (that is, subjects withdrawing from a study during data collection) and maturation (that is, subjects changing their characteristics during the study outside the parameters of the study) did not arise. Thus, we believe the extent of this threat to validity is limited.

External Validity. concerns the generalization of the results from our study. While insights can be drawn from our study, we do not claim that these results can be generalized in all instances. However, these results serve as the basis of using data driven approach for evaluating allocation of requests to workers effectively, leading to higher service quality.

7   Related Work

The problem of allocation of tasks to resources has been studied for some time now and there is a good body of literature dedicated to various aspects like routing work to teams and dispatching tasks to resources. In [9], the authors use mixed integer programming (MIP) and a heuristic algorithm to allocate tasks to the resources based on their workload and skill, with an objective of meeting service quality. There are similar such scheduling and skill based routing of calls been addressed in the call center domain [12]. However, in all these scenarios, the inherent variations in human behavior and efficiency is not considered. Simulation models to evaluate the skill requirements of the team for a SS in the context work types discuss the improvement in service time of a SW over time through on the job learning [2,6]. Service workers of a skill and expertise level are assumed to have similar characteristics and learning factors. Given the complexity characteristics of human resources, in our work, we learn the allocation of tasks that would lead to favorable outcome from historical data and use it to guide future allocations.

Learning based predictive models, like ours, has been used for routing or dispatching work in SS. In [3], tickets or service requests are classified and routed to the right group using historical data. An approach to route the requests to multiple teams for resolving an IT problem ticket or incident, is addressed by [17]. Historical data is used to mine the sequence of groups or teams involved to further build a markov model that generates ticket transfer recommendations for an new arriving ticket. These studies focus on identifying suitable teams or groups and do not evaluate operational efficiencies of teams or workers.

In [16], the authors present an approach that uses historical data and illustrate the variance in operational productivity of workers for requests with different priorities and complexities. The variances in efficiency of workers is used to define policies for dispatching and optimally staffing teams. Our approach further demonstrates that data-driven techniques can be used to implicitly learn the efficiency of service workers and help in driving better allocation of tasks.

8 Conclusion

In this paper, we have evaluated the use of learning based model to predict and assist in allocation of tasks to resources. We observe that within a team, service workers of similar competencies vary in their efficiencies and have deterioration in the quality of service at different workloads or queue lengths. The model based on historical data has a prediction accuracy between 65 % to 80 %. The simulation model further indicates that modeling all workers as similar, results in lower quality of service. Through this work, we demonstrate that using of data-driven techniques to evaluate efficiencies of service workers, similar to ours, can serve as the basis for effective dispatching or task allocation policies and better meet the contractual service levels (quality) of the service system.

References

1. Van der Aalst, W.M., Nakatumba, J., Rozinat, A., Russell, N.: Business process simulation: how to get it right
2. Agarwal, S., Sindhgatta, R., Dasgupta, G.B.: Does one-size-fit-all suffice for service delivery clients? In: ICSOC, pp. 177–191 (2013)

3. Agarwal, S., Sindhgatta, R., Sengupta, B.: Smartdispatch: enabling efficient ticket dispatch in an it service environment. In: KDD, pp. 1393–1401 (2012)
4. Banerjee, D., Dasgupta, G.B., Desai, N.: Simulation-based evaluation of dispatching policies in service systems. In: Winter Simulation Conference, pp. 779–791 (2011)
5. Borshchev, A.: The Big Book of Simulation Modeling. Multimethod Modeling with AnyLogic 6. Kluwer, AnyLogic North America, Hampton (2013)
6. Dasgupta, G.B., Sindhgatta, R., Agarwal, S.: Behavioral analysis of service delivery models. In: Basu, S., Pautasso, C., Zhang, L., Fu, X. (eds.) ICSOC 2013. LNCS, vol. 8274, pp. 652–666. Springer, Heidelberg (2013)
7. Diao, Y., Heching, A., Northcutt, D.M., Stark, G.: Modeling a complex global service delivery system. In: Winter Simulation Conference, pp. 690–702 (2011)
8. Field, A.: Discovering Statistics Using SPSS. SAGE Publications, London (2005)
9. Gupta, H.S., Sengupta, B.: Scheduling service tickets in shared delivery. In: Liu, C., Ludwig, H., Toumani, F., Yu, Q. (eds.) Service Oriented Computing. LNCS, vol. 7636, pp. 79–95. Springer, Heidelberg (2012)
10. IBM   (2008).   http://www-01.ibm.com/software/analytics/spss/products/modeler/
11. Maglio, P.P., Vargo, S.L., Caswell, N., Spohrer, J.: The service system is the basic abstraction of service science. Inf. Syst. E-Bus. Manag. 7(4), 395–406 (2009)
12. Mazzuchi, T.A., Wallace, R.B.: Analyzing skill-based routing call centers using discrete-event simulation and design experiment. In: Winter Simulation Conference, pp. 1812–1820 (2004)
13. Nakatumba, J., van der Aalst, W.M.P.: Analyzing resource behavior using process mining. In: Business Process Management Workshops, pp. 69–80 (2009)
14. Ng, A.Y., Jordan, M.I.: On discriminative vs. generative classifiers: a comparison of logistic regression and naive bayes (2001)
15. Ramaswamy, L., Banavar, G.: A formal model of service delivery. In: IEEE International Conference on Services Computing, SCC 2008, vol. 2, pp. 517–520, July 2008
16. Sindhgatta, R., Dasgupta, G.B., Ghose, A.: Analysis of operational data for expertise aware staffing. In: Sadiq, S., Soffer, P., Völzer, H. (eds.) BPM 2014. LNCS, vol. 8659, pp. 317–332. Springer, Heidelberg (2014)
17. Sun, P., Tao, S., Yan, X., Anerousis, N., Chen, Y.: Content-aware resolution sequence mining for ticket routing. In: Hull, R., Mendling, J., Tai, S. (eds.) BPM 2010. LNCS, vol. 6336, pp. 243–259. Springer, Heidelberg (2010)
18. Technologies, X.: (2011). http://www.xjtek.com/
19. Wetcher-Hendricks, D.: Analyzing Quantitative Data: An Introduction for Social Researchers. Wiley, Hoboken (2011)
20. Wickens, C., Hollands, J., Banbury, S., Parasuraman, R.: Engineering Psychology and Human Performance. Always learning, Pearson, Cape Town (2013). http://books.google.co.in/books?id=N3N0MAEACAAJ

Resource-Aware Process Model Similarity Matching

Michaela Baumann$^{(\boxtimes)}$, Michael Heinrich Baumann, Stefan Schönig,
and Stefan Jablonski

University of Bayreuth, Bayreuth, Germany
{michaela.baumann,michael.baumann,stefan.schoenig,
stefan.jablonski}@uni-bayreuth.de

Abstract. As business process models are widely used and essential
for most organizations, the problem of redundantly modeled processes
rises. This can happen when a process is modeled by different modelers
or when organizations merge. In order to cope with this issue, typically
process model similarity matching methods are used. Thereby, pure textual matching algorithms operating on single activities are often not
suitable. One alternative is to include further information like data and
resources and to check for M:N-matchings. The work at hand describes
how to use resource information to match process models, even if they
are modeled on different levels of granularity. The approach can be used
for both human and non-human resources. Furthermore, the differences
between intra- and inter-organizational matchings are pointed out.

Keywords: Process modeling · Process model similarity · Resource-
aware process matching · M:N-matching

1 Introduction

For documentation purposes as well as for the redesign of workflows and the
implementation of information systems [15], organizations typically rely on business process models. Thereby, several models for the same process may exist as
several modelers from different domains model more or less the same process
from different views [4] or after the merging of companies [5]. In order to avoid
expensive dublicates and inconsistencies, to improve processes, to identify patterns or to increase efficiency, correspondences between different models have to
be found [5].

For the matching of process models already a variety of approaches have
been proposed. Since they are usually based on the comparison of activity labels,
most of them do not take into account the resource perspective, see e.g. [6,11].
Furthermore, the bulk of these methods are only applicable for 1:1-matchings,
i.e., a single node in one process model is assigned to a single node in another
one. In [2] the authors introduced a M:N-matching technique, that matches sets
of activities to sets of activities. This approach allows for the consideration of

© Springer International Publishing Switzerland 2015
F. Toumani et al. (Eds.): ICSOC 2014, LNCS 8954, pp. 96–107, 2015.
DOI: 10.1007/978-3-319-22885-3_9

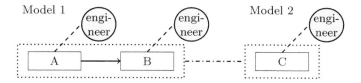

Fig. 1. Example process model similarity matching based on human resources: Set of nodes A and B of model 1 is mapped to set of node C of model 2 due to the role assignment "engineer"

human resources in case that each activity is assigned to exactly one agent who can be located on a conrete position of some hierarchical tree structure. If this requirement is fulfilled, the proposal of how to include the resource perspective in process matching as given in [2] should be preferred, as it considers all the available information. However, in most cases the requirements are too restrictive and the methods presented on the following pages should be applied instead. The work at hand gives answer to the question how information about resources can be taken into consideration during model matching if no further information about the resources' structure is available.

As described in [2] the possibility of constructing similarity measures for power sets of process activites and in this context the inclusion of further process information, i.e., not only activity labels, is crucial for the usability of process matching methods. Usually, such similarity measures have values in $[0, 1]$, with 0 meaning no similarity and 1 meaning full similarity. Therein, a value of, for example, 0.6 is not meaningful on its own, but the normalized interval $[0, 1]$ is very well suited for comparisons and threshold values.

The work at hand focuses on the resource information of process models and distinguishes between human and non-human resources as well as inter- and intra-organizational matchings. The latter distinction is important, because, as mentioned above, process models of one organization or models originating from different organizations can be matched. In both cases it is likely that the activity labels of the process models to be matched considerably deviate from each other, both in the used vocabulary as well as in the granularity of the documented activities, which may lead to low recall if only these labels are considered [11]. Taking into account the resources of processes may, as represented in Fig. 1, help to reduce computation time and to identify similar activities in process models that use different vocabulary and are modeled at different levels of granularity.

This paper defines process models with different perspectives, so-called extended process models, presents the idea of M:N-model matching and points out several ways of taking resource information into account depending on different prerequisites.

2   Background and Related Work

For a lot of modeling notations representing business processes, like Event-driven Process Chains (EPCs), UML Activity Diagrams or the Business Process

Modeling Notation (BPMN) [15], the task of matching those models or models of a general, more abstract form, has already been topic of various papers: For example, [7] and [5] present label matching techniques, [9] deals with label and behavioral similarity, [3] provides process structure trees for the behavioral perspective, [12] discusses different methods of model matching, [13] improves the label matching method, [10] uses ontologies, [1] presents methods based on so-called typical behavior and [8] provides behavioral and semantic matching for EPCs using a thesaurus. Typically the presented techniques are 1:1-matchings.

In [6] some possibilities to expand matching techniques and not only use the nodes' labels, as they might not lead to the desired results, but also their context with predecessor and successor relations, are described. In [5] only the idea of expanding this method to more than one node in a successive/iterative way is mentioned. Nevertheless, all methods described so far are based on mapping single nodes to single nodes. [14] introduces 1-to-n matchings, however, it does not imply other perspectives of business process models and only focuses on sequence flows during analysis. The authors of [7] and [5] apply the so called string-edit similarity to get a similarity measure that takes into account the number of mapped or deleted nodes and edges. In doing so the matching problem is reduced to a definition of similarity measure between two given process models G_1 and G_2, called graph-edit similarity. In [2], this idea was extended to M:N-mappings under consideration of more perspectives than just the nodes' labels (see Definitions 2 and 3 in the next section). In this context, the work at hand can be seen as a generalization or an addition that can be applied if resource informaton in the process models is given without predetermined structure.

Briefly summarized, one calculates a number of similarities, or distances respectively, for each perspective (e.g. activity labels, deleted nodes, data perspective) and uses these results for calculating a measure $GSim_M(G_1, G_2)$ for the similarity of G_1 and G_2 under mapping M. By maximizing this value with respect to M, one gets $GSim(G_1, G_2)$.

Definition 1 (Graph-edit similarity). *For two models G_1 and G_2 and weights $weight_i$ with $\sum_{i=1}^{k} weight_i = 1$ and $weight_i > 0$ or $weight_i \geq 0$ the graph-edit similarity $GSim$ is given through*

$$GSim(G_1, G_2) = \max_{M}\{1 - \sum_{i=1}^{k} weight_i \cdot fnd_{i,M}(G_1, G_2)\},$$

where M describes a mapping between G_1 and G_2, i is the index for the ith perspective and $fnd_{i,M}(G_1, G_2)$ is a fractional normalized distance for the ith perspective between G_1 and G_2 under mapping M.

For the implementation of this maximization problem, efficient algorithms are used, like Greedy or A*-Algorithms (see e.g. [7]).

If the problem of finding process models that describe the same process among a large set of such models has to be solved, a clustering algorithm can be applied. The clustering method can run 1-dimensional with respect to $GSim(G_1, G_2)$ or directly use the partial normalized distances

$$fnd_i(G_1, G_2) = \min_M fnd_{i,M}(G_1, G_2)$$

without computing $GSim(G_1, G_2)$ in the first place.

In the following section, similarity measures for the resource perspective, or the corresponding partial normalized distances, respectively, are derived. For similarity definitions of other perspectives see [2].

3   Resource-Aware Similarity

In the first step, a process model and the further requirements that should be fulfilled have to be defined. Furthermore, a definition of a mapping between two process models is given.

Definition 2 (Extended process model). *Let $\mathfrak{B} \subset \{s_1 s_2 \ldots s_{n_\mathfrak{B}} \mid s_i \text{ is a}$ character $\forall i \in \{1, \ldots, n_\mathfrak{B}\}, n_\mathfrak{B} \in \mathbb{N}_0\}$ be a set of descriptions, $\mathfrak{D} = \{d_1, \ldots, d_{n_\mathfrak{D}}\}$ a finite set of data objects, $\mathfrak{A} = \{a_1, \ldots, a_{n_\mathfrak{A}}\}$ a finite population (human resources), and $\mathfrak{W} = \{w_1, \ldots, w_{n_\mathfrak{W}}\}$ a finite set of machines (non-human resources). Then, a process graph G is a tuple (N, E, λ) with*

- *N being a set of nodes,*
- *$E \subseteq N \times N$ a set of edges and*
- *$\lambda : N \rightarrow \mathfrak{B} \times \mathcal{P}(\mathfrak{D}) \times \mathcal{P}(\mathfrak{A}) \times \mathcal{P}(\mathfrak{W})$ a function, that maps nodes to entities.*

For all process models to be matched, the sets $\mathfrak{B}$, $\mathfrak{D}$, $\mathfrak{A}$, and $\mathfrak{W}$ have to be the same. Note, that $\mathcal{P}(\cdot)$ indicates the power set.

For intra-organizational matchings $\mathfrak{A}$ and $\mathfrak{W}$ are sets of IDs, for inter-organizational ones

$$\mathfrak{A} = \mathfrak{A}_1 \cup \mathfrak{A}_2, \tag{1}$$

where $\mathfrak{A}_i$ is the set of IDs in the respective organization, analogously for $\mathfrak{W}$. That means, from the resource point of view the difference between intra- and inter-organizational process models arises out of the fact, if agents come from one population or more than one and if non-human resources belong to one pool or more. This can be extended to k organizations straight forward.

Definition 3 (Mapping between two process models). *Given two process models $G_i = (N_i, E_i, \lambda_i)$, $i = 1, 2$, and $P_i \subset \mathcal{P}(N_i) \ni \emptyset$ a complete and disjoint partition of N_i (i.e. $\bigcup_{p \in P_i} p = N_i$ & $\forall p, p' \in P_i : p \cap p' = \emptyset, p \neq p'$), $i = 1, 2$. Further on, let $M : P_1 \rightarrow P_2$ be a bijective function ($\emptyset \mapsto p_2$ and $p_1 \mapsto \emptyset$ means, that p_2 and p_1 are deleted, respectively, $p_1 \in P_1$, $p_2 \in P_2$), where $\neg(\emptyset \mapsto \emptyset)$.*

Such mappings as defined in Definition 3 are called M:N-mappings, because they are defined on powersets of the respective nodes.

3.1   Human Resource

For a closer look on similarity concerning the human resource perspective a distinction between several possibilities has to be made. In case that each node of the process models is assigned to one unique agent and all occurring agents can be located in a hierarchical tree, the similarity measure described in the following subsection as presented in [2] may be applied. For other application scenarios, e.g., sets of agents or roles are assigned to each node, a second possibility of computing a similarity measure is introduced. The second method is suitable for the general case of resource specification.

Single Agents in Hierarchical Trees. In this section we assume that all $A \in \mathcal{P}(\mathfrak{A})$ in the image of λ_i have $|A| = 1$, i.e., exactly one agent is assigned to each node (explicit assignment). A similarity value has to be found that is 1 if the executing agents in the compared sets of nodes are the same and decreases to 0 the more organizational distance lies between the involved agents. Figure 2 (on page 9) shows how a hierarchical tree may look like with the letters referring to conrete agents. As one can easily guess, the assumption of agents being arranged in a hierarchical tree is very restrictive and quite visionary. This is why a generalization is given afterwards.

In comparing the agents of two nodes of a given hierarchical tree it is possible to find a minimal number of edges, $\tilde{k}$, that have to be passed to get from one position in the tree to the other and the number of levels, $\tilde{e}$, that lie between them. Two agents on the same level have $\tilde{e} = 0$. To transform these two values into a similarity value, we set

$$ksim(A, B) := \frac{1}{\tilde{k} + 1} \text{ and } esim(A, B) := \frac{1}{\tilde{e} + 1},$$

with A and B being two concrete agents. Therefore, by comparing an agent with itself, we get a value of 1 for both similarities, that means maximal similarity, and a value tending to 0, the more edges and levels are between two tree positions. To combine these two similarity measures, we define

$$HSim(A, B) = \alpha ksim(A, B) + (1 - \alpha)esim(A, B),$$

with $\alpha \in [0, 1]$ being a weight factor, that allows to display some preferences for the position similarity. This value $HSim$ has to be extended to work for sets of nodes, that means a set of positions. This is done the following way:

Definition 4 (Similarity for single agents). *Let $H_{p_i} \subset \mathfrak{A}$ be the set of agents occurring in $p_i \in P_i$, $i = 1, 2$, i.e.,*

$$H_{p_i} = \bigcup_{n \in p_i} (\lambda(n))_3. \tag{2}$$

Then, for $p_i \in P_i$, it is

$$HSim(p_1, p_2) = \frac{\sum_{h_1 \in H_{p_1}, h_2 \in H_{p_2}} HSim(h_1, h_2)}{|H_{p_1}| \cdot |H_{p_2}|}.$$

Hence, we compute the similarity of every pair of positions from the two sets, add this values up and divide through the number of pairings to get an average value for position similarity. Note, that if there is more than one tree representing the hierarchical structure of an organization, a comparison of positions from different trees leads to a similarity value of 0.

Now, the fractional normalized distance under a certain mapping M, as required in Definition 1, can be computed:

$$fnd_{h,M} = \begin{cases} \dfrac{\sum_{(p_1,p_2)\in M|p_1\neq\emptyset\neq p_2}(1-HSim(p_1,p_2))}{\sum_{(p_1,p_2)\in M|p_1\neq\emptyset\neq p_2}1}, & \text{if } \exists(p_1,p_2)\in M|p_1\neq\emptyset\neq p_2 \\ 1, & \text{else} \end{cases}$$

Sets of Agents. In the following, the more general case of having sets of agents assigned to each node, e.g., roles, will be regarded. The idea of constructing a similarity measure for the human resource perspective for two given process models G_1 and G_2 is to, at first, define a similarity measure for two sets of agents $A_1, A_2 \subset \mathfrak{A}$ and then, in step two, extend this definition to sets of nodes. Note, that in each node a set of agents is given. In step three, $fnd_{a,M}(G_1, G_2)$, the fractional normalized distance for the human resource perspective for the two process models under mapping M is derived.

Definition 5 (Similarity for two sets of agents). *Let $A_1, A_2 \subset \mathfrak{A}$ be two non-empty sets. The similarity between these sets is:*

$$ASim(A_1, A_2) = \frac{|A_1 \cap A_2|}{|A_1 \cup A_2|} \tag{3}$$

For $p_i \in P_i$, $i = 1, 2$ the sets of agents, that are responsible for the respective, mapped sets of tasks, are defined as

$$A_{p_i} = \bigcap_{n\in p_i} (\lambda(n))_3. \tag{4}$$

Note, that the use of the intersection symbol in (4) is essential, because it reduces the chance of overfitting. Furthermore, the determination of A_{p_i} corresponds to the idea of M:N-mappings, because nodes that may be executed by approximately the same agents are to be combined. The concrete underlying agents are, however, replacable as we just count the number of agents in the sets and look at the process models at a certain point of time with a specific mapping of agents to agent sets which is the same for all models at that point of time.

Getting together the two Definitions (3) and (4), the resource based similarity for two sets of nodes, that are mapped under M, can be computed.

Definition 6 (Human resource-aware similarity for two sets of nodes). *Let $p_i \in P_i$, $i = 1, 2$, then*

$$ASim(p_1, p_2) = \begin{cases} ASim(A_{p_1}, A_{p_2}), & \text{if } A_{p_1} \neq \emptyset \neq A_{p_2}, \\ 0, & \text{else.} \end{cases} \tag{5}$$

To get the normalized distance of the human resources, as it is needed for the computation of $GSim(G_1, G_2)$ (see Definition 1), some kind of average over all elements of M is calculated:

$$fnd_{a,M} = \begin{cases} \frac{\sum_{(p_1,p_2)\in M|p_1\neq\emptyset\neq p_2}(1-ASim(p_1,p_2))}{\sum_{(p_1,p_2)\in M|p_1\neq\emptyset\neq p_2}1}, & \text{if } \exists(p_1,p_2)\in M|p_1\neq\emptyset\neq p_2 \\ 1, & \text{else} \end{cases}$$

This $fnd_{a,M}$ is element of $[0,1]$ whereby a value of 0 means no distance, as $ASim(p_1,p_2)=1$, which is full similarity, for all $(p_1,p_2)\in M$ with regard to the human resource perspective.

Alternative Method for Sets of Agents. The definition of $ASim$ in the above section follows the idea of mapping sets of nodes of one process model to sets of nodes of another process model. That means, in order to get a proper set of agents for one of the mapped sets of nodes, an intersection over all responsible agents of these nodes was made. In doing so it is secured that no agent is assigned to a task among the set of nodes he is not responsible for. Although this follows the idea of the M:N-mapping presented in [2], one can imagine cases where the above definition of $ASim$ does not lead to satisfying results. Imagine the following situation:

P_1 is a partition of the nodes of G_1 and P_2 a partition of the nodes of G_2 with G_1 and G_2 being two process models. $p_1 \in P_1$ and $p_2 \in P_2$ where p_1 consists of two nodes, n_{11}, n_{12}, of G_1 and p_2 consists of two nodes, n_{21}, n_{22} of G_2. The corresponding agents for these nodes are $(\lambda(n_{11}))_3 = \{A\} \cup X_1$, $(\lambda(n_{12}))_3 = \{A\} \cup X_2$, $(\lambda(n_{21}))_3 = \{A\} \cup X_3$ and $(\lambda(n_{22}))_3 = \{A\} \cup X_4$ where $X_1, \ldots, X_4$ are pairwise disjoint sets of agents not containing agent A. For the assignment $(p_1, p_2) \in M$, M being a mapping $G_1 \rightarrow G_2$, the similarity of the resource perspective $ASim(p_1, p_2)$ would be 1 as all X_i, $i = 1, \ldots, 4$, are cut away in the first intersection step according to (4) and only agent A remains in both A_{p_1} and A_{p_2}.

To take into account the cut away agents, e.g., the X_i, $i = 1, \ldots, 4$, of the above example, an alternative method, $\tilde{A}Sim$, is presented. For this, formula (5) is modified:

Definition 7 (Alternative human resource-aware similarity for two sets of nodes). *Let $p_i \in P_i$, $i = 1, 2$, then with H_{p_i} like in (2) it is*

$$\tilde{A}Sim(p_1, p_2) = \begin{cases} \frac{|A_{p_1} \cap A_{p_2}|}{|H_{p_1} \cup H_{p_2}|}, & \text{if } H_{p_1} \neq \emptyset \neq H_{p_2}, \\ 0, & \text{else.} \end{cases}$$

The numerator is the same as in (5), so it is $ASim \geq \tilde{A}Sim$. Using $\tilde{A}Sim$ as a similarity measure for the resource perspective would mean, that the sets of nodes have to be much more similar with respect to the resource perspective to gain high similarity values than the measuring method $ASim$, as this alternative definition considers all occurring agents of the respective nodes. But after all it does not completely follow the idea of mapping suitable sets of nodes (as mentioned after (4)) and will therefore not be taken into consideration in the ongoing work at hand.

Intra- vs. Inter-organizational Matching. Note, that the sets $A \subset \mathfrak{A}$ can be defined in two different ways. One possibility is to define them explicitly, that means $A = \{a_1, a_2, \ldots, a_l\}$. Another possibility would be an implicit definition, that is $A = \{a \mid a$ is fulfilling a QUERY$\}$. Furthermore, this implicit definition can be done organization-specific or general, e.g. $A = \{a \mid a$ works in department III$\}$ or $A = \{a \mid a$ is an engineer$\}$. Note that such a general version can be used across multiple organizatons, that means refer to a set of agents from different organizations. The organization-specific definition on the other hand does not allow for overlappings. Evaluating a QUERY will transform an implicit set definition into an explicit one.

If one wants to calculate a similarity value of two models of the same organization, it is not crucial how the sets are defined. If the models originate from different organizations, all definitions of resource sets have to be implicit and as general as possible. For performing such a matching generate $\mathfrak{A}$ and $\mathfrak{W}$ as mentioned in (1) first and then evaluate the QUERY, e.g. by using a database. Otherwise the intersection in (3) will be empty.

3.2 Practicability and Limitations of the Different Approaches and Examples

The techniques presented in the work at hand are not to be divided into better and worse techniques. Obviously the tree-based value $HSim$ makes use of more information about the process but also needs stricter preliminaries than the set-based value $ASim$. Table 1 shows the application possibilities of the different methods.

Table 1. Application fields for the two presented resource similarity matching methods

		Definition of performing agents		
		single agent in one hierarchical tree	explicit	implicit (organization-specific)	implicit (general)
context	intra-organizational	tree-based[a] and set-based	set-based	set-based	set-based
	inter-organizational	×	×	×	set-based

[a] Tree-based similarity is preferred as information about resource structure is used

The following example illustrates the different resource similarity methods and why the tree-based technique should to be preferred if its preliminaries are fulfilled.

Example 1. Two process models G_1 and G_2, as shown in Fig. 3 are given, the hierarchical structure of the agents is as shown in Fig. 2. Following partitions for G_1 and G_2 are made: $p_{11} = \{n_{11}\}$, $p_{12} = \{n_{12}, n_{13}\}$, $p_{13} = \{n_{14}\}$ and

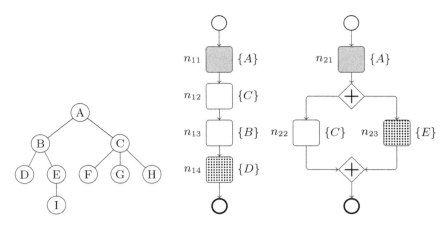

Fig. 2. Agents organized in a hierarchical tree

Fig. 3. Two (incomplete) process models with single agents assigned to each node: G_1 on the left, G_2 on the right

$p_{21} = \{n_{21}\}$, $p_{22} = \{n_{22}\}$, $p_{23} = \{n_{23}\}$. Mapping M is indicated with different fillings of the activity nodes and given as $M = \{(p_{11}, p_{21}), (p_{12}, p_{22}), (p_{13}, p_{23})\}$. The nodes' names and the corresponding agents are recognizable in Fig. 3. In this setting, the fractional normalized distances for the tree-based (with $\alpha = 0.5$) and the set-based methods are

$$fnd_{h,M} = \frac{(1-1) + \left(1 - \frac{5}{6}\right) + \left(1 - \frac{2}{3}\right)}{3} = \frac{1}{6} \text{ and } fnd_{a,M} = \frac{(1-1) + (1-0) + (1-0)}{3} = \frac{2}{3}.$$

During the calculation it is obvious, that the tree-based method uses more information about the agents' relations. As this information gets lost in the set-based method, the similarity value is less than that one of the tree-based method. Hence, for process models with exactly one agent assigned to each node, the set-based method often returns $ASim$-values of 0 and is therefore not recommended. Otherwise, calculating $HSim$ requires more operations than $ASim$, so the calculation time of $ASim$ and thus of the whole graph similarity $GSim$ is less than that of the tree-based method. In the following example that does not fulfill the preliminaries of the tree-based approach it is shown why one mapping M is preferred to another mapping M' for the same two process models.

Example 2. Given two process models G_1 and G_2 as shown in Fig. 4 and two different mappings M and M' between them, the respective similarity values are calculated. Thereby the two mappings are defined on different partitions of the process graphs: $P_1 = \{p_{11}, p_{12}\}$, $p_{11} = \{n_{11}\}$, $p_{12} = \{n_{12}, n_{13}\}$, $P_2 = \{p_{21}, p_{22}\}$, $p_{21} = \{n_{21}, n_{22}\}$, $p_{22} = \{n_{23}\}$ and $M = \{(p_{11}, p_{21}), (p_{12}, p_{22})\}$ as well as $P'_1 = \{p'_{11}, p'_{12}\}$, $p'_{11} = \{n_{11}, n_{21}\}$, $p'_{12} = \{n_{13}\}$, $P'_2 = \{p'_{21}, p'_{22}\}$, $p'_{21} = \{n_{21}\}$, $p'_{22} = \{n_{22}, n_{23}\}$ and $M' = \{(p'_{11}, p'_{21}), (p'_{12}, p'_{22})\}$. One calculates:

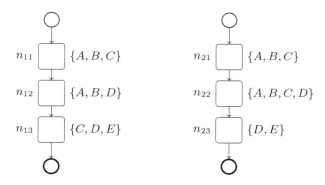

Fig. 4. Two (incomplete) process models with explicitly defined sets of agents assigned to each node: G_1 on the left, G_2 on the right

$$fnd_{a,M} = \frac{(1-1)+\left(1-\frac{1}{2}\right)}{2} = \frac{1}{4} \text{ and } fnd_{a,M'} = \frac{\left(1-\frac{2}{3}\right)+\left(1-\frac{1}{3}\right)}{2} = \frac{1}{2}$$

With respect to the human-resource perspective mapping M is preferred to mapping M'.

3.3   Non-human Resource

Non-human resources are treated the same way as human resources, if similarity values are computed using the set-based $ASim$. The non-human resource-based similarity for two sets of nodes therefore is given through:

$$WSim(p_1, p_2) = \begin{cases} WSim(W_{p_1}, W_{p_2}), & \text{if } W_{p_1} \neq \emptyset \neq W_{p_2}, \\ 0, & \text{else,} \end{cases}$$

with

$$WSim(W_1, W_2) = \frac{|W_1 \cap W_2|}{|W_1 \cup W_2|}, \quad W_1, W_2 \subset \mathfrak{W}, \ W_1 \neq \emptyset \neq W_2$$

and

$$W_{p_i} = \bigcap_{n \in p_i} (\lambda(n))_4.$$

This leads to the following normalized distance of the non-human resources:

$$fnd_{w,M} = \begin{cases} \dfrac{\sum_{(p_1,p_2) \in M \,|\, p_1 \neq \emptyset \neq p_2} (1 - WSim(p_1,p_2))}{\sum_{(p_1,p_2) \in M \,|\, p_1 \neq \emptyset \neq p_2} 1}, & \text{if } \exists (p_1, p_2) \in M \,|\, p_1 \neq \emptyset \neq p_2 \\ 1, & \text{else} \end{cases}$$

The results about intra- and inter-organizational matching as shown in the corresponding part of Sect. 3.1 may analoguosly be applied for $W \subset \mathfrak{W}$.

3.4 Exclusion Criterion

The techniques given in the work at hand can be used to extend existing process matching algorithms. To save computing time, in [2] it is suggested to use the data/dataflow perspective as an exclusion criterion, i.e., if under a certain mapping M the similarity between two sets of nodes with respect to the data/dataflow perspective is 0 then the whole mapping M gets a similarity value of 0 and is rejected. In doing so, a lot of possibilities that would have to be exercised for getting the best mapping M can be rejected without computing $GSim_M$. Now, the resource perspective based on resource sets can serve the same purpose, as the calculation of its fractional normalized distance as shown in the work at hand is a modification of that one of the data/dataflow perspective. That means, every M with $fnd_{a,M} = 1$ or $fnd_{w,M} = 1$ can be rejected during the optimization process to improve the runtime of the chosen algorithm.

4 Conclusion and Future Work

The work at hand shows how information about resources may be applied in process matching procedures and specifically deals with such process models where no information about the agents' and non-human resources' structure is available. The main application field is to use the resulting similarity measures or the fractional normalized distances for clustering process models. Future work may concentrate on extending and refining multi-perspective M:N-matching methods. Research focus may thereby lie on improving similarity measures for the several perspectives as well as on an improvement of the global graph-edit similarity. Concerning the resource perspective it is conceivable to merge the set-based and the tree-based techniques.

For testing the resulting similarity measures one can take k textual process models and l modelers and have each of them modeling all k textual models in BPMN. After calculating the similarity between all $k \cdot l$ BPMN-models, a clustering method can be applied to check if the detected clusters correspond to the k textual models.

Acknowledgement. The presented work is developed and used in the project "Kompetenzzentrum für praktisches Prozess- und Qualitätsmanagement", which is funded by "Europäischer Fonds für regionale Entwicklung (EFRE)".

The work of Michael Heinrich Baumann is supported by a scholarship of "Hanns-Seidel-Stiftung (HSS)" which is funded by "Bundesministerium für Bildung und Forschung (BMBF)".

References

1. van der Aalst, W.M.P., de Medeiros, A.K.A., Weijters, A.J.M.M.T.: Process equivalence: comparing two process models based on observed behavior. In: Dustdar, S., Fiadeiro, J.L., Sheth, A.P. (eds.) BPM 2006. LNCS, vol. 4102, pp. 129–144. Springer, Heidelberg (2006)

2. Baumann, M.H., Baumann, M., Schönig, S., Jablonski, S.: Towards multi-perspective process model similarity matching. In: Barjis, J., Pergl, R. (eds.) EOMAS 2014. LNBIP, vol. 191, pp. 21–37. Springer, Heidelberg (2014)
3. Castelo Branco, M., Troya, J., Czarnecki, K., Küster, J., Völzer, H.: Matching business process workflows across abstraction levels. In: France, R.B., Kazmeier, J., Breu, R., Atkinson, C. (eds.) MODELS 2012. LNCS, vol. 7590, pp. 626–641. Springer, Heidelberg (2012)
4. Dijkman, R.: A classification of differences between similar businessprocesses. In: 11th IEEE International Enterprise Distributed Object Computing Conference, EDOC 2007, p. 37 (2007)
5. Dijkman, R., Dumas, M., García-Bañuelos, L., Käärik, R.: Aligning business process models. In: IEEE International Enterprise Distributed Object Computing Conference, EDOC 2009, pp. 45–53 (2009)
6. Dijkman, R., Dumas, M., van Dongen, B., Käärik, R., Mendling, J.: Similarity of business process models: metrics and evaluation. Inf. Syst. **36**(2), 498–516 (2011)
7. Dijkman, R., Dumas, M., García-Bañuelos, L.: Graph matching algorithms for business process model similarity search. In: Dayal, U., Eder, J., Koehler, J., Reijers, H.A. (eds.) BPM 2009. LNCS, vol. 5701, pp. 48–63. Springer, Heidelberg (2009)
8. van Dongen, B.F., Dijkman, R., Mendling, J.: Measuring similarity between business process models. In: Bellahsène, Z., Léonard, M. (eds.) CAiSE 2008. LNCS, vol. 5074, pp. 450–464. Springer, Heidelberg (2008)
9. Dumas, M., García-Bañuelos, L., Dijkman, R.M.: Similarity search of business process models. IEEE Data Eng. Bull. **32**(3), 23–28 (2009)
10. Ehrig, M., Koschmider, A., Oberweis, A.: Measuring similarity between semantic business process models. In: Proceedings of the Fourth Asia-Pacific Conference on Comceptual Modelling, APCCM 2007, vol. 67, pp. 71–80. Australian Computer Society, Inc. (2007)
11. Klinkmüller, C., Weber, I., Mendling, J., Leopold, H., Ludwig, A.: Increasing recall of process model matching by improved activity label matching. In: Daniel, F., Wang, J., Weber, B. (eds.) BPM 2013. LNCS, vol. 8094, pp. 211–218. Springer, Heidelberg (2013)
12. Kunze, M., Weidlich, M., Weske, M.: Behavioral similarity – a proper metric. In: Rinderle-Ma, S., Toumani, F., Wolf, K. (eds.) BPM 2011. LNCS, vol. 6896, pp. 166–181. Springer, Heidelberg (2011)
13. Leopold, H., Smirnov, S., Mendling, J.: On the refactoring of activity labels in business process models. Inf. Syst. **37**(5), 443–459 (2012)
14. Weidlich, M., Dijkman, R., Mendling, J.: The ICoP framework: identification of correspondences between process models. In: Pernici, B. (ed.) CAiSE 2010. LNCS, vol. 6051, pp. 483–498. Springer, Heidelberg (2010)
15. Weske, M.: Business process management: concepts, languages, architectures. Springer Science & Business Media (2012)

Supporting Rule-Based Process Mining by User-Guided Discovery of Resource-Aware Frequent Patterns

Stefan Schönig[(✉)], Florian Gillitzer, Michael Zeising, and Stefan Jablonski

University of Bayreuth, Bayreuth, Germany
{stefan.schoenig,florian.gillitzer,michael.zeising,
stefan.jablonski}@uni-bayreuth.de

Abstract. Agile processes depend on human resources, decisions and expert knowledge and are especially versatile and comprise rather complex coherencies. Rule-based process models are well-suited for modeling these processes. There exist a number of process mining approaches to discover rule-based process models from event logs. However, existing rule-based approaches are typically based on a given set of rule templates and predominately consider control flow aspects. By only considering a given set of templates, contemporary approaches underlie a representational bias. The usage of a fixed language frequently ends into insuffcient languages. In this paper we propose an approach to automatically suggest adequate resource-aware rule templates for a given domain by pre-processing the provided event log using frequent pattern mining techniques. These templates can then be instantiated and checked by process mining methods.

Keywords: Rule-based process mining · Resource-aware process mining · Frequent pattern mining

1 Introduction

The success of an organization primarily depends upon its ability to accomplish its tasks in a structured and reliable manner. A well accepted method for structuring an organization is business process management (BPM). BPM usually involves modeling, executing and analyzing processes [10]. As already recognized about 20 years ago, two different types of processes can be distinguished [12]: well-structured routine processes of which the exact flow is in focus and less structured, i.e., agile processes of which the exact flow cannot be determined completely a priori.

Agile processes heavily depend on human participants, decisions and their expert knowledge [15]. Participants have a higher degree of freedom when performing these processes. As a consequence, these processes are especially versatile and comprise rather complex coherencies. Agile processes such as healthcare processes can often be captured more easily using a rule-based rather than a

© Springer International Publishing Switzerland 2015
F. Toumani et al. (Eds.): ICSOC 2014, LNCS 8954, pp. 108–119, 2015.
DOI: 10.1007/978-3-319-22885-3_10

procedural modeling approach [3,17]. While a procedural model describes how a process has to work exactly, a rule-based model describes only the essential characteristics of the process. To this end, constraints, i.e., rules are specified that restrict possible actions that can be taken during process execution. The more constraints are added to the model the less paths remain. Moreover, a rule-based model focuses on crosscutting relations instead of the flow of activities [11]. Hence, a rule-based approach is well-suited for modeling agile processes [21].

For purposes of compliance and process improvement, organizations are interested in the way their processes are de facto executed. Since processes are often supported and executed by information systems, process events like starts and completions of activities or write events of documents are recorded in so-called event logs. Process mining aims at discovering and improving real-life processes by extracting knowledge from event logs. Given an event log, process discovery techniques can be used to automatically produce a process model reflecting the recorded behaviour [1]. Over the last years, rule-based languages such as Declare [3], Sciff [8], or DPIL [19] have been developed. There exist a number of process mining approaches and tools to discover rule-based process models from event logs. Examples are the Declare Maps Miner [14] the MINERful tool [9], the SciffMiner [8] or the CMMN Miner [18].

Rule-based base languages can typically be extended individually by user-defined templates in order to express specific relations of the corresponding domain adequately. This is not the case for process mining approaches. Mining methods are all based on a given set of rule templates and therefore on a predefined language library. Initially, the given rule templates are instantiated with every possible combination of parameters. Most of the generated constraints have often no domain significance and are uninteresting for analysts [6]. One of the main reasons for this is that existing approaches have mainly focused on mining control-flow dependencies [6,13] such as the "response" constraint ("if A occurs, B must occur afterwards") of Declare, and do not consider additional perspectives like resources or group affiliations. Hence, resulting models lack insights into the role of humans and user groups during the execution of processes. Human resources are important in agile processes, since decisions, collaboration and knowledge of process participants are the main drivers during the process [22]. Here, some rules do not hold in any case but for certain originators or user groups, i.e., under certain resource-based conditions ("if A occurs and is performed by originator of group g_1, B must occur afterwards"). Hence, mining with basic rule templates possibly leads to incomplete models that are only an approximation of actual underlying relations. This limitation is typically called "representational bias" [2]. Finding a suitable representational bias for process discovery is one of the big challenges in process mining [2].

In order to discover resource-based coherencies additional types of rules are needed. Therefore, in this work we focus on the set of language constructs, i.e., the set of rule templates that should be comprised when discovering models. Traditionally, rule templates are developed and organized by technical experts [8]. To the best of the authors knowledge, there is no mining approach that is engaged in, at least semi-automatically supporting users with suggestions of reasonable rule templates. Figure 1 shows our approach to suggest resource-aware rule templates by pre-processing the provided event log using frequent pattern mining techniques.

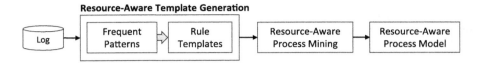

Fig. 1. Support of rule-based process mining by the approach of the work at hand

In a first step frequently occurring resource-aware patterns are extracted. In a second step, rule templates are derived of patterns with a common structure. Finally, these templates can be instantiated and checked. The approach has been implemented as a part of the *Process Workbench*[1] platform. First experiments with real life event logs of agile university processes showed that the technique can discover resource-aware patterns and suggest rule templates that describe the underlying coherencies more adequately than basic rule templates. Due to space limitations we cannot provide details here. The remainder of this paper is organized as follows. Section 2 discusses related work and some issues in contemporary approaches. Section 3 presents the basic and enhanced frequent pattern mining concepts. Section 4 presents our approach to extract frequent process patterns. In Sect. 5 we describe how these patterns can be transformed to templates. The paper is finally concluded in Sect. 6.

2   Background and Related Work

Automated process discovery aims at constructing a process model from an event log consisting of traces, such that each trace corresponds to one execution of the process. Almost all process discovery techniques, e.g., [4,16,23] aim to discover flow-oriented, i.e., procedural models. In this paper, we aim to discover rule-based, i.e., declarative models from event logs. A rule-based process model typically consists of a set of rules, i.e., constraints, which are based on so-called rule templates. A rule template defines a particular type of rules and can be seen as a modeling construct definition. Therefore, a set of templates defines the language library used within the domain. Templates have formal semantics specified through logical formulae and are equipped with user-friendly graphical representations like in Declare or abbreviations in textual languages like DPIL that make the model easier to understand [3]. Techniques for the automated discovery of rule-based process models from event logs have been proposed in several papers, e.g., in [9,14,18]. These approaches are all based on a given set of

---

[1] Process Workbench is a process management system that consists of a modeling, execution as well as a mining module. See *workbench.kppq.de* for more information.

rule templates and therefore on a predefined language library that only considers control flow related dependencies. Several of todays event logs contain rich information corresponding to the data, resource, and time perspectives [6]. In [6,13] the authors proposed post-processing approaches to take this additional information into account and to discover event correlations and data conditions in order to extend already discovered Declare models with meaningful annotations and to increase comprehensibility of discovered models. Here, the need for more complex modeling constructs becomes obvious. Both approaches take a model and an event log as an input and produce an annotated model. Rules that only hold within special circumstances regarding the performing human resources and group memberships are not discovered. Furthermore, resource-aware rule templates that could adequately represent the observed behaviour are not suggested.

The contribution of this paper is twofold. First of all, we propose a *preprocessing* instead of a post-processing approach to discover resource-aware frequent patterns. This way, we limit the observed language to important, i.e., only frequently occurring rules and therefore avoid performance issues. Furthermore, many extracted patterns of the same structure can result in the suggestion of a new resource-aware rule template, i.e., a new modeling construct. These rule templates are obviously important within the observed domain and should be checked by rule-based process mining in ongoing analysis.

3   Frequent Pattern and Association Rule Mining

3.1   Traditional Approach and Applicability for Process Mining

In this section, we introduce frequent pattern mining and its applicability in the field of process mining. Given a set of transactions, where each transaction is a set of items, an association rule is an implication $X \to Y$, where X and Y are sets of frequent items. The meaning of such a rule is that transactions which contain the items in X tend to also contain the items in Y. An example of such a rule might be that 98 % of customers who purchase tires and auto accessories also buy some services. Here, 98 % is called *confidence* of the rule.

Definition 1 (Support and Confidence). *Let $|D|$ be total number of transactions of the data basis. Let T_{xy} be the set of transactions that contain a set of items $X \cup Y$ and T_x be the set of transaction that contain a set of items X. Then, the support and the confidence of a rule $X \to Y$ are defined as*

$$Support := \frac{|T_{xy}|}{|D|}, \qquad Confidence := \frac{|T_{xy}|}{|T_x|} \qquad (1)$$

The *support* of the rule $X \to Y$ is the percentage of transactions that contain both X and Y. The problem of mining association rules is to find all rules that satisfy a user-specified minimum *support* and *confidence*. The Apriori algorithm by Agrawal is a well-studied method that is able to discover frequent itemsets and association rules efficiently [5].

Similar to procedural as well as rule-based process mining methods the algorithm traverses the data basis looking for certain patterns. Given that association rules in its basic form do not consider the exact ordering of items and do not aim to build an overall process model, association rules are obviously not suitable for mining procedural process models [1]. A rule-based model on the contrary consists of a set of rules and only describes the essential characteristics of the process. The exact step-by-step execution order is evaluated during runtime. Therefore, extracted association rules can discover unknown relations and indeed support and extend rule-based process mining. The fundamental difference to previous approaches of checking rule template instatiations is that there is no need to provide rule templates. Therefore, the discovery target is not predetermined.

3.2   Extensions: Generalization, Negations and Intertransactionality

In its basic form, association rule mining only aims at discovering $intra-transactional, positive$ patterns that do not consider the presence of taxonomies ($is-a$ hierarchies). Many interesting patterns hidden in real-life event logs of agile processes typically cannot be expressed that way. In many cases there are $inter-transactional$ relations that additionally comprise $negations$ ("activity a_2 must not be performed directly after activity a_1") and take background knowledge, e.g., in form of taxonomies into account ("activity a_1 must be performed by a resource who is member of group g_1"). That's why the basic method needs to be extended by further concepts to be applicable in fields of rule-based process mining.

Generalization. In most cases, background knowledge in form of taxonomies over items are available [5]. In this work we especially focus on resources involved in the process. Therefore, a taxonomy is given by an organigram of resource-group memberships. By adding the different levels of a given organigram to a transaction it is possible to discover rules that addionally take group affiliations into account.

Negative Association Rules. In order to express the diverse characteristics of a process, rules can involve negative terms which indicate negative associations between items, i.e., process elements. The $negation$ of an itemset A is indicated by $\neg A$. The support of $\neg A$ is $supp(\neg A) = 1 - supp(A)$. In particular, for an itemset $\{i_1, \neg i_2, i_3\}$, its support is $supp(i_1 \neg i_2 i_3) = supp(i_1 i_3) - supp(i_1 i_2 i_3)$ [24].

Intertransactional Association Rules. Traditional association rule mining discovers patterns among items within the same transaction, i.e., intra- transactional rules that are limited to express $static$ patterns. Rules in rule-based process models typically also relate process entities from different events, i.e., from different transactions. Here, $inter-transactional, dynamic$ patterns need to be extracted. In [20] the authors introduced a method to extract inter-transactional association rules by combining the items of closely spaced transactions to so-called *megatransactions*. A megatransaction is built by running through the transaction data basis with a sliding window of size w. Then, it contains all the items of the merged transactions within an interval w annotated with its positions in w. This way at least *local* dynamic patterns like e.g., $i_1(0) \rightarrow i_2(1)$ ("if i_1 occurs then i_2 occurs in the next position") can be discovered directly using the Apriori approach.

4   User-Guided Discovery of Resource-Aware Frequent Process Patterns

In this section, we make use of association rule mining to extract frequently occuring, resource-aware patterns from event logs. Combined with the extensions described above, extracted patterns suggest a set of rules that can adequatly represent the frequently occurring relations given in the event log. Note, that there is no need to provide rule templates to initialize the discovery process.

4.1   Preliminaries: Rule-Based Process Models and Event Logs

In this subsection we provide a formal definition for some basic concepts, i.e., rule-based process models and process event logs.

Definition 2 (Rule-based process model). *A rule-based process model M is defined by the tuple $M = (A, D, O, G, R)$ where the basic process model elements include $A = \{a_1, a_2, ..., a_n\}$ that denotes the finite set of all activities, $D = \{d_1, d_2, ..., d_m\}$ that defines the finite set of data objects, $O = \{o_1, o_2, ..., o_k\}$ that represents the finite set of human resources and $G = \{g_1, g_2, ..., g_l\}$ that stands for the finite set of user groups. R defines the set of rules specifying the relations and constraints for the process.*

During the execution of a process different events can be observed. Contemporary information systems store a multitude of information about these events in a structured way in so-called *event logs*. In addition to process-aware information systems focusing on activities there is a significant amount of organizations that use document-driven, i.e., data-centric information systems. Therefore, an event can be of a specific type, e.g., the start $ev_s(a_i)$ or completion $ev_c(a_i)$ of an activity a_i or the write $ev_w(d_j)$ of a data object d_j and is performed by a human resource o_k who is a member of a set of user groups $\{g_1, g_2, ..., g_n\} \in G$ defined in an organigram.

Definition 3 (Event, Trace and Event log)

- *An event $e = \{id, i, ev, el, o, t\}$ is a tuple specified by a unique identifier id, corresponds to exactly one process instance i, has a specific event type ev with $ev \in E = \{ev_s, ev_c, ev_w\}$, concerns a specific process element el with el being an activity $el \in A$ or a data object $el \in D$ and was performed by a resource $o \in O$ at a specific time t.*

- A trace $\sigma = \langle e_1, e_2, ..., e_n \rangle$ denotes an ordered set of events generated during execution of a single process instance with $|\sigma_i|$ being the length of the trace.
- An event log $\Phi = \{\sigma_1, \sigma_2, ...\sigma_k\}$ finally consists of a set of traces and precisely describes the execution of all process instances within a certain timeframe.

4.2   Extracting Static, Local and Global Resource-Aware Patterns

Rules defined in rule-based process models can typically be classified in different types [3,7]. *Static* patterns express properties regarding a single process event, e.g., a role-based allocation rule. *Dynamic* patterns, i.e., history-based or future constraining, deal with relations between process elements of different events regarding the sequential execution order. *Local dynamic* patterns define relations between process model elements in a certain time window, e.g., the *"chain succession"* constraint of Declare. *Global dynamic* patterns define sequential relations concerning a process instance as a whole, e.g., the *"succession"* constraint of Declare. *Global existence* patterns also describe relations concerning a whole process instance but do not comprise a sequential order, e.g., the *"co − existence"* constraint of Declare. Except for global dynamic rules all types of patterns can be extracted by the extended Association Rule Mining approach directly and without any predefined rule template. Contrary to classic approaches that check the log for counterexamples, the Apriori approach discovers frequently occurring coherencies contained within the provided transactions directly. It is obvious that for each rule type a transaction needs to be defined differently. In order to extract static patterns, a transaction contains elements regarding a single event, e.g., the event type, the activity and the performing originator (*static* transaction). Regarding local patterns a transaction consists of elements of a interval of events, e.g., two directly sequenced events (*local* transaction). For discovering global patterns on the other hand a transaction comprises elements of process instances as a whole, e.g., all activities and originators that occurred within a trace (*global* transaction). In order to support the understandability of discovered results, analysts can guide the rule discovery process by selecting the type of information they are interested in. This way, transactions only comprise the selected information. This limits the number of extracted rules to a manageable quantity. The possible set screws are: incorporating originators, comprising generalization, i.e., group memberships of originators as well as comprising negations of human resources, groups or events. Given three different types of transaction sets, i.e., static, local, and global transaction sets generated as described above, the Apriori approach is feasible to extract patterns that satisfy a $minSupp$ and rules that satisfy a $minConf$ threshold. Figure 2 shows an example transformation of an event log excerpt to the different transaction sets in consideration of exemplary information selections.

Static Patterns. In the context of static rules we are interested in patterns that frequently occur between the process elements of a single event of the process. Here, a single transaction comprises elements of a single event, e.g., $s_1 = \{ev_s(a_1), o_1, g_1, g_2, \neg g_3\}$ of Fig. 2. We define the *Static Rule Support (SRS)* value as follows.

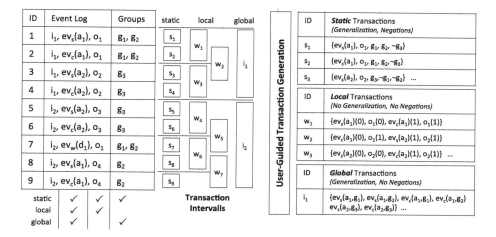

Fig. 2. Example transformations of event log to transactions

Definition 4 (Static Rule Support). *Let $|\sigma_i|$ be the number of events of a trace i and $|\Phi|$ be the number of traces in Φ. Let $(T_{xy})_S$ be the set of static transactions that contain a set of items $X \cup Y$. Then, the SRS of a rule $X \to Y$ is defined as*

$$SRS := \frac{|(T_{xy})_S|}{\sum_{i=1}^{|\Phi|} |\sigma_i|} \qquad (2)$$

Given the SRS definition, the algorithm discovers all the static rules whose items satisfy the user-defined $minSupp_S$ and $minConf_S$ thresholds. By comprising group affiliations as well as negative group affiliations, i.e., negative items for all groups that the performing resource has not been member of, examples for discovered resource-aware static rules are:
$ev_w(d_1) \to o_1$ (direct originator allocation rule), $ev_c(a_2) \to g_3$ (group-based allocation rule), $ev_w(d_1) \to \neg g_3$ (prohibited group-based allocation rule)

Local Dynamic Patterns. Here, a transaction consists of the elements of a megatransaction, i.e., a sliding window, e.g., $w_1 = \{ev_s(a_1)(0), o_1(0), ev_c(a_1)(1), o_1(1)\}$ in Fig. 2. Therefore, we define the *Local Rule Support* (LRS) value as follows.

Definition 5 (Local Rule Support). *Let $|\sigma_i|$ be number of events of a trace i, $|\Phi|$ be the number of traces in Φ and w be the predefined size of sliding windows. Let $(T_{xy})_L$ be the set of local transactions that contain a set of items $X \cup Y$. Then, the LRS of a rule $X \to Y$ is defined as*

$$LRS := \frac{|(T_{xy})_L|}{\sum_{i=1}^{|\Phi|} (|\sigma_i| - w + 1)} \qquad (3)$$

Given the *LRS* definition, the algorithm discovers all the local dynamic rules whose items satisfy the user-defined $minSupp_L$ and $minConf_L$ thresholds. Examples for resource-aware discovered local dynamic rules are: $ev_c(a_1)(0), o_1(0) \rightarrow ev_s(a_2)(1)$ (originator-based chain response), $ev_c(a_1)(0), g_1(0) \rightarrow ev_s(a_2)(1)$ (group-based chain response), $ev_s(a_2)(1), g_3(1) \rightarrow ev_c(a_1)(0)$ (group-based chain precedence),

Global Existence Patterns. Here, a transaction consists of elements of a whole process instance, e.g., $i_1 = \{ev_s(a_1, g_1), ev_c(a_1, g_1), ev_s(a_1, g_2), ev_c(a_1, g_2), ev_s(a_2, g_3), ev_c(a_2, g_3)\}$ in Fig. 2. Note, that in global transactions we have to merge event type, entity and additional process elements like originators or groups to one single item in order to be able to trace them back. We define the *Global Rule Support* (*GRS*) value as follows.

Definition 6 (Global Rule Support). *Let $|\Phi|$ be number of traces in Φ. Let $(T_{xy})_G$ be the set of global transactions that contain a set of items $X \cup Y$. Then, the GRS of a rule $X \rightarrow Y$ is defined as*

$$GRS := \frac{|(T_{xy})_G|}{|\Phi|} \tag{4}$$

Given the *GRS* definition, the algorithm discovers all the global existence rules whose items satisfy the user-defined $minSupp_G$ and $minConf_G$ thresholds. Examples for discovered resource-aware global existence patterns are: $ev_c(a_1, g_2)$ (group-based existence), $ev_s(a_2, o_2)$ (originator-based existence), $ev_c(a_1, g_2) \rightarrow ev_s(a_2, g_3)$ (group-based responded existence).

5   Transformation of Patterns to Rule Templates

In this section, we describe how to create pattern templates for frequently extracted patterns of the same type. Subsequently, these pattern templates are transformed to logical formulae used in commonly known rule-based process modeling languages and are therefore applicable to contemporary rule-based process mining approaches.

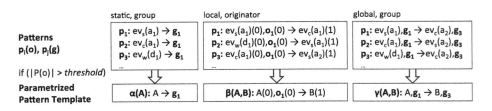

Fig. 3. Composition of pattern templates for frequent pattern types

Table 1. Transformation of some resource-aware patterns to logical rule templates

Type	Description	Pattern/Itemset	FOL/LTL semantics
static	orig.-based allocation	$A \rightarrow o_1$	$A \rightarrow o_1$
	group-based allocation	$A \rightarrow g_1$	$A \rightarrow g_1$
	prohibited group-based allocation	$A \rightarrow \neg g_1$	$A \rightarrow \neg g_1$
local	orig.-based chain response	$A(0), o_1(0) \rightarrow B(1)$	$\Box(A \wedge o_1 \rightarrow \bigcirc B)$
dynamic	orig.-based chain precedence	$B(1), o_1(1) \rightarrow A(0)$	$\Box(\bigcirc B \wedge o_1 \rightarrow A)$
	group-based chain response	$A(0), g_1(0) \rightarrow B(1)$	$\Box(A \wedge g_1 \rightarrow \bigcirc B)$
	group-based not chain succession	$A(0), g_1(0) \rightarrow \neg B(1)$	$\Box(A \wedge g_1 \rightarrow \bigcirc(\neg B))$
global	orig.-based existence	A, o_1	$\Diamond(A \wedge o_1)$
existence	group-based existence	A, g_1	$\Diamond(A \wedge g_1)$
	group-based absence	$\neg A, g_1$	$\neg\Diamond(A \wedge g_1)$
	orig.-based resp. existence	$A, o_1 \rightarrow B, o_2$	$\Diamond(A \wedge o_1) \rightarrow \Diamond(B \wedge o_2)$
	group-based resp. existence	$A, g_1 \rightarrow B, g_2$	$\Diamond(A \wedge g_1) \rightarrow \Diamond(B \wedge g_2)$
	group-based co-existence	$(A, g_1 \rightarrow B, g_2) \wedge$ $(B, g_2 \rightarrow A, g_1)$	$\Diamond(A \wedge g_1) \leftrightarrow \Diamond(B \wedge g_2)$
	group-based not co-existence	$A, g_1 \rightarrow \neg B, g_2$	$\neg(\Diamond(A \wedge g_1) \rightarrow \Diamond(B \wedge g_2))$

Figure 3 exemplarily illustrates the procedure of finding frequent types of patterns. First, extracted patterns are sorted by their type, i.e., static, local or global coherency and by the concerning resources or groups. Since each pattern can be seen as a function $p_i(o)$ or $p_j(g)$ they are assigned to sets $P(o)$ and $P(g)$ for each type. Finally, if $|P(o)|$ or $|P(g)|$ goes beyond a user-defined threshold, a parametrized pattern template, e.g., $\alpha(A) : A \rightarrow g_1$ with A being an event is composed. In order to be usable in contemporary rule-based process mining approaches, these pattern templates need to be transformed to logical rule formulae. For static pattern templates, i.e., coherencies regarding a single process event where the time aspect is not crucial, rules can be expressed in First-Order Logic (FOL). For expressing dynamic and existence patterns between events that refer to a process instance as a whole we use First-Order Linear Temporal Logic (LTL-FO) which is the first-order extension of LTL. Here, a basic LTL semantics is extended by an additional condition on resources to hold. This formalizm has already been introduced in [13] for Declare constraints and additional data conditions. In the work at hand we focus on human resources where the additional condition is a first-order formula considering originators and group memberships. Since details regarding LTL are out of the scope of this paper, we refer to [3] for a detailed explanation. Table 1 shows the exemplary transformation of extracted pattern templates to rule templates expressed in FOL as well as LTL-FO formulae. The "group-based chain response" template e.g., claims that every event A must be directly followed by an event B in case that A is performed by an originator of group g_1. Note, that A and B are parameters whereas g_1 is a special user-group like, e.g., trainees or secretaries. These extracted resource-aware rule templates can finally be checked by existing rule-based process mining approaches.

6   Conclusion, Limitations and Future Work

This paper presented an approach to automatically suggest adequate resource-aware rule templates for a given domain by pre-processing the provided event log using frequent pattern mining techniques. Therefore, first of all frequently occurring resource-aware patterns have been extracted. Subsequently, rule templates can be derived of patterns with a common structure. Since the approach can be seen as a pre-processing step to traditional process mining, we limit the observed language to important, i.e., only frequently occurring rules and therefore avoid performance issues. First experiments using real-life logs of agile university processes showed that the technique can discover resource-aware patterns that describe the underlying coherencies more adequately. The limitation of the approach clearly consists in its inability to discover global dynamic resource-aware patterns, like e.g., a resource-based "response" constraint. Global dynamic patterns need to be inferred by traditional mining methods and can then be enriched by resource information. As future work, we will first of all enable the approach to deal with global dynamic patterns. Furthermore, we will carry out a more extensive validation comprising more event logs and use cases.

Acknowledgement. The presented work is developed and used in the project "Kompetenzzentrum für praktisches Prozess- und Qualitätsmanagement", which is funded by "Europäischer Fonds für regionale Entwicklung (EFRE)".

References

1. van der Aalst, W.: Process Mining: Discovery, Conformance and Enhancement of Business Processes. Springer, Heidelberg (2011)
2. van der Aalst, W., et al.: Process mining manifesto. In: Daniel, F., Barkaoui, K., Dustdar, S. (eds.) BPM Workshops 2011, Part I. LNBIP, vol. 99, pp. 169–194. Springer, Heidelberg (2012)
3. van der Aalst, W., Pesic, M., Schonenberg, H.: Declarative workflows: Balancing between flexibility and support. Comput. Sci.- Res. Deve. **23**(2), 99–113 (2009)
4. van der Aalst, W., Weijters, T.: Process mining: a research agenda. Comput. Ind. **53**(3), 231–244 (2004)
5. Agrawal, R., Srikant, R.: Mining generalized association rules. Future Gener. Comput. Syst. (FGCS) **13**(2), 161–180 (1997)
6. Bose, R.P.J.C., Maggi, F.M., van der Aalst, W.M.P.: Enhancing declare maps based on event correlations. In: Daniel, F., Wang, J., Weber, B. (eds.) BPM 2013. LNCS, vol. 8094, pp. 97–112. Springer, Heidelberg (2013)
7. Caron, F., Vanthienen, J., Baesens, B.: Advances in Rule-Based Process Mining: Applications for Enterprise Risk Management and Auditing. SSRN (2013). http://www.ssrn.com/abstract=2246722

8. Chesani, F., Lamma, E., Mello, P., Montali, M., Riguzzi, F., Storari, S.: Exploiting inductive logic programming techniques for declarative process mining. In: Jensen, K., van der Aalst, W.M.P. (eds.) Transactions on Petri Nets and Other Models of Concurrency II. LNCS, vol. 5460, pp. 278–295. Springer, Heidelberg (2009)
9. Ciccio, C.D., Mecella, M.: MINERful: a mining algorithm for declarative process constraints in MailOfMine. Technical report, Sapienza University of Rome. Department of Computer and System Sciences (2012)
10. Dumas, M., Rosa, M.L., Mendling, J., Reijers, H.A.: Fundamentals of Business Process Management. Springer, Heidelberg (2013)
11. Fahland, D., Lübke, D., Mendling, J., Reijers, H., Weber, B., Weidlich, M., Zugal, S.: Declarative versus imperative process modeling languages: the issue of understandability. In: Halpin, T., Krogstie, J., Nurcan, S., Proper, E., Schmidt, R., Soffer, P., Ukor, R. (eds.) Enterprise, Business-Process and Information Systems Modeling. LNBIP, vol. 29, pp. 353–366. Springer, Heidelberg (2009)
12. Jablonski, S.: MOBILE: A modular workflow model and architecture. In: International Working Conference on Dynamic Modelling and Information Systems. Delft University Press (1994)
13. Maggi, F.M., Dumas, M., García-Bañuelos, L., Montali, M.: Discovering data-aware declarative process models from event logs. In: Daniel, F., Wang, J., Weber, B. (eds.) BPM 2013. LNCS, vol. 8094, pp. 81–96. Springer, Heidelberg (2013)
14. Maggi, F.M., Mooij, A., van der Aalst, W.: User-guided discovery of declarative process models. In: IEEE Symposium on Computational Intelligence and Data Mining (CIDM), pp. 192–199. IEEE (2011)
15. Marin, M., Hull, R., Vaculín, R.: Data centric BPM and the emerging case management standard: a short survey. In: La Rosa, M., Soffer, P. (eds.) BPM Workshops 2012. LNBIP, vol. 132, pp. 24–30. Springer, Heidelberg (2013)
16. de Medeiros, A.K.A., Weijters, T., van der Aalst, W.: Genetic process mining: an experimental evaluation. Data Min. Knowl. Disc. 14(2), 245–304 (2007)
17. Pichler, P., Weber, B., Zugal, S., Pinggera, J., Mendling, J., Reijers, H.A.: Imperative versus declarative process modeling languages: an empirical investigation. In: Daniel, F., Barkaoui, K., Dustdar, S. (eds.) BPM Workshops 2011, Part I. LNBIP, vol. 99, pp. 383–394. Springer, Heidelberg (2012)
18. Schönig, S., Zeising, M., Jablonski, S.: Supporting collaborative work by learning process models and patterns from cases. In: Bertino, E., Georgakopoulos, D., Srivatsa, M., Nepal, S., Vinciarelli, A. (eds.) CollaborateCom, pp. 60–69. ICST / IEEE (2013)
19. Schönig, S., Zeising, M., Jablonski, S.: Towards location-aware declarative business process management. In: Abramowicz, W., Kokkinaki, A. (eds.) BIS 2014 Workshops. LNBIP, vol. 183, pp. 40–51. Springer, Heidelberg (2014)
20. Tung, A., Lu, H., Han, J., Feng, L.: Efficient mining of intertransaction association rules. IEEE Trans. Knowl. Data Eng. (TKDE) 15(1), 43–56 (2003)
21. Vaculín, R., Hull, R., Heath, T., Cochran, C., Nigam, A., Sukaviriya, P.: Declarative business artifact centric modeling of decision and knowledge intensive business processes. In: EDOC, pp. 151–160. IEEE Computer Society (2011)
22. Vaculín, R., Hull, R., Vukovic, M., Heath, T., Mills, N., Sun, Y.: Supporting collaborative decision processes. In: IEEE SCC, pp. 651–658. IEEE, June 2013
23. Weijters, T., de Medeiros, A.K.A.: Process mining with the heuristics miner-algorithm. Eindhoven University of Technology, Technical report (2006)
24. Wu, X., Zhang, C., Zhang, S.: Efficient mining of both positive and negative association rules. ACM Trans. Inf. Syst. 22(3), 381–405 (2004)

Optimizing Resource Utilization by Combining Running Business Process Instances

Christine Natschläger[(✉)], Andreas Bögl, and Verena Geist

Software Competence Center Hagenberg GmbH,
Hagenberg im Mühlkreis, Austria
{christine.natschlaeger,andreas.boegl,verena.geist}@scch.at

Abstract. Efficient business processes are a critical success factor for organizations in a competitive market environment. One of the key potentials to increase efficiency of business processes is the optimization of resource utilization. The contribution of this paper is a novel approach for combining activities across running process instances to optimize resource utilization; i.e., resources are shared across different process instances. The main benefits of the suggested approach are the identification, disclosure, and application of optimization potentials.

1 Introduction

The execution of business processes is typically managed by some workflow management system which is able to handle multiple instances of a business process. Given such a workflow management system, we subsequently present the *Combined-Instance Approach* that exploits the current state of running process instances to reveal optimization potentials of resources associated with process activities. Typically, organizations pursue two ways to increase efficiency of their business processes. The first way is achieved by specifying an "optimal" sequence of activities to accomplish a given process goal. By contrast, the second way addresses efficiency by increasing productivity and by optimizing the use of resources associated with activities in running process instances. While the first attempt reveals optimization endeavors on the process schema level, the second attempt reflects resource optimization on the process instance level (but only individual instances are considered). The idea of this paper is to bridge the gap between optimization potentials on the schema and on the instance level (and in-between instances). In particular, we suggest sharing resources across running process instances thereby considering restrictions defined in the process schema.

The proposed approach can be applied to almost all types of resources including physical, human, organizational, and financial resources. Concrete examples for processes that can potentially share resources are, e.g., delivery processes, production processes, (business) travel processes, ordering processes, and so on. Considering production processes, the suggested approach can also deal with the problem of small batch sizes and combine activities until a minimum-cost batch size is reached. Hence, with our approach we address the goals of the Industry

© Springer International Publishing Switzerland 2015
F. Toumani et al. (Eds.): ICSOC 2014, LNCS 8954, pp. 120–126, 2015.
DOI: 10.1007/978-3-319-22885-3_11

4.0 project of the German government, which especially emphasizes the demand for adaptable processes and resource efficiency in traditional industries.

2   The Combined-Instance Approach

In this section, we present our approach for combining activities across process instances to optimize resource utilization. An overview of the approach applied to a running example is shown in Fig. 1 and consists of four steps: (1) defining business processes with data objects and constraints, (2) identifying possible combinations, (3) determining the optimization potential, and (4) combining business process instances.

2.1   Business Processes with Data Objects and Constraints

In the first step, the required business process definitions are provided. The *business process schema* $\mathcal{S}$ defines the business process with its data objects and resources and is the basis for all process instances. For our approach, $\mathcal{S}$ is extended with (a) *meta-information* (mi) describing, e.g., resources and their capacities, (b) *type-level constraints* (tc) specifying general restrictions that

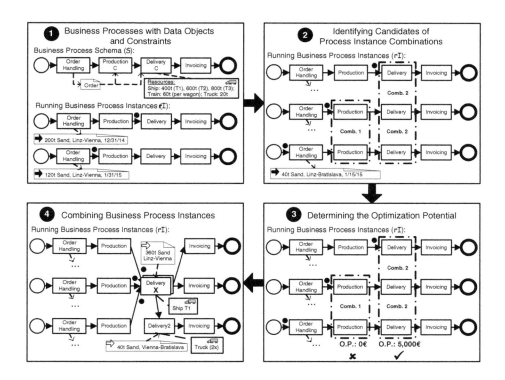

Fig. 1. Combined-instance approach

apply to all process instances either emerging from given data or being specified manually, and (c) *combinable activities* ($\mathcal{C}$) which comprise a *combinable condition* (*cc*) that defines the required matching of two instance activities for a possible combination and an *optimization function* (*of*) that determines the optimization potential of a combination. Every combinable activity is marked with a 'C' in the process diagram. Considering type-level constraints, we further distinguish hard and soft constraints, where the latter may not be satisfied depending on the optimization function. All constraints must be formally specified (e.g., based on the *Object Constraint Language* (OCL)) to support business process execution.

In our running example, $\mathcal{S}$ defines an order execution process comprising activities for order handling, production, delivery, and invoicing with corresponding data objects (e.g., order, product, and invoice) and resources (e.g., production and transportation means). Due to space limitations not all of them are shown in Fig. 1. $\mathcal{S}$ is then extended with meta-information like possible transportation means and their capacity (Ship T1: 400t, ...), constraints like the capacity of a ship (*tc* based on *mi*) or that a ship can only be used for cities with a harbor that are connected by a river (manually specified *tc*), and combinable conditions, e.g., for a possible combination of delivery activities the routes must be overlapping. In our example, the production activity and the delivery activity specify a *cc* and an *of*, so these two activities are combinable.

An instantiation of $\mathcal{S}$ is called a business process instance $\mathcal{I}$. During the execution of $\mathcal{I}$, data objects and corresponding constraints defined in $\mathcal{S}$ are instantiated and provide concrete instance-specific data and restrictions. A running process instance $r\mathcal{I}$ further comprises one or more tokens that mark the current position(s) in the process flow (shown by a black-filled circle in Fig. 1).

In our example, the order execution process is instantiated three times. In the first process instance ($\mathcal{I}1$), 200t of sand are ordered and must be sent from Linz to Vienna until 12/31/14. The order of $\mathcal{I}2$ has the same route but with 120t of sand that must be delivered until 1/31/15. Finally, $\mathcal{I}3$ (shown in step 2) comprises an order with 40t of sand that must be sent from Linz to Bratislava until 1/15/15. All three process instances are running but the current positions differ.

Finally, we require some auxiliary functions that return all $r\mathcal{I}$, the current position(s) of $r\mathcal{I}$, the state of $\mathcal{C}$ (open, running, or completed), whether $\mathcal{C}$ is still reachable, and the expected costs and execution time of activities.

2.2   Identifying Candidates of Process Instance Combinations

Inputs to the second step are all definitions of $\mathcal{S}$ and a set of $r\mathcal{I}$. The goal then is to identify candidate pairs of $\mathcal{C}$ that satisfy all constraints. The search for candidate pairs is initiated whenever a token reaches a $\mathcal{C}$ and the triggering $\mathcal{C}$ is compared with the corresponding activity of every other $r\mathcal{I}$. If the other $\mathcal{C}$ is open and reachable (auxiliary functions) and all hard constraints and the *cc* are satisfiable, then the two $\mathcal{C}$ are a candidate pair. Several candidate pairs may be combined to sets of higher cardinality.

In our running example, searches are triggered by the production activity of $\mathcal{I}2$ and the delivery activity of $\mathcal{I}1$. Candidate pairs are the production activities of $\mathcal{I}2$ & $\mathcal{I}3$ (in $\mathcal{I}1$ already completed) and the delivery activities of $\mathcal{I}1$ & $\mathcal{I}2$ and $\mathcal{I}1$ & $\mathcal{I}3$ (which can further be combined to $\mathcal{I}1$ & $\mathcal{I}2$ & $\mathcal{I}3$).

The actual combination of candidates depends on three further conditions:

1. If the "other" (not-triggering) $\mathcal{C}$ will ever receive a token (after a preceding split an alternative path may be taken).
2. If waiting for the "other" (not-triggering) $\mathcal{C}$ will cause a currently satisfiable constraint to be violated (e.g., a deadline).
3. If the combination provides an improvement (optimization potential). This condition is evaluated within the next step.

2.3   Determining the Optimization Potential

Inputs to the third step are sets of combinable candidates. The goal then is to identify whether a possible combination is economically worthwhile by applying the *optimization function* (*of*) defined for every $\mathcal{C}$. Instructions for defining an *of* are provided by the mathematical domain under the terms *multi-objective optimization* and *constrained optimization* (see Sect. 3). In our case, the *of* must identify an optimal approach for the separate solution and the combined solution (e.g., choose fitting production and transportation means) and calculate a value for comparison (e.g., costs, time). Note that there is the possibility that candidates satisfy the *cc* but can, nevertheless, not be fully merged, e.g., due to routes being overlapping but not identical. In this case, we can split an activity so that part of it can be combined and the remaining part is executed individually. Then both sub-activities must be considered in the optimization function.

In our running example, we assume that the optimal transportation means for $\mathcal{I}1$ is a ship of type T1, for $\mathcal{I}2$ two train wagons and for $\mathcal{I}3$ two trucks. For the combined solution, the *of* suggests a ship of type T1 from Linz to Vienna and two trucks from Vienna to Bratislava (activity of $\mathcal{I}3$ is split). Then the loading and transportation costs for both solutions are calculated and compared. We assume that we have an optimization potential of € 5,000 for the combined delivery activities and no optimization potential for the production activities.

2.4   Combining Business Process Instances

Inputs to the fourth step are sets of combinable candidates with optimization potential. The goal then is to combine the activities and update the process instances, thereby providing runtime validation and (manual) authorization of combinations for quality assurance. However, for combining activities of several process instances, we require a new business process element, which we call *Combined-Instance Activity* ($\mathcal{X}$). Syntactically, this element receives the data objects and resources of all merged activities and must satisfy all constraints. It will further be addressed by several incoming and outgoing flows coming from different process instances. The semantics is that $\mathcal{X}$ will consume a token from every participating process instance, execute the combined activity thereby using the recommended resource(s) and, finally, produce the same amount of tokens and return them to the process instances. For the graphical representation, we recommend two overlapping activities where the front activity is marked with a bold 'X'. A similar element with the required semantics is not available in any other business process modeling language (BPMN, UML, EPC, or YAWL).

For replacing the individual activities with $\mathcal{X}$ we use a deferred approach. The first activity already received a token which triggered the search. We now have to wait for further tokens to reach corresponding candidates in other $r\mathcal{I}$. The waiting is restricted either by a predefined amount of time, by not delaying the activity but considering the time before execution as implicit waiting, or by the deadline of the activity minus the expected execution time. When a second process instance reaches the required position in time, the two activities are replaced by an $\mathcal{X}$ (if necessary an activity is thereby split). When a further candidate receives a token, then the corresponding activity is also integrated in $\mathcal{X}$. The deferred approach is necessary, since some candidates may not be reached at all (preceding split with alternative path) or not reached in time. When all possible activities are integrated, $\mathcal{X}$ is executed and separately written in the log-file of every process instance (together with further split activities).

3   Related Work

Related research is provided by different domains. For example, in the mathematical domain, scheduling problems are studied and algorithms are defined that calculate the optimal solution. Of particular interest are the resource-constrained project scheduling problem, dynamic optimization problems, and constrained optimization problems (see e.g. [3,6]). If several objectives have to be optimized simultaneously, this issue is investigated within multi-objective optimizations [4].

In the business process domain, related research is available concerning optimization of resources (e.g., in the sub-field of business process intelligence [5]), typically based on goals or constraints. In addition, in the areas of service composition and dynamic resource allocation related work exists that deals with similar problems. However, the focus of the suggested approaches is either on the type-level (business process schema) or on individual running process instances (sometimes in combination with previously completed process executions).

A similar approach that also synchronizes running process instances but does not sufficiently address resource combination and optimization potentials is described in [8]. An example in the context of the healthcare domain is presented in [1] and supports instance-level adaption of workflow schemas to prevent repeating or overlapping activities. The paper builds on previous research on flexible workflow management systems (e.g., by [9]) and introduces interesting ideas but restricts the approach of activity crediting to a single workflow instance.

Finally, considering domains like logistics or production, applications and methods have been designed that optimize the utilization of resources in the specific domain (e.g., dynamic logistics process management problems [2,10]).

However, our goal is to dynamically address resource optimization on a higher level of abstraction, i.e., business processes, with the advantage that several resources from different domains can be considered within the same business process (e.g., optimization of production and transportation resources).

So, to the best of our knowledge, there is no other approach that suggested sharing resources across several running process instances.

4   Conclusion

In this paper, we presented a novel approach for resource optimization in business processes. The main idea is to combine activities with similar tasks of several running process instances, thereby sharing resources like transportation or production means. Thus, we address the demand for adaptable processes and resource efficiency identified by the Industry 4.0 project of the German government.

Our future goals are to implement a prototype and to extend the approach by providing exception handling for *Combined-Instance Activities*, by also waiting for future process instances with new combination possibilities (if the deadline is not violated), and by considering similar activities derived from different process schemas (e.g., based on the identification of similarities described in [7]).

Acknowledgements. This publication has been written within the project *Vertical Model Integration* (VMI) 4.0. The VMI 4.0 project is supported within the program "Regionale Wettbewerbsfähigkeit OÖ 2007-2013" by the European Fund for Regional Development as well as the State of Upper Austria. This work was also supported in part by the *AdaBPM* project, which is funded by the *Austrian Research Promotion Agency* (FFG) under the project number 842437.

References

1. Browne, E.D., Schrefl, M., Warren, J.R.: Activity crediting in distributed workflow environments. In: ICEIS (3), pp. 245–253 (2004)
2. Chow, H.K., Choy, K.L., Lee, W.B.: A dynamic logistics process knowledge-based system - an RFID multi-agent approach. Know.-Based Syst. **20**(4), 357–372 (2007)
3. Cruz, C., González, J., Pelta, D.: Optimization in dynamic environments: a survey on problems, methods and measures. Soft Comput. **15**(7), 1427–1448 (2011)
4. Deb, K.: Multi-objective optimization. In: Burke, E.K., Kendall, G. (eds.) Search Methodologies, pp. 403–449. Springer, US (2014)
5. Grigori, D., Casati, F., Castellanos, M., Dayal, U., Sayal, M., Shan, M.C.: Business process intelligence. Comput. Ind. **53**(3), 321–343 (2004)
6. Hartmann, S., Briskorn, D.: A survey of variants and extensions of the resource-constrained project scheduling problem. EJOR **207**(1), 1–14 (2010)
7. Leopold, H., Niepert, M., Weidlich, M., Mendling, J., Dijkman, R., Stuckenschmidt, H.: Probabilistic optimization of semantic process model matching. In: Barros, A., Gal, A., Kindler, E. (eds.) BPM 2012. LNCS, vol. 7481, pp. 319–334. Springer, Heidelberg (2012)

8. Pufahl, L., Weske, M.: Batch activities in process modeling and execution. In: Basu, S., Pautasso, C., Zhang, L., Fu, X. (eds.) ICSOC 2013. LNCS, vol. 8274, pp. 283–297. Springer, Heidelberg (2013)

9. Reichert, M., Rinderle, S., Dadam, P.: ADEPT workflow management system. In: van der Aalst, W.M.P., ter Hofstede, A.H.M., Weske, M. (eds.) BPM 2003. LNCS, vol. 2678, pp. 370–379. Springer, Heidelberg (2003)

10. Wang, Y., Caron, F., Vanthienen, J., Huang, L., Guo, Y.: Acquiring logistics process intelligence: methodology and an application for a chinese bulk port. Expert Syst. Appl. **44**, 195–209 (2014)

Knowledge Aware Service
Oriented Applications

A Planning-Based Service Composition Approach for Data-Centric Workflows

Carlos-Manuel López-Enríquez[2,4]([✉]), Víctor Cuevas-Vicenttín[3],
Genoveva Vargas-Solar[1,2], Christine Collet[2], and José-Luis Zechinelli-Martini[4]

[1] CNRS, Paris, France
genoveva.vargas@imag.fr
[2] Grenoble Institute of Technology, BP. 72,
38402 Saint Martin d'hères Cedex, France
{carlos.manuel.lopez}@gmail.com, christine.collet@grenoble-inp.fr
[3] Universidad Popular Autónoma del Estado de Puebla,
21 sur 1103 Barrio Santiago, 72410, Puebla, Puebla, Mexico
victorcuevasv@gmail.com
[4] Universidad de las Américas Puebla, Exhacienda Sta. Catarina Mártir s/n,
72820, San Andrés Cholula Puebla, Mexico
joseluis.zechinelli@udlap.mx

Abstract. This paper presents a planning-based approach for the enumeration of alternative data-centric workflows specified in ASASEL (Abstract State mAchineS Execution Language), which define the coordination of data and computation services for satisfying data requirements. The optimization of data-centric workflows is associated to the exploration of the parallelization of the workflow activities. We address the exploration of parallelism formalizing the enumeration problem in the DLV-K language. Together, our ASASEL language and enactment engine along with our enumeration approach provide the foundation for a highly flexible mechanism for managing data-centric workflows.

Keywords: Workflows · Services · Answer set planning · Logic programming

1 Introduction

We witness a proliferation of streaming and on-demand data services for accessing data pertaining to a multitude of domains, possibly involving temporal and mobile properties. The availability of data services is accompanied by a democratization in access to computational resources. Nevertheless, users typically must rely on proprietary applications that delegate data processing to their backend, which makes it difficult to share resources and add new features.

Therefore we propose ASASEL (Abstract State Machines Execution Language) to build up systems from shared resources accessible as services via data-centric workflow specifications. Our work considers both on-demand and streaming data services producing complex values, operations on these data,

© Springer International Publishing Switzerland 2015
F. Toumani et al. (Eds.): ICSOC 2014, LNCS 8954, pp. 129–143, 2015.
DOI: 10.1007/978-3-319-22885-3_12

and the ability to construct composite computation services to process them. In addition, we propose a workflow transformation framework based on planning techniques to meet quality of service goals. We present a concrete implementation of this framework covering parallelization through the workflow structure.

The remainder of this paper is structured as follows. Section 2 presents our workflow model and language, while Sect. 3 introduces our complex values data model and related operations. In Sect. 4 we present a planning-based workflow transformation framework, whose experimental results are presented in Sect. 5. Our system implementation is discussed in Sect. 6. Section 7 discusses related work. Finally, we present our conclusions and discuss future work in Sect. 8. The material in Sect. 2 is also presented in [3], which however does not cover the contents of Sect. 3 onwards.

2 Data-Centric Workflows

Consider a Friend Finder application in which multiple users carry mobile devices that periodically transmit their location. Assume that they have agreed to share some of their personal information. A user in this scenario may want to *Find friends recently located no more than 3 Km away from me, which are over 21 years old and that are interested in art*.

Data services produce data in one of two ways: on-demand in response to a given request, or continuously as a data stream. In either case, the data service exposes an interface, composed of several operations and supported by standardized protocols. The JavaScript Object Notation is used to represent the data. Accordingly, objects are built from atomic values, nested tuples, and lists.

For instance, in our scenario the users' location is available by a stream data service with the interface

$$\texttt{subscribe}() \rightarrow \lceil \texttt{location} : \langle \texttt{nickname}, \texttt{coor} \rangle \rceil$$

consisting of a subscription operation that after invocation will produce a stream of location tuples, each with a nickname that identifies the user and his/her coordinates. The rest of the data is produced by the next two on-demand data services, each represented by a single operation

$$\texttt{profile}(\texttt{nickname}) \rightarrow \texttt{person} : \langle \texttt{age}, \texttt{sex}, \texttt{email} \rangle$$
$$\texttt{interests}(\texttt{nickname}) \rightarrow [\texttt{s\_tag} : \langle \texttt{tag}, \texttt{score} \rangle]$$

The first provides a single person tuple denoting a profile of the user, once given a request represented by her nickname. The second produces, given the nickname as well, a list of s_tag tuples denoting the interests of the user by scored tags (*e.g.* 'music' with 8.5).

In order to obtain the desired result we need to give to it an executable form, in our case a workflow of activities implementing a service coordination. Workflows are built by the parallel and sequential composition of activities that are bound to data and computation services; the first provide the data, while the latter process them as required.

2.1   Workflow Model

The workflow is specified as an Abstract State Machine (ASM) [5], which can be represented as a series-parallel graph. The ASM specification of the service coordination corresponding to our example application is presented in Listing 1.1, while its workflow representation is given in Fig. 1. It includes the location, profile, and interests data services, as well as computation services for various relational operations such as selections, joins, and a time-based window bounding the location stream to recent data (e.g. location notifications obtained within the last 10 min).

```
seq
   par
      seq
         par
            seq
               location := l.location ()
               locWin := comp.timeWin(location ,10)
                  distSel := comp.funCallSel(locWin ,
                     d.dist(lat ,lon ,48.85 ,2.29) <3.0 )
            endseq
               profile := profile.profile ()
         endpar
         lp := comp.bindJoin(distSel ,profile ,nickname=nickname )
         ageSel := comp.selection(lp ,age > 21)
      endseq
      interests := i.interests ()
   endpar
   lip := comp.bindJoin(lp ,interests ,nickname=nickname )
   tagSel := comp.selection(lip ,tag='art ')
   output := comp.output(tagSel )
endseq
```

Listing 1.1. ASM specification for example application

A   workflow W is   modeled   as   a   directed   acyclic   graph $W =$ (V, E, in, out, A, C) where:

$$V \text{ is a set of vertices}$$
$$E \subseteq V \times V \text{ is a set of edges}$$
$$A \subseteq V \text{ is a set of activities}$$
$$\{in, out\} \subseteq A \text{ are the initial and final activities of } W$$
$$C \subseteq V \text{ is a set of composition operators } \{par_1, ..., par_n\}$$

There are three types of vertices: *activities* perform a service method invocation and always have ancestor and descendant vertices, *in* vertices have no ancestors and their only goal is to launch the first *activity* of the workflow, *out* vertices

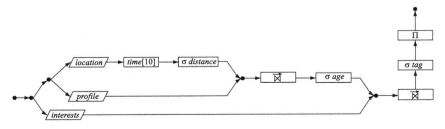

Fig. 1. Data-centric workflow for example application

have no descendants and stop the workflow execution after the last *activity*. A series of construction rules enable to generate a workflow graph from a given ASM, which are detailed in [2].

2.2   Computation Services

Two kinds of computation services form part of our approach: simple computation services and composite computation services specified in the ASASEL language.

Simple computation services involve a single service operation invocation to process data. For instance, a distance computation service that relies on a `geo-distance` service, which provides the capability to calculate the geographical distance between two points, e.g., by Vincenty's formula.

Composite computation services process data by multiple operation invocations, possibly from different services, and often also by the manipulation of local data. These tasks are organized in a service coordination specified in the ASASEL language and represented as a workflow, following a model in which we add data items as well as conditional and iteration constructs to our basic parallel and sequential composition workflow model illustrated in Fig. 1.

The specification of a time-based window composite service in ASASEL is presented in Listing 1.2, based on a simple `calendar-queue` service. It has a corresponding workflow representation as detailed in [2].

```
if( ctl_state = 'active')
  seq
     inTuple := readTuple()
     if(inTuple = nil)
        skip
     else
        seq
           oldTuple := cq.peekFirst()
           iterate(oldTuple != nil)
              if(oldTuple.ts + range < inTuple.ts)
                 seq
                    oldTuple.sign := −1
                    oldTuple.ts := oldTuple.ts + range
                    output(oldTuple)
                    cq.removeFirst()
                    oldTuple := cq.peekFirst()
                 endseq
           pq.enqueue(inTuple)
           output(inTuple)
        endseq
  endseq
```

Listing 1.2. ASM specification for the time-based window

3   Complex Values Data Model

Our workflow model is complemented by a data model consisting of complex values and operations to flexibly manipulate them. Due to space restrictions we only specify two representative operators while the full specification and semantics of the model is given in [2]. Concretely, we first define complex values and then present a recursive operator and a nesting operator over them.

The set $\mathbf{T}$ of all complex value types over a set $\mathbb{A}$ of type names is defined inductively as follows.

1. if D is a domain, then $A : D$ is an atomic type named A, where $A \in \mathbb{A}$;
2. if $\hat{t}$ is a type, then $A : \{\hat{t}\}$ is a set type named A;
3. if $\hat{t}_1, ..., \hat{t}_n$ are types with distinct names, then $A : \langle \hat{t}_1, ..., \hat{t}_n \rangle$ is a tuple type named A and each $\hat{t}_i$ is an attribute type.

3.1 Recursive Complex Value Operators

Inspired in the traditional relational operators, they apply to complex values in a recursive manner; meaning that through an expression it is possible to apply the operator to structures nested within a complex value. In particular, we present next the specification of the projection operator.

Projection. Enables to retrieve certain data elements in a complex value instance. Such data elements may be nested and multivalued. The data elements to retrieve are specified in a (possibly recursive) projection expression π_{exp}, which is applied to the input complex value instance s.

- *Notation:* $\pi_{exp}(s)$
  Projection expressions π_{exp} are constructed as follows, we use A to represent type names that occur in the complex value instance

$$
\begin{aligned}
\pi_{exp} &\quad ::= \quad \pi \;(\; list \;) \\
list &\quad ::= \quad term \;\mid\; term \;,\; list \\
term &\quad ::= \quad A \;\mid\; \pi_{exp}
\end{aligned}
$$

- *Operation type:* $\pi : \hat{t} \rightarrow \hat{t}'$, where $\hat{t}'$ is defined below
- *Semantics:* $\pi_{exp}(s)$ is defined as follows.
  First, we define the function $eval(A : v, L)$, where $A : v$ is a tuple complex value of the form $A : \langle ..., A' : v', ... \rangle$ and L an expression term (as defined by the notation third rule above).
  1. If L is of the form A' then $eval(A : v, L) = A' : v'$
  2. If L is of the form $\pi(A', L'_1, ..., L'_n)$ then $eval(A : v, L) = \pi(A', L'_1, ..., L'_n)(A' : v')$
  The value of $\pi_{exp}(s)$ is then given by
  1. If $s = A : \langle A_1 : v_1, ..., A_n : v_n \rangle = A : v$, i.e. s is a tuple complex value, and $\pi_{exp} = \pi(A, L_1, ..., L_n)$, then
     $\pi_{exp}(s) = A : \langle eval(A : v, L_1), ..., eval(A : v, L_n) \rangle$ and
     $\hat{t}'$ is $A : \langle type(eval(A : v, L_1)), ..., type(eval(A : v, L_n)) \rangle$
  2. If $s = A : \{A' : v_1, ..., A' : v_m\}$, i.e. s is a set complex value, and $\pi_{exp} = \pi(A, \pi_{exp'})$ with $\pi_{exp'}$ of the form $\pi(A', L'_1, ..., L'_n)$, then
     $\pi_{exp}(s) = A : \{\pi_{exp'}(A' : v_i) \mid A' : v_i \in val(s)\}$ and
     $\hat{t}'$ is $A : \{type(\pi_{exp'}(A' : v_j))\}$ for an arbitrary $A' : v_j \in val(s)$

Consider the following complex value

$s = person:\langle$ *sex:'M', nick:'Charles', email:'charles@gmail.com', age:40,*
          interests:{stag: $\langle$*tag:* *'art', score:* 6.5$\rangle$*, stag:* $\langle$*tag 'sports', score:* 7.5$\rangle$*}*$\rangle$

The expression $\pi(person, nick, age, \pi(interests, \pi(stag, score)))(s)$ produces the value

person:$\langle$ *nick:'Charles', age:40, interests:* { *stag:*$\langle$ *score:6.5* $\rangle$*, stag:*$\langle$*score:7.5* $\rangle$*}*$\rangle$

3.2   Nesting and Unnesting Operations

These operators take into consideration common values occurring in several tuples, therefore facilitating grouping or ungrouping them (which gives the operators their names). The specification of the group operator is presented next.

Group. Intuitively, grouping a set of tuple complex values R over a set of attributes X implies aggregating the tuples that are equal in all attributes except those in X to create a single tuple. This tuple will contain a new set attribute with new tuples containing all of the X-values of the aggregated input tuples. This set attribute is given a new name, as are the tuples built from the X attributes that are contained in it; both of which are specified in the group expression.

– *Notation*: $group_{exp}(R)$
  Group expressions exp are constructed as follows, we use A to represent the type names that occur in the complex value instances, and B and B' to represent the new names of the grouped tuples set and its constituent tuples, respectively

$$\begin{aligned} exp &\quad ::= \quad group\ (A,\ B:list\ [B']\ ) \\ list &\quad ::= \quad A\ |\ A\ ,\ list \end{aligned}$$

– *Operation type*:
  $group:\ \{A:\langle \hat{a}_1, ..., \hat{a}_m, \hat{b}_1, ..., \hat{b}_n \rangle\} \rightarrow \{A:\langle \hat{a}_1, ..., \hat{a}_m, B:\{B':\langle \hat{b}_1, ..., \hat{b}_n \rangle\}\rangle\}$
– *Semantics*:
  $group\_exp(R) =$
  $\{A:\langle A_1:v_1, ..., A_m:v_m, B:w\rangle\ |\ ($
  $\exists t \in R\ |\ \forall_{i|1 \le i \le m}\ t.A_i = v_i \wedge w =$
  $\{B':\langle B_1:u_1, ..., B_n:u_n\rangle | A:\langle A_1:v'_1, ..., A_m:v'_m, B_1:u_1, ..., B_n:u_n\rangle$
  $\{B':\langle B_1:u_1, ..., B_n:u_n\rangle | A:\langle A_1:v'_1, ..., A_m:v'_m, B_1:u_1, ..., B_n:u_n\rangle$
  $\in R \wedge \forall_{i|1 \le i \le m}\ t.A_i = v'_i\}$
  $)\}$
  where all values $A_i:v_i$ and $A_i:v'_i$ are of type $\hat{a}_i$ and all values $B_i:u_i$ are of type $\hat{b}_i$.

Consider the following set of tuple complex values

$R = \{$ *person:*$\langle$ *nickname:'Bob', tag:'sports', score:6.5* $\rangle$
       person:$\langle$ *nickname:'Bob', tag:'cars', score:8.0* $\rangle$

person: ⟨ *nickname:'Alice', tag:'fashion', score:7.0* ⟩
person:⟨ *nickname:'Alice', tag:'novels', score:8.5* ⟩ }

The expression *group(person, interests : tag, score[s_tag])(R)* thus yields:

$R' = \{$ *person:*⟨ *nickname:'Bob',*
                 interests:{*s_tag:*⟨ *tag:'sports', score:6.5* ⟩,
                          s_tag:⟨*tag:'cars', score:8.0* ⟩ },
              person:⟨ *nickname:'Alice',*
                 interests:{*s_tag:*⟨ *tag:'fashion', score:7.0* ⟩,
                          s_tag:⟨*tag:'novels', score:8.5* ⟩ } }

4   Workflow Enumeration

This section decribes the process of enumerating all the equivalent workflows that satisfy the same functional requirements given by an ASASEL specification. The enumeration leads to a search space of workflows with increasing levels of parallelism in their structure. The levels of parallelism can privilege the cost preferences such as response time or the communication cost. The enumeration is subject to constraints for composing the required activities by the ASASEL specification. In order to make a proof of concept, we model these constraints as action rules in the language DLV-K[1].

In DLV-K, planning problems have a set of facts that represent the problem domain named background knowledge. The facts are predicates of static knowledge and are the input of the planning problem. Planning problems are modeled as state machines described by a set of fluents and a set of actions. A fluent is a property of an object in the world and is part of the states of the world. Fluents may be true, false or unknown. An action is executable if a precondition holds in the current state. Once an action is executed, the fluents and thus the state of the plan are modified. The action rules define the subset of fluents that must be held before the execution of an action (*i.e.* pre-conditions) and the subset of fluents to be held after the execution (*i.e.* post-conditions). Finally, a goal is a set of fluents that must be reached at the end of the plan. A goal is expressed by the conjunction of fluents and by a plan length $l \in \mathbb{Z}^+$.

The mapping from workflow enumeration to a planning problem is shown in Table 1. The APIs and the required activities by the ASASEL specification are modeled as facts of the background knowledge. The execution state of a workflow is modeled as fluents and the activities to perform as actions.

Next we show, through an example, how we represent the background knowledge for workflow enumeration. Afterwards, we show how the workflow state and activities are expressed in DLV-K rules. Given such rules, the DLV-K engine performs the workflow enumeration.

---

[1] http://www.dbai.tuwien.ac.at/proj/dlv/k.

Table 1. Mapping to a planning problem

Workflow	Planning problem
APIs, required activities	Facts (background knowledge)
Workflow states	Fluents
Workflow activities	Actions
Result delivery	Goal: finished? $(l \in \mathbb{Z}^+)$

4.1 Background Knowledge

The background knowledge contains a set of facts of the form fact/# where # is the arity of the fact. Facts serve as the input for the workflow enumeration. It includes (1) the service methods and (2) the required activities derived from the ASASEL specification.

Service methods are represented by the facts method/2. The bound and free attributes associated to such a method are represented by the facts bound_p/4 and free_p/4. The rule att/4 represents the normal form of an attribute.

```
method(p,profl).
bound_a(p,profl,nickname,str).
free_a(p,profl,age,int).
free_a(p,profl,sex,str).
free_a(p,profl,email,str).

att(DSN,ON,PN,T):- bound_a(DSN,ON,PN,T).
att(DSN,ON,PN,T):- free_a(DSN,ON,PN,T).
```

Required activities are derived from the ASASEL workflow specification and represented through facts (with the underscore at the end). The required activities derived from a workflow implementing *"What are the interests of my friend Joe?"* are represented by the following facts.

```
project_(p1,nickname,n).
project_(i1,score,s).
project_(i1,tag,t).
retrieve_(p,profl,p1).
retrieve_(i,interests,i1).
filter_(p1,nickname).
join_(p1,nickname,i1,nickname).
```

These required activities express the need over the methods p:profl and i:interests. Both data are retrieved by retrieve_/3 and represented by p1 and i1. The nickname attribute of the profile is filtered by filter_/2 and correlated by join_/4 interests through the nickname attribute. The attributes nickname, score and tag are projected. Observe that the filter over the nickname attribute is only indicated as the equality operators are not relevant for the workflow transformation.

4.2   Workflow Activities

Workflow activities are represented as actions in DLV-K. Such actions are predicates that require facts from the background knowledge to be true. There are also activities that are independent from facts.

init and finish. These activities have the special purpose to initialize and terminate the workflow execution. Thus their semantics is not associated with the application and there is no dependency with the background knowledge.

data_service establishes a connection with a data service method. It requires from the knowledge base a service method and the expressed need to retrieve data from it.

```
data_service(DS)  requires  method(DSN,ON),  retrieve_(DSN,ON,DS).
```

bind_selection invokes a service method and retrieves data from it. The invocation is done by providing a bound attribute.

```
bind_selection(DS,BP)  requires  method(DSN,ON),
    retrieve_(DSN,ON,DS),   bound_a(DSN,ON,BP,_),  filter_(DS,BP).
```

bind_join correlates data from two service methods w.r.t. an attribute from each one. The attribute from the outer method must be bound. This activity is analogous to **bind_selection** but it takes the value from another method attribute.

```
bind_join(DS1,P1,DS2,BP2)  requires
    method(DSN1,ON1),  retrieve_(DSN1,ON1,DS1),
    att(DSN1,ON1,P1,_),  method(DSN2,ON2),  retrieve_(DSN2,ON2,DS2),
    bound_a(DSN2,ON2,BP2,_),  join_(DS1,P1,DS2,BP2).
```

filter performs the filtering over an attribute of a required service method.

```
filter(DS,P)  requires  method(DSN,ON),  retrieve_(DSN,ON,DS),
                        att(DSN,ON,P,_),  filter_(DS,P).
```

project projects an attribute of a service method.

```
project(DS,P)  requires  project_(DS,P,_).
```

The semantics of these activities is completed with constraints that define their pre-conditions and post-conditions.

4.3   Workflow Constraints

The workflow constraints define the pre-conditions and post-conditions associated to the execution of the workflow activities. A condition is a state of knowledge modifiable by the execution of activities. Through the satisfaction of such conditions, the workflows are transformed. In the following, we present the intuition of these constraints along with their rules in DLV-K.

init and finish. The **init** activity has no previous activity and its pre-condition is that the workflow has not been **initiated**. As post-condition, it produces the state **initiated**. The last activity is **finish** and there is no other activity to be executed afterwards. Its pre-condition is that there is not evidence that the workflow is **finished** and the result has been **delivered** (See **output** activity below for details about **delivered**). The post-condition of **finish** is **finished** and this is the goal to be reached for the workflow transformation.

```
executable  init if    -initiated.
caused      initiated after init.
executable  finish if not finished, delivered.
caused      finished after finish.
```

data_service. Once initiated the workflow, the data services must be **connected(DS)**. This fluent is produced by the execution of the **data_service(DS)** activity.

```
executable  data_service(DS) if initiated.
caused      connected(DS) after data_service(DS).
```

In order to retrieve all the required data, all data services should be connected. The fluent **all_connected** that is false if there is not evidence that a data service is connected. Otherwise, it is true.

```
caused  -all_connected if not connected(DS).
caused  all_connected if not -all_connected.
```

bind_selection. It is only executable if there is not evidence that data from the data service **DS** have been retrieved and if there is a connection with **DS**. Once the bind selection is executed, the fluent **retrieved(DS)** is true.

```
executable  bind_selection(DS,BP) if not retrieved(DS), connected(DS).
caused  retrieved(DS) after bind_selection(DS,BP).
```

filter. It is executable if there is not evidence that the attribute **P** of **DS** has been filtered. It is required that the data from **DS** have been retrieved and the activity **select_(DS,P)** must be required. The execution of the filter makes the fluent **filtered(DS,P)** true.

```
executable  filter(DS,P) if not filtered(DS,P),
            retrieved(DS), filter_(DS,P).
caused  filtered(DS,P) after filter(DS,P).
```

As might several filter activities over **DS** are required, the **all_filtered_from** becomes true if there is no other attribute pending to be filtered.

```
caused  -all_filtered_from(DS) if not filtered(DS,P), filter_(DS,P).
caused  all_filtered_from(DS) if not -all_filtered_from(DS),
                                   retrieved(DS).
```

There is the fluent **all_filtered** that becomes true if there is no other attribute of the method **DS** pending to be filtered.

```
caused  -all_filtered if -all_filtered_from(DS), filter_(DS,P).
caused  -all_filtered if -all_filtered_from(DS), not filter_(DS,P),
                         att(DSN,ON,P,_), retrieve_(DSN,ON,DS).
```

project. This activity is executable if there is not evidence that the attribute P of DS has been projected. The execution of projection makes the fluent `projected` true.

```
executable  project(DS,P)  if  not  projected(DS,P),retrieved(DS),
                            project_(DS,P,_).
```

During the workflow execution, all the projection activities have to be performed. For the method DS, the fluent `all_projected_from` is true if there is no other attribute from DS pending to be projected. The fluent `all_projected` is true if there is no other DS with an attribute pending to be projected.

```
caused  −all_projected_from(DS)  if  not  projected(DS,P),  project_(DS,P,_).
caused   all_projected_from(DS)  if  not  −all_projected_from(DS)
                            after  project(DS,P).
caused  −all_projected  if  −all_projected_from(DS),  project_(DS,P,_).
```

output. Once all the required activities are performed, the result is delivered by the activity `output`. To model this pre-condition, the fluent `activities_performed` is true if all the required activities have been processed. Otherwise, the fluent is false `-activities_performed`.

```
caused   all_projected  if  not  −all_projected.
caused  −activities_performed  if  not  all_connected,not  all_retrieved,
                            not  all_filtered,  not  all_projected.
caused   activities_performed  if  not  −activities_performed.
```

Once the result is delivered by `output`, the fluent `delivered` becomes true and the workflow can be finished (*cf.* `finish` pre-conditions).

```
executable  output  if  activities_performed,  not  delivered.
caused  delivered  after  output.
```

5   Experiments

We performed experiments to measure the amount of alternative workflows with sequential compositions and with parallel compositions for a given ASASEL workflow. We setup seven different ASASEL workflows $WF^1, ..., WF^7$ with increasing number of activities and different potential grades of parallelism.

The generated workflows were classified by analyzing the data dependencies among activities and their structures. A workflow whose independent activities

(a) par^+ workflow   (b) seq^+ workflow

Fig. 2. Classification of alternative workflows

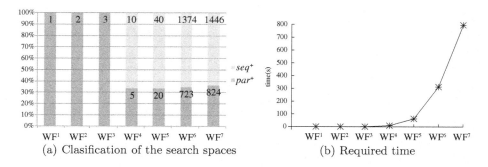

Fig. 3. Enumeration of the space of alternative workflows with different grade of parallelism

are composed in parallel is classified as par^+, *cf.* Fig. 2a; otherwise it is classified as seq^+, *cf.* Fig. 2b. The charts in Fig. 3 show the search spaces with the classification of workflows and the required time for each ASASEL workflow $WF^1, ..., WF^7$.

In Fig. 3a, the search spaces of the workflows $WF^1 - WF^3$ only contain par^+ workflows because they have few activities and there are no independent activities. The search spaces of the workflows $WF^4 - WF^7$ have ~1/3 of par^+ workflows and ~2/3 seq^+ workflows. This correspondence is not constant and depends on the data dependencies among activities, *e.g.* a workflow with many activities may have only sequential alternatives if there are no independent activities.

The par^+ workflows represent good opportunities for improving time related costs while the seq^+ ones privilege the resource usage. This classification can be used for improving the enumeration performance (*cf.* Fig. 3b) by incorporating user's preferences over the costs or QoS measures associated to the workflow execution.

6 System Implementation

The ASASEL system was developed on the Java platform. Workflows are entered textually via a GUI illustrated in Fig. 4 and their corresponding visualization is generated. The system interacts with DLV-K through intermediate input and output files generated and parsed as required. The enactment of a selected workflow is supported by two main components. First, a scheduler determines which service is executed at a given time according to a predefined policy. Second, composite services are executed by an interpreter that implements the full ASASEL language. Computation service workflows can also be visualized through the GUI, as shown at the right part of the screenshot in Fig. 4.

During the execution of a workflow, data flows from the data services to complex value operators as well as several computation services via queues, as determined by the ASASEL specification. These computation services run on a Tomcat container supported by the JAX-WS reference implementation, which enables to create stateful services. Additional output services can be specified to

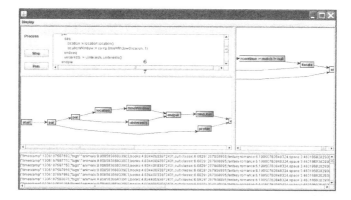

Fig. 4. Caption of the ASASEL GUI

output data in textual form in the GUI or to transmit it to another application. For instance, in our example application we output as a result a data stream that denotes the tuples that are added and the tuples that are removed from the result dataset.

We implemented two test scenarios and their corresponding data and computation services. The first one is the location-based application introduced in Sect. 2. The second scenario is an adaptation of the online auctions NEXMark benchmark[2] for XML stream query processing which we employed to obtain performance measurements. In brief, the measurements indicated a tolerable overhead for the use of services, which we consider outweighed by the advantages.

7   Related Work

Data-centric workflows involving services share some similarities with queries over Web services as presented in [10]. There the authors propose an optimization approach by ordering the service calls in a pipelined fashion and by tuning the size of service call batches. An algebraic approach for the optimization of workflows with relational and map-reduce operations is presented in [8]. Our approach is to enable workflows with a broader variety of operations defined through service compositions, thus requiring alternative optimization techniques.

Planning techniques have been applied for automatic service composition, for instance in [7] and [9]. The problem addressed in those works is to create a service composition from atomic actions (services) based on a propositional goal. The Roman Model [1] alternatively employs finite state transition system descriptions for the available and target services, but with the same basic objective in mind. However, we use planning techniques instead for the optimization of a workflow that includes possibly composite computation services.

Alternative formalisms for the specification of workflows include, for example, process algebras [4] and petri nets [6]. The use of ASMs provides a formal

---

[2] http://datalab.cs.pdx.edu/niagara/NEXMark/.

semantics, as in the aformentioned formalisms, but also fully compatible text and workflow representations that are easy to specify. Although ASMs have been used to study and model the properties of workflows, less effort has been given to using them in a fully operational manner.

8 Conclusions and Future Work

In this paper we presented a language and system for the specification and enactment of data-centric workflows based on service composition. In addition, we introduced a planning-based approach for the enumeration of the search space of workflows implementing requirements specifications. Concretely, we proposed a set of constraints modeled in an action language, specifically DLV-K, in order to characterize the transformation of workflows with sequential and parallel compositions. This work is envisaged to be a foundation for incorporating a full cost model that covers the specification of composite computation services, leading to the selection of the most suitable workflow w.r.t. the user's preferences. Future work also includes validating the practicality of ASASEL for the specification of data-centric workflows for diverse users, which would require a more sophisticated GUI-based editing tool than our current prototype.

References

1. Calvanese, D., De Giacomo, G., Lenzerini, M., Mecella, M., Patrizi, F.: Automatic service composition and synthesis: the roman model. IEEE Data Eng. Bull. **31**(3), 18–22 (2008)
2. Cuevas-Vicenttín, V.: Evaluation of hybrid queries based on service coordination. Ph.D. thesis, University of Grenoble, May 2005. http://tel.archives-ouvertes.fr/tel-00630601
3. Cuevas-Vicenttín, V., Vargas-Solar, G., Collet, C., Ibrahim, N., Bobineau, C.: Coordinating services for accessing and processing data in dynamic environments. In: Meersman, R., Dillon, T.S., Herrero, P. (eds.) OTM 2010. LNCS, vol. 6426, pp. 309–325. Springer, Heidelberg (2010)
4. Curcin, V., Missier, P., De Roure, D.: Simulating taverna workflows using stochastic process algebras. Concurr. Comput. : Pract. Exper. **23**(16), 1920–1935 (2011)
5. Gurevich, Y.: Evolving Algebras 1993: Lipari Guide. In: Specification and Validation Methods, pp. 9–36. Oxford University Press Inc., New York (1995)
6. Hidders, J., Kwasnikowska, N., Sroka, J., Tyszkiewicz, J., Van den Bussche, J.: Dfl: A dataflow language based on petri nets and nested relational calculus. Inf. Syst. **33**(3), 261–284 (2008)
7. McIlraith, S.A., Son, T.C.: Adapting golog for composition of semantic web services. In: Proceedings of the Eights International Conference on Principles and Knowledge Representation and Reasoning (KR 2002), 22–25 April, 2002, Toulouse, France, pp. 482–496 (2002)
8. Ogasawara, E.S., de Oliveira, D., Valduriez, P., Dias, J., Porto, F., Mattoso, M.: An algebraic approach for data-centric scientific workflows. PVLDB **4**(12), 1328–1339 (2011)

9. Sirin, E., Parsia, B., Wu, D., Hendler, J., Nau, D.: Htn planning for web service composition using shop2. Web Semant. **1**(4), 377–396 (2004)
10. Srivastava, U., Munagala, K., Widom, J., Motwani, R.: Query optimization over web services. In: Proceedings of the 32nd International Conference on Very Large Data Bases, VLDB 2006, pp. 355–366. VLDB Endowment (2006)

Discovering and Categorizing Goal Alignments from Mined Process Variants

Karthikeyan Ponnalagu[1,3]([✉]), Aditya Ghose[3], Nanjangud C. Narendra[2], and Hoa Khanh Dam[3]

[1] IBM Research India, Bangalore, India
karthikeyan.ponnalagu@in.ibm.com
[2] Cognizant Technology Solutions, Bangalore, India
ncnaren@gmail.com
[3] University of Wollongong, Wollongong, Australia
aditya.ghose@gmail.com, hoa@uow.edu.au

Abstract. With the emergence of contextual enterprise, organizations increasingly tend to analyze the adherence of the day to day execution of internal business processes with their stated goals. This is needed so that they can continuously evaluate and readjust their operating models and corresponding business strategies. However organizations often find it very difficult to discover and categorize the process variants in terms of their stated goal adherence from process execution logs. This is due to the challenges in resolving the extent of goal compliance as it necessitates the classification of process variants first in terms of the contextual factors associated with the process execution. In this paper, we propose our approach for discovering goal adherence of process variant instances mined from event logs. We first generate goal-service alignment models to establish correlation of process fragments with specific sub-goals of the organization's goal model. Subsequently we discover the extent of goal adherence of individual process instances by the composition of correlated sub-goals. We also associate the contextual factors with each process instance that are goal preserving in nature. Leveraging the difference in correlation and association of contextual factors we classify the instances as goal preserving executed process variants. This bottom-up approach enables the organizations to study the depth and breadth of goal adherence in their organizations. Also the impact of any specific change in the goal decomposition models and the associated contextual factors can be studied with our approach. We evaluate our approach using a real industrial case study in IT Incident Management using a event log of 25000 records.

Keywords: Variability · Reuse · SOA · Process mining · Event logs

1 Introduction

Today, organizations tend to continuously adapt their operation strategies due to changing business dimensions. One aspect of this adaptation is continuous

© Springer International Publishing Switzerland 2015
F. Toumani et al. (Eds.): ICSOC 2014, LNCS 8954, pp. 144–157, 2015.
DOI: 10.1007/978-3-319-22885-3_13

evolution of the goal models governing the internal business processes. This necessitates assessment of such evolutionary changes in their internal operations mostly characterized as business process models. From the history of past execution of a given process in the form of event logs, assessing the alignment of executed process instances for a proposed change/deviation in their current strategies is an important business need. On the other hand, the emergence of adaptive Process Management Systems (PMSs) [12], have contributed to arising challenges of non-conformance and misalignment to organization goals and strategies [7]. The goal of this paper is to discover and categorize goal adherence information of process variants from transaction logs. This we see as an important aspect of *variability management (VM)* [13]. VM has received considerable research and industry attention over the past decade [3] due to increasing need for differing alignments to organization's strategies and goals. Process mining techniques focus on extracting process execution insights from event logs [2]. While the existing body of work contains useful results in the space of leveraging schema and ontology [4] to discover and differentiate process capabilities, much remains to be done in the space of mining goal alignments from process logs and thereby improvising process designs as discussed in the IEEE Task Force Manifesto on Process Mining [18]. In the context of organization's goal alignment, an adequate (and formal) definition of what makes a process instance a variant of another has remained elusive [9]. There is also considerable challenge in mining process varaints from event logs, as they are generally scattered across different business units of the organization. Also most often these logs have differing maturity levels of data completeness leading to difficulty in discovering patterns of non-compliance [16]. This has meant that there is considerable room for improvement in the support that many existing approaches to VM offer for key functions such as context-driven variant substitution [20], variant validation, variant identification from process log.

A goal is basically a formal assertion (a condition or a partial state description) that an organization seeks to realize. This paper argues that the notion of a *goal* must underpin any process variability mining framework . Goals provide an adequate basis for a formal definition of *variation* at the time of process design and engineering. We argue that an artifact is a variant of another if and only if it realizes the same goal (but in possibly different ways). In this paper, we propose our approach for discovering goal adherence of process instances mined from event logs. We assume the following inputs to our proposed approach: (a) a goal model (e.g., as depicted in Fig. 1) with goals and associated decomposition of sub goals (AND, OR) represented as a collection of boolean conditions in conjunctive normal form (CNF) [10]. For our evaluation, we have developed a goal modeling eclipse plugin to design a goal model with end effect annotations; (b) a process event log containing a set of event records. The event log contains multiple process instance execution data along with association state transitions and associated contextual factors, (c) a standard list of state transition events that are represented as end effect annotations and (d) a semantically annotated process design created with the composition of services, said process design adhering to the goal model. We first generate Process Instance Goal

`Alignment` `(PIGA)` model to discover the extent of goal adherence at the process instance level by formalizing it as truth satisfaction in propositional logic. We also associate the environmental factors with each process instance that are goal preserving in nature. From such discovered goal preserving process instances, we categorize the instance variants based on the extent of goal adherence and associate with a contextual reasoning of environmental factors.

This paper is organized as follows. Section 2 discusses our case study example, which is drawn from the IT Ticket Management domain. In Sect. 3 we discuss how we leverage goal models for variability analysis to generate process instance goal alignment and categorization of process instances. In Sect. 4, we evaluate our proposed approach by running experiments on an real world industrial case study. We discuss the related work in this area in Sect. 5 and conclude the paper in Sect. 6.

2   Running Example

Our running example is based on an actual industrial case study of IT incident resolution process. This is illustrated in Fig. 4. The goals and derived sub-goals of this process are depicted in Fig. 1. As Fig. 1 illustrates, when a new incident is reported, it needs to be determined whether there was an earlier reported incident matching with the newly reported incident. If so, then the new incident is linked with the problem ticket of the matched incident. Depending on the status of the linked problem ticket being closed or pending, the new incident is kept open or closed. If there exists no similar incident, then the new incident is subjected to a standard list of diagnostic tests to enrich the data. Then based on the identified level of complexity, corresponding known fixes are tried to solve the incident. If the incident is solved, it is closed. Otherwise, it is escalated to the next level of support. Once the escalation happens, the steps of identifying level of complexity, trying out the known fixes to solve the incident or to escalate to the next level are repeated. The different paths of activity flows are also best captured by differentiating the links between the goals as either being AND or XOR types, as depicted in Fig. 1. An AND link in Fig. 1 specifies that all sub-goals of a goal need to be satisfied for the goal to be satisfied; an XOR link specifies that the sub-goals are mutually exclusive, and only one is needed to satisfy the goal. For example, the goal of Incident and Problem management fulfills the goals Fix Problem, Detect Problem and Verify Problem, viz., a case of AND relationship. If we consider the goals Isolate Problem or Escalate Problem they share an XOR Relationship as in any given situation only one of the goals can be fulfilled and they are mutually exclusive in nature.

We collected and consolidated process logs consisting of 25000 records. Each of the records signify a specific state transition of ticket. A ticket in `start` state signals the initiation of Incident resolution process. A ticket in `closed` state signifies the conclusion of the process. We used PROM [15] process miner to identify 1500 process instances from this log. As illustrated in Fig. 2, the number of state transitions is not constant among the process instance executions.

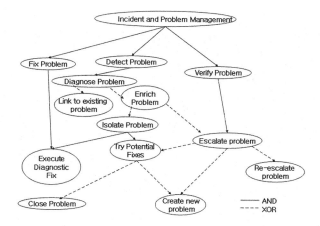

Fig. 1. Goals & Sub-goals

This indicates that a significant percentage of process instances have higher execution cycles for achieving incident resolution. We identified two scenarios for the difference in execution among the process instances: One contributed by the contextual factors such as incident complexity, unavailability of customer, resource constraints and so on as illustrated in Fig. 3; The other contributed by varying levels of adherence to the goals stated in Fig. 1. In the rest of this paper, we focus on addressing both of these scenarios.

3   Goal Aligned Process Variant Mining

In this section, we argue for the centrality of goals in mining, categorizing and reasoning of process variants in terms of goal alignment and associated contextual factors. The effectiveness of our approach relies on a correct and complete goal decomposition model as illustrated in Fig. 1. For a given goal decomposition model, we assert the following:

- A1: a set S of sub-goals will achieve a parent goal G(entailment);
- A2: S $\models$ G will never be incorrect (consistency).
- A3: S will be the smallest set of sub-goals to achieve G (minimality);

The key idea is to leverage such a goal model to organize and categorize the process variants to identify the extent of goal adherence in an organization. This involves the following as depicted in Fig. 5: We start with discovering unique process instances from event logs using a process mining tool. Each process instance contributes to a varying number of events generated as part of its execution. Using the assertion A1 and A2, we tend to identify "faultly executed instances". That is, if a given process instance does not satisfy the set S, it violates entailment of G. We subsequently categorize the process instances as variants based on the alignment to the OR-refinements of sub-goals in S and

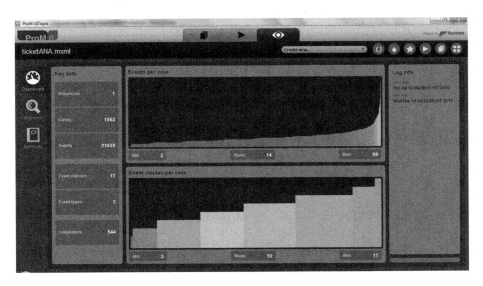

Fig. 2. State transitions of incident tickets

satisfying the assertion A3. For each category of variant instances, we initiate reasoning based on contextual factors by leveraging association rule mining approaches. The rest of this section discusses each of these steps in detail.

3.1   Process Instance Goal Alignment (PIGA)

In this section, we discuss our approach for generating goal correlation based identification of "valid" process instances. We achieve it through the generation of what we call **Process Instance Goal Alignment**. In Sect. 2, we discussed how we mined around 1562 process instances on incident resolution management. The objective is to evaluate each of such mined instance against the root goal correlated with the given process model. This is achieved by positioning a subset of state transitions in the process instance as a correlation to one of the sub goals realizing the root goal. Each sub goal in the goal model is annotated with an intended end effect resulting from the realization of the goal. Then leveraging a standard semantic matching tool such as [6], we begin from the initial state transition and iterate with the succeeding state transitions till we identify correlation with atleast one mandatory sub goal of G. For this, we assume a standard ontological schema specific to the domain (such as Insurance, Health Care) is used to express the end effect annotations. For our evaluation we have considered ITIL's Common Information Model (CIM). We leverage the cumulative similarity match score to identify the closest correlated goal for a given task in the process. Once we identify a correlation, we group all of its preceding state transitions and call this as *maximally refined correlation group* for that goal. Like this we split the process instance into one or more such groups as follows:

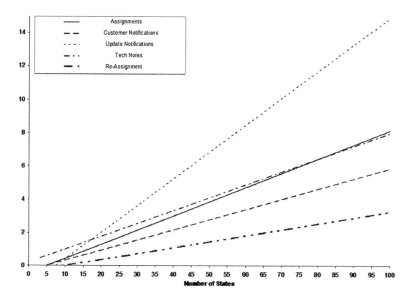

Fig. 3. Process instance characteristics

Given a goal model (AND-OR goal graph) $\mathcal{G}$, a group of state transitions ST will be referred to as the *maximally refined correlation group* for a sub-goal $G1$ if and only if all of the following hold:

- C1: A group ST is always correlated with one mandatory sub goal $G1$ only. $ST \models G1'$ is always false
- C2: There exists no state transition e in a given goal correlation group ST that is part of another group correlating a different sub-goal If $e \subseteq ST$ the, $e \subset ST'$ does not arise.
- C3: The number of state transitions in the group ST is the smallest set of state transitions that are required to entail the goal $G1$.

At the end of this exercise, if any of the mandatory sub goals of root goal G is not correlated, it implies that the process instance P is not correlated with the goal G and is rejected. We repeat this evaluation for each of the mined process instance to identify the "valid process instances". The expression of the process instance in terms of list of goal correlation groups, along with the correlated mandatory sub-goal constitutes the Process Instance Goal Alignment. In this technique, we can observe that two aspects are ignored: One, we did not discuss the state transitions that are not part of any *maximally refined correlation group*. Two, we have only focused on the correlation of mandatory sub-goals $G1..Gn$ of G, without focusing on the actual entailment of a particular OR-refinement of a given sub goal $G1$. This we will discuss in the next section. Figure 6 depicts the distribution of state transitions across the 1562 process instances in our running example. We illustrate the generation of PIGA with a small number

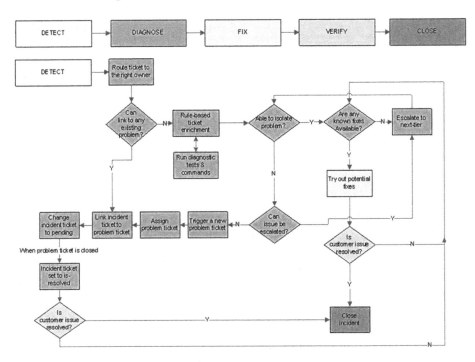

Fig. 4. Incident resolution process

of process instance data from the running example as depicted in Table 1. We observe that the process instance INS0001 is split into three groups GR1, GR2 and GR3 respectively. Each group correlates with one of the mandatory sub-goals in the goal model in Fig. 1. This leads to the conclusion that INS0001 is a valid goal preserving process instance of Fig. 4 as it satisfies the conditions C1 and C2. The complete validation of condition C3 is subjective to identifying similar groups that correlate the goal `Fix Problem` from other process instances. In the case of instance INS0024, even though logically the ticket is closed, there is no entailment of the mandatory sub-goals `Fix Problem, Verify Problem`. This violates condition C1 and therefore, INS0024 is not a valid instance. The instance INS0033 is also not a valid instance as it has not have a group correlating the goal `Verify Problem`, even though the problem is actually fixed. The verification of fix was not performed in this instance. This is an interesting scenario, as without the notion of goal adherence, the instance INS0033 would have been confirmed as a successful execution of the incident resolution process.

3.2   Process Instance Variants Categorization

A process instance P' (with a set of effect scenarios E' observed from its state transition events) will be deemed to be a *variant* of another process variant P (with a set of final effect scenarios E) if and only if any one of the following hold:

Table 1. PIGA generation for goal alignment and categorization

Event groups	State transitions	Instance ID	Correlated goal
GR1	(Start, Open Notification, ticket opened, Acknowledge Notification, Investigation Started, problem identified)	INS0001	Detect Problem
GR2	(Tech Note identified, solution identified, Fixing Started, Pending Customer, Incorrect Solution, Tech Note identified, solution identified, Fixing Started, Pending Customer, problem fixed)	INS0001	Fix Problem
GR3	(Service Restored, Ticket Closed)	INS0001	Verify Problem
GR4	(Start, Open Notification Not Sent, System Alerted, Notification Sent, ticket opened, Acknowledge Notification, Investigation Started, problem identified)	INS0024	Detect Problem
GR5	(Tech Note Identified, Solution Identified, Customer System Not ready, Ticket Closed)	INS0024	Not correlated
GR6	(Start, Open Notification Not Sent, System Alerted, Notification Sent, ticket opened, Acknowledge Notification, Investigation Started, problem identified)	INS0033	Detect Problem
GR7	(Tech Note Identified, Solution Identified, Fixing Started, Problem Fixed)	INS0033	Fix Problem
GR8	Ticket Closed	INS0033	Not correlated
GR1	(Start, Open Notification, ticket opened, Acknowledge Notification, Investigation Started, problem identified)	INS0034	Detect Problem
GR9	(Reassigned-Additional Work, Solution Identified, Customer Notified)	INS0034	Fix Problem
GR10	Customer Confirmed, Ticket Closed	INS0034	Verify Problem

- **Post-condition entailment (C1):** For every $e' \in E'$, there exists an $e \in E$ such that $e' \models e$ and for every $e \in E$, there exists an $e' \in E'$ such that $e' \models e$.
- **Goal entailment (C2):** For some maximally refined correlated goal G of P, $e' \models G$ for every $e' \in E'$.

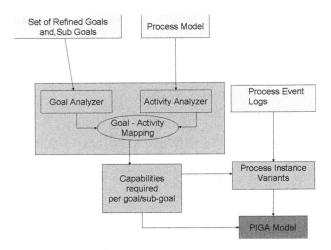

Fig. 5. Systematic view of proposed approach

- **Disjunctive entailment (C3):** A maximally refined correlated goal G' of P' is an OR-alternative of a maximally refined correlated goal G of P or obtained via a series of OR-refinements of an OR-alternative of G.

Given the process instances P and P', if a maximally refined correlated goal G' of P' can be obtained via a series of OR-refinements of a maximally refined correlated goal of P, then condition **C2** (goal entailment) holds. This also applies to the maximally refined correlation groups of the process instances that we have discussed in the previous section. We start by leveraging the PIGA model that constructs the correlation groups and perform the initial categorization of "Valid vs invalid" process instances. In PIGA Model, if two process variants share the same set of event groups, then we establish that they are similarly executed instances. If they are expressed respectively by different set of event groups, we initiate variation categorization and create a new category. Any subsequent process instance from the event log is first matched with all existing variant categories before creating a new category. This is achieved in an iterative manner till we complete categorization of all the process instances discovered from the event log. We illustrate with our running example as follows: Let us compare the process instances INS0001 and INS0034 in Table 1. By observing their correlation groups alignment to mandatory sub-goals, we establish that both are valid process instances that adhere to the root goal in 1. We can express INS0001 as $GR1, GR2, GR3 \sqsubseteq INS0001$, and INS0034 as $GR1, GR9, GR10 \sqsubseteq INS00341$. We can obviously infer that these two instances are not executed similarly. In the case of INS0001, the identified solution is locally applied by the support executive and only confirmed by the user. But in the case of INS0034, given the nature of the customer system, the customer is instructed to follow the guidelines to apply the fix and fixing is subsequently confirmed. These two are two different

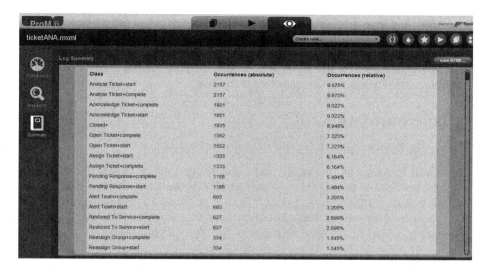

Fig. 6. List of state transitions and occurances

realizations of the goal and belong to two categories (Remote fix, Local fix with guidance) of process variations. If we refine the goal correlation, we can establish that the group GR1 of INS0001 can be aligned with the child goal `Execute Diagnostic Fix`, which is the OR-refinement of the goal `Fix Problem`. But the group GR9 of INS0034 is aligned with the goal `Fix Problem`. On reflection, we can further establish that the instance INS0001 is a derived variant customization of the instance INS0034. These are useful insights from understanding the functional relationships of process instances from a goal adherence perspective and to assess the ripple effects when the associated goals are changed.

Subsequent to the categorization of valid process instances into different data sets, we proceed to reason the categorization by applying association rule mining(ARM). For this, we have used a simple ARM mining tool [17]. We start by identifying a list of candidate contextual factors using which we want to mine the association rules. For each category of adherence to an OR-refinment sub goal, the contextual factors with maximum support and confidence will be associated at the end of this exercise. In addition to that, the same confidence factors affecting different such goal adherence will also be discovered. This further enables deriving dependency insights between a pair of goals that are not necessarily the OR-refinements from the same parent goal. For example, as depicted in Table 1, the instances INS0034 and INS0001 align with the goals `Fix Problem` and `Execute Diagnostic Fix` respectively. For the instance INS0034, we identify `Email Notification, Remote Connection Issues and Manual Solution Fix` as the associated contextual factors. Similarly for the instance INS0001, we identify `Email Notification, Wrong Assignment` as the associated contextual factors. A simple inference by just comparing these two instances (before evaluating the support and confidence against the entire data set of 1534 instances) is the factors `Remote Connection Issues and Manual Solution Fix` leads to adherence of goal `Fix Problem`. Given that `Fix Problem` is a parent goal of textttExecute Diagnostic Fix, such observations can eventually lead to augmenting the current goal model with creating additional OR-Refinement child goals for the goal `Fix Problem`.

4   Experimentation

The purpose of the evaluation is to establish the following:

- The Goal Refinement procedure and semantic end effect annotations of state transitions enable reasonably correct identification of goal preserving valid instance variants for a given process from a large pool of event records.
- Our proposed approach can also leveraged to categorize the valid process variants in terms of the goal alignments for a given goal model.

Therefore, our evaluation will primarily demonstrate the scalability and correctness of our approach. A prototype implementation supporting list of state transitions of a process instance and using them as effect annotation of goal models is implemented an Eclipse-based plugin called VAGAI (Variability Analysis with Goal Annotations and Integration). Also for the sake of simplicity, we have restricted the annotations to the same domain schema based on CIM[1]. We have extracted the process instances using PROM [15] from the event record data with 23124 event records. As depicted in 6, using PROM we extracted 15000 records along with associated events. The evaluations were done on a 64 bit Windows 7 machine with Intel Celeron @ 1.07 Ghz, 4 GB RAM. We ran the events with the VAGAI tool, taking the list of events and annotated goal model to generate PIGA. As depicted in Table 2, the generated PIGA for all the 1562 event instances contains a total of 74 event correlation groups. Out of which, 55 groups were correlating with a mandatory sub-goal from the goal model depicted in Fig. 1. This resulted in 681 instances being categorized as valid instances out of the total set. The distribution of the valid instances across different categories based on respective goal adherence is depicted in Table 3. As we observe for example, most of customer self-help fixes have been contributed by remote system connection issues. Also issues due to third party software have been raised taking considerable effort in diagnosing and closing the problem. Most of the escalation issues have been contributed by either wrong email address or avoidable human errors on wrong ticket assignments. These operational insights thus provide different contextual aspects on execution of process instances and help improvising overall goal adherence.

5   Related Work

The area of Process mining has gained relatively recent research focus and is cross disciplined in nature [1,5]. It leverages data mining techniques on one

---

[1] dmtf.org/standards/cim.

Table 2. View of goal correlated groups in an industrial data set

Instances	Total correlated groups	Goal aligned groups	Valid instances
1562	74	55	681

Table 3. Categorization of goal adherence

Goal aligned groups	Category	Contextual factor		
		Name	Max. Support	Max. Confidence
5	Fix Problem	Remote Connection Issues	.07	.9
10	Execute Diagnostic Fix	Known Solution	.08	1.0
9	Close Problem	Third party Vendor Issues	.09	0.9
10	Create New Problem	Event Trace Missing	.07	.8
1	Escalate Problem	Wrong Ticket Assignment	.009	0.6
6	Enrich Problem	Additional Diagnostics	.05	0.7
1	Detect Problem	Known Solution	.008	0.6
9	Verify Problem	Email Sent	.09	0.9
4	Re-escalate Problem	Wrong Email Note	0.06	.9

hand, and process modeling and analysis techniques on the other hand. The existing works in the area of process mining have mostly focused on the data mining aspects [18] such as control flow discovery and model conformance. But aspects such as concept and goal conformance drift that arises with evolutionary changes in process executions have been mostly ignored [7]. The emergence of adaptive Process Management Systems (PMSs) while providing some flexibility by enabling dynamic process changes during run time have also widely contributed to such non-conformance and mis-alignment issues [2,8,12]. This is not necessarily applicable in practical considerations of processes adhering to different domain standards and changing business requirements.

Our proposed approach complements works such as [11], where the mined variation instances are only utilized to construct a common reference model without validation and proper categorization of such mined variants. Our work can lead to constructing multiple reference model variants, each preserving the intended organization's objective in its own way. In [7], the authors provide an approach for mining process changes from execution logs, but without subjecting to conformance or goal-alignment validation. Our work complements these, in mining such functional variants at the process level, but also focuses on categorizing variants in terms of the contextual aspects. On similar lines, [14] describes an approach to quantitatively calculate similarity between any two variants of a business process, so that activities such as process reuse, analysis and discovery can be facilitated. This is done via the modeling of process constraints on tasks, such as which tasks should (or should not) execute together. Such methods undoubtedly possess effective variability management techniques, but without the notion of alignment and conflict resolution with the governing goal model and underlying service models. In [19], the authors discuss approaches for representing goal models and transformations to variability modeling representations such as feature models, component-connector views and state charts. They propose identifying alternate functionality from AND/OR dependency relationships between goals and sub-goals. But all such alternate functionality identified from goal models may not necessarily be supported due to variability constraints with the process and underlying service design models. Our proposed work enables the identification of specific goals in the goal model that are subjected to higher degree of realization based on the mined variants.

6 Conclusion

Organizations increasingly tend to analyze the adherence of the day to day execution of internal business processes with their stated goals. The emergence of adaptive Process Management Systems have enabled dynamic ad-hoc changes even in a single process instance. But such approaches have also contributed to arising challenges of non-conformance and misalignment to organization goals and strategies. In this paper, we have proposed a goal oriented process variability mining and categorization approach. This bottom-up approach enables the organizations to study the depth and breadth of goal adherence in their organizations. In our future work, we would like to study the impact of any specific change in the goal decomposition models and the associated contextual factors based as an hind sight assessment based on historical data. We also would like to focus on leveraging the reasoning of goal adherence categorization for refining a given goal model in terms of adding or deleting OR-refinement sub goals.

References

1. Van der Aalst, W.M.P., Weijters, T., Maruster, L.: Workflow mining: discovering process models from event logs. IEEE Trans. Knowl. Data Eng. **16**(9), 1128–1142 (2004)
2. Van der Aalst, W.M.P., Weijters, A.: Process mining: a research agenda. Comput. Ind. **53**(3), 231–244 (2004)
3. Czarnecki, K., Grünbacher, P., Rabiser, R., Schmid, K., sowski, A.: Cool features and tough decisions: a comparison of variability modeling approaches. In: Proceedings of the Sixth International Workshop on Variability Modeling of Software-Intensive Systems, pp. 173–182. ACM (2012)
4. Derguech, W., Bhiri, S.: Business process model overview: determining the capability of a process model using ontologies. In: Abramowicz, W. (ed.) BIS 2013. LNBIP, vol. 157, pp. 62–74. Springer, Heidelberg (2013)

5. van Dongen, B.F., de Medeiros, A.K.A., Verbeek, H.M.W.E., Weijters, A.J.M.M.T., van der Aalst, W.M.P.: The ProM framework: a new era in process mining tool support. In: Ciardo, G., Darondeau, P. (eds.) ICATPN 2005. LNCS, vol. 3536, pp. 444–454. Springer, Heidelberg (2005)
6. Giunchiglia, F., Shvaiko, P., Yatskevich, M.: S-Match: an algorithm and an implementation of semantic matching. In: Bussler, C.J., Davies, J., Fensel, D., Studer, R. (eds.) ESWS 2004. LNCS, vol. 3053, pp. 61–75. Springer, Heidelberg (2004)
7. Günther, C.W., Rinderle, S., Reichert, M., van der Aalst, W.M.P.: Change mining in adaptive process management systems. In: Meersman, R., Tari, Z. (eds.) OTM 2006. LNCS, vol. 4275, pp. 309–326. Springer, Heidelberg (2006)
8. Gunther, C.W., Rinderle-Ma, S., Reichert, M., Van Der Aalst, W.M.P.: Using process mining to learn from process changes in evolutionary systems. Int. J. Bus. Proc. Integr. Manage. 3(1), 61–78 (2008)
9. Heath, D., Singh, R., Shephard, B.: Approaching strategic misalignment from an organizational view of business processes. In: 2013 46th Hawaii International Conference on System Sciences (HICSS), pp. 4055–4064. IEEE (2013)
10. Carbonell, J.: Context-based machine translation. In: Proceedings of the 7th Conference of the Association for Machine Translation in the Americas, pp. 19–28 (2006)
11. Li, C.: Mining process model variants: Challenges, techniques, examples. University of Twente (2010)
12. Li, C., Reichert, M., Wombacher, A.: Discovering reference models by mining process variants using a heuristic approach. In: Dayal, U., Eder, J., Koehler, J., Reijers, H.A. (eds.) BPM 2009. LNCS, vol. 5701, pp. 344–362. Springer, Heidelberg (2009)
13. Lu, R., Sadiq, S.K.: Managing process variants as an information resource. In: Dustdar, S., Fiadeiro, J.L., Sheth, A.P. (eds.) BPM 2006. LNCS, vol. 4102, pp. 426–431. Springer, Heidelberg (2006)
14. Lu, R., Sadiq, S.W., Governatori, G.: On managing business processes variants. Data Knowl. Eng. 68(7), 642–664 (2009)
15. Medeiros, A., Weijters, A., Aalst, W.M.P.: Genetic process mining: an experimental evaluation. Data Min. Knowl. Disc. 14(2), 245–304 (2007)
16. Messai, N., Bouaud, J., Aufaure, M.-A., Zelek, L., Séroussi, B.: Using formal concept analysis to discover patterns of non-compliance with clinical practice guidelines: a case study in the management of breast cancer. In: Peleg, M., Lavrač, N., Combi, C. (eds.) AIME 2011. LNCS, vol. 6747, pp. 119–128. Springer, Heidelberg (2011)
17. Stoecker-Sylvia, Z.: Merging the association rule mining modules of the weka and arminer data mining systems. Undergraduate Thesis. WPI (2002)
18. van der Aalst, W.M.P., et al.: Process mining manifesto. In: Daniel, F., Barkaoui, K., Dustdar, S. (eds.) BPM Workshops 2011, Part I. LNBIP, vol. 99, pp. 169–194. Springer, Heidelberg (2012)
19. Yu, Y., Lapouchnian, A., Liaskos, S., Mylopoulos, J., Leite, J.C.S.P.: From goals to high-variability software design. In: An, A., Matwin, S., Raś, Z.W., Ślęzak, D. (eds.) Foundations of Intelligent Systems. LNCS (LNAI), vol. 4994, pp. 1–16. Springer, Heidelberg (2008). http://dl.acm.org/citation.cfm?id=1786474.1786476
20. Zhou, Z., Sellami, M., Gaaloul, W., Barhamgi, M., Defude, B.: Data providing services clustering and management for facilitating service discovery and replacement. IEEE Trans. Autom. Sci. Eng. 10(4), 1131–1146 (2013)

Supporting Enterprise Changes Using Actor Performance Assessment

Marwen Jabloun[1(✉)], Yemna Sayeb[1], Henda Ben Ghezala[1],
and Khaled Gaaloul[2]

[1] Riadi–GDL Laboratory, Manouba University, Manouba, Tunis, Tunisia
{marwenjabloun,yemna.sayeb}@gmail.com,
hhbg.hhbg@gnet.tn
[2] Public Research Centre Henri Tudor, Esch-sur-Alzette, Luxembourg
khaled.gaaloul@tudor.lu

Abstract. In an evolutionary environment, many changes can be triggered by enterprise in order to cope with increased development. These changes can be critical if they are not well identified and addressed. In this context, Enterprise Architecture (EA) operates to provide holistic and coherent enterprise vision and aims to guide enterprise change. One of these changes depends on competence which is related to actors' performance assessment. In doing so, we define a formal approach that accompanies changes and provides strategic guidance based on actors performance assessments. Then, we identify the multilevel character of changes using hierarchical linear model (HLM) to compute linear correlation coefficient. Our method is based on the prediction and helps in anticipating the changing impacts. Finally, a prototype is developed to evaluate this approach in a case study.

Keywords: Actor · Change · Competence · Enterprise architecture · Performance

1 Introduction

Enterprises are increasingly aware that their existences depend on their ability to adapt in a rapidly changing environment. So enterprises need an efficient management of resources and competencies [1]. This allows the enterprises to address complex social and environmental problems, provide better customer service and to deal with advances in information technology and communication that create both opportunities and challenges for the enterprise [2]. Then, the EA is positioned as one of the best management practices that can provide a consistent view in all areas of programs and services to support planning and decision making. EA standards promote the success of changes' mission thanks to the promotion of functional integration and the resource optimization [3]. EA has to deal not only with technical difficulties because of the complex information system (IS) that becomes a constellation of different applications, architectures, infrastructure (operating system, network, databases), but also with actor attitude to change. In fact, the human factor issues are often more difficult and less predictable. Thus any process change within EA should take into account the actors'

© Springer International Publishing Switzerland 2015
F. Toumani et al. (Eds.): ICSOC 2014, LNCS 8954, pp. 158–170, 2015.
DOI: 10.1007/978-3-319-22885-3_14

reaction and impact otherwise the risks to fail [4]. Actors are essential to support changes' mission, also to maintain the skills and abilities and to contribute to the continuous improvement process. Actors' negative attitudes to change are often based on fears of downsizing, loss of status or previous failures of changing application. This reaction is generally due to a lack of impacts' consideration on actors by managers when planning the transformation process [1]. So, it is a priority to clearly explain the reasons for change and to communicate proposed changes to actors at all levels. Certainly, technical problems may provide considerable challenges but the human factor and cultural issues are often more difficult and less predictable, which requires attention at the different phases of change.

In this context, we are interested in supporting enterprise change based on actors performance. The core contribution of this paper is to support EA by offering a guideline process approach to support change. This process aims to carry decision making by performance assessment based on actors' competence. The idea is to study the impact of changes in order to anticipate an appropriate action plan. To that end, we develop methods of explanation using hierarchical linear model (HLM) to compute linear correlation coefficient. This will help us in the prediction, classification and correlation analysis in anticipating enterprise changes.

The remainder of this paper is structured as follows. Section 2 presents the context and the problem statement. Section 3 introduces the approach and explains the different steps in the changing process based on the actors' performance assessment, including the mathematical methods to anticipate changes. Section 4 validates our work. In Sect. 5, we conclude and discuss future directions.

2 Context and Problem Statement

2.1 Enterprise Architecture (EA)

The EA can be defined as: "the set of artifacts and primitive descriptions that constitute the enterprise's knowledge infrastructure" [5]. EA is generally considered to be an engineering discipline with systemic view of the enterprise [6, 7]. Several EA frameworks exist for example the Zachman Framework, TOGAF and a French EA approach entitled "urbanization" [8]. The role of an EA is to help facilitate and support a common understanding of enterprise needs, help formulate recommendations to meet those needs, and facilitate the development of a plan of action that should not only meet needs but is also implementable within financial, political, and organizational constraints. In addition, enterprise architects have an important role to play in the investment, implementation, and performance measurement activities and decisions that result from this planning [3]. So, success in accomplishing the EA's mission requires a coherent and consistent understanding of the existing situation, planning changes, and target situation. Thus, Enterprise models are claimed to be crucial not only for understanding and/or engineering the enterprise but also for adequately developing on top a supportive software system. The Unified Enterprise Modelling Language (UEML) project leads to an unified modelling language [9]. UEML has a "meta-model" that depends on content and specific area of enterprise modelling.

UEML proposes a consensus in the scientific community, both at the terminology and conceptual structures used to represent an enterprise. In this context, some researches try to work on complementary language for competencies 'modelling such as the Unified Enterprise Competence Modeling Language (UECML). UECML is mainly considered as an extension of UEML. UECML is an enterprise modeling approach based on competences presents specific requirements. UECML is based on a set of core constructs and sets of additional constructs. These additional constructs are specialized constructs required by the competence and resource based enterprise modelling needs [10]. Despite the competence extension, UECML is still lacking of a systematic approach for the evaluation of competences based on resources. Moreover, there is the Model for the Organization and the Validation of Enterprise Structures (MOVES), which considers the underlying concepts of both competence modeling and the enterprise process performance estimation approach. Moves can link qualitative aspects associated with competence classes and quantitative aspects such as competence patterns or performance evaluation. MOVE is the result of an analysis of a set of enterprise meta-models (IDEF3, GRAI, CIMOSA, MECI, and UEML) and collaboration with industrial partners. Actor is defined in MOVES as an enterprise object. There is a distinction between human and material actor. Human actor is composed of group and individual, whereas the material is composed of software and machine. Competence is linked to human actor and capacity is linked to material [11].

2.2 Change Management

Transition from one stage to the next requires substantial investment of time and money in process management, technology and cultural change (people) over a number of years. Opt' land et al. position enterprise architecture explicitly as a means for informed governance of enterprise transformation, requiring indicators and controls to govern enterprise transformations [12]. The EA can show the way the company should operate and what transformation should be done. It helps to control the transformation. It provides a target, a gap analysis and a migration plan (roadmap) [13]. Consequently, the need to manage change is one of the EA's success keys. Change management is generally divided into three steps [14]: (i) the change definition, (ii) the change implementation by following a chosen implementation strategy, and (iii) the change consolidation to guarantee change assimilation.

These three steps represent the life cycle of a change process [15]. To facilitate the realization of these steps, there are several approaches for managing change such as: The socialized approaches integrate the changes 'recognition as a social activity involving people from different social groups. And the rationalist approaches that integrate the analysis, planning and management of change and give a great importance in the controllability of change [16]. In this paper, we will be interested in the rationalist approach.

2.3 Performance Measurement in EA

EA play a pivotal role in governing the continuous improvement process of an enterprise [17]. The continuous improvement is one of the basics of quality managed by a set of standard such as the ISO 9000, ISO 9001, ISO 9004, ISO 10011 that describe the requirements for a system of quality management [18, 19]. The ISO 9001 emphasizes the continuous improvement of the overall performance of the company. This principle means that management must measure performance due to quality. Performance measurement methods are attractive to researchers. As stated by Phusavat et al. [20]. ISO 9001:2008 clearly specifies performance measurement as part of its requirement no. 8. Performance measurement helps to bring more scientific analysis into a decision-making process. It underlines the change towards management by information and knowledge, instead of primarily relying on the experiences and judgment [21]. Several studies have highlighted the importance of human resource management in controlling enterprise performance [22]. Since 1980s, the focus of performance measures shifted from purely financial factors to a combination of financial and non-financial ones. The factors affecting performance measurement in different research studies are based on one, or a combination of some criteria like finance, operations, quality, safety, personnel and customer satisfaction. Effective strategies to motivate and enhance employee competency are of urgent need for companies. Literature does not show much work on employee performance. Medlin and Green examined the relationship between the constructs of employee engagement and employee optimism, as a means to improve employee performance [23]. The competence concept is multifaceted and many definitions exist. The definition that has been adopted for the development of UECML describes the competence as the ability to combine in an efficient manner a number of non-material resources (knowledge, know-how and social attitude) and material resources (instruments, machines, etc.) in order to respond to the need of an activity [24]. This definition has been considered as the best suited in our context because it provides clear boundaries between resources and competences, concepts that are known to be difficult to distinguish [25, 26]. The process of competence management aims to improve the enterprise performance through the effective deployment of resources mobilized in the business process. Competence management involved several steps: (i) Analysis of existing data; (ii) Analysis of decision change, and (iii) The design of the new organization.

2.4   Synthesis

The lack of guidance approaches in EA implies the need to develop an accompanying change process. However, there is a lack of change management methods that consider the actors' impact when making decision. Thus, we aim to elaborate a support change process that focuses on actors' impact. We notice that actors' behaviour in a changing situation is an important factor that contributes greatly to ensure alignment between the various IS's components and so ensures the success of the change management in the enterprise. Indeed, evolution is obsolete without an investment in the affected actors. Thus, this process is based on performance assessment oriented competence. Considering competencies can provide a consistent view across all program and service areas to support planning and decision-making.

3 Proposed Approach

A consistent approach to improve and manage actors' competencies within an enterprise can lead to significant improvements at the operational level of the enterprise and can also lead to new opportunities. An enterprise that adopts a competence management approach needs to acknowledge that competence cut across organisational boundaries, both internal and external. This approach aims to guide transformations triggered in EA context. It aims to improve the ability of enterprise to respond to new requirements quickly and effectively by providing a clear definition of desired change, identifying the impacted component and measuring the actor performance. The approach consists on an actor-centered Process to Support Changes called "PSC" based on performance assessment. The performance assessment is driven by actor's competencies. In this section we will present the sequence of steps of "PSC" to facilitate progression towards the target and a mathematical equation used for performance assessment.

3.1 Construction of Accompanying Change Process

The process of supporting change (PSC), shown in Fig. 1 is a simple, repeatable process that consists of impact analysis that results in recommendations to guide changes.

The PSC consists of three phases detailed in several steps inspired from competence management process and performance assessment process:

- Change Definition Phase: In order to understand change concept we are interested in Regeves's taxonomy based on flexibility. It focuses on changes that may occur during the life cycle of a business process [27]. The change is presented in several dimensions such as the change's subject for instance the change may involve process activities (functional dimension), the control flows (behavioural dimension), process data (informational dimension) or the various protocols used in the process (operational level), etc. And The change's properties for example the degree of change that can be partial, total or radical when creating a new process, the duration of change that can be temporary or permanent, and the swiftness of change's implementation that can be either immediate or deferred and the anticipation of change that can be planned or ad hoc. This first phase serves a key role facilitating the definition of the change. This phase aims to clearly identify the subject, the nature and the type of the change. This stage needs collaboration between leadership and various stakeholders to clearly identify and prioritize needs of change and to formulate the set of change plans. So, the change definition phase contains three steps: (i) the identification of the change's type that specifies the type of action to perform: update, addition, deletion; (ii) the identification of the change's nature which includes a description of change's properties and (iii) and the identification of the subject to change that identifies the various aspects involved in the change. So once the change is identified, the impact assessment phase starts.
- Impact assessment Phase: In general, the change occurs in intentional level (business objectives) to the operational level (enterprise business processes) which is supported by the information system. This means that a change occurs on one of the

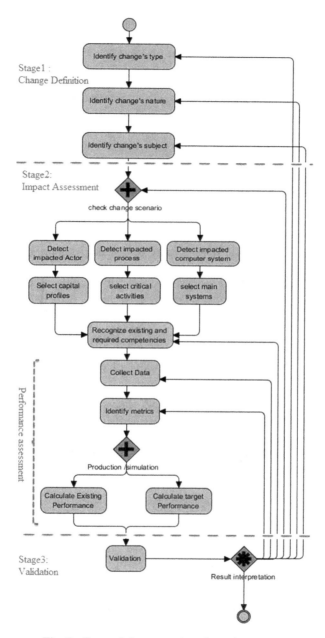

Fig. 1. Steps of the supporting change's process

three levels and will affects the remaining levels. The impact assessment is based on the knowledge of the existing level of actors' competence and the target level required because of changes which influences the strategies and/or business process and/or computer system. Thus, regardless of the trigger level of change (business, infrastructure or strategic), an assessment of the change's impact should be implemented to facilitate the success of this change. This phase is composed of a first analysis activity that clarifies all impacted entities according to the existing situation. This activity is based on the identification of the impacted stakeholders processes and computer Systems; recognizing required and acquired competence and the performance assessment. At this level we will detail the steps of assessing performance. For that we are oriented to Performance Measurement Process. A performance measure is composed of a number and a unit of measure. The number gives us a magnitude (how much) and the unit gives the number a meaning (what). Performance measures are always tied to a goal or an objective (the target). This step involves performing several activities. Each performance measurement consists of a defined unit of measure and collected raw data. These allow computing performance as follows: (i) collect the necessary data; (ii) identify metrics; (iii) Calculate existing performance and (iv) Calculate target performance.

- Validation Phase: Validation is an activity of decision support. In this phase, the quantification of the change's impact is performed. The validation is based on mathematical models to make predictions about the impact on performance. Predictions identify a set of proactive actions based on the obtained results. The mathematical model adopted will be explained in the next section.

3.2   Performance Assessment Based on Actor's Competence

In order to determine the relation between competence, actor and performance, we focus on enterprise models. We notice that there is an evolution with regards to actors' considerations in enterprise models. We estimated that every model was interested in actors in a definite point of view. The construction of enterprise models oriented competence is motivated by practical needs such as a better definition of enterprise modeling concepts, engineering methods and competence oriented business processes, clarification of the role of competence and its components and direct integration of human resources aspects with the objective to manage and control competence. These findings have allowed us to identify the elements that should be considered to define the performance of the actors. So, The performance of the actor is well connected with the actor's entity and especially the actor's roles and the required/acquired competences. The performance of the actor is also linked to the business component via the "role" entity. This entity assigns an actor to a business process activity. This assignment depends on required competence for a given role. Another aspect related to the actors must be taken into consideration regarding actors' interactions. We can identify two main types of interactions: Horizontal interactions based on the concept of teamwork and vertical interactions based on hierarchical relations. These interactions lead us to the collective dimension of competence. In order to emerge and develop, collective competence involves conditions for the creation of appropriate combinations of individual competencies.

So the actor performance depends on:

- The actor type: So we suggest to consider a coefficient "**v**" that reflects the actors' type (individual or team; internal or external). This coefficient value varies depending on the enterprise type.
- The assigned role: we suggest presenting the importance rate of each actor's role by the coefficient "**η**". It is based on the extent and nature of the activity.
- The competence concept: So we suggest considering various factors such as:
  - A value "**θ**" that reflects the type of competence (collective, individual, etc.).
  - A competence's importance rate "**σ**" is determined according to the competences' family rates. EMSI [28] present for instance 5 competence families related to the design, operations, the infrastructure, the business and the management.
  - A competence's level of an actor such as: novice, junior, expert, etc. is presented by the variable "**μ**".

The global actor performance Pc can be presented as shown in the Table 1.

Table 1. Performance description

Equation	Description
$$Pc = v \sum_{k=0}^{n} \theta_k Pa_k \quad (1)$$	For a set of k acquired actor's competence $\{ C_k \}$ with n>0 and $0 \le k \le n$ ○ θ_k represents the value of the competence 's type (individual , collective, unit). ○ Pa_k represents the performance of the actor according to a given **acquired competence**
$$Pa_k = \eta \sum_{l=0}^{m} \mu_l \, \overset{k}{Ac_l} \, Pac_l \quad (2)$$	○ η represents the importance's rate value of the assigned actor role. ○ μ_l represents the value of actor's competence level {1(novice), 2 (junior), 3 (senior), 4 (expert) ○ $\overset{k}{Ac_l}$ is a bivalent variable associated with the set of m **required competence** with m> 0 and $0 \le l \le m$. In fact, if the actor "Ac" have the competence then $\overset{k}{Ac_l} = 1$ else $\overset{k}{Ac_l} = 0$ ○ Pac_l is the value of competence's performance.
$$Pac_l = F(Ac_l, \sigma_l, \mu_l) \quad (3)$$	This function calculates the actor's performance according to the given competencies. Calculating is based on a set of business rules that depends on the value of actor's competence level μ_l and the value of the competence's importance rate σ_l.

Pac_l depends on the considered change's scenario, change level and change features. In addition, it is based on a set of business rules specific to each enterprise. These business rules are based on a set of a given KPIs and metrics. So in order to measure competence performance, we agree to implement business rules and to deploy them as services. Depending on changing scenario the invocation of a set of services will allow us to get a performance value.

(1), (2) and (3) allow us to define the global actor performance as follows:

$$Pc = \eta v \sum_{k=0}^{n} \sum_{l=0}^{m} Ac_{l}^{k}\ \theta_k \mu_l F(Ac_l, \sigma_l, \mu_l)$$

3.3   Validation

In the EA context, our approach aims to help managers who intended to make decisions about change's applications. The main basis for a good management is anticipation. We recognize tow type of anticipation prediction (anticipation in space) and prevision (anticipation in time). Hierarchical linear model (HLM) allows us to study the relationship between an explained variable y and an explanatory variable x within a group of individuals.

For an actor "i" with a performance Pc_i inferred from competence we have a global actor performance Pac_i. So, we aim to determine the linear regression. Regression is used to create mathematical models and make forecasts on the change's impact on performance. Linear regression attempts to model the relationship between two variables by fitting a linear equation to observed data. One variable is considered to be an explanatory variable, and the other is considered to be a dependent variable [29]. In our case, we think that the global actor's performance is an explained variable and the competence's performance is the explanatory variable. So we propose the following equation:

$$Pc_i = aPac_i + b$$

The estimation of a and b allows us to draw regression lines for a set of actor performance assessment. The relevance and significance of this regression line consist in the verification of the calculated performance pertinence using the proposed mathematical model and the credibility of forecast based on this model.

4   Developed Prototype

4.1   Prototype and Developed Interfaces

The prototype development is done in the context of an internship in a shipping company. The architecture of the solution as shown in Fig. 2 includes a web component that sets the desired change's scenario; a business component consists of business rules which can perform calculations of performance and an integration component consists of a mediation which provides a set of service to be consumed by the developed prototype. All these components interact with a given database in which we save the computed values in order to perform regression calculations.

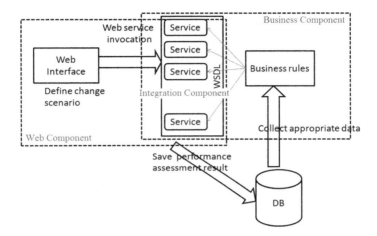

Fig. 2. Prototype overall architecture

The user can define the change scenario in a web form. This description represents the input of the PSC. The form allows the user to define the type, the subject and the nature of the change scenario. In this Table 2 we will present some services used in our use case.

In order to get responses, the SCP runs and invokes the appropriate Web services. In fact each business rules used in performance assessment is exposed by a web service in order to make easier its exploitation. By doing that we minimize the impact of business rules modification because we have separated web services.

4.2   Results Interpretation

For a set of actors we calculate the global performance and the competence's performance. These values allow us to calculate for each actor the slope b and the intercept a of the regression line. These lines are presented in the Fig. 3.

For this, the linear correlation coefficient is calculated.

$$\rho_i = \frac{\mathrm{cov}(Pac_i, Pc_i)}{\sqrt{\mathrm{var}(Pc_i)\mathrm{var}(Pac_i)}}$$

The interpretation of ρ allows us to plan the actions to take:

- If $\rho = 0$ then there is no impact.

Table 2. Services' description

Service	Input/Output	Business rules
Getactorratebyexperience (id,y)	The Input is composed of an actor identifier (id) and the years of work experience (Y) The Output is an Actor rate	For every year of work we add 10 % to the actor rate. If the work period exceeds 10 years than the actor rate is 100 %
Getcompetencerate(, idcompetence, IdFamily)	The Input is composed of a competence identifier (Idcompetence) and the competence family identifier (Idfamily) The Output is a competence rate	For each competence family we assign a rate value: infrastructure 20 %, design 50 %, business 90 % and management 100 %
SelectEligiblector (Idactivity)	The Input is composed of an activities' identifier (Idactivity) Output: a Set of actor Id	Every actor that has the suitable competence can be assigned to the activity. An actor cannot be assigned to more than 4 activities in a week

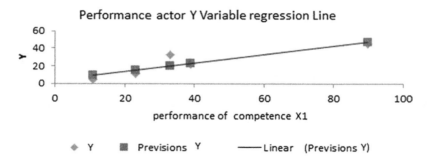

Fig. 3. Regression lines

- If ρ tends to 1 then the change is beneficial.
- If ρ tends to −1 then preventive action must be planned such as training, recruitment or outsourcing, depending on the situation.

5   Conclusion

At present, there is no other management best practice, other than EA, that can serve as a context for enterprise-wide planning and decision making. The EA becomes a catalyst for consistent methods of analysis and design, which are needed for the organization to remain agile and effective with limited resources. The proposed approach is to build a process in order to support change. This process is based on performance assessment. We have defined a relation between the performance of the actor and his competencies. We consider that the actor, the role and the competence are the key elements that allow us to predict the impact of change. We also think that knowledge of existing and/or the target competence of all involved actors in a business process greatly facilitate the management of all improvement approaches especially in the EA context. The proposed approach in this paper will be improved. We are implementing a BPEL Process in order to synchronize web service used in the calculation of the competence's performance and we are treating semantic dimension of collected data by developing an ontology oriented competence. The ontology Integration in the process will guarantee a semantic interoperability.

References

1. Australian Government Information Management Office AGIMO: The Australian Government Business Process Interoperability Framework. Technical report (2007)
2. Bos, B., Delattre, S., Cha, M., Denis, B.: Les métiers de l'informatiques en développement un domaine à découvrir. Blue-Search conseil, cabinet de conseil en recrutement et ressources humaines. Aster, cabinet-conseil en organisation, RH et management (2005)
3. Executive office of the president of the USA EOPUSA: The common approach to federal enterprise architecture. Technical report (2012)
4. Gagnon, Y-C.: Les trois leviers stratégiques de la réussite du changement technologique (2008)
5. Zachman, J.: Enterprise Architecture vs Application Development Artifacts. ZIFA report (2005)
6. IEEE Computer Society: IEEE recommended practice for architecture description of software-intensive systems. IEEE Std 1471–2000 (2000)
7. van Gils, B.: Strategy and architecture – reconciling worldviews. In: Proper, E., Harmsen, F., Dietz, J.L.G. (eds.) PRET 2009. LNBIP, vol. 28, pp. 181–196. Springer, Heidelberg (2009)
8. Longépé, C.: Démarche de conception d'une cible urbanisée et du plan de convergence. Actes du colloque Urbanisation Sorbonne (2002)
9. Petit, M., Doumeingts, G.: UEML – WP1- Report on the State of the Art in Enterprise Modelling UEML: Unified Enterprise Modelling Language. Technical report (2001)
10. Pépiot, G., Cheikhrouhou, N., Furbringer, J-M., Glardon, R.: UECML: Unified Enterprise Competence Modelling Language. Ecole Polytechnique Fédérale de Lausanne (2006)
11. Bennour, M., Crestani, D.: Using competencies in performance estimation: From the activity to the process. Université Montpellier 2, Laboratoire d'Informatique, de Robotique et de Microélectronique de Montpellier (2006)
12. Op't Land, M., Proper, H.A., Waage, M., Cloo, J., Steghuis, C.: Enterprise Architecture – Creating Value by Informed Governance. Springer, Berlin (2008)
13. CIGREF: L'Architecture d'Entreprise Un cadre global de coopération pour les acteurs de l'entreprise. Livre Blanc (2008)
14. Autissier, D., Moutot, J-M.: Pratiques de la conduite du changement: Comment passer du discours à l'action (2003)
15. Nurcan, S., Barrios, J., Rolland, C.: Une méthode pour la définition de l'impact organisationnel du changement. INFORSID (2002)

16. Mamadou Samba, C.: Gestion proactive du changement dans les projets de réingénierie des processus métiers. L'Université de Paris 8, Vincennes-Saint-Denis (2009)

17. Proper, H.A., Greefhorst, D.: Principles in an enterprise architecture context. J. Enterp. Archit (2011)

18. Létrat Pyltak, J.: Le passage d'une certification ISO 9001 à un management par la qualité totale. Université des sciences sociales, Toulouse (2002)

19. Bouamane, A., Talbi, A., Tahoni, C., Bouami, D.: Contribution à la modélisation de la compétence. In: MOSIM (2006)

20. Phusavat, K., Photaranon, W.: Productivity/performance measurement, case application at the government pharmaceutical organization. Ind. Manage. Data Syst. **106**(9), 1271–1287 (2006)

21. Phusavat, K., Anussornnitisarn, P., Helo, P., Dwight, R.: Performance measurement: roles and challenges. Ind. Manage. Data Syst. **109**(5), 646–664 (2009)

22. McEwan, A.M., Sackett, P.: The human factor in CIM systems: worker empowerment and control within a high-volume production environment. Comput. Ind. (1998)

23. Medlin, B., Green, K.W.: Enhancing performance through goal setting, engagement, and optimism. Ind. Manage. Data Syst. **109**(7), 943–956 (2009)

24. Bhaskar, K., Srinivasan, G.: Static and dynamic operator allocation problem in cellular manufacturing systems. Int. J. Prod. Res. **35**(12), 3467–3481 (2008)

25. Arditi, D., Tokdemir, O.B., Suh, K.: Effect of learning on line balancing scheduling. Int. J. Project Manage. **19**, 236–277 (2001)

26. Mosheiov, G.: Scheduling problem with learning effect. Eur. J. Oper. Res. **13**, 687–693 (2001)

27. Boukhebouze, M.: Gestion de changement et vérification formelle de processus métier: une approche orientée règle. Laboratoire d'Informatique en Image et Systèmes d'information, l'institut national des sciences appliquées de Lyon (2010)

28. EMSI: L'évolution des compétences les Systèmes d'Information. Livre blanc, École de Management des Systèmes d'Information de Grenoble (2009)

29. Arrègle, J-L.: Les modèles linéaires hiérarchiques: principes et illustration. EDHEC Campus de Nice (2003)

Towards a Framework for Semantically-Enabled Compliance Management in Financial Services

Amal Elgammal[1(✉)] and Tom Butler[2]

[1] Faculty of Computers and Information, Cairo University, Giza, Egypt
a.elgammal@fci-cu.edu.eg
[2] Governance, Risk and Compliance Technology Centre (GRCTC),
University College Cork, Cork, Ireland
TButler@ucc.ie

Abstract. Following the crisis in 2008, the financial industry has faced growing numbers of laws and regulations globally. The number and complexity of these regulations is creating significant issues for governance, risk and compliance management in almost all industrial sectors; however some of these sectors are characterized by being heavily-regulated including the financial industry. This paper proposes a semantically-enabled compliance management framework. In the heart of the framework is an integrated semantic repository incorporating regulatory, business and compliance knowledge; i.e., *CMKB*. The approach is underpinned by legal Subject Matter Experts (SMEs) interpreting financial regulations and encoding them in the Semantics of Business vocabulary and Business Rule (SBVR) standard. As a proof-of-concept, we have integrated the SBVR and CMKB repositories with a validated compliance solution for design-time compliance verification. However, the approach could be integrated with other compliance solutions at different phases of the business process lifecycle.

Keywords: Business process compliance management · Financial services · Semantic compliance management · Compliance patterns · SBVR

1 Introduction

The global regulatory environment has grown in complexity and scope since the financial crisis in 2008. This is causing significant problems for organisations in the financial industry, as the complexity of hard and soft regulations little understood or appreciated [1]. Take, for example, that the Dodd-Frank Wall Street Reform and Consumer Protection Act of 2010 has an estimated 1,500 provisions and 398 rules, which are being drafted by relevant regulatory agencies—approximately 40 % of these rules are in force in 2013 at the time of writing[1]. The U.S. Bank Secrecy Act Anti-Money Laundering (AML) rules are equally complex and far-reaching, with a raft

---

[1] http://www.usatoday.com/story/money/business/2013/06/03/dodd-frank-financial-reform-progress/2377603/.

© Springer International Publishing Switzerland 2015
F. Toumani et al. (Eds.): ICSOC 2014, LNCS 8954, pp. 171–184, 2015.
DOI: 10.1007/978-3-319-22885-3_15

of major banks found not to be in compliance in 2012. Standard Chartered Bank, London, for example, was fined a total of $459 million by U.S. regulators in December 2012. Worse still HSBC Holdings Plc. had pay a record $1.92 billion in fines to U.S. regulators for similar anti-money laundering offences.

In a broader perspective, compliance is about unambiguously ensuring conformance to a set of prescribed and/or agreed upon rules [2]. These rules may originate from various sources, including laws and regulations, standards, public and internal policies, partner agreements and jurisdictional provisions. To address this emergent *business need*, many organizations typically achieve compliance on a *per-case basis* resulting into myriad *ad-hoc* solutions. In practice, these solutions are generally handcrafted for a particular compliance problem, which creates difficulties for *reuse* and *evolution*. Furthermore, compliance and business concepts may be treated differently by different stakeholders, this *ambiguity* results in inconsistency, which makes it infeasible to *share* and *re-use* business and compliance specifics. All these problems make it infeasible for automated compliance checking and analysis at any of the phases of the BP lifecycle; design-time, runtime and off line monitoring.

In this paper, we draw our ongoing research to propose a generic semantically-based compliance management framework, which addresses a number of important compliance challenges:

- *Compliance Requirements Interpretation:* Compliance requirements embedded in regulatory sources are often high-level, vague and sometimes ambiguous [1]. Hence, they require interpretation by legal subject matter experts (SMEs) in collaboration with business SMEs. We have developed and field-tested an approach to capturing compliance requirements in a *structured natural* language using the Semantics of Business Vocabulary and Business Rules (SBVR) standard [3]. This interpretation approach is integrated into a semantic compliance management framework. Encoding interpreted regulations in a structured natural language significantly improves *communications* between different stakeholders, removes any potential *ambiguity* in interpreting regulations and enables the *sharing* and *reuse* of compliance knowledge.

- *Compliance Management Knowledge Base:* The need to manage regulatory and compliance data especially in the financial industry exceeds the abilities of current information systems. Our research indicates that a framework for compliance management should be founded on a semantic knowledge base that incorporates and integrates a set of ontologies capturing the different perspectives of the compliance and business spheres (cf. [4]). In the heart of the framework is a uniform conceptualization of the process and compliance space, enabling the *sharing* and *re-use* of compliance and business knowledge, the elimination of any *ambiguity*, and improves the level of *automation*.

- *Proof of Concept* implementation: As a PoC, we have applied the SBVR interpretation approach on an Anti-Money Laundering (AML) case study relevant to the financial industry. And we have integrated CMKB to a well-recognized approach [5] in the compliance research community for automated design-time compliance verification. Our results show that the SBVR interpretation approach and CMKB could be smoothly instantiated and integrated with the compliance verification approach proposed in [5], which utilizes a pattern-based compliance language as an intermediate layer between SBVR statements and their formal representations (LTL). This ascertains the feasibility and applicability of our framework. It is worth noting that the framework is generic and we are working on its realization for runtime compliance monitoring.

The rest of this paper is organized as follows: The semantic compliance management framework is presented in Sect. 2. A simplified AML BP model, which we have also developed (based on the Financial Action Task Force (FATF) 40 recommendations[2]) is presented in Sect. 3, and acts as a running scenario throughout this paper. Section 4 applies the approach on the running scenario. Section 5 presents the status of our implementation and validation efforts. Related work is discussed in Sect. 6. Finally conclusions and future work are highlighted in Sects. 7.

2 Semantic Design-Time Compliance Management Framework

Figure 1 presents a high-level view of the generic semantic compliance management framework. As shown in Fig. 1, the CMKB knowledge base represents the backbone of the framework, which incorporates and integrates a set of ontologies to capture the different perspectives of the compliance and business spheres. There are two primary abstract roles (SMEs) involved: (i) a business expert, who is responsible for defining and managing BP in an organization, and (ii) a compliance/legal expert, who is responsible for refining, interpreting, specifying and managing compliance requirements in close collaboration with the business expert. Given the semantic knowledge base and the SMEs involved, there are four major iterative steps:

1. The refinement and interpretation of relevant compliance sources and then encoding interpreted regulations in a Structured Natural Language (SNL); SBVR.
2. The specification of interpreted SNL statements in a formal language to enable their automated verification and analysis against impacted BP models.
3. The definition of new business processes or the re-use of existing ones.
4. The automated compliance checking of formally-represented compliance requirements against the impacted business process models.

Figure 2 represents one possible refinement of the generic sematic framework, which instantiates each of the major compliance-related steps described in Fig. 1. The top right hand-side of Fig. 2 represents the CMKB, highlighting one of the main contributions of this paper. CMKB incorporates two main ontologies, represented in the Ontology Web Language (OWL2.0). As a PoC, we have focused on the financial domain. Therefore, these ontologies capture the regulatory and the financial business domain; i.e. the Financial Industry Regulatory Ontology (FIRO) and the Financial Industry Business Ontology (FIBO)[3].

---

[2] FATF recommendations: http://www.fatf-gafi.org/topics/fatfrecommendations/.

[3] FIBO: http://www.omg.org/hot-topics/fibo.htm.

FIBO is a collaborative initiative led by industry members of the Enterprise Data Management Council (EDMC) in collaboration with the Object Management Group (OMG). FIBO aims to bridge the language gap between business and technology by capturing business meanings, rather than being a mere data dictionary. The main components of FIBO are: (i) a Business Conceptual Ontology (FIBO-BCO), (ii) a web-accessible business presentation layer, (iii) a set of operational ontologies, and (iv) the FIBO Object Management Group Specifications. The web-accessible business presentation layer is the EDM Council Semantics Repository. It presents FIBO-BCO, alongside its OWL representation, in a business readable format that avoids technical representations or the need to learn new languages.

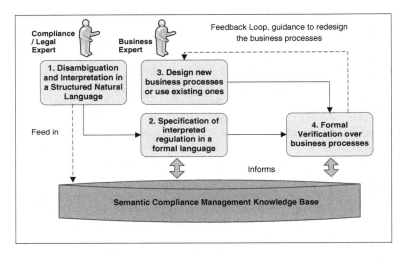

Fig. 1. Generic semantic design-time compliance management framework

FIBO is an adopted OMG standard. The development of FIRO is paralleling that of FIBO and is also intended to be submitted to OMG for standardization. However, FIRO is focusing on capturing the semantics and regulatory rules from regulations focusing on the AML domain, in line with the problems being experienced in the industry. As shown in Fig. 2, FIRO and FIBO represent the Terminological part (TBox) of the CMKB. Instances of FIRO and FIBO populate the Compliance Requirements Repository (CRR), and Business Process Repository (BPR), representing the Assertional part (ABox) of the knowledge base. Figure 2 integrates the design-time compliance management in [5] as one possible realization of the generic semantic framework (Fig. 1).

Compliance practices may commence with the *interpretation* of compliance constraints into a set of organization specific compliance requirements ('Step 1' in Fig. 2). This step is achieved by following the SBVR interpretation approach we propose and is detailed in Sect. 4.1 for interpreting regulations and encoding them in SBVR. Following [5], the approach enables automated design-time compliance verification.

This includes checking interpreted compliance requirements (represented in SBVR as proposed in this paper), against BP designs. 'Step 2' of the framework addresses this significant challenge. This can be basically achieved by utilizing formal reasoning and verification techniques. However, formal languages are well-known of their difficulty and complexity, therefore in [5] a pattern-based graphical compliance language (CRL) is introduced, which enables the abstract specification of compliance constraints. CRL is formally grounded on Linear Temporal Logic (LTL), therefore, from CRL expressions capturing SBVR statements, corresponding LTL formulas are automatically generated for automated verification by means of model checkers.

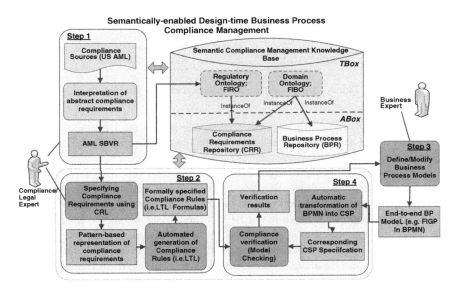

Fig. 2. Semantically-enabled design-time compliance management framework

'Step 3' involves the design of relevant BP models. As a PoC, we adopt BPMN v2.0. As shown in 'Step 4' of Fig. 2, BPMN models is then mapped into a formal representation (Promela code as proposed in [5]) and SPIN model-checker is adopted for compliance checking. Having the verification results from the model-checker, the SMEs can then alter the BP model to resolve any detected compliance violation.

3 Money-Laundering Detection Process: Running Scenario

Anti-money laundering is a pressing concern to any organization operating in the financial industry, as it is tightly adjunct to terrorism and proliferation financing. Despite the fact that it is not possible to precisely quantify the amount of money laundered every year, in [6], it has been shown that billions of US dollars certainly are. On-going work in GRCTC in collaboration with respectable Irish financial organizations focuses on

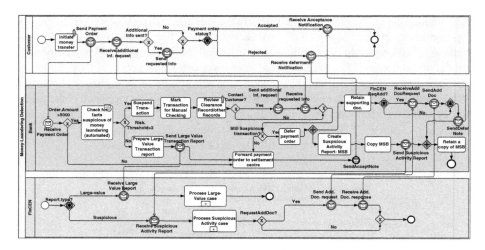

Fig. 3. Money laundering detection BPMN process

developing an end-to-end AML business process encoded in the BPMN v2.0 standard, which is established based on best practices and the Financial Action Task Force (FATF) 40 recommendations.

Figure 3 presents the money laundering detection and reporting BPMN process. The process proceeds as follows: it starts by a customer initiating a money transfer. Once the order is received by the bank, and if the order amount is greater than a given threshold (interpreted as 5 k Euros in our BPMN model), an automated check is carried out to detect if the transaction is suspicious. If the automated module detects that the transaction is suspicious, an authorized personnel is required to re-check the transaction manually by reviewing clearance records and all other available records, and contacting the customer for further information, if necessary. If the transaction is proved to be suspicious, the transaction is flagged as suspicious and then deferred, and a Suspicious Activity Report (MSB) is sent to FinCEN[4]. The customer will be notified in both cases on the status of her transaction, while retaining all supporting documents in case they are requested by FinCEN during its investigation. Next, Sect. 4 presents some of the AML compliance requirements of the U.S. Patriot act of 2001 that are relevant to this BPMN model.

4   Application on the Case Study

As outlined in Sect. 2, the design-time compliance management practices commence with legal experts (SMEs) interpreting and refining relevant compliance requirements to produce a set of concrete organization-specific constraints that a financial services organization has to comply with. Figure 3 introduced a part of the AML BPMN

---

[4] Financial Crimes Enforcement Network: http://www.fincen.gov/.

process. Next in Sect. 4.1, the adopted refinement methodology that is followed by our legal SMEs is summarized, and the SBVR representations of some of these constraints are presented. Then, the representation of the SBVR specifications as pattern-based expressions (in CRL) is discussed in Sect. 4.2.

4.1   Interpretation and Refinement of the AML Financial Regulations

Legal SMEs play an important role in addressing the complexity of regulations and more precisely in consolidating and making sense of regulatory text. SMEs follow an interpretation methodology consisting of the following tasks:

- Follow reference chains in regulations and produce self-contained sentences.
- Define terms iteratively until all confusions are clarified.
- Identify, describe and constrain relationships between terms.
- Capture regulatory requirements using the vocabulary from previous steps.

Table 1 presents four interpreted compliance requirements of the U.S. Patriot act of 2001 that are relevant to the BPMN model in Fig. 3 (*R4* below is coming from the Bank's internal policy). SBVR [3] is an OMG specification for a Business Natural Language. SBVR defines a *Concept* as a 'unit' of knowledge created by a unique combination of characteristics.

Table 1. SBVR specification of the AML compliance requirements

ID	SBVR Specification
R1	It is **obligatory** that each money services business ***reports*** a suspicious transaction that ***involves*** or ***aggregates*** funds ***of*** at least $5,000
R2	and It is **obligatory** that the identification ***of*** the suspicious transaction ***is identified from a review of*** clearance record or other record ***of*** money order that ***are sold*** and ***processed***
R3	It is **obligatory** that each money services business ***maintains*** each copy of each Suspicious Activity Report-MSB ***filed*** and original record or business record equivalent ***of*** any supporting documentation
R4	It is **obligatory** that each money services business ***notify*** the Customer with either the acceptance or deference of the money order

The two main categories of concepts in the SBVR meta-model are *Noun* and *Verb*:

- *Noun Concepts* are a group of things in the domain of discourse or the domain of interest. For example: regulator, financial institution, etc. *Individual Noun Concepts* are a particular type of *Noun Concepts* representing actual entities or individuals. E.g., Wells Fargo Bank (Regulated Entity).
- *Verb Concepts* (or *Fact Types*) capture the relationships between *Noun Concepts*. For example, the *Verb Concept* '*money services business submits suspicious activity report*' captures the submission relationship between a money services business and a suspicious activity report.

Typically an SBVR document has two parts: a Vocabulary and a Rulebook. An SBVR Vocabulary is a Terminological Dictionary where entries are *Noun Concepts* and relationships represented by *Verb Concepts*. It also contains *Definitional Rules*—which constrain, in the form of *alethic modalities* (modifiers such that 'it is necessary that', etc.)—and related *advices of possibility*. An SBVR Rulebook is a set of guidance statements containing *behavioural rules* in the form of *deontic modalities* (e.g. it is obligatory that, must, etc.) and *advices of permission/prohibition*.

SBVR relies on *text styles* to visually identify elements from the SBVR Meta-model. In Table 1, Noun Concepts are underlined with a single line. Individual Noun Concepts are doubled underlined. The **verb part** of a *verb concept* is in italic-bold font face. **Keywords** are in a bold font face.

4.2   Pattern-Based Specification of SBVR Statements

After the refinement of compliance constraints and encoding them in SBVR as a structured natural language-such that concepts and verbs used in SBVR specifications are coming for the underlying CMKB ontologies-the underpinning ontologies and SBVR specifications could be used as the backbone of any compliance solution at any of the BP lifecycle phases; design-time, runtime and offline monitoring. As a PoC, we have integrated our approach to the design-time verification framework proposed in [5]. To facilitate the work of the compliance experts as proposed in [5], they may apply and combine *compliance patterns*. This serves as an auxiliary step to represent interpreted compliance requirements into their formal statements (as LTL formulas for our case).

Table 2. Representing SBVR specifications in CRL and generated LTL rules

ID	Textual CRL	Generated LTL formulas
R1	(Order.Amount > 5000 **And** StillSuspiciousTransaction = 'Yes') **LeadsTo**(SendSuspiciousActivityReport)	$G(((Order.Amount > 5000) \wedge (StillSuspiciousTransaction = 'Yes')) \rightarrow F(SendSuspiciousActivityReport))$
R2	(ReviewClearanceRecord **And** ReviewClearanceRecord.Manual = 'Yes')**Precedes** (SendSuspiciousActivityReport)	$((\neg SendSuspiciousActivityReport) U (ReviewClearanceRecord \wedge ReviewClearanceRecord.Manual = 'Yes')) \vee (G(ReviewClearanceRecord \wedge ReviewClearanceRecord.Manual = 'Yes'))$
R3	R3.1:(StillSuspiciousTransaction = 'Yes') **LeadsTo** (RetainCopySuspiciousReport **And** RetainSupportingDoc)	$G(StillSuspiciousTransaction = 'Yes' \rightarrow F(RetainCopySuspiciousReport \wedge RetainSupporting Doc))$
	R3.2: DeleteSuspiciousTransactionRecords **IsAbsent**	$G(\neg DeleteSuspiciousTransactionRecords)$
R4	InitiateMoneyTransfer **LeadsTo** (SendAcceptNote **MutexChoice** SendDeferNote)	$G(InitiateMoneyTransfer F((F(SendAcceptNote) \wedge G(\neg SendDeferNote)) \vee (F(SendDeferNote) \wedge G(\neg SendAcceptNote))))$

These CRL expressions are automatically transformed into LTL formulas. Due to space limitations, we will explain CRL by applying it on the SBVR specifications produced in Table 1. Table 2 presents the textual representation of these SBVR specifications using compliance patterns, and the automatically generated LTL rules [7]. *G, F, U, X* in Table 2 correspond to '*always*', '*eventually*', '*until*' and '*next*' temporal modalities, respectively. *LeadsTo, isFollowedBy* and *MutexChoice* are examples of the compliance patterns used in Table 2. The mapping scheme of the compliance patterns used to represent compliance requirements *R1-4* into LTL formulas are presented in Table 3. *P* and *Q* in Table 3 (and their instances in Table 2) are basically compliance and/or financial business concepts coming from the CMKB Knowledge base (cf. Figure 2).

Table 3. A subset of CRL's compliance patterns and their mapping rules into LTL

Compliance pattern	Description	LTL representation
P LeadsTo Q	P must always be followed by Q	$G(P \rightarrow F(Q))$
P Precedes Q	Q must always be preceded by P	$(\neg Q\ U\ P) \vee G(P)$
P IsAbsent	P should not exist throughout the BP model	$G(\neg P)$
P isFollowedBy Q	P is directly followed by Q	$G(P \rightarrow X(Q))$
P MutexChoice Q	Either P or Q exists but not any of them or both of them	$(F(P) \wedge G(\neg(Q))) \vee (F(Q) \wedge G(\neg(P)))$

LeadsTo, Precedes and isAbsent compliance patterns and their mapping rules are based on Dwyer property specification patterns [8]

5   Implementation

The implementation of an integrated tool-suite as a PoC and an instantiation artefact of the semantic compliance management approach proposed in this paper is a first key step towards its validation and evaluation. Figure 5 shows a high-level architecture view of the interacting components of the prototypical implementation. Designs for Management™ (DesignsForManagement.com) is an SBVR-based application that is used to ensure that the SBVR regulatory business vocabulary, and the regulatory guidance rules content are complete, consistent and compliant with SBVR standard.

Having interpreted compliance requirements encoded in SBVR using concepts from the CMKB, compliance experts can then use the graphical Compliance Rule Manager (CRM) [5] to build pattern-based CRL compliance expressions[5]. The upper left-hand side part of Fig. 2 depicts the internal architecture of the CRM, its

---

[5] http://eriss.uvt.nl/compas/.

components, and their interaction with the semantic compliance management knowledge base. The CRM comprises two sub-components: Compliance Rule Modeller and Text Template Transformation Toolkit. The Compliance Rule Modeller is a graphical modeller that is used to visually design and create pattern-based expressions of compliance requirements in a drag-and-drop fashion.

Operands used in building CRL expressions constitute instances of concepts defined in the compliance and financial business ontologies (FIRO and FIBO as described in Sect. 2). Figure 4 presents a snapshot of EDM's implementation of the FIBO business entities ontology[6].

From graphical CRL expressions capturing interpreted compliance requirements in SBVR, corresponding formal rules (i.e. LTL rules) and other meta-data information are automatically generated by CRM.

As shown in Fig. 5, the WSAT[7] tool will then be used to map BP models into promela code, and SPIN model Checker will check the compliance between the LTL rules (capturing compliance requirements) and the promela code (capturing the BP model).

Several experiments are ongoing to validate the feasibility and utility of the approach presented in this paper. This includes an experiment that concerns itself with encoding

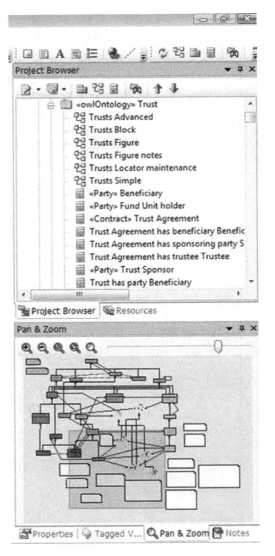

Fig. 4. EDM implementation of FIBO business entities ontology

the U.S. Bank Secrecy Act Anti-Money Laundering (AML) in SBVR. Future experiments will involve the application of the approach on large scale case-studies provided by GRCTC's industrial partners. Another experimental direction is the integration of our

---

[6] https://www.youtube.com/watch?v=bNeHmvdX69E.

[7] http://www.cs.ucsb.edu/~su/WSAT/.

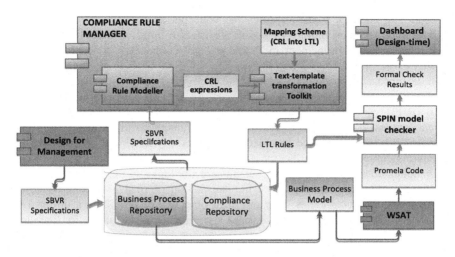

Fig. 5. A high-level architectural view of the implementation

semantic compliance approach with dominant frameworks for runtime and offline compliance monitoring. This will allow us to validate the applicability and utility of our approach, and detect the limitations and possible enhancement and extension points.

6 Related Work

With the increase in attention paid to the role of compliance in organizations, several work efforts have been produced in the area of compliance management, attempting to address the current needs of organizations. Since the main contributions of this paper are: (i) providing a set of business and compliance ontologies as the backbone of any compliance solution; CMKB, and (ii) using a structural natural language for encoding refined regulations that are interpreted by legal SMEs, who use concepts and relationships from the CMKB; therefore, the next discussion will focus on related-work efforts in these two areas, by aligning them to the work in this paper.

Notably, the COSO framework is an early work introduced as a key guidance to establish internal control systems in organizations. The COSO framework does not propose concrete model to describe compliance concepts, however, it elucidates the way the organization progresses from objectives, abstract requirements, to controls instituted into the processes. Other initiatives, such as COBIT and OCEG's GRC provide a governance model with control objectives for particular domains.

In [9], a compliance conceptual model is introduced to manage and connect compliance and business process concepts. The authors identified a set of first class entities and relations in business process compliance. The set of relationships among these entities are also identified and structurally represented. Similarly, a compliance conceptual model is proposed in [10] based on OCEG's GRC framework. The REALM model is proposed in [11], which constitutes (among others) a concept model and metadata. The concept model captures the concepts and relationships related to a certain domain (domain ontology), which are used to build up compliance rules. In [2, 12] a compliance refinement methodology and compliance conceptual model is proposed based on the COSO framework.

These approaches particularly address the management of compliance specifics, but no refinement methodology is proposed (except for [2, 12]). Furthermore, we consider the SBVR [3] standard as an integral part of a semantically-based compliance management framework. SBVR is a structured natural language that enables the sharing and re-usability of compliance knowledge, removes any ambiguity, which facilitates the communication between different stakeholders.

A parallel stream of research uses semantic technologies to model the business and compliance space and possibly check the satisfaction of *structural* compliance constraints. Semantic technologies have the main objective of providing a uniform representation of an organization process space at a semantic level mainly for knowledge sharing and reusability. The core idea is to use an ontology language, e.g. the Ontology Web Language (OWL) standard to represent relevant process and compliance ontologies. OWL is formally grounded on Description Logic (DL); therefore, compliance requirements can also be specified in DL or a semantic rule language such as SWRL. Then OWL automated reasoning tools, e.g. FaCT++, Pellet, can be used to check the compliance. Prominent work efforts in this direction are [13–16]. However, as pointed out in [15] ontology languages, such as OWL and DL can only capture the structural part of a specific domain. They are not particularly suited to capture the dynamic behaviour, which concerns itself with how the flow proceeds within a process. Behavioural aspects can be better captured using formal languages for workflow, such as petri-nets and state machines.

The semantic compliance management framework proposed in this paper utilizes semantic technologies to provide a uniform conceptualization of the process and compliance space; facilitates the interpretation of compliance requirements and encodes interpreted regulations in the SBVR standard. As a PoC, we have integrated the SBVR interpretation methodology and the semantic CMKB to a well-experimented design-time compliance verification approach in [5], which is capable of specifying and verifying structural and the behavioural compliance constraints.

The body of research on compliance management has been intensive especially after the financial crisis in 2008, and many research projects have been/are running to fill in this gap, e.g. COMPAS, SeaFlows…etc. Providing a compliance verification/checking solution is not the main focus of the paper, therefore, we have integrated the design-time checking approach in [5], due to the maturity of the approach and its recognition by the research community. Other prominent work examples addressing design-time compliance management include: [11, 17–19]. For a detailed analysis of design-time and runtime compliance management approaches, we refer the reader to [20, 21], respectively.

7 Conclusions and Future Work

Business process compliance management is an emergent *business need*, as it has been witnessed that without explicit BP definitions, effective and expressive compliance frameworks, organizations may face litigation risks and even criminal penalties. Financial institutions usually operate in highly-regulated environments and are governed by large number of regulatory requirements, which raise many complex research and development problems. These problems became more challenging after the financial crisis due to the enactment of a broad body of strict financial regulations.

It is worth noting that the approach presented in this paper is also applicable on compliance problems in other industrial sectors rather than the financial industry. This can be enabled by building relevant business ontologies; e.g., healthcare ontology, manufacturing ontology...etc. This paper contributes by an integrated semantic management framework focusing on the financial industry. This can serve as the backbone of any financial compliance solution at any of the stages of the BP lifecycle; design-time, runtime and offline monitoring. CMKB provides a uniform *conceptualization* of the regulatory and business compliance space, enables the sharing and reusability of this knowledge, and improves the level of automation. Furthermore, the interpretation of financial regulations and encoding interpreted regulations in a structured natural language using concepts from CMKB, i.e., the SBVR standard, removes any ambiguity and significantly facilitates the communication between different stakeholders.

As a PoC, we have incorporated our sematic approach to the design-time compliance verification framework proposed in [5]. This approach adopts a pattern-based compliance specification language, which significantly facilitate the work of the experts. The expressive power, efficiency and the computational complexity of the approach will depend heavily on the underlying formal languages and reasoning techniques. While it takes some time and effort to build relevant business and compliance ontologies, and to interpret relevant regulatory bodies in SBVR, however, it is one time investment, which will pave the way for subsequent analysis and reasoning techniques, and eliminate much potential for errors and mistakes.

Future work involves the further evaluation and validation of the approach proposed in this paper by its application on large-scale case studies provided by GRCTC's financial partners. Future work also focuses on the integration of the semantic design-time compliance management approach proposed in this paper with the subsequent runtime and offline monitoring phases.

References

1. Brummer, C.: How international financial law works (and how it doesn't). GEO. L.J. **99**, 272–273
2. Turetken, O., Elgammal, A., van den Heuvel, W.J., Papazoglou, M.: Enforcing compliance on business processes through the use of patterns. In: 19th European Conference on Information Systems (ECIS 2011), Finland (2011)

3. OMG: Semantics of Business Vocabulary and Business Rules (SBVR), version 1.0 (2008)
4. Sheth, A.: Enterprise applications of semantic web: the sweet spot of risk and compliance. In: IASW2005, pp. 25–27 (2005)
5. Elgammal, A., Turetken, O., van den Heuvel, W.J., Papazoglou, M.P.: Formalising and appling compliance patterns for business process compliance. J. Syst. Softw. Model. (SoSym) 1–28 (2014)
6. Reuter, P., Truman, E.M.: Chasing Dirty Money: The Fight Against Money Laundering. Institute for International Economics, Washington, D.C. (2004)
7. Pnueli, A.: The temporal logic of programs. In: 18th IEEE Symposium on Foundations of Computer Science, pp. 46–57 (1977)
8. Dwyer, M., Avrunin, G., Corbett, J.: Property specification patterns for finite-state verification. In: 2nd International Workshop on Formal Methods on Software Practice, pp. 7–15 (1998)
9. Namiri, K., Stojanovic, N.: Towards a formal framework for business process compliance. In: International Multikonferenz Wirtschaftsinformatik, pp. 1185–1196, Germany (2008)
10. Vicente, P., Silva, M.: A conceptual model for integrated governance, risk and compliance. In: 23rd International Conference on Advanced Information Systems Engineering, pp. 199–213 (2011)
11. Giblin, C., Liu, A., Muller, S., Pfitzmann, B., Zhou, X.: Regulations expressed as logical models. In: 18th International Annual Conference of Legal Knowledge and Information Systems, pp. 37–48, Belgium (2005)
12. Turetken, O., Elgammal, A., van den Heuvel, W., Papazoglou, M.: Capturing compliance requirements: a pattern-based approach. IEEE Softw. Spec. Issue Softw. Eng. Compliance 29, 28–36 (2012)
13. Gordon, T.F.: Constructing legal arguments with rules in the legal knowledge interchange format (LKIF). In: Casanovas, P., Sartor, G., Casellas, N., Rubino, R. (eds.) Computable Models of the Law. LNCS (LNAI), vol. 4884, pp. 162–184. Springer, Heidelberg (2008)
14. Hepp, M., Roman, D.: An ontology framework for semantic business process management. Business and Information Systems Engineering- BISE (Wirtschaftsinformatik) (2007)
15. Di Francescomarino, C., Ghidini, C., Rospocher, M., Serafini, L., Tonella, P.: Reasoning on semantically annotated processes. In: Bouguettaya, A., Krueger, I., Margaria, T. (eds.) ICSOC 2008. LNCS, vol. 5364, pp. 132–146. Springer, Heidelberg (2008)
16. De Leenheer, P., Cardoso, J., Pedrinaci, C.: Ontological representation and governance of business semantics in compliant service networks. In: Falcão e Cunha, J., Snene, M., Nóvoa, H. (eds.) IESS 2013. LNBIP, vol. 143, pp. 155–169. Springer, Heidelberg (2013)
17. Halle, S., Villemaire, R., Cherkaoui, O.: Specifying and validating data-aware temporal web service properties. IEEE Trans. Softw. Eng. 35, 669–683 (2009)
18. Awad, A., Weidlich, M., Weske, M.: Specification, verification and explanation of violation for data aware compliance rules. In: Baresi, L., Chi, C.-H., Suzuki, J. (eds.) ICSOC-ServiceWave 2009. LNCS, vol. 5900, pp. 500–515. Springer, Heidelberg (2009)
19. Sadiq, W., Governatori, G., Namiri, K.: Modeling control objectives for business process compliance. In: Alonso, G., Dadam, P., Rosemann, M. (eds.) BPM 2007. LNCS, vol. 4714, pp. 149–164. Springer, Heidelberg (2007)
20. Elgammal, A.: Towards a Comprehensive Framework for Business Process Compliance. Information Management Department, Ph.D. Dissertation, p. 284. Tilburg University, Tilburg University Press (2012). ISBN:9789056683139
21. Linh Thao, L., Maggi, F.M., Montali, M., Rinderle-Ma, S., van der Aalst, W.M.P.: A framework for the systematic comparison and evaluation of compliance monitoring approaches. In: EDOC 2013, pp. 7–16 (2013)

Reasoning on Incomplete Execution Traces Using Action Languages – A First Report

Chiara Di Francescomarino[1]([⊠]), Chiara Ghidini[1], Sergio Tessaris[2],
and Itzel Vázquez Sandoval[2]

[1] FBK-IRST, Via Sommarive 18, 38050 Trento, Italy
{dfmchiara,ghidini}@fbk.eu
[2] Free University of Bozen–Bolzano,
Piazza Università, 1, 39100 Bozen-Bolzano, Italy
{tessaris,vazquezsandoval}@inf.unibz.it

Abstract. In this paper we tackle the problem of reconstructing information about incomplete business process execution traces proposing an approach based on action languages.

1 Introduction

In the last decades, the use of IT systems for supporting business activities has notably increased, thus opening to the possibility of monitoring business processes and performing on top of them a number of useful analysis. This has brought to a large diffusion of tools that offer business analysts the possibility to observe the current process execution, identify deviations from the model, perform individual and aggregated analysis on current and past executions, thus supporting process model re-design and improvement.

Unfortunately, a number of difficulties may arise when exploiting information system data for monitoring and analysis purposes. Among these, data may bring only partial information in terms of which process activities have been executed and what data or artefacts they produced, due to e.g., manual activities that are scarcely monitorable and therefore not present in within the information system data.

To the best of our knowledge, none of the current approaches has tackled the latter problem. Only recently, the problem of dealing with incomplete information about process executions has been faced by few works [1,2]. However, either the approach proposed in these works relies on statistical models, as in [1] or it relies on a specific encoding of a particular business process language, with limited expressivity, as in [2].

In this paper we tackle the problem of reconstructing information about incomplete business process execution traces, proposing an approach that, leveraging on the model, aims at recovering missing information about process executions using action languages. In order to address the problem we exploit the similarity between processes and automated planning [3], where activities in a process correspond to actions in planning. A (complete) process execution corresponds to a sequence of activities which, starting from the initial condition,

F. Toumani et al. (Eds.): ICSOC 2014, LNCS 8954, pp. 185–191, 2015.
DOI: 10.1007/978-3-319-22885-3_16

leads to the output condition satisfying the constraints imposed by the workflow. Analogously, a total plan is a sequence of actions which, starting from the initial state, leads to the specified goal.

Given a workflow and an observed trace, we provide an algorithm to construct a planning problem s.t. each solution corresponds to a complete process execution and vice versa. In this way, by analysing all the possible plans we can infer properties of the original workflow specification. The advantage of using automated planning techniques is that we can exploit the underlying logic language to ensure that generated plans conform to the observed traces without resorting to an ad hoc algorithm. In the literature different languages have been proposed to represent planning problems and in our work we use the language $\mathcal{K}$ based on the Answer Set Programming engine $DLV^{\mathcal{K}}$ (see [4]). The language is expressive enough for our purposes and the integration within an ASP system enables a flexible and concise representation of the problem.[1] On the other hand, the main ideas behind the encoding are general enough to be adapted to most of the expressive planning languages.

We focus on *block structured* workflows which, broadly speaking, means that they are composed of blocks, where every split has a corresponding matching type join, and of loops with a single entry and exit points ([5,6]). This assumption rules out pathological patterns that are notoriously hard to characterise (e.g. involving nested OR joins); but they provide coverage for a wide range of interesting use cases.

2   The Problem and Its Encoding Using Planning

In this section we report a description of the problem and its encoding in $\mathcal{K}$.

The Problem. We aim at understanding how to reconstruct information of incomplete process execution traces, given some knowledge about the process model. The input to our problem consists of an instance-independent component, the process model, and an instance-specific component, i.e., the (partial) input trace.

Process models we deal with in this paper are described in the YAWL language [5]. YAWL is a workflow language inspired by Petri Nets, whose main constructs are reported in Fig. 1.

As a simple explanatory example of the problem we want to solve, consider the process described in YAWL in Fig. 2. The process takes inspiration from the procedure for the generation of the Italian fiscal code: the registration module is created (CRM), the personal details of the subject are added (APD) and, before assigning the fiscal code, according to whether it is for a foreigner or for a newborn, either the passport/stay permit information ($APPD$) or the parents' data ($APARD$) are added respectively. Once the data

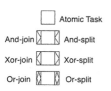

Fig. 1. YAWL

------

[1] A brief introduction of $\mathcal{K}$ is available as appendix after the bibliography.

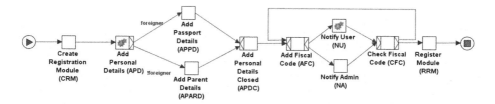

Fig. 2. A simple process for the generation of the Italian fiscal code.

$(APDC)$ and the fiscal code (AFC) are added, both the user (NU) and the administrative offices (NA) are notified in parallel, in order to see whether they have objections; only at this stage, the fiscal code is checked once again (CFC). If no problem occurs, the module can be registered (RRM), otherwise the fiscal code has to be added again and the notification and validation procedure iterated until successful.

We can suppose that a run-time monitoring system has been able to trace some knowledge about the execution of this process, by logging only the *observable activities ADP* and *NU*, marked in Fig. 2 by using small engine icons. An example of partial trace listing 3 executions of observable activities and their observed data, enclosed in curly brackets, is:

$$APD\ \{name : JohnSmith, foreigner : FALSE\}$$
$$NU\ \{name : JohnSmith, foreigner : FALSE, FC : xyz\}$$
$$NU\ \{name : JohnSmith, foreigner : FALSE, FC : xxz\}$$

Exploiting the available knowledge about the process model and the observed trace, we would like to know whether it is possible (and how) to reconstruct the missing information of the partial trace. For instance, being aware of the process control flow in the example and of the fact that the APD and the NU activities have been executed, suggests that (i) the CRM and the $APDC$ activities have also been executed; (ii) either the $APPD$ or the $APARD$ activity has been executed; (iii) AFC, NU, NA and CFC have also been executed at least once. By inspecting the value of the condition variable $(foreigner)$ after the split activity, it is possible to understand which branch has been taken among the two alternative paths, i.e., the one passing through the $APARD$ activity. Moreover, since the observable activity NU has been executed twice, it is possible to understand that the loop has been executed two times.

Although in this simple example understanding how to fill "gaps" in the incomplete trace is relatively easy, this is not the case for real world examples. For lack of space in this paper we do not include the general encoding but we aim at providing the intuition on how it is possible to encode complex workflows so as to understand how to reconstruct the missing information.[2]

---

[2] The example is not presenting the OR-join which has a rather involved semantics which we capture in the general case. Full details and proofs are included in [7].

Translation of Workflows. The key of the bisimulation of the workflow processes using an action language lays in the fact that the semantics of YAWL is provided in terms of transition systems, where states are defined in terms of conditions connected to activities. Conditions may contain one or more tokens and the execution of activities causes the transition between states by moving tokens from incoming to outgoing conditions according to their type (AND/OR/XOR join or split). Moreover, block structured workflows are *safe* in the sense that no more than one token accumulates in a single condition; therefore we do not need to keep track of the number of tokens in each condition.

To each activity it corresponds an action with the same identifier. The states are represented by the inertial fluent enabled(·) ranging over the set of conditions in the workflow. Intuitively, the executability of an action depends on join conditions over the enabled(·) fluents whose values are manipulated according to the split conditions.

The encoding is based on the activities in the workflow; each activity with input and output conditions corresponds to a set of statements. The kind of join determines the executability of the corresponding action according to the input conditions; while splits induce a set of causation rules involving the terms associated to output conditions.

Figure 2 introduces two kinds of patterns: AND and XOR split/join representing parallelism and decision respectively. In the translation below implicit conditions are named using the starting and ending activities. Parallelism makes sure that all the alternative branches are activated by activating all the output conditions and waiting for all the input conditions before enabling the closing activities:

caused enabled(afc_nu) **after** afc.
caused enabled(afc_na) **after** afc.
executable cfc **if** enabled(nu_cfc), enabled(na_cfc).

All tokens in input conditions are "consumed" by the activities and this is captured by using strong negation; e.g. for *CFC*:

caused −enabled(nu_cfc) **after** cfc.
caused −enabled(na_cfc) **after** cfc.

Decision patterns (XOR) select *only one* condition on the basis of a split predicate associated to the edge and the corresponding join expects just one of the input conditions to be activated:

caused enabled(apd_appd) **if** foreigner, **not** enabled(apd_apard) **after** apd.
caused enabled(apd_apard) **if not** foreigner, **not** enabled(apd_appd) **after** apd.
executable apdc **if** enabled(appd_apdc).
executable apdc **if** enabled(apard_apdc).

The workflow contains two special conditions called start and end respectively. These are encoded in the initial state and goal specification:

initially: enabled(start).
goal: enabled(end)?

Encoding of Traces. Activities are divided in observable and non-observable. Traces are sequences of observed activities and generated plans should conform to these sequences in the sense that observable activities should appear in the plan only if they are in the traces and in the exact order.

In order to generate plans in which observable activities appear in the correct order we introduce a set of fluents of the form observed $(\cdot,\cdot)$ where the first argument is the name of the activity and the second one an integer representing the order in the sequence. An additional fluent observed (end, $k+1$) is included to indicate the end of a trace of length k. The additional fluents are used to "inhibit" observable actions unless they are in the right sequence. The trace *APD, NU, NU* of the example corresponds to the sequence of fluents

observed(apd,1), observed(nu,2), observed(nu,3), observed(end,4)

The additional integer argument is necessary to account for multiple activations of the same activity in the trace.

All the pre-conditions of the executability conditions for observable actions are augmented with the corresponding trace fluents:

executable nu **if** observed(nu,_), enabled(afc_nu).

The execution of an observable action should enable the following action in the sequence and disable the previous one to avoid multiple activations:

caused observed(nu,2) **after** observed(apd,1), apd.

caused −observed(apd,1) **after** observed(apd,1), apd.

The value of the flag `foreign` is not set by any of the activities, but it is necessary to understand which branch should be activated. Note that, according to the trace, its value is *observed* by the first action *apd*. This fact is encoded by the causation statement

caused foreign **if** observed(apd,1).

Finally the initial status and goal should be modified in order to enable the first observable action and ensure the completion of the whole trace:

initially: enabled(start), observed(apd,1).

goal: enabled(end), observed(end,_)?

With the additional constraints related to the observed trace, the planner will select only plans that conform to the observation among all the possible ones induced by the workflow specification. In particular, even without any knowledge about the predicates governing the loop, only plans where the loop is executed twice are produced.

3   Conclusions and Related Works

The paper aims at supporting business analysis activities by tackling the limitations due to the partiality of information often characterising the business activity monitoring. To this purpose, a novel reasoning method for reconstructing incomplete execution traces, that relies on the formulation of the issue in terms of a planning problem, is presented.

The problem of incomplete traces has been faced in the field of process mining, where it still represents one of the challenges [8]. Several works (e.g., [9]) have addressed the problem of aligning event logs and procedural models.

In our case, however, both goal and preconditions are different since we assume that the model is correct.

The reconstruction of flows of activities of a model given a partial set of information on it can be related to several fields of research in which the dynamics of a system are perceived only to a limited extent and hence it is needed to reconstruct missing information. We can divide the existing proposals into quantitative and qualitative approaches.

The former rely on the availability of a probabilistic model of execution and knowledge. For example, in a very recent work [1], the authors exploit stochastic Petri nets and Bayesian Networks to recover missing information (activities and their durations).

The latter stand on the idea of describing "possible outcomes" regardless of likelihood; hence, knowledge about the world will consist of equally likely "alternative worlds" given the available observations in time. Among these approaches [2], the same issue of reconstructing missing information in execution traces given the process model, has been faced in [2], where the problem has been tackled by reformulating it in terms of a Boolean Satisfiability Problem (SAT), rather than by applying a planning approach.

Planning techniques have already been applied to process models in YAWL [10], by translating workflow tasks into plan actions and task states into causes and effects, similarly to our approach though with a different planning technique and purpose. To the best of our knowledge, indeed, planning approaches have not yet been applied to specifically face the problem of incomplete execution traces.

Although preliminary experiments with significantly more complex workflows than the one used in the paper show that the approach can cope with real workflows, we plan to perform an exhaustive empirical evaluation to understand whether the planner can scale up to workflows deployed in practice. Another aspect to investigate is the different kind of data used in workflows and their interaction with the observed traces in order to discriminate relevant plans by augmenting the workflow with annotations.

Overview of Action Language $\mathcal{K}$. The main elements of action languages are *fluents* and *actions*. The formers represent the state of the system which may change by means of actions. Causation statements describe the possible evolution of the states and preconditions associated to actions describe which action can be executed according to the current state. A planning problem in $\mathcal{K}$ is specified using a Datalog-like language where fluents and actions are represented by literals (not necessarily ground). A problem specification includes the list of fluents, actions, initial state and goal conditions; moreover a set of statements specifies the dynamics of the planning domain using causation rules and executability conditions.

A *causation rule* is a statement of the form

caused f **if** $b_1, \ldots, b_k$, **not** $b_{k+1}, \ldots,$ **not** b_ℓ **after** $a_1, \ldots, a_m$, **not** $a_{m+1}, \ldots,$ **not** a_n.

where f is either a classical literal over a fluent or **false** (representing absurdity), the b_i's are classical literals (atoms or strongly negated atoms, indicated using –)

over fluents and background predicates and the a_j's are positive action atoms or classical literals over fluent and background predicates. Informally, the rule states that f is true in the new state reached by executing (simultaneously) some actions, provided that the condition of the after part is true with respect to the old state and the actions executed on it, and the condition of the if part is true in the new state.

An *executability condition* is a statement of the form

executable a **if** $b_1, \ldots, b_k$, **not** $b_{k+1}, \ldots,$ **not** b_ℓ.

where a is an action atom and $b_1, \ldots, b_\ell$ are classical literals (known as preconditions in the statement). Informally, such a condition says that the action is eligible for execution in a state, if $b_1, \ldots, b_k$ are known to hold while $b_{k+1}, \ldots, b_\ell$ are not known to hold in that state.

A fluent can be declared `inertial`, expressing the fact that it should stay true, unless it explicitly becomes false in the new state.

References

1. Rogge-Solti, A., Mans, R.S., van der Aalst, W.M.P., Weske, M.: Improving documentation by repairing event logs. In: Grabis, J., Kirikova, M., Zdravkovic, J., Stirna, J. (eds.) PoEM 2013. LNBIP, vol. 165, pp. 129–144. Springer, Heidelberg (2013)
2. Bertoli, P., Di Francescomarino, C., Dragoni, M., Ghidini, C.: Reasoning-based techniques for dealing with incomplete business process execution traces. In: Baldoni, M., Baroglio, C., Boella, G., Micalizio, R. (eds.) AI*IA 2013. LNCS, vol. 8249, pp. 469–480. Springer, Heidelberg (2013)
3. Nau, D., Ghallab, M., Traverso, P.: Automated Planning: Theory & Practice. Morgan Kaufmann Publishers Inc., San Francisco, CA, USA (2004)
4. Eiter, T., Faber, W., Leone, N., Pfeifer, G., Polleres, A.: A logic programming approach to knowledge-state planning, II: the DLVK system. Artif. Intell. **144**, 157–211 (2003)
5. van der Aalst, W.M.P., ter Hofstede, A.H.M.: YAWL: yet another workflow language. Inf. Syst. **30**, 245–275 (2005)
6. Kiepuszewski, B., ter Hofstede, A.H.M., Bussler, C.J.: On structured workflow modelling. In: Krogstie, J., Bubenko, J., Pastor, O., Pernici, B., Rolland, C., Sølvberg, A. (eds.) Seminal Contributions to Information Systems Engineering, pp. 241–255. Springer, Berlin, Heidelberg (2013)
7. Sandoval, I.V.: Automated reasoning support for process models using action language. Master's thesis, Faculty of Computer Sciences, Free University of Bozen-Bolzano (2014)
8. van der Aalst, W., et al.: Process mining manifesto. In: Daniel, F., Barkaoui, K., Dustdar, S. (eds.) BPM Workshops 2011, Part I. LNBIP, vol. 99, pp. 169–194. Springer, Heidelberg (2012)
9. Adriansyah, A., van Dongen, B.F., van der Aalst, W.M.P.: Conformance checking using cost-based fitness analysis. Proc. EDOC **2011**, 55–64 (2011)
10. Marrella, A., Mecella, M., Russo, A.: Featuring automatic adaptivity through workflow enactment and planning. In: CollaborateCom 2011 (2011)

Semantic Web Services Approach for Collaboration in E-Gov Context

Amal Latrache$^{(\boxtimes)}$, El habib Nfaoui, and Jaouad Boumhidi

LIIAN Laboratory, Sidi Mohamed Ben Abdellah University, Fez, Morocco
{amal.latrache, elhabib.nfaoui,
jaouad.boumhidi}@usmba.ac.ma

Abstract. The main objective of e-government information systems is to provide integrated, transparent, and efficient services to citizens by exploiting the potential of new information and communication technologies. The current trend in this field is the use of semantic technologies, especially semantic web services (SWS) which enable enriching E-Gov services description with additional semantic information. However, besides making available e-services, a number of gaps must be filled such as services discovery, integration and collaboration. In this paper, we propose a SWS approach to overcome these gaps in government-to-government (G2G) context which is distributed environment.

Keywords: E-Gov · Semantic web services · Semantic web services discovery · Matchmaking · Mobile agent

1 Introduction

To face the problems of traditional public administrations such as high costs, poor quality services and the time consuming tasks, E-government have now been considerably developed to cover the basic services that should be delivered to citizens and enterprises. For that, Moroccan Government has launched the strategic plan "Digital Morocco 2013" in October 2009. Its main objective is to provide efficient e-government services which meet the expectations and the needs of the business sector and the population at large. The realized projects fall into two categories; the first category is related to particular sectors such as e-justice, e-finance, e-health, e-consulate ...etc. The second category concerns transverse projects such as the National Portal and the e-Wilaya.

However, the most exiting E-Gov projects deal with different issues such as the high costs of development, the complexity of maintenance, the difficulty of integrating an external e-service, and the exchange and collaboration between different administration e-services is almost impossible. Semantic technologies and semantic web services remains as the suitable solution to tackle these issues, thanks to their interoperability and reusability.

The main advantages of combining semantics technologies and web services are an explicit semantic description of their functionality understood by software agents as well as by human users, also a correct interpretation of information sent and received. On the other hand, finding the suitable SWS that satisfy the user request is an emergent and challenging research problem especially if the SWSs are published in different hosting sites.

© Springer International Publishing Switzerland 2015
F. Toumani et al. (Eds.): ICSOC 2014, LNCS 8954, pp. 192–197, 2015.
DOI: 10.1007/978-3-319-22885-3_17

In this work we propose to use the advantages of SWS to tackle the issues of E-Gov exiting systems. Thus, Developing SWS oriented systems instead of developing or using complex software and systems allow an administration to link its applications with those of other administrations via the Internet. Also, administrations can view and use partners' information as if it were their own (SWS which is developed in agency "X" can be easily used in an agency "Y" without facing the interoperability issues). Not only that but administrations also can link their own applications within the administration, even those coded in different programming languages, to reduce redundancy and increase efficiency. This paper is organized as follows. Section 2 discusses some related works to semantic technologies in E-Government field. Section 3 describes our proposed approach while the last section outlines the conclusions and future works.

2   Background Review

2.1   Background Review of Semantic Web Services

Semantic Web technologies, such as ontology, can be used for describing and reasoning the capabilities of a Web service. The existing SWS description languages can be basically grouped under two main categories, which are the languages modeling SWS from the top by defining high-level conceptual models of SWS such as OWL-S [1], and the languages modeling SWS from the bottom by defining semantic elements for WSDL descriptions of a Web service. On the other hand, SWS vision highlights the need of SWS discovery tools and mechanisms that can extract and exploit these semantic descriptions.

The SWS discovery process depends on the location of the web services descriptions. It may be a centralized repository such as UDDI (Universal Description Discovery and Integration) or web portals (www.webservicelist.com, www.xmethods.com). This mechanism has several limitations as discussed in [2].

Peer-To-Peer(P2P) networks provide a scalable alternative to centralized systems by distributing data (web services) and load among all peers, this architecture is complicated (difficulties in implementation) and sharing web services information among peers is not practical due to lack of trust among peers [3]. Another alternative is the internet based architectures in which a web crawler or search engine is used to gather web services. For more efficient result, intelligent agents can be used in the web services discovery process.

Semantic web services in distributed environment is becoming a challenging research problem, the authors in [4] propose an approach to find SWS in distributed environment but it is limited just to SWAM enabled sites. This highlighted the need of an approach to discover SWS in different hosting sites which is one of the main motivations of our approach.

2.2   Background Review of Semantic Technologies in E-Gov

Many e-gov projects have been developed and various architectures have been proposed for the development of e-gov semantic information systems. Table 1 illustrates the most relevant projects in this field.

Table 1. Semantic projects and Approaches in E-GoV

Project/Approach	SWS?	Objectives
OntoGov [5]	No	Platform that facilities the configuration, the compostion and the evaluation of e-gov web services
An e-gov case study [6]	No	Platform that can be used to integrate Government services across different service providers
SWS in an E-Gov knowledge network [7]	Yes	A framework to improve services matching process in the context of IRS-II SWS infrastructure
Public administration services access [8]	No	Infrastructure that help the public administration clients to find the services that fulfill their needs

Such projects and approaches have demonstrated the add-value of integrating semantic technologies in E-Gov but they didn't explore the possibility of using SWS for the interoperability and integration of different services (expect [7] which is IRS-II based). Also, the major part of the proposed approaches is government-to-citizens (G2C) driven; however there is a need for a tool to facilitate the interaction and the collaboration among heterogeneous government organizations services (G2G collaboration), the development of such tool is the objective of our proposed approach.

3 Agent and SWS Based Approach for Collaboration in E-Gov Context

The lack of collaboration between E-Gov agencies can contribute to a significant waste of financial and material resources. For example, developing taxes payment as SWS requires the collaboration with the property conservation administration as shows in Fig. 1.

Finding the requested SWS among several services published in different hosting sites is the principal objective of our approach which is based on our previous work [9]. The main components of this architecture are illustrated in Fig. 2.

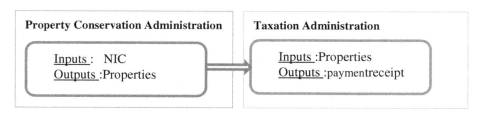

Fig. 1. Taxes payment SWS

User interface provides a set of features that can help the developer to better express his request. This interface has several fields: the web service's name in which the user enters the desired value. Then, he selects the requested inputs (NIC code) and

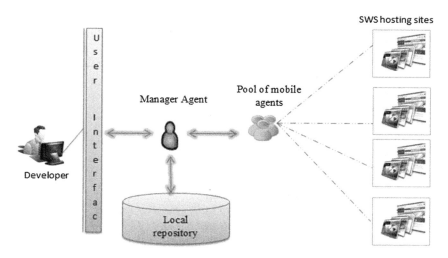

Fig. 2. Proposed architecture for SWS discovery

outputs (properties list) on the basis of predefined domain ontology (in our case is an E-Gov ontology). After gathering user requirements, an OWL-S request is automatically generated according to the OWL-S profile sub-ontology.

Manager agent analyzes the owl-s request that contains the semantic description of the user request. This agent has the following roles:

Decide if an index of the requested service is in the local repository of the taxation administration.

If the requested service is not found in the local repository, the manager agent sends the request to the pool of mobile agents to search for the requested service in different sites (other E-Gov hosting sites).

Update the data included in the repository.

Local repository contains a set of useful information related to the collected web services (by previous crawling) such as the semantic description, the provider site link, etc. These information aren't stored arbitrarily but according to a specific categorization to facilitate the access and the update process.

Mobile agents collect the semantic web services that fulfill the manger agent request; this is done by crawling the web and finding the E-Gov web sites that contains the required SWS. To accomplish this task, we have proposed a focused web crawler by adapting the crawler proposed in [10]. The main enhancements we have proposed are the use of matching algorithm [11] that measure similarities between owl-s request and the founded SWS based on their inputs, outputs and domain. Also, the use of mobile agents instead of using a web crawler. This choice is recommended by [12] since it has several advantages.

The proposed crawler selects a random link from the URLs queue (the E-Gov web sites); then for each valid link i.e. a link which doesn't exist in robots.txt and it is not an image or PDF document, the crawler verifies if it contains SWS that may satisfy the user's request. The main steps of the proposed algorithm are as follows:

Inputs: (starting URL in queue, user' request)
Begin:
  While (URLs queue is not empty){
  Get first URL from queue
  If (the actual link is valid){
    Visiting the actual link
    If (the OWL_S descriptions exist){
      For each SWS {
        Invoke matchmaking algorithm
        If the SWS is a candidate to satisfy the user request
          Store an index of the selected SWS} } }
  Else {Extract links from the actual page
  Add linked URLs in queue}}
End;

In our case, only three services (as illustrated in Table 2) are selected in the discovery process with different degrees of similarities; the adequate SWS to satisfy the user request is the one with the highest score.

Table 2. Administrations SWSs discovery result

Property conservation administration SWSs			Matchmaking score
SWS name	Inputs	Outputs	
Land list	NIC	Land	5
Properties list	NIC	properties	6
Estate list	Code	Estate	3

The main advantages of our approach are:

It enables collaboration between public administration services

It can be applied successfully in other domains such as E-business.

It's a distributed architecture that enables the discovering of web services over several hosting sites. Thus, it's not limited to the UDDI which has several limits [2]. And it's not just to SWAM enabled sites [4].

It's based on mobile agents that increase the crawling speed and minimize the network overhead [12].

It does not enforce the providers or the consumers of SWS to use a specific annotations or technologies, either than OWL-S, to perform their tasks.

Several functionalities are provided in a convivial user interface which helps the user to better express his request using predefined domain-ontologies.

4   Conclusion and Future Work

In this paper we have presented a mobile agent approach to discover SWS in a distributed environment. The few approaches that takes into account the distribution of the web services require the use of a specific annotations to describe the web service or to find it, while we can't enforce the web service' publisher to use these specific annotations, the only annotation to consider for him is the standard semantic one and in our approach is the OWL-S.

The E-Government information systems deal with several problems such as services integration and interoperability. SWSs are an efficient solution to overcome these issues; it provides interoperability within and between administrations. For that, we have applied our approach in the E-Gov context.

Sometimes web services requesters need the use of several atomic web services to achieve their requests, thus the composition of web services - taking advantage of currently existing web services to provide a new service that does not exist on its own- will be taking into account in our future work.

References

1. Semantic Markup for Web Services. http://www.w3.org/Submission/OWL-S/
2. Al-Masri, E., Qusay, M.: Discovering web services in search engines. IEEE Int. Comput. **12** (3), 74–77 (2008)
3. D'Mello, D.A., Ananthanarayana, V.S.: A Review of Dynamic Web Service Description and Discovery Techniques. In: First International Conference on Integrated Intelligent Computing, pp. 246 − 251 (2010) doi:10.1109/ICIIC.2010.57
4. Crasso, M., Mateos, C., Zunino, A.: SWAM: A logic-based mobile agent programming language for the Semantic Web. Expert Syst. Appl. J. **38**(3), 1723–1737 (2011)
5. Tambouris, E., Gorilas, S., Kavadias, G., Apostolou, D., Abecker, A., Stojanovic, L., Mentzas, G.: Ontology-enabled E-Gov service configuration: an overview of the OntoGov project. In: Wimmer, M. (ed.) KMGov 2004. LNCS (LNAI), vol. 3035, pp. 122–127. Springer, Heidelberg (2004)
6. Drumm, C., Cabral, L.: An eGovernment case study: integrating governmental services using semantic web technology. In: Semantic Web Services: Concepts, Technologies, and Applications, pp. 365–380 (2007)
7. Sell, D., Cabral, L., Gonçalves, A., Motta, E., Pacheco, R.: A framework to improve semantic web services discovery and integration in an E-Gov Knowledge Network. In: Motta, E., Shadbolt, N., Stutt, A., Gibbins, N. (eds.) EKAW 2004. LNCS (LNAI), vol. 3257, pp. 509–510. Springer, Heidelberg (2004)
8. Evangelos, T.: Semantic Web-Services for e-Government: Application to Public Administration Services. Ph.D. thesis, university of Southampton (2010)
9. Latrache, A., Nfaoui, E., Boumhidi, J.: A mobile agent based approach for automating a discover-compose process of semantic web services. J. Compt. Sci. **10**, 1628–1641 (2014)
10. Batzios, A., Dimou, C., Symeonidis, A.L.: BioCrawler: An Intelligent Crawler for the Semantic Web. Expert Syst. Appl. J. **35**(2), 524–530 (2008)
11. Berdjouh, C., Okba, K.: An agent-based approach to web services discovery. UBiquitous comput. Commun. J. **4**(3), 509–515 (2009)
12. Kumari, V., Rajput, P.: web crawler based on secure mobile agent. Res. J. Comput. Syst. Eng. **3**(3), 419–423 (2012)

Intelligent Service Clouds

Contextualised Security Operation Deployment Through MDS@run.time Architecture

Wendpanga Francis Ouedraogo[1]([✉]), Frédérique Biennier[1], and Philippe Merle[2]

[1] Université de Lyon, CNRS INSA-Lyon, LIRIS UMR 5205,
20 avenue Albert Einstein, 69621 Villeurbanne Cedex, France
{wendpanga-francis.ouedraogo,frederique.biennier}@liris.cnrs.fr
[2] Inria Lille - Nord Europe, Parc Scientifique de la Haute Borne,
40 avenue Halley, 59650 Villeneuve d'Ascq, France
philippe.merle@inria.fr

Abstract. The fast development of Cloud-based services and applications have a significant impact on Service Oriented Computing as it provides an efficient support to share data and processes. The deperimeterised vision involved by these Intelligent Service Clouds lead to new security challenges: providing a consistent protection depending on the business environment conditions and on the deployment platform specific threats and vulnerabilities. To fit this context aware protection deployment challenge, we propose a MDS@run.time architecture, coupling Model Driven Security (MDS) and Models@run.time approaches. By this way, security policies (that can be generated via a MDS process) are interpreted at runtime by a security mediator depending on the context. This proposition is illustrated thanks to a proof of concept prototype plugged on top of the FraSCAti middleware.

1 Introduction

The fast development of Cloud-based services and applications provides an efficient support to share data and processes, leading to deperimeterised Information Systems. The flexibility and agility provided by these so-called Intelligent Service Clouds enables new styles of inter-enterprises Collaborative Business, taking advantage of service reusability to create new collaborative workflows and of the Cloud plasticity allowing to use different access devices. This deperimeterised and evolving vision of Information Systems leads to enforce the call for protection mechanisms to mitigate potential vulnerabilities or threats related to any potential business (i.e. the specification of the organizations and workflow in which the service may be involved) or deployment context (namely access device, interconnection network or deployment platform configuration information). To avoid a systematic and costly over-protection deployment, we propose a context-aware security architecture to select at runtime the security policy rules that fit the current business and technical execution context. To this end, we couple the MDS [6] and Models@run.time approaches to set a MDS@run.time architecture. In brief, security policies (defining the different protection services depending on environmental conditions) are seen as an abstract

© Springer International Publishing Switzerland 2015
F. Toumani et al. (Eds.): ICSOC 2014, LNCS 8954, pp. 201–212, 2015.
DOI: 10.1007/978-3-319-22885-3_18

Models@run.time specification used to select, compose and orchestrate security services depending on the current execution context. This architecture plugged on hosting middleware allows outsourcing security concerns from the business services. The service invocation is captured and processed to compose and orchestrate the convenient security services depending on the execution context. We call this process Security Mediation as it is built in a similar perspective of the classical outsourced mediation components. A proof of concept prototype plugged on FraSCAti is used to evaluate the "execution cost" of the dynamic security deployment. We first present the context and a motivating example before defining the way MDS is extended in a MDS@run.time vision (Sect. 2). The related architecture and its implementation plugged on the FraSCAti middleware is detailed in Sect. 3 and its performance are evaluated in Sect. 4. We lastly confront our proposal with related work (Sect. 5).

2   Context and Motivating Example

The openess and deperimeterized information system organization involved by intelligent service clouds takes advantage of service reusing abilities to support new business processes. A dynamic supply chain organisation can be seen as a motivating example of such service ecosystem. In this use case a food product tracking process (see Fig. 1) relies on a dynamic workflow interconnecting the business services of the different partners, sharing products production, storage and transport information. Such collaborative workflow combines services and personal workflows from both companies, challenging new security features such as partner authentication, access control on the product storage information, non repudiation features. While setting *on the fly* collaborative organisations, taking advantage of the dynamic service selection provided by the service ecosystem, each partner can compose shared services to create ad-hoc workflows. This involves that a business service can be invoked *on the fly* by different own partner workflows. To provide end to end consistent protection of a given service, one has to take context into account related to the business workflow in which the service takes part and to the end to end execution platform configuration (namely the hosting platform, the access devices and the interconnetion network). Thus, the consistent security services must be composed and orchestrated depending on the execution context. For example, a secured transport is required while accessing logistics information via the unsecured Internet network whereas it is useless while using the safer logistics company LAN, authentication/access control must integrate new partners. Differents methods (EBIOS, MEHARI, OCTAVE, SNA)[1] can be used to identify perceived security risks/system vulnerabilities. Based on the ISO/IEC 27002, the OASIS Service Reference Model[2] defines different security requirements (confidentiality and privacy management, integrity, authentication, authorization, availability and non repudiation) that require the

---

[1] https://www.enisa.europa.eu/activities/risk-management/current-risk/risk-management-inventory/rm-isms.

[2] http://docs.oasis-open.org/soa-rm/v1.0/soa-rm.html.

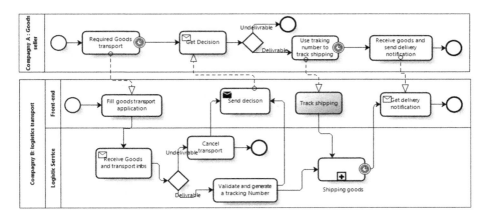

Fig. 1. This collaborative business process is organized in different lanes associated to the different supply chain participants. Services such as *Track shipping* are tagged depending on their patrimonial value. Global information on the collaborative environment is also attached to the different lanes. Restricted access control features can also be defined while defining the collaboration agreement between partners.

deployment of security means from the network layer, which is rather focused on the availability requirement and protection against deny of service attacks, and transport layer, which has to provide secured confidential channels between transmitters and receivers, to the application layer, which manages most of the security requirements such as authentication, authorization, non repudiation, confidentiality and privacy. Different standards such as WS-Security, SAML, XACML, BSLA, etc. have been developped to support and implement these security requirements. Such protection means can either be deployed directly in the service operation or "attached" to the service interface specification.

Based on the way the OASIS service reference model organizes the different security services, we have proposed in previous work [7] an XML extension to define these security services and protection requirements in the service security policy using exiting standards such as SAML, XACML.

Focusing on the service attached to the logistic application form, a security policy can be set to define the different protection means to be deployed (see Fig. 2). This service includes an operation named TrackShipping, which is considered as a resource (Line 2 in Fig. 2). Its protection requires an authentication (lines 2–9) using a simple login/password process (Line 4) refering to a checking file defined in Line 5. Besides authentication, according to the user network domain (public at Line 14) or company B private network at Line 19) access control rules have to be performed (lines 10–22). If a public network is used, ACL (Line 12), should be applied to this resource. Figure 3 describes the contents of the authorization file allowing only *user1* and *user2* of the company A to access the resource whereas any user of B can access it freely from the B's local network.

```
1.   <policies>
2.       <policy id="1" resource="/logisticService/trackShipping/" type="Authentication" metric="0.5">
3.           <policyRule>
4.               <pattern layers="Service" metric="0.5" name="LoginPwd" type="Technique">
5.                   <setting key="userRegistry" value="Registry/Users.xml"/>
6.                   <context type="Device" value="{smartphone,PC}"/>
7.               </pattern>
8.           </policyRule>
9.       </policy>
10.      <policy id="2" resource="/logisticService/trackShipping/" type="Authorization">
11.          <policyRule >
12.              <pattern layers="Service" metric="0.25" name="ACL" type="Technique">
13.                  <setting key="accessFile" value="resources/acl/AccessControlList.xml"/>
14.                  <context type="Network" value="public"/>
15.              </pattern>
16.          </policyRule>
17.          <policyRule >
18.              <pattern layers="Service" metric="0" name="" type="">
19.                  <context type="Network" value="private{compagnyB.com}"/>
20.              </pattern>
21.          </policyRule>
22.      </policy>
23.  </policies>
```

Fig. 2. Security policies associated to the *Logistic* resource.

```
1.   <acl xsi:noNamespaceSchemaLocation="AccessListSchema.xsd">
2.       <resource name="/logisticService/trackShipping/compagnyA/">
3.           <grant user="user1@compagnyA.com" ></grant>
4.           <grant user="user2@compagnyA.com" ></grant>
5.       </resource>
6.   </acl>
```

Fig. 3. *AccessControlList.xml* authorization file.

As these business services can be invoked dynamically by ad-hoc collaborative workflows,or via different devices such as smartphone or classical computing environment, protection services must be deployed according to the execution context paying attention on both organisational (i.e. which partner, trusted or not, invokes the service) and technical (which kind of cloud hosts the collaborative workflow, which kind of transport service is provided, etc.) environment. The protection requirements are defined globally in the security policies attached to the different business services (for example see Fig. 4, Line 3). These security policies are seen as security models at runtime that will be used at runtime by the security mediator to select, compose and orchestrate the security services depending on the execution context.

In our example, the tracking service and the related information must be protected in the new *opened* context as it can be accede by partners, with differnt access devices (smartphone for executive members, or PC). This confidentiality requirement impacts both application layer, which is in charge of the access control, i.e., authentication and authorization management, and transport layer (see Fig. 2). The systematic composition of the authentication and authorization services may be costly. Table 1 shows a comparison of service execution time with/without authentication and authorization, testing conditions and environment are detailed in Sect. 4.

To avoid this costly over protection or risky under protection depending on the runtime environment vulnerability, we propose to turn these security

```
1.   <wsdl:binding name="LogisticSoapBinding" type="tns:LogisticServicePortType">
2.       <soap:binding style="document" transport="http://schemas.xmlsoap.org/soap/http"/>
3.         <wsdl:operation name="trackShipping " mds:policyRef="resources/data/policies.xml"
4.   xmlns:mds="http://mds.org">
5.           <soap:operation soapAction="" style="document"/>
6.           <wsdl:input name="trackShippingData">
7.             <soap:body use="literal"/>
8.           </wsdl:input>
9.           <wsdl:output name="trackShippingDataResponse">
10.            <soap:body use="literal"/>
11.          </wsdl:output>
12.        </wsdl:operation>
13.  </wsdl:binding>
```

Fig. 4. Link policy file with the *TrackShipping* operation of the *Logistic* service.

Table 1. Service execution time.

Executed components	Execution time (ms)	
	1-100	101-201
Business service	71	58
Business service + Authentication	82	68
Business service + Authentication + Authorization	85	70

policies as Models@run.time so that they can be analysed to select, compose and orchestrate the most convenient security services depending on the exact runtime environment. This requires a new architecture to *outsource* the security management as a new high-level service that can be plugged on the hosting middleware. In next sections, we present this new architecture and a proof of concept based on the FraSCAti middleware.

3   MDS@run.time with FraSCAti

Our architecture is plugged on the traditional service/middleware/hosting platform architecture (see Fig. 5(a)). In order to avoid under or over protection depending on the runtime context, we propose to outsource the security management thanks to our MDS@run.time architecture (see Fig. 5(b)) which consists in:

- A middleware specific `Interceptor` component plugged on the middleware intercepts each service/middleware interaction (Step 1) and routes this interaction to the `MDS@run.time` component (Step 2).
- The `MDS@run.time` component is the core component to achieve the dynamic security deployment. It consists in three sub components:
  - The `policy manager` parses the service description, extracts and loads the associated policy files before launching the context acquisition process.
  - The `context manager` collects information associated to the execution context (steps 3 and 4). It transfers the results to the `security mediator`.

- The **security mediator** parses the security policy to get the protection level associated to each security service. Depending on the execution context, it selects and composes security services to implement the required protection. Then it orchestrates the security service invocations (steps 5 and 6) and if succeeded, it routes back the business service/middleware interaction to the middleware (steps 7 and 8).
- The **Security as a Service** component gathers implementation of various security services (authentication, authorization, integrity controls, etc.).

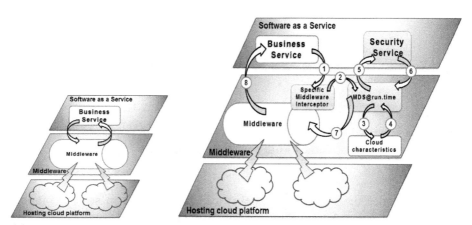

(a) Multi-layer architecture.   (b) Multi-layer architecture with MDS@run.time.

Fig. 5. MDS@run.time architecture.

FraSCAti[3] [10] is an open source middleware framework to build, program, deploy, and execute adaptable service-oriented business applications. FraSCAti is based on the OASIS Service Component Architecture (SCA) standard[4]. FraSCAti applications can be deployed in different clouds (Amazon EC2, Amazon Elastic BeanTalk, Google App Engine, CloudBees, etc.) [8,9]. The adaptability at design time is based on the fact that the FraSCAti platform was designed as a plugin-based architecture to adapt it to different execution environments and to select on demand the required application functionalities composing a FraSCAti instance [1]. The adaptability at execution time is based on the FraSCAti reflective features, which encompass introspection and reconfiguration of applications at runtime [11]. For dealing with web services and REST, FraSCAti embeds Apache CXF[5], a well-known open source services framework.

To ensure the BP security deployed on cloud infrastructures, we propose a MDS@run.time framework based on SCA components, which can be plugged to

---

[3] http://frascati.ow2.org.

[4] http://www.oasis-opencsa.org/sca.

[5] http://cxf.apache.org.

the FraSCAti platform. Our prototype takes advantage of Aspect Oriented Programming (AOP) features and of the SCA model, both provided by FraSCAti, to deploy the three `Interceptor`, `MDS@run.time` and `Security as a Service` components shown in Fig. 6.

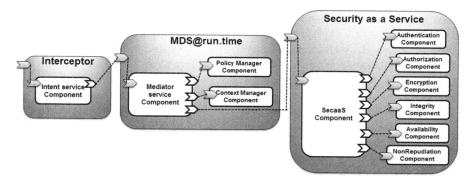

Fig. 6. MDS@run.time with FraSCAti.

3.1 FraSCAti Intent for MDS@run.time

SCA provides the notion of intent, which is an abstraction for designating a non-functional property such as security, transaction, logging, etc. With FraS-CAti, SCA intents are implemented as SCA components, then both business and non-functional concerns are designed then implemented in the same framework aka SCA.

The `Intent` component is responsible for detecting and intercepting business services invoked by clients. This component uses AOP techniques provided by FraSCAti to perform actions before, during and after each business service invocation. These techniques use the Apache CXF interception mechanism. The `Intent` component creates a `Request` object, which plays the intermediary role between the FraSCAti middleware and security services. This object provides a bidirectional interface that allows the `Intent` component to formalize the interaction messages received from Apache CXF and also to specify orders towards Apache CXF. The `Request` object ensures a total independence between our MDS@run.time components and the underlying service-oriented middleware, allowing on one hand the security services to be able to deploy and run on any other middleware and on another hand to deploy on a specific platform just the required security services.

3.2 Composite MDS@run.time

The `MDS@run.time` composite[6] is invoked by the `Intent` component of the `Interceptor` composite. It includes:

---

[6] An SCA composite is an SCA component containing a set of SCA components.

- The `Mediator` component is responsible for analyzing called service requests intercepted by the `Intent` component and encapsulated into a `Request` object. It also identifies the security policy rules associated to business services invoked by clients. Thus, through the `Request` object, the `Mediator` receives information of the services involved in the interaction. This information is used to get policies associated to resources (the business services functionality implemented by the service operation). These policies are then analyzed and orchestrated by the `Mediator` to call the required security services.
- The `PolicyManager` component manages the policies. It receives from the `Mediator` the resource or service reference requested and the link to the policy file. It returns to the `Mediator` the list of security policies to apply.
- The `ContextManager` component analyses security policies associated to services and identifies the different policies to be applied according to the user context, the execution environment and security policies associated to the client and service provider. It also provides to the `Mediator` component information such as policies and policy rules related to the execution context. These policy rules are used by the `Mediator` component to call the technical security services.

3.3   Composite SecaaS

The `Security as a Service` (SecaaS) composite is invoked by the `Mediator` component. It includes various security services, which allow protecting resources and business services according to a *security as a service* approach. This composite contains the following components:

- The `SecaaS` component is the composite entry point. It receives from the `Mediator` component the security policies to be applied. It is responsible for analyzing these policies, to identify the type of security services (authentication, authorization, etc.) to call.
- The `Authentication` component is used to prove the user identity (of human or other service). This component receives from the `SecaaS` component the policy rule to apply, extracts information about the security pattern and invokes the security mechanism to be applied. It can be a weak authentication mechanism such as login/password or strong authentication such as One Time Password (OTP) or two factors authentication. This `Authentication` component includes subcomponents such as `SSORegistry` (Single Sign On Registry) component used to store information about authentication of sessions and to allow to retrieve user information without restarting authentication.
- The `Authorization` component allows managing access to resources and services, and allows grant or deny the user access to them. As the `Authentication` component, it receives the security policy rule and invokes the authorization mechanism to be applied. This mechanism can be based on an authorization by role (RBAC) implemented by the XACML authorization protocol or a simple Access Control List (ACL).

- The `Encryption` component provides data and messages encryption/decryption mechanisms and secure communication protocols (SSL).
- The `Integrity` component ensures the integrity of exchanged data and messages by using message signatures or hash functions.
- The `NonRepudiation` component is responsible for recording user actions (authentication, access to data or service, data modification/destruction, etc.). This information can then be used for auditing and monitoring.
- The `Availability` component is responsible for the services' availability providing access to the service or a clone (redundant service) if the original target service is unavailable. This component also provides backup mechanism to restore system data and services after disaster.

The `Encryption`, `Integrity` and `NonRepudiation` components can use security protocols such as WS-Security XML Encryption and XML Signature, which provide encryption and signing exchanged message mechanisms.

4   Evaluation

Our performance evaluation is based on the use case presented in Fig. 1, focusing on the *TrackShipping* operation. This operation is implemented thanks to a service associated to a security policy including authentication (see Fig. 2, lines 2–8) by login/password (Line 4) and access control (lines 9-16) using ACL (Line 11) combined with a used network constraint (Line 13). As far as the collaborative service is concerned, the business service is encapsulated in an *LogisticService*, which is associated to the convenient security policy and refers to the `MDS@run.time` composite (Fig. 7, Line 6). By this way, the business service can be intercepted and MDS@run.time is invoked before invoking the business service itself.

To evaluate the impact of our *MDS@run.time with FraSCAti* prototype on the service execution time, we set a test environment using FraSCAti version 1.6 with Oracle Java Virtual Machine 1.7.0_51 on Microsoft Windows 7 Professional (32 bit) using a 2,54 GHz processor Intel(R) Core(TM)2 Duo CPU with 4Go of memory. We set different types of measures: A first execution invokes the business service without invoking our security architecture (measure 1 used to set a reference time), the time between the intent invocation and the MDS@run.time

```
1.   <composite xmlns="http://www.osoa.org/xmlns/sca/1.0" xmlns:cxf="org/ow2/frascati/intent/cxf"
2.   xmlns:frascati="http://frascati.ow2.org/xmlns/sca/1.1"
3.   xmlns:wsdli="http://www.w3.org/2004/08/wsdl-instance" name="logistic" >
4.      <service name="logisticService" promote="LogisticComponent/TrackShipping">
5.         <interface.java interface="compagnyB.api.logisticService"/>
6.         <binding.ws requires="MDSatRuntime" uri="/logistic-ws-mds"
7.   wsdlElement="http://api.compagnyB/#wsdl.port(logisticService/LogisticServicePort)"
8.   wsdli:wsdlLocation="resources/wsdl/logistic.wsdl"/>
9.         <frascati:binding.rest requires="MDSatRuntime" uri="/logistic-rest-mds"/>
10.     </service>
```

Fig. 7. Link the *Logistic* component with **MDS@run.time**.

Table 2. Mean execution time of **MDS@run.time** components.

No	Component	Average execution time (ms) time (ms)		Average execution time/ Total execution time	
		1–100	101–201	1–100	101–201
1	FraSCAti + Apache CXF + Business service	63	53	74 %	75 %
2	FraSCAti Interceptor	1	1	2 %	2 %
3	MDS@run.time	7	4	8 %	6 %
4	Authentication	11	10	13 %	14 %
5	Authorization	3	2	4 %	3 %
	Total	85	70	100 %	100 %

invocation measures the cost for the service interception. Then, the time required to get the policy file and parsed it is expressed by the mediation measure. Lastly execution times related to the authentication process and to the authorization process are given. We manage a test loop to compute an average time for the first request to evaluate the setup time and on 200 client requests, so that extra factor impacts can be smoothed, such as bootstrapping effects, Just-In-Time compilation, etc.

The main result is that the interception and mediation process represents only 8 % (101–201 requests) of the total execution. This overhead could certainly reduced within an industrial implementation of **MDS@run.time**. However this demonstrates that our **MDS@run.time** approach, i.e. interpretation of security policies at runtime, introduces a small overhead compared to over protecting services (Table 2).

5   Related Work

Different strategies can be used to provide a consistent protection on distributed information systems, paying attention on both organisational and infrastructure related risks.

On one hand, *Security by Design* approaches integrate protection requirements while designing the information system. To this end, different frameworks have been defined to manage security annotations on UML diagrams (such as the multi-purpose UMLSec or the rather access control oriented Secure UML domain specific languages) or BPMN diagrams [12]. Taking advantage of such high-level specification, MDS [5] adapts the Model Driven Engineering (MDE) approach to the security field. Several studies have focused on the use of the MDS approach to secure BP and led to frameworks definition like OpenPMF [4], and SECTET [2]. Nevertheless, none of them support the full transformation process. While BPSec is focused on the requirement engineering part (it includes CIM and PIM models), SECTET and Open PMF provide PIM, PSM and code generation features. Moreover, the generation process is achieved according to a static environment vision (perimetrised information system and well-known deployment platform). This does not fit the dynamic service ecosystem context.

On the other hand, the security stack defined in the OASIS Service reference model defines the way protection requirements should be implemented in a multi-layer architecture (application/Middleware-Transport/network) to improve the global protection consistency while deploying security features associated to a standardized security policy. Nevertheless, this coarse-grain model does not integrate any platform dependent risks/protection models (such as works achieved for cloud based infrastructure by the Cloud Security Alliance (CSA)[7], Intrusion Detection System [6], vulnerabilities checking [3], etc.) nor any governance loop so that the execution context can be taken into account while deploying the required protection. This can lead to either over or under protection. To overcome this limit, our MDS@run.time approach takes advantage of the OASIS security model and of the MDS approach to generate security policies depending on the collaborative BP organisational context so that services can be secured on demand. Moreover, it provides a fully oursourced security environment that can be plugged on any service-oriented middleware. Thanks to the execution platform information, collected by the `Mediator` component, security services are selected, composed and orchestrated in a transparent and consistent way, avoiding the costly over protection and the risky under protection.

6   Conclusion

Securing collaborative business processes deployed on cloud systems requires paying attention on both organisational and platform-related vulnerabilities. Taking advantage of the intrinsic flexibility provided by the association of security policies to services, we propose to use them as Models@run.time to select, compose and orchestrate security services depending on the required protection and on the execution context. To this end, a MDS@run.time component is plugged on the middleware, intercepting service invocation and capturing context information. The experiment reported in this paper shows how our MDS@run.time architecture can be plugged on the FraSCAti middleware and evaluate its performance level. Further works will focus on the integration of more detailed platform models and on vulnerability monitoring loops so that our coarse-grained vision of the execution context will be refined to increase the protection efficiency.

References

1. Acher, M., Cleve, A., Collet, P., Merle, P., Duchien, L., Lahire, P.: Reverse engineering architectural feature models. In: Crnkovic, I., Gruhn, V., Book, M. (eds.) ECSA 2011. LNCS, vol. 6903, pp. 220–235. Springer, Heidelberg (2011). http://hal.inria.fr/inria-00614984

---

[7] http://www.cloudsecurityalliance.org/guidance/csaguide.v3.0.pdf.

2. Alam, M., Hafner, M., Breu, R.: Constraint based role based access control in the SECTET-framework a model-driven approach. J. Comput. Secur. **16**(2), 223–260 (2008)

3. Avgerinos, T., Cha, S.K., Rebert, A., Schwartz, E.J., Woo, M., Brumley, D.: Automatic exploit generation. Commun. ACM **57**(2), 74–84 (2014). http://doi.acm.org/10.1145/2560217.2560219

4. Lang, U.: OpenPMF SCaaS: authorization as a service for cloud SOA applications. In: 2010 IEEE Second International Conference on Cloud Computing Technology and Science (CloudCom), pp. 634–643, November 2010

5. Lucio, L., Zhang, Q., Nguyen, P.H., Amrani, M., Klein, J., Vangheluwe, H., Traon, Y.L.: Chapter 3 - advances in model-driven security. In: Memon, A. (ed.) Advances in Computers, vol. 93, pp. 103–152. Elsevier, Newyork (2014). http://www.sciencedirect.com/science/article/pii/B9780128001622000038

6. Modi, C., Patel, D., Borisanya, B., Patel, A., Rajarajan, M.: A novel framework for intrusion detection in cloud. In: Proceedings of the Fifth International Conference on Security of Information and Networks (SIN 2012), pp. 67–74. ACM, New York (2012). http://doi.acm.org/10.1145/2388576.2388585

7. Ouedraogo, W.F., Biennier, F., Ghodous, P.: Adaptive security policy model to deploy business process in cloud infrastructure. In: 2nd International Conference on Cloud Computing and Services Science (CLOSER 2012), pp. 287–290 (2012)

8. Paraiso, F., Haderer, N., Merle, P., Rouvoy, R., Seinturier, L.: A federated multi-cloud paas infrastructure. In: 5th International Conference on Cloud Computing (CLOUD 2012), pp. 392–399. IEEE (2012)

9. Paraiso, F., Merle, P., Seinturier, L.: soCloud: A service-oriented component-based PaaS for managing portability, provisioning, elasticity and high availability across multiple clouds. Special Issue on Cloud Computing, Computing Journal, Springer (To appear) (2015)

10. Seinturier, L., Merle, P., Fournier, D., Dolet, N., Schiavoni, V., Stefani, J.B.: Reconfigurable SCA applications with the FraSCAti platform. In: IEEE International Conference on Services Computing (SCC 2009), pp. 268–275. IEEE (2009)

11. Seinturier, L., Merle, P., Rouvoy, R., Romero, D., Schiavoni, V., Stefani, J.B.: A component-based middleware platform for reconfigurable service-oriented architectures. Softw. Pract. Exp. **42**(5), 559–583 (2012)

12. Wolter, C., Menzel, M., Schaad, A., Miseldine, P., Meinel, C.: Model-driven business process security requirement specification. J. Sys. Archit. (JSA) **55**(4), 211–223 (2009)

Domain Specific Monitoring of Business Processes Using Concept Probes

Adrian Mos[✉]

Xerox Research, 6 chemin de Maupertuis, Meylan, France
adrian.mos@xerox.com

Abstract. This paper proposes a monitoring framework that has business concepts at its core. Rather than relying on generic mechanisms to provide monitoring data, it proposes the notion of concept probes that fully match the business concepts used in the definition of business processes. These concept probes combine monitoring information from business process execution as well as service execution into aggregate information that makes sense from a business concept point of view. The approach has far-reaching implications: firstly, it provides superior understanding of the various execution parameters of the business concepts used in processes (including performance, correctness and context), with potential to aid Business Process Management (BPM) and Service Oriented Architecture (SOA) governance. Secondly, it helps with setting application-wide alarms and constraints potentially corresponding to Service-Level-Agreements, on a concept-level. For a given concept, such constraints can be set-up with immediate effect in all the business processes that use it. Thirdly, this approach gives technical users a deep understanding of the contribution of each of multiple application layers (BPM, SOA, operating system, various other technical layers) to the combined performance of a particular business concept. This can lead to faster reaction time in fixing problems, changes in business partners (that provide better services) or improvements in the underlying infrastructure or application parameters.

Keywords: BPM · Monitoring · SOA

1 Introduction and Scope

Business Process Management (BPM) and Service Oriented Architecture (SOA) are two important paradigms in today's enterprise solutions. They each bring a level of agility to business applications. BPM addresses the methodology and tools that enable the management of business processes (BPs) including their evolutions throughout their lifecycle. BPM Suites (BPMS) are complex software stacks that execute business processes and connect them to various enterprise resources such as the personnel directory, the various legacy applications and potentially the organization's SOA. An enterprise SOA typically manages the reusable technical services used to execute tasks that occur in business processes and it is often hosted in a cloud environment. Their functionality, granularity and interfaces define their level of reuse across a multitude of business processes. In general, the closer the SOA services match the business requirements, the faster it is to implement new business processes. In practice, SOA has

© Springer International Publishing Switzerland 2015
F. Toumani et al. (Eds.): ICSOC 2014, LNCS 8954, pp. 213–224, 2015.
DOI: 10.1007/978-3-319-22885-3_19

often drifted away from its initial promise of matching IT with business and has evolved in the IT domain, enabling a certain kind of agility at the IT solution level, i.e. making it faster for IT departments to implement new applications, much like previous paradigms such as component-based software or object-oriented development.

The typical approach to develop business applications using BPM and SOA with today's state of the art tools involves the definition of business processes using a generic language such as the widely-used Business Process Model and Notation (BPMN) [1]. This language contains elements such as "activity", "gateway", "signal" or "flow". Users need to describe their BPs by assigning textual labels such as "payment" or "customer registration" to the generic BPMN elements. Users who design BPs are generally users with good business knowledge and understanding of the various roles in the organization.

In contrast, users who design and create SOA services are typically architects and developers with much less business know-how. There is a certain connection between these two classes of users (business and technical) as, naturally, the SOA must eventually fulfil some useful functionality for the business applications, yet they have fundamentally different concerns. This translates into a disconnect between BPM and SOA which is solved through manual "glue" in the form of SOA connectivity parameters in the BP descriptions. This connectivity typically translates into configuration forms that are associated to certain BPMN activities.

Once the BPs are designed and fully configured, they can be run by the BPMS. The BPMS will manage their execution and will also direct SOA calls to the appropriate SOA services, as required. It is very important to be able to extract information related to the execution of the BPs. Such information can be used to understand what really happens with the various activities, whether they execute correctly or not, how long it takes to execute them, what data is passed around and whether pre-established thresholds for various parameters are exceeded or not. Such information is extracted using monitoring infrastructure that connects to the BPMS and collects data as the BPs execute. The monitoring infrastructure is typically tightly woven into the BPMS. Similarly, for SOA data collection, the monitoring infrastructure can leverage the execution environment, such as a specific Enterprise Service Bus in order to collect metrics of interest.

The fundamental problem with the state-of-the-art approaches is that they collect and present data at the level of process definition, which is generic. The fact that BPs have been designed and deployed using a generic language such as BPMN inherently means that monitoring data is collected in a generic way, with respect to the business domain. Therefore, reusing the example above, monitoring data will be collected for elements such as "activity", "gateway", "signal" or "flow" with no correlation to the business concepts of "payment" or "customer registration" apart from the simple matching of the textual labels to the monitored generic elements. This causes a number of problems:

- It is hard to make use of the monitoring data in order to present meaningful metrics to business users, without significant configuration efforts for each BP.
- It is difficult to correlate the execution of business concepts to the execution of services in the SOA layer as well as to the parameters of the runtime infrastructure.

- It is difficult to set wide-ranging Service-Level-Agreements (SLA) that affect all BPs equally. For instance it may be necessary to specify that all "payment" operations, regardless of the BP in which they occur, must execute in less than 20 s. In today's BPM solutions this would typically imply manually changing each of the BPs in which the payment activity occurs in order to establish this SLA, or refactoring all BPs to use the "payment" activity as a sub-process and then setting the SLA to the sub-process.

In summary, the above-mentioned problems with today's monitoring approaches are due to the fact that most existing solutions are domain-independent and technology-dependent. In contrast, the approach presented in this paper is domain-dependent and technology-independent with a focus on BPM/SOA environments.

2   Overview of the Approach

This proposal aims to address the shortcomings of today's monitoring capabilities for BPMS/SOA applications. It does so by adding a layer of abstraction on top of existing capabilities, rather than replacing them. This ensures compatibility with a wide range of existing systems and platforms. In fact the proposed approach is technology-independent. The approach entails the creation of Concept Probes (CPs) that are monitoring entities corresponding directly to business concepts. These CPs provide an aggregated view of the various execution layers involved in the execution of a particular business concept present in BPs. Once the CPs are created, they need to be bound to the monitoring capabilities of the existing infrastructure, effectively acting as an extra monitoring layer on top of BPMS and SOA monitoring capabilities. In addition to the CPs, this approach introduces the notion of Business Process Probe (BPP) which corresponds to each deployed business process and which is essentially a composition of the CPs that correspond to the concepts used in the BP.

Figure 1 below uses an example to illustrate the conceptual placement of the probes in the context of a typical BPM/SOA environment. The figure illustrates a simple business process deployed into the BPMS and connected to the SOA services by links from activities **Aa** and **Ac**, with **Aa** requiring services **S1** and **S3**, and **Ac** requiring **S6** respectively. These links represent regular web service calls such as SOAP or RESTful invocations. The rectangle represented above the BPMS represents the monitoring capabilities that are available for the respective BPMS. Usually these capabilities include the generation of events when activities execute, the computation of execution times for activities and generally the reporting of various states in which the BPs operate. The rectangle below the SOA Runtime represents the monitoring capabilities of the SOA environment (which is typically an Enterprise Service Bus or other forms of SOA-based middleware such as an SCA runtime [2]). These capabilities typically include monitoring the service invocations, computing execution times for various service operations and general reporting of the states in which the services operate.

To reduce clutter, the image above does not present other monitoring layers that may be available in an enterprise environment, such as cloud monitoring, operating

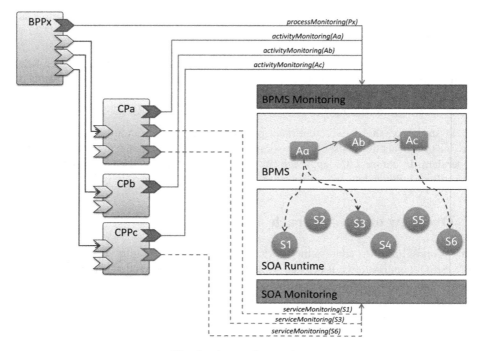

Fig. 1. Approach overview

system monitoring or network monitoring. These are however taken into account and mentioned in the description of the probe structure below.

Figure 1 presents three concept probes **CPa**, **CPb** and **CPc** that correspond to the business concepts **a**, **b** and **c**, used in the illustrated BP through the activities **Aa**, **Ab** and **Ac**. In addition to the CPs, the image also shows a business process probe, the **BPPx**. This corresponds to the example BP and it uses the three CPs to aggregate BP-level information. The outgoing lines from the CPs represent their connections to the BPMS and SOA monitoring systems. For example, since **CPa** is a probe specifically generated for concept **a**, it will interrogate the BPMS monitoring system with regard to the activity **Aa** and the SOA monitoring system with regard to services **S1** and **S3**. These connections are generated based on the knowledge that concept **a** is used in activity **Aa** and it requires services **S1** and **S3**. This knowledge comes from concept mappings described in the section below. The lines are labeled with abstract functions that simply illustrate what kind of data they collect from the monitoring systems.

The CPs therefore leverage existing monitoring capabilities using specific bindings related to the concepts they need to match. They aggregate the required data from the various BPMS and SOA monitoring systems into meaningful information that matches the business concepts used throughout a business application. Similarly, the BPPs aggregate the monitoring data from CPs corresponding to the monitored BP with additional BP-specific monitoring information that is generated by the BPMS monitoring system (such as timestamps and duration for the process execution, user roles and other process-specific data). Note that the information provided by a BPP is significantly richer than that provided by BPMS monitoring systems for a given BP because it includes the breakdown of monitoring information for each of the concepts used in the BP as well as the aggregated BP-level data. Naturally, modern BPMS monitoring systems can make the correlation between a BP and it composing activities but this approach consolidates monitoring information in a conceptual layer that adds the semantics of the contained concepts.

3 Concept Mappings

In their simplest form, concept mappings are connections between business concepts and the SOA services that are used by them. The concepts are then used in all of the BPs in various combinations, resulting in a variety of BPs.

The starting point is the following sets that are known:

1. Set of services $S = \{s_1, s_2, \ldots s_q\}$
2. Set of processes $P = \{p_1, p_2, \ldots p_m\}$
3. For each process p_k, a set of activities $Ak = \{a_{k1}, a_{k2}, \ldots a_{ky}$ where y depends on the complexity of $p_k\}$.
4. The set of all activities in all the processes $A = A_1 \cup A_2 \cup \ldots \cup A_{|P|}$

The goal of concept mapping operations is to determine the following sets

1. Set of concepts $C = \{c_1, c_2, \ldots c_n\}$
2. $CM = \{(c_j, S_j): \forall c_j \in C; S_j \subseteq S\}$ which contains for each concept its list of services, e.g. $(c_4, (s_1, s_3, s_8))$
3. $AM_k = \{(a_{ki}, c_j): \forall a_{ki} \in A_k; c_j \in C\}$ which contains for process p_k its activities and the concepts they map to
4. $AM = AM_1 \cup AM_2 \cup \ldots \cup AM_{|P|}$ which contains for each activity in all processes the concept it maps to

This paper does not make a claim about a particular method of obtaining concept mappings. However, this section briefly discusses this aspect in order to demonstrate feasibility of the entire approach. The existence of the sets described above is a requirement for the proposed method to function. There are two important aspects to be discussed about concept mappings, namely concept identification and concept use, which can be seen as two required stages in the application of the method.

3.1   Concept Identification and Use

Obtaining the sets C and CM, described above, requires that the business concepts that are used over and over again in the business processes be clearly identified together with their required usage of the SOA. There are three main potential approaches for concept identification:

- Automatic Top-Down: this approach corresponds to the desirable approach for modern organizations that will create new business processes in the future.

It assumes that the concepts are defined by business experts and eventually bound to SOA services in a deployment stage where their service requirements are mapped to available SOA assets. An in-depth discussion of this approach is presented in [3].

- Automatic Bottom-Up: this approach assumes existing legacy BPs are already deployed and functional in an organization, so it is best suited for existing BPs deployed in BPMS/SOA environments. It leverages extraction capabilities from execution logs to cluster and identify commonly used concepts and their correlations to SOA services. Many such approaches are possible, for instance [4, 5].
- Manual Top-Down: this approach is a downgraded version of the first approach (Automatic Top-Down) and it can be applied in organizations that do not use a deployment stage for BPs that connects them automatically with the SOA. It has the same characteristics as the first approach but it requires the manual annotation of concepts with SOA services, rather than using the service binding information that the first approach has.

The three approaches can be used in combination in some cases, for instance the Automatic Bottom-Up may need help from Manual Top-Down to increase quality of the results. In all cases the result is a list of concepts with their related SOA services.

After concepts are identified, it is necessary to obtain the **AM** set by mapping the BPs (existing or future) to the concepts. This involves matching BP activities to concepts. Such matching is closely related to the method for identifying concepts. When using Automatic Top-Down, the BPs are in fact composed of activities directly matching concepts, so there is no ambiguity, each activity corresponds to a clearly identified concept. When using Automatic Bottom-Up identification, the concepts are extracted from BP activities so matching activities to concepts requires simply storing the correlations between the activities and the extracted concepts. When the Manual Top-Down approach is used, BPs need to be annotated with the concepts manually, this requires the manual creation of the connection between activities and concepts (i.e. **Aa** activity to concept **a** in the example above).

When all the required mappings are available, the probes need to be created, instantiated and deployed. The specific technical means for generating and running monitoring probes are out of the scope of this proposal. The generation can be done using a variety of existing methods such as code generation or template instantiation for instance. Once they are generated they need to be executed as they need to be running entities managed by a monitoring framework. There exist a variety of monitoring frameworks that can be used for managing these probes and this proposal does not aim to propose a new monitoring system. Rather it proposes a new layer of monitoring probes that can be executed in any extensible monitoring system. A very common technology that can be employed for merging the proposed approach with existing monitoring frameworks is Java Management Extensions,[1] supported by a large variety of infrastructures, both commercial and open-source.

---

[1] http://en.wikipedia.org/wiki/Java_Management_Extensions.

4   Probe Structure and Functionality

The concept probes are capable of collecting an arbitrary number of metrics, such as execution time or execution status. The approach described here does not focus on a particular metric, as the same approach can be used to measure several metrics. For illustration purposes, execution time is used when an example is required. In the description of the structure of the probe, metrics are identified by Greek symbols such as Metric α or Metric β...

The connections of the probe to the various existing monitoring infrastructures are explained in the paragraphs below. All CPs contain the same three main components, illustrated in Fig. 2. The first, **Raw Data Collection** is charged with collecting data for any given metric from any of the collection points, represented in the image to the right edge of the CP composite structure. For a given concept c_j, its corresponding data collection points are:

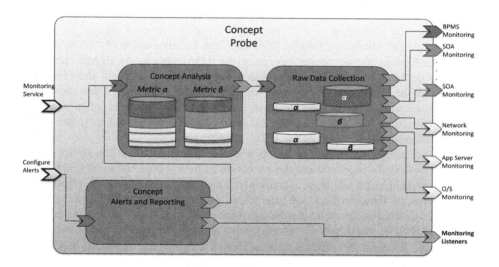

Fig. 2. Concept probe structure

- One BPMS monitoring point that collects data from the BPMS with regard to activities that map to this concept, i.e. $CA_j = \{a_{xy}: (a_{xy}, c_j) \in AM\}$. This effectively means that there is one probe per concept regardless of the number of activities that correspond to this concept. The reason for this is that the approach emphasizes the value of monitoring each individual concept regarding of where it is used in the business processes. So each time an activity is executed, the concept probe corresponding to the concept associated to the activity is notified.
- Several SOA collection points that each map to the SOA Runtime monitoring capabilities for each of the SOA services that this concept maps to, i.e. S_j. These points extract execution information for the services that are related to the concept.
- Several other collection points that can collect information potentially to be correlated with the above-mentioned collection points. This includes Network

Monitoring, App Server Monitoring and Operating System Monitoring. These extra collection points can give useful information regarding the context of the metric values. For instance, a service execution can be perceived as slow if network latency is very high. Similarly, if the OS processes are not scheduled properly by the OS or if the Application Server is not scalable, these can impact the execution of the BPMS and the SOA layers. Therefore, these extra collection points can potentially be very useful, although they are not essential. They are given here as an example of extra aggregation capabilities of the probes.

The second component, **Concept Analysis**, is tasked with aggregating raw data obtained from the collection component into composite metrics. These composite metrics are data structures that present the aggregate monitoring information combining the individual metric data for the BPMS, SOA and other collection points, for the concept.

The data structures give an aggregate value if appropriate (such as *total execution time*), as well as a breakdown of this value or contextual information pertaining to this value for the individual collection points. This can include the individual execution time of services and of the process activity in the BPMS, as well as values for network latency, resource utilization in the application server or process scheduling in the operating system. Similarly, cloud-related data can be obtained such as the virtual machine utilization for the server executing the SOA services or BPMS elements. Individual methods for obtaining these values are out of the scope of the presented approach, as the approach is concerned with the architectural entities that the monitoring framework has, not their detailed implementation which is often straightforward. This concept is also queried by outside entities for metric values (represented as the Monitoring Service port of the CP).

The third component, **Concept Alerts and Reporting** relates to the ability of the probe to give specific reports about the execution of the concept and most importantly to register alerting rules and react accordingly. This component allows the registration of SLA requests through the Configure Alerts port and uses the Concept Analysis component to constantly compare the aggregated metric values with the required thresholds. If SLA thresholds are exceeded it can notify registered Monitoring Listeners. These listeners are external entities (out of scope of the presented approach), which can be connected to the monitoring probe and notified of important alerts and events.

There is one **Business Process Probe (BPP)** per business process deployed. Similarly to the concept probe, the business process probe contains a set of three components with distinct responsibilities, as illustrated in Fig. 3.

The **Raw Data Collection** component collects the monitoring data from the CPs that correspond to the activities of the business process monitored by the BPP.

For the BPP_k corresponding to a process p_k, the data collection points are:

- One BPMS collection point that collects monitoring data for the execution of p_k in the BPMS. This can include contextual information (e.g. user name) for the required metric as well as metric values for the business process (e.g. execution time of p_k as seen from the BPMS).
- Several connections to each of the CPs required by the BPP_k. These are the CPs that correspond to the set of process concepts $PC_k = \{c_i \in C: \forall (a_{kx}, c_i) \in AM_k\}$.

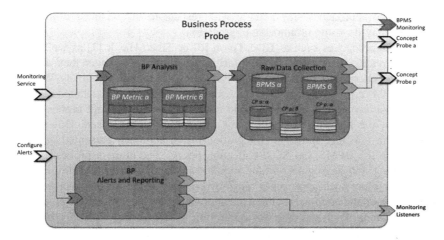

Fig. 3. Business process probe

These are used in the aggregation of monitoring data corresponding to each concept used by the P_k. If a concept appears several times in the process (due to several process activities mapping to the same concept), this concept will count several times in the aggregation. This is part of the logic of the **BP Analysis** component.

The **BP Analysis** component is very similar in functionality to the Concept Analysis component of the CP, except that it aggregates data from the BPMS and the various CPs, rather than from the BPMS, SOA and the extra monitoring collection points. To this end it aggregates the BPMS-collected data corresponding to the execution of the process together with the already aggregated data of each of the CPs it connects to. The CPs correspond to monitoring data for the individual activities that compose the process so a simple way to visualize their composition is putting them side by side, under the complete process data. An example is the total execution time of a process composed by the sum of the individual execution times of its activities. It may be useful to understand why a process executes in a given amount of time, and the composed metric would be able to show its individual components, highlighting the concepts that take the most amount of time. This can be decomposed further by showing why the individual concepts take so long to execute, by drilling down into individual services that are used for the concepts as well as the other monitoring data collected. The last component, **BP Alerts and Reporting** has identical functionality to the CP-level component, Concept Alert and Reporting, but refers to the entire BP.

5 Related Work

There are many commercial tools and academic approaches to monitoring business processes and services in a BPM/SOA setting. Some of them tackle only BPM while other only SOA, with a number of them tackling both, however without providing the same level of monitoring as the proposal presented here. This is because the vast majority of the approaches stay generic with respect to the business domain, even though they may do some monitoring aggregation.

Industrial approaches such as IBM Tivoli [6] or Tibco Hawk [7] as well as many others do provide a wide array of monitoring capabilities. However they are tightly bound to the generic capabilities of the BPMS they are targeting, namely Websphere and Tibco BPM respectively for these two examples. They provide detailed monitoring data from a variety of sources but they do not offer domain concept probes or monitoring data at the level of abstraction that business designers need. However such approaches are typically suited for integration in the approach presented in this proposal, through the BPMS and SOA collection points. The domain probes would use JMX to extract and aggregate runtime monitoring data from such monitoring infrastructure. Therefore such approaches are fully complementary to this proposal.

Among academic approaches, there are approaches that recur to aggregation mainly to compose events from a low-level monitoring source (using Complex Event Processing queries) in order to extract more meaningful data out of the raw events. For instance they may aggregate events such as "process starts" with "process ends" in order to extract the aggregated metric "process execution time". Such approaches [8–12] use a variety of techniques to derive better understanding of raw events but they fundamentally still stay at a generic level with regard to the business domain. As with the commercial approaches outlined above, the presented proposal is complementary and could interact with such approaches using them as data collection points. There are also approaches that try to correlate execution events to the originating processes using some forms of traceability between model elements and execution events. For instance in [13] the authors argue for the existence of domain-specific patterns for interpreting events, without giving a complete solution. Their suggestion is in line with the proposal here in that they promote the idea of presenting information corresponding to domain elements, but they focus mostly of interpreting CEP events, while our proposal targets structured probes that connect directly with monitoring APIs. In addition, this proposal presents in detail the structure of the probes while the authors of [13] simply state that it would be useful to have domain understanding of events.

In summary all of these approaches ultimately recur to generic event analysis and do not provide a "native" monitoring probe layer that directly corresponds to the business concepts.

Lastly there are approaches (such as [14]) that try to trace the execution events back to modeling entities using unique correlation IDs. Similarly to the above-mentioned approaches, this remains generic with respect to the business domains and does not benefit from concept-level aggregation presented in our approach. Therefore it does not allow the creation of concept-based SLAs, nor does it offer concept-based metrics that span across the business processes. Like the other approaches above, it can correlate data back to business processes without further aggregation into business concepts.

The approach presented in this proposal provides the same level of functionality that a generic approach offers, but at the domain-element level using probes that correspond on a 1-to-1 basis with business concepts. These probes hook into the existing monitoring systems regardless of the technology they use to extract and represent events. These elements ensure that the approach offers the advantages explained in the previous sections and constitute important differentiating factors.

6 Summary and Conclusion

Existing monitoring solutions are typically technology-specific and generic with respect to the business domains. In contrast, the approach presented here is generic with respect to technology and domain-specific with respect to the business. This brings several interesting advantages. Having concept monitoring probes gives unprecedented insight into the execution of applications. Business users can understand how the processes execute in terms that are ideally suited to them. In addition, they can specify constraints and alerts for particular concepts that have immediate effect across the entire spectrum of the deployed business processes. Setting a Service-Level-Agreement for a concept would instantly translate into the constraint being applied to all the activities of all the processes using it. Similarly, specifying alerts or simply observing the concept behavior would apply to any execution of the activities related to it. In addition, each execution monitoring of such activities would be complemented by monitoring of the SOA services that are associated to the concept. Beside performance metrics, this approach brings important benefits in understanding whether a concept executes successfully.

For technical users or system administrators, this would give a breakdown of responsibilities for performance problems showing the individual contribution of each of the layers involved and each of the entities (e.g. services) that compose the concept execution. Similarly, when monitoring process execution, this approach promotes the use of process-level probes composed of concept probes. Each BPP would correspond to a particular process and it would provide the same benefits as described above, but at process-level. Therefore business users could understand how a process performs in terms of the business concepts that it comprises, while technical users could understand the impact of the various layers and entities involved in fulfilling the end-to-end process. This can help pinpoint SOA services that cause bottlenecks for individual processes, or explain why certain processes do not execute correctly, by showing the concepts whose execution fails.

A full prototype of the presented framework is in advanced stages of implementation, using Stardust BPMS [15] and Fuse ESB [16] as the target BPM and SOA layers, respectively. The implemented probes correspond to the concepts of a sample domain chosen for validation. They correlate data for BP activity execution with data for service execution and give a breakdown of each layer's contribution to various performance metrics. The data is then sent for display to Eclipse graphical editors where it is presented in the appropriate context alongside process design elements [17]. Such usage helps validate the added value of the approach and its two main components: domain-level concept mapping of monitoring data; and technology independence where existing BPM/SOA environments can be augmented to benefit from the collection and graphical display of relevant monitoring information.

References

1. Object Management Group, Business Process Model and Notation. http://www.bpmn.org/
2. OASIS Service Component Architecture. http://www.oasis-opencsa.org/sca/
3. Mos, A., Jacquin, T.: A platform-independent mechanism for deployment of business processes using abstract services. In: 6th International Workshop on Evolutionary Business Processes, EDOC, Vancouver, Canada (2013)
4. Pérez-Castillo, R., García-Rodriguez de Guzmán, I., Piattini, M., Weber, B., Places, A.S.: An empirical comparison of static and dynamic business process mining. In: ACM Symposium on Applied Computing, ACM, New York (2011)
5. Wang, J., Tan, S., Wen, L., Wong, R.K., Guo, Q.: An empirical evaluation of process mining algorithms based on structural and behavioral similarities. In: 27th Annual ACM Symposium on Applied Computing (2012)
6. IBM Tivoli. http://www-01.ibm.com/software/tivoli/
7. Tibco Hawk. https://docs.tibco.com/products/tibco-hawk-4-9
8. Pedrinaci, C., Lambert, D., Wetzstein, B., van Lessen, T., Cekov, L., Dimitrov, M.: SENTINEL: a semantic business process monitoring tool. In: First International Workshop on Ontology-Supported Business Intelligence (OBI 2008). ACM, New York, NY, USA (2008)
9. Pedrinaci, C., Domingue, J., Alves de Medeiros, A.K.: A core ontology for business process analysis. In: 5th European Semantic Web Conference on the Semantic Web (2008)
10. Mos, A., Pedrinaci, C., Rey, G.A., Gomez, J.M., Liu, D., Vaudaux-Ruth, G., Quaireau, S.: Multi-level monitoring and analysis of web-scale service based applications. In: Dan, A., Gittler, F., Toumani, F. (eds.) ICSOC/ServiceWave 2009. LNCS, vol. 6275, pp. 269–282. Springer, Heidelberg (2010)
11. Hummer, W., Inzinger, C., Leitner, P., Satzger, B., Dustdar, S.: Deriving a unified fault taxonomy for event-based systems. In: 6th ACM International Conference on Distributed Event-Based Systems (2012)
12. Mulo, E., Zdun, U., Dustdar, S.: An event view model and DSL for engineering an event-based SOA monitoring infrastructure. In: 4th ACM International Conference on Distributed Event-Based Systems (2010)
13. Ammon, R.V., Silberbauer, C., Wolff, C.: Domain specific reference models for event patterns for faster developing of business activity monitoring applications. In: VIPSI (2007)
14. Mulo, E., Zdun, U., Dustdar, S.: Monitoring web service event trails for business compliance. In: Service-Oriented Computing and Applications (SOCA) (2009)
15. Stardust BPMS. http://www.eclipse.org/stardust/
16. Jboss Fuse ESB. http://www.jboss.org/products/fuse
17. EclipseCON Talk: Modeling and Monitoring Business Processes with Mangrove, BPMN2 Editor and Stardust. https://www.eclipsecon.org/na2014/session/modeling-and-monitoring-business-processes-mangrove-bpmn2-editor-and-stardust

Towards a Model for Resource Allocation in API Value Networks

James Houghton[1(✉)], Michael Siegel[1], and Maja Vukovic[2]

[1] MIT SLOAN, Cambridge, MA, USA
{houghton,msiegel}@mit.edu
[2] IBM T.J. Watson Research Center, Yorktown Heights, NY 10598, USA
maja@us.ibm.com

Abstract. REST APIs have brought the power of reuse within reach of individuals and enterprises at Internet-scale through extreme consumability. An effective API strategy must consider not just how the API will be built, but how it will be sold and offered in the Cloud environments. Traditional models of software marketing omit the complexity associated with the multiple parties involved in the API value chain. New models are needed to help platform providers allocate resources for optimum return. This paper extends traditional software marketing models to include this multi-party complexity, and contrasts optimal strategies over a variety of possible model parameters. Our results show that system models can be used to differentiate platform marketing strategies. We expect that there is a wide range of application once such models are parameterized with measured platform adoption and marketing data.

1 Introduction

In traditional software marketing, sales are made directly to the end user of a platform. The end user then provides business value either through upfront payment or through ongoing subscription. It is common, however, for a platform API to be provided free of charge to a third party developer, who provides a product to the final user. The final user then provides business value to both the third party developer and the platform provider (Fig. 1).

In traditional software marketing we expect the system to exhibit a market penetration lag as end users discover and adopt the platform. Marketing a platform through an API introduces additional lag as the API penetrates the market of developers and is adopted into new third party software. As such, the return on investment profile for API development does not map directly to more traditional models. Additionally, the new complexity associated with marketing to two groups of individuals requires that platform promoters consider how to best allocate their marketing resources at different times in the API lifecycle.

Traditional models of software marketing [1] are unable to account for this lag or give guidance as to how platform providers can optimize their marketing allocations for optimum return on investment. In the sections that follow, we review how these models are structured, their qualitative behavior, and how they apply to a single, differentiated software platform. Building on this knowledge, we extend the models to account for the new complexity associated with the API value chain.

© Springer International Publishing Switzerland 2015
F. Toumani et al. (Eds.): ICSOC 2014, LNCS 8954, pp. 225–235, 2015.
DOI: 10.1007/978-3-319-22885-3_20

Fig. 1. Traditional software development (Left): a product is delivered to the end user in exchange for business value. API model (Right): an API is provided to a third party developer, who then provides a product to the end user, who returns business value.

While several groups have qualitatively enumerated the various strategies for marketing APIs [19, 20], there has to date been little model-based analysis of how these marketing strategies behave from a performance perspective over time. This work begins to address that lack, and seeks to establish theory that future observational data may confirm or disprove.

The models presented in this paper employ the System Dynamics methodology; which tracks stocks of quantities and the flows that govern their growth and decay, and accounts for reinforcing and balancing feedback loops that drive behavior. This methodology has successfully been applied to applications in software development, maintenance and marketing [2, 3]. The main contribution of this work is a model that considers the implications of the complex networks of providers and consumers in the API ecosystem, which drives the marketing and pricing strategy.

2   Model 1: Software Direct Sales, Upfront Payments

We begin our analysis with the direct sale model of software marketing. In this case we can use a standard Bass Diffusion model [4] with discard and potential re-adoption [5]. This model considers the total number of possible users of a platform to be fixed in time, and at any given point divided between those who are currently using the platform, and those who may choose to use the platform in the future. We model a stock of each of these categories, and assert that they move from one to another either by adopting the platform or discarding it, as seen in Fig. 2.

The rate at which individuals move from the 'Potential End Users' stock to the 'Active End Users' is driven by two types of factors: the first an external influence with no dependence on the existing installed base, typically summarized as 'Marketing' related adoption; the second an endogenous influence which is driven by the size of the installed base. This may include increased platform utility due to network effects, but is generally summarized as 'Word-of-Mouth' related adoption.

The flow of individuals from 'Active End Users' back to 'Potential End Users' is modeled as being simply proportional to the total number of 'Active End Users', and produces an exponential type decay behavior dependent upon the average platform discard rate.

The general behavior of this structure is 'S-shaped' growth, in which marketing drives the initial adoption, after which word-of-mouth effects drive exponential growth

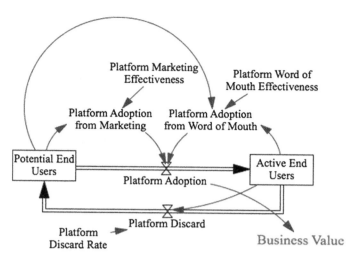

Fig. 2. The bass diffusion model with discard and re-adoption. The flow of individuals from 'Potential' to 'Active' users is driven by marketing and word-of-mouth effects, while discard is a constant fractional rate.

for a time. The market eventually saturates and reaches a steady state condition in which the number of new adopters in a given month is balanced by the number of active users discarding the platform.

In Fig. 3 we see this S shaped growth for a set of model parameters specifically chosen to make the qualitative behavior as apparent as possible. In this run of the simulation, the platform is in use by about 70 % of the possible population in the final steady state. Changes to the model parameters influence this final level, and the distinctiveness of the s-shaped behavior.

Optimal business strategy in this situation is to increase sales – not active users – and may involve encouraging discard of the product (with the assumption that this discard will not affect the rate of re-adoption). We see this behavior exhibited in many

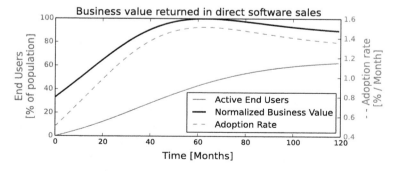

Fig. 3. In the traditional model of software marketing, business value is returned through new sales, and so peaks along with the process of platform adoption and declines to a steady state as the market saturates.

products that are designed to be used once and then thrown away (or better, recycled) such as paper towels or disposable coffee cups.

In the world of software, however, discard is more commonly due to the platform no longer meeting the needs of the user, and so is more likely to affect the rate of re-adoption. Because of this, many software platform providers have switched to a model of time-limited licensing, or provision of software-as-a-service.

3   Model 2: Software Licensing, Service Contracts, or Software as a Service

A slight departure from the traditional model is the one in which firms provide software, software functionality, or support guarantees to their customers in exchange for ongoing service payments. In this case, returned business value is dependent not on the total number of sales made, but upon the total user base, as seen in Fig. 4.

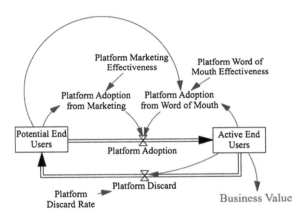

Fig. 4. In this model, business value is returned not from the sale of software, but through its ongoing use.

We see that business value tracks here with the number of active users, instead of with platform adoption, as can be seen in Fig. 5. While it may not achieve the same peak in revenue, a service model is able to sustain return of business value as the market saturates. The optimal state of this system is one that maximizes the end state adoption of the product, instead of churn and new sales.

This changes a platform provider's strategy, and gives them additional levers for influencing business value: reducing platform discard, and improving business value returned per active user. It also allows for a broader definition of business value – eyeballs on advertising may be as valid a strategy as monetary payments.

Under this model, providers work to maximize the active user base of their platform, and business value generated by that user base, by influencing the leverage points of marketing, retention, and value. At its best, an API strategy works to increase the power of these levers in a cost-effective manner.

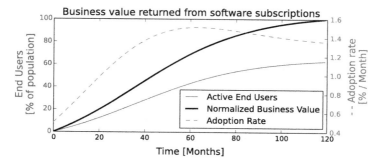

Fig. 5. In a service-based model, business value track with the platform installed base, or the number of active users; and avoids the peak and decline seen in the direct sale model.

4 Model 3: Service Through APIs and Third Party Developers

APIs allow the functionality of a platform to be accessed through third party applications. These applications can benefit a provider by improving the three levers for returned business value that we discussed in the previous section. By creating their own marketing and outreach, they improve a provider's visibility to the pool of potential adopters. By adding value to the platform for end users, they can reduce platform discard. By providing additional mechanisms for interacting with the platform, they can improve business value returned per user.

These benefits, however, are not immediately realized to the platform provider upon release of an API, as it takes time for third party developers to become aware of the API and produce applications for it. In fact, this process of adoption parallels the adoption process we saw in the previous two examples, and we can use the same Bass diffusion model with discard and re-adoption to model the adoption of an API by third party developers into their own product offerings, as seen in Fig. 6.

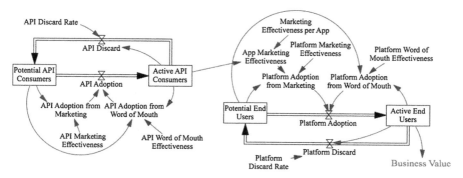

Fig. 6. An additional diffusion model is added to simulate the adoption of a platform API into third party applications. Those applications in turn influence adoption of the platform itself - but only after they have been implemented.

For simplicity, we only show the influence of third party applications on adoption of the underlying platform. The model generalizes easily to show an influence of these applications on the platform discard rate or the business value returned per user.

We choose here to model not the (potentially unbounded) number of third party applications, but the number of application developers, as these are the entities which respond to marketing and word of mouth, and make decisions to adopt or discard an API. As third party applications require ongoing development and maintenance of their own, developers who are actively consuming the API serve as a valid proxy for active applications in our generalized model.

In Fig. 7, we show a simulation in which the API strategy is implemented after 36 months of development under the previous (service) model. As in Fig. 6 we simplify to say that the third party application has influence solely on marketing-based adoption.

In Fig. 8 we compare the impact of the API offering on adoption rate as compared to the baseline. The release of applications contributes to a spike in new adoption of the platform, which levels off as the system reaches a new steady-state equilibrium.

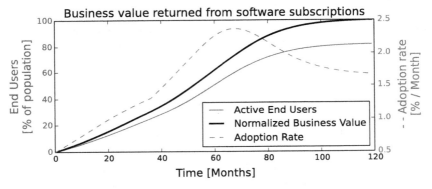

Fig. 7. After 36 months of offering the platform according to Model 2, the provider implements an API and begins to attract third party developers. Increased exposure leads to an uptick in platform adoption, and bends the S curve to of 'Active Users'.

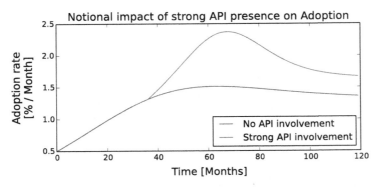

Fig. 8. Implementation of the API improves long run adoption rates over the baseline, representing an improvement in both first-time adoption and re-adoption after discard.

In Fig. 9, we show how the steady state business value returned per month reaches a higher level when third party applications contribute to marketing-related adoption of the service.

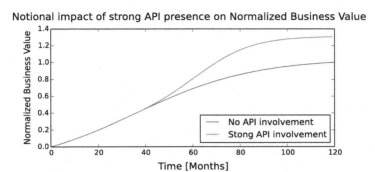

Fig. 9. Business value returned per month levels off at a higher steady-state value with the API offering than without.

5 Going Deeper

Up until this point, we have selected parameters for our models that best show the qualitative behavior of the models over time. We have shown how these models can behave at their best, and in doing so we run the risk of implying that any API strategy will lead to improvements over the traditional software model. This is not the case, and depends strongly on the relative strength of the word-of-mouth vs. the marketing loops. Intuitively, as the marketing loop strength increases, the more important it becomes to find a proper balance between marketing to API developers and marketing to end users.

We'll demonstrate this in a case where we have fixed word-of-mouth influence to be equal to the total influence that the platform provider can have through marketing to either end users or third party developers. In Fig. 10 we plot the decision space of a platform provider who must choose how to allocate their marketing budget between marketing to API developers and marketing to platform end users. The right hand side of the graph represents a decision to allocate the entire marketing budget to marketing the API to third party developers, and the left hand side represents the choice to devote the entire budget to marketing towards end users. The vertical axis represents a quantity outside the control of the platform provider, but crucial to his decision: the secondary ability of third party developers to market their applications (and therefore the platform) to end users.

When the average secondary marketing ability of third party developers is low, optimal strategy is to allocate a smaller fraction of the platform's total marketing budget to attracting third party developers, as can be seen in Fig. 10. This corresponds intuitively to the case where third party applications have poor reach to end users, or are inefficient at converting potential users to active users. When third party marketing effectiveness increases the marketing budget goes further when allocated toward

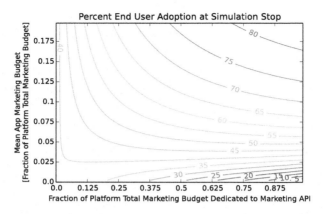

Fig. 10. Mapping the optimal marketing allocation strategy as a function of the average marketing effectiveness of third party applications.

recruiting third party developers to consume the API and provide applications to the end user, as their reach acts as a multiplier on platform marketing spending.

6 Related Work

Rapid growth and consumption of REST APIs [6] is generating new types of service marketplaces, which are dynamic and complex networks of providers and consumers. As enterprises continue to expose their core capabilities through APIs and enable co-creation of novel business capabilities this opens up a set of challenges in the understanding the value across the network of providers. Researchers have recognized the need for research in marketing and pricing of complex Cloud, API-based, services [7, 8]. Gallego and Stefanescu [9] discuss the need for real options, bundling and unbundling and versioning to help broaden and segment markets in the services domain. Service Value Networks (SVNs) [10–12] is an area of research that emerged with adoption the Service Oriented Architectures (SOA) and Software as a Service (SaaS) models, which focuses on providing business value through the agile and market-based composition and pricing of complex services from an open pool of complementary, as well as substitutive standardized service modules [10]. Conte et al. [11] and Speiser et al. [12] examine business models for platform providers of service networks, and study network formation together with incentives mechanisms to foster the evolution of desired networks.

Yet, in the context of APIs, which are characterized by extreme loose-coupling and extensibility, the efforts so far have primarily focused on understanding the structure and dynamics of API ecosystems. Yu and Woodard [13] investigate behavior patterns on Programmable Web [14], identifying linear growth in APIs over the period of two years, by analyzing the relative frequency with which APIs are used in mashups. They find that the cumulative API use follows a power law distribution, where a large number of APIs is used in a few mashups and a small number of APIs is used by many mashups. Weiss and Gangadharan [15] validate this power law relationship of API usage and identify that complexity of mashups is the key driver for the development of mashup platforms. Huang et al. [16] present a methodology to quantitatively characterize API ecosystems, that an increasing number of APIs inspires new compositions, which should drive ecosystem providers to support corresponding growth. A number of graph based approaches to representing and analyzing API ecosystems emerged [17, 18]. Dojcinowski et al. [17], create complex graph in which users are socially connected, which mashups users create, which APIs these mashups use, and categories of APIs. Wittern et al. [18] present a graph designed to continuously collect data as users interact with an API ecosystem, enabling real time insights through its expressiveness and extensibility. One can envision that the API graph can be employed to predict API consumption trends based on the knowledge of API networks, user social networks, expertise, and usage history, and thereby further influence marketing models for atomic and composite APIs.

7 Conclusions and Future Work

We have demonstrated the limits of traditional models of software marketing in application to API value chains, and have proposed a modification that allows adoption of the API by third party developers to be included in our system understanding. We have shown that analysis of this model can provide insight into optimal resource allocation strategies for platform providers.

Future work with this model would benefit from strong collaboration with a platform provider who was interested in assessing the impact of their API offering on business value, using internal data on API adoption, third party application offerings, and user behavior through direct platform access and as mediated by third party applications. As examples, the models could then be used to do sensitivity analysis to marketplace parameters, suggest time-based strategies for marketing platforms and compare outcomes over different scenarios.

This model could be further extended to consider multiple firms in competition for the same semi-differentiated market segment, such as map or weather API providers. Simulation could then suggest optimal strategies for both maximizing business value return and achieving satisfactory market position. Further extensions could study the influence of multiple API versions and features on third party application development and end user adoption.

Acknowledgments. Authors thank Kerrie Holley and Jim Laredo for discussions about API state of the art in the industry.

Appendix

If you wish to replicate the model used in this analysis, this system of differential equations are sufficient to calculate the derivative of all stocks - the state of the system. A number of methods exist to integrate these equations. Alternately, models, software, and analysis scripts necessary to recreate this analysis are available at www.github.com/JamesPHoughton/APIs.

```
platform_marketing_effectiveness = 0.005
marketing_effectiveness_per_app = 0.001
app_marketing_effectiveness = marketing_effectiveness_per_app*active_api_consumers
platform_adoption_from_marketing = potential_end_users*
      (app_marketing_effectiveness+platform_marketing_effectiveness)
api_kickoff_time = 36
api_word_of_mouth_effectiveness = 0.1
api_adoption_from_word_of_mouth = api_word_of_mouth_effectiveness*potential_api_co
nsumers*active_api_consumers/(active_api_consumers+potential_api_consumers)
api_marketing_effectiveness = 0.1
api_adoption_from_marketing = potential_api_consumers*step(api_marketing_effective
ness, api_kickoff_time, t)
api_adoption = api_adoption_from_marketing+api_adoption_from_word_of_mouth
api_discard_rate = 0.01
api_discard = api_discard_rate*active_api_consumers
dactive_api_consumers_dt = api_adoption-api_discard
platform_word_of_mouth_effectiveness = 0.05
platform_adoption_from_word_of_mouth = platform_word_of_mouth_effectiveness*active
_end_users*potential_end_users/(active_end_users+potential_end_users)
platform_discard_rate = 0.02
platform_discard = active_end_users*platform_discard_rate
dpotential_api_consumers_dt = api_discard-api_adoption
platform_adoption = platform_adoption_from_marketing+platform_adoption_from_word_o
f_mouth
dpotential_end_users_dt = platform_discard-platform_adoption
business_value_returned_per_user = 0.5
business_value = business_value_returned_per_user*active_end_users
dactive_end_users_dt = platform_adoption-platform_discard
```

References

1. Geroski, P.A.: Models of technology diffusion. Res. Policy **29**(4), 603–625 (2009)
2. Abdel-Hamid, T.K., Madnick, S.E.: Lessons learned from modeling the dynamics of software development. Commun. ACM **32**(12), 1426–1438 (1989)
3. Goldsmith, D., Siegel, M.: Managing and Valuing a Corporate IT Portfolio Using Dynamic Modeling of Software Development and Maintenance Processes (2010)
4. Bass, F.M. (n.d.). A new product growth for model consumer durables. Manage. Sci. **15**(5) (1969)
5. Sterman, J.D.: Business Dynamics: Systems Thinking and Modeling for a Complex World, vol. 19. Irwin/McGraw-Hill, Boston (2000)

6. Pautasso, C., Zimmermann, O., Leymann, F.: Restful web services vs. big'web services: making the right architectural decision. In: Proceedings of the 17th International Conference on World Wide Web. ACM (2008)
7. Weinhardt, C., Anandasivam, A., Blau, B., Borissov, N., Meinl, T., Michalk, W., Stoesser, J.: Cloud computing – a classification, business models and research directions. Bus. Inf. Syst. Eng. 1(5), 391–399 (2009)
8. Buyya, R., Yeo, C.S., Venugopal, S.: Market-oriented cloud computing: vision, hype, and reality for delivering it services as computing utilities. In: High Performance Computing and Communications (2008)
9. Gallego, G., Stefanescu, C.: Services Engineering: Design and Pricing of Service Features. Oxford Handbooks Online, Oxford (2012)
10. van Dinther C., Blau B., Conte, T.: Strategic behavior in service networks under price and service level competition. In: Proceedings of the 9th International Conference on Business Informatics (2009)
11. Conte T., Blau B., Satzger G., van Dinther, C.: Enabling service networks through contribution-based value distribution. In: Proceedings of the 15th Americas Conference on Information Systems (2009)
12. Speiser, S., Blau, B., Lamparter, S., Tai, S.: Formation of service value networks for decentralized service provisioning. In: Proceedings of the 6th International Conference on Service-Oriented Computing, pp. 517–523 (2008)
13. Yu, S., Woodard, C.J.: Innovation in the programmable web: characterizing the mashup ecosystem. In: Feuerlicht, G., Lamersdorf, W. (eds.) ICSOC 2008. LNCS, vol. 5472, pp. 136–147. Springer, Heidelberg (2009)
14. ProgrammableWeb. http://www.programmableweb.com
15. Weiss, M., Gangadharan, G.A.: Modeling the mashup ecosystem: structure and growth. Res. Dev. Manage. 40(1), 40–49 (2010)
16. Huang, K., Fan, Y., Tan, W.: an empirical study of programmable web: a network analysis on a service-mashup system. In: Proceedings of the IEEE 19th Conference on Web Services (ICWS), pp. 552–559 (2012)
17. Zaremba, M., Dojchinovski, M., Kuchar, J., Vitvar, T.: Personalised graph-based selection of web APIs. In: Cudré-Mauroux, P., Heflin, J., Sirin, E., Tudorache, T., Euzenat, J., Hauswirth, M., Parreira, J.X., Hendler, J., Schreiber, G., Bernstein, A., Blomqvist, E. (eds.) ISWC 2012, Part I. LNCS, vol. 7649, pp. 34–48. Springer, Heidelberg (2012)
18. Wittern, E., Laredo, J., Vukovic, M., Muthusamy, V., Slominski, A.: A graph-based data model for API ecosystem insights. In: Proceedings of the 21 IEEE International Conference on Web Services (2014)
19. Potluri, T.: Business Models for APIs. https://developer.ibm.com/api/docs/api-101/business-models-apis/. Accessed 17 Apr 2014
20. Santos, W.: How to choose the right business model to win the API economy. http://www.programmableweb.com/news/how-to-choose-right-business-model-to-win-api-economy/2013/10/26. Accessed 26 Oct 2013

Using COBIT 5 for Risk to Develop Cloud Computing SLA Evaluation Templates

Onyeka Illoh[1,2(✉)], Shaun Aghili[1], and Sergey Butakov[1]

[1] Concordia University of Edmonton,
7128 Ada Boulevard, Edmonton, AB T5B 4E4, Canada
o.illoh@yahoo.com,
{shaun.aghili,sergey.butakov}@concordia.ab.ca
[2] Information Systems Assurance Management,
Concordia University of Edmonton, Edmonton, Canada

Abstract. The use of cloud services as a business solution keeps growing, but there are significant associated risks that must be addressed. Despite the advantages and disadvantages of cloud computing, service integration and alignment with existing enterprise architecture remains an ongoing priority. Typically, quality of services provided is outlined in a service level agreement (SLA). A deficient template for evaluating, negotiating and selecting cloud SLAs could result in legal, regulatory, and monetary penalties, in addition to loss of public confidence and reputation. This research emphasizes (or advocates) the implementation of the proposed SLA evaluation template aimed at cloud services, based on the COBIT 5 for Risk framework. A gap analysis of existing SLAs was done to identify loopholes, followed by a resultant template where identified gaps were addressed.

Keywords: Cloud computing · Cloud users · Cloud providers · Service level agreements · Software as a service · Platform as a service · Infrastructure as a service · Everything as a service · COBIT 5 for risk

1 Introduction

1.1 Background

Cloud computing remains a hot topic among vendors, enterprises and end users. Different authors and industry experts advocate a variety of approaches to realize benefits at optimal costs, and reduce associated risks from cloud computing [1, 2]. Some of the key benefits include: pay-as-you-go model, scalable solution that supports rapid business growth, cost transparency to the end user or business, outsourcing of competencies that are not core to the business, as well as mirrored solutions to minimize the risk of downtime [1, 2].

For users, the cloud computing industry promises tremendous prospects of market growth, but a wide range of potential risks and safety issues remain prominent [16]. Cloud challenges ranges from data privacy issues, responsibilities for security breach, loss of physical control, availability concerns, cloud data backup and recovery, implications for e-discovery, compromised system security, inaccurate billing, greater dependency on third parties, to the inability of enterprises to satisfy audit/assurance

© Springer International Publishing Switzerland 2015
F. Toumani et al. (Eds.): ICSOC 2014, LNCS 8954, pp. 236–249, 2015.
DOI: 10.1007/978-3-319-22885-3_21

charter and requirements of regulators or external auditors [1, 2, 18]. Well known incidents with cloud services include: Amazon's EC2 cloud service partial outage, the security breaches of Sony's PlayStation Network and Qriocity music service [19]. These events emphasized that customers' inability to control their data remains a key issue of the cloud computing model [19].

The Institute of Internal Auditors indicated that today's auditors are faced with increasingly new-and-improved technologies (including cloud computing) that are transforming the business environment but introduces new risks that must be managed [11]. Hence, through this research, an SLA evaluation template aimed at cloud computing services, based on the COBIT 5 for Risk framework was developed.

(a) Cloud Computing Defined

According to the National Institute of Standards and Technology (NIST) and Cloud Security Alliance (CSA), *"Cloud computing is a model for enabling convenient, on-demand network access to a shared pool of configurable computing resources (e.g., networks, servers, storage, applications, and services) that can be rapidly provisioned and released with minimal management effort or service provider interaction"*. Cloud is composed of five essential characteristics, three service models, and four deployment models [20, 21].

1.2   Problems with Cloud SLAs

Gartner's 2010 EXP Worldwide Survey of nearly 1,600 Chief Information Officers, indicates that spending on IT cloud services is expected to grow almost threefold over the next five years [14]. Although cloud computing has evolved as a business solution, there are significant associated risks that must be addressed. As enterprises implement this technology, the integration and alignment of the services delivered by the Cloud Service Provider (CSP) remains an ongoing priority.

1.3   Research Questions and Scope

This research attempts to answer these cloud related questions and concerns:

- How can potential cloud users effectively evaluate and select the best suitable CSP for their business needs while minimizing potential risks (what standard or reference SLA parameters can be used to measure CSP's performance)?
- How can cloud users rely on cloud providers to secure and protect their data and information assets (what assurance do cloud users have about cloud services and who will provide this assurance)?

2   Discussion and Analysis

2.1   Literature Review

The related works reviewed are categorized into: Cloud Governance, Cloud Computing Market Maturity, Service level agreements (SLAs), as well as Security, Compliance and Data Privacy. The various categories are discussed in subsequent sections.

(a) Cloud Governance

According to Gartner, good governance practices, the ability to choose a suitable cloud computing environment, as well as security and privacy are the key challenges in cloud computing.[1] Boards of Directors are advised to guide the cloud investments to ensure optimization of risk, control of associated costs and creation of enterprise value [15].

Jirasek highlighted the importance of establishing and enforcing good governance practices for cloud computing projects [5]. To realize strategic, economic and operational benefits from cloud computing, enterprise goals and objectives must be aligned with adoption drivers [3]. Flexibility, reduced initial investment cost, faster deployment and virtualization are some of the cloud characteristics that may demand more governance considerations so that benefits are realized within the enterprise's risk appetite [3]. The enterprise's ability to buy only what it uses was reinforced as one of the goals of cloud computing [3]. ISACA advised focusing on using competition among cloud service providers as a bargaining chip to negotiate the best prices since the core can be provisioned and modified as needed [3].

According to ISACA, in order to discern whether cloud services will meet board's expectations, there should be an initial alignment between the enterprise strategy and expectations [3]. For effective cloud governance, the establishment of a mutual understanding of expected benefits, as well as tracking and measuring tools should be prioritized [3]. ISACA proposed COBIT 5 as a tool for governing and managing cloud investments, in addition to implementing consistent practices to maximize value and control risk [3]. Hence, it is evident that governance is a key area in cloud computing that helps ensure alignment with business strategy and priorities. Thus, the importance of SLA management in the governance framework cannot be overemphasized.

(b) Cloud Computing Market Maturity

Although cloud computing is still in its early stages of maturity, significant concerns will continue to be addressed [6, 7]. Cloud computing should be seen more as a business enabler and less as a technology issue so that the technology can progress in its maturity levels and enterprises can derive promised benefits [7].

The need for executive management to gain an understanding and appreciation for cloud by seeing it as a source of innovation was also highlighted [7]. Furthermore, cloud risks should be addressed at the enterprise level rather than as a technical issue [7]. Hence, to ensure cloud computing progresses through its maturity levels and benefits are maximized, an enterprise should address risk areas like security, privacy, data ownership, etc. These can be negotiated with the provider through SLAs.

(c) Security, Compliance and Data Privacy

According to Awad, cloud computing is best implemented through a phased-in approach [10]. Security, application type to be transitioned, as well as the CSP's proven track record, financial stability, and allowance for negotiating suitable terms are the key considerable factors in selecting the right cloud partner [10].

---

[1] http://www.gartner.com/technology/topics/cloud-computing.jsp.

Long-term viability, privileged user access, data segregation, recovery, vulnerability to attack or breaches, and regulatory compliance were also among customers' security concerns listed [8]. Jurisdictional issues, whereby the cloud user needs to comply with both laws governing its own country and that of the country where its data is stored was highlighted [8]. Where there is a conflict of laws, further consideration should be given to security levels at the physical location where cloud services will be deployed and managed [8]. Since cloud providers are required to physically separate backup data from production data, location of the offsite backup data becomes a compliance issue as it could be stored outside the client's legal/regulatory jurisdictions. While vendors may not disclose city, state, or country the backup data is stored, they should be willing to work with the client to provide, and prove compliance of the offsite backup data location [17].

A survey of IT executives by IDC eXchange, highlighted that security, availability and performance[2] are key challenges facing cloud services. The work done by Symantec to help enterprises make the right decisions in evaluating CSPs affirmed that security, compliance and data privacy remain areas of concern when considering the use of cloud services [12]. This paper focused on how CSPs could leverage secure sockets layer (SSL) certificates to deliver desired security levels for enterprises. Gartner Research identified seven areas of security risk associated with cloud computing that should be evaluated by enterprises when selecting a cloud hosting provider: privileged user access, compliance, data location, data segregation, recovery, investigative support and viability [13].

For secure and confidential data, enterprises are under regulations. Outsourcing services to CSPs does not relinquish consumer's responsibility for compliance. As due diligence, cloud users should ensure CSPs are preventing unauthorized third-party access or modification to address compliance risks [12]. As an added layer of protection, SSL deployed in backup and recovery ensures that backup data accessed is encrypted in transit, and servers accessed for backup data are authenticated as legitimate sources [12]. SSL is the proven technology for cloud security as it helps in developing trust between cloud user and provider [12].

According to Wei, Murugesan, Kuo, Naik and Krizanc, CSPs must implement strategies that enhance data integrity and privacy to address users' security concerns [24]. New data auditing and encryption techniques to protect cloud users' data from cyber-attacks while assuring a high level of data availability were also proposed [24]. Hence, addressing security and compliance issues in SLAs remain paramount.

(d) SLAs

According to Gartner, establishing the right SLA prior to the cloud user-vendor relationship is essential [14]. In a survey, CSA and ISACA affirmed that SLAs form the basis for clear definition and enforcement of user expectations, in addition to adequately documenting expectations of what the cloud provider will offer [7]. Based on related work, different but overlapping components or concerns to be addressed in an SLA are summarized in Table 1.

Table 1. Summary of existing work related to SLA components

SLA component	References
Business requirements for availability, response time for incidents and additional computing resources, change and patch management	[1, 4, 7, 9]
Provisions for disaster recovery, business continuity and physical access controls	[4, 8, 9, 13, 14]
Penalties for non-compliance to SLAs	[1, 14]
SLAs for security (Sec-SLAs)	[8]
CSP and cloud user's responsibilities for data and security, alignment of security metrics with industry standards and practices	[4, 8, 9, 14]
Confidentiality agreement, exit strategies, and portability (moving from one CSP to another)	[1, 9, 13]
Data retention and disposal policies and procedures	[4, 13]
Controls to satisfy legal, compliance and jurisdictional requirements	[4, 8, 13, 24]
Monitoring and performance measurements	[1, 8]

Therefore, inadequately defined SLAs contribute to a risky relationship between the cloud user and service provider [7]. As more enterprises leverage cloud computing, some of the service providers are offering competitive prices while others are being distinguished by quality of service through availability, and enhanced security.

2.2   Research Methodology

An initial comprehensive search for existing cloud SLA evaluation templates was carried out. Next, a list of the ten most important cloud computing companies was looked at, but the top five CSPs were critically compared, as well as their respective SLAs: Amazon, VMware, Microsoft, Salesforce and Google [25]. Public cloud vendors (Amazon, Microsoft and Google) were asked questions related to the infrastructure and platform services as suggested by cloud analysts and consultants [26]. Note that at the time of this research, Amazon had created a unique niche market where their larger cloud consumers are given the opportunity to customize cloud SLAs, thereby defining terms that best meet their business needs. The comparison is summarized in Table 2 and this is not conclusive due to rapid change of CSP offerings.

The study and analysis by Cloud Spectator compared five large cloud IaaS providers (Amazon, Rackspace, HP Cloud, SoftLayer and Windows) to determine their price-performance value, and Microsoft Windows topped the list in terms of customer satisfaction (performance) [27].

(e) Findings and Results

Cloud SLA concepts adapted from NIST, SLA terms and parameters from ISACA and CSA were used to formulate a scorecard prototype of SLA components that should be negotiated and documented in cloud SLAs [4, 21, 22]. According to Tschinkel, security in addition to data privacy and availability concerns are to be addressed as these are some of the most critical areas of risk management for the cloud [17]. A vendor market survey was carried out to justify the selection of cloud providers and at the time of

Table 2. Top 5 SLAs analysis - side by side comparison

	Amazon	VMware	Microsoft	Salesforce	Google
Availability/uptime guarantee	99.95 %	99.9 %	99.95 %	N/A	99.95 %
Custom cloud SLA	Yes	N/A	No	N/A	No
Compensation for downtime	Service credit	Service credit	Service credit	N/A	Service credit
Reporting uptime	Public dashboard	N/A	Public dashboard	N/A	Public dashboard
Publicly post audits	Limited	N/A	Limited	N/A	Limited
Audits of controls by customers/potential customers	No	N/A	No	N/A	No
Customer-led penetration testing (simulate cyber-attack)	Yes	N/A	Yes	N/A	No
Response-time to notify customers of breach	Based on applicable law	N/A	Promptly	N/A	Per contractual terms
Customers choose cloud storage location	Yes	N/A	Yes	N/A	Yes

research, Amazon and Microsoft emerged at the top for the following reasons: customization of cloud SLAs and customer satisfaction. Hence, these best practice SLA terms were grouped in five areas, though some are applicable in more than one area: Confidentiality, Integrity, Availability, Auditability and Customer Satisfaction. Case in point is the 'Interoperability and Portability' component that fits into Integrity and Customer Satisfaction.

Patel, Ranabahu and Sheth proposed the Web Service Level Agreement (WSLA) framework as a mechanism for managing SLAs in a cloud computing environment, in addition to being developed for SLA monitoring and enforcement in a Service Oriented Architecture (SOA) [23]. The third party support feature of WSLA was used to delegate monitoring and enforcement tasks, in addition to presenting a real world use case to validate their proposal [23]. However, a risk-based approach in alignment with COBIT 5 for Risk was not adapted or mentioned.

At the time of research, no existing cloud computing SLA evaluation template aligned with the COBIT 5 for Risk framework was found. So, these key SLA terms were mapped to COBIT 5 for Risk and the resultant scorecard prototype was used to test Amazon's SLA.

The scorecard prototype becomes the basis of risk analysis for the IT Risk Scenarios in COBIT 5 for Risk framework for cloud SLAs. An IT Risk scenario is an event that can lead to loss and has a business impact, when and if it occurs [28]. These IT Scenarios were adapted to the cloud environment and embedded into the gap analysis.

Table 4 shows the mapping of the SLA components to COBIT 5 for Risk. The complete analysis table shows the twenty example scenarios that were adapted from

Table 3. Testing the scorecard prototype (SLA components) based on best practices from NIST, ISACA and CSA with Amazon's SLA

Scorecard prototype		Amazon elastic compute cloud (Amazon EC2) SLA'		
SLA components		*Addressed*	*Not addressed*	*Vague*
Confidentiality	SSL, Encryption based on data classification (data at rest and in transit)		√	
	Data (Information) Dispersion		√	
	Secure Disposal (data security lifecycle)		√	
	User Management, Access Control/Authorization		√	
	Human Resources/NDAs		√	
	Identity and Access Management		√	
	Segregation of Duties (SoD)		√	
	Third Party Access		√	
	Security controls		√	
Integrity	Interoperability and Portability - must not affect data in any way		√	
	Data segregation (per multi-tenancy)		√	
Availability	Uptime	√		
	Contingency Planning (IR, DR, BC)			√
	Data Retention, Backup and Recovery		√	
	Response time		√	
	Source code escrow		√	
Auditability	Independent Audits; sub-categories: Type of audit (type I or II), Frequency (annual/semi-annual), scope/quality (is CIA covered), credibility/reputation of the auditing firm		√	
	Change Management, Configuration Management and Patch Management		√	
	Audit Logging and Monitoring			√
	Penalty for noncompliance	√		
	Cross-border issues/Compliance with Jurisdictional laws on Data Location		√	
	Security breach disclosure responsibilities		√	
	Third party certification (ISO/IEC 27001/27017, SAS 70, PCI, etc.): sub-categories-Type, Frequency and CIA Components should be part of the report		√	

(Continued)

Table 3. (*Continued*)

Scorecard prototype		Amazon elastic compute cloud (Amazon EC2) SLA		
SLA components		*Addressed*	*Not addressed*	*Vague*
	System of internal controls (e.g. Policies and Procedures)		√	
	Review of SLA metrics and compliance		√	
	Right to audit clause		√	
Customer Satisfaction (UnixBench components)	Pricing Plans		√	
	Performance (usage, load balancing, delivery, quality, etc.)	√		
	Maintenance and Service Support	√		
	Flexibility to Customers' Request		√	
	Scale Up/Scale Out - Interoperability and Portability		√	

COBIT 5 for Risk and tailored to cloud computing. These Risk Scenario Categories are high level descriptions of the category, while Risk Type are types to which scenarios derived from the gap analysis will fit (using three risk types which could be primary fit (higher degree)-P/secondary fit (lower degree)-S/blank for non-related risk scenario). The three risk types are [28]:

- *IT benefit/value enablement risk* (resulting from lost opportunities to leverage technology for new business initiatives or improve the efficiency or effectiveness of business processes).
- *IT programme and project delivery risk* (related to the contribution of IT to new or improved business solutions, through projects and programmes).
- *IT operations and service delivery risk* (as a result of operational stability, availability, protection and recoverability of IT services that can destroy or reduce enterprise value).

Amazon's publicly available SLA - Elastic Compute Cloud (Amazon EC2) was tested against the scorecard prototype and results are shown in Table 3 above. The rating scale in three categories are: Addressed (where the SLA component is clearly stated), Not Addressed (if not stated) and Vague (if it's unclear how the SLA component is addressed). According to the test, majority of the SLA components fall into the 'Not Addressed' category and are gaps to be discussed or negotiated with the CSP. This is just an example of how the scorecard prototype can be applied to any SLA.

This initial audit helps in identifying gaps and risks the enterprise needs to manage. If an SLA component is not stated in the SLA, it becomes the customer's responsibility. Where the SLA component is important, the cloud consumer should see if it can be negotiated with the CSP to reduce risk and cost. The importance of evaluating the amount of risk being shared cannot be overemphasized. This evaluation should also identify the risk either the consumer or CSP are responsible for. Any risk that cannot be

Table 4. Mapping of SLA components to COBIT 5 for risk - cloud SLA evaluation template

Risk scenarios based on COBIT 5 for Risk

#	Risk scenario category	Risk Type (P/S)			SLA components from Table 3	Example scenarios
		IT benefit/value enablement	IT Program and project delivery	IT Operations and service delivery		
1	Portfolio Establishment and Maintenance	P	P	S	N/A	Ensure selected cloud services are aligned with business strategy and priorities. Prior to adoption, cloud services should be assessed for compatibility with existing architecture
2	Program/projects life cycle management (program/projects initiation, economics, delivery, quality and termination)	P	P	S	Performance (usage, load balancing, delivery, quality, etc.) Change management Maintenance and Service Support	Cloud projects are within scope, allocated budgets and delivered on time without deteriorating quality. Stakeholders are actively involved from initiation to the end to avoid failure. Change management is deployed to keep stakeholders informed and future users trained
3	IT investment decision making	P		P	N/A	There's alignment between business and IT when making cloud investment decisions. Business case is drawn up to justify cloud investments
4	IT expertise and skills	P	P	P	Human Resources/NDAs User Management, Access Control/Authorization Identity and Access Management, SoD Third Party Access	Due diligence and screening of candidates involved either at the cloud consumer's end or vender's to ensure appropriate skills and competences in the recruitment process. Security education, training and awareness (SETA) to ensure staff are up to date with the latest cloud developments. Segregation of duties and job rotation to ensure no single employee knows the entire system. Suitable staff with appropriate skills and competences are attracted to support business objectives, service and value delivery. Staff and 3rd party access or authorization is granted based on Least Privilege and Need-to-Know principles
5	Staff operations (human error and malicious intent)	P	S	P	Configuration, Patch, Identity and Access Management, Uptime, Contingency Planning (IR, DR, BC), Backup and Recovery Response time, System of internal controls, Security controls Logging and Monitoring	Configuration management is leveraged to elude errors. Avoid authorization creep so that access rights from prior roles are not abused. Coordination between HR and IT Administration to ensure timely removal of access rights to deter abuse. For security, two separate individuals should approve before actions are taken (the 4-eye principle) especially in the areas of backup, information entry, system maintenance and upgrades. Data centre is secured, monitored for irregularities and only authorized staff are granted access. Ensure appropriate security controls are in place to deter theft. Ensure monitoring for performance, availability and other irregularities, in addition to prompt response to alerts

(Continued)

Table 4. (*Continued*)

Risk scenarios based on COBIT 5 for Risk

#	Risk scenario category	Risk Type (P/S)			SLA components from Table 3	Example scenarios
		IT benefit/value enablement	IT Program and project delivery	IT Operations and service delivery		
6	Information (data breach: damage, leakage and access)	P	S	P	SSL, Encryption based on data classification (data at rest and in transit) Data (Information) Dispersion Secure Disposal (data security lifecycle) Data Retention. Data segregation (per multi-tenancy) NDAs Contingency Planning (IR, DR, BC), Backup and Recovery Security breach disclosure responsibilities	Contingency planning to ensure that if database is corrupted or hardware components are damaged, data would be available. Backup procedures based on data classification levels are in place, in addition to testing backups and protecting backup media. Through continuous network monitoring and firewalls, sensitive information on cloud provider or consumer's site is protected. SETA to ensure staff do not accidentally disclose sensitive information through social media or email. To protect data, portable media are secured and encrypted. Intentional modification of information is prevented through the 4-eye principle. Regular update of the data retention policy to avoid inefficient archiving, retaining or disposal of information. Non-disclosure agreements and intellectual property clauses are factored into contracts to avoid leakage information or trade secrets and loss of competitive advantage
7	Architecture (architectural vision and design)	P	S	P	Scale Up/Scale Out	Cloud consumer's architecture should be flexible to support adoption of newly acquired cloud services in a timely manner
8	Infrastructure (hardware, operating system and controlling technology) (selection/implementation, operations and decommissioning)	P	S	P	Scale Up/Scale Out Performance (usage, load balancing, delivery, quality, etc.)	Newly acquired cloud services should not make consumer's systems unstable leading to operational incidents. Underlying infrastructure should allow for scale up/scale out in case user volumes increase or handle system load when new cloud services are deployed. Cloud services should be tested prior to deployment into the production environment to ensure system availability and proper functionality. Hardware and utilities should be protected from failures, in addition to putting standby measures in place to support continual execution of critical business transactions
9	Software	P		S	Source code escrow Change and configuration Management Backup and Recovery	For SaaS models, contingency planning should include source code and data escrow to assure business continuity regardless of what happens to the SaaS provider. SaaS customers could enter into an agreement with the 3rd party hosting provider to continue hosting the application in case the SaaS vendor goes out of business.

(*Continued*)

Table 4. (*Continued*)

Risk scenarios based on COBIT 5 for Risk

#	Risk scenario category	Risk Type (P/S)			SLA components from Table 3	Example scenarios
		IT benefit/value enablement	IT Program and project delivery	IT Operations and service delivery		
						Change control and change management should be in place to reduce incident resolution time and problem management. Roll-back procedures are in place in case of operational issues, in addition to establishment of backup and restore points in accordance with business needs
10	Business ownership of IT	P	S	S	Review of SLA metrics and compliance	Cloud initiatives should not be a sole responsibility of the technical team, enterprises should assume accountability to ensure alignment with business strategy. Business requirements should be adequately defined and reviewed to ensure effective SLAs. Cloud investments are within the procurement process and weighed based on cost vs. benefits
11	Supplier selection/performance, contractual compliance, termination of service and transfer		S	P	Review of SLA metrics and compliance; Performance (usage, load balancing, delivery, quality, etc.); Maintenance and Service Support; Flexibility to Customers' Request; Penalty for noncompliance; Interoperability and Portability	Prior to a strategic partnership, enterprises should exercise due diligence in selecting the CSP; check the financial viability, delivery capability, as well as sustainability of the CSP. Cloud services and support should be reviewed to ensure they're in accordance with the SLA. Defined key performance indicators (KPIs) should be linked to rewards and penalties to ensure adequate service delivery and support. If the partnership ceases to exist, there should be measures that allow for interoperability and portability (exit strategies). To avoid service integration issues with existing services, the enterprise should consult/involve IT before purchasing cloud services
12	Regulatory compliance	P	S	P	Independent Audits, Credibility/reputation of the auditing firm, Third party certification, Review of SLA metrics and compliance, Right to audit clause, Cross-border issues/Compliance with Jurisdictional laws on Data Location	Independent audits and 3rd party certification should be carried out to assure compliance with regulatory standards. The consumer can request for a right to audit clause in contractual agreements and ensure the CSP is willing to work with the consumer to comply with regulations that prohibit cross-border dataflow

(Continued)

Table 4. (*Continued*)

Risk scenarios based on COBIT 5 for Risk

#	Risk scenario category	Risk Type (P/S)			SLA components from Table 3	Example scenarios
		IT benefit/value enablement	IT Program and project delivery	IT Operations and service delivery		
13	Geopolitical			P	Cross-border issues/Compliance with Jurisdictional laws on Data Location	Ensure that compliance to national, support of local initiatives and government interference does not affect the partnership between cloud consumers and their service providers, in addition to service capabilities
14	Infrastructure theft or Destruction	S	S	P	Contingency Planning (IR, DR, BC) Security controls Logging and Monitoring	Security controls and contingency planning should address theft of servers or devices with sensitive data, in addition to destruction or sabotage of data centres. Access to data centres should be logged, monitored and restricted only to authorized personnel
15	Malware	S		P	Contingency Planning (IR, DR, BC) Security controls Logging and Monitoring	Through firewalls, security controls, contingency planning and continuous monitoring of network, cloud infrastructure should be protected against malware, logical bombs, and loss of data through phishing attacks
16	Logical attacks	S		P	Contingency Planning (IR, DR, BC), Security controls Logging and Monitoring Identity and Access Management	Through firewalls, security controls, contingency planning and continuous monitoring of network, cloud infrastructure should be protected against hacking, unauthorized access to systems, industrial espionage and service interruption due to denial-of-service attacks
17	Industrial action	S	S	P	Contingency Planning (IR, DR, BC)	Through contingency planning, alternate solutions where critical business tasks can be executed should be planned for in case the 3rd party or primary location becomes unavailable due to strike
18	Environmental	S	S	P	Contingency Planning (IR, DR, BC)	Ensure that equipment used at data centres is environmentally friendly (e.g., power consumption)
19	Acts of nature	S	S	P	Contingency Planning (IR, DR, BC)	Contingency planning should take into consideration the impact of natural disasters on cloud services, if and when they occur
20	Innovation	P		S	Security controls Pricing plans	New and important technology trends in cloud computing that have been identified should be timely assessed for business impact and adopted if required. The security controls and cost of the new trends should be considered

negotiated with the CSP must be addressed by the consumer through various risk management practices. The goal is to realize benefits from cloud initiatives while optimizing resources and managing risks.

3 Conclusion

In this paper, a scorecard prototype was developed to effectively help cloud users evaluate and select the best suitable CSP for its business needs while minimizing potential risks. Best practices from NIST, ISACA and CSA were identified as reference SLA parameters that can be used in SLAs and measurement of provider's performance. Incorporating these terms in SLAs (either as standard or negotiated terms), assures cloud users of their providers' commitment and responsibility in securing and protecting their data, as well as information assets.

Though the initial evaluation template has been generalized, this paper is the first in its direction for future work where each SLA component can be further addressed. Recommendations for future work also includes taking a company considering moving to the cloud as a case study, specifically tailoring the template for the company, and testing the template prior to acquiring cloud services.

Acknowledgement. The first author will like to thank Concordia University of Edmonton's research team for their guidance and support in the completion of this work. Their efforts, knowledge and experience were instrumental in making this paper a success. She acknowledges the Academic Research Council for the Student Research Grant awarded to her. She is also thankful to God Almighty, her family and friends; this has been a journey and she is very grateful for their love, support and encouragement.

References

1. Information Systems Audit and Control [ISACA]: Cloud computing management audit/assurance program (2010)
2. Gadia, S.: Cloud computing: an auditor's perspective. ISACA J. **6**, 1–2 (2009). http://www.isaca. org/Journal/Past-Issues/2009/Volume-6/Pages/Cloud-Computing-An-Auditor-s-Perspective1. aspx
3. ISACA: Cloud governance: questions boards of directors need to ask (2013)
4. ISACA: Security considerations for cloud computing (2012)
5. Jirasek, V.: Cloud governance done right: examples from the trenches. BrightTALK (2013)
6. Sinnett, W.M: In the Cloud and Beyond. Financial Executive (February 2012)
7. CSA and ISACA: Cloud computing market maturity: study results (2012)
8. de Chaves, S. A., Westphall, C.B., Lamin, F.R.: SLA perspective in security management for cloud computing. In: IEEE ICNS, pp. 212–217 (2010)
9. Subbiah, S., Muthukumaran, S.S., Ramkumar, T.: Enhanced survey and proposal to secure the data in cloud computing environment. In: IJEST, vol. 5, no. 01 (2013)
10. Awad, R.: Considerations on cloud computing for CPAs. CPA J. **81**(9), 11 (2011)
11. Jackson R.A.: Audit in a digital business world. In: The Internal Auditor Magazine, pp. 36–41 (2013)

12. Symantec Corporation: Choosing a cloud hosting provider with confidence: Symantec SSL certificates provide a secure bridge to trusted cloud hosting providers (2012)
13. Heiser, J., Nicolett, M.: Assessing the security risks of cloud computing. Gartner Research, ID G00157782 (2008)
14. Smith, D.M, Plummer, D.C, Bittman, T.J, Bova, T, Basso, M, Lheureux, B.J, Prentice, B.: Predicts 2013: cloud computing becomes an integral part of IT. Gartner, ID: G00230929 (2012)
15. Gartner. http://www.gartner.com/technology/topics/cloud-computing.jsp
16. Wu, J., Shen, Q., Wang, T., Zhu, J., Zhang, J.: Recent advances in cloud security. J. Comput. 6(10), 2156–2163 (2011)
17. Tschinkel, B.: Cloud computing security understanding risk areas and management techniques (2011)
18. Gordon, M.: The compliant cloud. BrightTALK (2009)
19. Moore, J.: [CNBC]: Reducing security risks in cloud computing. http://www.cnbc.com/id/43139361/Reducing_Security_Risks_in_Cloud_Computing
20. Badger, L., Grance, T., Patt-Corner, R., Voas. J.: Cloud computing synopsis and recommendations. In: NIST, vol. 800, p. 146. Special Publication (SP) (2011)
21. CSA: Security guidance for critical areas of focus in cloud computing v3.0 (2011)
22. NIST: NIST US government cloud computing technology roadmap, Release 1.0 (Draft) - In: NIST, vol. 500, p. 293. Special Publication (SP) (2011)
23. Patel, P., Ranabahu, A., Sheth, A.P.: Service level agreement in cloud computing (2009)
24. Wei, D.S.L., Murugesan, S., Kuo, S., Naik, K., Krizanc, D.: Enhancing data integrity and privacy in the cloud: an agenda. IEEE Comput. Soc. 46, 87–90 (2013)
25. Bort, J.: The 10 most important companies in cloud computing. Business Insider (2013)
26. Loftus, T.: Public cloud vendors side by side by side. Wall Street J. 1–3 (2013). http://blogs.wsj.com/cio/2013/02/26/public-cloud-vendors-side-by-side-by-side/
27. Cloud Spectator: Cloud server performance: a comparative analysis of 5 large cloud IaaS providers (2013)
28. ISACA: COBIT 5 for risk framework, pp. 67–74 (2013)

A Non-Parametric Data Envelopment Analysis Approach for Cloud Services Evaluation

Chunxiang Xu, Yupeng Ma$^{(\boxtimes)}$, and Xiaobo Wang

XinJiang Technical Institute of Physics and Chemistry CAS, Beijing, China
chunxiangxu@gmail.com, {ypma,wangxb}@ms.xjb.ac.cn

Abstract. Due to advantages of cloud computing, services are increasingly deployed in cloud. It is a challenge to choose a proper service. Besides QoS requirements, customers expect more efficient services which provide better performance but with minimum cost. In this paper, we propose a non-parametric method to evaluate relative efficiency of cloud services based on Data Envelopment Analysis. It can classify cloud services into different efficiency levels and tell how to improve less efficient services. We illustrate the method with a case study.

Keywords: Cloud service · Relative efficiency · QoS · Data envelopment analysis

1 Introduction

With the fast development of cloud computing, numerous services with similar functions have been presented to cloud customers at different prices and performances, therefore it is a challenge for customers to select the most "worthy" cloud services. Often, there may be trade-off between cost and performance which makes it difficult to evaluate services from different cloud providers in an objective way.

Lots of work have been done for comparing different cloud services. Some researchers specified factors or attributes important for evaluating cloud computing models [5,10], such as security, availability, performance, cost, etc. Based on these attributes, cloud services are compared and ranked for selection.

Some of existing works [8,11,15,16] compared services only based on performances while the cost was not considered. Some researchers considered both. Brebner [3] used statistical graphs to compare cost of different cloud scenarios. Li [9] proposed Cloudcmp to compare public cloud providers on different aspects separately. The work in [13] analyzed the application of different multicriteria decision analysis (MCDA) methods to cloud services selection, including AHP, TOPSIS and other methods taking multiple QoS attributes and cost into account. Saurabh [6] introduced a framework named SMICloud using AHP

Supported by the West Light Foundation of Chinese Academy of Sciences (Project No. XBBS201319).

F. Toumani et al. (Eds.): ICSOC 2014, LNCS 8954, pp. 250–255, 2015.
DOI: 10.1007/978-3-319-22885-3_22

method. It is parametric and requires customers to define the preference value for each factor first. However, sometimes we might only care about the minimum performance and the maximum cost, while the preference of QoS attributes is of little concern. In this case, the AHP method might not be appropriate, because different preference values will give different results.

DEA is a non-parametric method suitable for situation without user's preference. In this paper, we introduce how to apply DEA to evaluate and compare a group of cloud services according to their prices and performances. According to features of DEA models and characteristic of cloud services, we combine results of C^2R [4] and BC^2 [2], and define several efficiency levels for cloud services based on their relative efficiency scores and slacks. Thereby customers can select services of higher efficiency level. Moreover, for less efficient services, we show how they should be improved in order to be more efficient.

2   Classifying Cloud Services with DEA Models

2.1   DEA Models

Here we introduce how to construct DEA models for calculating relative efficiency scores and slacks. The problem can be defined as following: given n cloud services, each having s QoS attributes and m cost items, finding out which service's QoS value could be improved with the cost remaining the same. The cloud services, QoS attributes and cost items are modeled as DMUs, output variables and input variables respectively.

The C^2R and BC^2 models are used to calculate efficiency scores. The C^2R model is designed with the assumption of constant returns to scale, meaning that if all inputs are doubled, the outputs are also expected to double. The BC^2 model takes into account that the performance at the most efficient point may not be attainable and thus assumes variable returns to scale.

The C^2R model $D_{C^2R}^I$ is given in Eq. 1, where x_{ij} and y_{rj} are constants representing the ith input and rth output for the jth service, and θ and λ_j are variables of the LP problem. The BC^2 model $D_{BC_2}^I$ is similar to $D_{C^2R}^I$ with one more constraint $\sum_{j=1}^{n} \lambda_j = 1$. The optimal values of the two models $h_{C^2R}^I$ and $h_{BC^2}^I$ are called technical and scale efficient score (TSE score) and technical efficient score (TE score) respectively. It can be inferred that if TSE score is 1, then TE score is 1, but not vice versa.

$$D_{C^2R}^I \begin{cases} \min \theta = h_{C^2R}^I \\ \sum_{j=1}^{n} \lambda_j x_{ij} \leq \theta x_{i0} & i = 1, \ldots, m \\ \sum_{j=1}^{n} \lambda_j y_{rj} \geq y_{r0} & r = 1, \ldots, s \\ \lambda_j \geq 0 & j = 1, \ldots, n \end{cases} \tag{1}$$

Because of the existence of weak efficient point which is on the efficient frontier but still possible to be improved, we apply the slack-based method [12] to calculate slacks. The model $\bar{D}_{C^2R}^I$ expressed by Eq. 2 can be used to check if a service is weak technical and scale efficient (W-TSE). Accordingly, a similar model $\bar{D}^I_{BC^2}$ with one more constraint ($\sum_{j=1}^n \lambda_j = 1$) can check weak technical efficient (W-TE). Here, λ_j, s_i^- and s_r^+ are variables of the equations. s_i^{*-} and s_r^{*+} are values of s_i^- and s_r^+, the sum of which is the optimal value (called slack) of the model. If the slacks for the two models are greater than 0, the cloud service is called W-TSE and W-TE respectively.

$$\bar{D}^I_{C^2R} \begin{cases} \max \sum_{i=1}^m s_i^- + \sum_{r=1}^s s_r^+ = \sum_{i=1}^m s_i^{*-} + \sum_{r=1}^s s_r^{*+} \\ \sum_{j=1}^n \lambda_j x_{ij} + s_i^- = h^I_{C^2R} x_{i0} & i = 1, \ldots, m \\ \sum_{j=1}^n \lambda_j y_{rj} - s_r^+ = y_{r0} & r = 1, \ldots, s \\ \lambda_j \geq 0 & j = 1, \ldots, n \\ s_i^- \geq 0 & i = 1, \ldots, m \\ s_r^+ \geq 0 & r = 1, \ldots, s \end{cases} \quad (2)$$

Table 1. Service efficiency types and levels

Level	Type	$h^I_{C^2R}$	Slack_C^{2}R	$h^I_{BC^2}$	Slack_BC^2	Improvement
1	TSE	1	0	1	0	no
2	TE	<1	-	1	0	not sure
3	W-TSE	1	>0	1	-	yes
4	W-TE	<1	-	1	>0	yes
5	inefficient	<1	-	<1	-	yes

2.2 Efficiency Levels

Table 1 shows different efficiency types and their levels, where level 1 is the most efficient and level 5 is the least. Consider the cases of the second and the third row, if a cloud service is W-TSE, it can be improved by the distance of the slack. However, a TE service might not be able to be improved, because its improvement requires moving along the frontier of the C^{2}R model and the efficient target might be an impossible situation for a cloud service. For example, the percent of SLA agreement is bounded to the range of [0,1] and it cannot be greater than 1 in order to be efficient. Therefore, if a cloud service is TE, we believe that its efficiency is better under current cloud services group. The order of efficiency level of 3, 4 and 5 is obvious. According to the above discussion, we can have the efficiency order defined in Table 1.

2.3 Method Implementation

Now we give detailed steps to evaluating cloud services' efficiency with DEA.

The first step is preparing data for the model. One thing is to check non-numeric value and missing value. Non-numeric value should be transformed to numeric value according to its definition. For example, if a service's security protection level is specified as *poor*, *average* or *extensive*, these values can be transformed to integer values of 1, 2 and 3, with larger value meaning better performance. Missing value can be filled with the average value of the attribute or predict its value with a precise assumption [7,14]. The other thing is to check QoS attributes. DEA generally minimizes "inputs" and maximizes "outputs". In other words, smaller levels of the former and larger levels of the latter represent better efficiency. Therefore, for attribute having smaller value for better performance, such as response time, we use the reciprocal of the variable instead.

The second step is to determine efficiency level of a cloud service based on its efficiency scores and slacks. First we calculate the TSE score with the model $D_{C^2R}^I$. If it is equal to 1, the model $\bar{D}_{C^2R}^I$ is used to obtain the slack. If the slack is 0, then the cloud service is of level 1, otherwise it is of level 3. If the TSE score is smaller than 1, we continue to solve the model $D_{BC^2}^I$. If the TE score is smaller than 1, the service is inefficient and of level 5. Otherwise, the model $\bar{D}_{BC^2}^I$ is applied to get the slack of BC^2 model. The service is of level 2 if the slack is 0, otherwise it is of level 4.

The last step is to obtain the improving targets of less efficient cloud services by calculating their projections on frontier of either $D_{C^2R}^I$ model or $D_{BC^2}^I$ model. If a cloud service's efficiency is of level 2 or 3, its projection can be obtained according to Eq. 3, where s_i^{*-} and s_r^{*+} are from the optimal value of model $\bar{D}_{C^2R}^I$. If the efficiency level of the cloud service is 4 or 5, its projection can be obtained according to Eq. 4, where s_i^{*-} and s_r^{*+} are from the optimal value of model $\bar{D}_{BC^2}^I$.

$$(\mathrm{P}-j_0) \begin{cases} \hat{x}_{i0} = h_{C^2R}^I x_{i0} - s_i^{*-}, \text{ for } i = 1, \ldots, m \\ \hat{y}_{r0} = h_{C^2R}^I y_{r0} + s_r^{*+}, \text{ for } r = 1, \ldots, s \end{cases} \tag{3}$$

$$(\mathrm{P}-j_0) \begin{cases} \hat{x}_{i0} = h_{BC^2}^I x_{i0} - s_i^{*-}, \text{ for } i = 1, \ldots, m \\ \hat{y}_{r0} = h_{BC^2}^I y_{r0} + s_r^{*+}, \text{ for } r = 1, \ldots, s \end{cases} \tag{4}$$

3   Case Study

We illustrate our method by evaluating relative efficiency of a group of IaaS services from an online data set [1]. Due to limited pages, we select 15 services from three cloud providers. The input data and analysis results are listed in Table 2, where p1s1 corresponds to the first service from the first provider, and (0.12,1,2,3.75,410) represents values of price/hour, number of virtual cores, compute units, memory(GB) and disk(GB).

It can be seen that services from the first and second providers are more efficient. Projections for services of level 1 are the same as their original values, while others are targets for improving services' performance in order to become efficient. For example, the projection of service p2s2 is (0.12,4,4,4,80), whose

Table 2. Case study result

Service	$h^I_{C^2R}$	$h^I_{BC^2}$	Slack_C^{2}R	Slack_BC^2	Input data Projection	Level
p1s1	0.9982	1.0000	-	0.1304	(0.12,1,2,3.75,410) (0.1198,1.0797,2.0507,3.75,410)	4
p1s2	1.0000	1.0000	0.0000	-	(0.24,2,4,7.5,840)	1
p1s3	1.0000	1.0000	0.0000	-	(0.48,4,8,15,1680)	1
p2s1	1.0000	1.0000	0.0000	-	(0.03,1,1,1,20)	1
p2s2	1.0000	1.0000	2.0000	-	(0.12,2,4,4,80) (0.12,4,4,4,80)	3
p2s3	1.0000	1.0000	4.0000	-	(0.24,4,8,8,160) (0.24,8,8,8,160)	3
p3s1	0.8476	0.8476	-	2.9513	(0.12,1,1,3.35,123) (0.1017,1.8854,3.0660,3.35,123)	5
p3s2	0.9908	0.9908	-	3.0248	(0.24,2,2,7.5,738) (0.2378,2.5075,4.5174,7.5,738)	5
p3s3	0.9904	1.0000	-	6.7783	(0.48,4,4,15,1467) (0.4754,5.6978,9.0804,15,1467)	4
p4s1	0.7500	0.7500	-	0.0000	(0.04,1,1,1,20) (0.03,1,1,1,20)	5
p4s2	0.8063	0.9667	-	0.1875	(0.08,2,2,2,60) (0.0773,2,2.05,2.1375,60)	5
p4s3	0.7500	1.0000	-	0.0000	(0.16,4,4,4,80) (0.12,4,4,4,80)	2
p5s1	0.3113	0.3115	-	0.0481	(0.1,1,1,1,25) (0.0312,1,1.0129,1.0353,25)	5
p5s2	0.3675	0.4267	-	0.5625	(0.2,2,2,2,100) (0.0853,2,2.15,2.4125,100)	5
p5s3	0.4150	0.5467	-	0.1875	(0.3,4,4,4,100) (0.164,4,4.05,4.1375,100)	5

input data is (0.12,2,4,4,80), thus its number of virtual cores should be changed from 2 to 4, and the distance between the two value (4−2=2) is slack for virtual cores. From all the slack values, we can see that services from the third provider need more improvement.

4   Conclusion and Future Work

In this work, non-parametric method based on DEA model is applied to evaluate the relative efficiency of cloud services, which is the ratio of performance and price. The method can evaluate and classify cloud services by analyzing their efficiency, and further show how to improve inefficient services.

Our work can classify a group of cloud services according to their efficiency levels, but services of the same level cannot be distinguished yet. Next, we will study how to distinguish services of the same efficiency level so as to offer more support for user's decision.

References

1. Iaas cost snapshot, 29 May 2014. https://docs.google.com/spreadsheet/fm?id=t9fsKqXYKmIQ6LFvmVkHTCQ.04776183464924915040.7277648387216344348&fmcmd=420
2. Banker, R.D., Charnes, A., Cooper, W.W.: Some models for estimating technical and scale inefficiencies in data envelopment analysis. Manag. Sci. **30**(9), 1078–1092 (1984)

3. Brebner, P., Liu, A.: Performance and cost assessment of cloud services. In: Maximilien, E.M., Rossi, G., Yuan, S.-T., Ludwig, H., Fantinato, M. (eds.) ICSOC 2010. LNCS, vol. 6568, pp. 39–50. Springer, Heidelberg (2011)
4. Charnes, A., Cooper, W.W., Rhodes, E.: Measuring the efficiency of decision making units. Eur. J. Oper. Res. **2**(6), 429–444 (1978)
5. Consortium, C.S.M.I.: Service measurement index framework version 2.0 (2014). http://csmic.org/wp-content/uploads/2014/01/SMI_Overview_140113.pdf
6. Garg, S.K., Versteeg, S., Buyya, R.: A framework for ranking of cloud computing services. Future Gener. Comput. Syst. **29**(4), 1012–1023 (2013)
7. Goldman, A., Ngoko, Y.: On graph reduction for qos prediction of very large web service compositions. In: 2012 IEEE Ninth International Conference on Services Computing (SCC), pp. 258–265 (2012)
8. Huang, K., Yao, J., Fan, Y., Tan, W., Nepal, S., Ni, Y., Chen, S.: Mirror, mirror, on the web, which is the most reputable service of them all? In: Basu, S., Pautasso, C., Zhang, L., Fu, X. (eds.) ICSOC 2013. LNCS, vol. 8274, pp. 343–357. Springer, Heidelberg (2013)
9. Li, A., Yang, X., Kandula, S., Zhang, M.: Cloudcmp: comparing public cloud providers. In: Proceedings of the 10th Annual Conference on Internet Measurement, pp. 1–14 (2010)
10. Parhizkar, B., Abdulhussein, A.A., Joshi, J.H., Twinamatsiko, A.M.: A comman factors analysis on cloud computing models. Int. J. Comput. Sci. Issues **10**(2), 523–529 (2013)
11. Park, J., Jeong, H.Y.: The QoS-based MCDM system for SaaS ERP applications with social network. J. Supercomput. **66**(2), 614–632 (2012)
12. Tone, K.: A slacks-based measure of efficiency in data envelopment analysis. Eur. J. Oper. Res. **130**(3), 498–509 (2001)
13. Whaiduzzaman, M., Gani, A., Anuar, N.B., Shiraz, M., Haque, M.N., Haque, I.T.: Cloud service selection using multicriteria decision analysis. Sci. World J. **2014**, 10 (2014)
14. Xie, Q., Wu, K., Xu, J., He, P., Chen, M.: Personalized context-aware QoS prediction for web services based on collaborative filtering. In: Cao, L., Zhong, J., Feng, Y. (eds.) ADMA 2010, Part II. LNCS, vol. 6441, pp. 368–375. Springer, Heidelberg (2010)
15. Zheng, Z., Wu, X., Zhang, Y.: QoS ranking prediction for cloud services. IEEE Trans. Parallel Distrib. Syst. **24**(6), 1213–1222 (2013)
16. Zheng, Z., Zhang, Y., lyu, M.R.: Cloudrank: a qos-driven component ranking framework for cloud computing (2010)

Self-Managing Pervasive Service Systems

A Lightweight User State Monitoring System on Android Smartphones

Weishan Zhang[1](✉) and Xun Wang[2]

[1] Department of Software Engineering, China University of Petroleum,
No. 66 Changjiang West Road, Qingdao 266580, China
zhangws@upc.edu.cn
[2] School of Software, China University of Science and Technology, Hefei, China

Abstract. Smartphones are widely used around the world, which are also equipped with some sensors that can be used for the awareness of their users' state. These sensors include GPS, accelerometer, and microphone among others. In this paper, we present an empirical way to identify user's state including daily activity like walking, running, accidental threats like falling-down, and emotional status like sadness, joy, and anger. The monitoring should be realized in a non-intrusive way. We realize this idea by the design and implementation of a comprehensive run time user state monitoring system on Android smartphones, as less instructive as possible. The experiments show that it has good performance in terms of both monitored state accuracy and footprint incurred while conduct monitoring. The evaluations also show that the power consumption of the monitoring system is even neglectable which proves the usability of the proposed monitoring system.

1 Introduction and Motivation

Smartphones are becoming increasing popular all over the world. Besides the increasing processing power and storage capabilities, the smartphones are equipped with various sensors, which can be used for identifying its user's state. These sensors include GPS, accelerometer, and microphone among others. It is becoming natural to make use of these sensors to conduct the awareness of smartphone user's state, including his activity (like walking, running, still), his accidental threats (like sudden falling down), and emotional status (like in sadness, joy, anger). Then these states can be used to provide location based services, such as recommending food and hotels. Furthermore, health care strategies can be applied based on the monitored states like suggestions of exercises after monitoring long time still states, and reporting to healthcare center during emergencies like a falling-down detected in a senior/patient monitoring situation.

As Android[1] based smartphones are gaining the majority of the market[2] and also due to its openness for research and development, Android based mobile

---

[1] http://developer.android.com.
[2] http://arstechnica.com/gadgets/2012/06/android-market-share-stalls-version-4-0-s ees-a-7-percent-install-base/.

© Springer International Publishing Switzerland 2015
F. Toumani et al. (Eds.): ICSOC 2014, LNCS 8954, pp. 259–269, 2015.
DOI: 10.1007/978-3-319-22885-3_23

sensing become popular. There are some research work gearing towards the monitoring of user activities, such as [5–7]. But none of the existing work provides comprehensive user state monitoring that covers both physical activity and mental activity. For example, [6] is specialized in the detecting of falling-down, [5] and [7] cover the monitoring of running, walking and other physical states, but not including the falling down states which are vital for health care applications. Also, for the health care applcations, it is preferable to get user states in a real time manner in order to take appropriate actions for handling serious situations.

On the one hand, user state monitoring system should be as accurate as possible. On the other hand, resource consumption must be taken into consideration due to the fact that mobile phones have limited battery and processing capabilities [3]. From the user point of view, a monitoring system should be as less intrusive as possible. Therefore, it is preferable that user will not notice they are being monitored. Following the philosophy of 'the simpler, the better', and from the power and resource consumption point of view, a algorithm of identifying user states should be as simple as possible, with the restrictions of acceptable accuracy of identifying.

Considering all these issues, we propose an empirical approach to design the algorithms of identifying user states. We then implement these identifying algorithms in a comprehensive user state monitoring system on Android smartphones, which conducts sensing and monitoring at real time. We have extensively evaluated the monitoring system in terms of both monitored state accuracy and footprint incurred while conduct monitoring to show its usefulness.

The rest of the paper is structured as follows: Sect. 2 presents how we design algorithms for the recongnition of user phsical and mental status in an empirical way. Then in Sect. 3, we present the design and implementation of the monitoring system using the proposed algorithms. Section 4 presents our tests on the recognitioin accuracy and also the performance of the monitoring system, and power consumption of the monitoring system. We compare our work with the related work in Sect. 5. Conclusions and future work end the paper.

2   Design of the Identifying Algorithms

There are various sensors coming with a smartphone, such as GPS, accelerometer, proximity, microphone, camera, light, and other sensors. According to our own experiences and the ones from the related work [5,7], accelerometers, GPSs, and microphones are useful in terms of non-intrusive sensor usage, acceptable power consumption when conduct sensing. In this paper, we will try to use these sensors to conduct the monitoring and identifying of still, walking, take stairs, driving, running for our daily activities, and also the mental states including anger, joy, sadness, fear, and normal.

2.1   Outdoor Activity Recognition with GPS

The outdoor activities can be conveniently recognized by measuring the user's speed by a GPS sensor. After the outdoor GPS positioning intialized, we took 11 measurements for the four activities, namely still, walking, running, and running in a car/bus. The results are shown in Fig. 1. From the chart, we can see that the speed for still state is always 0 (in m/s), no fluctuation is obtained; for walking, the speed measurements all fall in the range between 0 and 2; for running, the velocity is between 2 and 5; and usually the driving speed is greater than 5. Therefore, it is easy to design the algorithm for outdoor activity recognition.

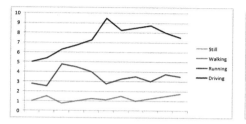
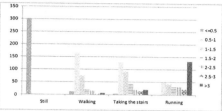

Fig. 1. Measured speed for outdoor activities

Fig. 2. Distribution of accelerations for various physical behaviors

2.2 Indoor Activity Recognition

According to some experimental measurements, in the same time duration, if there is no mechanical shock, diffrent physical acitivity will show different acceration features. The 'still' state will have the least acceleration fluctuations; while in walking, there will be a greater acceleration fluctuation than that in the still state; Similarly, if a user is in the running state, the fluctuations of the acceleration in a certain time will be even greater than the walking state. Based on this idea, we first investigate the threshhold values of linear acceleration fluctuations in the following state: stationary, walking, taking stairs and running.

For Andoid, the coordinate-system is defined relative to the screen of the phone in its default orientation: The X axis is horizontal and points to the right, the Y axis is vertical and points up and the Z axis points towards the outside of the front face of the screen[3]. In this system, coordinates behind the screen have negative Z values. Please note that although the measured acceration by a phone is divided into three axes, the specific location of the mobile phone and how a user carries it, can be ignored, i.e. it does not matter whether the mobile is in pocket or in a bag, whether the screen is facing up or its rear is facing up. The detection process are synchronized for values from all the three axes, and these values are equally important in the identifying algorithm.

To explore how the acceleration is sensed by the accelerometer and in what frequency it is sensed, we have done some preliminary tests with a Motorola ME 600. We found that the phone measures the linear acceleration around 10 times per second. We then do some more tests to check the distribution of the values of linear acceleration at different scale. Figure 2 shows the distribution of acceleration scales for different physical activities, including still, walking,

---

[3] http://developer.android.com/reference/android/hardware/SensorEvent.html.

running and walking stairs, with a 30 s measurement. In this 30 s duration, we obtained 303, 293, 318, 310 measurement respectively for the activity of still, walking, taking the stairs, and running. In Fig. 2, The vertical axis represents the number of detected values in the current range of distribution for a respective activity.

From the chart in Fig. 2, we found that for the still state, the majority (301 out of 303 measurements) of the absolute acceleration values for all the three axes are less than 0.5 (in m/s^2). For the walking activity, the majority of the the acceleration values are between 0.5 and 2.5 (273 out of 293 measurements). Looking at the running state, it is found that the largest proportion of acceleration values are greater than 2.5 (154 out of 310 measurements).

After this analysis, we can conclude that using a linear acceleration sensor to identify still, walking, running is possible by counting the number of the acceleration value ranges. Therefore using three flag variables to record the number of these ranges (one variable for the case of acceleration value less than 0.5, the other one for the situation of acceleration value greater than 0.5 and less than 2.5, the last one for the case of acceleration value greater than 2.5) obtained within a certain time is the key in the algorithm to differentiate what activity it is, as can be seen from Fig. 2.

It seemingly difficult to differentiate walking and taking the stairs as the differences of chart segments (Fig. 2) are not obvious. But walking is a one-dimensional movement, and walking the stairs is a two dimentional activity: besides the horizontal movement as walking, some fluctuations will occur for the vertical direction. A careful analysis of the chart in Fig. 2, we will find that the acceleration value between 1 to 2, there is big difference between walking and taking the stairs (92 vs. 134). Therefore, we use this to distinguish between these two activities. The corresponding algorithm is shown in Fig. 3.

We show in Fig. 4 the distibution of these four flags: flag1, flag2, flag3, and flag4 are used to represent the occurence of the activity of still, walking, running and taking the stairs respectively. As expected, in the still state, flag1 is the majority; in the walking state, the number of flag2 accounts for the majority; for the running activity, flag3 takes the biggest proportion. For taking the stairs, flag4 holds the highest proportion.

To help the senior citizens and those with walking faltering, the detecting of sudden falling down is of great importance in order to avoid accidental hurting from the falling, which paves the way for providing timely assistance from care centers and hospitals. We did some experiments with respect to the fluctuation of acceleration during the falling, and we found that the result is perfectly matching with the result from [6]. We show the measurements in Fig. 5. During the fall process, there is a big acceleration fluctuation returned from the acceleration sensor, and the peak of the fluctuations can be used as a basis to determine whether there is a fall. For simplicity, we can say that as long as the instantaneous peak of the acceleration is more than 4, there is a fall.

```
if (abs(x)<=0.5&&abs(y)<=0.5&&abs(z)<=0.5)
  {
  flag1++; //the number of 'still' state
  k++;
  } else
if (abs(x)>0.5&&abs(x)<=0.5||abs(y)>0.5
  &&abs(y)<=2.5||abs(z)>0.5&&abs(z)<= 2.5)
  {
  if ((abs(x)>1&&abs(y)>2)||(abs(y)>1&&abs(z)> 2)
  || (abs(x) > 1 && abs(z) > 2))
    {
    flag4++; //the number of 'taking the stairs'
    flag2 —;
    }
  flag2++; //the number of 'walking'
  k++;
  } else
if (abs(x)>2.5||abs(y)>2.5|| abs(z)>2.5)
  {
  flag3++; //the number of 'running'
  k++; //the number of total measurements
  }
if (k > 10)
  {
  if (flag1 >flag2&&flag1 >flag3&&flag1 >flag4)
  {
  IN STILL STATE
  } else
  if (flag2 >flag1&&flag2 >flag3&&flag2 >flag4)
    {
    IN WALKING STATE
    } else
  if (flag3 >flag1&&flag3 >flag2&&flag3 >flag4)
  {
  IN RUNNING STATE
  } else
  if (flag4 >flag1&&flag4 >flag2&&flag4 >flag3)
  {
  IN TAKING STAIRS STATE
  }
}
```

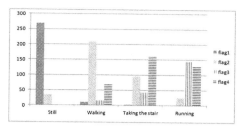

Fig. 4. Distribution of flags for various physical activities

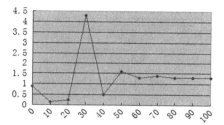

Fig. 3. Algorithm for identifying physical behaviors

Fig. 5. Fluctuation of accelerations while falling down

2.3 Mood Recognition

The recongnition of user's mental status is very important for helping users to keep good mood in order to recover from some chronic diseases, like ulcerative colitis. For the sensors equipped with an smartphone, there can be some choices on realizing the recognition of users' mood. The first choice is using the microphone to sense the speaking of the user, and then we analyze the speaking sigal to check what mood the user is in. The second choice is using the camera to check the pulse through measuring the absorbance of red light, which will vary when oxygenated blood is passing through the fingertips. But the second choice is not fairly reliable, since it requires good lighting conditions. Also this measurement is not convenient for a user to use. This leads us to choose the use of microphone as the sensor to recongnize users' mood.

Figure 6 shows the white noise for different mood. Based on the decision tree of mood recognition in the Chinese speaking environment [8] as shown in 7, we can design the corresponding mood recognition algorithm as shown in Fig. 8. The proportion of white noise values with respect to the total will be used to determine which branch to go along. The joy state has the highest white noise percentage, the percentage for anger mood is relatively high, in fear mood the percentage is at a medium level, the normal mood has relatively low percentage, with sadness mood has the lowest percentage.

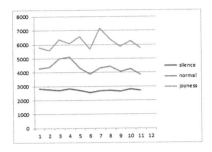

Fig. 6. White noise for different mood

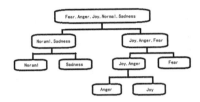

Fig. 7. Decision tree for mood recognition

```
if (flag1/kk>= 0.2) {
        if (flag1 / kk < 0.4) {
                IN FEAR
        } else
        if (flag1 /kk >= 0.4&& average >= 4500
                        && average <= 5500)
                {
                        IN ANGER
        } else
        if (flag1 / kk >= 0.4&& average >= 5500)
        {
                IN JOY
        } else {
                NOT RECOGNIZABLE
        }
} else {
        if (flag2 / kk >= 0.4|| flag3 / kk >= 0.4
                        && average >= 3800)
        {
                NORMAL
        } else
        if (flag3 / kk >= 0.5&& average <= 3800) {
                IN SADNESS
        } else {
                NOT RECOGNIZABLE
        }
}
```

Fig. 8. Algorithm for mood recognition

3   Design and Implementation of the User State Monitoring System

We adopted the MVC (Model-View-controller) style in the design of the user state monitoring system in order to provide a low coupling and easily maintainable system to increase its reusability. The Model components contain data variables for the monitory system, the controller is responsible to conduct a series of logical operations by calling these data variables, and then display the corresponding results in a variety of Android 'Activity's which serve as the View component in the MVC style (Fig. 9).

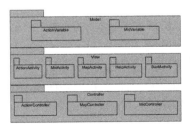

Fig. 9. Design of the user state monitoring system

Fig. 10. Activity recognition with accelerometer

Android provides a SensorManager class to facilitate the usage of various physical sensors, including accelerometers. To use a concrete type of sensor, the first thing is to get this type of sensor service from the SensorManager, and then to register a sensor event listner using an object of SensorEventListener class. The retrieving of sensor data resides in a onSensorChanged method specified in the SensorEventListener interface. The usage of microphone and GPS is similar. Figures 10, 11 and 12 shows the running results of monitoring and recognition.

4   Evaluations of the User State Monitoring System

To make evaluations, we used the Motorola ME600 phone is the primary test bed. We then checked these measurements on Sony Ericsson X10, which is consistent with the running results.

The first thing we need to check is how accurately that the moniting system can obtain user states. The tests are shown in Table 1. We can see that the monitoring system can get satisfied results with accuracy around 85 %.

Table 1. Accuracy of the monitored physical acitivities

											Accuracy
Still	y	y	y	y	y	y	y	y	y	y	100 %
Walking	y	y	y	y		y	y	y	y	y	90 %
Go stairs	y	y	y	y	y	y	y		y	y	90 %
Running	y		y		y	y	y	y	y	y	80 %

Table 2. Accuracy of mood monitoring

							Accuracy
Joy	y	y	y	y		y	83.33 %
Anger	y	y			y		50.00 %
Fear	y	y	y		y	y	83.33 %
Normal			y	y	y		50.00 %
Sadness	y	y		y		y	66.66 %

As we are aiming at using the monitoring system at run time, therefore it is important that the monitoring system has little incurrence of footprints at run time, especially during the time of the switching of phsical activity, for example from still to walking. We have tested the performance of the activity switching in Table 3, showing in milleseconds. We can that it takes less than 1 s for the monitoring system to notice the changing of physical activies (the total average time is).

We also measured the accuracy of mood recognition as shown in Table 2. We can see that the accuracy of mood recognition is at an OK level of identifying the correct type of mood, which will be one of the main focus areas for us to improve the recognition algorithm.

To be usable as a service running on smartphones, the monitoring system should consume as less battery as possible. Therefore we also measured the battery consumption (in terms of Joule) for our system as show in Table 4, where Acc. stands for the power consumption of accelerometer based physical activity recognition, followed by are the LCD and CPU power consumptions respectively when the accelerometer is working; and Mic stands for the power consumptoins for the microphone based mood recognition, again the power consumptions of

Table 3. Time taken to recognize switched phsical acitivity

	Still	Walking	Taking stairs	Running
Still		368	622	501
		193	698	98
		297	354	298
		301	436	293
		94	188	101
Average		250.6	459.6	258.2
Walking	205		532	398
	201		299	165
	297		165	100
	100		301	100
	196		298	499
Average	199.8		319	252.4
Running	894	307	765	
	698	300	587	
	1800	200	309	
	802	402	679	
	895	697	319	
Average	1017.8	381.2	537.8	
Taking stairs	288	375		638
	451	531		454
	399	831		521
	657	342		437
	621	426		528
Average	483.2	501		515

Table 4. Battery consumption of the monitoring system

Acc	LCD	CPU	Mic	LCD	CPU	GPS	LCD	CPU
61.1	54.6	5.5	61.7	58.5	3.2	56.2	54	2.2
55.2	50.3	4.9	61.2	57.6	3.6	53.3	52.1	1.2
55.5	50.4	5.1	63.1	59.4	3.7	57.6	55.8	1.8
58.4	53.1	5.3	60.2	56.7	3.4	53.3	52.1	1.2
62	56.7	5.3	61.2	57.6	3.6	55.5	53.6	1.9
59.4	54	5.4	62.4	58.7	3.7	56.2	54	2.2
60.4	54.9	5.5	60.2	56.7	3.4	56.7	54.9	1.8
57.5	52.2	5.3	55.3	52.2	3.1	55.8	54	1.8
58.9	54	4.8	58.9	55.8	3.1	57.2	55.6	1.6
59.4	54	5.3	55.2	52.2	3	53.2	52	1.2
58.78	53.42	5.24	59.94	56.54	3.38	55.5	53.81	1.69

LCD and CPU follow. The last line of the table is the average of the measureed values. These measurements were done in one minutes (60 s). Therefore, the monitoring system consums around 1 W (including the power consumption for LCD, which accouts for the majority of the power consumption), which is usable for a long time and everyday usage. We have used PowerTutor[4] for measuring power consumption. Please note if the monitoring is running as a service, which will rule out the power consumption from the LCD mostly, then the power consumption of the monitoring system is more or less neglectalbe, which is advantageous to be used to monitor physical activities and mental status in everyday life.

5   Related Work

Due to the importance of user state monitoring in the domain of context-aware service provisioning, e-health, and so on, there are increasingly more work on using smartphones to conduct this monitoring.

---

[4] http://ziyang.eecs.umich.edu/projects/powertutor/.

 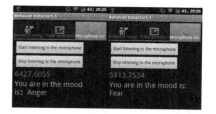

Fig. 11. Activity recognition with GPS sensor

Fig. 12. Mood recognition running results

The work on monitoring physical activities using machine learning techniques [7], where it can achieve 97.7 % percentage of correct recognition of the activities. It used offline monitoring by measuring 5 to minutes and then use machine learning to identify activities. We are targetting real time monitoring for both physical activities and mental states. Due to the simplicity of our algorithms and approach, we believe that our monitoring system consume less battery that the machine learning approach, though there is no mention of power consumption aspect in [7].

In [6], the detection of falling is the main contribution using the accelerometer. Our experiments are consistent with this work, and the same parameters are used for detecting the falling down state. We go beyond this work by providing a comprehensive set of tools for monitoring both physical and mental states. We also provide comprehensive evaluations to test the usability of our monitoring system. Considering the resource limitations on smartphones, we did not consider the complex machine learning techniques for the recognition of users' mood as in [8], which would be not practical on resource scarce devices to realize real time requirements.

Similarly, accelerometers are used to in [5] to identify user physical activities. The recognition approach is divided into data collection, feature extraction and activity recogniton phases. This is similar to what we are doing in this work. But the work in [5] is conduct monitoring in an offline way, we are doing online recognition instead. Both our work and the work in [5] achieve the same level of accuracy. but as we are conduct recognition at run time, besides we are monitoring more user states that include mental states.

In [2], data of daily activities such as walking, climbing stairs, sitting, and standing, are transferred to an Internet-based server where a static model is generated offline. This may incur security problems for a user due to the privacy is not completely guarantted. This approach is different to what are doing in our work for online monitoring. Due to the complexity of the recognition of users' mood, this may become a choice for us to pursue in the near future in order to improve the accuracy of the mood recognition in the proposed monitoring system.

On the contrary to the work using offline static classification models as in [1, 2] proposed Mobile Activity Recognition System (MARS), where an on-board classifier for mobile devices to conduct acitivity recognition is used. It provides also adaptation of the model as the user's activity profile changes. In our work, we are not using any machine learning techniques (yet), but simple empirical way to design recognition algorithms, where 'the simpler, the better' philosophy is adopted in order to save resources and power consumption for the monitoring system. From the evaluations of MARS, we can see that it consumes a lot of battery (within an hour, battery level from 70 % drops to 0). We can see that MARS is not suitable for long time usage as a daily service, which is the very target of our work.

There are some work that make use external sensors to monitor the bio-environmental tracking for users, for example the BEAT system [4] using a blue-tooth wrist sensor to monitor heart rate.s The power consumption of the BEAT system is around 550 mW, which is a problem for draining battery as said by the authors. In our work, we do not want to use any other devices at all to facilitate the monitoring and relieve users from the trouble of wearing extra devices.

6   Conclusions and Future Work

In this paper, we have presented a lightweight but comprehensive user state monitoring system based on some algorithms using empirical expriments. Extensive evaluations show that our work consumes neglectable battery, with acceptable accuracy of state recognition, including both physical activities and mental activities. The monitoring system is usable at real time with little incurrence of footprints for user state changes. Compared with existing work, the main contributions lie in the lightweight of the monitoring system for real time and long time usage, with acceptable accuracy of state recognition.

In the future, we will expand the current work by improving mood recognition accuracy using some machine learning techniques. Compared to the physical activiy monitoring, the mental activity monitoring do not need a fast response, some lag during recognition is allowed in order to improve the accuracy of recognition. We will also add some adaptation features as done in [1] in order to cater for the varieties of characteristics of different users. The monitoring system will be further tested by more device types and user groups, which will be connected with our e-health research prototype. Another direction we are going to work is to make use the pervasive cloud infrastructure we have developed [9–11] to make the recognition of user states more precise, based on the storage and computing capabilities from the backend cloud nodes.

References

1. Gomes, J.B., Krishnaswamy, S., Gaber, M.M., Sousa, P.A.C., Menasalvas, E.: Mobile activity recognition using ubiquitous data stream mining. In: Cuzzocrea, A., Dayal, U. (eds.) DaWaK 2012. LNCS, vol. 7448, pp. 130–141. Springer, Heidelberg (2012)

2. Kwapisz, J., Weiss, G., Moore, S.: Activity recognition using cell phone accelerometers. ACM SIGKDD Explor. Newsl. **12**(2), 74–82 (2011)
3. Lane, N., Miluzzo, E., Lu, H., Peebles, D., Choudhury, T., Campbell, A.: A survey of mobile phone sensing. IEEE Commun. Mag. **48**(9), 140–150 (2010)
4. Mitchell, M., Sposaro, F., Wang, A., Tyson, G.: Beat: bio-environmental android tracking. In: IEEE Radio and Wireless Symposium (RWS) 2011, pp. 402–405. IEEE (2011)
5. Sönercan, M., Dinçer, S.: User state tracking using smartphones
6. Sposaro, F., Tyson, G.: iFall: an android application for fall monitoring and response. In: Annual International Conference of the IEEE Engineering in Medicine and Biology Society, EMBC 2009, pp. 6119–6122. IEEE (2009)
7. Sun, L., Zhang, D., Li, N.: Physical activity monitoring with mobile phones. In: Abdulrazak, B., Giroux, S., Bouchard, B., Pigot, H., Mokhtari, M. (eds.) ICOST 2011. LNCS, vol. 6719, pp. 104–111. Springer, Heidelberg (2011)
8. Zhang, S.: Emotion recognition by speech signal in madarin. Doctorate Degree dissertation of China University of Science and Technology (2007)
9. Zhang, W., Chen, L., Liu, X., et al.: An osgi-based flexible and adaptive pervasive cloud infrastructure. Sci. China Inf. Sci. **57**(3), 1–11 (2014). http://dx.doi.org/10.1007/s11432-014-5070-3
10. Zhang, W., Chen, L., Lu, Q., et al.: Towards an osgi based pervasive cloud infrastructure. In: 2013 IEEE International Conference on and IEEE Cyber, Physical and Social Computing. pp. 418–425. IEEE (2013)
11. Zhang, W., Chen, L., Lu, Q., Zhang, P., Yang, S.: Flexible component migration in an OSGi based pervasive cloud infrastructure. In: Lomuscio, A.R., Nepal, S., Patrizi, F., Benatallah, B., Brandić, I. (eds.) ICSOC 2013. LNCS, vol. 8377, pp. 505–514. Springer, Heidelberg (2014)

Developing Service Platform for Web Context-Aware Services Towards Self-Managing Ecosystem

Hiroki Takatsuka[✉], Sachio Saiki, Shinsuke Matsumoto,
and Masahide Nakamura

Graduate School of System Informatics, Kobe University, Kobe, Japan
tktk@ws.cs.kobe-u.ac.jp, sachio@carp.kobe-u.ac.jp,
{shinsuke,masa-n}@cs.kobe-u.ac.jp

Abstract. The convergence of cloud/service computing and M2M/IoT systems provides real-world sensing and actuation as globally distributed Web services. Context-aware services using such Web services (we call them *Web Context-Aware Services, Web-CAS*) are promising in many systems. However, definition of contexts and Web services to be used highly depend on individual environments and preferences. Therefore, it is essential to have a place for self-management, where individual users can efficiently manage their own Web-CAS by themselves. In this paper, we develop a service platform, called *RuCAS platform*, which works as PaaS for self-managing Web-CAS. In the platform, contexts and actions are defined by adapting the distributed Web services, and every Web-CAS is managed in form of an *ECA (Event-Condition-Action) rule*. Through Web-API of RuCAS, individual clients can rapidly create, update, delete and execute custom contexts and services. To support non-expert users, we implement a GUI front-end of the RuCAS platform, called *RuCAS.me*. A case study of sustainable air-conditioning demonstrates practical feasibility. Finally, we discuss how the RuCAS platform works to achieve self-managing ecosystem of Web-CAS.

Keywords: Web services · Context-awareness · Self-management · Event-condition-action rule · Home network system

1 Introduction

A *context* refers to situational information derived from dynamic data of a sensor or a system. A *context-aware service* is a service that automatically detects a change of contexts and performs appropriate actions corresponding to the context change [7]. For instance, a context Hot can be derived from information that "the value of a temperature sensor in a room is higher than 28 degrees". An example of context-aware service, say "Automatic Air-conditioning", turns on an air-conditioner when the context Hot holds. Traditionally, such context-aware services had been studied extensively in ubiquitous/pervasive computing,

© Springer International Publishing Switzerland 2015
F. Toumani et al. (Eds.): ICSOC 2014, LNCS 8954, pp. 270–280, 2015.
DOI: 10.1007/978-3-319-22885-3_24

where each contexts was defined using situated sensors [15] or hand-held devices (e.g., smartphone) within a local smart space [4].

However, cloud/service computing [13] and IoT/M2M technologies [14] dramatically extend the scope of context-aware services. Cloud/service computing abstracts heterogeneous computing resources and data, and provides them as interoperable Web services. IoT/M2M allow various devices to communicate with each other without human intervention. The combination of both technologies provides real-world sensing and actuation as globally distributed Web services. Relevant studies include *LinkSmart middleware* [6], *service-oriented home network system* [10], and *sensor service framework* [9]. Using such Web services to build context-aware services is a promising approach, since a wide variety of contexts and actions can be seamlessly defined over distributed and heterogeneous resources. In this paper, we refer to such context-aware services with Web services as *Web context-aware services* (or simply *Web-CAS*).

A major challenge of Web-CAS lies in how to manage unstable and complex relations among Web services, defined contexts, and actions caused by the contexts. In general, definition of contexts and Web services to be used highly depend on individual environments and preferences. For instance, in the Automatic Air-conditioning service, which temperature sensor and air-conditioner should be used depends on the room where the service is operated. The definition of Hot context with 28 degree may not be reasonable in winter. A user may prefer to turn on a fan instead of the expensive air-conditioner. To meet various requirements and preferences, every Web-CAS should not be hard-coded. Instead, it is essential to have a place for self-management, where individual users can efficiently manage own Web-CAS by themselves.

In this paper, we develop a service platform, called *RuCAS platform*. Intuitively, it works as PaaS (Platform-as-a-Service), which provides self-managing Web-CAS capabilities for various clients. The RuCAS platform is designed specifically based on the following three requirements: (**R1**) every context-aware service can be defined by arbitrary Web services in an intuitive and systematic manner, (**R2**) individual client can dynamically create, update, delete and execute custom contexts, actions and services, (**R3**) even non-expert users can develop and manage their own context-aware services. As far as we know, there exists no service platform satisfying all the requirements.

To satisfy requirement R1, RuCAS manages every Web-CAS in form of an *ECA (Event-Condition-Action) rule*. The event is a context that triggers a service. The condition refers to a guard condition to execute the service. The action is a Web service executed by the service. As for requirement R2, we implement the platform with five layers: *Web service layer, adapter layer, context layer, action layer* and *ECA rule layer*. Each layer exhibits Web-API (REST or SOAP) so that individual clients can manage their own elements. Finally, to meet requirement R3, we implement a GUI front-end of the RuCAS platform, called *RuCAS.me*. Based on an intuitive user interface, a user can easily create and manage adapters, contexts, actions, and ECA rules within the RuCAS platform.

To evaluate practical feasibility, we conduct a case study using the RuCAS platform and RuCAS.me. Integrating an external Web service with our home network system [10], we implement a sustainable air-conditioning service, which contributes to peak shaving of regional energy consumption. We also discuss how the RuCAS platform works to achieve *self-managing ecosystem* of Web-CAS.

2 RuCAS: Rule-Based Management Framework for Web Context-Aware Services

RuCAS (Rule-based management framework for Web Context-Aware Service) is a service framework, specifically designed to help individual clients (human users and software applications) to easily create and manage their own Web-CAS.

2.1 Event-Condition-Action (ECA) Rule

The *ECA rule* is an important design decision of RuCAS, which defines every Web-CAS as a triplet of [Event, Condition, Action]. This design decision is to implement Web-CAS by *loose coupling* of Web services as data sources, contexts defined with the data sources, and actions to be performed by the contexts.

A context-aware service can be described by a rule that "when a context becomes true, do something". Intuitively, the part "when a context becomes true" corresponds to the *event*, whereas "do something" corresponds to the *action*. However, the above rule lacks flexibility, because the action always fires when the context becomes true. Therefore, we extend the rule a bit such that "when a context becomes true, if a condition is satisfied, do something". The part "if a condition is satisfied" corresponds to the *condition*. More specifically,

- A *context* is a situational information defined by a logical expression over data obtained from a Web service. Depending on the value of the data, every context is evaluated to true or false. A context can be also defined by a composition of the existing contexts.
- An *event* is a context triggering the execution of a context-aware service.
- A *condition* is a guard condition enabling the execution of a context-aware service. A condition is defined as a conjunction of one or more contexts.
- An *action* is a set of operations executed by a context-aware service. An action is defined by one or more Web services.
- *ECA Rule:* Let $c_1, c_2, ...$ be contexts, and let $a_1, a_2, ...$ be invocations of Web services. An ECA rule r is defined by $r = [E : c_i, C : \{c_{j_1}, c_{j_2}, ..., c_{j_m}\}, A : \{a_{k_1}, a_{k_2}, ..., a_{k_n}\}]$, where E is an event, C is a condition, A is an action. For r, we say "event E occurs" if the value of context c_i moves from false to true. When E occurs, if all contexts $c_{j_1}, c_{j_2}, ..., c_{j_m}$ are satisfied, we say "r is executed". When r is executed, all Web services $a_{k_1}, a_{k_2}, ..., a_{k_n}$ are invoked.

For instance, a context-aware service "when it is hot, if a user is present in a room, turn on an air-conditioner" can be described by an ECA rule: $[E : Hot, C : \{PresentUser\}, A : \{AC.on\}]$. Thus, the ECA rules give an intuitive but systematic foundation to define Web-CAS, which satisfies the requirement R1.

2.2   RuCAS Platform: RuCAS as Service Platform

To allow various clients to dynamically manage their own contexts, actions and ECA rules via network, we implement RuCAS as a service platform. The implementation is deployed in a cloud as PaaS (Platform-as-a-Service).

Figure 1 represents a system architecture of the RuCAS platform. To build ECA rules from loosely-coupled components, the platform consists of five layers: Web service layer, adapter layer, context layer, action layer and ECA rule layer.

Web Service Layer: This layer contains existing Web services used as *input* or *output* of Web-CAS. The input Web service is a Web service that can return a certain value (e.g., numeric, Boolean, string, etc.) for defining a context. Typical examples include a value from a sensor service, status of a device, dynamic Web information (e.g., weather, stock price), RSS, clock, system logs. The output Web service is a Web service that can yield an action. Examples include an operation of home network system (e.g., switch on/off, voice announce, etc.) and a request to an information system (e.g., send an email, post a comment to SNS, etc.).

Adapter Layer: To obtain data from an input Web service, a client needs to invoke Web-API and extract necessary data by parsing the return value. However, Web-API and the return value vary from one service to another. Hence, this layer creates an *adapter* that normalizes the heterogeneous interface. Specifically, every Web-API used to obtain data is adapted to `getValue()`. For example, we can create `TempAdapter`, with a temperature Web-API, say http://www. hns/TemperatureSensorService/getTemperature. RuCAS adapts the Web-API so that `TempAdapter.getValue()` returns the temperature.

Context Layer: This context layer manages contexts defined by data from Web services via the adapter layer. Every context is defined by *context ID* and *context*

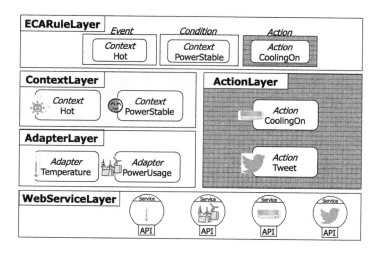

Fig. 1. Architecture of RuCAS platform

expression. The context ID is a label to identify every context. The context expression is a logical formula, in the form of `Adapter.value comp_op const`, where `comp_op` is a comparison operator and `const` is a constant value. For example, to define `Hot` context to be "the temperature is more than 28 degrees", RuCAS describes it by `[Hot: TempAdapter.value > 28]`. Similarly, to define `Humid` to be "the humidity is more than 70 percent", RuCAS describes it by `[Humid: HumidAdapter.value > 70]`. Each context can be associated with a *refresh interval*, by which RuCAS periodically evaluates the context expression. For example, when the refresh interval of `Hot` is one minute, RuCAS obtains a new value from `TempAdapter` and evaluates `Hot` every minute.

RuCAS can define two types of contexts: *atomic* and *compound.* The atomic context is a context directly defined by a single Web service. The compound context is a context defined by the existing contexts combined with logical operators (`!`: NOT, `&&`: AND, `||`: OR). For example, a compound context `Muggy` can be defined by combining `Hot` and `Humid` such that `[Muggy: Hot && Humid]`.

Action Layer: This layer manages actions, each of which wraps an output Web service. An action is defined by an endpoint, a method name, and parameters of the Web service. Each action is associated with *action ID*, by which RuCAS invoke the Web service as an action. For example, we create an action `CoolingOn`, by using an air-conditioner service, say http://www.hns/ACService/on?mode=cooling. When RuCAS invokes `CoolingOn`, the Web service is executed to turn on an air-conditioner with a cooling mode.

ECA Rule Layer: The ECA rule layer defines context-aware services as ECA rules. An ECA rule can be created as follows:

1. Define an event by choosing a single context from the context layer.
2. Define a condition by choosing one or more contexts from the context layer.
3. Define an action by choosing one or more actions from the action layer.

The created ECA rules are *executed* based on the semantics (see Sect. 2.1).

To meet the requirement R2, each layer exhibits Web-API to create, update, delete and execute the custom elements. Using REST or SOAP protocol, clients in various platforms can execute the Web-API to self-manage their Web-CAS. The RuCAS platform was implemented with the following technologies: **Language:** Java 1.7.0_21, **Database:** MongoDB 2.4.3, **Web server:** Apache Tomcat 7.0.39, **Web service engine:** Apache Axis2 1.6.2.

2.3   RuCAS.me

We have also developed a Web application, called *RuCAS.me*, to support non-expert users who are unfamiliar with Web service programming (see the requirement R3). RuCAS.me works as a GUI front-end of the RuCAS platform.

Figure 2 shows screenshots, with which a user can easily create, edit and delete own RuCAS elements (adapter, context, action, ECA rule) using a Web browser. Figure 2 (a) shows the index page of RuCAS.me consisting of four

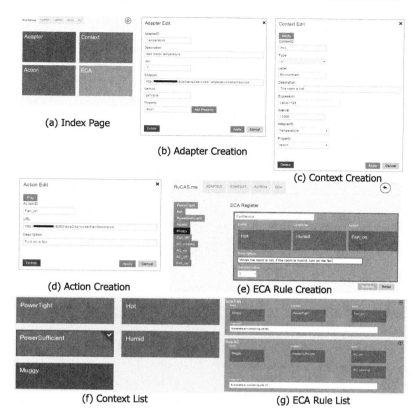

(a) Index Page

(b) Adapter Creation

(c) Context Creation

(d) Action Creation

(e) ECA Rule Creation

(f) Context List

(g) ECA Rule List

Fig. 2. Screenshots of RuCAS.me

buttons to manage the four elements. Figure 2 (b) shows an adapter creation page. By filling the form and pressing the apply button, a new adapter is created within the RuCAS platform. Figure 2 (c) shows a context creation page. By filling the form and pressing the apply button, a new context is created within the RuCAS platform. A created context is enumerated in a context list page (see Fig. 2 (f)), where a user can manage the existing contexts. As shown in the figure, a context that currently holds appears as a checked box. This helps a user understand the current situation. Figure 2 (d) shows an action creation page. By filling the form and pressing the apply button, a new action is created within the RuCAS platform.

Figure 2 (e) shows an ECA rule creation page. The list in the left side of the page enumerates contexts and actions that are already registered in the platform. From the list, a user just selects a preferred context for an event, one or more contexts for a condition and one or more actions. The selected elements appear in the rule pane (in the right side), in the form of ECA rule. In this figure, a user creates an ECA rule to implement a context-aware service *FanService*: "when

Table 1. Parameters for creating adapters

Adapterid	Endpoint	Method	Property
Temperature	http://www.cs27-hns/sensor/temperature	getValue	return
Humidity	http://www.cs27-hns/sensor/humidity	getValue	return
PowerDemand	http://setsuden.yahooapis.jp/Setsuden	latestPowerUsage	{usage,capacity}

Table 2. Parameters for creating contexts

Contextid	Type	Adapter	Expression	Interval	Description
Hot	A	Temperature	value>=28	5000	It is hot in lab
Humid	A	Humidity	value>=80	5000	It is humid in lab
Muggy	C	—	Hot&&Humid	5000	It is muggy in lab
PowerSufficient	A	PowerDemand	value<20000000	1800000	Power demand is sufficient in Kansai region
PowerTight	A	PowerDemand	value>=20000000	1800000	Power demand is tight in Kansai region

Table 3. Parameters for creating actions

Actionid	url	Description
Fan_on	http://www.cs27-hns/appliance/fan/on	Turn on a fan
AC_on	http://www.cs27-hns/appliance/AC/on	Turn on an AC
AC_cooling	http://www.cs27-hns/appliance/AC/cooling	Drive an AC in cooling mode

the room is hot, if the room is humid, turn on the fan". A created ECA rule is enumerated in an ECA list page (see Fig. 2 (g)) to manage existing rules.

RuCAS.me was implemented with the following technologies: **Language:** JavaScript, HTML5, **JavaScript Library:** jQuery 2.0.3, **CSS framework:** TwitterBootstrap v3.0.3, bootmetro, **Tested Browser:** Google Chrome 33.0.

3   Case Study: Sustainable Air-Conditioning Service

To illustrate the practical feasibility of the developed system, we create the *sustainable air-conditioning service*. This service performs automatic air-conditioning in our laboratory (CS27), when the lab becomes muggy. For this, if the regional power demand (in Kansai area) is sufficient, turn on an air-conditioner. However, if the demand is tight, use a fan that consumes much lower energy. To implement the service, we use the following Web services:

- **Temperature/Humidity Sensor Services** [9]: Web services that obtain room temperature and humidity of in CS27.
- **Power Demand API** [3]: External Web service that obtains the current power demand in Japan Kansai region, provided by Yahoo Japan.
- **Appliance Control Service** [10]: Web service that controls appliances in the lab, including the air-conditioner and the fan.

Table 4. Parameters for creating ECA

ecaid	Event	Condition	Action	Description
Sus_AC	Muggy	PowerSufficient	{AC_on, AC_cooling}	Air-conditioning with an AC
Sus_Fan	Muggy	PowerTight	Fan_on	Air-conditioning with a fan

Using RuCAS.me, we create the service based on the following recipe:

Step 1 (Creating Adapters): We first create three adapters `Temperature`, `Humidity` and `PowerDemand`, using the temperature/humidity sensor services and the power demand API. The parameters are summarized in Table 1.

Step 2 (Creating Contexts): Using the adapters, we then create five contexts `Hot`, `Humid`, `Muggy`, `PowerSufficient` and `PowerTight`. In this case study, `Hot` (or `Humid`) is defined as a situation that `Temperature` (or `Humidity`) is greater or equal to 28 degrees (or 80 percent, respectively). `Muggy` is defined as a compound context `Hot && Humid`. These three contexts are refreshed every 5 seconds. Using `PowerDemand`, we also create two contexts `PowerSufficient` and `PowerTight`. Here, the threshold of the tight demand is set to 20,000,000 kW, and refresh interval is set to 30 min. Parameters for each context are summarized in Table 2. Figure 2 (f) shows RuCAS.me where the five contexts are registered.

Step 3 (Creating Actions): Using the appliance control service, we create three actions `Fan_on` (turn on a fan), `AC_on` (turn on an air-conditioner) and `AC_cooling` (drive an air-conditioner in cooling mode), as shown in Table 3.

Step 4 (Creating ECA Rule): Finally, we create two ECA rules `Sus_AC` and `Sus_Fan` to implement the sustainable air-conditioner service. `Sus_AC` corresponds to the scenario: "when it is muggy in the lab, if the power demand is sufficient, turn on an air-conditioner". `Sus_Fan` corresponds to the scenario where the demand is tight and the service uses a fan. The parameters for each rule are summarized in Table 4. Figure 2 (g) shows the two rules are created.

4   Discussion

4.1   Operating RuCAS Platform for Self-Managing Ecosystem

The RuCAS platform can be a key component for *self-managing ecosystem*, which alleviates increasing complexity, scale and development/operation cost of Web-CAS. Figure 3 shows a block diagram involving the RuCAS platform and related components. A solid arrow represents a manual (or proprietary) operation performed by a user, while a dotted arrow represents an autonomic operation.

First, individual users create custom contexts and ECA rules (with RuCAS.me or proprietary client software). For given rules, the RuCAS platform periodically pulls current status from distributed Web services, and actuates designated Web services. This forms a small ecosystem as depicted by a

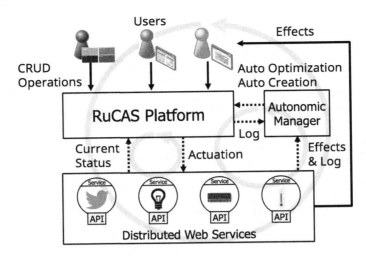

Fig. 3. RuCAS platform as component of self-management ecosystem

left-small circle. The actuation of the Web service yields some *effects* within the global/local environment. The users monitor the effects, and update contexts and rules if needed. This forms a global ecosystem depicted by a large circle.

It is also promising to integrate an external *autonomic manager*, which conducts autonomic creation and optimization of contexts and ECA rules. This causes an extra ecosystem depicted as a right-small circle in Fig. 3. The integration is quite easy, since the RuCAS platform is interoperable with any other system via Web-API. We are currently developing an autonomic manager for our home network system with referring to related studies (e.g., [5,16]).

4.2   Related Work

As for self-managing pervasive systems, Zhang et al. proposed a semantic web based approach [16], and Ada et al. [5] proposed extension of iPOJO. They aim to satisfy four aspects of self-management [8] (i.e., self-configuration, self-optimization, self-healing and self-protection), by managing all pervasive objects under a proprietary middleware. On the other hand, RuCAS coordinates existing distributed Web services, for which we cannot enforce a specific middleware.

Several studies of context-awareness with Web services exist. Rasch et al. proposed a context-driven personalized service discovery system [12]. Niu et al. proposed *CARSA* [11], a context-aware AI planning of Web service composition. These studies use contexts to improve an accuracy of Web service discovery and composition. Whereas, RuCAS aims the systematic self-management of custom context-aware services using Web services. Thus, the targets are different.

Practical services for self-managing context-aware services recently come onto the market. *IFTTT* [1] coordinates various network services (e.g., Gmail, Twitter, RSS feeds, etc.) based on a rule of "if this then that". *WigWag* [2] defines custom context-aware services based on "when then" logic over proprietary sensors and control devices. These services basically use *ready-made* data source (called channel) to define events and actions. RuCAS differs in using custom data sources by creating adapters for arbitrary Web services. Also IFTTT and WigWag basically use an event and an action only, while our ECA rule uses a condition together with them. This makes RuCAS more expressive.

5   Conclusion

In this paper, we have developed the RuCAS platform for self-managing context-aware services with distributed Web services (Web-CAS). In the platform, contexts, actions and services are systematically managed by five layers: Web service, adapter, context, action and ECA rule. Using Web-API, individual clients can manage their own context-aware services efficiently and flexibly. To support non-expert users, We also developed a GUI front-end, RuCAS.me. A case study demonstrated the practical feasibility. Finally, we discussed how the RuCAS platform work within the self-managing ecosystem of Web-CAS.

Our future work includes development of the autonomic manager discussed in Sect. 4.1, investigation of self-healing and self-protection aspects of Web-CAS.

Acknowledgments. This research was partially supported by the Japan Ministry of Education, Science, Sports, and Culture [Grant-in-Aid for Scientific Research (C) (No. 24500079, No. 24500258), (B) (No. 26280115), Young Scientists (B) (No. 26730155)] and Kawanishi Memorial ShinMaywa Education Foundation.

References

1. IFTTT. https://ifttt.com. Accessed 30 July 2014
2. Wigwag. http://www.wigwag.com. Accessed 30 July 2014
3. Yahoo JAPAN Web API. http://developer.yahoo.co.jp/webapi/shinsai. Accessed 30 July 2014
4. Chon, Y., Cha, H.: Lifemap: a smartphone-based context provider for location-based services. Trans. Pervasive Comput. 10(2), 58–67 (2011)
5. Diaconescu, A., Bourcier, J., Escoffier, C.: Autonomic iPOJO: towards self-managing middleware for ubiquitous systems. In: IEEE International Conference on Wireless and Mobile Computing, Networking and Communications, pp. 472–477 (2008)
6. Eisenhauer, M., Rosengren, P., Antolin, P.: Hydra: a development platform for integrating wireless devices and sensors into ambient intelligence systems. In: Giusto, D., Iera, A., Morabito, G., Atzori, L. (eds.) The Internet of Things, pp. 367–373. Springer, New York (2010)
7. Gu, T., Pung, H.K., Zhang, D.Q.: A service-oriented middleware for building context-aware services. J. Netw. Comput. Appl. 28(1), 1–18 (2005)
8. Kephart, J., Chess, D.: The vision of autonomic computing. Computer 36(1), 41–50 (2003)
9. Nakamura, M., Matsuo, S., Matsumoto, S., Sakamoto, H., Igaki, H.: Application framework for efficient development of sensor as a service for home network system. In: International Conference on Services Computing, pp. 576–583 (2011)

10. Nakamura, M., Tanaka, A., Igaki, H., Tamada, H., Matsumoto, K.: Constructing home network systems and integrated services using legacy home appliances and Web services. Int. J. Web Serv. Res. **5**(1), 82–98 (2008)

11. Niu, W., Li, G., Tang, H., Zhou, X., Shi, Z.: CARSA: a context-aware reasoning-based service agent model for AI planning of Web service composition. J. Netw. Comput. Appl. **34**(5), 1757–1770 (2011)

12. Rasch, K., Li, F., Sehic, S., Ayani, R., Dustdar, S.: Context-driven personalized service discovery in pervasive environments. World Wide Web **14**(4), 295–319 (2011)

13. Velte, T., Velte, A., Elsenpeter, R.: Cloud Computing, A Practical Approach, 1st edn. McGraw-Hill Inc, New York (2010)

14. Wu, G., Talwar, S., Johnsson, K., Himayat, N., Johnson, K.: M2M: from mobile to embedded internet. IEEE Commun. Mag. **49**(4), 36–43 (2011)

15. Yamamoto, S., Kouyama, N., Yasumoto, K., Ito, M.: Maximizing users comfort levels through user preference estimation in public smartspaces. In: International Conference on Pervasive Computing and Communications Workshops, pp. 572–577 (2011)

16. Zhang, W., Hansen, K.: Semantic web based self-management for a pervasive service middleware. In: Second IEEE International Conference on Self-Adaptive and Self-Organizing Systems, pp. 245–254 (2008)

Retrieving Sensors Data in Smart Buildings Through Services: A Similarity Algorithm

Claudia Foglieni, Mirjana Mazuran, Giovanni Meroni,
and Pierluigi Plebani[✉]

Politecnico di Milano – Dipartimento di Elettronica, Informazione e Bioingegneria,
Piazza Leonardo da Vinci 32, 20133 Milano, Italy
foglieni.claudia@gmail.com,
{mirjana.mazuran,pierluigi.plebani}@polimi.it,
giovanni2.meroni@mail.polimi.it

Abstract. This paper proposes a semantic-based retrieval algorithm
that allows the pervasive service system to find services able to return
data about specific physical phenomenon (e.g. temperature, humidity), in
a given location, with particular timeliness. This retrieval algorithm can
be used to increase the capabilities of a self-managing pervasive systems,
with specific focus on smart buildings, by providing a flexible solution
to find sensors similar to a one that failed, or to find sensor data able to
control actuators.

1 Introduction

The diffusion of wireless and wired sensor networks led to the development of
pervasive systems. An example are *smart buildings*, where sensors are deployed
in residential, commercial and industrial buildings to monitor and control the
installed devices. Service oriented architectures have been adopted to implement
these pervasive systems and to hide the technical heterogeneity and the complexity of the deployed devices [1]. In this way, sensors are seen as services and
the communication with them can be performed as a service invocation. Especially when heterogeneous sensor networks are considered, this pervasive service
system can overcame the limitations caused by the vendor lock-in problem.

Goal of this paper is to propose an algorithm for retrieving sensors, seen
as services, able to return data about a specific phenomenon, in a given location, with particular timeliness. This algorithm is based on (i) a semantic-based
service description model that extends OWL-S[1] with SensorML[2] and information about the sensor location, and (ii) a similarity function that compares the
output of the services with the characteristics of the needed data. Generally
speaking, with this retrieval algorithm we aim to increase the capabilities of a
building-related pervasive service system with the possibility to find sensors similar to another one by comparing the services that represent such sensors. Indeed,

---

[1] http://www.w3.org/Submission/OWL-S/.
[2] http://www.opengeospatial.org/standards/sensorml.

© Springer International Publishing Switzerland 2015
F. Toumani et al. (Eds.): ICSOC 2014, LNCS 8954, pp. 281–291, 2015.
DOI: 10.1007/978-3-319-22885-3_25

in case a sensor recording the temperature fails or is not present, with the proposed algorithm it is possible to find the closer temperature sensor and to use the data recorded by it, thus overcoming the lack of the desired information.

The rest of the paper is organized as follows. Section 2 introduces an overview of the approach. Section 3 focuses on the retrieval algorithms that represents the core of this paper. The validation of the algorithm is discussed in Sect. 4. Finally, after a discussion of related work in Sects. 5 and 6 concludes the work and outlines some possible future work.

2   The Overall Approach

In this work we assume that a pervasive system is composed of many heterogeneous sensors and actuators that are spatially distributed. These devices belong to different technologies, have different semantics, and are characterized by different complexity levels. Therefore, in order to manage the gathering and processing of data we need a middleware that will hide the complexity of this scenario while allowing users to exploit all its potential. To reach this goal we use PerLa [2] to manage the data through a database abstraction, that is, the data gathered by sensors are seen as if arranged into a database and the final user is provided with a user-friendly language, featuring an SQL-like syntax, to handle it. On top of this middleware, a "Sensors as a Service" layer exposes only the data that are defined as externally accessible, thus the user or application that invokes the services relies only on the methods specified in the service interfaces without knowing the data model or the storage technology.

In this scenario, a proper service description is crucial, as it is the only way to know what a service offers and how to interact with it and, in this work, such a service description is based on a semantic characterization. In particular, we describe each available service in terms of the information that can be useful to the users to express the requirements that have to be satisfied during the retrieval process. We consider fundamental the following three dimensions: (i) *sensor*, services are related to sensors or actuators and have different characteristics (e.g., type, measure unit, etc.); (ii) *location*, sensors providing services are bound to a physical location. By knowing this location we can answer queries in a context-aware fashion; (iii) *device*, it is our aim to monitor consumption flows, thus, we need to have some information about the devices (considering the sensors themselves) that consume or produce energy.

To support these requirements, we adopt a service ontology. We start from the well-known OWL-S ontology and extend it with information related to our needs and application domain. Therefore, as shown in Fig. 1, we enrich OWL-S with three more ontologies, each one describing one of the three dimensions introduced above. In particular, notice that each service is described in terms of:

- its temporal output (i.e. *timeOutput* relation): data returned by a service may be: (i) the current data reading (*Last One*), (ii) all the readings in a specific interval of time (*Interval*) or (iii) the last X readings (*Last X*, where X depends on the service);

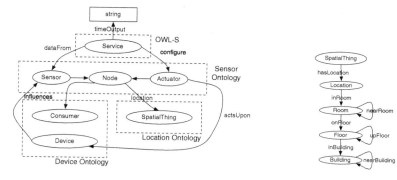

Fig. 1. Service Ontology extending OWL-S specification with sensor-specific concepts.

Fig. 2. Location Ontology made of hierarchies of elements in space.

- the features of the node in the sensor network to which the service is associated (described by the *Sensor* ontology)
- the physical location of the sensor providing the service (described by the *Location* ontology as shown in Fig. 2): a hierarchy (*Location* → *Room* → *Floor* → *Building*) is used to support different granularities and different relations (*nearRoom*, *upFloor* and *nearBuilding*) are used to understand if the concepts of same granularity are somehow near one to the other;
- the features of the devices that influence or are influenced by the node to which the service is associated (described by the *Device* ontology): we specify the energy they consume or produce.

This semantic representation allows us to describe the structure of services and to reason on the data we have, in order to infer some new knowledge that might be useful during the query answering process. To better understand, let consider the following example: suppose that a user wants to know the temperature in Room 23 but that one does not have a sensor installed, yet Room 24, the one next to Room 23, has one. By having this information expressed in the location ontology, our retrieval algorithm will be able to suggest to the user the service returning the temperature in Room 23, even though a penalty will be applied to this one since it does exactly satisfy the user request.

3   Retrieval Algorithm

There are many approaches supporting the service retrieval process (as discussed in Sect. 5). For our purposes, we assume that the users' needs are expressed in terms of a desired service, i.e., using the same description model used to describe a service the user can define the features of a service that the user is looking for. Then the description of the desired service is compared with all the available services. Formally, we introduce the following definitions:

- $\Sigma = \{\sigma_i\}$ is the set of available services, where each σ_i is described in terms of the service ontology discussed before. Moreover, $\sigma_i.values$ is the set of values that have been sensed by the sensor associated to the service σ_i.
- $\overline{\sigma} = \langle type, location, time, output \rangle$ is the desired service, defined in terms of one or more concepts and properties of the service ontology. More precisely:
  - *type* is associated to the nature of the sensor, i.e., what the sensor measures (e.g., temperature, power, and so on).
  - *location* defines where the data have been sensed using one of the *SpatialThing* related concept in the location ontology.
  - *time* = $\{LastOne, LastX, Interval\}$ specifies the nature of the sensed data returned as output of the service. In case of *time* = *LastOne*, this means that the user is interested in the more recent sensed value, whereas *time* = *LastX* in a set of more recent values. Finally, in case of *time* = *Interval* the user specifies the time range in which the sensed values are considered relevant.
  - Depending on the value of *time*, *output* specifies the value of $X \in \mathbf{N}$, or the initial and final hours and dates, and the granularity.
- $\overline{\Sigma} \subseteq \Sigma$ is the set of services relevant with respect to the desired service.

With respect to the traditional approaches our algorithm considers the location as a first class citizen and the similarity algorithm strongly depends on it. Moreover, having the *time* and *output*, allows the user to insert in query elements that makes more expressive the request in the reference scenario.

In our approach, we provide a similarity function $sim(\overline{\sigma}, \sigma_i) \rightarrow [0, 1]$ that compares two service descriptions and the higher the returned value the more similar the two services.

Listing 1. Similarity algorithm overview

```
Σ̄ = ∅
for all σᵢ ∈ Σ do
   if σᵢ.type = σ̄.type then
      sim = 1.0
      if σ̄.location ≠ ∅ then
         sim = sim * (1-location_penalty(σᵢ.location, σ̄.location))
      end if
      if σ̄.time ≠ ∅ then
         sim = sim * (1-time_penalty(σᵢ.time, σ̄.time))
         sim = sim * (1-output_penalty(σᵢ.time, σᵢ.output, σ̄.time, σ̄.output))
      end if
      if sim > th then
         Σ̄ = Σ̄ ∪ σᵢ
      end if
   end if
end for
return Σ̄
```

The resulting algorithm is presented, in its main steps, in Listing 1. Here the functions *location_penalty*, *time_penalty*, and *ouput_penalty* are in charge of computing the distance between the request and the offer with respect to a specific aspect. The similarity is computed as the product of all the penalties. In this way, a good value of similarity can be obtained only if all the requirements are matched at least partially. Indeed, it is enough that at least one of the requirements is not properly supported to significantly reduce the similarity. Finally, as also reported in the algorithm, as the elements composing $\bar{\sigma}$ are not mandatory, the corresponding penalty function could not be invoked.

3.1   Location Penalty

The computation of the location penalty identifies the distance between the concepts $\bar{\sigma}.location$ and $\sigma_i.location$ in the location ontology and it is based on the following assumptions:

- If $\bar{\sigma}.location = \sigma_i.location$ no penalty is applied.
- The more distant $\bar{\sigma}.location$ to $\sigma_i.location$, the grater the penalty.
- The wider the location $\bar{\sigma}.location$ with respect to the location $\sigma_i.location$, the greater the penalty. For instance, if the user asks for a temperature in a room and the service monitors the entire floor, then the penalty will be lower than that of a service returning the temperature of the entire building.
- If the location $\bar{\sigma}.location$ is more narrow than the location $\sigma_i.location$ no penalty is applied.

Listing 2. Location algorithm

```
award=1
for all edge: edges in shortest path between σ_i.location and σ̄.location do
    if edge.from is more specific σ̄ then
        award = award * λ
    end if
end for
location_penalty = 1 - award
```

Based on these assumptions, Listing 2 shows the complete algorithm for computing the location penalty. First, the shortest path between the concepts $\bar{\sigma}.location$ and $\sigma_i.location$ is computed. As the penalty depends on the edges from less specific concepts to less specific concepts, we firstly count the opposite to compute the award. Then, the penalty is given by the opposite. The parameter λ quantifies the amount of award (penalty) to be given for each relevant hop and its value is defined after a tuning phase, that is presented in the next section.

3.2   Time Penalty

Time penalty depends on the degree of compatibility between services having different time output property values. For example, if $\bar{\sigma}.time = LastX$ a service

σ_i is fully compatible if $\sigma_i.time = LastX$ but, we also consider a compatibility (with a penalty) also in case $\sigma_i.time = Interval$. Indeed, the time range can cover the required more recent values. On the contrary, if $\sigma_i.time = LastOne$ cannot be considered compatible as it returns only the most recent value over the required X values. Accordingly, we defined three levels of compatibility, i.e., Mismatch ($penalty = 1.0$), Close ($penalty = \tau$), Exact ($penalty = 0.0$) and Table 1 reports how these penalties are associated to each possible combination of $\sigma_i.time$ and $\overline{\sigma}.time$, where the value of τ is set during the tuning phase.

Table 1. Time compatibility matrix

		$\sigma_i.time$		
		Last One	**Last X**	**Interval**
$\overline{\sigma}.time$	**Last One**	Exact	Close	Close
	Last X	Mismatch	Exact	Close
	Interval	Mismatch	Close	Exact

3.3 Output Penalty

The last computed penalty is related to timeliness, that is defined as the extent to which data are timely for their use or as the property of information to arrive early or at the right time [3].

In our case, timeliness depends on the distance between when the sensed data is available with respect to when it is required, so the penalty depends on how much the timeliness is not satisfied. As the user with $\overline{\sigma}.time$ when the required data is relevant in three different ways (i.e., $LastOne$, $LastX$, and $Interval$) three different approaches for computing penalties are proposed. Differently from the previous penalties, the computation of the output penalty requires the interaction with the services. Indeed, the information available in the service description is not enough as we need to have information on the data returned by the services which can be obtained only bu invoking them. As a consequence, in this phase the services need to be invoked and the returned data analyzed. We remind that $\sigma_i.values$ represents these values and each of them is a pair of a timestamp (when the values is sensed) and the sensed value.

LastOne. If $\overline{\sigma}.time = LastOne$ then the user is interested in services that return the most recent values. Here the discussion is on the meaning of "recent value": is it with respect to when the user submits the query, or is it the most recent among the data returned by the services? As both the solutions are valid, we consider both the situation and, using a weighted sum, we leave to the user the possibility to specify which is the best interpretation. This results in the algorithm reported in Listing 3. First of all, we assume that the $current\_date$ is given (for instance, by invoking a system call); then, the $more\_recent$ and $less\_recent$ dates are obtained by calling the services available and considering the lower and higher values for the returned timestamps. Then, the penalty in both the cases is calculated as a proportion of the distance between the date of the returned value and the reference date.

Listing 3. Last One algorithm

---

for all $\sigma_k \in \Sigma$ **do**
    $max(\sigma_k.values.timestamp)$ = date of the more recent sampled data
    if $max(\sigma_k.values.timestamp)$ < less_recent **then**
        less_recent = $max(\sigma_k.values.timestamp)$
    end if
    if $max(\sigma_k.values.timestamp)$ > more_recent **then**
        more_recent = $max(\sigma_k.values.timestamp)$
    end if
end for
pen_current $= 1 - (max(\sigma_i.values.timestamp) - less\_recent)/(current\_date - less\_recent))$
pen_morerec $= 1 - (max(\sigma_i.values.timestamp) - less\_recent)/(more\_recent - less\_recent))$
output_penalty $= w_{curr}$ * pen_current $+ w_{morerec}$ * pen_morerec

---

Last X. In case of $\overline{\sigma}.time = LastX$ the user also specifies in the query the desired number (e.g., $\overline{\sigma}.output.X$) of output values. On this basis, two main aspects will be considered in the computation of the penalty:

- The number of returned values (*pen_number*): a σ_i able to retrieve at least $\overline{\sigma}.output.X$ values has lower penalty than a σ_i that satisfies the user request only partially returning a number of values lower than $\overline{\sigma}.output.X$: i.e., $pen\_number = \text{count}(\sigma_k.values) / \overline{\sigma}.output$.
- The timeliness of the returned values (*pen_recent*): a σ_i returning values that are more recent has lower penalty than a σ_i that returns values with lower timestamps: i.e., $pen\_recent = \text{lastOne}(\sigma_i)$

Having these values: $output\_penalty = 0.5 \cdot pen\_number + 0.5 \cdot pen\_recent$

Interval. The third possible kind of query on the output is $\overline{\sigma}.time = Interval$, i.e., the user wants services that have sampled data in a specified time range ($\overline{\sigma}.output.start\_date$, $\overline{\sigma}.output.end\_date$). Here, the more covered is the interval, the more similar the service. To properly consider also a homogeneous coverage of the interval, a third input parameter named $\overline{\sigma}.output.granularity$ is required that specifies the sampling time inside the time range. For instance, having a time range of $10mins$ with a granularity of $60secs$, means that the ideal service should have at least 10 sampled data distributed every $1\,min$. Listing 4 reports the details of the adopted algorithm. First of all, given the time range, the number of subintervals is computed. Then, for each of them, we verify how many intervals are covered by the $\sigma_i.values$. Finally, the higher the number of not covered intervals, the higher the penalty.

Listing 4. Interval algorithm

```
interval = σ̄.output.end_date − σ̄.output.start_date
subintervals= interval /σ̄.output.granularity
covered_subintervals = 0
for all subintervals in interval do
    if count(σ_i.values ∈ subinterval) > 0 then
        covered_subinterval ++
    end if
end for
output_penalty = 1- (covered_subinterval / subintervals)
```

Table 2. Tuning and test queries.

Query	$\overline{\sigma}$.location	$\overline{\sigma}$.time	$\overline{\sigma}$.output
$\overline{\sigma}_1^{tuning}$	-	Interval	Range: from 28/2/2004 6:30 AM to 28/2/2004 2:30 PM Granularity: 1 hour
$\overline{\sigma}_2^{tuning}$	Floor22	LastX	Samples: 14
$\overline{\sigma}_3^{tuning}$	Room27	LastOne	-
$\overline{\sigma}_1^{test}$	-	Interval	Range: from 28/2/2004 10:30 AM to 28/2/2004 6:30 PM Granularity: 1 hour
$\overline{\sigma}_2^{test}$	Floor12	LastX	Samples: 11
$\overline{\sigma}_3^{test}$	Room111	LastOne	-

4   Validation

To validate the proposed algorithm, we based our tests on a testbed containing data collected from 54 sensors deployed in the Intel Berkeley Research lab[3]. The sensors collected timestamped values of humidity, temperature, light and voltage, producing 2.3 million readings in a period of a month and a half.

Before running the test cases to validate the approach, a proper tuning of the parameters th, λ, and τ is required. To this aim, the first three queries reported in Table 2 have submitted to the testbed varying, for each run, the values of these three parameters. For each of these queries, the list of relevant services is manually created to be used for computing the precision and recall.

Based on the obtained results, the better precision and recall values for these queries is given for the following values: $th = 0.5$; $\lambda = 0.9$; $\tau = 0.8$. The corresponding precision recall chart for this tuning set is shown in Fig. 3. With this configuration, a second set of queries (some of them are reported in the lower part of Table 2) has been used to calculate the final precision and recall graph. As shown in Fig. 4, the proposed algorithm properly responds to the queries with a good precision for all the percentage of recall. Indeed, when all the relevant services are returned (i.e., recall equals to 100 %) the precision remains greater

---

[3] http://db.csail.mit.edu/labdata/labdata.html.

than 60 %. To the best of our knowledge, there are no comparable approaches, thus, a comparison with existing methods is not possible at this stage.

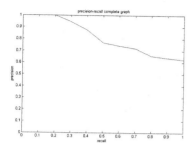

Fig. 3. Performances with the tuning set queries.

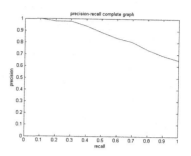

Fig. 4. Performances with the test set queries.

5   Related Work

Different similarity algorithms have been proposed that allow to compare sensors. In [4] a methodology to discover service similarity is based on testing and requires the evaluation of the outputs produced by the services after invoking them. With respect to this work, we are interested in introducing a semantic dimension into the matchmaking process. Research has put much effort in developing ontology-based models to support pervasive systems [5] which mostly adopt ad hoc solutions that depend on the application domain but also bring up the need for ontologies to describe sensors [6] and locations [5] in particular. Among sensor ontologies it is worth pointing out the Semantic Sensor Web, a framework to support semantic annotation of sensor data through the use of ontologies to elicit the features of the sensors. In this work we make use of such an ontology to extend the OWL-S ontology with useful domain-dependent information similarly to what has been done in the context of the SemsorGrid4Env EU project[4].

Other works [7,8] enrich services description by associating their inputs and outputs with the concepts in a domain ontology and adopt a hybrid strategy that exploits both logic-based reasoning and content-based information retrieval techniques. Authors in [9] adopt an ontology to describe the interactions between the processes in a service and then compute the similarity by keeping into account: (i) the structural similarity, based on the outputs of the services and (ii) the semantic similarity, based on the data in the ontology.

As for structural similarity, in [10] and [11] two approaches are described that dynamically select and recommend services to users. However, both approaches are based on historical data and thus they assume that the similarity computed in the past can be used to refine the future rankings.

---

[4] http://www.semsorgrid4env.eu.

On the other hand, different approaches have been proposed that exploit an ontology to determine semantic similarity between services. The most common approaches are distance metrics, information-based measures and more complex ontology frameworks. In [12] authors propose a information-based similarity measure that also takes into account reasoning, that is, the semantic similarity of an object depends on how many new objects it can generate. In [13] the authors take a similar road but propose a weighted algorithm that takes into account the frequency of words appearing the in semantic description of services. In this work we focus on a simpler semantic similarity, that is based on the evaluation of the distance between the features of a service and the features requested by a user, in terms of the amount of edges that separates the two semantic concepts in the ontology.

6   Conclusion

In this paper we have presented a semantic-based approach for retrieving services that refer to sensors installed in buildings. The approach has been validated and the results highlights the good performances of the algorithm in terms of precision and recall. Future work will focus on reducing the number of service invocations and optimizing the number of comparisons in the retrieval algorithm, in order to improve the response time performance and the scalability of the solution.

Acknowledgement. This work has been partially funded by Italian project "Industria 2015-Sensori" Grant agreeement n. 00029MI01/2011.

References

1. Chehri, A., Mouftah, H.T.: Service-oriented architecture for smart building energy management. In: Proceedings of IEEE International Conference on Communications, pp. 4099–4103 (2013)
2. Schreiber, F.A., Camplani, R., Fortunato, M., Marelli, M., Rota, G.: Perla: A language and middleware architecture for data management and integration in pervasive information systems. IEEE Trans. Software Eng. **38**(2), 478–496 (2012)
3. Cappiello, C.: Data Quality and Multichannel Services. Ph.D. thesis, Politecnico di Milano (2007)
4. Church, J., Motro, A.: Discovering service similarity by testing. In: Proceedings of the IEEE International Conference on Services Computing, SCC 2011, pp. 733–734. IEEE Computer Society, Washington, DC (2011)
5. Ye, J., Coyle, L., Dobson, S., Nixon, P.: Ontology-based models in pervasive computing systems. Knowl. Eng. Rev. **22**(4), 315–347 (2007)
6. W3C: Review of Sensor and Observations Ontologies. http://www.w3.org/2005/Incubator/ssn/wiki/Review_of_Sensor_and_Observations_Ontologies
7. Klusch, M., Fries, B., Sycara, K.: Automated semantic web service discovery with owls-mx. In: Proceedings of the 5th International Joint Conference on Autonomous Agents and Multiagent Systems, pp. 915–922. ACM, New York (2006)

8. Bianchini, D., Antonellis, V.D., Melchiori, M.: Capability matching and similarity reasoning in service discovery. In: CAiSE International Workshop on Enterprise Modeling and Ontologies for Interoperability, EMOI 2005, pp. 285–296 (2005)
9. Günay, A., Yolum, I.: Structural and semantic similarity metrics for web service matchmaking. In: Psaila, G., Wagner, R. (eds.) EC-Web 2007. LNCS, vol. 4655, pp. 129–138. Springer, Heidelberg (2007)
10. Manikrao, U., Prabhakar, T.V.: Dynamic selection of web services with recommendation system. In: International Conference on Next Generation Web Services Prac. (2005)
11. Li, Z., Bin, Z., Jun, N., Liping, H., Mingwei, Z.: An approach for web service qos prediction based on service using information. In: International Conference on Service Sciences (ICSS), pp. 324–328 (2010)
12. Hau, J., Lee, W., Darlington, J.: A semantic similarity measure for semantic web services. In: Web Service Semantics Workshop at WWW (2005)
13. Liu, M., Shen, W., Hao, Q., Yan, J.: An weighted ontology-based semantic similarity algorithm for web service. Expert Syst. Appl. **36**(10), 12480–12490 (2009)

Formal Modeling and Verification
of Service-Based Systems

An EXPTIME Algorithm for Data-Aware Service Simulation Using Parametrized Automata

Walid Belkhir[1]([⊠]), Yannick Chevalier[2], and Michael Rusinowitch[1]

[1] INRIA Nancy–Grand Est and LORIA, Villers-lès-Nancy, France
walid.belkhir@inria.fr, particle.mania@gmail.com, rusi@loria.fr
[2] Université Paul Sabatier and IRIT Toulouse, Toulouse, France
ychevali@irit.fr

Abstract. The service composition problem asks whether, given a client and a community of available services, there exists an agent (called the mediator) that suitably delegates the actions requested by the client to the available community of services. We address this problem in a general setting where the agents communication actions are parametrized by data over an infinite domain and possibly subject to constraints. For this purpose, we define *parametrized automata* (PAs), where transitions are guarded by conjunction of equalities and disequalities. We solve the service composition problem by showing that the simulation preorder of PAs is decidable.

1 Introduction

Service Oriented Architectures (SOA) consider services as self-contained components that can be published, invoked over a network and combined with other services through standardized protocols in order to dynamically build complex applications [19]. Service composition is required when none of the existing services can fulfill some client needs but a suitable coordination of them would satisfy the client requests. How to find the right combination and how to orchestrate this combination are among the key issues for service architecture development.

Service composition has been studied in many works e.g. [6,15,18]. The related problem of system synthesis from libraries of reusable components has been thoroughly investigated too [17].

In this paper we address the composition synthesis problem for web services in which the agents are *parametrized*, i.e. the client and the available services exchange data ranging over an infinite domain and they are possibly subject to some *data constraints*. More precisely, the composition synthesis problem we consider can be stated as follows: (e.g. [7,18]): given a client and a community of available services, compute a mediator which will enable communication between the client and the available services in such a way that each client request is forwarded to an appropriate service.

As usual (e.g. [6]), this problem is reduced to the computation of a simulation relation between the target service (specifying an expected service behaviour

© Springer International Publishing Switzerland 2015
F. Toumani et al. (Eds.): ICSOC 2014, LNCS 8954, pp. 295–307, 2015.
DOI: 10.1007/978-3-319-22885-3_26

for satisfying the client requests) and the asynchronous product of the available services. If such a simulation relation exists then it can be easily used to generate a mediator, that is a function that selects at each step an available service for executing an action requested by the client.

One of the most successful approaches to composition abstracts services as finite-state automata (FA) and apply available tools from automata theory to synthesize a new service satisfying the given client requests from an existing community of services. However it is not obvious whether the automata-based approach to service composition can still be applied with infinite alphabets since simulation often gets undecidable in extended models like Colombo ([1]). Starting from the approach initiated in [2] our objective is to define expressive classes of automata on infinite alphabets which are well-adapted to the specification and composition of services and enjoy nice closure properties and decidable simulation preorder. Compared to our previous work [2] we introduce a strictly more expressive service specification formalism thanks to the use of guarded transitions.

1.1 Contributions

In this paper we rely on automata-based techniques to tackle the problem of composition synthesis of parametrized services. We introduce an extension of automata called *parametrized automata* or PAs, that allows a natural specification and decidable synthesis of parametrized services. In PAs, the transitions are labeled by letters or variables ranging over an infinite alphabets and guarded by conjunction of equalities and disequalities. Besides, some variables can be refreshed in some states: their value is reset, and they can be bound later to an arbitrary letter. Refreshing mechanism is particularly useful when computation starts a new sessions or to simulate calls to functions with local variables.

We introduce a simulation preorder for PAs and show its decidability. The proof relies on a game-theoretic characterization of simulation. We show how this result can be applied to the synthesis of a mediator for web services. Although not detailed here, the simulation decision procedure can help to solve language containment problems which are important ones in formal verification. The potential applicability of our model in verification also follows from the fact that PAs are closed under intersection, union, concatenation and Kleene operator.

1.2 Related Work

Logic-based techniques for the synthesis problem (e.g. [10]) have been considered in the literature. In the *Roman* model web services behaviours are specified with activity-based finite state automata. The corresponding services composition problem was reduced to PDL satisfiability (e.g. [5,7]). Thanks to the relation between PDL and Description Logic (DL), several DL reasoning tools can be applied in the latter case. The composition problem can also be reduced to computing a simulation preorder as in [6]. This approach cannot be extended to the data-centric Colombo [4] model of services for which, as we mentionned above, simulation is undecidable. Known decidable cases of the composition synthesis problem in Colombo framework need restrictions such as determinism or finite domain for values.

For instance, the Colombo^{k,b} model is a restriction of the Colombo model in which suitable hypotheses ensure that only a finite number of domain values (and thus a finite number of different records) are considered. In [4] the composition problem for this model was proven decidable when the clients are represented as deterministic guarded automata. Besides, the proof provided relies on (a priori) bounding two parameters of the synthesised mediator. More precisely, they assume that the mediator is (p, q)-bounded, where p is the number of states, and q is the number of variables representing records in its global store. It is conjectured that this decidability result can be obtained without mentioning these bounds. We believe our result, though in a different setting, justifies this conjecture as we need to bound neither the number q of variables in the mediator nor its number p of states.

In [8], the authors address a related problem of synthesizing a controller generator from which one can compute new controller when the environment or the available services change. The controller implements a fully controllable target behaviour by suitably coordinating available partially controllable behaviors that are to execute within a shared, fully observable, but non-deterministic environment. The behaviours and the environment are represented as finite state transition systems. They construct a table of states related in a simulation, and are able to update this table on the fly when the available services change. For efficiency reasons they also consider *safety games* for generating a new controller from this table. Though our results only address the synthesis of one controller in an unmutable setting, our underlying model is more general than finite transition systems as it allows the exchange of data from an infinite domain. Though our simulation game also uses a bounded number of constants, it is worth mentionning that an unbounded execution of the synthesized controller can handle an unbounded number of different constants.

In [14] the authors also obtain an interesting positive result for the case where services are described by finite state machines but the number of instances of existing services that can be used in a given composition is not bounded a priori.

Several automata models have been designed recently for infinite alphabets. However they have not been applied to service composition. Usages nominal calculus ([9]) is a computational model based on infinite alphabets and dynamic creation of resources. PAs are incomparable with Usages.

A service behaviour can be expressed by a Petri net too (see [13]), where actions are modeled by transitions and the state is modeled by places. However it seems hard to extend our synthesis result to Petri nets service specification because of the negative result of [16]. On the other hand, simulation between finite state machines and well-structured transition systems (and so Petri nets) is decidable as shown in [11].

1.3 Paper Organization

Section 2 recalls standard notions. Section 3 introduces the new class of parametrized automata. Section 3.2 studies closure properties and the complexity of Nonemptiness for PAs. Section 4 uses the parametrized automata to solve the composition synthesis problem, more precisely, Sect. 4.1 introduces the simulation preorder of PAs, Sect. 4.2 shows its decidability, Sect. 4.3 applies these results to service composition by sketching a procedure for mediator synthesis, and future work directions are given in Sect. 5. All proofs and further details can be found in [3].

2 Preliminaries

Let $\mathcal{X}$ be a finite set of variables, Σ an infinite alphabet of letters. A substitution σ is an idempotent mapping $\{x_1 \mapsto \alpha_1, \ldots, x_n \mapsto \alpha_n\} \cup \bigcup_{a \in \Sigma} \{a \mapsto a\}$ with variables $x_1, \ldots, x_n$ in $\mathcal{X}$ and $\alpha_1, \ldots, \alpha_n$ in $\mathcal{X} \cup \Sigma$. We call $\{x_1, \ldots, x_n\}$ its *proper domain*, and denote it by $dom(\sigma)$. We denote by $Dom(\sigma)$ the set $dom(\sigma) \cup \Sigma$. We denote by $codom(\sigma)$ the set $\{a \in \Sigma \mid \exists x \in dom(\sigma) \text{ s.t. } \sigma(x) = a\}$. If all the $\alpha_i, i = 1 \ldots n$ are letters then we say that σ is ground. The empty substitution *i.e.*, with an empty proper domain) is denoted by $\emptyset$. The set of substitutions from $\mathcal{X} \cup \Sigma$ to a set A is denoted by $\zeta_{\mathcal{X}, A}$, or by $\zeta_{\mathcal{X}}$, or simply by ζ if there is no ambiguity. If σ_1 and σ_2 are substitutions that coincide on the domain $dom(\sigma_1) \cap dom(\sigma_2)$, then $\sigma_1 \cup \sigma_2$ denotes their union in the usual sense. As a special case, if $dom(\sigma_1) \cap dom(\sigma_2) = \emptyset$ we emphasize the disjointness by denoting $\sigma_1 \uplus \sigma_2$ the union. We define the function $\mathcal{V} : \Sigma \cup \mathcal{X} \longrightarrow \mathcal{P}(\mathcal{X})$ by $\mathcal{V}(\alpha) = \{\alpha\}$ if $\alpha \in \mathcal{X}$, and $\mathcal{V}(\alpha) = \emptyset$, otherwise. For a function $F : A \to B$, and $A' \subseteq A$, the restriction of F on A' is denoted by $F_{|A'}$.

Definition 1. *A two-players game is a tuple* $\langle \mathrm{Pos}_E, \mathrm{Pos}_A, M, p^\star \rangle$, *where* $\mathrm{Pos}_E, \mathrm{Pos}_A$ *are disjoint sets of positions: Eloise's positions and Abelard's positions.* $M \subseteq (\mathrm{Pos}_E \cup \mathrm{Pos}_A) \times (\mathrm{Pos}_E \cup \mathrm{Pos}_A)$ *is a set of moves, and* $p^\star$ *is the starting position. A strategy for the player Eloise is a function* $\rho : \mathrm{Pos}_E \to \mathrm{Pos}_E \cup \mathrm{Pos}_A$, *such that* $(\wp, \rho(\wp)) \in M$ *for all* $\wp \in \mathrm{Pos}_E$. *A (possibly infinite) play* $\pi = \langle \wp_1, \wp_2, \ldots \rangle$ *follows a strategy* ρ *for player Eloise iff* $\wp_{i+1} = \rho(\wp_i)$ *for all* $i \in \mathbb{N}$ *such that* $\wp_i \in \mathrm{Pos}_E$. *Let* $\mathcal{W}$ *be a (possibly infinite) set of plays. A strategy* ρ *is winning for Eloise from a set* $S \subseteq \mathrm{Pos}_E \cup \mathrm{Pos}_A$ *according to* $\mathcal{W}$ *iff every play starting from a position in* S *and following* ρ *belongs to* $\mathcal{W}$.

3 Parametrized Automata

In this section we define formally the class of PAs. Firstly, we illustrate the practical use of PAs through a service composition problem.

3.1 A Motivating Example

In Fig. 1 we have an e-commerce Web site allowing clients to open files, search for items in a large domain that can be abstracted as infinite and save them to an appropriate file depending on the type of the items (whether they are in promotion or not). The three agents: CLIENT, FILE and SEARCH communicate with messages ranging over a possibly infinite set of terms. The problem is to check whether FILE and SEARCH can be composed in order to satisfy the CLIENT requests. Following [6] the problem reduces to find a simulation between CLIENT and the asynchronous product of FILE and SEARCH. We emphasize that the variables x and y are refreshed (i.e. freed to get a new value) when passing through the state p_0. In the same way variables z and w are refreshed at p_2. The variables m and n are refreshed at q_0; the variables i and j are refreshed at r_0. For saving space, a transition labeled by a term, say `write(m,n)`, abbreviates successive transitions labeled by the root symbol and its arguments, here `write`, `m` and `n`, respectively. We notice that this example cannot be handled within the subclass of fresh-variable automata [2] since they do not have guards.

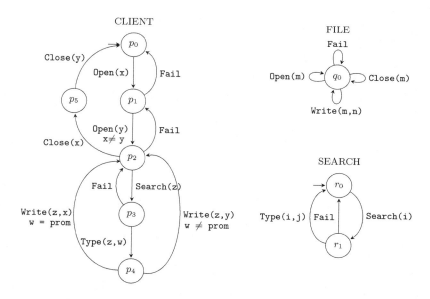

Fig. 1. PROM example.

Before introducing formally the class of PAs, let us first explain the main ideas behind them. The transitions of a PA are labeled with letters or variables ranging over an infinite set of letters. These transitions can also be labeled with guards consisting of equalities and disequalities. Its guard must be true for the transition to be fired. We emphasize that while reading a guarded transition some variables of the guard might be free and we need to *guess* their value. Finally, some variables are refreshed in some states, that is, variables can be *freed* in these states so that new letters can be assigned to them. Firstly, we introduce the syntax and semantics of guards.

Definition 2. *The set $\mathbb{G}$ of guards over $\Sigma \cup \mathcal{X}$ is inductively defined as follows:*

$$G := \mathbf{true} \mid \alpha = \beta \mid \alpha \neq \beta \mid G \wedge G,$$

where $\alpha, \beta \in \Sigma \cup \mathcal{X}$. We write $\sigma \models g$ if a substitution σ satisfies a guard g.

We notice that adding the disjunction operator to the guards would not increase the expressiveness of our model. A guard is atomic iff it is either $\mathbf{true}$, an equality, or a disequality. Let $g_i, i = 1, \ldots, n$, be atomic guards. Then we define the *free* variables of a guard by extending the function $\mathcal{V}$ to a mapping $\Sigma \cup \mathcal{X} \cup \mathbb{G} \to \mathcal{P}(\mathcal{X})$ as follows: $\mathcal{V}(\bigwedge_{i=1,n} g_i) = \bigcup_{i=1,n} \mathcal{V}(g_i)$ and $\mathcal{V}(\alpha \sim \beta) = \mathcal{V}(\alpha) \cup \mathcal{V}(\beta))$, where $\sim$ belongs to $\{=, \neq\}$ and $\alpha, \beta \in \Sigma \cup \mathcal{X}$. The finite set of letters of a guard g can be defined similarly and it will be denoted by Σ_g. The application of a substitution γ to a guard g, denoted by $\gamma(g)$, is defined in the usual way. We shall write $\sigma \vdash g$ if there exists a substitution γ s.t. $\sigma \uplus \gamma \models g$. The formal definition of PAs follows.

Definition 3. *A PA is a tuple $\mathcal{A} = \langle \Sigma, \mathcal{X}, Q, Q_0, \delta, F, \kappa \rangle$ where*

- *Σ is an infinite set of letters,*
- *$\mathcal{X}$ is a finite set of variables,*
- *Q is a finite set of states,*
- *$Q_0 \subseteq Q$ is a set of initial states,*
- *$\delta : Q \times (\Sigma_{\mathcal{A}} \cup \mathcal{X} \cup \{\varepsilon\}) \times \mathbb{G} \to 2^Q$ is a transition function where $\Sigma_{\mathcal{A}}$ is a finite subset of Σ,*
- *$F \subseteq Q$ is a set of accepting states, and*
- *$\kappa : \mathcal{X} \to 2^Q$ is called the refreshing function.*

A run of a PA is defined over *configurations*. A configuration is a pair (γ, q) where γ is a substitution such that for all variables x in $dom(\gamma)$, $\gamma(x)$ is the current value of x, and q is a state of the PA. Intuitively, when a PA $\mathcal{A}$ is in state q, and (γ, q) is the current configuration, and there is a transition $q \xrightarrow{\alpha, g} q'$ in $\mathcal{A}$ then:

i) if α is a free variable (i.e. $\alpha \in \mathcal{X} \setminus dom(\gamma)$) then α stores the input letter and some values for all the other free variables of $\gamma(g)$ are *guessed* such that $\gamma(g)$ holds, and $\mathcal{A}$ enters the state $q' \in \delta(q, \alpha, g)$,

ii) if α is a bound variable or a letter (i.e. $\alpha \in Dom(\gamma)$) and $\gamma(\alpha)$ is equal to the input letter l then some values for all the free variables of $\gamma(g)$ are *guessed* such that $\gamma(g)$ holds, and $\mathcal{A}$ enters the state $q' \in \delta(q, \alpha, g)$.

In both cases when $\mathcal{A}$ enters state q' all the variables which are refreshed in q' are freed. Thus the purpose of guards is to compare letters and to guess new letters that might be read afterward.

For a PA $\mathcal{A}$, we shall denote by $\Sigma_{\mathcal{A}}$ the finite set of letters that appear in the transition function of $\mathcal{A}$. We shall denote by $\kappa^{-1} : Q \to 2^{\mathcal{X}}$ the function that associates with each state of the PA the set of variables being refreshed in this state. That is, $\kappa^{-1}(q) = \{x \in \mathcal{X} \mid q \in \kappa(x)\}$.

The formal definitions of run and recognized language follow.

Definition 4. *Let* $\mathcal{A} = \langle \Sigma, \mathcal{X}, Q, Q_0, \delta, F, \kappa \rangle$ *be a PA. We define a transition relation over the configurations as follows:* $(\gamma_1, q_1) \overset{a}{\Rightarrow} (\gamma_2, q_2)$, *where* $a \in \Sigma \cup \{\varepsilon\}$, *iff there exists a substitution* σ *such that* $dom(\sigma) \cap dom(\gamma_1) = \emptyset$ *and either:*

i) $a \in \Sigma$ *and in this case there exists a label* $\alpha \in \Sigma \cup \mathcal{X}$ *such that* $q_2 \in \delta(q_1, \alpha, g)$, $(\gamma_1 \uplus \sigma)(\alpha) = a$, $(\gamma_1 \uplus \sigma) \models g$ *and* $\gamma_2 = (\gamma_1 \uplus \sigma)_{|D}$, *with* $D = Dom(\gamma_1 \uplus \sigma) \setminus \kappa^{-1}(q_2)$. *Or,*

ii) $a = \varepsilon$ *and in this case* $(\gamma_1 \uplus \sigma) \models g$ *and* $\gamma_2 = (\gamma_1 \uplus \sigma)_{|D}$, *with* $D = Dom(\gamma_1 \uplus \sigma) \setminus \kappa^{-1}(q_2)$.

We denote by $\overset{*}{\Rightarrow}$ *the reflexive and transitive closure of* $\Rightarrow$. *For two configurations* $\mathbf{c}, \mathbf{c}'$ *and a letter* $a \in \Sigma$, *we write* $\mathbf{c} \overset{a}{\to} \mathbf{c}'$ *iff there exists two configurations* $\mathbf{c}_1$ *and* $\mathbf{c}_2$ *such that* $\mathbf{c} \overset{\varepsilon}{\Rightarrow^*} \mathbf{c}_1 \overset{a}{\Rightarrow} \mathbf{c}_2 \overset{\varepsilon}{\Rightarrow^*} \mathbf{c}'$. *A finite word, or a trace,* $w = a_1 a_2 \ldots a_n \in \Sigma^*$ *is recognized by* $\mathcal{A}$ *iff there exists a run* $(\gamma_0, q_0) \overset{a_1}{\to} (\gamma_1, q_1) \overset{a_2}{\to} \ldots \overset{a_n}{\to} (\gamma_n, q_n)$, *such that* $q_0 \in Q_0$ *and* $q_n \in F$. *The set of words recognized by* $\mathcal{A}$ *is denoted by* $L(\mathcal{A})$.

Fig. 2. Two PAs $\mathcal{A}_1$ and $\mathcal{A}_2$ where the variable y_1 is refreshed in the state p, and the variables x_2, y_2 are refreshed in the state q.

Example 1. Let $\mathcal{A}_1$ and $\mathcal{A}_2$ be the PAs depicted above in Fig. 2 where the variable y_1 is refreshed in the state p, and the variables x_2, y_2 are refreshed in the state q. That is, $\mathcal{A}_1 = \langle \Sigma, \{x_1, y_1\}, \{p, p'\}, \{p\}, \delta_1, \{p'\}, \kappa_1 \rangle$ with

$$\begin{cases} \delta_1(p, y_1, (y_1 \neq x_1)) = \{p\} \text{ and } \delta_1(p, x_1, \mathtt{true}) = \{p'\}, \text{ and} \\ \kappa_1(y_1) = \{p\} \end{cases}$$

And $\mathcal{A}_2 = \langle \Sigma, \{x_2, y_2\}, \{q, q'\}, \{q\}, \delta_2, \{q'\}, \kappa_2 \rangle$ with

$$\begin{cases} \delta_2(q, x_2, \mathtt{true}) = \{q'\} \text{ and } \delta(q', y_2, (y_2 \neq x_2)) = \{q\}, \text{ and} \\ \kappa_2(x_2) = \kappa_2(y_2) = \{q\}. \end{cases}$$

We notice that while making the first loop over the state p of $\mathcal{A}_1$, the variable x_1 of the guard $(y_1 \neq x_1)$ is free and its value is guessed. Then the variable y_1 is refreshed in p, and at each loop the input letter should be different than the value of the variable x_1 already guessed. More precisely, the behaviour of $\mathcal{A}_1$ on an input word is as follows. Being in the initial state p, either:

– Makes the transition $p \to p'$ by reading the input symbol and bounding the variable x_1 to it, then enters the state p'. Or,
– Makes the transition $p \to p$ by:
  1. Reading the input symbol and bounding the variable y_1 to it.
  2. Guessing a symbol in Σ that is different than the input symbol (i.e. the value of x_1) and bounds the variable y_1 to the guessed symbol, then enters the state p.
  3. From the state p, refresh the variable x_1, that is, it is no longer bound to the input symbol. Then, start again.

We illustrate the run of $\mathcal{A}_1$ on the word $w = abbc$, starting from the initial configuration $(\emptyset, p)$ as follows:

$$(\emptyset, p) \xrightarrow{a} (\{y_1 \mapsto c\}, p) \xrightarrow{b} (\{y_1 \mapsto c\}, p) \xrightarrow{b} (\{y_1 \mapsto c\}, p) \xrightarrow{c} (\{y_1 \mapsto c\}, p')$$

Hence, the language $L(\mathcal{A}_1)$ consists of all the words in $\Sigma^\star$ in which the last letter is different than all the other letters. By following similar reasoning, we get $L(\mathcal{A}_2) = \{w_1 w_1' \cdots w_n w_n' \mid w_i, w_i' \in \Sigma, n \geq 1, \text{ and } w_i \neq w_i', \forall i \in [n]\}$.

3.2   Properties of Parametrized Automata

Closure properties are important for the modular development of services. PAs enjoy the same closure properties as finite automata except for complementation:

Theorem 1 *[3]. PAs are closed under union, concatenation, Kleene operator and intersection. They are not closed under complementation.*

For the main decision procedures we have that:

Theorem 2. *[3]. For PAs, Membership is NP-complete, Universality and Containment are undecidable. Nonemptiness is PSPACE-complete.*

To argue that Nonemptiness is PSPACE, given a PA $\mathcal{A}$, it is sufficient to show that $\mathcal{A}$ recognizes a non-empty language over Σ iff $\mathcal{A}$ recognizes a non-empty language over a finite set of letters. For this purpose, and in order to relate the two runs of $\mathcal{A}$ (the one over an infinite alphabet and the one over a finite alphabet) we introduce a *coherence* relation between substitutions.

Definition 5. *Let C be a finite subset of Σ. The coherence relation $\bowtie_C \subseteq \zeta \times \zeta$ between substitutions is defined by $\bar{\sigma} \bowtie_C \sigma$ iff the three following conditions hold:*

1. *$dom(\bar{\sigma}) = dom(\sigma)$,*
2. *If $\bar{\sigma}(x) \in C$ or $\sigma(x) \in C$ then $\bar{\sigma}(x) = \sigma(x)$, for any $x \in dom(\sigma)$, and*
3. *for any variables $x, y \in dom(\sigma)$, $\bar{\sigma}(x) = \bar{\sigma}(y)$ iff $\sigma(x) = \sigma(y)$.*

Thus, the fact the Nonemptiness of PAs is PSPACE follows from the following lemma.

Lemma 1. *Let* $\mathcal{A}$ *be a PA over* Σ *with* k *variables and* m *letters* $\Sigma_{\mathcal{A}} = \{c_1, \ldots, c_m\}$. *Let* $\boldsymbol{\Sigma} = \{a_1, \ldots, a_k, c_1, \ldots, c_m\}$. *Then,* $\mathcal{A}$ *recognizes a non-empty language over* $\Sigma^\star$ *if, and only if, it recognizes a non-empty language over* $\boldsymbol{\Sigma}^\star$.

To show that the Nonemptiness of PAs is PSPACE-hard, we reduce the reachability problem for bounded one-counter automata [12] (known to be PSPACE-hard) to the Nonemptiness problem of PAs [3].

4   Service Synthesis with Parametrized Automata

We define and study the simulation preorder for PAs, an extension of the simulation preorder for FAs. Then we show how to synthesis a mediator (i.e. a PA) allowing the communication between a client and the community of available services. To simplify the presentation, we shall only consider in this section PAs without ε-transitions and in which there is a unique initial state and all the states are accepting.

4.1   Simulation Preorder for PAs, and Symbolic Games

Simulation-preoder for PAs is a relation defined over pairs of configurations instead of pairs of states as it is the case for FAs.

In order to show the decidability of simulation for PAs we shall provide a game-theoretic formulation of simulation in terms of *symbolic simulation games*. Roughly speaking, the arena of a symbolic game is a PA in which each state is controlled by one of the two players, Eloise or Abelard. From a state under his control, the player chooses an outgoing transition and instantiates the (possible) free variable that labels this transition and all the free variables in the constraint of this transition. Firstly, we introduce symbolic games in Definition 6 and their concretisation in Definition 7. Then, we show in Definition 8 how to formulate the simulation preorder for PAs as a symbolic game.

Definition 6 (Symbolic games). *A symbolic game is a pair* $(\mathcal{A}, \lambda)$ *where* $\mathcal{A} = \langle \Sigma, \mathcal{X}, Q, q_0, \delta, F, \kappa \rangle$ *is a PA and* $\lambda : Q \to \{E, A\}$ *is the labeling function. The states labeled by* E *(resp.* A*) correspond to* Eloise *(resp.* Abelard*) states.*

The concretisation of a symbolic game amounts to instantiate its variables from a (possibly infinite) set of letters. The resulting game is a two-players game in the sense of Definition 1. The formal definition follows.

Definition 7 (Concretisation of symbolic games). *Let* $(\mathcal{A}, \lambda)$ *be a symbolic game where* $\mathcal{A} = \langle \Sigma, \mathcal{X}, Q, q_0, \delta, F, \kappa \rangle$. *Let* $S \subseteq \Sigma$ *be a set of letters. The concretisation of the symbolic game* $(\mathcal{A}, \lambda)$ *with letters in* S, *denoted by* $\mathcal{G}(\mathcal{A}, \lambda, S)$, *is the two players game* $\langle \text{Pos}_E, \text{Pos}_A, M, p^\star \rangle$ *where the initial position is* $p^\star = (\emptyset, q_0)$ *and the set of positions* $\text{Pos} = \text{Pos}_A \cup \text{Pos}_E$ *is the set of positions containing* $p^\star$ *and reachable from the moves:* $M = \{(\sigma, q) \to (\sigma', q') \text{ where } (\sigma, q) \xrightarrow{a} (\sigma', q') \text{ for all } a \in \Sigma\}$. *Finally,* $\text{Pos}_E = \{(\sigma, q) \in \text{Pos where } \sigma \in \zeta_{\mathcal{X},S} \text{ and } \lambda(q) = E\}$, *and* $\text{Pos}_A = \{(\sigma, q) \in \text{Pos where } \sigma \in \zeta_{\mathcal{X},S} \text{ and } \lambda(q) = A\}$.

Definition 8 (Symbolic games for simulation). *Let* $\mathcal{A}_1 = \langle \Sigma, \mathcal{X}_1, Q_1, q_0^1, \delta_1, F_1, \kappa_1 \rangle$ *and* $\mathcal{A}_2 = \langle \Sigma, \mathcal{X}_2, Q_2, q_0^2, \delta_2, F_2, \kappa_2 \rangle$ *be two PAs and let* $S \subseteq \Sigma$ *be a set of letters. The symbolic simulation game of* $\mathcal{A}_1$ *by* $\mathcal{A}_2$ *is the symbolic game* $(\mathcal{M}, \lambda)$ *where* $\mathcal{M} = \langle \Sigma, \mathcal{X}, Q, q_0, \delta, F, \kappa \rangle$ *is defined by:*

$$Q = \quad Q_1 \times Q_2 \quad \cup \quad Q_1 \times Q_2 \times (\Sigma_{\mathcal{A}_1} \cup \mathcal{X}_1)$$
$$q_0 = q_0^1 \times q_0^2$$
$$\delta = \Delta_0 \cup \Delta_1, \quad where$$

$$\begin{cases} \Delta_0 &= \left\{ (q_1, q_2) \xrightarrow{\alpha_1, g_1} (q_1', q_2, \alpha_1), \qquad \text{for all } q_1 \xrightarrow{\alpha_1, g_1} q_1' \in \delta_1 \right\} \\ \Delta_1 &= \left\{ (q_1, q_2, \alpha_1) \xrightarrow{\alpha_2, g_2 \wedge (\alpha_1 = \alpha_2)} (q_1, q_2'), \qquad \text{for all } q_2 \xrightarrow{\alpha_2, g_2} q_2' \in \delta_2 \right\} \end{cases}$$

$$\kappa = \kappa_1 \times \kappa_2$$

and the labeling function λ *is defined by* $\lambda((q_1, q_2)) = A$ *and* $\lambda(q_1, q_2, \alpha) = E$, *for every* $(q_1, q_2), (q_1, q_2, \alpha) \in Q$.

The simulation game of $\mathcal{A}_1$ *by* $\mathcal{A}_2$ *over letters in* S, *denoted by* $\mathcal{G}_S(\mathcal{A}_1, \mathcal{A}_2)$, *is the concrete game* $\mathcal{G}(\mathcal{M}, \lambda, S)$.

Finally, any infinite play in $\mathcal{G}(\mathcal{M}, \lambda, S)$ *is winning for* **Eloise**, *and any finite play is losing for the player who cannot move.*

The simulation problem for PAs is the following: given two PAs $\mathcal{A}_1$ *and* $\mathcal{A}_2$, *is* $\mathcal{A}_1 \trianglelefteq \mathcal{A}_2$? *This amounts to asking whether player* **Eloise** *has a winning strategy in the concrete game* $\mathcal{G}_\Sigma(\mathcal{A}_1, \mathcal{A}_2)$.

The following lemma states an immediate property of the symbolic games.

Lemma 2. *Let* $(\mathcal{M}, \lambda)$ *be a symbolic game and* $S \subset \Sigma$. *If* S *is finite then the concrete game* $\mathcal{G}_S(\mathcal{M}, \lambda)$ *is finite too.*

4.2 Decidability of the Simulation Problem

We show that the simulation problem is decidable by showing that solving symbolic games is decidable. The idea is that the problem of solving a symbolic game can be reduced to solving the same game in which the two players instantiate the variables from a *finite* set of letters, see Proposition 1. In order to relate these two games we need to adapt the notion of coherence between substitutions given in Definition 5 to the coherence between game positions. The definition of the coherence between game positions, still denoted by $\bowtie_C$, follows.

Definition 9. *Let* $\mathcal{M}$ *be a PA and* q *be a state of* $\mathcal{M}$. *Let* S_1, S_2 *be subsets of* Σ *where* $C = S_1 \cap S_2 \neq \emptyset$. *Let* $(q, \sigma)_P$ *(resp.* $(q, \gamma)_P$ *) be a position of player* $P \in \{E, A\}$ *in the two-players game* $\mathcal{G}_{S_1}(\mathcal{M}, \lambda)$ *(resp.* $\mathcal{G}_{S_2}(\mathcal{M}, \lambda)$*). Define* $(q, \sigma)_P \bowtie_C (q, \gamma)_P$ *iff* $\sigma \bowtie_C \gamma$.

Let $(\mathcal{M}, \lambda)$ be a symbolic game where $\mathcal{M} = \langle \Sigma, \mathcal{X}, Q, q_0, \delta, F, \kappa \rangle$ is a PA. Let $k = |\mathcal{X}|$. We define C_0 to be the finite set of letters:

$$C_0 = \Sigma_A \uplus \{c_1, \ldots, c_k\} \tag{1}$$

Let us take the abbreviations $\mathcal{G}_\Sigma = \mathcal{G}_\Sigma(\mathcal{M}, \lambda)$ and $\mathcal{G}_{C_0} = \mathcal{G}_{C_0}(\mathcal{M}, \lambda)$. Now we are ready to show that the games $\mathcal{G}_\Sigma$ and $\mathcal{G}_{C_0}$ are equivalent. For the direction "$\Rightarrow$" we show that out of a winning strategy of Eloise in $\mathcal{G}_\Sigma(\mathcal{M}, \lambda)$ we construct a winning strategy for her in $\mathcal{G}_{C_0}(\mathcal{M}, \lambda)$. For this purpose, we show that each move of Abelard in $\mathcal{G}_{C_0}(\mathcal{M}, \lambda)$ can be mapped to an Abelard move in $\mathcal{G}_\Sigma(\mathcal{M}, \lambda)$, and that Eloise response in $\mathcal{G}_\Sigma(\mathcal{M}, \lambda)$ can be actually mapped to an Eloise move in $\mathcal{G}_{C_0}(\mathcal{M}, \lambda)$. Formally, we

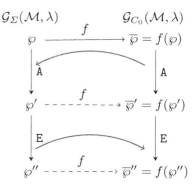

need to define a function $f : \mathrm{Pos}(\mathcal{G}_\Sigma(\mathcal{M}, \lambda)) \to \mathrm{Pos}(\mathcal{G}_{C_0}(\mathcal{M}, \lambda))$ in order to make possible this mapping as shown in the Diagram on the right. It follows that this is sufficient to argue that if there is an infinite play in $\mathcal{G}_\Sigma(\mathcal{M}, \lambda)$ then we can construct an infinite play in $\mathcal{G}_{C_0}(\mathcal{M}, \lambda)$ as well. We show in Lemma 3 that it is possible to construct the function f. The proof of the direction ($\Leftarrow$) is similar to the one of ($\Rightarrow$) by following the same construction.

Lemma 3. *Let $(\mathcal{M}, \lambda)$ be a symbolic game. Let $\mathcal{G}_\Sigma(\mathcal{M}, \lambda)$ (resp. $\mathcal{G}_{C_0}(\mathcal{M}, \lambda)$) be the concrete game in which the variables are instantiated from the infinite set Σ (resp. finite set C_0 defined in Eq. (1)). Let $\wp^\star$ and $\overline{\wp}^\star$ be their starting position respectively. Then, there is a function $f : \mathrm{Pos}(\mathcal{G}_\Sigma(\mathcal{M}, \lambda)) \to \mathrm{Pos}(\mathcal{G}_{C_0}(\mathcal{M}, \lambda))$ with $f(\wp^\star) = \overline{\wp}^\star$ and $\wp \bowtie_C f(\wp)$ for all $\wp \in \mathrm{Pos}(\mathcal{G}_\Sigma(\mathcal{M}, \lambda))$, such that the following hold:*

i) *for all $\overline{\wp} \in \mathrm{Pos}_A(\mathcal{G}_{C_0}(\mathcal{M}, \lambda))$, if $\overline{\wp} \to \overline{\wp}'$ is a move of Abelard in $\mathcal{G}_{C_0}(\mathcal{M}, \lambda)$ and $f(\wp) = \overline{\wp}$ for some position $\wp$ in $\mathcal{G}_\Sigma(\mathcal{M}, \lambda)$ then there exists a position $\wp'$ in $\mathcal{G}_\Sigma(\mathcal{M}, \lambda)$ such that the move $\wp \to \wp'$ is possible in $\mathcal{G}_\Sigma(\mathcal{M}, \lambda)$ and $f(\wp') = \overline{\wp}'$. And,*

ii) *for all $\wp \in \mathrm{Pos}_E(\mathcal{G}_\Sigma(\mathcal{M}, \lambda))$, if $\wp \to \wp'$ is a move of Eloise in $\mathcal{G}_\Sigma(\mathcal{M}, \lambda)$ then the move $f(\wp) \to f(\wp')$ is possible in $\mathcal{G}_{C_0}(\mathcal{M}, \lambda)$.*

Therefore,

Proposition 1. *Let $(\mathcal{M}, \lambda)$ be a symbolic game and let C_0 be the finite set of letters defined in Eq. (1). Then, Eloise has a winning strategy in $\mathcal{G}_\Sigma(\mathcal{M}, \lambda)$ iff she has a winning strategy in $\mathcal{G}_{C_0}(\mathcal{M}, \lambda)$.*

It follows from Lemma 2 and Proposition 1 that the simulation problem for PAs is decidable. We argue next that this problem is in EXPTIME.

Theorem 3. *The simulation problem for PAs is decidable in EXPTIME.*

4.3   Synthesis of a Mediator

It is possible to synthesize a mediator (as a PA) allowing the communication between a client C and a community of available services $S_1, \ldots, S_n$ by relying on a winning strategy for `Eloise` in the simulation game $\mathcal{G}_{C_0}(C, S_1 \otimes \ldots \otimes S_n)$ [3], where C_0 is the finite set of letters defined in Eq. (1). It is worth mentioning that it is possible to devise an algorithm that generates all possible mediators.

5 Conclusion

We introduced an extension of automata that provides us with both a natural specification style as shown by examples and a composition synthesis algorithm for parametrized services. To our knowledge PAs is one of the largest class of automata on infinite alphabet to admit a decidable simulation algorithm.

References

1. Akroun, L., Benatallah, B., Nourine, L., Toumani, F.: On decidability of simulation in data-centeric business protocols. In: La Rosa, M., Soffer, P. (eds.) BPM Workshops 2012. LNBIP, vol. 132, pp. 352–363. Springer, Heidelberg (2013)
2. Belkhir, W., Chevalier, Y., Rusinowitch, M.: Fresh-variable automata: applicationto service composition. In: SYNASC 2013, pp. 153–160. IEEE C.S (2013)
3. Belkhir, W., Chevalier, Y., Rusinowitch, M.: Parametrized automata simulation and application to service composition. J. Symbolic Comput. **69**, 40–60 (2014)
4. Berardi, D., Calvanese, D., De Giacomo, G., Hull, R., Mecella, M.: Automatic composition of transition-based semantic web services with messaging. In: Proceedings of the 31st International Conference on Very Large Data Bases, VLDB 2005, pp. 613–624 (2005)
5. Berardi, D., Calvanese, D., De Giacomo, G., Lenzerini, M., Mecella, M.: Automatic composition of E-services that export their behavior. In: Orlowska, M.E., Weerawarana, S., Papazoglou, M.P., Yang, J. (eds.) ICSOC 2003. LNCS, vol. 2910, pp. 43–58. Springer, Heidelberg (2003)
6. Berardi, D., Cheikh, F., Giacomo, G.D., Patrizi, F.: Automatic service composition via simulation. Int. J. Found. Comput. Sci. **19**(2), 429–451 (2008)
7. Cheikh, F.: Composition de services: algorithmes et complexité. Ph.D. thesis, Université Paul Sabatier, Thèse de doctorat (2009). http://thesesups.ups-tlse.fr/712/1/Cheikh_Fahima.pdf
8. De Giacomo, G., Patrizi, F., Sardiña, S.: Automatic behavior composition synthesis. Artif. Intell. **196**, 106–142 (2013)
9. Degano, P., Ferrari, G.-L., Mezzetti, G.: Nominal automata for resource usage control. In: Moreira, N., Reis, R. (eds.) CIAA 2012. LNCS, vol. 7381, pp. 125–137. Springer, Heidelberg (2012)
10. Feuillade, G., Pinchinat, S.: Modal specifications for the control theory of discrete event systems. Discrete Event Dyn. Syst. **17**(2), 211–232 (2007)
11. Finkel, A., Schnoebelen, P.: Well-structured transition systems everywhere!. Theor. Comput. Sci. **256**(1–2), 63–92 (2001)
12. Haase, C., Ouaknine, J., Worrell, J.: On the relationship between reachability problems in timed and counter automata. In: Finkel, A., Leroux, J., Potapov, I. (eds.) RP 2012. LNCS, vol. 7550, pp. 54–65. Springer, Heidelberg (2012)
13. Hamadi, R., Benatallah, B.: A Petri net-based model for web service composition. In: Database Technologies, ADC 2003, pp. 191–200 (2003)

14. Ragab Hassen, R., Nourine, L., Toumani, F.: Protocol-based web service composition. In: Bouguettaya, A., Krueger, I., Margaria, T. (eds.) ICSOC 2008. LNCS, vol. 5364, pp. 38–53. Springer, Heidelberg (2008)
15. Hull, R., Su, J.: Tools for composite web services: a short overview. SIGMOD Rec. **34**(2), 86–95 (2005)
16. Jancar, P.: Undecidability of bisimilarity for Petri nets and some related problems. Theor. Comput. Sci. **148**(2), 281–301 (1995)
17. Lustig, Y., Vardi, M.Y.: Synthesis from component libraries. In: de Alfaro, L. (ed.) FOSSACS 2009. LNCS, vol. 5504, pp. 395–409. Springer, Heidelberg (2009)
18. Nourine, L., Toumani, F.: Formal approaches for synthesis of web service business protocols. In: ter Beek, M.H., Lohmann, N. (eds.) WS-FM 2012. LNCS, vol. 7843, pp. 1–15. Springer, Heidelberg (2013)
19. Reisig, W.: Towards a theory of services. In: UNISCON 2008, pp. 271–281 (2008)

Optimal Virtual Machine Placement in a Multi-tenant Cloud

Hana Teyeb[(✉)], Ali Balma, Nejib Ben Hadj-Alouane, and Samir Tata

National Engineering School of Tunis, OASIS,
University of Tunis El Manar, Tunis, Tunisia
hana.teyeb@gmail.com, ali.balma@tunisietelecom.tn,
nejib_bha@yahoo.com, samir.tata@it-sudparis.eu

Abstract. In this work, we focus on the problem of virtual machines (VMs) placement in geographically distributed data centers, where tenants may require a set of networking VMs. The aim of the present work is to plan and optimize the placement of tenant's VMs requests in a geographically distributed Cloud environment while considering location and system performance constraints. Thus, we propose ILP formulations which have as objective the minimization of traffic generated by networking VMs and circulating on the backbone network. The different experiments conducted on the proposed formulations show the effectiveness of our model for large-scale Cloud systems in terms of convergence time and computational resources.

Keywords: Cloud computing · Virtual machine · Data center · Linear programming

1 Introduction

With the rise of the popularity of Cloud Computing services, the number of applications having high demand on networking resources has increased significantly. In the IaaS, which is the focus of this paper, tenants can benefit from on-demand provisioning of compute, storage and networking resources. Currently, IaaS providers do not offer guaranteed performance to tenants [9]. Therefore, application performance may varies unpredictably which leads to a decrease of the application productivity and customer satisfaction [3]. In fact, performance metrics such as propagation delay and Quality-of-Service (QoS) are important for many applications and services (e.g. video streaming servers, data intensive applications, ...). Although centralized data centers provide efficiency, the latency between user and data center may hurt user experience. So geographic locations of data centers would be a balance of centralization and proximity to users [8,25]. In a geographically distributed Cloud environment, several DCs are

---

A. Balma is with Tunisie Telecom, Jardins du Lac II, 1053, Tunis, Tunisia.
S. Tata is with the Institut TELECOM SudParis, CNRS UMR Samovar, 9 rue Charles Fourier, 91011 EVRY Cedex, France.

© Springer International Publishing Switzerland 2015
F. Toumani et al. (Eds.): ICSOC 2014, LNCS 8954, pp. 308–319, 2015.
DOI: 10.1007/978-3-319-22885-3_27

interconnected via an IP over wavelength-division-multiplexing (WDM) backbone network (*IP-over-WDM*); in such an environment, traffic between DCs is quite significant [7]. Tenants may require services from different regions. As a result, Cloud service providers face two fundamental problems in order to achieve a trade-off between operational costs and performance:

- Finding the optimal placement schema for several VMs while considering proximity and location constraints which will ensure application performance.
- Reducing the inter-DCs traffic produced by the different communicating VMs to prevent from eventual network congestion problems and reduce energy consumption.

To solve this problem, this paper consider exact methods to plan and optimize the placement of VMs among geographically distributed DCs. We propose an Integer Linear Programming model (ILP) that solves optimally the VM placement problem in a large-scale Cloud system while considering location constraints. The objective of our formulation is to minimize the traffic between DCs. We aim to minimize the traffic in order to prevent from possible network congestion problems and reduce the energy consumption. For that purpose, we present a well-known formulation proposed in [17]. This formulation had been largely used in the literature as being the most efficient formulation for the problem of Hub Location [1].

This work makes the following contributions:

- An ILP formulation is presented inspired from a well known formulation [17] to deal with the VM placement problem in distributed Clouds with traffic awareness.
- A simplified reformulation is proposed in which a variable aggregation methods is considered in order to reduce the problem size and speed up the exact resolution compared to the classical formulation.
- We note that generally communicating-VMs belong to the same tenant. Thus, the tenant request is modeled by considering clusters of networking VMs of different sizes.
- Simulation results show that our proposed model provide optimal solutions for the placement of communicating VMs in large-scale Cloud systems with traffic-aware consideration even for large instance sizes compared to the classical formulation.

The remainder of this paper is organized as follows: In Sect. 2, we present a literature survey and we position our contribution. We then give in Sect. 3, a detailed problem statement with the assumptions. In Sect. 4, we provide a mathematical formulation of the VM placement problem across a distributed infrastructure. Section 5, discusses the simulation results showing the effectiveness of our model. Finally, we conclude.

2   Related Work

The problem of VM placement in a Cloud environment has received particular attention in recent years. Many researches have studied this problem from different perspectives. The VM placement problem within a single DC has been extensively studied in literature. In particular, managing communication traffic generated by communicating VMs within a DC is of a practical concern that has attracted significant attention. In [5], the authors propose a network-aware VM placement approach that satisfies traffic demands of the VMs in addition to hardware requirements. For that purpose, they present different heuristics to solve this problem. In [15], a VM placement algorithm is proposed in order to reallocate VMs in DC servers based on traffic matrix and hardware resources usage. In [10], the authors consider the placement problem of VMs hosting applications with intense bandwidth requirements. To solve this problem, they present a polynomial-time constant approximation algorithm. In [27], the authors consider the objective of minimum communication traffic in a DC. They propose a heuristic algorithm based on clustering methods for solving the optimization problem. The main limitation of the aforementioned works is the fact that they do not consider the geographically distributed DCs. They only study the VMs placement problem within a single DC. Moreover, they propose heuristics for solving the problem. Heuristics solve the problem but they do not provide the optimal solution, they provide only an approximate solution. There are only few researches that have studied the problem of VM placement within geographically distributed DCs. Some recent works tried to reduce power consumption or service delay of geographically distributed data centers by optimizing the location of DCs [20,24]. In [21], the authors propose both an offline and an online solution based on scheduling techniques to solve the problem of energy efficiency and load balancing for a geographically distributed Cloud infrastructure. However, to reduce energy costs, most of the existent works focus on minimizing the power consumption, or maximizing resource usage. In order to achieve these goals, it is crucial to consider one practical aspect which is the traffic transmission within the backbone network. By minimizing the amount of traffic exchanged between different DCs nodes, the energy costs including data transport costs will be also reduced [2]. The present work is different from traditional VM placement proposals since it considers resource allocation for VMs and traffic demands satisfaction across a geographically distributed Cloud architecture. In addition, it addresses a traffic-aware VM placement problem in large-scale Cloud systems while considering exact mathematical methods which provide the optimal solution.

3   Problem Description

The VMs placement problem in geographically distributed DCs (VMP) can be seen as a variant of the hub location problem where DCs are considered as hubs [1,11,18]. In fact, we aim to plan and optimize the assignment of different VMs that exchange data to geographically distributed DCs as we minimize the overall flow over the backbone network. By minimizing the traffic between DCs, we minimize the energy consumption and we reduce time delay. In this work, we present a well-known formulation proposed in [17]. This formulation was cited in [12] as being the best computationally effective. It has been proved as efficient for many variants of the Hub Location problem [22, 26], the transportation problem [13] and many other problems. We adapt this formulation to our problem by considering DCs as hubs nodes. In fact, the formulation proposed in [17] is a general formulation. The authors consider that all nodes could be considered as a hub. However, in our case, we consider that only DCs are hub nodes. Moreover, as explained in the assumptions section, DCs cannot generate traffic, but they are intermediary nodes. The traffic is generated and exchanged only between pairs of VMs. All these facts have contributed to the effectiveness of the formulation. In fact, the main advantage of this formulation is related to the reduced number of variables which is considerably low compared to existing formulations in the literature. In fact, the number of DCs is always very small compared to the number of VMs which makes the formulation efficient and suitable for our problem. For instance, suppose that we have $|D| = 10$ DCs and $|V| = 1000$ VMs, the number of variables of the formulation of [6] is $|V|^2 \times |D|^2$ which is equal to 10^8 variables. However, the formulation of [17] has only $|V| \times |D|^2$ which is equal to 10^5 variables.

Proposition 1. *The VMP problem is NP-Hard.*

Proof. The proof is based upon reduction of VMP to a capacitated multicommodity flow problem by considering DCs as hubs and where the flows are unsplittable, since each demand node must be assigned to a single DC (hub) then to a single path. The capacities on the DC can be considered as capacities on virtual links by splitting the DCs into two connected virtual nodes. The capacity of this virtual link is the same capacity of the DC. This problem is well known as being NP-hard [19].

In this work, we make the following assumptions:

- We assume that each VM may have a location constraint. Therefore, it can be only assigned in two particular DCs. But only one DC is effectively assigned to each VM.
- We suppose that different DCs are connected with a complete graph. This assumption aims to determine the demand matrix between each pair of DCs so it constitutes a basis for dimensioning the capacities of the backbone network links.
- Data center hardware capacities are supposed to be known and fixed a priori. We assume that DCs capacities are able to satisfy all VMs requests so we can achieve feasible solutions.
- We suppose that only VMs can exchange traffic between each other, DCs are considered as intermediary nodes that are not able to generate traffic to other nodes. There is also no traffic exchanged between VMs and DCs.
- We assume that each VM is characterized by an instance type. Every instance type has a fixed set of hardware configuration (CPU, memory and storage).

In next section, we present the ILP formulations of the problem of VM placement in large-scale Cloud system.

4   Problem Formulation

In this section, we formally define the VMs placement problem across multiple DCs as an ILP. We aim to optimally distribute VMs among different DCs in order to minimize inter-DCs traffic. The problem is considered as a complete graph $G = (N, E)$, where N is the set of the nodes constituted by VMs and DCs and E is the set of the edges. By considering a complete graph structure, we aim to estimate the amount of traffic exchanged between each pair of DCs so that we can dimension physical capacity links of the backbone network which will be the subject of our future work. We consider that VMs are connected to DCs by virtual links. We are given a traffic matrix that indicates the amount of communication traffic between each pair of VMs. We assume that each VM can be assigned into two possible DCs for geographical proximity considerations. But only one DC is effectively assigned to each VM. We denote by:

- D the set of DCs.
- V the set of virtual machines.
- R the set of hardware resources (CPU, RAM and storage).
- d_{ij} the amount of traffic exchanged between each pair of VMs.
- a_i^k takes 1 if the VM $i \in V$ can be placed in the DC $k \in D$, 0 otherwise.
- cap_r^k the capacity of the DC $k \in D$ in terms of resource $r \in R$.
- u_{ir} the amount of resource $r \in R$ consumed by the VM $i \in V$.

4.1   The Classical Formulation

We adapt a well-established classical formulation due to [17] for the CSAHLP problem. Although the two problems are quite different, they have many similarities that permits the adaptation of the formulation of [17] to our problem. In this formulation, we consider the following decision variables, similar to those of [17].

- z_i^h takes 1 if the VM $i \in V$ is placed in the DC $h \in D$, 0 otherwise.
- f_{kh}^i designates the amount of traffic generated by the VM $i \in V$ and circulating between DCs $h \in D$ and $k \in D$.

We denote by O_i the total flow emanating from a VM i. We have:

$$O_i = \sum_{j \in V} d_{ij} \quad \forall i \in V \tag{1}$$

The linear model denoted by (MF1) is described as follows:

$$\min \sum_{k \in D} \sum_{\substack{h \in D \\ h \neq k}} \sum_{i \in V} f_{kh}^i \tag{2}$$

Subject to:

$$z_i^h . O_i - \sum_{j \in V} d_{ij} . z_j^h = \sum_{k \in D} f_{hk}^i - \sum_{k \in D} f_{kh}^i \qquad \forall i \in V, \forall h \in D \qquad (3)$$

$$z_i^h \leqslant a_i^h \qquad \forall i \in V, \forall h \in D \qquad (4)$$

$$\sum_{h \in D} z_i^h = 1 \qquad \forall i \in V \qquad (5)$$

$$\sum_{i \in V} u_{ir} . z_i^h \leqslant cap_r^h \qquad \forall r \in R, \forall h \in D \qquad (6)$$

$$z_i^h \in \{0, 1\} \qquad \forall i \in V, \forall h \in D$$

$$f_{hk}^i \geqslant 0 \qquad \forall i \in V, \forall h, k \in D$$

The objective function (2) aims to minimize the amount of traffic generated by communicating VMs on the backbone network. The constraint (3) ensures the flow conservation. As for the constraint (4), it is a location constraint that indicates that the placement of different VMs must be restricted to a particular number of DCs that satisfy proximity constraint. This constraint aims to maintain service performance and to reduce time delay by placing high-communicating VMs in proximity of end-users. The matrix denoted by a_i^k is an input of the problem. It can be produced by measuring performance between each pair of nodes of the graph G. The constraint (5) ensures that every VM is running on only one DC. The final constraint (6) is a capacity constraint. It ensures that the amount of hardware resources consumed by different VMs placed in a given DC does not exceed the hardware capacities of this DC. The aim of this formulation is to solve optimally the problem of placing communicating VMs with correlated traffic in geographically distributed DCs for large-scale Cloud system. Unfortunately, with this formulation the convergence time to solve it optimally is very large and it may lead to an out of memory status for the commercial solver. Thus, we have reduced the resolution time of the linear program for large instances sizes by variables aggregation.

4.2 Variable Aggregation

We note that the formulation presented above, can be reformulated to another equivalent formulation that turns out to be more efficient as it reduces the number of the variables. In fact, we consider new decision variables:

- The first, designates the amount of traffic originated from a VM i and destined to a DC h.

$$v_{ih} = \sum_{k \in D} f_{kh}^i \quad \forall i \in V, \forall h \in D \qquad (7)$$

- The second decision variable designates the amount of traffic generated by VMs and sent to the backbone network.

$$\varphi_{ih} = \sum_{k \in D} f_{hk}^i \quad \forall i \in V, \forall h \in D \qquad (8)$$

Since we aim to minimize the amount of traffic circulating on the backbone network and we do not consider any associated cost, there is no need to consider the first decision variable in the objective function and in the flow conservation constraint. Thus, this reformulation reduce considerably the number of variables which becomes $|V|.|D|$ instead of $|V|.|D|^2$. A comparative experimentation will be provided in next section. Suppose that we have $|V| = 1000$ and $|D| = 10$, then the number of variables of the classical formulation (MF1) is equal to 10^5. However, when we adopt variable aggregation approach, the number of variables is reduced to 10^4. Hence, the new equivalent formulation denoted by (MF2) of the VMP problem is presented as follows:

$$\min \sum_{i \in V} \sum_{h \in D} \varphi_{ih} \tag{9}$$

Subject to:

$$O_i.z_i^h - \sum_{j \in V} d_{ij}.z_j^h \leqslant \varphi_{ih} \qquad \forall i \in V, \forall h \in D \tag{10}$$

$$z_i^h \leqslant a_i^h \qquad \forall i \in V, \forall h \in D \tag{11}$$

$$\sum_{h \in D} z_i^h = 1 \qquad \forall i \in V \tag{12}$$

$$\sum_{i \in V} u_{ir}.z_i^h \leqslant cap_r^h \qquad \forall r \in R, \forall h \in D \tag{13}$$

$$z_i^h \in \{0,1\} \qquad \forall i \in V, \forall h \in D$$

$$\varphi_{ih} \geqslant 0 \qquad \forall i \in V, \forall h \in D$$

The new objective function (9) aims to minimize the amount of traffic destined to the backbone network. In the flow conservation constraint 10, we replace the decision variables used in the first model by the new decision variables (8) and (7). The constraints (11), (12) and (13) are exactly the same constraints of the first model. In the next section, we present the details of different experiments conducted on the proposed formulations that show the effectiveness of this new formulation.

5   Experiments

In this section, we present the results of experiments performed. By these experiments, we show the effectiveness and the performance of our final model. We generated instances of different sizes in order to test the execution time of the linear program and the amount of traffic reduced within the backbone network. The different experiments were carried out on a machine that has an *Intel Xeon* 3,3 *GHz* CPU and 8 *Gb* of RAM. We have used the commercial solver CPLEX 12.5 [14] to solve, evaluate and compare different ILP formulations. In all tests, we have considered a complete graph representing the network topology. We denote by:

- S the value of the optimal solution provided by CPLEX and expressed in (Mb/s).

Table 1. Equivalence between the two formulations (MF1) and (MF2)

$(|V|, |C|)$	$(MF2)$			$(MF1)$		
	S	T	G	S	T	G
$(2000, 10)$	31713	2,176	0	31713	7,538	0
$(2000, 20)$	65287	2,262	0	65287	6,684	0
$(2000, 40)$	132221	2,047	0	132221	7,842	0
$(2000, 60)$	197789	2,568	0	197789	9,202	0
$(2000, 80)$	255693	2,663	0	255693	10,748	0
$(2000, 100)$	314895	2,683	0	314895	12,229	0

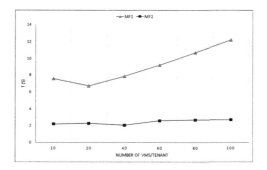

Fig. 1. Comparison between the two formulations $(MF1)$ and $(MF2)$

- T the convergence time, expressed in seconds.
- G the gap between S and the lower bound provided by CPLEX and expressed in %. $G = 0$ indicates that the optimal solution is reached.
- $|C|$ the number of VMs per tenant.

5.1 Data Input Characteristics

We consider that VMs have different hardware configuration. In particular, we choose three instance types (Small, Medium and Large) provided by Amazon Elastic Computing Cloud (EC2) [16]. Without loss of generality, we assume that all DCs have the same hardware capacities. We consider that the servers are hosted in racks. Every server has 8 cores and 16 GB of RAM. We consider that each rack host 30 server and each DC has an average of 500 racks. The traffic matrix represents traffic communication between each pair of VMs belonging to the same tenant. We have generated the traffic matrix randomly. The values of the traffic matrix range between 0 to 10 Gb/s. In fact, it is typically hard to obtain such data from real DCs [4,23] because of the required server level instruments.

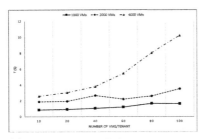
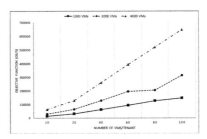

(a) Dependence of the convergence time of MF2 with the number of VMs per client

(b) Dependence of the objective function of MF2 with the number of VMs per client

Fig. 2. Simulation results.

5.2 Simulation Results

In this section, we present the simulation results conducted on the proposed formulation. We study the impact of different data input characteristics on the performance and convergence time of the linear program. We also present a case study with realistic data input sizes and discuss different configuration scenarios. For each simulation, we randomly generate 10 groups of tenant requests. All the simulation results are averaged by 10. The Table 1 shows the equivalence of the two formulations (MF1) and (MF2) as it provide exactly the same values of the objective function. We compare also the performance of the two formulations $(MF1)$ and $(MF2)$ for the same instances. We fix $|V| = 2000$ and we plot the convergence time for increasing number of tenant requests in Fig. 1. The results show the effectiveness of the variables aggregation approach we proposed, compared to the classical formulation (MF1). Moreover, the values of the convergence time (T) of (MF2) are more stable than those of (MF1) as the number of VMs per tenant increases.

We verify then the scaling properties of the final linear program denoted by $(MF2)$. First, we fix the number of DCs ($|D| = 6$), and plot the convergence time for increasing values of VMs ($|V| = 1000$ to 4000) and for different size of tenant requests in Fig. 2b which illustrates the variation of the convergence time with respect to the number of VMs. We note that the convergence time increase with the number of networking VMs. It is important also to study the dependence of the objective function with the increasing values of networking VMs per tenant. We remark that the amount of traffic increase with the number of VMs and also with the increasing number of networking VMs which is evident.

In real Cloud environment, demand size of networking VMs varies from a client to another. In order to study the impact of such granularity of the traffic matrix, we perform groups of experiments where we have fixed the number of DCs at 6 and have generated randomly the number of networking VMs for each client. The details of these simulations are presented in Tables 2, 3 and 4. We conclude that the convergence time is related to the number of networking VMs.

Table 2. Simulation results for granular traffic matrix for $|V| = 1000$ and $|D| = 6$

Inst.	S	T	G
1	870062	6,22	0
2	1293963	12,08	0
3	464183	2,96	0
4	1046745	7,78	0
5	473609	4,15	0
6	850318	6,91	0
7	526378	3,47	0
8	1573899	13,91	0
9	1534363	13,59	0
10	400959	3,92	0

Table 3. Simulation results for granular traffic matrix for $|V| = 2000$ and $|D| = 6$

Inst.	S	T	G
1	2389520	26,37	0
2	2360764	3,5	0
3	2509212	30	0
4	1905721	19,79	0
5	2789950	45,6	0
6	2391700	58,16	0
7	2942320	80,39	0
8	2093672	25	0
9	5826080	75,6	0
10	4135462	48,95	0

Table 4. Simulation results for granular traffic matrix for $|V| = 4000$ and $|D| = 6$

Inst.	S	T	G
1	452235	6,39	0
2	438499	7,16	0
3	428807	6,817212	0
4	447650	6,88	0
5	411661	6,56	0
6	445644	6,74	0
7	444393	6,84	0
8	432195	6,7	0
9	420983	6,66	0
10	460827	6,46	0

6   Conclusion

In this work, we have focused on the problem of VMs placement in a geographically distributed Cloud infrastructure where the DCs are interconnected over the backbone network. We have used and a well-known ILP formulation and have adapted it to fit our particular problem. We reduced the number of the variables by using variables aggregation methods. The different experiments that we have conducted show the effectiveness of the proposed linear model in terms of convergence time and computational resources for realistic instance sizes.

References

1. Alumur, S., Kara, B.Y.: Network hub location problems: The state of the art. Eur. J. Oper. Res. **190**(1), 1–21 (2008)
2. Amokrane, A., Zhani, M., Langar, R., Boutaba, R., Pujolle, G.: Greenhead: Virtual data center embedding across distributed infrastructures (2013)
3. Bari, M.F., Boutaba, R., Esteves, R., Granville, L.Z., Podlesny, M., Rabbani, M.G., Zhang, Q., Zhani, M.F.: Data center network virtualization: a survey. IEEE Commun. Surveys Tutorials **15**(2), 909–928 (2013)
4. Benson, T., Anand, A., Akella, A., Zhang, M.: Understanding data center traffic characteristics. ACM SIGCOMM Comput. Communi. Rev. **40**(1), 92–99 (2010)
5. Biran, O., Corradi, A., Fanelli, M., Foschini, L., Nus, A., Raz, D., Silvera, E.: A stable network-aware vm placement for cloud systems. In: 2012 12th IEEE/ACM International Symposium on Cluster, Cloud and Grid Computing (CCGrid), pp. 498–506 (2012)
6. Campbell, J.F.: Integer programming formulations of discrete hub location problems. Eur. J. Oper. Res. **72**(2), 387–405 (1994)
7. Chen, Y., Jain, S., Adhikari, V.K., Zhang, Z.L., Xu, K.: A first look at interdata center traffic characteristics via yahoo! datasets. In: 2011 Proceedings IEEE INFOCOM, pp. 1620–1628. IEEE (2011)
8. Church, K., Greenberg, A., Hamilton, J.: On delivering embarrassingly distributed cloud services. Hotnets VII 34 (2008)
9. Bitcurrent.   http://www.bitcurrent.com/download/cloud-performance-from-the-end-user-perspective/. Visited 04 February 2014
10. Cohen, R., Lewin-Eytan, L., Naor, J., Raz, D.: Almost optimal virtual machine placement for traffic intense data centers. In: 2013 Proceedings IEEE INFOCOM, pp. 355–359 (2013)
11. Contreras, I., Fernández, E.: General network design: a unified view of combined location and network design problems. Eur. J. Oper. Res. **219**(3), 680–697 (2012)
12. Correia, I., Nickel, S., Saldanha-da Gama, F.: The capacitated single-allocation hub location problem revisited: a note on a classical formulation. Eur. J. Oper. Res. **207**(1), 92–96 (2010)
13. Correia, I., Nickel, S., Saldanha-da Gama, F.: Single-assignment hub location problems with multiple capacity levels. Transp. Res. Part B: Methodol. **44**(8), 1047–1066 (2010)
14. Ibm corporation ilog cplex. http://www.ilog.com/products/cplex/. Visited: 04 February 2013
15. Dias, D., Costa, L.: Online traffic-aware virtual machine placement in data center networks. In: Glob. Inf. Infrastruct. Networking Symp. (GIIS) 2012, pp. 1–8 (2012)

16. Amazon elastic compute cloud amazon ec2. http://aws.amazon.com/ec2/. Visited 05 February 2014

17. Ernst, A.T., Krishnamoorthy, M.: Solution algorithms for the capacitated single allocation hub location problem. Ann. Oper. Res. **86**, 141–159 (1999)

18. Farahani, R.Z., Hekmatfar, M., Arabani, A.B., Nikbakhsh, E.: Hub location problems: a review of models, classification, solution techniques, and applications. Comput. Ind. Eng. **64**(4), 1096–1109 (2013)

19. Garey, M.R., Johnson, D.S.: Computer and intractability. A Guide to the NP-Completeness. WH Freeman and Company, New York (1979)

20. Goiri, I., Le, K., Guitart, J., Torres, J., Bianchini, R.: Intelligent placement of datacenters for internet services. In: 2011 31st International Conference on Distributed Computing Systems (ICDCS), pp. 131–142 (2011)

21. Goudarzi, H., Pedram, M.: Geographical load balancing for online service applications in distributed datacenters. In: 2013 IEEE Sixth International Conference on Cloud Computing (CLOUD), pp. 351–358. IEEE (2013)

22. da Graça Costa, M., Captivo, M.E., Clímaco, J.: Capacitated singleallocation hub location problema bi-criteria approach. Comput.Oper. Res. **35**(11), 3671–3695 (2008)

23. Kandula, S., Sengupta, S., Greenberg, A., Patel, P., Chaiken, R.: The nature of data center traffic: measurements & analysis. In: Proceedings of the 9th ACM SIGCOMM Conference on Internet Measurement Conference, pp. 202–208. ACM (2009)

24. Larumbe, F., Sansò, B.: Optimal location of data centers and software components in cloud computing network design. In: Proceedings of the 2012 12th IEEE/ACM International Symposium on Cluster, Cloud and Grid Computing (Ccgrid 2012), CCGRID 2012 pp. 841–844. IEEE Computer Society, Washington, DC (2012). http://dx.doi.org/10.1109/CCGrid.2012.124

25. Valancius, V., Laoutaris, N., Massoulié, L., Diot, C., Rodriguez, P.: Greening the internet with nano data centers. In: Proceedings of the 5th International Conference on Emerging Networking Experiments and Technologies, pp. 37–48. ACM (2009)

26. Yaman, H., Carello, G.: Solving the hub location problem with modular link capacities. Comput. Oper. Res. **32**(12), 3227–3245 (2005)

27. Zhang, B., Qian, Z., Huang, W., Li, X., Lu, S.: Minimizing communication traffic in data centers with power-aware vm placement. In: 2012 Sixth International Conference on Innovative Mobile and Internet Services in Ubiquitous Computing (IMIS), pp. 280–285. IEEE (2012)

Cloud Computing and Scientific Applications

A Validation Method of Configurable Business Processes Based on Data-Flow

Yiwang Huang[1,2] and Zaiwen Feng[1(✉)]

[1] State Key Laboratory of Software Engineering, School of Computer,
Wuhan University, Wuhan, China
{huangyw, zwfeng}@whu.edu.cn
[2] Institute of Information Engineering, Tongren College, Tongren, China

Abstract. In configurable business process model, an incorrect configuration may lead to behavioral issues. The researches of the configurable business process model focus on the control-flow perspective but lacking the perspective of the data-flow, which can't reflect the constraints of data-flow during the configuration. To overcome this shortage, this paper uses the CPN as a formalism model to express the business process model and extends the business process model by adding the data-flow, which enables it to deal with the data semantic in business process model, then transforms business process model into the configurable business process model by adding configuration operations. Finally, we use the logic ASK-CTL to express the data constraints of configurable business process model, and then we apply the corresponding toolset of CPN to analyzing and verifying the data semantic constraint properties of this model, and the results of experiment show the validation of the proposed method.

Keywords: Process configuration · CPN · Configurable business process model · Artifact · ASK-CTL

1 Introduction

It is a hot field for Software product line engineering (SPLE) [1–4] to promote reuse throughout the software lifecycle in order to benefit from economies of scale when developing several similar systems. Configurable business process model [9, 10] enable the sharing of common processes among different organizations in a controlled manner, thus they can be regarded as decision models. It restricts the possible behaviors of business process model by process configuration during the design-time of the process model. In a configurable business process model, the process configuration operation is achieved by hiding, blocking or allowing certain fragments of the configurable process model [5, 6], when an individual business process model is needed for particular users' requirements, it can be configured by three process operations under the certain guidelines or constraints from the configurable business process model. Although the configurable process models provide certain guidance to analyze during configuration, they do not guarantee that the individualized models are correct, whether syntactically or semantically. In fact, because of hiding some fragments and blocking some others,

© Springer International Publishing Switzerland 2015
F. Toumani et al. (Eds.): ICSOC 2014, LNCS 8954, pp. 323–335, 2015.
DOI: 10.1007/978-3-319-22885-3_28

the instances of a configured model may suffer from behavioral anomalies such as deadlocks and livelocks, so it is very important issue that analysis and verification the configurable process model.

Existing approaches [11–16] about the verification of the configurable process models are divided the several parts as follows: focusing on the control-flow perspective of configurable process models, but lacking the perspective of the data-flow processing semantic [12, 13]; discussing syntactical correctness related to configuration [14–16], but not providing techniques for ensuring the behavioral correctness of the configured models. This research focuses on studying the general business process model such as modifying the WF-net model not configurable business process model. In order to offset the shortcomings of previous researches, this paper exploits an approach which expends the configurable business process model with by the data-flow, it is not only reflects the control-flow but also the data-flow of the business process, enabling to deal with the data semantic in the configurable business process model. In this approach, we use the colored Petri-net (CPN) [17–19] to represent the business process model by adding the data, then transforms it to express the configurable business process model through process configuration; Following, it can analyze and verify the correctness of the control-flow and data-flow utilizing powerful toolset of CPN that support the designing and analysis of such processes.

2 Motivation

The basic idea of our work is to exploit an analysis and verification framework based on the data-flow in configurable business process model. This framework is shown as the Fig. 1. (1) the designer will design a CPN model in term of particular domain the basic of the CPN model; (2) the analyst extract the data model from the same domain, then add the data model to the designed CPN model; (3) we transform this model into the configurable business process model with data model by the process configuration; (4) this configurable process model will be analyzed and verified to satisfy the desired properties of data-flow which express by the ASK-CTL using the toolset of CPN.

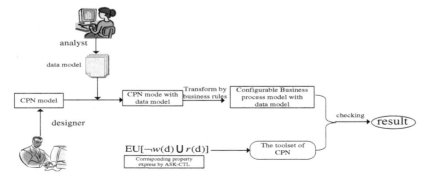

Fig. 1. The framework of verification of the configurable business process model with data-flow based on CPN

3   The Configurable Business Process Model with Data-Flow

3.1   Integrate the Data-Flow into the Business Process Model

In order to integrate the data-flow into the business process model, it is necessary to introduce the basic concepts of the data-flow, and add the data model to the CPN model, the formal definition is shown as follows:

Definition 1. Let D is the set of data element $(d_1, \ldots, d_2 \in D)$, assume the set of data expressions over D is $E_D = \{e_1, \ldots, e_n\}$, then give a function $l : E_D \rightarrow 2^D$ (2^D represents the power set of data element over D), in other words, mapping each data expression e_i ($e_i \in \Pi$) a set of data element depend on D.

For example $l(e) = \{d_1, \ldots, d_n\}$ ($e \in E_D$), then the data expression will be denoted as $e(d_1, \ldots, d_n)$, indicating the date expression e will depend on $\{d_1, \ldots, d_n\}$.

Definition 2. The CPN [18] based on data-flow is a tuple $CPN_D = (P, P_D, T, A, \Sigma, D, V, C, G, R, W, E, I)$, here: (1) P, T, A, Σ, E, the semantic of these symbols are the same as the regular CPN; (2) V is the set of variables; (3) P_D is the set of data places of business process; (4) D is the data set of business process model; (5) $C : (P \rightarrow \Sigma) \cup (P_D \rightarrow D)$ is color set function, mapping each place a color set (including data set); (6) $G : T \rightarrow EXPR_v \cup E_D$ is guard function, including the data expression, $Type[G(t)] = Bool$; (7) $R : P_D \times T \rightarrow E_D$ is read arc function, mapping each reading arc(read operation) a data expression; (8) $W : T \times P_D \rightarrow E_D$ is write arc function, mapping each write arc(write operation) a data expression; (9) $I : (P \rightarrow EXPR_\phi) \cup (P_D \rightarrow E_D)$ is initialization function, here, including the data expression; (10) and are satisfied the following conditions:

$$P \cup P_D \cup T \neq \emptyset$$
$$\wedge (P \cap T = \emptyset \wedge P \cap P_D = \emptyset \wedge P_D \cap T = \emptyset)$$
$$\wedge (A \subseteq (P \times T \cup T \times P) \wedge R \subseteq P_D \times T \wedge W \subseteq T \times P_D),$$
$$\wedge (dom(A) \cup cod(A) \cup cod(R) \cup dom(W) = P \cap T)$$
$$\wedge (dom(R) \cup cod(W_r) = P_D)$$

Here, *dom* and *cod* are precursor and successor set of dual relationship respectively, P_D is the set of data places, A is flow relation, R is read relation and W is write relation.

Figure 2 shows a CPN model based on the data-flow, in this figure, $dp_i \in P_D$ is the data place (represented by light-blue ellipse), $D_i \in D$ is color sets of the corresponding data place, $p_i \in P$ is the control-flow place and $C_i \in C$ is the corresponding color sets, $t_i \in T$ is the transition in this model CPN_D, t_2 is enabled when the guard expression $guard(v)$ evaluates true, otherwise, t_3 is enabled, the read arc is represented by an arrow with character "r", the write arc is represented by an arrow with the character "w", for example, the transition t_1 will read data of color set d_1 through the read arc from the data place dp_0, denoted as $r(dp_0, t_1) = d_1$, after the transition t_1 is triggered, the transition t_1 will produce the data d_2, denoted as $w(t_1, dp_1) = d_2$.

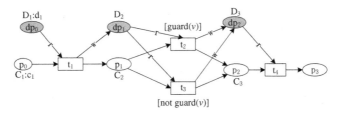

Fig. 2. The CPN model based on data-flow

Definition 3. Let CN is a colored Petri net over D CPN_D, then:

1. Marking: mapping each place a token multiset $M(p) \in C(p)_{MS}$, here $p \in P \cup P_D$; 2. Initial marking: $M_0(p) = I(p), \forall p \in P \cup P_D$; 3. Variable of transition: $Var(t) \subseteq V$; 4. Binding of transition: mapping each variable v ($v \in Var(t)$) a value $b(v)$ ($b(v) \in Type[v]$) for certain transition, all the variable bindings of transition is denoted as $B(t)$; 5. Binding element: is a pair $(t, b), t \in T, b \in B(t)$, all the set of binding element for transition t is marked as $BE(t) = \{(t, b)|b \in B(t)\}$, all the binding set of the transitions of model marked as BE; 6. Step: $Y \in BE_{MS}$.

Definition 4. A binding element $(t, b) \in BE$ in the marking M is enabled if and only if:

1. $G(t)\langle b \rangle$; 2. $\begin{array}{l} \forall p \in P : E(p, t)\langle b \rangle \ll= M(p), \\ \forall dp \in P_D : R(p, t)\langle b \rangle \ll= M(p) \end{array}$;

3. When the $(t, b) \in BE$ occurs, the next marking M' will determinate by the following formula:

$$
M'(p) = \begin{cases} (M(p) - -E(p, t)\langle b \rangle) + +E(t, p)\langle b \rangle, \\ \qquad\qquad\qquad\qquad \text{if } p \in P; \\ (M(p) - -R(p, t)\langle b \rangle) + +W(t, p)\langle b \rangle, \\ \qquad\qquad\qquad\qquad \text{if } p \in P_D. \end{cases}
$$

The condition 1 shows all the guard expressions of transition t in binding b evaluate true; the condition 2 shows the tokens of each input places ($\forall p \in P \cup P_D$) of transition t suffice to enable the transition t, for example, the transition t_1 in Fig. 2 is enabled if and only if the tokens' number of place p_0 and data places dp_0 is not less than one respectively; the condition 3 shows the tokens' distribution M' after the transition is enabled, including two parts: the tokens' distribution of control-flow places $p \in P$ and the tokens' distribution of data-flow places $p \in P_D$.

3.2   The Configuration of Business Process Model

Only the variation point of the business process model integrating the data-flow is configurable transition, so these transitions of this model will divided two kinds: configurable transitions T_v and regular transitions T_r, here, the transitions T_r will be configured with three configurations: allowed, hidden or blocked, so the configurable business process model based on the data-flow can derive the different business process variants through configuration decisions to the variation transitions.

Definition 5. (Configurable CPN_D). Let CN is a CPN_D, CN^c is a configurable business process model, which is derived from CN by through assign a configuration to variation transitions of CN, here, there exists a configuration function $F_{CN} : T_v \rightarrow \{allowed, hidden, blocked\}$, then: (1) $F_{CN}(t) = allow$, $t \in T_v$ is allowed; (2) $F_{CN}(t) = blocked$, $t \in T_v$ is blocked; (3) $F_{CN}(t) = hidden$, $t \in T_v$ is hidden.

We can draw some conclusions:
(1) $T = (T_v \cup T_r) \wedge (T_v \cap T_r = \Phi)$;
(2) $A^c_{CN} = \{t \in T_v | F_{CN}(t) = allow\}$ is the set of all the variation transitions which is allowed;
(3) $H^c_{CN} = \{t \in T_v | F_{CN}(t) = hide\}$ is the set of all the variation transitions which is hidden;
(4) $B^c_{CN} = \{t \in T_v | F_{CN}(t) = block\}$ is the set of all the variation transitions which is blocked.

For example, in the Fig. 2, after the transition t_2 is enabled, its execution will produce a data $d_3 \in D_3$, the execution of the transition t_4 will be assign three configuration operations in terms of the value of data d_3, so the transition t_4 is a configurable transition, so $T_v = \{t_4\}$, $T_r = \{t_1, t_2, t_3\}$, the configurable model of the Fig. 2 is shown as Fig. 3 (the configurable transition represented by bold border), the transition t_4 is assigned the operation *hidden* in terms of the value of data d_3, then $F_{CN}(t_4) = hidden$, $H^c_{CN} = \{t_4\}$, the execution of this transition will *skip*, the others transitions are all regular transitions, so $A^c_{CN} = B^c_{CN} = \Phi$ (empty set).

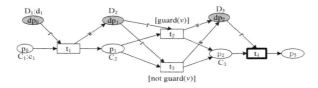

Fig. 3. The configurable CPN model based on data-flow

3.3   The Analysis and Verification of the Configurable Business Process Model with Data-Flow

There exist some researches [13–15] about correctness of control-flow, this paper will discuss the correctness of the configurable business process model with two stages: first, analyzes and verifies the soundness of the configurable business process model with data-flow; second, analyzes and checks the correctness of data-flow of business process model. Here, we use the similar CTL formulas to express the correctness of data-flow.

(1) **Temporal logic ASK-CTL** [16, 17]

The syntax of ASK-CTL: The state formula and transition formula of ASK-CTL be definition as follows.

Definition 6. The state formula of ASK-CTL Φ and the transitions formula of ASK-CTL Φ are generated by the following syntax:

$$\phi ::= T|\alpha|\neg\phi|\phi_1 \vee \phi_2|\langle\psi\rangle|\mathrm{EU}(\phi_1, \phi_2)|\mathrm{AU}(\phi_1, \phi_2),$$
$$\psi ::= T|\beta|\neg\psi|\psi_1 \vee \phi_2|\langle\phi\rangle|\mathrm{EU}(\psi_1, \psi_2)|\mathrm{AU}(\psi_1, \psi_2),$$

Here, α is a function from the CPN marking to Boolean, β is a function from the binding element of CPN transitions to Boolean, $\phi \in \Phi, \psi \in \Psi$. Based on the CTL, the ASK-CTL is extended the CTL with adding the transformation operations "$\langle\rangle$". It is enable to transform each other between the state formula and transition formula, vice versa. The "$\neg, \vee$" is logic operators, the operators "EU, AU" are combined by temporal operators "U(Until)" and path operators "E(Exist)" or "A(for A11)".

The semantics of ASK-CTL: Let Φ is a state formula, Ψ is transitions formula, we use the formula $\wp, s| =_{St} \phi$ ($\phi \in \Phi$, s is a state in model $\wp$) to interpret state formula, $\wp, \tau| =_{Tr} \psi$ ($\psi \in \Psi$, τ is a transition in model $\wp$) to interpret transition formula, the concrete semantic interpretation is shown as follows:

$$\wp, s| =_{St} T.$$
$$\wp, s| =_{St} \alpha, iff\, \alpha(s) = T.$$
$$\wp, s| =_{St} \neg\phi, iff\, M, s| =_{St} \phi \text{ is not true.}$$
$$\wp, s| =_{St} \phi_i \wedge \phi_j, iff\, (\wp, s| =_{St} \phi_i) \vee (\wp, s| =_{St} \phi_j).$$

$$\wp, s| =_{St} <\beta> , iff\, (\exists\alpha = (s, (t, b), s') \in \Phi) \wedge \wp,$$
$$\alpha| =_{Tr} \Psi, \text{the}(t, b) \text{ is a binding element.}$$
$$\wp, s| =_{St}\mathrm{EU}(\phi_1, \phi_2), iff\, \exists\sigma \in P_s.$$
$$(\exists n \leq |\sigma|.(\forall 0 \leq k < n.\wp, s_k| =_{St} \phi_1)$$
$$\wedge \wp, s_n| =_{St} \phi_2).$$
$$\wp, s| =_{St}\mathrm{AU}(\phi_1, \phi_2), iff\, \forall\sigma \in P_s.$$
$$(\exists n \leq |\sigma|.(\forall 0 \leq k < n.\wp, s_k| =_{St} \phi_1)$$
$$\wedge \wp, s_n| =_{St} \phi_2).$$

Here, P_s represents the path set which start from the state s, any path will be finite or infinite, for any finite path $\forall\sigma = s_0 b_1 s_1 \cdots s_{n-1} b_n s_n$, the length of the path $|\sigma| = n$, b_i

represent the edge from s_{i-1} to s_i. The interpretation of transitions formula is the same as the state formula. In this paper, the analysis and verification of the correctness focus on the data-flow of the business process model, we use the logic ASK-CTL to express the corresponding properties of correctness in the data-flow.

(2) **The correctness of the data-flow of business process model**

In this section, we use the logic ASK-CTL to define these data anti-pattern [16] as following.

Definition 7. (Missing Data). If there exist a path in the configurable business process model with data-flow that the data element d ($d \in D$) is not written before reading the data element d, then called the data element d is missing, use ASK-CTL to express this situation as follows (Fig. 4):

$$EU[\neg w(d) \cup r(d)] \tag{1}$$

The missing data is shown as the Fig. 5, the transition t_3 is enabled when the guard expression guard(v) evaluates the value false, then this transition will not produce the data $d_3 \in D_3$, however, the configurable transition t_4 isn't triggered until reading the data d_3, under this situation, the data d_3 is missing.

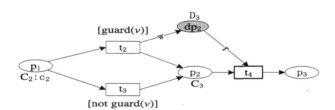

Fig. 4. Error of missing data in configurable business process model

Corollary 1. (The checking of missing data). Let $\wp$ is a configurable business process model with data-flow, here, the set of data object is D, assume $QS_\wp$ is all the complete path set over model $\wp$ (including start and termination transitions), then there isn't missing data in the process model if and only if the missing data errors doesn't exist in any path, formally:

$$\forall \sigma \in QS_\wp : \wp, \sigma| = \neg(EU[\neg w(d) \cup r(d)]), r \in R, w \in W, d \in D \tag{2}$$

The error of redundant data error refers to the situation some data elements which generated by some tasks aren't access by any task until the end of business process; these data elements are called redundant data.

Definition 8. (Redundant Data): If there exists a path in the configurable business process model with data-flow in which a data element d ($d \in D$) is not read forever after written by certain transition, then the data element d is redundant by generated, use the logic ASK-CTL to express as follows:

$$EU[w(d) \wedge EU[\neg r(d) \cup (w(d) \wedge \neg r(d))]] \tag{3}$$

It is shown as the Fig. 6, the data $d_2 \in D_2$ is produced by the transition t_1 will not be consumed by any transition for the remaining process, so the data d_2 is redundancy.

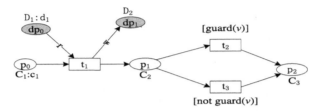

Fig. 5. Error of redundancy data in configurable business process model

Corollary 2. (The checking of redundancy data). Configurable business process model based on data-flow with the set of transitions T, D is the set of data objects, assume $QS_\wp$ is a completed trace generated over $\wp$ (including start activity and terminal activity), then there does not exist the redundancy data in the configurable business process model if and only if every trace does not exist redundancy data for $\wp$, formally:

$$\forall \sigma \in QS_S : M, \sigma| = \neg(EU[w(d) \wedge$$
$$EU[\neg r(d)w(d) \wedge \neg r(d))]]), r \in R, w \in W, d \in D \tag{4}$$

The errors of lost data update refers to a data object written by an activity is update by the subsequent activity, but without reading the data object by any activity between the twice writing operations, leading the result that the content of data object of the first writing operation is covered by the content of second writing operation before it is read by other activity needing its' content of data object.

Definition 9. (Lost data update): In the configurable business process model based on the data-flow, there exists a path such that a data element d ($d \in D$) is written twice before it is read by some activity, then the update of the data element d is missing, using the logical of ASK-CTL to expressed this definition as follows:

$$EU[w(d) \wedge EU[\neg r(d) \cup w(d)]] \tag{5}$$

It is shown as the Fig. 7, the data place dp_2 has been written two times by the transition t_1 and t_2 or t_1 and t_3, the data written by transition t_1 will be replaced by the

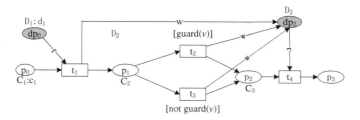

Fig. 6. Error of lost data update in configurable business process model

data written by transition t_2 or t_3 in data place dp_2, so the data generated by the transition t_1 is lost, this situation will be lost data update.

Corollary 3. (Checking of lost data update). Let M is a configurable business process model based on data-flow with the set of transitions T, D is the set of data objects, assume QS_M is a completed trace generated over M (including start activity and terminal activity), then there does not exist the errors of lost data update in the configurable business process model if and only if every trace does not exist lost data update in model M, formally:

$$\forall \sigma \in QS_S : M, \sigma| = \neg(EU[w(d) \wedge$$
$$EU[\neg r(d) \cup w(d)]]), r \in R, w \in W, d \in D \tag{6}$$

4   Case Study

Here, we use an example (logistics dispatching) to illustrate this basic idea which is shown as Fig. 8. In this configurable CPN model, there exists ten activities (bold & italic style): *GoodsChosing, submitPhoneOrder, submitPaperOrder, submitElectricOrder, InformationRecord, DuplicateDetection, Sortby Region, SortbyTime, SortbyPriority, Oder Storing* (represented by transitions with white box in the figure) and seven places (labeled by white ellipse in the figure) represent the corresponding state (italic style): *Start, GoodsChosed, RecordInformation, OrderSubmited, OrderConfirmed, Order Stored, End*. So, the control-flow of general business process model can be express with the white transitions and places. However, data dependencies between the activities will restrict the behavior of the business process model, so the data-flow research is also very important part of workflow. In the Fig. 8, the activity *GoodsChosing* will produce data GoodsProperty, this data element will include: GoodsID, GoodsQuantity, DeliveryPriority etc., then the data GoodsProperty take as the input data of Submitting activity, here, all of the data elements represent by places labeled with green in order to distinguish from the replaces represent the control-flow, such as: GoodsChoose, GoodsProperty, RecordForm, ElectricOrder, DeliveryRegion, Delivery Timesort, DeliveryBatch, OrderBooked.

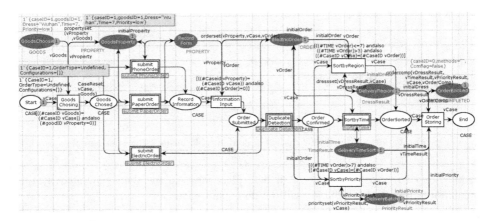

Fig. 7. Integrity configurable CPN_D model logistics dispatching

Here, we only verify the correctness of the errors of miss data information, the result is shown in the Fig. 8, in this figure, we define two function Node1 and Node2 to express two desired data states: "Choosing Goods" and "Order is created", using A1 and A2 to note these two states respectively, finally, we define a ASK-CTL formula **myASKCTLformula** to represent the property of the error of missing data, we can judge whether the model exists the error of missing data in term of the value of **myASKCTLformula**, we observe the ASK-CTL formula **myASKCTLformula** *InitNode* estimates **true** in the Fig. 8, so the designed model doesn't exist the error of missing data. This analysis and verification are fit the errors of redundancy data and lost data update, because of the paper's space, we don't discuss these properties with detail.

5   Related Work

There exists some research work about the modeling and ensuring correctness of configurable business process model [12–16], they are divided into two parts: on the one hand, focused on the informal modeling language of business process model, such as C-SAP, C-BPEL, C-EPC and C-iEPC etc. [4–8]; on the other hand, aim to model and analyze the configurable business process model using formal method, most of them are adapt the Petri nets and its variations. The theory is first developed in the context of Petri nets and then extended to a process modeling notation widely used in practice, namely Event-driven Process Chains. In the reference [8], it proposed Configurable EPC (C-EPC) as an extended reference modeling language which allows capturing the core configuration patterns. A formalization of this language as well as examples for typical configurations is provided. A program of further research including the identification of a comprehensive list of configuration patterns, deriving possible notations for reference model configurations and testing the quality of these proposed extensions in experiments. In the references [1–4], from the perspective of the Software Product Line Engineering, these works main to tackle those challenges at a fundamental level, it extend transition systems with features in order to describe the

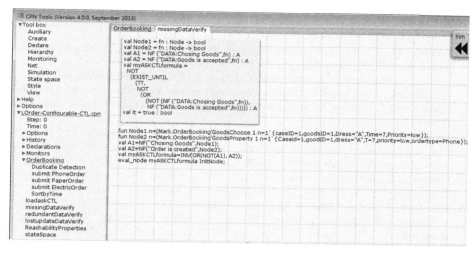

Fig. 8. The correctness verification of data-flow in the configurable CPN_D model

combined behavior of an entire system family, then define and implement a model checking technique that allows to verify such transition systems against temporal properties. For discuss the consistence between the goal model and the configurable business process model, some research works proposed an automated solution that relies on Description Logics and automated reasoning for validating mappings that describe the realization of goals by activities in business process models. The results are the identification of two inconsistency patterns: strong-inconsistency and potential-inconsistency, and the development of the corresponding algorithms for detecting inconsistencies in the references [16].

6   Conclusion and Future Work

In this paper, we proposed an analysis and verification method of configurable business process based on data-flow, the method is based on the Colored Petri net (CPN). We assume the CPN model designed in term of particular domain, then the analyst extract the data model from the same domain and add the data model to the designed CPN model, integrated the data model into the business process model, we can transform this model into the configurable business process model with data model by the process configuration, so the execution of the configurable business process model does abbey the constraints of data-flow and analyze and verify this configurable process model to satisfy the desired property which express by the ASK-CTL using the toolset of CPN.

Acknowledgment. This work is supported by the National Natural Science Foundation of China (61100017), the Fundamental Research Funds for the Central Universities under Grant (2042014kf0237), the united fund of science and technology department of GuiZhou province Municipal Science and Technology of Tongren Bureau and Tongren university (No. J&LKT [2012]02).

References

1. Webber, D.L., Gomaa, H.: Modeling variability in software product lines with the variation point model. Sci. Comput. Program. **53**(3), 305–331 (2004)
2. Classen, A., Heymans, P., Schobbens, P.Y., Legay, A., Raskin, J.F.: Model checking lots of systems: efficient verification of temporal properties in software product lines. In: 32th IEEE International Conference on Software Engineering, pp. 335–344. IEEE Press, New York (2010)
3. Classen, A., Cordy, M., Schobbens, P.Y., Heymans, P., Legay, A., Raskin, J.F.: Featured transition systems: foundations for verifying variability-intensive systems and their application to LTL model checking. IEEE Trans. Softw. Eng. **39**(8), 1069–1089 (2012)
4. Czarnecki, K., Helsen, S.: Staged configuration using feature models. In: Nord, R.L. (ed.) SPLC 2004. LNCS, vol. 3154, pp. 266–283. Springer, Heidelberg (2004)
5. Gottschalk, F., van der Aalst, W.M.P., Jansen-Vullers, H.M.: Configurable process models: a foundational approach. Reference Modeling: Efficient Information Systems Design through Reuse of Information Models, pp. 59–78. Springer, Heidelberg (2007)
6. Gottschalk, F., van der Aalst, W.M.P., Jansen-Vullers, H.M., la Rosa, M.: Configurable workflow models. Int. J. Coop. Inf. Syst. **17**(2), 177–221 (2008)
7. Gottschalk, F., Wagemakers, T.A., Jansen-Vullers, M.H., van der Aalst, W.M., La Rosa, M.: Configurable process models: experiences from a municipality case study. In: van Eck, P., Gordijn, J., Wieringa, R. (eds.) CAiSE 2009. LNCS, vol. 5565, pp. 486–500. Springer, Heidelberg (2009)
8. Rosemann, M., van der Aalst, W.M.P.: A configurable reference modeling language. Inf. Syst. **32**(1), 1–23 (2007)
9. La Rosa, M., Dumas, M., ter Hofstede, A.H.M., Mendling, J.: Configurable multi-perspective business process Models. Inf. Syst. **36**(2), 313–340 (2011)
10. La Rosa, M., van der Aalst, W.M.P., Dumas, M., terHofstede, A.H.M.: Questionnaire-based variability modeling for system configuration. Softw. Syst. Model. **8**(2), 251–274 (2009)
11. La Rosa, M., Dumas, M., ter Hofstede, A.H., Mendling, J., Gottschalk, F.: Beyond control-flow: extending business process configuration to roles and objects. In: Li, Q., Spaccapietra, S., Yu, E., Olivé, A. (eds.) ER 2008. LNCS, vol. 5231, pp. 199–215. Springer, Heidelberg (2008)
12. van der Aalst, W., Lohmann, N., La Rosa, M., Xu, J.: Correctness ensuring process configuration: an approach based on partner synthesis. In: Hull, R., Mendling, J., Tai, S. (eds.) BPM 2010. LNCS, vol. 6336, pp. 95–111. Springer, Heidelberg (2010)
13. van der Aalst, W.M.P., Dumas, M., Gottschalk, F., terHofstede, A.H.M., La Rosa, M., Mendling, J.: Preserving correctness during business process model configuration. Formal Aspects Comput. **22**(3–4), 459–482 (2010)
14. Wang, Z.X., Wang, J.M., Zhu, X.C., Wen, L.J.: Verification of workflow nets with transition conditions. J. Zhejiang Univ. Sci. C. **13**(7), 483–509 (2012)
15. Liu, D.S., Wang, J.M., Chan, S.C.F., Sun, J.G., Zhang, L.: Modeling workflow processes with colored petri nets. Comput. Indus. **49**(3), 267–281 (2002)
16. Sidorova, N., Stahl, C., Trčka, N.: Soundness verification for conceptual workflow nets with data: early detection of errors with the most precision possible. Inf. Syst. **36**(7), 1026–1043 (2011)
17. van der Aalst, W.M.P., Stahl, C., van der Westergaard, M.: Strategies for modeling complex processes using colored petri nets. In: Jensen, K., van der Aalst, W.M., Balbo, G., Koutny, M., Wolf, K. (eds.) ToPNoC VII. LNCS, vol. 7480, pp. 6–55. Springer, Heidelberg (2013)

18. Kurt, J., Lars, M.K.: Colored Petri Nets: Modelling and Validation of Concurrent Systems. Springer, Berlin (2009)
19. van Hee, K.M., Oanea, O., Sidorova, N.: Colored petri nets to verify extended event-driven process chains. In: Meersman, R., Tari, Z. (eds.) OTM 2005. LNCS, vol. 3760, pp. 183–201. Springer, Heidelberg (2005)

Exploiting the Parallel Execution
of Homology Workflow Alternatives
in HPC Compute Clouds

Kary A.C.S. Ocaña[1]([⊠]), Daniel de Oliveira[2], Vítor Silva[1],
Silvia Benza[1], and Marta Mattoso[1]

[1] Federal University of Rio de Janeiro - COPPE/UFRJ, Rio de Janeiro, Brazil
{kary, silva, silviabenza, marta}@cos.ufrj.br
[2] Computing Institute, Fluminense Federal University – UFF, Niterói, Brazil
danielcmo@ic.uff.br

Abstract. Homology modeling (HM) plays an important role in drug discovery. HM analysis aims at predicting a 3D model from a biological sequence in order to discover new drugs. There are several problems in executing an HM analysis in large-scale, such as multiple software to be evaluated, the management of the parallel execution, and results analysis, e.g. browsing manually all results to find which structure was derived from which program with good quality. Scientific Workflow Management System (SWfMS) with parallelism and provenance support can aid the large-scale HM executions by addressing the result analysis. However, before submitting the HM workflow for execution, it has to be specified along with its several alternatives (also called variants), as considered in this paper. Managing HM workflow variations is a complex task to be accomplished even with the help of a SWfMS. In this paper, we propose SciSamma (**S**tructural **A**pproach and **M**olecular **M**odeling **A**nalyses), an abstract representation of HM workflows inspired in the concept of software product lines (SPL). SciSamma models HM workflow variants to execute with parallel processing in the cloud using SciCumulus SWfMS. We evaluated SciSamma with two common variants using 100 protease enzymes of protozoan genomes. Both variations presented scalability with performance improvements (dropping from 8 h to 27 min using 32 Amazon's large virtual machines). While evaluating the two workflow variants, through provenance queries, they present the same quality in biological results, but the difference in execution time between them was around 40 %.

Keywords: Cloud · Workflow · Homology modeling · Provenance data

1 Introduction

Homology Modeling (HM) refers to the process of constructing an atomic-resolution model, i.e. a 3D structure, of a target sequence of interest [1]. HM is important for investigation of molecular targets, offering a deeper insight into the relationship

This work was partially sponsored by FAPERJ and CNPq.

F. Toumani et al. (Eds.): ICSOC 2014, LNCS 8954, pp. 336–350, 2015.
DOI: 10.1007/978-3-319-22885-3_29

between structure, stability, dynamics, and functions of orthologous protein alignment interpreted under constraints of natural selection [1]. Computer-based HM experiments have significant potential to contribute to biomedical and pharmaceutical research when results of simulations prove to be consistent with the outcome of conventional laboratory experiments (also called wet experiments).

Modeling and executing computer-based HM experiments is a complex and time-consuming task, since, in several cases, there is a large set of programs to explore in each execution (i.e. program alternatives). In summary, there are four main problems in conducting an HM experiment: (i) *Scaling*. The large-scale of data and the time-consuming homology programs demand parallelism and the use of HPC resources; (ii) *Analysis*. HM result analysis is complex, e.g. manually browsing all resulting files to find which structure was successfully produced by which program with good quality; (iii) *Variants*. There are different definitions for *Variants* in scientific workflows. In this paper, we consider a *variant* as one of the multiple possible specifications of the workflow. For example, for each implementation of an homology activity, there is a corresponding workflow variant. The choice of a software implementation (for a specific activity) can impact the resulting data or products [2]. This choice is not simple to be done before the execution. Multiple softwares have to be evaluated and configured according to the several steps of the HM analysis. There are variations in several levels, e.g. installation and configuration issues, parallel execution requirements, difference in performance and financial cost of the execution and the quality of 3D structures generated by different algorithms, etc. Exploring possible execution plans with variants and registering a corresponding specification is necessary; (iv) *Execution with variants*. Managing the execution of variants along HM experiments is far from trivial. Commonly programs are manually executed by scientists (via command line or Web services), which can introduce systematic errors in the experiment. Tracking and exploring these program variations along the results is commonly complex in large-scale science.

Using scientific workflow support addresses problems of *scaling* and *analysis*, but configuring workflow *variants* and managing their *executions* are important, yet open, problems. HM experiments can be modeled as scientific workflows, where each step refers to a workflow activity, which invokes a particular application. These workflows can be defined and managed by Scientific Workflow Management Systems (SWfMS) [2] in High Performance Computing (HPC) environments such as clouds. To address the HM result analysis problem, SWfMSs register the execution history of the workflow through provenance data [3]. This is important since provenance data contains valuable information about the entire experimentation process.

According to Gil et al. [2] representing workflow variants in scientific workflows is fundamental and understanding the impact that a choice has on the resulting data products is top priority. However, SWfMS only execute workflows with activities associated to a specific program not allowing variabilities. The Wings system [4] supports generic experiment definition in abstract levels and generates workflows ready to execute in Pegasus [5] and OODT workflow systems.[1] This a very important support

---

[1] http://oodt.apache.org/components/maven/workflow/.

in registering an experiment exploration plan and powerful in suggesting a workflow configuration ready to execute. However, even when all variations are identified, scientists should be able to identify which program is the best choice for a specific activity (or a specific input dataset), and avoid poor configurations. These workflows may take hours or days to execute; it is necessary to eliminate variants that are showing poor results during the execution. This is a complex task, especially in the HM domain, where several expertises are necessary. Moreover, sometimes, changes within variations are driven by the parallel execution environment and this decision must be done at runtime, based on the current workload of the system. This requires a runtime change on the configuration of the workflow being executed [6].

SciCumulus cloud workflow engine [7] has a dynamic tool that allows for scientists to perform changes of the workflow specification at runtime [6]. Scientists can choose the best program to implement a specific activity among a set of variabilities while complying with several criteria defined by scientists (e.g. deadlines, maximum financial cost, validation rules). Alternatively, it also lets scientists to change the workflow definition arbitrarily during the execution, for instance, changing the program that implements a specific workflow activity to an equivalent one, based on the current execution behavior. This way, SciCumulus implements the concept of workflow variants at runtime, without having to interrupt the workflow execution, change the program and start all over. The fourth problem of managing workflow execution with variants is also addressed by SciCumulus, which supports PROV-Wf [8], an extension of W3C PROV standard [9], which allows for querying on workflow variations related to runtime provenance data. SciCumulus has a rich provenance database that relates domain data with execution data (besides typical provenance) and allows for user steering during the execution.

To evaluate workflow variants in SciCumulus, we have modeled Sci*Samma*, (*Structural Approach and Molecular Modeling Analyses*), a workflow that represents variations in activities involved in the HM analysis. SciCumulus is able to map executable workflows from activities' variabilities in SciSamma's specification. We executed two traditional HM variants over protozoan cysteine protease (CP) [10] sequences of protozoan neglected tropical diseases (NTD) [11]. Both executable workflows mapped from SciSamma were executed in the Amazon Elastic Compute Cloud (EC2). Both variants presented scalability with performance improvements from approximately 8 h to 27 min (using 32 Amazon's large virtual machines).

The main contributions of this paper are: (i) to provide a specification of an HM workflow that represents several variations for each activity with associated validation rules and (ii) to assist scientists in analyzing their HM workflows by exploring and querying the provenance database, obtaining information about each HM workflow variation from the same database. With these experiments we show the potential and necessity of variants support at runtime in long running workflows. We also briefly present biological results from a real case study that reported a list of candidate 3D-models of CPs, suitable for antimalarial drugs investigation. To the best of the authors' knowledge, this is the first report of large-scale HM experiments for large datasets to construct 3D structures using scientific workflows in HPC clouds.

The remainder of this paper is organized as follows. Section 2 shows the benefits and potential of SciCumulus workflow engine tools to model and execute HM workflow variations. Section 3 presents HM experiments modeled as scientific work-flows and describes the specification of SciSamma and workflow variants evaluated with SciCumulus. Section 4 shows experimental results. Section 5 discusses related work and Sect. 6 concludes this paper.

2   SciCumulus: A Suite of Tools for Managing Scientific Workflow in Clouds

As stressed by Gil et al. [2], in their survey about the challenges of scientific work-flows, there is a need of approaches to support basic research in computer science to create a "science of workflows". These approaches should cover a list of requirements of scientific applications. According to Gil et al. they should support (non-exhaustive list): (i) *Scaling*: provide high performance capabilities since most of the large-scale workflows demand parallelism and the use of HPC environments; (ii) *Workflow Variants*: representing workflow variants since many scientific experiments explore the variants with alternative settings to understand the final effects on the generated results; (iii) *Monitoring*: support for monitoring since many workflows execute for weeks; (iv) *Fault Tolerance*: allow for re-executing failed activities or reuse partial executions; and (v) *Reproducibility*: support for capturing and querying provenance data associated to the several workflow executions. We have been improving SciCumulus' workflow engine to address these issues.

SciCumulus is a workflow engine that manages the parallel execution of large-scale scientific workflows in cloud environments, such as Amazon AWS or Microsoft Azure. Based on the workflow specification and the input datasets provided by scientists, SciCumulus is able to distribute activity executions on a set of VMs, mapping data to these activities, thus increasing parallelism. It has a 3-objective cost model where scientists can inform their preferences for scheduling: they can focus on maximizing reliability (i.e. minimizing errors), minimizing execution time or minimizing financial costs. This way, SciCumulus distributes the activity executions according to its esti-mated execution time to the most suitable VM. These estimations are provided by querying the PROV-Wf provenance repository. Differently from other SWfMS, Sci-Cumulus executes workflows in static or adaptive modes [12]. In the adaptive mode, it performs a horizontal scaling to overcome problems on the environment (i.e. if a VM has failed or restarted) or to meet scientists' requirements such as maximum execution time or maximum allowed financial cost. SciCumulus is able to add (or remove) VMs from the pool of available VMs during the workflow execution. Since HM workflows process hundreds or even thousands of input multi-fasta files, HPC adaptive mecha-nisms are essential to provide scalability.

SciCumulus provenance repository represents fine grained information about the experiment and the cloud environment. Statistics on previous executions of scientific workflows are obtained by querying this database. Provenance data is also the input to the cost model to estimate the execution time and adapt the scheduling. Execution information of the provenance model is captured at each VM involved in the execution and by the autonomous agent, which captures the information about the cloud envi-ronment. This provenance repository contains information about elements that represent: (i) processes executed in the cloud; (ii) artifacts consumed and produced by the workflow execution, (iii) the temporality of data and, (iv) information about the cloud environment. Besides reproducibility, the provenance repository of SciCumulus allows for monitoring, fault-tolerance and adaptation of the workflow execution, which is in sync with requirements in [2].

To support workflow variations, SciCumulus has a specific component that allows for dynamic changes in the workflow specification [6]. It queries the provenance repository to estimate the necessary execution time of each activity and chooses the best program to implement a specific activity following a specific weighted cost model. Each variant is evaluated following d different factors $F = \{f_1, f_2, ..., f_d\}$. Each factor is associated with a function that calculates the value of the factor. Each variant is associated with $\{v_1, ..., v_d\}$ values, corresponding to the F factors. Each factor has an associated weight α_i, for all d factors such that $\sum \alpha_i = 1$ For each variant program ap_x of an activity it calculates a value in the form $f(ap_x) = \alpha_1.v_1 + \alpha_2.v_2 + ... + \alpha_d.v_d$. Since for each factor it is assigned a weight α_i, the higher the α_i value, the more valuable is the factor for calculating $f(ap_x)$. Scientists may establish the criteria defining these weights, otherwise they can use default values. The idea is that scientists can adjust these weights both a priori and during workflow execution. Based on factor values and their weights, SciCumulus chooses (and adapts at runtime) the most appropriate program to a specific activity variant or uses the program selected by scientists. HM workflows can benefit from this type of mechanism due to the number of variabilities in their structure. Therefore, with the adaptive component, scientists are not forced to model several different independent workflows (one for each variability) for the same experiment, thus reducing the chance of errors and helping the management and analysis of the variabilities.

As for monitoring, SciCumulus has a notification mechanism that identifies pre-defined events, through queries on provenance data generated at runtime. Notification is a relevant alternative for long-term "black-box" executions since it is unviable for scientists to stay at a monitor for days or even weeks. Scientists define preconfigured events to be notified via message services in social networks (such as twitter) or via android mobile devices. Since SciSamma workflow variants can execute for days and produce a large variety of events (errors, activity termination, etc.), monitoring mechanisms are effectively required and were used.

3   Representing Homology Modeling as a Scientific Workflow

3.1   Background on Homology Modeling

Homology (or comparative) modeling [1] refers to the process of constructing a 3D-model of the (target) protein sequence and an experimental 3D structure of homologous proteins (i.e. template). HM relies on the identification of previously known protein structure to resemble the structure of the target sequence in order to produce an alignment that maps residues in both target and template sequences. The 3D structure of the template must be determined by reliable empirical methods (e.g. X-ray crystallography or Nuclear Magnetic Resonance, NMR) to provide the necessary high resolution and accuracy to build 3D-models. Two important factors influence the ability to predict accurate models for HM: the extent of structural conservation between target and template and the accuracy of alignments [1]. A HM experiment is composed by four main steps, as defined by Marti-Renom et al. [13] labeled from I to IV in Fig. 1, as follows:

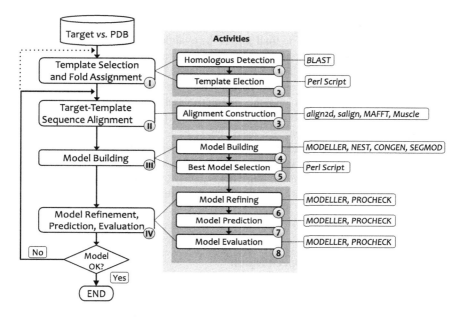

Fig. 1. HM workflow conceptual view

(I) **Template Selection and Fold Assignment.** Identifies previously known 3D structures of a related protein that can serve as a template for HM. Template protein structures are collected from databases such as Protein Data Bank (RCSB PDB), SCOP or CATH [14]. The most used software for searching homologous sequences is BLAST, but others (pHMMs-based) such as SAM, HMMER, and HHPred are also applied. If more than one template is found, it is recommended to select the template protein with the highest sequence identity to the target.

(II) **Target-Template Sequence Alignment.** Establishes correspondences between the residues of the target and the template using sequence alignment methods, such as Needleman-Wunsch and Smith-Waterman. However, programs relying on multiple sequence alignments (e.g. MAFFT) and structure information derived from homologous proteins (e.g. 2D-align) may produce better results. When the sequence identity value (calculated comparing the target and template) is high, the standard methods produce similar alignments. On the other hand, when this identity value is low (usually less than 40 %) more sophisticated alignment tools are needed and manual inspection of the alignment is suggested [13].

(III) **Model Building and Refinement.** It involves the prediction of the target structure atomic coordinates using residue equivalences defined in the sequence alignment. Methodologies for building 3D-models are based on five main approaches: rigid body assembly (e.g. COMPOSER, CONGEN, SWISS-MODEL, WHATIF), segment matching (e.g. SEGMOD), satisfaction of spatial restraints (e.g. MODELLER, DRAGON), artificial evolution (e.g. NEST), and self-consistent mean field approach (e.g. Builder).

(IV) **Prediction Evaluation.** The final step is the evaluation of predicted structures. It focuses on the model (as an entity) or specific segments. Some computational methods such as PROCHECK, AQUA, and MolProbity are used in the prediction/evaluation of the model for checking and assessing the target-template alignment and the geometry and stereochemistry. Alternative evaluation methods combine different structure-based scoring functions (e.g. QMEAN) and classical physics-based energies for molecular dynamic simulations (e.g. AMBER). After the evaluation and depending on the quality of the target structure, it is possible to go back to the previous steps (e.g. to select a better template or improve the alignment quality). In these cases, the prediction procedure is repeated until the final structure reaches an acceptable level of accuracy [13].

3.2 SciSamma Conceptual Specification

SciSamma is composed by the four steps, which are decomposed into one or more activities (each one associated to one or more programs), labeled from 1 to 8, as follows: (I) Template Selection and Fold Assignment, activities 1 and 2; (II): Target-Template Sequence Alignment, activity 3; (III): Model Building, activities 4 and 5; and (IV): Model Refinement, Prediction, Evaluation, activities 6 to 8.

Activity 1 executes BLAST [15] to compare an input sequence (target) against non-redundant sequences from PDB to detect the potentially homologous sequences of the known structures (template). It writes the matches into an output file. This output file is used as input for Activity 2, which executes a Perl script that parses and extracts important information such as the code of the PDB sequence that was aligned to the target sequence, the percentage identities between the target and PDB sequences, and the e-value of the alignment. This information is essential to elect the candidate(s) template(s). As a result, one or more potential template structures can be obtained, but only the most appropriate single template structure for the target sequence (from all possible templates) is elected using a custom Python script based on MODELLER [16]. Summarizing, with MODELLER, scientists are able to: (i) assess sequence and structure similarities between all candidate templates, (ii) create the structure alignment, (iii) calculate the root mean square (rms) and distance root mean square (drms) deviations, (iv) calculate a clustering tree with pairwise distances, and (v) allow for the visualization of differences among template candidates.

In Activity 3, the elected alignment program aligns the target sequence with the template and produces an alignment based on the structural information from the template. Activity 3 is called a variant activity, i.e. more than one program can implement it and scientists have to choose one of them. There are several programs (e.g. align2d, salign, MAFFT, Muscle) based on specific bioinformatics methods (e.g. general dynamic programming or progressive methods). Scientists do not know a priori which alignment program/method provides the best results for their input data. Therefore, they typically try each one of the programs in different workflow executions (i.e. trials). This approach is time consuming and can be financially unviable if executed in pay-as-you-go clouds.

Activity 4 builds the 3D-model of the target sequence based on template structure and alignment. This is a variant activity. There are several programs that build 3D-models (e.g. COMPOSER [17], CONGEN [18], MODELLER [16], NEST/Jackal [19], Builder [20]), and each one is based on distinct approaches (e.g. rigid body assembly, segment matching, spatial restraints satisfaction). If MODELLER is elected, as the replication number for building 3D-models should be fixed in five, then the outcome should be five PDB models obtained for the same target, assigned as "Target [1–5].pdb". Activity 5 elects the best PDB model by picking the previously produced model with the lowest value of the DOPE assessment score. Activities 6, 7 and 8, refine, predict and evaluate the selected best PDB model, respectively. These three activities can be executed using programs such as MODELLER and PROCHECK [21] as variant activities.

3.3 SciSamma Workflow Implementation in SciCumulus

A single SciSamma workflow specification in SciCumulus allows for creating workflow variants, which can be defined and changed at runtime according to decisions taken by scientists considering validation rules to indicate whether a program is compatible with another. SciSamma is structured as: Activities 1, 2 and 5 are implemented by fixed programs, Activities 3, 4, 6, 7 and 8 are variant activities. Activity 3 has four variations: align2d, salign, MAFFT and Muscle; Activity 4 has four variations: MODELLER, NEST, CONGEN, and 4SEGMOD; Activity 6, 7 and 8 have two possible implementations: MODELLER and PROCHECK. The difference among Activities 6, 7 and 8 is that each one is invoked with different parameters, which makes the same programs execute with different behavior. In the current structure, SciSamma could theoretically execute 96 different workflow variations. However, many of these possible variations do not comply with validation rules. For example, if we choose PROCHECK in Activity 6 we have to choose the same program in Activities 7 and 8. Figure 2 shows an excerpt of the specification of SciSamma (for Activity 3), which follows the SciCumulus XML schema.

Each activity using the tag *<SciCumulusActivity>* that contains files and parameter values associated is represented by the tags <File> and *<Field>*. Each variability is then represented using the tag *<Alternate>* where scientists define the programs that will be executed as alternatives to the *<SciCumulusActivity>*. This way, at runtime, SciCumulus can invoke one of them to implement the activity according to scientists' decision. When using this representation, scientists have to model just one workflow specification whose activities implementations can be explored as workflow variants.

```
<SciCumulus xmlns:xsi="http://www.w3.org/2001/XMLSchema-instance" xsi:noNamespaceSchemaLocation="f">
  <database name="***" password="***" port="***" server="***" username="***"/>
  <SciCumulusWorkflow description="Molecular Modeling" exectag="scisamma-113" expdir="/root/scisamma">
    <SciCumulusActivity tag="Alignment" description="Alignment Construction" type="MAP" activation="./mafft">
      <Relation filename="output_templateelection.txt" name="A" reltype="Input"/>
      <Relation filename="output_alignment.txt" name="C" reltype="Output"/>
      <File filename="experiment.cmd" instrumented="true"/>
      <File filename="aligncontr.py" instrumented="true"/>
      <Field input="A" name="FASTA_FILE" output="C" type="string"/>
      <alternative activation="./muscle.cmd" templatedir="/root/scisamma/template_align_muscle"/>
      <alternative activation="./salign.cmd" templatedir="/root/scisamma/template_align_salign"/>
      <alternative activation="./align2d.cmd" templatedir="/root/scisamma/template_align_align2d"/>
    </SciCumulusActivity>
  </SciCumulusWorkflow>
</SciCumulus>
```

Fig. 2. Specification of SciSamma in SciCumulus format

We executed two workflow variants (Fig. 3). The first one (Wf1) is implemented by the following programs (the activity number is in the parenthesis): (1) BLAST, (2) Perl Script, (3) align2d, (4) MODELLER, (5) Perl Script, (6) MODELLER, (7) MODEL-LER, and (8) MODELLER. The second workflow (Wf2) is implemented by: (1) BLAST, (2) Perl Script, (3) salign, (4) PROCHECK, (5) Perl Script, (6) PRO-CHECK, (7) PROCHECK, and (8) PROCHECK. We have chosen these two variations as case study since, according to Marti-Renom et al. [13], these two combinations are the most common and important in HM experiments.

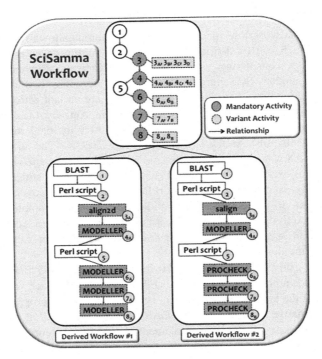

Fig. 3. Workflows variants of SciSamma: derived workflows #1 and #2

4   Experimental Results

In this section, we present an evaluation of SciSamma by deriving two workflows and analyzing their variations in scalability and benefits to obtain 3D-models for cysteine protease target sequences in order to develop anti-malarial chemotherapy.

4.1   Cloud Environment Setup

Following the results achieved in previous work [12], we chose to use large VMs in Amazon EC2 (m1.large – 7.5 GB RAM, 850 GB storage, 2 virtual cores) to execute the experiments. Each VM uses Linux Cent OS 5 (64-bit), configured with the necessary software and bioinformatics libraries. All instances were configured to be accessed using Secure Shell (SSH) on port 22.

4.2   Experiment Setup

We focused on cysteine proteases (CPs) as a candidate drug target for protozoan diseases. The input a dataset has 100 fasta files of target protein sequences of falcipain CPs from *Plasmodium* species, which were extracted from the RefSeq database [22]. This input dataset is composed by different CP sequences, since they are promising potential drug targets for anti-malarial chemotherapy. However, only few 3D-structures were built based on these sequences by crystallography or NMR, and consequently there are not yet available in structural databases e.g. RCSB-PDB. The importance of these 3D-structures construction for CP sequences is that they are used as input datasets in several CADD experiments of structural bioinformatics for drug design. The bio-informatics programs were used with default parameters, they are: BLAST 2.2.18, MAFFT v7.012b, Muscle v3.7, MODELLER 9-11, NEST (Jackal 1.5), CONGEN Version 2.2.1, SEGMOD v1.0, and PROCHECK v.3.5.4.

4.3   Experimental Results

We have evaluated the performance of the parallel execution of these two derived workflows. First, we measured the performance of executing the Wf1 and Wf2 on a single processor machine (with one core) to analyze the local optimization before scaling up the number of VMs. Next, we measured the performance and scalability by executing these derived workflows using from 2 up to 32 large size VMs (m1.large) (thus totalizing 64 virtual cores – 2 per VM). Figure 4 presents the measurements of the Total Execution Time (TET) of Wf1 and Wf2. As the number of VMs increases, the TET of both workflows decreases, as expected. For example, when the Wf1 processes 100 fasta files, the TET is reduced from 8.1 h (using 1 single virtual core) to 27.13 (using 64 virtual cores), which represents a time reduction of up to 94.53 % and for the Wf2 the TET was reduced from 7.0 h (using 1 single virtual core) to 16.27 min (using 64 virtual cores) with a performance improvement of up to 96.12 %. We can also verify that one single variability in the third activity (align2d in Wf1 and salign in Wf2)

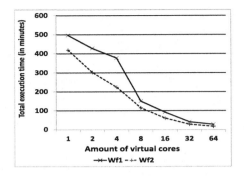

Fig. 4. Total execution time for SciSamma derived Wf1 and Wf2

produced a considerable TET variation. This was due to the use the dynamic programming algorithm since salign uses the weight matrix, which is considerably faster than gap penalty function used by align2d [30]. Even though the two variations present scalability, the difference in TET was around 40 % with 64 cores.

To evaluate the behavior of performance gain according to the number of processing units, we used a traditional metric of parallel computing that is speedup. The executions of the Wf1 and Wf2 have a similar behavior as observed in Fig. 5, since the speedup of both is acceptable (>50 %) and presented a discrete degradation (from 32 up to 64) due to the heterogeneity of activity durations, which led to overhead in the distribution mechanism of SciCumulus.

This result indicates that acquiring more than 32 VMs (64 virtual cores), for these workflow variations, may not bring the expected benefit, particularly if programs do not have features such as multi-thread execution and if financial costs are involved. For example, in the Wf2, salign benefits from multi-threading. We also observed that, when the number of activities becomes closer to the number of VMs, many cores of the VMs may remain idle, thus not producing a positive impact on the TET.

We also analyzed the results from the biological point of view. From the biological perspective, Wf1 and Wf2 present similar results, since both recover the same 3D

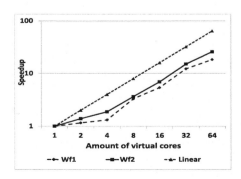

Fig. 5. Speedup for SciSamma derived Wf1 and Wf2

models from the replications in all inputs, with very similar values of quality. Both Wf1 and Wf2 executions consumed 100 Plasmodium CP sequences and generated 500 3D-models. The 100 best models were selected based on quality scores e.g. the lowest values of the DOPE assessment score, by querying the provenance database. Table 1 shows results of the 13 CP sequences, i.e. *Plasmodium* species and the PDB/accession number of the best structural models based on three assessment scores (moldpf, DOPE, GA341). PROCHECK and MolProbity scores confirmed that the 3D models that were generated ('pdb' files) are reasonable (*i.e.*, present good quality) and could be used in additional structural and chemoinformatics analyses (e.g. QSAR, CADD or molecular docking). Although, these models have to be validated and tested in further in vivo or in vitro experiments they represent a step forward to develop new anti-malarial drugs.

Table 1. Summary of the best 3D-models of 13 CPs obtained in *Plasmodium*.

Plasmodium Species	Cysteine Protease-PDB	Best 3D_models Acc. Number	moldpf	DOPE score	GA341 score	Procheck	MolProbity
P. falciparum	Falcipain 2-A	XP_001347836	4,428.13	-31,424.34	0.54	71.0%	81.6%
	Falcipain 2-B	XP_001347832	4,485.77	-31,903.35	0.78	68.6%	75.4%
	Falcipain 3	XP_001347833	5,943.31	-31,770.01	0.14	69.9%	78.4%
P. vivax	Falcipain-like	XP_001615274	3,739.38	-32,688.98	0.79	77.0%	85.98%
	Falcipain-like	XP_001615273	5,827.03	-31,924.03	0.60	75.2%	82.47%
	Falcipain-like	XP_001615272	4,932.57	-32,851.41	0.15	70.8%	77.08%
P. cynomolgi	Falcipain-like	XP_004222378	4,241.46	-31,999.42	0.61	77.6%	82.56%
	Falcipain-like	XP_004222377	4,940.49	-32,589.03	0.32	72.5%	82.64%
P. knowlesi	Falcipain-like	XP_002259152	4,650.63	-30,134.75	0.47	68.5%	76.73%
	Falcipain-like	XP_002259153	5,154.38	-29,993.30	0.49	72.9%	82.78%
	Falcipain-like	XP_002259151	5,548.87	-27,827.77	0.49	69.1%	77.26%
P. berghei	Falcipain 2 pre	XP_680416	4,560.20	-31,188.33	0.36	71.3%	79.06%
P. yoelii	Falcipain-like	XP_726900	5,640.04	-30,920.02	0.32	70.2%	77.02%

5 Related Work

Most of the HM workflows are based on individual scripts or simple Web applications [16, 23]. There is to this date no published work reporting the integrated management of HM workflow variants or other bioinformatics workflow variants. MHOLline is a comparative modeling workflow that combines BLAST, T-Coffee, BATS, MODEL-LER, and PROCHECK. It is encapsulated as a Web service and uses BPEL to formally specify the workflow. BPEL allows the automatic execution of MHOLline (i.e. no human interaction); however, MHOLline has a fixed structure and does not allow scientists for choosing the most suitable structure for their experiment. SWISS-MODEL [16] workspace is a Web-based integrated service dedicated to protein structure homology modeling. SWISS-MODEL is one of the most important approaches used by scientists in HM experiments; however, it has very similar characteristics to MHOLline, since it was encapsulated as a Web service and presents a fixed structure and does not provide parallelism that is required for large-scale experiments. In comparison, SciSamma presents the advantage of structuring HM experiments using SciCumulus, as workflow variations to be executed in parallel, with associated provenance management, which allows for dynamic changes on the workflow specification, notifications and fault-tolerance. Execution data is available for analysis at runtime via SciCumulus provenance online queries at the cloud database. Some provenance query templates, based on scientists' typical analytical queries, are made available as pre-defined parameterized queries.

6 Conclusions and Final Remarks

This paper explores the workflow variation concept to assist the specification and execution of large-scale scientific workflows for HM experiments. SciSamma workflow, modeled in SciCumulus, enables the exploration of a set of workflow variants in HM experiments, allowing scientists to explore different methodologies to build 3D-models. We performed computational and biological studies and provided an illustration of SciSamma's execution in the cloud. From the computational perspective, both SciSamma workflow variants Wf1 and Wf2 process 100 fasta files as input with several hundreds of tasks and data files producing several gigabytes of data. Using provenance data from SciCumulus at runtime, it was possible to query information from this large volume of tasks and data files, allowing scientists to query results obtained using BLAST retrieved 3D structures from PDB. Depending on the results, scientists could decide to re-execute the workflow exploring other parameters, or use another workflow variation, or stop the current execution. By analyzing the overall performance, we can state that parallel techniques improved the performance of the two workflow variations of SciSamma using up to 64 cores, in cloud VMs. TET reaches improvements around 95 % when compared to a sequential workflow execution in one single VM. Both variants presented scalability with performance improvements (dropping from 8 h to 27 min using 32 Amazon's large VMs). While evaluating the two variants, through provenance queries, they show the same quality in biological results, but the difference in execution time between them was around 40 %. From the biological perspective, it obtained 100 3D-models of *falcipains* by executing Wf1 and Wf2, evidencing that for a larger number of models, executing workflow with variants is a fundamental support.

References

1. Cavasotto, C.N., Phatak, S.S.: Homology modeling in drug discovery: current trends and applications. Drug Discov. Today. **14**, 676–683 (2009)
2. Gil, Y., Deelman, E., Ellisman, M., Fahringer, T., Fox, G., Gannon, D., Goble, C., Livny, M., Moreau, L., Myers, J.: Examining the challenges of scientific workflows. Computer **40**, 24–32 (2007)
3. Freire, J., Koop, D., Santos, E., Silva, C.T.: Provenance for computational tasks: a survey. Comput. Sci. Eng. **10**, 11–21 (2008)
4. Gil, Y., Ratnakar, V., Deelman, E., Mehta, G., Kim, J.: Wings for Pegasus: creating large-scale scientific applications using semantic representations of computational workflows. In: The National Conference on Artificial Intelligence, pp. 1767–1774, Vancouver, BC, Canada (2007)

5. Deelman, E., Mehta, G., Singh, G., Su, M.-H., Vahi, K.: Pegasus: mapping large-scale workflows to distributed resources. In: Taylor, I.J., Deelman, E., Gannon, D.B., Shields, M. (eds.) Workflows for e-Science, pp. 376–394. Springer, London (2007)
6. Santos, I., Dias, J., Oliveira, D., Ogasawara, E., Ocaña, K., Mattoso, M.: Runtime dynamic structural changes of scientific workflows in clouds. In: Proceedings of the IEEE/ACM 6th International Workshop on Clouds and (eScience) Applications Management – CloudAM, pp. 417–422. Dresden, Germany (2013)
7. Oliveira, D., Ogasawara, E., Baião, F., Mattoso, M.: SciCumulus: a lightweight cloud middleware to explore many task computing paradigm in scientific workflows. In: Proceedings of the 3rd International Conference on Cloud Computing, pp. 378–385. IEEE, Washington, DC, USA (2010)
8. Costa, F., Silva, V., de Oliveira, D., Ocaña, K., Ogasawara, E., Dias, J., Mattoso, M.: Capturing and querying workflow runtime provenance with PROV: a practical approach. In: Proceedings of the Joint EDBT/ICDT 2013 - Workshops on EDBT 2013, pp. 282–289. ACM Press, NY, USA (2013)
9. Moreau, L., Groth, P.: Provenance: an introduction to PROV. In: Synthesis Lectures on the Semantic Web: Theory and Technology, vol. 3(4), pp. 1-129. Morgan & Claypool Publishers, San Rafael (2013)
10. Shah, F., Mukherjee, P., Desai, P., Avery, M.: Computational approaches for the discovery of cysteine protease inhibitors against Malaria and SARS. Curr. Comput. Aided-Drug Des. **6**, 1–23 (2010)
11. Lindoso, J.A.L., Lindoso, A.A.B.P.: Neglected tropical diseases in Brazil. Revista do Instituto de Medicina Tropical de São Paulo. **51**, 247–253 (2009)
12. Oliveira, D., Ocaña, K., Baião, F., Mattoso, M.: A provenance-based adaptive scheduling heuristic for parallel scientific workflows in clouds. J. Grid Comput. **10**, 521–552 (2012)
13. Martí-Renom, M.A., Stuart, A.C., Fiser, A., Sánchez, R., Melo, F., Sali, A.: Comparative protein structure modeling of genes and genomes. Annu. Rev. Biophys. Biomol. Struct. **29**, 291–325 (2000)
14. Rose, P.W., Bi, C., Bluhm, W.F., Christie, C.H., Dimitropoulos, D., Dutta, S., Green, R.K., Goodsell, D.S., Prlic, A., Quesada, M., Quinn, G.B., Ramos, A.G., Westbrook, J.D., Young, J., Zardecki, C., Berman, H.M., Bourne, P.E.: The RCSB protein data bank: new resources for research and education. Nucleic Acids Res. **41**, D475–D482 (2013)
15. Altschul, S.F., Madden, T.L., Schäffer, A.A., Zhang, J., Zhang, Z., Miller, W., Lipman, D.J.: Gapped BLAST and PSI-BLAST: a new generation of protein database search programs. Nucleic Acids Res. **25**, 3389–3402 (1997)
16. Eswar, N., Eramian, D., Webb, B., Shen, M.-Y., Sali, A.: Protein structure modeling with MODELLER. Methods Mol. Biol. **426**, 145–159 (2008)
17. Sutcliffe, M.J., Haneef, I., Carney, D., Blundell, T.L.: Knowledge based modelling of homologous proteins, part I: three-dimensional frameworks derived from the simultaneous superposition of multiple structures. Protein Eng. **1**, 377–384 (1987)
18. Li, H., Tejero, R., Monleon, D., Bassolino-Klimas, D., Abate-Shen, C., Bruccoleri, R.E., Montelione, G.T.: Homology modeling using simulated annealing of restrained molecular dynamics and conformational search calculations with CONGEN: application in predicting the three-dimensional structure of murine homeodomain Msx-1. Protein Sci. **6**, 956–970 (1997)
19. Xiang, J.Z., Honig, B.: Jackal: a Protein Structure Modeling Package. Columbia University and Howard Hughes Medical Institute, New York (2002)
20. Koehl, P., Delarue, M.: A self consistent mean field approach to simultaneous gap closure and side-chain positioning in homology modelling. Nat. Struct. Biol. **2**, 163–170 (1995)

21. Laskowski, R.A., MacArthur, M.W., Moss, D.S., Thornton, J.M.: PROCHECK: a program to check the stereochemical quality of protein structures. J. Appl. Crystallogr. **26**, 283–291 (1993)
22. Pruitt, K.D., Tatusova, T., Klimke, W., Maglott, D.R.: NCBI reference Sequences: current status, policy and new initiatives. Nucleic Acids Res. **37**, D32–D36 (2009)
23. Arnold, K., Bordoli, L., Kopp, J., Schwede, T.: The SWISS-MODEL workspace: a web-based environment for protein structure homology modelling. Bioinformatics **22**, 195–201 (2006)

Vertical Scaling Capability of OpenStack

Survey of Guest Operating Systems, Hypervisors, and the Cloud Management Platform

Marian Turowski and Alexander Lenk[(✉)]

FZI Forschungszentrum Informatik, Friedrichstr. 60, 10117 Berlin, Germany
{Turowski,Lenk}@fzi.de

Abstract. With the emergence of cloud computing, resources can be dynamically scaled. A common scaling approach is the addition and removal of virtual machines, known as horizontal scaling. Horizontal scaling can take several minutes but erratic and sudden changes in demand take place within seconds. Therefore, vertical scaling has been introduced, changing the resources of an existing virtual machine during run time and within one second or less. At the same time, more and more private clouds and cloud providers apply the open-source platform OpenStack. Hence, this paper evaluates the vertical scaling capability of OpenStack. For this purpose, we examine whether and to what extent common guest operating systems, popular hypervisors, and OpenStack itself support vertical scaling. Altogether, the considered operating systems and hypervisors support vertical scaling of almost all considered resources while OpenStack does not support vertical scaling at all. Based on our findings, we finally suggest steps to improve OpenStack.

Keywords: Cloud computing · Scalability · Operating system · Hypervisor · OpenStack · Vertical scaling

1 Introduction and Motivation

Through the increasing popularity of the internet, the scientific community but also more and more small and medium enterprises benefit from offering their services as web applications. These web applications face a volatile demand due to scheduling, seasonal changes, temporary trends, and momentary effects [11]. Examples include experiments, time-of-day patterns as well as breaking news, marketing activities, and posts on social media such as Twitter [21]. As a consequence, applications' demand for resources is unstable and hardly predictable. In the past, the common strategy to handle the uncertain resource demand was to provide enough resources for peak workloads. This overprovision led to mostly idle resources and thus high expenses [10].

With the emergence of cloud computing, resource provision strategies changed fundamentally. Cloud computing enables on-demand provisioning of resources for experimentation [29], disaster recovery [35,36], scaling, and so on.

© Springer International Publishing Switzerland 2015
F. Toumani et al. (Eds.): ICSOC 2014, LNCS 8954, pp. 351–362, 2015.
DOI: 10.1007/978-3-319-22885-3_30

This flexible provision and release of resources based on customer demand is an essential feature of cloud computing and known as elasticity [41]. Together with the pay-per-use billing model, clouds allow customers to pay only for the resources they are actually using and hereby to avoid over- and underprovisioning [11]. Nevertheless, adding and removing resources according to the actual demand while minimizing cost and maintaining a constant service level is a crucial issue in cloud computing [37]. A common approach for adequate scaling of resources in literature [12, 18, 62] and practice [8, 24] is the addition and removal of virtual machines (VMs), known as horizontal scaling.

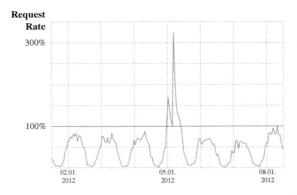

Fig. 1. Peak in the request rate of gloveler.de after the release of a newspaper article and its dissemination in social media

However, horizontal scaling comes with flaws. In scientific computing Galante et al. [23] point out that the scaling size of a whole virtual machine is not sufficient and fine-grained scaling techniques are necessary. Also erratic and sudden changes in demand take place within seconds [21] (see Fig. 1) but provisioning an additional VM requires about 50 to 800 seconds and starting multiple VMs at once may take longer than starting a single VM [39]. In these situations, horizontal scaling could lead to a decreased throughput [19], an increased response time, or even the outage of the whole system [28]. As a consequence, horizontal scaling is more appropriate for situations where changes in demand take place gradually or can be foreseen. Furthermore, additional VMs could lead to additional licensing costs [68]. For each VM, an operating system is required, which limits the additional capacity usable by the application [50]. Since VMs function as scaling unit, horizontal scaling can also cause unnecessary overprovisioning [19] and high resource wastage in case of a slight workload increase [68]. In Fig. 2, such a situation is visualized, where VMs are horizontally scaled because of a demand peak. Lastly, horizontal scaling requires a running load balancer and is limited to stateless applications [19].

In order to avoid these shortcomings, vertical scaling has been introduced as a new approach. In contrast to horizontal scaling, it changes the resources

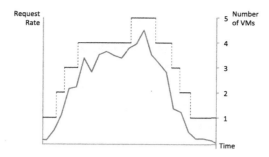

Fig. 2. Overprovision and resource wastage with horizontal scaling

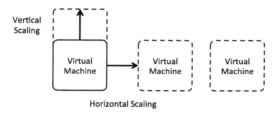

Fig. 3. Horizontal scaling and vertical scaling

of an existing VM, such as CPU cores or memory, during run time [50] (see Fig. 3). Additionally, vertical scaling can be done within one second or less [22,67]. Hereby, vertical scaling reduces violations of a certain service level [19].

In practice, however, only few cloud providers (e.g. ProfitBricks [50]) support vertical scaling whereas big providers such as Amazon Web Services[1] have not implemented vertical scaling yet [23]. Since private clouds and cloud providers such as Rackspace[2] and HP[3] apply the open-source platform OpenStack[4], it has become more and more prominent. Hence, this paper evaluates the feasibility of vertical scaling for OpenStack. For this purpose, this paper examines to what extent common guest operating systems, popular hypervisors, and OpenStack itself support vertical scaling.

The remainder of this paper is structured as follows. Section 2 presents related work before Sect. 3 assesses the support of vertical scaling by guest operating systems, hypervisors, and OpenStack. Finally, Sect. 4 presents a conclusion and discusses the fields of further research related to this work.

2 Related Work

We want to give an overview of OpenStack's vertical scaling capability. Yet, no literature exists that examines whether and to which extent OpenStack supports

---

[1] https://aws.amazon.com.

[2] http://www.rackspace.com.

[3] http://www.hpcloud.com.

[4] https://www.openstack.org.

vertical scaling. However, several work has been done on horizontal and vertical scaling as well as combinations of both, often with respect to auto-scaling. Generally, authors use different approaches to scale a VM according to the current demand. Lorido-Botrán et al. classify the available auto-scaling approaches in the following way: 1. static, threshold-based policies, 2. reinforcement Learning, 3. queuing theory, 4. control theory, and 5. time-series analysis [37].

For vertical scaling, one example is the work of Dawoud et al. who propose an architecture based on CPU utilization [19]. Similarly, Lu et al. present a tool for automatic vertical scaling of VMs based on throughput, average response time, and percentile response time [38]. Yazdanov and Fetzer apply reinforcement learning in their autonomic scaling framework [68]. Shen et al. propose a time-series-based system for vertical scaling of CPU and memory that considers VM migration and resource efficiency [58]. As presented by Rodero-Merino et al., vertical scaling is also possible through replacing an underlying server by a more powerful one [56]. Svärd et al. take vertical scaling even further by aggregating and pooling the resources that can be scaled vertically [61].

Other authors combine horizontal and vertical scaling. Caballer et al. suggest an architecture for horizontal and vertical scaling that adapts resources automatically to the requirements of scientific applications [13]. The framework from Dutta et al. uses a combination of horizontal and vertical scaling in order to optimize resource usage and incurring cost [22] while scaling decisions in the approach of Wang et al. are based on availability [66].

3   Vertical Scaling with OpenStack

In order to assess the support of vertical scaling in OpenStack, we examine the components (see Fig. 4) that are required to enable vertical scaling in OpenStack. Ideally, an administrator can use the dashboard of the cloud management platform in order to scale a running VM vertically. OpenStack as the *Cloud Management Platform* provides such a dashboard. The dashboard is connected to Open Stack's resource management that controls the *Hypervisor*. In the case of vertical scaling, the resource management that administers CPU, memory, disks, and network interfaces would prompt the hypervisor to provide a *Virtual Machine* more resources. The VM again would pass the resources to the *Guest Operating System (OS)* that runs within the VM. As a consequence, the applied guest OS, the used hypervisor, and OpenStack itself have to support vertical scaling, which is also known as hot plugging of resources, i.e. adding and removing of resources to or from a running VM [67]. Therefore, our assessment starts with the hypervisor (see Sec. 3.1) before we continue with the guest OS (see Sec. 3.2). Finally, we examine OpenStack as cloud management platform that coordinates the scaling process with its dashboard (see Sec. 3.3).

Regarding the considered resource categories, we reviewed Amazon Web Services, Rackspace, Profitbricks, OpenStack[5] itself, and market places like the

---

[5] https://www.openstack.org/software/openstack-compute/.

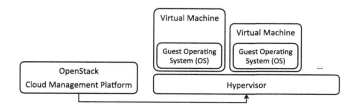

Fig. 4. Overview of interaction between OpenStack, a hypervisor, virtual machines, and guest operating systems

Deutsche Börse Cloud Exchange[6]. Knowing that other resource categories might be interesting for future work, we decide to consider the most important resources in this work and therefore focus our review on adding and removing computing power, memory space, and storage space as well as extending and shrinking the network. In this context, we distinguish between adding or removing an additional disk and extending or shrinking an existing disk because for the first case, the used hard drive might have to be changed for applications running inside the OS. Since the introduction of plug and play as well as of the universal serial bus (USB), adding and removing disks and network devices has become a common action. However, adding and removing disks and network devices is still important in this context because hypervisors have to support the addition and removal as well.

3.1 Vertical Scaling Capabilities of Guest Operating Systems

We use the most common operating systems, namely CentOS 6.5[7], SUSE Linux Enterprise Server 11 SP3[8], and Debian 7.4.0[9] as well as Ubuntu Server 14.04 LTS[10], and Microsoft Windows Server 2012 R2[11]. Our literature review is mainly based on websites, documentations, release notes, and blog entries in order to identify whether and to which extent an OS supports vertical scaling. Thereby, we classify the OS's support in four categories: yes, partly, no, and unknown. The results are shown in Table 1.

In general, all considered operating systems support vertical scaling with almost all considered types of resources. For CentOS, extending and shrinking is only possible for unmounted disks. SUSE Linux Enterprise Server does not offer the addition and removal of a CPU core as a full virtualization guest. While a user cannot shrink a disk with SUSE Linux Enterprise, the user can extend a disk depending on the file system. Debian supports both extending and shrinking a disk depending on its file system. Ubuntu Server supports vertical scaling of all resources except shrinking a disk, which works for unmounted

---

[6] http://www.dbcloudexchange.com.
[7] https://www.centos.org.
[8] https://www.suse.com/products/server/.
[9] https://www.debian.org/index.en.html.
[10] http://www.ubuntu.com/server.
[11] http://www.microsoft.com/en-us/server-cloud/products/windows-server-2012-r2/.

Table 1. Comparison of resources that can be vertically scaled with CentOS 6.5, SUSE Linux Enterprise Server 11 SP3, and Debian 7.4.0 as well as Ubuntu Server 14.04 LTS and Microsoft Windows Server 2012 R2

		CentOS	SUSE	Debian	Ubuntu	Windows Server
CPU core	Add/ Remove	Yes[53]/ Yes [53]	No[60]/ No[60]ᵃ	Yes[3]/ Yes[3]	Yes[3]/ Yes[3]	Yes[64]/ ?
Memory	Add/ Remove	Yes[52]/ Yes[52]	Yes[60]/ Yes[60]	Yes[64]/ Yes[2]	Yes[64]/ Yes[2]	Yes[64]/ ?
Disk	Add/ Remove	Yes[51]/ Yes[51]	Yes[60]/ Yes[60]	Yes[6]/ Yes[20]	Yes[7]/ Yes[7]	Partly [45]/ Yes[45]
	Extend/ Shrink	Partly [54]/ Partly [54]	Partly [46]/ No [46]	Partly [5]/ Partly [5]	Yes[15]/ Partly [15]	Yes[43]/ Partly [43]
Network	Add/ Remove	Yes[51]/ Yes[51]	Yes[60]/ Yes[60]	Yes[9]/ Yes[9]	Yes[59]/ Yes[14]	Yes[44]/ Yes[44]

ᵃ [60] distinguishes SUSE running as paravirtualized guest and full virtualization guest. We focus on full virtualization here.

file systems only. For Microsoft Windows Server, we cannot determine whether it supports the removal of a CPU core and memory. Furthermore, Microsoft Windows Server only supports the addition of SCSI disks during run time and shrinking previously expanded disks.

The aforementioned review is based on certain assumptions. First, we focus on adding or removing hardware to or from a guest and not to or from the host. Second, if the addition or removal works for one architecture such as x86, our assumption is that it is also possible with other architectures. Third, we assume that an OS supports adding or removal of a certain hardware if we find that the OS is able to do so with a specific hypervisor. Furthermore, if an older version of an OS offer a certain functionality, we infer that newer versions offer the same functionality. Similarly, we consider the edition of an OS that offers the most functionalities, which often refers to the 64 bit version of an OS. Moreover, we do not require the considered OS to detect the changed hardware on its own but at most through a command in the command-line interface. Lastly, we make use of the fact that CentOS builds on the repository of Red Hat Enterprise Linux[12] by determining the functionality supported by CentOS through the functionality that Red Hat Enterprise Linux offers [17].

3.2   Vertical Scaling Capabilities of Hypervisors

As a next step, we review the most common hypervisors, namely KVM[13], VMware vSphere Hypervisor[14], Xen Project Hypervisor[15], and Microsoft Hyper-V[16].

---

[12] http://www.redhat.com/products/enterprise-linux/.
[13] http://www.linux-kvm.org.
[14] http://www.vmware.com/products/vsphere-hypervisor.
[15] http://www.xenproject.org/developers/teams/hypervisor.html.
[16] http://technet.microsoft.com/en-us/library/hh831531.aspx.

Table 2. Comparison of resources that can be vertically scaled with KVM, VMware vSphere Hypervisor, Xen Project Hypervisor, and Microsoft Hyper-V

		KVM	VMware	Xen	Hyper-V
CPU core	Add/	Yes[30]/	Yes[65]/	Yes[26]/	No[34]/
	Remove	No[30]	No[65]	Yes[26]	No[34]
Memory	Add/	Yes[31,33]/	Yes[65]/	Yes[25]/	Yes[42]/
	Remove	Yes[31,33]	No[65]	Yes[25]	No[42]
Disk	Add/	Partly [32]/	Partly [4]/	Yes[27]/	Partly [55]/
	Remove	?	Yes[4]	Yes[27]	Partly [55]
	Extend/	No[57]/	Yes[65]/	Partly [40]/	Partly [43]/
	Shrink	No[57]	Partly [65]	No[40]	Partly [43]
Network	Add/	Yes[32]/	Yes[65]/	Yes[1]/	No[34]/
	Remove	?	Yes[63]	Yes[1]	No[55]

Using the same four categories and similar sources as in Sect. 3.1,we determine whether and to which extent the hypervisors support vertical scaling. The results are shown in Table 2.

Generally, the considered hypervisors support vertical scaling with all considered resources. With KVM, removing a CPU core and altering disk size do not work. Furthermore, only SCSI disks can be added while we cannot determine the support for removing a disk and a network. Similarly, VMware does not support the removal of a CPU core and of memory. The addition of a disk also only works for SCSI disks. Additionally, while shrinking a disk, the VM stops responding. Xen enables vertical scaling with almost all resources. One exception is that Xen does not allow shrinking a disk and that extending a disk works only for certain file systems. For Hyper-V, the addition and removal of a CPU core and a network as well as the removal of memory are not available. Furthermore, only SCSI disks can be added and removed. Lastly, Hyper-V requires two functionalities in order to extend or shrink a virtual disk: Firstly, the disk has to be of a certain file format, i.e. the way how the disk's data and file format are stored. Secondly, the relevant disk has to be attached to a SCSI controller.

The aforementioned review is based on certain assumptions. When increasing or decreasing the memory assigned to a guest OS, KVM and Xen use memory ballooning, which takes memory from the guest OS and gives the memory to the host or vice versa [16]. Since memory ballooning is one method of vertical scaling, we consider it as equivalent to the addition and removal of memory. Lastly, we assume that tools that manage the interaction between the OS and the host (e.g. VMware Tools) are installed on the OS.

3.3 Vertical Scaling Capabilities of the Cloud Management Platform

Finally, we examine whether OpenStack supports vertical scaling. According to the OpenStack Operations Guide, OpenStack only supports horizontal scaling in order to match the cloud paradigm of "cloud-based applications that typically request more, discrete hardware". Consequently, the ideal for OpenStack is to add a VM and to load balance among the existing VMs in case of increasing resource demand [48].

However, OpenStack allows altering the size of an existing server during run time by changing the flavor [47]. A flavor is a hardware templates that defines a number of CPU cores, a memory size, a root disk size, and a data disk space. An administrative user can create, edit, and delete flavors. The default installation provides five different flavors [49]. Nevertheless, the question is whether changing the flavor is as quickly as hot plugging of resources. Therefore, we examine the source code of OpenStack. In the compute API file[17], we find that OpenStack resizes a VM by initiating a migration process. Shutting down the VM and moving it to a new host requires some time. Consequently, OpenStack does not provide vertical scaling within few seconds as provided by hot plugging and as presented in the introduction.

4   Conclusion and Future Work

This paper evaluates the vertical scaling capability of OpenStack. More specifically, this paper assesses whether the components that are relevant for enabling vertical scaling with OpenStack support vertical scaling. Based on an literature review, we evaluate common guest operating systems, popular hypervisors, and OpenStack regarding vertical scaling. Hereby, the paper gives a current overview of the resources supported for vertical scaling and allows for comparisons between the considered operating systems and between the hypervisors regarding vertical scaling.

In this paper, we identified that guest operating systems and hypervisors are in general capable of vertical scaling. OpenStack however does not support vertical scaling at all and is rather designed for horizontal scaling. Therefore, we recommend that future work focuses on how to implement vertical scaling in OpenStack. Possible solutions could be the removal of the flavor system or the automatic creation of flavors during run time as needed. In any case, the vertical scaling mechanism should be changed from migration to hot plugging. Additionally, we could not completely determine the vertical scaling capabilities of operating systems and hypervisors, which is thus left for future work. Furthermore, our work concentrated on the qualitative assessment of vertical scaling capabilities on a scale with yes, partial, and no. On these grounds, we suggest that future research performs a qualitative assessment of vertical scaling capabilities of operating systems, hypervisors, and OpenStack and defines metrics for the degree of support. Moreover, future research should examine how hypervisors, operating systems, and the implementation of vertical scaling in OpenStack influence the quality of vertical scaling in terms of spin-up time, speed, reliability etc. Lastly, vertical scaling is not always possible since the vertical scaling capacity is limited due to the limited resources of a VM. Therefore,

---

[17] https://github.com/openstack/nova/blob/master/nova/compute/api.py.

our immediate future work will combine horizontal and vertical scaling in order to deal with demand changes more efficiently.

Acknowledgment. This work is part of the project CLoUd Services Scalability (CLUSS) that is funded by the German Federal Ministry of Education and Research (funding code 01IS13013A-D). We also would like to thank Andreas Sperber from the gloveler GmbH for providing us with Fig. 1.

References

1. Xen : Adding and removing NICs on virtual machines — linux - storage - virtualization. http://linux.cloudibee.com/2009/04/xen-adding-and-removing-nics-on-virtual-machines/
2. (2007). https://www.kernel.org/doc/Documentation/memory-hotplug.txt
3. Linux Hotplug a CPU (2009). http://www.cyberciti.biz/faq/debian-rhel-centos-re dhat-suse-hotplug-cpu/
4. Vmware Linux Guest Add a New Hard Disk Without Rebooting Guest - nixCraft (2010). http://www.cyberciti.biz/tips/vmware-add-a-new-hard-disk-without-reb ooting-guest.html
5. Chapter 12. Advanced Administration (2013). http://debian-handbook.info/ browse/stable/advanced-administration.html
6. How to add a new hard disk or partition using UUID and ext4 filesystem (2014). http://www.debiantutorials.com/how-to-add-a-new-hard-disk-or-partition-using-uuid-and-ext4-filesystem/
7. QemuDiskHotplug - Ubuntu Wiki (2014). https://wiki.ubuntu.com/QemuDisk Hotplug
8. Amazon Web Services: Auto Scaling. https://aws.amazon.com/autoscaling/
9. Aoki, O.: Debian GNU/Linux Reference - 10.8.2 Triggering network configuration - hotplug (2005). http://www.linuxtopia.org/online_books/linux_system_administration/debian_linux_guides/debian_linux_reference_guide/ch-gateway.en_024.html
10. Armbrust, M., Fox, A., Griffith, R., Joseph, A.D., Katz, R., Konwinski, A., Lee, G., Patterson, D., Rabkin, A., Stoica, I., Zaharia, M.: A view of cloud computing. Commun. ACM **53**(4), 50–58 (2010)
11. Baun, C., Kunze, M., Nimis, J., Tai, S.: Cloud Computing: Web-Based Dynamic IT Services. Springer, Heidelberg (2011)
12. Bodík, P., Griffith, R., Sutton, C., Fox, A., Jordan, M., Patterson, D.: Statistical machine learning makes automatic control practical for internet datacenters. In: Proceedings of the 2009 Conference on Hot Topics in Cloud Computing (2009)
13. Caballer, M., García, A., Moltó, G., de Alfonso, C.: Towards SLA-driven management of cloud infrastructures to elastically execute scientific applications. In: 6th Iberian Grid Infrastructure Conference (IberGrid), pp. 207–218 (2012)
14. Canonical: Ubuntu Manpage: ifconfig - configure a network interface. http:// manpages.ubuntu.com/manpages/precise/man8/ifconfig.8.html
15. Canonical: Ubuntu Manpage: resize2fs - ext2/ext3/ext4 file system resizer (2010). http://manpages.ubuntu.com/manpages/precise/en/man8/resize2fs.8.html
16. Capitulino, L.: Automatic ballooning. Technical report (2013). http://www. linux-kvm.org/wiki/images/f/f6/Automatic-ballooning-slides.pdf

17. CentOS: About - CentOS Wiki (2012). http://wiki.centos.org/About
18. Chieu, T.C., Mohindra, A., Karve, A.A., Segal, A.: Dynamic scaling of web applications in a virtualized cloud computing environment. In: 2009 IEEE International Conference on e-Business Engineering, pp. 281–286 (2009)
19. Dawoud, W., Takouna, I., Meinel, C.: Elastic virtual machine for fine-grained cloud resource provisioning. In: Krishna, P.V., Babu, M.R., Ariwa, E. (eds.) ObCom 2011, Part I. CCIS, vol. 269, pp. 11–25. Springer, Heidelberg (2012)
20. Debian Help: Mount Umount Harddisk Floppy CDROM under Debian. http://www.debianhelp.co.uk/mount.htm
21. Douglas, P.: How Stephen Fry takes down entire websites with a single tweet — News — TechRadar (2010). http://www.techradar.com/news/internet/how-stephen-fry-takes-down-entire-websites-with-a-single-tweet-674170
22. Dutta, S., Gera, S., Verma, A., Viswanathan, B.: SmartScale: automatic application scaling in enterprise clouds. In: 2012 IEEE Fifth International Conference on Cloud Computing, pp. 221–228 (2012)
23. Galante, G., De Bona, L.C.E.D., Mury, A.R., Schulze, B.: Are public clouds elastic enough for scientific computing? In: 3rd International Workshop on Cloud Computing and Scientific Applications (CCSA) (2013)
24. Google: Web Apps Articles & Tutorials - Google Cloud Platform. https://cloud.google.com/developers/articles/auto-scaling-on-the-google-cloud-platform
25. Herron, K.: How to Hot Add/Remove Memory from a Xen Domain — Backdrift. http://backdrift.org/xen-memory-hot-add-and-remove
26. Herron, K.: How to Hot Add/Remove VCPUs from a Xen Domain — Backdrift. http://backdrift.org/how-to-hot-addremove-vcpus-from-a-xen-domain
27. Herron, K.: Xen Disk Hot Add (Block Device) Howto — Backdrift. http://backdrift.org/xen-disk-hot-add-block-device-howto
28. Islam, S., Keung, J., Lee, K., Liu, A.: Empirical prediction models for adaptive resource provisioning in the cloud. Future Gener. Comput. Syst. 28(1), 155–162 (2012)
29. Klems, M.: Experiment-driven quality assessment and optimization of cloud-based distributed database systems. Soft. Qual. Prof. Mag. 15(4), 1–2 (2013)
30. KVM: CPUHotPlug - KVM. http://www.linux-kvm.org/page/CPUHotPlug
31. KVM: FAQ - KVM. http://www.linux-kvm.org/page/FAQ
32. KVM: Hotadd pci devices - KVM. http://www.linux-kvm.org/page/Hotadd_pci_devices
33. KVM: NetworkingTodo - KVM. http://www.linux-kvm.org/page/NetworkingTodo
34. Laverick, M.: Hyper-V R2eality: VMs not so hot after all. http://www.mikelaverick.com/2014/02/hyper-v-r2eality-vms-not-so-hot-after-all/
35. Lenk, A., Pallas, F.: Modeling quality attributes of cloud-standby-systems. In: Lau, K.-K., Lamersdorf, W., Pimentel, E. (eds.) ESOCC 2013. LNCS, vol. 8135, pp. 49–63. Springer, Heidelberg (2013)
36. Lenk, A., Tai, S.: Cloud standby: disaster recovery of distributed systems in the cloud. In: Villari, M., Zimmermann, W., Lau, K.-K. (eds.) ESOCC 2014. LNCS, vol. 8745, pp. 32–46. Springer, Heidelberg (2014)
37. Lorido-Botrán, T., Miguel-Alonso, J., Lozano, J.A.: Auto-scaling techniques for elastic applications in cloud environments. Technical report, Department of Computer Architecture and Technology University of the Basque Country (2012). http://www.sc.ehu.es/ccwbayes/isg/administrator/components/com_jresearch/files/publications/autoscaling.pdf

38. Lu, L., Zhu, X., Griffith, R., Padala, P., Parikh, A., Shah, P., Smirni, E.: Application-driven dynamic vertical scaling of virtual machines in resource pools. In: IEEE/IFIP Network Operations and Management Symposium (NOMS 2014) (2014)
39. Mao, M., Humphrey, M.: A performance study on the VM startup time in the cloud. In: 2012 IEEE Fifth International Conference on Cloud Computing, pp. 423–430 (2012)
40. McWilliams, G.: Grant McWilliams - Resize Disk Image used as Xen DomU partition (2009). http://grantmcwilliams.com/item/265-resize-disk-image-used-as-xen-domu-partition
41. Mell, P., Grance, T.: The NIST Definition of Cloud Computing. Special Publication 800–145, National Institute of Standards and Technology (NIST) (2011). http://csrc.nist.gov/publications/nistpubs/800-145/SP800-145.pdf
42. Microsoft: Hyper-V Dynamic Memory Overview. http://technet.microsoft.com/en-us/library/hh831766.aspx
43. Microsoft: Online Virtual Hard Disk Resizing Overview. http://technet.microsoft.com/en-us/library/dn282286.aspx
44. Microsoft: Networking (2008). http://technet.microsoft.com/en-us/library/cc772351(v=ws.10).aspx
45. Microsoft: Manage Server Storage in Windows Server Essentials (2014). http://technet.microsoft.com/en-us/library/dn550731.aspx
46. Novell: Linux Enterprise Server 11 SP2 (2012). http://doc.opensuse.org/products/draft/SLES/SLES-storage_sd_draft/biuymaa.html/#biuynjy
47. OpenStack Foundation: Change the size of your server - OpenStack End User Guide - current. http://docs.openstack.org/user-guide/content/nova_cli_resize.html
48. OpenStack Foundation: Chapter 5. Scaling - OpenStack Operations Guide. http://docs.openstack.org/trunk/openstack-ops/content/scaling.html
49. OpenStack Foundation: Manage flavors - OpenStack Admin User Guide - current. http://docs.openstack.org/user-guide-admin/content/dashboard_manage_flavors.html
50. ProfitBricks: Live Vertical Scaling. Technical report (2014). https://www.profitbricks.co.uk/sites/default/files/documents/LiveVerticalScalingbyProfitBricks.pdf
51. Red Hat: Red Hat Enterprise Linux 6 6.0 Release Notes. Technical report (2010). https://access.redhat.com/site/documentation/en-US/Red_Hat_Enterprise_Linux/6/pdf/6.0_Release_Notes/Red_Hat_Enterprise_Linux-6-6.0_Release_Notes-en-US.pdf
52. Red Hat: Red Hat Enterprise Linux 5 5.0 Release Notes. Technical report (2012). https://access.redhat.com/site/documentation/en-US/Red_Hat_Enterprise_Linux/5/pdf/5.0_Release_Notes/Red_Hat_Enterprise_Linux-5-5.0_Release_Notes-en-US.pdf
53. Red Hat: Red Hat Enterprise Linux 6 6.5 Release Notes, Technical report (2013). https://access.redhat.com/site/documentation/en-US/Red_Hat_Enterprise_Linux/6/pdf/6.5_Release_Notes/Red_Hat_Enterprise_Linux-6-6.5_Release_Notes-en-US.pdf
54. Red Hat: Red Hat Enterprise Linux 6 Storage Administration Guide. Technical report (2013). https://access.redhat.com/documentation/en-US/Red_Hat_Enterprise_Linux/6/pdf/Storage_Administration_Guide/Red_Hat_Enterprise_Linux-6-Storage_Administration_Guide-en-US.pdf

55. Remde, K.: Kevin Remde's Full of I.T., where we discuss Windows Server, System Center, Cloud, Virtualization, and all things Microsoft for the IT Professional and IT Manager. http://blogs.technet.com/b/kevinremde/archive/2013/03/05/you-want-to-hot-add-what-20-days-of-server-virtualization-part-2-of-20.aspx
56. Rodero-Merino, L., Vaquero, L.M., Gil, V., Galán, F., Fontán, J., Montero, R.S., Llorente, I.M.: From infrastructure delivery to service management in clouds. Future Gener. Comput. Syst. **26**(8), 1226–1240 (2010)
57. Server Fault: linux - KVM online disk resize? - Server Fault. http://serverfault.com/questions/122042/kvm-online-disk-resize
58. Shen, Z., Subbiah, S., Gu, X., Wilkes, J.: Cloudscale: elastic resource scaling for multi-tenant cloud systems. In: Proceedings of the 2nd ACM Symposium on Cloud Computing (SOCC 2011) (2011)
59. Slonka, K.J.: /public/slonkak (2013). http://www.kevinslonka.com/index.php?section=1&blog=305
60. SUSE: SUSE Linux Enterprise Server: Supported Virtualization Technologies. Technical report (2013). http://www.novell.com/docrep/2009/09/SUSE_Linux_Enterprise_Server_Virtualization_Technology_Support_en.pdf
61. Svärd, P., Hudzia, B., Tordsson, J., Elmroth, E.: Hecatonchire: enabling multi-host virtual machines by resource aggregation and pooling. Technical report, UmeåUniversity (2014). http://www8.cs.umu.se/research/uminf/reports/2014/011/part1.pdf
62. Urgaonkar, B., Pacifici, G., Shenoy, P., Spreitzer, M., Tantawi, A.: An analytical model for multi-tier internet services and its applications. In: Proceedings of the 2005 ACM SIGMETRICS International Conference on Measurement and Modeling of Computer Systems, pp. 291–302 (2005)
63. VMware: vSphere Networking vSphere 5.5. Technical report (2013). http://pubs.vmware.com/vsphere-55/topic/com.vmware.ICbase/PDF/vsphere-esxi-vcenter-server-55-networking-guide.pdf
64. VMware: Guest OS Compatibility Guide. Technical report (2014). http://partnerweb.vmware.com/comp_guide2/pdf/VMware_GOS_Compatibility_Guide.pdf
65. VMware: vSphere Virtual Machine Administration ESXi 5.5. Technical report (2014). http://pubs.vmware.com/vsphere-55/topic/com.vmware.ICbase/PDF/vsphere-esxi-vcenter-server-551-virtual-machine-admin-guide.pdf
66. Wang, W., Chen, H., Chen, X.: An availability-aware virtual machine placement approach for dynamic scaling of cloud applications. In: 2012 9th International Conference on Ubiquitous Intelligence and Computing and 9th International Conference on Autonomic and Trusted Computing, pp. 509–516 (2012)
67. Yazdanov, L., Fetzer, C.: Vertical scaling for prioritized VMs provisioning. In: 2012 Second International Conference on Cloud and Green Computing, pp. 118–125 (2012)
68. Yazdanov, L., Fetzer, C.: VScaler: autonomic virtual machine scaling. In: 2013 IEEE Sixth International Conference on Cloud Computing, pp. 212–219 (2013)

PhD Symposium Track

A Description-Based Service Search System

Isaac B. Caicedo-Castro[1,2,3,4](✉), M.-C. Fauvet[1,2], and H. Duarte-Amaya[4]

[1] LIG (MRIM), Univ. Grenoble Alpes, 38000 Grenoble, France
isaac-bernardo.caicedo-castro@imag.fr
[2] LIG, CNRS, 38000 Grenoble, France
[3] Univ. de Córdoba, Montería, Colombia
[4] Univ. Nacional de Colombia, Bogotá, Colombia

Abstract. This paper presents S^2niffer (Service Sniffer), a query-based system for discovering services. S^2niffer is a part of a broader project whose goal is, given mobile users' needs (e.g., buying airplane tickets, booking a hotel room, renting a car, etc.) expressed in a text query, to discover and compose services to be executed. Behind the service discovery system is the idea to match the users' queries with a set of documents in a corpus such that each document contains a service description given in free text, obtained from its corresponding profile given in a OWL-S file. A preliminary evaluation reveals that S^2niffer outperforms Latent Semantic Indexing and Vector Space Model.

Keywords: Web services · Discovery · Service retrieval

1 Introduction and Problem Statement

This paper presents a system for discovering services based on queries submitted by mobile users as they are seeking for services. This study is conducted as a part of a broader project, whose main goal is to design and implement a system that provides mobile users with services to book a hotel room, or for reserving a table in a restaurants located in a certain city, etc [9]. Figure 1 depicts the overall architecture of the system, which is built on the top of four components: (1) User interaction and query management, (2) User management System, (3) Discovery system, and (4) Composition and orchestration system. This paper focuses only on the issues raised by the design and implementation of the third component.

In prior works, discovering services have been dealt with Information Retrieval (IR) models, considering a corpus composed by WSDL documents. A WSDL document contains a syntactically-based description including service name, operations name and signature, and sometimes descriptions in natural language that are commentaries written by programmers. In spite of that WSDL is the standard service description language, currently, is not practical to assume that most of the services have WSDL descriptions because of the increasing adoption of REST-ful services. Hence, in this study is adopted

© Springer International Publishing Switzerland 2015
F. Toumani et al. (Eds.): ICSOC 2014, LNCS 8954, pp. 365–370, 2015.
DOI: 10.1007/978-3-319-22885-3_31

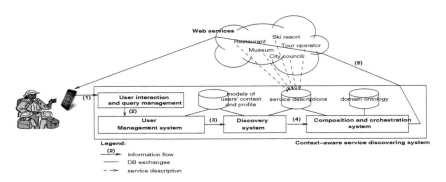

Fig. 1. A context-aware discovering system for mobile users

```
<profile:Profile  rdf:ID="CHEAPCAR1 ... ">
...
<profile:serviceName xml:lang="en">
   CheapCar 1PersonBicycle MaxPrice service
</profile:serviceName>
<profile:textDescription xml:lang="en">
   This service returns max purchase prices of the given pair
   of a cheap car model and one person bicycle model.
</profile:textDescription>
...
</profile:Profile>
```

Fig. 2. Profile of a Web service in a OWL-S document

OWL-S [1] (a.k.a., DAML-S), which is an OWL ontology for description, discovery, invocation, composition, and monitoring of services. With OWL-S is possible to describe either WSDL-based services and those based on REST-ful.

The structure of an OWL-S ontology is designed to provide the knowledge about three aspects of a Web service, i.e., (1) What does it provide? (2) How is it used? (3) How is the interaction with it? The answer to the first question is given in the profile of a service in a OWL-S ontology. Indeed, the functionality description of a service is given in the profile in a way that is suitable for a service searching agent to determine whether the service meets its needs [1]. Figure 2 shows an instance of a service profile described in a OWL-S document. Tags <profile:serviceName> and <profile:textDescription> provide the name of the service and its description in free text, respectively. The problem is to measure the extent to this information matches a query, which is the mean utilized as an attempt to communicate a need to a system designed for discovering services. In Computer Science, this is known as an IR problem.

In the context of this study, descriptions of the services are briefer than documents (e.g., books) in other contexts. This makes bigger the semantic gap between the query (which communicates the needed functionality) and the description of the desired services (which describe their functionalities). This semantic gap is due to synonym and homonym problems. Synonym problems avoid that a user finds the needed services when s/he uses terms in the query which are not included in the descriptions of the required services, despite of the terms in the query and in the descriptions have a similar semantics. In a document like a book there are more terms with their respective synonyms than in a brief service description. As a consequence, in this context, synonym problems are worse than other domains. On the other hand, homonym problems causes that users discover undesired services, which descriptions contain the same terms issued in the query, but with different semantics. Both kind of problems decrease the accuracy of an IR-based service discovery system.

In current stage of this study, we have analyzed the related work on IR-based service discovery, and we have proposed S^2niffer in order to fill the gap in the state-of-the-art.

2   Proposed Solution: S^2niffer

S^2niffer is a software system for IR-based service discovery. The discovering services process involves the following tasks: preprocessing of services profiles in OWL-S files, indexing, and ranking. Each task is handled by a S^2niffer component as a follows:

- **OWLS2Corpus**: This component is in charge of extracting terms from tags <profile:serviceName> and <profile:textDescription>. In this study is assumed that the content of the first tag is codified according the camel case convention (e.g., nonNegativeMatrixFactorization). Besides, it is assumed the terms in first tag to be separated by spaces or underscore character (cf., Figure 2). Thereafter, this component removes punctuation and symbols, transforms terms to lower case, lemmatizes the terms, and removes stop words. In this study was used the lemmatizer called MorphAdorner[1].
- **Service Descriptions Indexer**: This component creates an index by computing the Term Frequency and Inverse Document Frequency (TF-IDF).
- **Service Ranker**: This component assigns a score to the services given a user's query. The scoring task involves three procedures: (1) injection of synonyms into the query, (2) applying boolean retrieval, and (3) measuring the cosine similarity between the query and service descriptions. Injection of synonyms into the query is frequently effective to increase recall. Nevertheless, thesaurus-based query expansion might significantly decrease the accuracy, in especial when a query has ambiguous terms, e.g., in a query like book a room, if the term *book* is considered a noun, it may be expanded through WordNet with synonyms likewise: record, ledger, lever, etc. If all these synonyms are included into the query, the system will retrieve services which are not related to the user's need, i.e., reserving a room. However, if the same term is correctly identified as a verb, it may be expanded through WordNet with the following

---

[1] MorphAdorner, http://devadorner.northwestern.edu/maserver/lemmatize.

synonyms: hold and reserve. In the last case, the system will retrieve services for booking a room, although these ones might be described with terms such as *reserve* or *hold* instead of *book*. Thus, the accuracy might be increased.

Therefore, the problem consists of tagging parts of speech of the query. Thereafter, the synonyms associated with the term are sought in WordNet but considering if such term is an adverb, verb, noun or adjective. S^2niffer uses Apache OpenNLP[2] library to tag the parts of speech of a query. This library uses a probability model to predict the tag of a term based on its corresponding word type and its context in the query sentence. Finally, these synonyms are injected into the query. Through boolean retrieval, only the descriptions that fulfill the condition presented in the query are scored by means of cosine similarity, as a result, unnecessary matching are avoided.

3   Discussion and Future Work

In this section we aim to place the current version of S^2niffer in the state-of-the-art. This version has been designed in order to:

Table 1. Retrieval performance of S^2niffer, LSI and VSM

S^2niffer NDCG: 0.7645		NDCG	p-value (t-student)	Is statistically significant?
	LSI	0.7142	2.318×10^{-2}	Yes
	VSM	0.5435	7.728×10^{-6}	Yes

1. **Address synonymy and homonymy problems** by using WordNet lexicon, which is similar to the approaches proposed by Wang et al. [18] and Kokash et al. [5]. Nonetheless, S^2niffer injects the synonyms only into the query, while Wang's et al. system injects them also into the index. Kokash et al. used the algorithm proposed by Seco et al. [15] to measure the semantic similarity of concepts in WordNet. Another remarkable difference between S^2niffer and the approaches proposed by Wang et al. [18] and Kokash et al. [5], is that S^2niffer identifies the tag of parts of speech before the injection of synonyms with the purpose to avoid affect the accuracy of the retrieval process. On the other side, we have not adopted Latent Semantic Indexing (LSI) to overcome synonymy and homonymy problems, which is the model used by Sajjanhar et al. [14], Ma et al. [7], and in [19], because vector space model (VSM) scales better than LSI, and in the latter is not possible enforcing negations or boolean conditions. Moreover, Manning et al. [8, pg. 382] state there are studies which have revealed some modes where LSI failed to match the effectiveness of traditional indexes and score computations. Indeed, Table 1 shows that S^2niffer outperforms LSI (which has its better performance with

---

[2] Apache OpenNLP, http://opennlp.apache.org/.

161 latent factors during its evaluation) in experiments carried out over the fourth version of the OWL-S service retrieval test collection named OWLS-TC4[3]. It contains the descriptions of 1083 Web services from 9 domains. Each description is written in OWL-S 1.1. This collection includes 42 queries associated with their relevance judgment provided by several users. During the experiments, the Normalized Discounted Cumulative Gain (NDCG) has been used instead of Mean Average Precision (MAP) to measure the overall ranking accuracy of each approach.

2. **Handle negations and boolean condition included in the user's query**. This is a missing feature in prior works [2,4–7,10–14,17–19]. To realize why this feature is important, lets consider, for instance, a user interested in finding a service for booking an Italian restaurant table but not Arab.

3. **Support inexact matching**. This is another advantage of S^2niffer over prior works [2,4–7,10–14,17–19]. In fact, S^2niffer uses the query syntax of Apache Lucene that supports: Wildcard characters and Fuzzy search query based on the Damerau-Levenshtein similarity. This is useful when a user is not sure how to spell a word.

4. **Be independent of human experts of the domain**. Besides LSI, the another way to overcome synonym problems is by making an ontology for the specific domain, this approach was adopted by Paliwal et al. [10,11], Pan and Zhang [12]. Nevertheless, we have not adopted this approach due to the creation of ontologies is an expensive, time-consuming, tedious, and error-prone task [3,16].

For future work, we plan to compare S^2niffer with LSI based on other matrix factorization techniques (e.g., Non-negative Matrix factorization). Furthermore, we will consider other knowledge sources (e.g., Wikipedia) and techniques to expand the query.

Acknowledgment. Isaac B. Caicedo-Castro is a PhD student supported by Colciencias-Colfuturo (convocatoria 528 de 2011) scholarship, besides, he is founded by the Univ. de Córdoba (Colombia).

References

1. Burstein, M., Hobbs, J., Lassila, O., Mcdermott, D., Mcilraith, S., Narayanan, S., Paolucci, M., Parsia, B., Payne, T., Sirin, E., Srinivasan, N., Sycara, K.: OWL-S: Semantic markup for web services. Technical report (2004). http://www.w3.org/Submission/2004/SUBM-OWL-S-20041122/
2. Crasso, M., Zunino, A., Campo, M.: Easy web service discovery: a query-by-example approach. Sci. Comput. Program. **71**(2), 144–164 (2008)
3. Gomez-Perez, A., Corcho-Garcia, O., Fernandez-Lopez, M.: Ontological Engineering. Springer-Verlag New York Inc, Secaucus (2003)

---

[3] OWL-S Service Retrieval Test Collection, http://projects.semwebcentral.org/projects/owls-tc/.

4. Hao, Y., Zhang, Y., Cao, J.: Web services discovery and rank: an information retrieval approach. Future Gener. Comput. Syst. **26**(8), 1053–1062 (2010)
5. Kokash, N., van den Heuvel, W.-J., D'Andrea, V.: Leveraging web services discovery with customizable hybrid matching. In: Dan, A., Lamersdorf, W. (eds.) ICSOC 2006. LNCS, vol. 4294, pp. 522–528. Springer, Heidelberg (2006)
6. Lee, K.H., Lee, M.Y., Hwang, Y.Y., Lee, K.C.: A framework for xml web services retrieval with ranking. In: International Conference on Multimedia and Ubiquitous Engineering, (MUE 2007), pp. 773–778. IEEE Computer Society (2007)
7. Ma, J., Zhang, Y., He, J.: Web services discovery based on latent semantic approach. In: ICWS, pp. 740–747. IEEE Computer Society (2008)
8. Manning, C.D., Raghavan, P., Schütze, H.: Introduction to Information Retrieval. Cambridge University Press, New York (2008)
9. Na Lumpoon, P., Lei, M., Caicedo-Castro, I., Fauvet, M.C., Lbath, A.: Context-aware service discovering system for nomad users. In: 7th International Conference on Software, Knowledge, Information Management and Applications (SKIMA 2013), Chiang Mai, Thailande (2013)
10. Paliwal, A.V., Adam, N.R., Bornhövd, C.: Web service discovery: Adding semantics through service request expansion and latent semantic indexing. In: IEEE International Conference on Services Computing (IEEE SCC), pp. 106–113. IEEE Computer Society (2007)
11. Paliwal, A.V., Shafiq, B., Vaidya, J., Xiong, H., Adam, N.R.: Semantics-based automated service discovery. IEEE Trans. Serv. Comput. **5**(2), 260–275 (2012)
12. Pan, S.L., Zhang, Y.X.: Ranked web service matching for service description using owl-s. In: International Conference on Web Information Systems and Mining (WISM 2009), pp. 427–431 (Nov 2009)
13. Platzer, C., Dustdar, S.: A vector space search engine for web services. In: Proceedings of the 3rd European IEEE Conference on Web Services (ECOWS 2005, pp. 14–16. IEEE Computer Society Press (2005)
14. Sajjanhar, A., Hou, J., Zhang, Y.: Algorithm for web services matching. In: Yu, J.X., Lin, X., Lu, H., Zhang, Y. (eds.) APWeb 2004. LNCS, vol. 3007, pp. 665–670. Springer, Heidelberg (2004)
15. Seco, N., Veale, T., Hayes, J.: An intrinsic information content metric for semantic similarity in WordNet. In: Proceedings of the 16th European Conference on Artificial Intelligence (ECAI 2004) 4, pp. 1089–1090 (2004)
16. Shamsfard, M., Barforoush, A.A.: Learning ontologies from natural language texts. Int. J. Human-Comput. Stud. **60**, 17–63 (2004)
17. Stroulia, E., Wang, Y.: Structural and semantic matching for assessing web-service similarity. Int. J. Coop. Inf. Syst. **14**, 407–437 (2005)
18. Wang, Y., Stroulia, E.: Semantic structure matching for assessing web-service similarity. In: Orlowska, M.E., Weerawarana, S., Papazoglou, M.P., Yang, J. (eds.) ICSOC 2003. LNCS, vol. 2910, pp. 194–207. Springer, Heidelberg (2003)
19. Wu, C., Potdar, V., Chang, E.: Latent semantic analysis — the dynamics of semantics. In: Dillon, T.S., Chang, E., Meersman, R., Sycara, K. (eds.) Advances in Web Semantics I. LNCS, vol. 4891, pp. 346–373. Springer, Heidelberg (2008)

Dynamic Composite Web Service Execution by Providing Fault-Tolerance and *QoS* Monitoring

Rafael Angarita[1]([⊠]), Marta Rukoz[1,2], and Maude Manouvrier[1]

[1] Université Paris-Dauphine, Paris, France
{rafael.angarita,marta.rukoz,manouvrier}@lamsade.dauphine.fr
[2] Université Paris Ouest Nanterre La Défense, Nanterre, France

Abstract. One of the major goals of the Service Oriented Architecture is to support automatic Web Service (WS) composition and execution, allowing a user query to be satisfied by a Composite WS (CWS). User queries express functional and non-functional (*QoS*) requirements. *QoS* requirements indicate, for example, the maximum execution time or price allowed for a CWS execution. In this work, we propose a model to support CWS executions while maintaining the *QoS* requirements, even in presence of failures. *QoS* monitoring is performed during the entire execution of a CWS in order to satisfy *QoS* requirements, influencing the choice of the fault-tolerance strategy selection in case of failures.

Keywords: Composite web service · Dynamic fault-tolerance · *QoS*

1 Introduction and Problem Statement

In the Service Oriented Architecture (SOA), Web Services (WS) and semantic technologies have emerged to create an environment where users and applications can search, compose, and execute WSs in an automatic and seamless manner [1]. SOA is expected to be a place where a big number of WSs compete to offer a wide range of similar functionalities. This way, WSs from distributed locations can be composed to create new value-added Composite WS (CWS), which resolves complex user queries [2].

Different situations can cause a WS to fail during the execution of a CWS. A fault-tolerant CWS is the one that, upon a WS failure, ends up the whole CWS (e.g., by retrying, substituting, or replicating the faulty WS) or leaves the execution in a safe state (e.g., by rolling back or compensating the faulty WS and the related executed WSs). In this sense, reliable execution of CWSs becomes a key mechanism to cope with challenges of open-world applications in dynamic, changing, and untrusted operating environments, ensuring the consistent state of the whole system even in presence of failures [3].

PSL, Universit Paris-Dauphine, 75775 Paris Cedex 16, France
CNRS, LAMSADE UMR 7243.

F. Toumani et al. (Eds.): ICSOC 2014, LNCS 8954, pp. 371–377, 2015.
DOI: 10.1007/978-3-319-22885-3_32

In this context, failures during the execution of a CWS can be repaired by backward or forward recovery processes. Backward recovery implies to undo the work done until the failure and to go back to the initial consistent state (before the execution started) by using roll-back or compensation techniques. Forward recovery tries to repair the failure and continues the execution; retry and replacement are some techniques used. Backward and forward recovery ensure the all-or-nothing transactional property[1]; however, for some queries, partial responses may have sense for users; thus, checkpointing techniques can be implemented to relax the all-or-nothing transactional property and still provide fault-tolerance [4,5].

The highly dynamic nature of Internet and the compositional nature of WSs makes static CWS executions unpractical in real-world environments, providing a challenge for optimal fault-tolerance strategy determination and *QoS* monitoring. Hence, our research focuses on providing a general model to support CWS executions while maintaining required *QoS* and providing dynamism regarding the selection of fault-tolerance strategies.

The rest of this paper is structured as follows. Section 2 discusses the current literature. Section 3 exposes the main research challenges addressed in this work, while Sect. 4 introduces our proposed solution. Finally, Sect. 5 outlines the conclusions and future research.

2   Related Work

Some works consider transactional properties of component WSs to ensure the classical all-or-nothing properties in CWSs [6–9]. In this context, failures during a CWS execution can be repaired by backward or forward recovery processes. Other works consider WS replication, instead of transactional properties, to provide forward recovery [10–12]. Moreover, checkpointing techniques can be implemented to relax the all-or-nothing transactional property, and can be implemented as an alternative technique independent of transactional properties [4,5], allowing users to have partial results and resume the execution later.

There exist some works that implement combinations of fault-tolerant strategies [10,13,14]. In [10], a replication strategy is used and a rollback workflow is automatically created considering the WS dependencies. An actively replicated platform is implemented transparently to users and independent to WS implementation, in which all replicas of a WS are simultaneously invoked. Backward and forward approaches are combined in [13], based on re-execution, compensation, and WS or subdigraph substitution; for subdigraph substitution, it is necessary to pre-calculate best ranked subdigraph for the CWS and substitution may consider successfully executed WSs, which must be compensated. The strategy described in [14] takes into account user guidance to propose several recovery plans and users manually choose the desired one among those automatically proposed by the system. None of these works consider the dynamism of

---

[1] The all-or-nothing transactional property states that each component WS in a CWS must either complete successfully or have no effect whatsoever.

CWS executions to decide which recovery strategy is the most appropriate and to verify if the CWS execution satisfies the required *QoS* even during execution free of failures.

As far as we know, only [15] proposes an adaptive and dynamic solution for fault-tolerant WS executions. It is based on execution time, failures probability, and resource consumption parameters. Users specify weights that represent their requirements over those three parameters, deciding about the recovery strategy that complies the user needs; however, it is meant for the fault-tolerance of single WSs instead of entire CWSs.

3   Research Focus

Backward recovery can imply long waiting times and lost work due to compensation of previously successfully executed WSs, while users do not get any output, even if partial outputs can be useful. Forward recovery can also cause long waiting times, and the deterioration of other *QoS* parameters, such as price and reputation, due to WS replacement or replication. Moreover, even during failure free executions, the CWS *QoS* can surpass the required *QoS* due to, for example, long waiting times for WSs responses or dynamic changes in other WS *QoS* parameters.

To overcome the aforementioned issues, we focus our research on conceiving a model to support dynamic CWS execution by providing fault-tolerance and *QoS* monitoring; therefore, the main question addressed in this work is:

> *Given that CWS are executed in dynamic and unpredictable environments, how can we provide fault-tolerant CWS executions and, at the same time, comply with user QoS requirements?*

We tackle this question by formulating the following more specific questions:

1. If a WS fails, which fault-tolerance strategy is the most appropriate to choose to satisfy the *QoS* requirements? Can it be chosen dynamically?
2. Which would be the most suitable WS substitute in case of WS replacement?
3. Even during failure free executions, is it possible to finish the execution while maintaining *QoS* requirements, for example, by preventive replication?

By providing answers to these questions, our research aims to contribute to the field of Service Oriented Computing, specifically in the area of fault-tolerance for CWSs.

4   Our Approach to Dynamic CWS Execution

To present our approach, we are going to follow the research path we have pursued with the objective of developing a fault-tolerant CWS execution system [16–18]. At first, we have proposed a distributed execution system [16] based on transactional properties that aims to solve the problem of reliable CWS execution through providing scalable, fault-tolerant, and correct execution of CWSs by: *(i)* ensuring that sequential and parallel WSs will be executed according to the execution flow depicted by the CWS; and *(ii)* in case of failures, leaving the system in a consistent state by executing backward or forward recovery strategies. It also provides scalability as the number of WSs in CWSs grows. Later on, we have extended it to provide checkpointing as an alternative strategy [17,18], enabling users to get partial results, even in the presence of failures, while maintaining the CWS transactional property. Figure 1 shows the recovery strategies implemented by our execution system regarding the moment of the execution when they can be applied.

At the time of conceiving our fault-tolerant CWS execution system [16–18], it was distinguished from and ameliorated existing works because it provided automatic fault-tolerant execution based on transactional CWSs; its execution control followed the defined CWS dependency flow during execution to ensure that sequential and parallel executions satisfy the global transactional property; its framework architecture and execution control were distributed and independent of its implementation, since they could be implemented in distributed or shared memory platforms; CWS executions were totally transparent to users and WS developers, while most of existing works were based on WS-BPEL and/or execution controls have to be managed by developers; and finally, it was formally modeled using Petri Nets.

So far, we have presented our solution to the problem of reliable CWS execution; however, it does not provide dynamism regarding fault-tolerant strategy

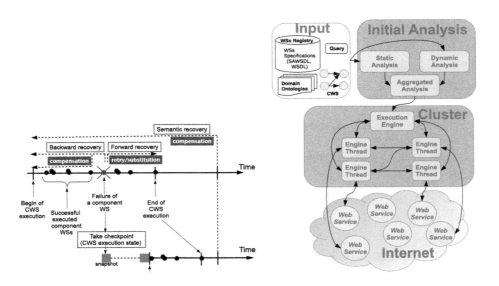

Fig. 1. Recovery techniques.   **Fig. 2.** Execution system.

selection and *QoS* monitoring: forward recovery is chosen if it is possible; if it is not possible, backward recovery is chosen; and checkpointing is selected if the user chose it as an alternative to backward recovery. Even though these strategies ensure system consistency, they have the disadvantages presented at the beginning of Sect. 3; therefore, with the aim of tackling these disadvantages, we strive to create a model to manage **dynamic CWS executions**, which we have presented as a preliminary study [19] and then extended to create a more complete approach for dynamic CWS executions [20].

We illustrate our approach with the help of Fig. 2. The `Input` of the `Execution System` is comprised by the WS Registry (WSDL and semantic documents); the query expressing functional requirements, required *QoS* and transactional property; and finally, the CWS. Prior to the start of the execution, two analyses are performed: one static; another dynamic. The `Static Analysis` produces the CWS estimated *QoS* (e.g., CWS estimated execution time, price, and reputation), whilst the `Dynamic Analysis` verifies the state of the network connectivity with each WS of the CWS. Then, the `Static Analysis` and `Dynamic Analysis` are combined to form the `Aggregated Analysis`, which is composed by tuned up CWS estimations. CWS executions are managed by an `Execution Engine`, which is a collection of `Engine Threads`, one per WS in the CWS. `Engine Threads` are responsible for the actual execution of WSs; monitoring their execution; triggering fault-tolerance mechanisms; and forwarding results to their peers to continue the execution. With the `Aggregated Analysis` and the required *QoS*, the `Execution Engine` deduces the *extra QoS* that can be afforded during the execution to not surpass the required *QoS*. During the actual execution, `Engine Threads` monitor the *QoS* in a distributed fashion, verifying if the required *QoS* is exceeded. When a failure occurs, *QoS* monitoring allows `Engine Threads` to dynamically choose which recovery strategy is the best choice in terms of its impact on the required *QoS*. In case of WS replacement, the choice of a WS substitute depends on the *QoS* at the moment of the failure. Users are able to give importance degrees to the CWS outputs, supporting the decision making between checkpointing and backward or forward recovery. This dynamic strategy selection addresses questions 1 and 2 of Sect. 3. Additionally, even during failure free executions, preventive replication or WS replacement can be used to maintain the required *QoS*; or the CWS execution can be aborted if it does not longer satisfies it, addressing question 3 of Sect. 3.

5   Conclusions and Future Work

We have proposed a novel approach to support dynamic CWS executions while maintaining the required *QoS* even in the presence of failures. We have built it on top of our execution system [16–18], which was a novel solution due to its automatic and distributed fault-tolerant CWS execution based on transactional properties. Preliminary results of dynamic fault-tolerance for CWSs show the validity of our solution regarding its efficiency and effectiveness [19, 20]. We continue to perform experimental evaluations and developing a more usable prototype, since this is ongoing research. By the end of this research, we expect to achieve the formalization of a detailed model to support dynamic CWS execution; as well as a prototype implementation, making our software components and artifacts available to the research community.

References

1. Issarny, V., Georgantas, N., Hachem, S., et al.: Service-oriented middleware for the future internet: state of the art and research directions. JISA **2**(1), 23–45 (2011)
2. Syu, Y., Ma, S.P., Kuo, J.Y., et al.: A survey on automated service composition methods and related techniques. In: Services Computing (SCC), pp. 290–297 (2012)
3. Sheng, Q.Z., Qiao, X., Vasilakos, A.V., et al.: Web services composition:a decades overview. Inf. Sci. **280**(1), 218–238 (2014)
4. Brzeziński, J., Danilecki, A., Hołenko, M., Kobusińska, A., Kobusiński, J., Zierhoffer, P.: D-ReSerVE: distributed reliable service environment. In: Morzy, T., Härder, T., Wrembel, R. (eds.) ADBIS 2012. LNCS, vol. 7503, pp. 71–84. Springer, Heidelberg (2012)
5. Sindrilaru, E., Costan, A., Cristea, V.: Fault tolerance and recovery in grid workflow management systems. In: CISIS 2010, pp. 475–480 (2010)
6. El Haddad, J., Manouvrier, M., Rukoz, M.: TQoS: transactional and QoS-aware selection algorithm for automatic web service composition. IEEE Trans. Serv. Comput. **3**(1), 73–85 (2010)
7. Bushehrian, O., Zare, S., Rad, N.K.: A workflow-based failure recovery in web services composition. JSEA **5**, 89–95 (2012)
8. Cardinale, Y., Rukoz, M.: A framework for reliable execution of transactional composite web services. In: MEDES, pp. 129–136 (2011)
9. Lakhal, N.B., Kobayashi, T., Yokota, H.: FENECIA: failure endurable nested-transaction based execution of composite web services with incorporated state analysis. VLDB J. **18**(1), 1–56 (2009)
10. Behl, J., Distler, T., Heisig, F., Kapitza, R., Schunter, M.: Providing fault-tolerant execution of web-service based workflows within clouds. In: CloudCP (2012)
11. Nascimento, A., Rubira, C., et al.: A systematic review of design diversity-based solutions for fault-tolerant SOAs. In: Proceedings of EASE 2013, pp. 107–118 (2013)
12. Zhou, W., Wang, L.: A byzantine fault tolerant protocol for composite web services. In: International Conference on Computational Intelligence and Software Engineering, pp. 1–4 (2010)
13. Saboohi, H., Kareem, S.A.: Failure recovery of world-altering composite semantic services - a two phase approach. In: Proceedings of the iiWAS 2012, pp. 299–302 (2012)
14. Simmonds, J., Ben-David, S., Chechik, M.: Guided recovery for web service applications. In: Proceedings of ACM SIGSOFT, pp. 247–256 (2010)
15. Zheng, Z., Lyu, M.R.: An adaptive QoS-aware fault tolerance strategy for web services. Empir. Softw. Eng. **15**(4), 323–345 (2010)
16. Angarita, R., Cardinale, Y., Rukoz, M.: FaCETa: backward and forward recovery for execution of transactional composite ws. In: Simperl, E., Norton, B., Mladenic, D., Valle, E.D., Fundulaki, I., Passant, A., Troncy, R. (eds.) The Semantic Web: ESWC 2012 Satellite Events. Lecture Notes in Computer Science, vol. 7540, pp. 343–357. Springer, Heidelberg (2012)

17. Rukoz, M., Cardinale, Y., Angarita, R.: Checkpointing for transactional composite web service execution based on petri-nets. Procedia Comput. Sci. **10**, 874–879 (2012). MobiWIS 2012

18. Cardinale, Y., Rukoz, M., Angarita, R.: Modeling snapshot of composite ws execution by colored petri nets. In: Lacroix, Z., Ruckhaus, E., Vidal, M.-E. (eds.) RED 2012. LNCS, vol. 8194, pp. 23–44. Springer, Heidelberg (2013)

19. Angarita, R., Cardinale, Y., Rukoz, M.: Reliable composite web services execution: towards a dynamic recovery decision. ENTCS **302**, 5–28 (2014)

20. Angarita, R., Cardinale, Y., Rukoz, M.: Dynamic recovery decision during composite web services execution. In: Proceedings of MEDES 2013, pp. 129–136. ACM (2013)

Dynamic QoS Requirement Aware Service Composition and Adaptation

Ajaya Kumar Tripathy[1,2]($\boxtimes$), Manas R. Patra[3], and Sateesh K. Pradhan[2]

[1] Department of CSE, SIT, Bhubaneswar, India
`ajayatripathy1@silicon.ac.in`
[2] Department of Computer Science, Utkal University, Bhubaneswar, India
[3] Department of Computer Science, Berhampur University, Berhampur, India

Abstract. With the prevalence of SOA, an increasing number of Web Services(WS) are created and composed to construct Web-Service Based Systems(SBS). WSs are independent of formulation of complex business process by multiple WS composition. With the steadily growing number of service providers the competition becomes more and more intense. In order to compose a SBS selecting appropriate service from among a collection independently developed services with the same functionality but different cost and Quality of Service (QoS) properties is essential to meet the client preferences. The existing planning and selection algorithms are mostly designed for service discovery. To our knowledge, there are only a few works that incorporate service selection with respect to end user's dynamic QoS requirements. Further, in case of QoS variation of composed SBS at provisioning-time due to QoS variation of one or more component services, a proactive adaptation strategy is required to maintain the required overall QoS. In this ongoing PhD work we propose complete, flexible solution for the "Dynamic QoS requirement aware automatic service selection and provisioning-time adaptation". This approach is a graph based multi-grain clustering and selection model for service composition.

Keywords: Web services · Quality of services · Composition · Run-time SBS adaptation

1 Introduction

Web Service Based Systems (SBS) are formed by composition of one or more Web Services called component services. Composed SBS should fulfil the user's requirements, and the service also needs to be provided with the desired level of quality defined by the service requester. For each component service there is a steady growth in the number of service providers. Selecting a well combination of component services for a SBS to obtain the most optimal result (with client QoS

Initial version of this article had been published in "Work in Progress track of *21st IEEE International Conference on Web Services 2014*: ICWS2014, Alaska USA" [9].

F. Toumani et al. (Eds.): ICSOC 2014, LNCS 8954, pp. 378–385, 2015.
DOI: 10.1007/978-3-319-22885-3_33

requirements) is a NP-hard problem [4]. Further, the QoS requirements varies from client to client. This research problem known as "Dynamic QoS requirement aware service selection", aims to effectively generate service composition workflows which satisfy QoS constraints and optimize certain QoS criteria. In service selection approaches, it is important to consider the service compatibility dependencies on the QoS of SBS. There is a possibility to improve the QoS of overall SBS by introducing an intermediate connector service between two incompatible component services.

Adaptation play an important role in SBS considering its heterogeneous and dynamic nature that is composed of Web Services called component services. Adaptation is necessary in the life cycle of an SBS due to various reasons such as new business goals, dynamic QoS requirements, dynamic nature of QoS of component services, and infrastructure problem or failure of any component service involved in composition.

To address the issue of "Client's required QoS oriented service selection for composition and run-time adaptation", this PhD work introduces a novel approach that introduces QoS aware service clustering [5] for grouping services with similar functionalities (single class of services) into clusters according to their QoS properties. A single cluster inside a class of services represents services of nearly similar QoS properties. This clustering will help us to reduce the time complexity of the searching algorithm. The incompatibility issue is also addressed in this approach. A service cluster graph (weighted directed graph) scheme is introduced to formally represent possible ways to formulate the SBS where each node represents a service cluster. An efficient service selection algorithm based on Bellman Ford's single source shortest path graph algorithm is designed to find end user's QoS requirement oriented component service selection to form the required SBS. Further, a SBS run-time adaptation scheme is designed based on service reselection approach.

2   Problem Statement

We present a "Online Parcel Delivery: OPD" scenario to illustrate the problem of "Dynamic QoS requirement aware service selection and run-time adaptation". OPD is a SBS combination of (*i*) a Short Messaging Service SMS, (*ii*) a Location Locator Service LLS, (*iii*) an Online Payment Service OPS, and (*iv*) a Parcel Delivery Service PDS.

Let us consider the QoS matrices are *Cost*: cost of the service, *Time*: time required to deliver the parcel, *Safety*: the packing quality for delivering goods, *Reliability*: the surety of delivery in proper address. Even if this is a very simple scenario there may be different QoS requirement for different clients. For example, *Client 1:* delivering Passports to foreign consulate and *Client 2:* delivering daily newspapers. *Client 1* needs delivery with high percentage of Safety and Reliability where as *Client 2* needs delivery in time and low cost. Therefore the QoS requirement of *Client 1* is: (*Cost*-10 %, *Time*-30 %, *Safety*-70 % and *Reliability*-90 %) and that of *Client 2* is: (*Cost*-90 %, *Time*-50 %, *Safety*-20 % and *Reliability*-20 %). These two example shows, QoS requirement varies from client to client for same SBS.

Problem 1: Existing service selection approaches mostly designed for service discovery with respect to achieving SBS composition with best QoS. Thus, they neglect the dynamic nature of client's QoS requirements. To avoid this we must understand the impact of a change in QoS requirement, which have its own characteristic and constraints.

Further, on the scenario we would like to show some adaptation example to motivate our adaptation problems: At run time a sub part of the SBS may be malfunctioning or degrades its QoSs. For example, the LLS component service provider of SBS suddenly decides to increase/decrease a particular QoS (e.g., increase/decrease of *Cost*) and consult the business analyst. In order to avoid this problem, business analyst decides to switch to a different (LLS). However, there is a problem with the new LLS. It provides client's location in geographical coordinates instead of full address. While during SBS application design, the designer uses full address as the input message to the PDS. To solve this new data mismatching problem, the service composition is adapted by a mediator service in the process, which converts geographical coordinates into the full addresses. Yet it triggers a new problem: We notice that the new service we introduced for data modification is too costly and in fact increases the overall cost in an unforeseen way.

Problem 2: Most of the adaptation schemes perform adaptation at a single component service level, which may hamper the desired QoS requirement of the whole SBS. Thus, they tend to propose local solution to local problems in a way that is isolated from the overall performance of the SBS. Further, most of them assume the QoS of component services are static, but in reality they may vary at run-time. To avoid this we must understand the impact of dynamic QoS of component services on whole SBS and need to design adaptation scheme considering the impact of adaptation on whole SBS performance.

To handle the above discussed problems we need a novel approach with following two features:

- QoS requirement oriented service selection.
- Component service's dynamic QoS oriented SBS adaptation.

3   Proposed Solution

A service cluster graph (weighted directed graph) scheme is introduced to formally represent possible ways to formulate the SBS where each node represents a service cluster. An efficient service selection algorithm based on Bellman Ford's single source shortest path graph algorithm is designed to find the near optimal combination of Web Services to form the required SBS. Further, a SBS run-time adaptation scheme is designed based on service reselection approach.

Service Graph Construction: Required SBS workflow is divided into sub atomic independent functional units which are denoted by *Job*. For each atomic *Job* unit, select a Web Service to perform that *Job*. And by collecting and composing services for all the atomic *Job*s create complete SBS.

To divide the available services and the SBS workflow, a weighted directed graph is used. The classifications of services and SBS workflows are:

- The services are divided into different classes according to their functionality and compatibility nature with the preceding *Jobs* in the business flow requirements of the SBS.
- QoS matrices based intra class cluster formation and intra class cluster based service graph construction.
- Client requirement and QoS oriented service graph edge's weight estimation.

Service Classification: Assuming that the SBS is a simple collection of n number of atomic *Jobs*, the SBS can be expressed as $Start \rightarrow Job_1 \rightarrow Job_2... \rightarrow Job_n \rightarrow End$. Therefore we can write the *Job* set $J = \{J_1, J_2, ..., J_n\}$. Collection of available services for a particular *Job* is called *Service Class* of the *Job*. Therefore the *Service Class* set $C = \{C_1, C_2, ..., C_n\}$, where C_i is the *Service Class* for J_i.

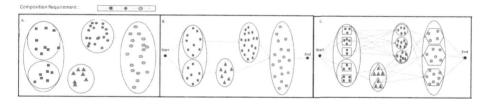

Fig. 1. A. Service classification. B. Service class level graph. C. Service Cluster Level Graph.

In case of any subset of services in a *Service Class* C_i is not compatible with the SBS design or with the services of succeeding *Service Class* C_{i+1}, another intermediate *Job* is needed to make them compatible, then the *Service Class* C_i is divided into sub classes i.e., $C_i \rightarrow \{C_{i.1}, C_{i.2}, ..., C_{i.m}\}$, where m is the number of division in the class due to compatibility problem. And the intermediate *Service Class* for the intermediate *Job* is added in the *Service Class* set.

Figure 1.A shows an example of *Service Class* level directed graph of an example SBS. Any path from *Start* to *End*, with selecting a service from the *Service Classes* at each node can form the required SBS with different QoS matrices. Services in a *Service Class* have different QoS. To select the best possible combination of services from each node to meet client's QoS constraint requirements is a real challenge.

To minimize the search space, considering the QoS parameters of services in *Service Classes*, services are further divided into sub classes to form number of clusters using *K-means* clustering algorithm [5]. Intra cluster services have nearly equal QoS parameters. Members of same cluster have almost same weightage to participate in the composition to form the SBS. So the search space of searching one service from a *Service Class* is reduced to number of clusters. More the cluster number, intra cluster distance is less and more optimal result in service selection, but the search space is proportionally increases. So there is a tread off in deciding the number of clusters needed to form.

Service Class Clustering: Services of each class are divided into K clusters using K-means clustering algorithm [5]. Services in one cluster can substitute each other with similar functionality as well as QoS. Let a *service class* $C = \{s_1, s_2, ..., s_n\}$ where n is the number of services available in the *service class* C. Let $Q_i = < q_{i1}, q_{i2}, ..., q_{im} >$ is the QoS matrices vector of service s_i which represent the features based on which clustering is to be performed and m is the number of QoS parameters considered for service selection. We use the Euclidean distance function to evaluate the distance between two QoS matrices vectors Q_i & Q_j.

Once the clusters are formed, each class nodes in the graph becomes k nodes. The class level graph converted to cluster level graph and particularly the cluster representative (cluster center) becomes node in the graph.

The service graph $SG = (S, E, W)$, is a weighted directed acyclic graph. Where,

- The vertex set $S = \{S_1, S_2, ...S_n\} \cup \{S_0, S_f\}$ represent the vertex set such that S_i, $i=1$ to n represents all cluster center. Two extra vertex S_0, S_f represent starting and ending points of composition.
- The edge set $E = \{(S_i, S_j) :$ there is a predecessor & successor relation between service S_i & S_j as per the composition requirement to achieve the business flow requirement for the composition.$\}$

Figure 1 demonstrates total process of cluster level graph design.

Graph Edge Weight Estimation: The weight set $W = \{w_{ij}, \forall (S_i, S_j) \in E\}$

$$w_{ij} = \begin{cases} EQM_j \text{ If } S_j \neq S_f \\ 0 \quad \text{ If } S_j = S_f \end{cases}$$

Where, EQM_j is the Estimated QoS Matrix of S_j. EQM_j is a function of QoS matrices Q_i and user requirement, which we will discuss in detail further.

EQM Estimation: EQM is a function of quality of service matrices of the available services and the user requirements. The specification of QoS matrices and user requirements are as follows.

- $Q_i = < q_{i1}, q_{i2}, ..., q_{im} >$ is the QoS matrices of service S_i, where m is the number of QoS matrices collected.
- $U_i = < u_{i1}, u_{i2}, ..., u_{im} >$ is the upper limit of the matrices.
- $L_i = < l_{i1}, l_{i2}, ..., l_{im} >$ is the lower limit of the matrices.
- $P_i = < p_{i1}, p_{i2}, ..., p_{im} >$ is the projection of Q_i into the range of 0 to 1.

$$p_{ij} = \frac{q_{ij} - l_{ij}}{u_{ij} - l_{ij}}$$

- $T = <t_1, t_2, ..., t_m>$ is the QoS matrix type.

$$t_i = \begin{cases} -1 & \text{If } i^{th} \text{ QoS matrix} \propto \text{preference of service} \\ 1 & \text{If } i^{th} \text{ QoS matrix} \propto \text{dislike of service} \end{cases}$$

- $I_i = <i_{i1}, i_{i2}, ..., i_{im}>$ is the importance % of the matrices for service class C_i.

$$EQM_i = \sum_{j=1}^{m} \frac{i_{ij} * p_{ij} * t_j}{m},$$

Service Selection for Composition: The *"Service Selection Algorithm"* selects services for single execution plan for the required SBS in such a way that the overall QoS of the composed services is as per the requirements. This algorithm is designed based on Bellman Ford's single source shortest path algorithm. The service *Selection Algorithm* is described in Algorithm 1.

ALGORITHM 1. Service Selection

- Using composition requirement construct the service graph as described in Sect. 3.
- Calculate EQM for all the edges of the constructed graph using Q, U, L, T and I as described in Sect. 3.
- Find the shortest path between S_o to S_f using Bellman Ford's single source shortest path algorithm.
- Service representative in the shortest path are recommended for composition to meet composition requirement with client's QoS matrices constraints.

---

4 SBS Adaptation

Keeping the adaptation needs, we categorize the monitoring properties into two broad categories.

Category 1. One of the component services in the SBS is down/ malfunctioning.
Category 2. An atomic service's QoS is degraded at run-time.

Adaptation scheme: In case of **Category 1**, remove the service from the corresponding service cluster and choose a new cluster representative. Then again run the *Service Selection* algorithm for run-time automatic composition.

But in case of **Category 2**, update the current QoS of the service. Based on that find the new cluster centers. Finally run the *Service Selection* algorithm for reselection of services for composition.

5 Related Work

QoS based service selection has been increasingly investigated recently [6,7] and proposed approaches can be categorized as three types (*i*) QoS-aware service selection based on functional workflow to optimize execution plan [1–3]. (*ii*) Traditional optimization algorithm based QoS optimization [10,12]. (*iii*) QoS constraints based service selection [4,11,13,14]. Most of them, however assume that the QoS matrices are static, which is unfortunately not true [15]. Thus, these kind of approaches are not useful in case of dynamic QoS requirements. In this PhD work, we proposed a novel approach for QoS-aware service selection with automatic adaptation to dynamic QoS matrices of component services.

Our expected research impact with respect to the state of the art is in two ways: First, existing service selection schemes mostly focus on achieving best composition with respect to achieve specific QoS [1,3]. However, in reality the SBS client's QoS requirements are heterogeneous in nature. Our solution aims to align and coordinate the client's dynamic requirements with service selection. Secondly, there are few approaches in literature that uses adaptation with respect to dynamic nature of QoS of the component services available [4,13,14]. Our approach properly aligns the dynamic nature of QoS of component services with the client's QoS requirements using automatic adaptation scheme.

6   Conclusion and Future Work

In this work, we have proposed a graph and clustering based service selection approach to support dynamic QoS requirement with automatic adaptation with respect to changing nature of QoS of component services. In the remaining one year of this PhD work, we will work on the formalization of the research problem and enhancement of implementation of proposed solution. We will integrate our SBS monitoring framework [8] with this approach to get run-time QoS matrices of the component services. Eventually, we would like to evaluate our approach by studying the usability of our approach in real life service based systems.

References

[1] Bartalos, P., Bieliková, M.: Qos aware semantic web service composition approach considering pre/postconditions. In: IEEE International Conference on Web Services (ICWS), pp. 345–352. IEEE (2010)
[2] Canfora, G., Di Penta, M., Esposito, R., Villani, M.L.: A lightweight approach for qos-aware service composition. In: Proceedings of 2nd International Conference on Service Oriented Computing (ICSOC04) (2004)
[3] Chiu, D., Deshpande, S., Agrawal, G., Li, R.: A dynamic approach toward qos-aware service workflow composition. In: IEEE International Conference on Web Services, ICWS 2009, pp. 655–662. IEEE (2009)
[4] Feng, Y., Ngan, L.D., Kanagasabai, R.: Dynamic service composition with service-dependent qos attributes. In: ICWS, pp. 10–17. IEEE (2013)
[5] Hartigan, J.A., Wong, M.A.: Algorithm as 136: a k-means clustering algorithm. J. R. Stat. Soc. Series C 28(1), 100–108 (1979)
[6] Kritikos, K., Plexousakis, D.: Requirements for qos-based web service description and discovery. IEEE Trans. Serv. Comput. 2(4), 320–337 (2009)
[7] Strunk, A.: Qos-aware service composition: a survey. In: IEEE 8th European Conference on Web Services (ECOWS), pp. 67–74. IEEE (2010)

[8] Tripathy, A.K., Patra, M.R.: An event based, non-intrusive monitoring framework for web service based systems. In: 2010 International Conference on Computer Information Systems and Industrial Management Applications (CISIM), pp. 547–552. IEEE (2010)

[9] Tripathy, A.K., Patra, M.R., Khan, M.A., Fatima, H., Swain, P.: Dynamic web service composition with qos clustering. In: 2014 IEEE International Conference on Web Services (ICWS), pp. 678–679. IEEE (2014)

[10] Wada, H., Champrasert, P., Suzuki, J., Oba, K.: Multiobjective optimization of sla-aware service composition. In: IEEE Congress on Services-Part I, pp. 368–375. IEEE (2008)

[11] Wagner, F., Ishikawa, F., Honiden, S.: Qos-aware automatic service composition by applying functional clustering. In: IEEE International Conference on Web Services (ICWS), pp. 89–96. IEEE (2011)

[12] Wan, C., Ullrich, C., Chen, L., Huang, R., Luo, J., Shi, Z.: On solving qos-aware service selection problem with service composition. In: Seventh International Conference on Grid and Cooperative Computing, GCC 2008, pp. 467–474. IEEE (2008)

[13] Xia, Y., Chen, P., Bao, L., Wang, M., Yang, J.: A qos-aware web service selection algorithm based on clustering. In: 2011 IEEE International Conference on Web Services (ICWS), pp. 428–435. IEEE (2011)

[14] Yao, L., Sheng, Q.Z., Segev, A., Yu, J.: Recommending web services via combining collaborative filtering with content-based features. In: 2013 IEEE 20th International Conference on Web Services (ICWS), pp. 42–49. IEEE (2013)

[15] Zheng, Z., Ma, H., Lyu, M.R., King, I.: Wsrec: A collaborative filtering based web service recommender system. In: IEEE International Conference on Web Services, ICWS 2009, pp. 437–444. IEEE (2009)

MobiDisc: Semantic Web Service Discovery Approach in Mobile Environments

Cheyma Ben Njima[1,2]([✉]), Chirine Ghedira Guegan[2], and Lotfi Ben Romdhane[1]

[1] Modeling of Automated Reasoning Systems Research Group,
FSM/University of Monastir, Monastir, Tunisia
bennjimacheima@yahoo.fr
[2] Magellan, IAE, Université Lyon 3, Lyon, France

Abstract. Over the last decades, Internet has grown dramatically. As a result of this growth, a huge amount of Web services and applications have emerged to fulfill consumer's requirements. At the same time, the mobile network industry has become ubiquitous as most consumers are now inseparable from their mobile terminals. The combination of mobile technology and web services provides new paradigm called mobile web services. In order to find services fulfilling the client's requirement, a discovery mechanism is needed. However, discovering services from devices is still a significant challenge due to terminal constraints such as screen resolution, smaller memory, CPU, mobility of consumers and the lack of service descriptions. Thus, the challenge is to increase the accuracy of the relevant discovered services that meet the user's need. In this paper, we present MobiDisc, our mobile web service discovery approach.

Keywords: Mobile web service discovery · OWL-S · Context · QoWS

1 Introduction

With the emergence of new generations of smart phones and mobile devices, consumers run more and more applications and web services anytime and anywhere. The combination of mobile technology and web services provide new paradigm called Mobile web services. Mobile web services has seen an explosion in interest [1], especially the discovery of relevant web services in such environment that still presents a challenge due to terminal constraints, the lack of enriched semantic web service description, the mobility of consumers while invoking web services. To our Knowledge, in the discovery process, researchers customize query by adding only mobile constraints or QoWS properties, if not, customize the web service description. In this paper we lay out the foundations of MobiDisc approach that allows mobile web service discovery according to context and QoWS-awareness. The ultimate objective is to enhance web service composition in mobile environment which constitute the second part of our work. In this paper, we only discuss MobiDisc which is based on three main contributions: the first one, is to extend the query and the web service description not only by

© Springer International Publishing Switzerland 2015
F. Toumani et al. (Eds.): ICSOC 2014, LNCS 8954, pp. 386–391, 2015.
DOI: 10.1007/978-3-319-22885-3_34

semantic enrichement but also by contextual informations. This is done using the OWL-S ontology integrating QoWS, terminal constraints and user profile. The second one is to perform a matching algorithm based on an exact comparison between ontologies. Finally, Mobile web service will be developed to enhance the discovery of Mobile web services by ranking services according to service provider's reputation. The remainder of the paper is organized as follows: Sect. 2 introduces the related work, Sect. 3 discusses the proposed approach, Sect. 4 presents an implementation of the approach, finally, conclusion and future work are given in Sect. 5.

2 Related Works

Several approaches in the literature have addressed the subject of discovery of web services in mobile environments. We have classified theses approaches into two categories according to Context-awareness and QoWS-Context awareness. In the first category, Doulkeridis's [5] defined context as *"the implicit information related to both the requesting user and service provider that can affect the usefulness of the returned results"*. [2,5] identified three types of context: (i) user context which includes user profile, user preferences and location; (ii) Service context that contains provider identity, cost, payment method and (iii) physical context that includes terminal constraints: memory, screen resolution, OS, process speed, audio display, video display, bandwidth and battery. Peng et al. [4] wrote the query as service profile ontology of OWL-S by adding user profile and terminal constraints (terminal type, screen size, screen resolution, video display capability, audio capability). However, in this approach, researchers did not consider QoWS properties and some important terminal constraints like bandwidth and localization which are neglected. In [1], authors proposed MobiEureka, a WSDL syntactic description exploiting the standard CC/PP defined by W3C. Services are then ranked using DaRF [1]. This approach has used a syntactic description which suffers from expressiveness, additional to the lacks that CC/PP presents: Extensibility, expressiveness and automatic discovery. Finally,work in [6] proposed a mechanism called SeMoSD. It uses WSMO to describe semantically services and terminal constraints, but QoWS is not in their consideration.

In the second category, Mobile web service discovery Context and QoWS-awareness, approaches attempts to address the issue of discovery from two perspectives, functional and non-functional properties. This already presents a challenge. Non-functional properties are QoWS which are divided in [7] into two categories: runtime quality and business quality. Runtime Quality includes the response time, reliability, availability, accessibility and integrity. Business Quality refers to the cost, reputation and payment method. Mobile web service approaches QoWS-context awareness, take into consideration, QoWS, user context, physical context and service context to find relevant services. Work in [8] extends semantic description WSMO to WSMO-M integrating functional and non functional properties, without insisting on terminal constraints and QoWS used, in addition, WSMO is an ontology that is heavy to execute. In [9], authors propose an approach which exploits CC/PP into an ontology called PBCO based on OWL (Ontology web Language) and DCO (Delivery Context Ontology). Even, this approach presents the advantage of the adaptive display on mobile devices. The construction of an ontology seems to be handmade and not standardized which poses problem of interoperability. Work in [12] extends the ontology OWL-S into two representations: EASY-Language and EASY-Matching. The EASY approach offers an efficient mechanism for service discovery only applied in a pervasive environment In order to fulfill the aforementioned gaps, we introduce our context and QoWS awareness approach. In addition to the enrichement of ontologies with QoWS properties and terminal capabilities, this approach adds an historization step to accelerate web service discovery.

3   Semantic Web Service Discovery Approach in Mobile Environment

As stated, our approach MobiDisc aims at increasing the accuracy of web service discovery process in mobile environment. To this end, our proposal is based on four steps. The first step is dedicated to the rewriting of the user query. Indeed, the discovery of adequate mobile web services suffers from a lack of environmental information regarding the user and the used device. Thereby, initial user query should be rewrited by adding for instance its terminal constraints, its profile and the expected QoWS properties as depicted in Fig. 1. In fact, the rewritten query adopts the service profile schema of OWL-S in order to facilitate the matching of the user query and mobile web service characteristics. In the second step, Web services are described using functional and non-functional properties. Functional properties represents especially physical context(service context and terminal context) and non functional properties represents QoWS features. We used and extended OWL-S service profile to describe the personalization of the web service description. Figure 2 is a snapshot of the enriched ontology. The third step is intended to perform a matching algorithm based on a comparaison of exact similarities between charateristics of the ontologies. The fourth step consists in a customization but also an enhancement of the mobile discovery process. Indeed, nowadays it's difficult to have confidence in all services given the large number of providers and of provided web services. In this context, our idea is to also consider the web service provider reputation and let user choose his/her criteria.Thereto, we base the computing and evaluation of web service providers reputation according to performance, security, quality of the services but also feedbacks and social networks. Knowing that those collected information are in constant change and frequently incomplete, we plan to use Bayesian networks. Indeed, Bayesian learning takes a probability-based approach to reason and infer results. Each training example that is encountered can change the probability that an hypothesis is correct. Moreover, rather than using knowledge from the current data set or training examples only, prior knowledge can be combined with the observed and incomplete data to meaningful achieve better results [11].

Select ?ServiceName,?ServiceURL		Select ?ServiceName, ?ServiceURL	
Where		Where	
{		{	
?BookName	&xsd:#string	?BookName:	&xsd:#string
?Author	&xsd:#string	?Author	&xsd:#string
?DateEdition	&xsd:#Date	?DateEdition	&xsd:#Date
}		!Battery	&xsd:#Concept
		!Audio_display	&xsd:#Concept
		!video_display	&xsd:#Concept
		!screen_resolution	&xsd:#Concept
		!screen_size	&xsd:#Concept
		!process_speed	&xsd:#Concept
		!Memory	&xsd:#Concept
		!OS	&xsd:#Concept
		Filter	
		!response_time <5s	
		!Cost<30euro	
		!Latitude ???	
		!longitude???	
		!bandwidth>100 Mbps and bandwidth<500Mbps	

Fig. 1. Rewriting user's request example

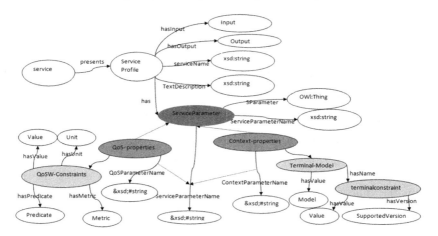

Fig. 2. Partial representation of the enriched OWL-S description with terminal constraints and QoWS

4   MobiDisc Architecture

In this section, we introduce MobiDisc architecture that takes advantage of the aforementioned features. The ultimate goal is to decrease the number of candidate web services to find the most relevant service that responds to user's requirements. Our architecture shown in Fig. 3 is composed of three layers. Each layer uses the result of the previous one. In this paper, we will introduce the first layer. To do this, we were inspired b the work in [3, 10] that handles the discovery of web services QoWS awareness in a static environment. Thus, we developed an OWL-S extension of a QoWS-context aware web service description for both request and advertised services. In order to support semantic QoWS and context matchmaking, we differentiate between request profile of a user and an advertisement profile provided by a specific service provider. Meanwhile, a profile advertised by a service provider, should have the following characteristics: QoWS properties such

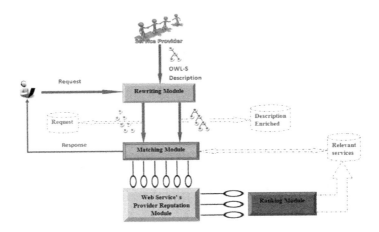

Fig. 3. MobiDisc's architecture

as reliability, cost, response time and disponibility, context properties related to terminal caracteristics includes OS, AudioDisplay, VideoDisplay, ScreenResolution, MemorySize, ProcessSpeed, Battery, Bandwidth. Therefore, upper profile ontology which satisfy the above requirements can be seen in Fig. 2. To implement the ontologies, we used Protege 3.5, including OWL-S tab editor. Then, OWL-S is connected to QoWS ontology and context ontology. To design this, QoWS-properties and Context-properties are two subclasses of OWL-S ServiceParameter. The service provider provides such an offer ·profile in its advertisement like: (response time, equal, 300, millisecond). Also, terminalModel is a subclass of ContextProperties which have also a subclass called TerminalConstraints. Service provider would provide such an offer profile in its advertisement service like: (iphone5S, ScreenResolution (1 136 × 640, Ecran Retina 4 pouces)). Request profile ontology is prepared in the same way, adding a third subclass of ServiceParameter which is UserProfile. This class contains a set of subproperties: login, password, payementmethod and localisation. After enriching of the query and the service description, a matching algorithm is needed to calculate similarities between the two ontologies and decrease the number of advertisement services. Also, the matching algorithm compare the enriched query with relevant service description based on a calculation of exact similarities. This is an historization step which aim at accelerating the discovery process and to constantly update relevant web service repository. Finally, Our architecture contains a third layer designed to rank web services based on bayesian networks. This is done by increasing the accuracy of relevant web services according to the evaluation of the web service provider's reputation.

5   Summary and Future Works

This paper has introduced MobiDisc, which is a new approach for web service discovery in mobile environment. This approach aims at finding the most relevant web service by extending OWL-S Ontology with functional and non functional properties, matching request and web service description, then ranking the resulting services after evaluating provider's reputation. The matching algorithm and the Ranking web service are under implementation, and a timing comparative study between mobile web service approaches will be done in the next work.

References

1. Al-Masri, E., Mahmoud, Q.H.: MobiEureka: an approach for enhancing the discovery mobile web services. Pers. Ubiquit. Comput. **14**(7), 609–620 (2009)
2. Saadon, N.A., Mohamad, R.: A comparative evaluation of web service discovery approaches for mobile computing. In: Abd Manaf, A., Sahibuddin, S., Ahmad, R., Mohd Daud, S., El-Qawasmeh, E. (eds.) ICIEIS 2011, Part IV. CCIS, vol. 254, pp. 238–252. Springer, Heidelberg (2011)
3. Ben Abboud, R., Maamri, R., Sahnoun, Z.: Agents and OWL-S based semantic web service discovery with user preference support. Int. J. Web Semant. Technol. **4**(2) (2013)
4. Peng, R., Mi, Z., Wang, L.: An OWL-S based adaptive service discovery algorithm for mobile users. In: 4th International Conference on Wireless Communications, Networking and Mobile Computing. IEEE (2008)
5. Doulkeridis, C.: CASD: management of a context-aware service directory. Pervasive Mob. Comput. **4**(5), 737–754 (2008)
6. Besen, R., Siqueira, F.: A mechanism for semantic web service discovery in mobile environment. In: ICN 2011 the Tenth International Conference on Networks (2011)
7. Yu, Q., Liu, X., Bouguettaya, A., Medjahed, B.: Deploying and managing web services: issues, solutions, and directions. VLDB J. **17**, 537–572 (2006)
8. Saadon, N., Mohamad, R.: Web Service Discovery Approach for Mobile Computing. In: Communications in Computer and Information Science (2011)
9. Niazi, R., Mahmoud, Q.H.: An ontology-based framework for discovering mobile services. In: 2009 Seventh Annual Communication Networks and Services Research Conference, pp. 178–184. IEEE, May 2009
10. Lin, L., Kai, S., Sen, S.: Ontology-based QoS-aware support for semantic web services, Technical report at Beijing University of Posts and Telecommunications (2008)
11. Nedia, B., Khouloud, B., Chirine, G: A trust management solution in the context of hybrid clouds. In: International Workshops on Enabling Technologies: Infrastructures for Collaborative Enterprises. IEEE (2014)
12. Mokhtar, S., Preuveneers, D., Georgantas, N., Issarny, V., Berbers, Y.: EASY: efficient semAntic service discoverY in pervasive computing environments with QoS and context support. J. Syst. Softw. **81**(5), 785–808 (2007)

Monitoring and Checking Privacy Policies of Cloud Services Based on Models

Eric Schmieders[(✉)]

paluno (The Ruhr Institute for Software Technology),
University of Duisburg-Essen, Essen, Germany
`eric.schmieders@paluno.uni-due.de`

Abstract. Data geo-location policies constrain the geographical locations at which personal data may be stored or processed. Data storage and processing locations are dynamically changed by cloud elasticity that migrates and replicates cloud services across data centers. Thus, cloud elasticity as well as data transfers of interacting services may re-locate data, which potentially violates data geo-location policies. To detect these violations, we develop a policy checking approach based on runtime models. We examine monitoring and model updating mechanisms for reflecting service composition and deployment changes caused by elasticity. Based on the updated runtime model we derive potential data transfers and check them against policies. Initial results indicate the effectiveness and high-performance of our approach.

Keywords: Privacy · Cloud platform management · Decentralized cloud platform architectures · Runtime verification · Data-geo-location

1 Introduction

For processing and storing data industry increasingly integrates cloud services in their IT-landscapes, thereby addressing availability and cost goals at low up-front investments [4]. These goals are accomplished by cloud elasticity. Cloud elasticity replicates and migrates virtual machines that contain cloud services across data centers, which impacts on service compositions and deployments. Dynamically changed service compositions and deployments may transfer personal data to locations excluded by policies. As unknown during design time, excluded locations and related violations must be detected during runtime.

In our research, we investigate a runtime model based approach for detecting data geo-location violations. We explore where and how to probe cloud services in order to observe composition and deployment changes. Observed changes need to be reflected in the runtime model. Thus, we investigate the utilization of updating mechanisms able to cope with complex model updates. We derive potential data transfers from the updated model that are checked for data geo-location compliance. To this end, we combine runtime models with reachability graphs, which furnishes high-performant policy checks and timely responses.

Supervised by Prof. Dr. Klaus Pohl and Dr. Andreas Metzger

© Springer International Publishing Switzerland 2015
F. Toumani et al. (Eds.): ICSOC 2014, LNCS 8954, pp. 392–398, 2015.
DOI: 10.1007/978-3-319-22885-3_35

2   Background and Research Challenges

Cloud services may store data and may interact with each other across data centers [2]. Table 1 discusses the combination of the two data usage dimensions - storage (sto.) and service interaction (int.) - with respect to data re-location.

The investigation of *cases 1–3* allows for systematically determining the information required for detecting policy violations, which is information on: service interactions, stored data, service deployments, and geo-locations of data centers. The privacy check itself and the provisioning the required information leads to several challenges and questions. As service providers restrict the access to service internals, it is challenging to *probe and monitor the observed cloud service as well as integrated third-party services to become aware of service composition and deployment changes (RC1)*. Service composition and deployment information have to be updated based on collected monitoring data. Due to heterogeneous monitoring facilities operating at different levels of detail the *analysis of monitoring data for updating the information required to check cases 1–3 (RC2)* is challenging. Cloud services may involve several hundreds of virtual machines (e.g., in Hadoop-systems), but service users and providers have a stake in rapidly becoming aware of policy violations. Therefore, it is a challenge to *check cloud services with respect to cases 1–3 in order to provide timely responses (RC3)*.

Table 1. Combinations of the storage and interaction dimension

sto.	int.	Combination description
✓	–	The replication or migration of a cloud service *S1* across data centers (e.g. a DBaaS), replicates or migrates data inside the service as well (*case 1*)
–	✓	*S1* accesses data stored at a remote cloud service *S2*. After migration or replication of *S1*, data may be transferred to the new location of *S1* directly (*case 2*) or transitively via intermediate cloud services (*case 3*)
✓	✓	This combination can be mapped to a combination of *case 1* and *case 2* or *case 1* and *case 3*
–	–	This combination does not involve any transferred, stored, or processed data

3   Related Work

In this section, we analyze (i) whether existing runtime model approaches update models based on observed service composition and deployment changes, and (ii) how far existing policy checks cover the identified *cases 1–3*.

(i) Work such as [6, 8, 12] *update parameterized models* based on observed service interfaces. Single observations, e.g., a service response time, are mapped to parameters of related model entities. Updating model parameters is not sufficient to reflect changes caused by elasticity, as elasticity changes the structure of service compositions. Approaches on model extraction and process mining, e.g., [3], *update the structure of runtime models* based on observed component interactions. The work exploits information of nested method executions to update information on component interactions. Inserting or deleting edges between given model elements is not sufficient to reflect complex compositional changes of the observed service. Moreover, existing runtime models, e.g., [3,6,8,12], lack information on processed or stored data, data meta-information as well as geo-location information of data centers required for checking *cases 1–3*.

(ii) *Policy checks based on access control*, e.g., [1,9], utilize mechanisms that permit or grant data access after matching the client characteristics with data policies. Access control neither covers elasticity (*case 1*) nor transitive data transfers (*case 3*) that may lead to undetected policy violations. *Elasticity rules are defined during design time* [14] in order to control the replication and migration of multiple services qualities and have not been applied to privacy yet. However, their application to data geo-location requires knowledge of data stored by a service (*case 1*) as well as the service interactions (*case 2* and *case 3*). This information is not available during design time. *Policy checks based on event processing* [15] may detect violations based on information provided by a migration or replication event. *Case 1* may be detected by mapping the geo-location policy to the geo-location of the target center. However, data transfers from direct (*case 2*) or transitive (*case 3*) service interactions would remain undetected as this requires information about the composition of the service.

To summarize, current runtime models fall short in monitoring (RC1) and updating information (RC2) required to cover *cases 1–3*. None of the existing policy checking approaches detect all violations described in *case 1–3* (RC3).

4   Research Plan

The research plan aims for tackling the identified gaps. It starts with research on the policy-check itself and the required runtime model (RC3). Once the runtime model entities and relations are specified, we are able to identify the model elements that need to be updated for reflecting changed service compositions and deployments (RC2). The research on model updates (RC2) allows for identifying the monitoring data (RC1) required for triggering the updates. Finally, we elaborate the service monitoring concept (RC1) providing the required data. Our plan includes an evaluation of each RC contribution as well as an evaluation of the integrated overall approach. We aim for investigating the effectiveness and efficiency in a realistic cloud environment instrumented with, e.g., OpenStack and Hadoop. However, there are different options for designing and arranging the evaluation, which are going to assess with respect to feasibility.

With the applied "reversed order" (from RC3 to RC1), we transfer the idea of goal-driven monitoring [11] to our research plan. We consider the detection of *cases 1–3* as the goal and the policy check (RC3), model update (RC2), and service monitoring (RC1) as hierarchically organized tasks. This allows for (i) specifying a tailored set of monitoring probes and monitoring information required for updating the runtime model and (ii) for identifying requirements towards monitoring solutions.

5   Overall Approach

In the following, we introduce the main concepts of our approach that we plan to develop. We describe the essential artifacts and activities based on an established service life cycle [10] (shown in Fig. 1).

To enable policy checks during runtime the required information described in Sect. 2 has to be modeled, cf. step (1) in Fig. 1. The model G reflects the initial composition of the developed service as well as the used third-party services (see Fig. 2). For instance, the runtime model reflects an application running on a virtual machines as well as attached databases. In step 2, the service is developed and instrumented with probes via aspects (cf. [7]). A set of data geo-location policies P is created. Each $p \in P$ is defined as triple $p = (s, c, l)$, including a data classification s, a data content description c, and a geo-location l. For instance, personalized (s) health care data (c) must not be processed in the USA (l) (see the policy meta-model in Fig. 2 and for further details [13]).

After being deployed, the service is continuously monitored, cf. steps (3) and (4). We propose to instrument every component of the developed service in order to monitor replications or migrations of owned components (RC1). Changes of third party services are retrieved from monitoring APIs of cloud providers that utilize established monitoring-tools such as Nagios or advancements discussed in [2]. The probes emit low level monitoring information M about the applied cloud elasticity. In order to update the model (RC2), we create a set of model transformations R. We define a mapping function $c \in C$ for each of the heterogenous monitoring facilities serving as adapter. c maps monitoring data $M' \subseteq M$ to a model transformation r, such that $c(M', r) : M' \times \{r\} \to \{true, false\}, M' \mapsto r$. When a mapping is possible, the function value is *true*, otherwise it is *false*. Each model transformation $r \in R$ alternates the structure of the runtime model in accordance to the observed changes (e.g., a new data base node has been added), specified as $r(G) : G \overset{r}{\Rightarrow} G'$.

Every model update triggers a policy check (RC3), cf. step (5). The runtime model includes current data geo-locations as well as information on service interactions, which allows for deriving potential data transfers. Thus, the proposed check detects policy violations resulting from transferring personal data inside a service (*case 1*), as well as from direct (*case 2*) and transitive (*case 3*) data transfers. We propose to treat the check as an st-connectivity problem, which enables checks with high-performance. To this end, we consider the runtime model G as a reachability graph. The proposed checking algorithm selects a subset V_s of

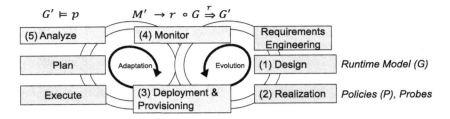

Fig. 1. Artifacts and activities along the service life-cycle

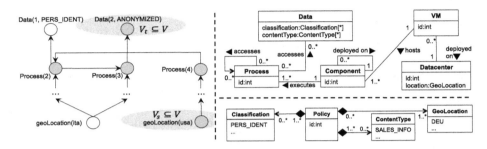

Fig. 2. Reachability graph, runtime meta model, and policy meta model

geo-location nodes from the runtime model specified by l in the checked policy p and selects a subset V_t of data nodes specified by s in p (see Fig. 2). After defining both subsets, the algorithm checks whether there is a path H_{v_s,v_t} for any combination in $V_s \times V_t$. The existence of H_{v_s,v_t} indicates a potential data transfer violating the checked policy. Given a graph G and a policy p, we define the model check $G \models p$ as function $f(G, p) : G \times \{p\} \rightarrow \{true, false\}$, which returns $true$, if $\neg \exists v_s \exists v_t : H_{v_s,v_t}$, with $v_s \in V_s \wedge v_t \in V_t$ and otherwise returns $false$. We can now formally specify the overall approach as $\forall m : c(m, r) \rightarrow (r \circ f)(G, p)$ with $m \in M'$. The expression indicates a policy violation in case of becoming $false$.

6 Conclusion and Future Work

With our research, we address the problem of detecting policy violations that result from elastic interacting cloud services. So far, we addressed RC3 by developing a policy checking approach that covers *cases 1–3*. We performed a validation of the checking algorithm based on an SOA-version of CoCoME. The evaluation indicates that the algorithm checks large models (with more than 800 virtual machines as in the case of Hadoop-Clusters) in less than a second.

Currently, we work on RC1 and RC2. We explore the utilization of monitoring and updating mechanisms to realize and enhance our model updating concept. We investigate how to exploit low level monitoring data that cloud monitoring infrastructures typically emit. For the model updates we may utilize a standard technique such as graph transformation (e.g. [5]). We aim for evaluating the overall approach on third-party cloud infrastructures.

Acknowledgements. This work was partially supported by the DFG (German Research Foundation) under the Priority Programme "SPP1593: Design For Future – Managed Software Evolution" (grant PO 607/3-1).

References

1. Comparative analysis of access control systems on cloud. In: International Conference on Software Engineering, Artificial Intelligence, Networking and Parallel Distributed Computing
2. Aceto, G., Botta, A., de Donato, W., Pescap, A.: Cloud monitoring: a survey. Comput. Netw. **57**(9), 2093–2115 (2013)
3. Brosig, F., Huber, N., Kounev, S.: Automated extraction of architecture-level performance models of distributed component-based systems. In: 26th IEEE/ACM International Conference on Automated Software Engineering (ASE) (2011)
4. Copil, G., Moldovan, D., Truong, H.-L., Dustdar, S.: Multi-level elasticity control of cloud services. In: Basu, S., Pautasso, C., Zhang, L., Fu, X. (eds.) ICSOC 2013. LNCS, vol. 8274, pp. 429–436. Springer, Heidelberg (2013)
5. Ehrig, H., Ermel, C., Runge, O., Bucchiarone, A., Pelliccione, P.: Formal analysis and verification of self-healing systems. In: Rosenblum, D.S., Taentzer, G. (eds.) FASE 2010. LNCS, vol. 6013, pp. 139–153. Springer, Heidelberg (2010)
6. Epifani, I., Ghezzi, C., Mirandola, R., Tamburrelli, G.: Model evolution by runtime parameter adaptation. In: 31st ICSE (2009)
7. Jung, R., Heinrich, R., Schmieders, E.: Model-driven instrumentation with kieker and palladio to forecast dynamic applications. In: Symposium on Software Performance: Joint Kieker/Palladio Days 2013. CEUR (2013)
8. von Massow, R., van Hoorn, A., Hasselbring, W.: Performance simulation of runtime reconfigurable component-based software architectures. In: Crnkovic, I., Gruhn, V., Book, M. (eds.) ECSA 2011. LNCS, vol. 6903, pp. 43–58. Springer, Heidelberg (2011)
9. Park, S., Chung, S.: Privacy-preserving attribute distribution mechanism for access control in a grid. In: 21st International Conference on Tools with Artificial Intelligence, ICTAI 2009 (2009)
10. Pernici, B.: Methodologies for design of service-based systems. In: Nurcan, S., Salinesi, C., Souveyet, C., Ralyt, J. (eds.) Intentional Perspectives on Information Systems Engineering, pp. 307–318. Springer, Heidelberg (2010)
11. Ramirez, A.J., Cheng, B.H.C.: Automatic derivation of utility functions for monitoring software requirements. In: Whittle, J., Clark, T., Kühne, T. (eds.) MODELS 2011. LNCS, vol. 6981, pp. 501–516. Springer, Heidelberg (2011)
12. Schmieders, E., Metzger, A.: Preventing performance violations of service compositions using assumption-based run-time verification. In: Abramowicz, W., Llorente, I.M., Surridge, M., Zisman, A., Vayssière, J. (eds.) ServiceWave 2011. LNCS, vol. 6994, pp. 194–205. Springer, Heidelberg (2011)
13. Schmieders, E., Metzger, A., Pohl, K.: A runtime model approach for data geolocation checks of cloud services. In: Franch, X., Ghose, A.K., Lewis, G.A., Bhiri, S. (eds.) ICSOC 2014. LNCS, vol. 8831, pp. 306–320. Springer, Heidelberg (2014)

14. Suleiman, B., Venugopal, S.: Modeling performance of elasticity rules for cloud-based applications. In: 2013 17th IEEE International Enterprise Distributed Object Computing Conference (EDOC), September 2013
15. Wu, E., Diao, Y., Rizvi, S.: High-performance complex event processing over streams. In: Proceedings of the 2006 ACM SIGMOD International Conference on Management of Data, SIGMOD 2006, pp. 407–418. ACM, New York (2006)

Service Map: A Service Hierarchy for Satisfying User's Requirement of Multiple Granularities

Chu Du[(✉)] and ZhangBing Zhou

China University of Geosciences, Beijing, China
duchusac@gmail.com

Abstract. With huge and ever-increasing number of services available on the Web, more non-domain experts are willing to chaining services for fulfilling their specific requirements. Users may get known more about their requirements gradually, which requires the solution identification at different levels of granularity. To address this challenge, we propose a remedy called *service map*, which aims to (i) organize services in a hierarchical fashion, such that different levels represent the functionalities of services in a different granularity, and (ii) to provide service chaining at a certain level of granularity with respect to user's requirement.

1 Introduction

Nowadays more and more services are being developed and applied for supporting many real applications, and we are moving to the era of Big Services [6]. In this setting, how to organize the huge amount of services efficiently and thus, to support the service chain recommendation according to specific requirements of certain users, is a challenge. To mitigate this issue, services are grouped into clusters [8], which are building a service network [7] and further forming a service ecosystem [2]. Services in the clusters nearby are usually similar in their functionalities, and thus may be replaced by each other in certain situations. On the other hand, services in the clusters "far away" are usually much different in their functionalities, but they may be chained together through other services in the clusters in "between", to fulfill the requirements that cannot be implemented by means of any single service. Consequently, techniques that can facilitate the chaining (or composition) procedure of services across clusters is essential. Currently, service composition is relatively mature and most are trying to chaining service operations into a value-added service [5]. They can be used somehow as the base of composing services in the service clusters, where a cluster is to be represented in terms of a service description.

With the wide applicability of services, more and more non-domain experts achieve their goals through chaining (composing) existing services into value-added ones. It is usual that normal users can hardly identify their requirements clearly, completely, and in detail at the service operation level at the beginning. Instead, users may specify their requirements at a high-level, and examine the solutions at the same granularity. Based on which, users may delve into the

© Springer International Publishing Switzerland 2015
F. Toumani et al. (Eds.): ICSOC 2014, LNCS 8954, pp. 399–405, 2015.
DOI: 10.1007/978-3-319-22885-3_36

requirements and examine the solutions at a finer granularity. This procedure may iterate until a solution, which is a chaining or composition of service operations, is determined. To support the solution identification at different granularities, services should be grouped in a hierarchical fashion, where the upper level is coarse-grained, whereas the lower level is fine-grained. Therefore, users can try to identify a solution of coarse-grained on the upper level of service abstraction initially, and can identify the solution of fine-grained finally. Consequently, how to organize services hierarchically and thus to facilitate the solution identification at a certain granularity with respect to users' requirements is a challenge. Current techniques are mainly focused on services grouping into clusters [8], the identification of usage patterns for service operations from the history of service compositions and executions [2], or interactive business process maps mined from the event log [3], in order to enable the reusability of best practices for facilitating service composition and execution. However, how to support the solution identification of multiple granularities is not explored extensively.

To address the challenges mentioned above, we propose a technique called *service map* in the thesis, which aims to organize services in a hierarchical fashion, where the upper level represents the coarse-grained functionalities of services contained in a cluster, while the lower level is to represent the finer-grained functionalities, and the leaf correspond to the clusters of service operations. Given a user's requirement, a solution can be determined at the certain level of functional granularity. It is worth mentioning that our service map is different from ServiceMap proposed by Wei et al. [2] and TomTom4BPM by Aalst [3] in that, both ServiceMap and TomTom4BPM organize service operations and activities in business processes at a single level, and they can hardly support the discovery of solutions when the requirement of certain users is represented in different level of granularity, whereas our service map aims to mitigate this problem.

2   Service Map: A Conceptual Model

Inspired by the physical map which is used for GPS guidance from the source area to the target area crossing multiple areas in between, our service map is purposed for guiding the service chaining from the source to the target service clusters. These clusters may be neighboring or far away in functionalities provided. In the physical map, physical areas are given names and organized into a logical hierarchy, where a city is composed of multiple districts, a province is composed of multiple cities, and so on. As shown by an example in Fig. 1, a service map can be organized in the similar fashion, where in the logical service hierarchy, the upper level represents more coarse-grained functionalities like "Trip" and "Entertainment", while the lower lever represents finer-grained functionalities like "Hotel" and "Sightseeing", and the leaf represent services or their operations that can be chained and invoked, like "Check In" and "Room Services". As an example, Fig. 1 illustrates a two-layer abstraction of service clusters, and much finer granularity can be achieved in real data sets.

When a non-domain expert would like to use existing services for achieving her goal (like planning a trip to a city for sightseeing), her initial requirement

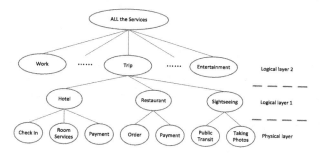

Fig. 1. An example of Service Map.

should match the "Trip" at the logical level 2, and she observes that a trip mainly includes three components: "hotel", "restaurant", and "sightseeing". Then, she is guided to give her requirements of finer-grained about these three components, and delve into possible solutions respectively. This procedure iterates until she can give her requirements clearly, completely, and in detail. A chain of services (or their operations) is composed, which is executable for fulfilling her requirement.

3 Service Map Construction Procedure

After introducing the concept of service map, this section presents the construction procedure of a service map. Generally, a service map can be generated from service compositions or process models (like *BIT-ProcessLibrary-Release2009*[1], and scientific workflows in myExperiment), or event logs. In this paper we show this construction procedure based on the process models provided by *BIT-ProcessLibrary-Release2009*, where the name of activities is anonymized. That is why we do not use the service map generated from these process models as the example in the previous section. We use *service composition* and *business process*, and *service* and *activity*, interchangeably in this paper. The construction procedure includes the following three steps: (i) service network construction, (ii) community determination and service map generation, and (iii) functionality identification of communities, as explained in the following sections.

3.1 Service Network Construction

We firstly construct a service network from the set of service compositions. Generally, a service network presents services, and invocation relationship between them [7]. We model a service network as follows:

$$G = (S, E) \tag{1}$$

$$s = (Ip, Op, Des) \in S \tag{2}$$

$$e = (sSvc, tSvc, freq) \in E \tag{3}$$

---

[1] http://www.zurich.ibm.com/csc/bit/downloads.html.

where G corresponds to a service network, which is composed of services (or their operations) S, and the edges E specifying invocation possibilities between these services. A service s includes its input (Ip), output (Op) and description in text (Des). Note that s can include more elements, such as spatial and temporal attributes. e represents the invocation relation between the source service $sSvc$ and the target service $tSvc$, while $freq$ reflects the invocation frequency for $sSvc$ and $tSvc$. Note that the reader can refer to [7] for the formal definition and the detailed construction procedure of service network.

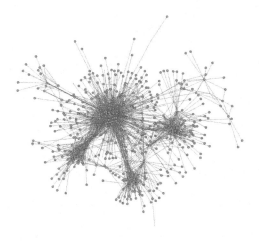

Fig. 2. Service network generated from *BIT-ProcessLibrary-Release2009*.

An example of service network is shown in Fig. 2, which is generated from the process models in *BIT-ProcessLibrary-Release2009*, where the nodes correspond to activities, the direct edges refer to the invocation relations between activities, while the thickness of edges reflects the invocation frequency of two activities. Given any two activities, the invocation frequency is proportional to the number of calling relation between these two activities in the set of process models.

3.2   Community Determination and Service Map Generation

We generate a service map based on the service network, where we group services into communities firstly. Intuitively, a community of services is a sub-graph of G, which reflects a higher-level, and coarser-gained functionality. We use a density-based graph clustering method, called *graph-skeleton-based clustering* [1], to detect communities. It is worth mentioning that a community can be regarded as a service somehow, and consequently, this community determination procedure iterates and a service map can be generated.

As an example, Fig. 3 illustrates the communities detected from the service network shown in Fig. 2. Note that the method [1] is able to detect communities,

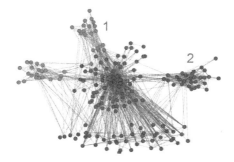

Fig. 3. Community determination for the service network shown in Fig. 2.

and also to identify bridges between communities and outliers in the graph. To get a clear illustration, we have screened off the outliers. Note that the red nodes at the bottom of Fig. 3 are not forming a community, instead, they are bridges. There are four communities as shown at the upper part of Fig. 3.

3.3   Functionality Identification of Communities

Fig. 4. Core process of *Area 1* in Fig. 3.   **Fig. 5.** Core process of *Area 2* in Fig. 3.

Given a community, the functionality is reflected by its core process, which is detected by a *graph skeleton extraction algorithm* [4]. Generally, a core process represents the part of the most important and most frequently used.

The functionality of the community is represented as a graph. We assume that users can specify their requirements formally in terms of a graph. Consequently, the matchmaking of the functionality of a community and the requirement of a user can be performed using a graph matching algorithm.

As examples, Figs. 4 and 5 illustrates the core processes for area 1 and 2 as shown in Fig. 3, respectively.

4   Conclusion and Future Directions

In this paper we have proposed the concept of *service map*, introduced the construction procedure of service map, and discussed how to use it for facilitating service chaining (or composition) when the requirements of users are given at coarse or fine levels of granularity. We argue that this technique should be beneficial to the users, since users, especially non-domain experts, can hardly give their requirement clearly, completely, and in detail at the beginning. There are key points to be explored further for realizing the vision of our service map:

- *Community functionality identification.* Currently, we represent the functionality of communities in terms of graphs, and assume that users can represent their requirements in terms of graphs as well. However, this may not hold in some situations and users may represent their requirements in text description. How to derive the functionality of communities from a graph and to represent it in terms of a service description (including an input, an output, and a text description for functionality) is a challenge.
- *Alignment of user's requirement and community functionality.* It is worth mentioning that users may hardly specify their requirements very clearly and completely. Consequently, the graph that a user gives may be incomplete since some nodes or edges may be hardly to be specified. In this setting, the alignment of user's requirement and community functionality leverages the matching of *incomplete graphs*, which is still a challenge in graph theory.

Acknowledgments. This work was supported partially by the National Natural Science Foundation of China (Grant No. 61379126), by the Scientific Research Foundation for Returned Scholars, Ministry of Education of China, and by the Fundamental Research Funds for the Central Universities (China University of Geosciences at Beijing).

References

1. Huang, J., Sun, H., Song, Q., Deng, H.: Revealing density-based clustering structure from the core-connected tree of a network. IEEE Trans. Knowl. Data Eng. **25**(8), 1876–1889 (2013)
2. Huang, K., Fan, Y., Tan, W.: Recommendation in an evolving service ecosystem based on network prediction. IEEE Trans. Autom. Sci. Eng. **11**(3), 906–920 (2014). doi:10.1109/TASE.2013.2297026
3. de Leoni, M., Suriadi, S., ter Hofstede, A.H.M., van der Aalst, W.M.P.: Turning event logs into process movies: animating what has really happened. Technical report, BPM Center Report, No. BPM-13-15 (2013)
4. Liu, W., Jiang, H., Bai, X., Tan, G., Wang, C., Liu, W., Cai, K.: Distance transform-based skeleton extraction and its applications in sensor networks. IEEE Trans. Parallel Distrib. Syst. **24**(9), 1763–1772 (2013)
5. Moustafa, A., Zhang, M.: Multi-objective service composition using reinforcement learning. In: 11th International Conference on Service Oriented Computing, pp. 298–312 (2013)
6. Zhang, L.J.: Big services era: global trends of cloud computing and big data. IEEE Trans. Serv. Comput. **5**(4), 467–468 (2012)

7. Zhou, Z., Cheng, Z., Li, W., Ning, K., Zhang, L.J.: A sub-chain ranking and recommendation mechanism for facilitating geospatial web service composition. Int. J. Web Serv. Res. **11**(3), 52–75 (2014)
8. Zhou, Z., Sellami, M., Gaaloul, W., Barhamgi, M., Defude, B.: Data providing services clustering and management for facilitating service discovery and replacement. IEEE Trans. Autom. Sci. Eng. **10**(4), 1131–1146 (2013)

Demo Track

WS-Portal an Enriched Web Services Search Engine

Mustapha Aznag[1]([⊠]), Mohamed Quafafou[1], and Zahi Jarir[2]

[1] Aix-Marseille University, CNRS, LSIS UMR 7296, 13397 Marseille, France
{mustapha.aznag,mohamed.quafafou}@univ-amu.fr
[2] LISI Laboratory FSSM, Cadi Ayyad University, Marrakech, Morocco
jarir@uca.ma

Abstract. With a growing number of web services, discovering services that can match with a user's query becomes a big challenging task. It's very tedious for a service consumer to select the appropriate one according to her/his needs. In this paper, we propose WS-Portal; An Enriched Web Services Search Engine which contains 7063 providers, 115 subclasses of category and 22236 web services crawled from the Internet. In WS-Portal, severals technologies are employed to improve the effectiveness of web services discovery (i.e. web services clustering, tags recommendation, services rating and monitoring).

Keywords: Web services · Discovery · Tags · Recommendation · Monitoring · Topic browsing · Topic models

1 Introduction

The Service Oriented Architecture (SOA) is a model currently used to provide services on the Internet. The SOA follows the find-bind-execute paradigm in which service providers register their services in public or private registries, which clients use to locate web services. SOA services have self-describing interfaces in platform-independent XML documents. Web Services Description Language (WSDL) is the standard language used to describe services. Different tasks like clustering, matching, ranking, discovery and composition have been intensively studied to improve the general web services management process. Thus, the web services community has proposed different approaches and methods to deal with these tasks. Nowadays, we are moving from web of data to web of services as the number of UDDI Business Registries (UBRs) is increasing. Moreover, the number of hosts that offer available web services is also increasing significantly. Consequently, discovering services which can match with the user's query is becoming a challenging and an important task. Recently, some web services portals and search engines as Biocatalogue[1] and Seekda![2] (Currently, the portal is no longer available.) and some other web services portals allows

---

[1] https://www.biocatalogue.org/.
[2] http://webservices.seekda.com/.

© Springer International Publishing Switzerland 2015
F. Toumani et al. (Eds.): ICSOC 2014, LNCS 8954, pp. 409–412, 2015.
DOI: 10.1007/978-3-319-22885-3_37

users to discover web services. In this paper we propose an enriched web service search engine called WS-Portal where we incorporate our research works to facilitate web services discovery task. our WS-Portal[3] contains 7063 providers, 115 sub-classes of category and 22236 web services crawled from the Internet. In WS-Portal, severals technologies, i.e., web services clustering, tags recommendation, services rating and monitoring are employed to improve the effectiveness of web services discovery. Specifically, probabilistic topics models are utilized for clustering, services/topics and tags recommendation [1–4]. We use probabilistic topic models to extract topic from semantic service descriptions and search for services in a topics space where heterogeneous service descriptions are all represented as a probability distribution over topics.

2   WS-Portal Functionalities

In this section, we describe some functionalities for our web services search engine:

1. **Service Clustering**: The number of web services created and published in a registry increases. Thus, searching services that can match with a user's query becomes a challenging task. Comparing a user's query to all services published in a service repository can be computationally expensive in large datasets. After our probabilistic model is trained [2], the distribution of words for each topic is known and all the services in the dataset can be described as a distribution of topics. A distribution over topics for a given service s is used to determine which topic best describes the service s. K clusters are created where K is the number of generated topics. More precisely, if a probability distribution over a specific z_j when given a web service s is high (i.e. $P(s|z_j)$), then the service s can be affected to the cluster C_j. If a service s has more than one topic, the service will be assigned to each of the clusters corresponding to these topics.

2. **Service Discovery**: By organizing service descriptions into clusters, services become easier and therefore faster to discover and recommend. Service Discovery and Selection aim to find web services with user required functionalities. A user query represented by a set of words is represented as a distribution over topics. The service discovery process is based on computing the similarity between retrieved topic's services and a user's query [1, 2, 4].

3. **Topics browsing**: We use topics browsing technique as another method search to discover the web services that match with users requirements. Users

---

[3] WS-Portal is available online:

- http://wvmweb.esil.univ-mrs.fr/wsportal.
- http://www.webvirtualmachine.fr/wsportal.
- http://wsportal.aznag.net.

can select the related topic to the their query and our system gives automatically the topic's services that match with user's query. The retrieved services are ranked in order of their similarity score to the query.

4. **Tags recommendation**: Tagging technique is widely used to annotate objects in Web 2.0 applications. This type of metadata provides a brief description of services and is utilized as another information source for service descriptions. In [3], we propose an automatic tagging technique for web services based on probabilistic topic models, in which both the WSDL documents and service tags are effectively utilized. The proposed system can work without existing tags, and works better when there exists manual tags. Our probabilistic approach based on LocLDA model, which is a latent variable model that exploits local correlation labels [3,5].

5. **Availability and performance monitoring**: The availability of Web Services is critical as more and more systems depend on them. WS-Portal monitor all registered services. In addition, after registering a service in our service registry its availability will be monitored automatically. Our system measures the availability by calling the service endpoints periodically. The time between two ping calls can be configured for each service individually. A popular method of online service availability is to calculate the fraction of the service's operational lifetime during which it has been accessible (i.e. $Availability = Uptime/[Uptime + Downtime]$).

6. **Services rating and comments posting**: Our system allows users to rate and post comments to enriche the service description.

7. **Dynamic service invocation**: Our system allows users to invoke the selected service using the html form generated automatically from the associated WSDL document for each service operations.

3   User Interface

Our web services search engine is available online (see footnote 3) and consumers can use it to discover, register or annotate web services. Figure 1(a) shows the search result page while using *Currency* as query term. As observed from this figure, we can find that each search result entity show a breif service description: (1) Web service name, (2) Service description, Tags given by users, (3) Service category, (4) Service provider, (5) Average rating score given by users, (6) Service availability. In addition we select a top five related topics to the user's query and its probabilities (i.e. $P(Q/z_f)$). When users select a disered service (i.e. *TourServices*), WS-Portal gives more details for selected service (i.e. Fig. 1(b)) such as service name, wsdl url, service documentation, provider, categories, country, availability, rating score, user's tags, recommended tags and WSDL cache. As Fig. 1(b) shows, our system gives also more details for service monitoring (availbity and response time values for each service endpoints). In addition, users can rate, annotate the selected service and post comments. Finally, users can invoke the selected service using the html form generated automatically from WSDL document for each service operations. Our system gives also two others important informations such as similar services and the related topics to the selected service. Indeed, we use the extracted topics from services descriptions to calculate the similarity between the selected service and others web services in our repository. For this, we compute the similarity score, using some probability metrics such as *Cosine Similarity* and *Symmetric KL Divergence* [4], between the vectors containing the service's distribution over topics. Finally, similar services are ranked in order of their similarity score to the selected service. Thus, we obtain automatically an efficient ranking of the services retrieved.

Fig. 1. (a) Search results page. (b) Web service details page.

References

1. Aznag, M., Quafafou, M., Jarir, Z.: Correlated topic model for web services ranking. Int. J. Adv. Comput. Sci. Appl. (IJACSA) **4**(6), 283–291 (2013)
2. Aznag, M., Quafafou, M., Rochd, E.M., Jarir, Z.: Probabilistic topic models for web services clustering and discovery. In: Lau, K.-K., Lamersdorf, W., Pimentel, E. (eds.) ESOCC 2013. LNCS, vol. 8135, pp. 19–33. Springer, Heidelberg (2013)
3. Aznag, M., Quafafou, M., Jarir, Z.: Multilabel Learning for Automatic Web Services Tagging. Int. J. Adv. Comput. Sci. Appl. (IJACSA) **5**(8), 182–191 (2014)
4. Aznag, M., Quafafou, M., Jarir, Z.: Leveraging formal concept analysis with topic correlation for service clustering and discovery. In: 21th IEEE International Conference on Web Services (ICWS), Alaska, USA, July 2014
5. Rochd, E.M., Quafafou, M., Aznag, M.: Encoding local correspondence in topic models. In: IEEE International Conference on Tools with Artificial Intelligence (ICTAI), Washington, DC, USA, 4–6 November 2013

SUPER: Social-Based Business Process Management Framework

Zakaria Maamar[1]([⊠]), Sherif Sakr[2], Noura Faci[3], Mohamed Boukhebouze[4], and Ahmed Barnawi[5]

[1] Zayed University, Dubai, U.A.E
`zakaria.maamar@zu.ac.ae`
[2] King Saud Bin Abdulaziz University for Health Sciences, Riyadh, Saudi Arabia
`sakrs@ksau-hs.edu.sa`
[3] Université Lyon 1, Lyon, France
`noura.faci@univ-lyon1.fr`
[4] Centre d'Excellence en Technologies de l'Information et de la Communication, Charleroi, Belgium
`mohamed.boukhebouze@cetic.be`
[5] King Abdulaziz University, Jeddah, Saudi Arabia
`ambarnawi@kau.edu.sa`

Abstract. In this demo paper, we present *SUPER* standing for *S*ocial-based b*U*siness *P*rocess manag*E*ment f*R*amework that leverages social computing principles for the design and development of social business processes (*aka* business processes 2.0). *SUPER* identifies task, person, and machine as the core components of a business process. Afterwards, *SUPER* establishes a set of execution and social relations to illustrate how tasks (also persons and machines) are connected together. The social relations help build configuration network of tasks, social network of persons, and support network of machines that capture the ongoing interactions during business process execution.

1 Motivation

Narrowing down the social-software view to social networks, only as per Gartner study, does not shed the light on other potential software systems like business process management systems that include multiple intrinsic social-elements [1]. Due to the variety of interactions that take place during the completion of business processes, different social relations can be modeled between these processes' three components that are task, machine, and person [2,3]. In principle, a task is a work unit that a person and/or machine complete. Tasks are put together to form processes, persons collaborate together on complex tasks, and machines replace each other in the case of failure, offer a glimpse of the social relations that business process management systems exhibit and hence, can be captured. Therefore, combining tasks together and machines together presents a lot of similarities with how people behave daily.

© Springer International Publishing Switzerland 2015
F. Toumani et al. (Eds.): ICSOC 2014, LNCS 8954, pp. 413–417, 2015.
DOI: 10.1007/978-3-319-22885-3_38

The development of *SUPER* exposes these social relations and promotes the social dimension of business processes. In particular, *SUPER* supports (*i*) identifying necessary execution and social relations between tasks (*t*), between executors (i.e., persons (*p*) and machines (*m*)), and between tasks and executors; and (*ii*) developing categories of networks upon these relations with respect to the intrinsic characteristics of each component.

2 Scenario

Figure 1 illustrates an example of business process in a medical facility. It includes multiple tasks such as t_1: scan documentation, t_2: update records, and t_i: prepare bill. Tasks connect to each other through input and output dependencies, e.g., patient's data from t_1 are sent to t_2 so that patient records are updated. However these dependencies are primarily meant for data exchange and thus, do not help much in enriching a business process with any social element nor in shedding the light on the potential relations between this process's components. Figure 1 also shows the execution nature of tasks. Some tasks are completely manual (p_j: cashier executing t_i) while others are either completely automated (m_2: ImageNow executing t_2) or semi-automated/semi-manual (p_1/m_1: operator/scanner taking turns in executing t_1).

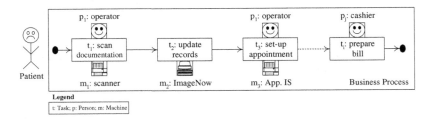

Fig. 1. Business process's components

In preparation for exposing the social dimension of business processes, we associate a task with *requirements* (e.g., t_2: update records must be done within one hour of scan receipt), a person with *capacities* (e.g., p_1: operate scanner), and a machine with *capacities* as well (e.g., m_1: produce high-resolution scan). Requirements impose restrictions on those who execute tasks in terms of execution nature (e.g., manual), necessary expertise level for persons, reliability level for machines, simultaneous involvement of persons and machines, etc. Table 1 summarizes the set of social relations, that are considered by *SUPER* between tasks, between machines, and between persons along with their respective preconditions, conditions, and post-conditions [2].

Table 1. Summary of social relations

	Relation type	Pre-conditions	Conditions	Post-conditions
t_i, t_j	**Coupling**	t_i and t_i participated in joint BP	review of BP design or concern over coupling level	BP design completion or coupling level satisfaction
	Interchange	t_i and t_j producing similar output in receipt of similar input	t_i lacking of executor who satisfies its requirements	executor found for t_j
m_i, m_j	**Backup**	m_i and m_j having similar capacities	m_i unexpected failure or concern over m_i reliability	backup/replacement machine found for m_i
	Cooperation	m_i and m_j having similar capacities	concern over machine collective performance	collective performance level satisfaction
	Partnership	m_i and m_j having complementary capacities	concern over machine collective performance	collective performance level satisfaction
p_i, p_j	**Substitution**	p_i and p_j having similar capacities	p_i expected unavailability (e.g., annual leave and sick leave) or concern over p_i availability	substitute found for p_i
	Delegation	p_i and p_j having similar capacities	p_i unexpected unavailability (e.g., call-in-sick, urgent tasks to complete, and risk of overload)	delegate found for p_i
	Peering	p_i and p_j having similar or complementary capacities	concern over peering appropriateness	peer found for either p_i or p_j

3   Architecture and Implementation

Figure 2 illustrates the architecture of *SUPER* which is built upon multiple components as follows. For the design phase, the BP modeling component is an exten-

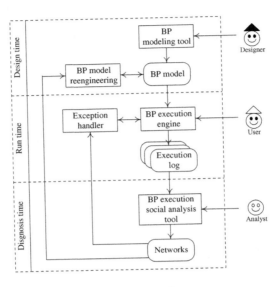

Fig. 2. SUPER architecture

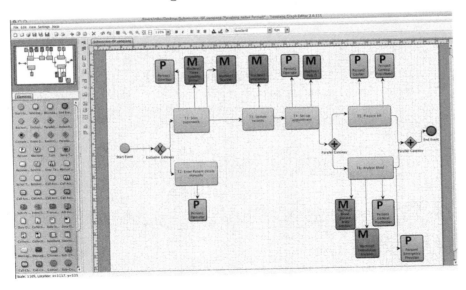

Fig. 3. Screenshot of Yaoqiang BPMN editor

sion of the Yaoqiang BPMN editor[1] with new operations that help for instance, assign executors (persons and/or machines) to tasks. Figure 3 shows a screenshot of our Yaoqiang BPMN editor extension in which a part of the business process in Fig. 1 is modeled. At run time, business process execution traces accumulated during the execution of process instances are stored in a log file. These traces contain information about events referring to the execution of tasks in terms of execution time (timestamp) and executors. *SUPER* adopts the representation of the traces using XES (eXtensible Event Stream) format[2] which represents the de facto standard for process execution log expression. At diagnosis time, a BP execution social analysis component is implemented to discover and build the networks of social relations between the business process components (task, machine, person) based on process execution logs as well as the BP model. This component is developed as a plugin of the popular process mining framework, ProM[3], and represents the discovered networks using a well-known XML-based format for representing graphs, GraphML[4]. Our demonstration[5] will show different examples of networks related to Fig. 1 that are generated using the social analysis component.

Acknowledgements. This work was partially supported by King Abdulaziz City for Science and Technology (KACST) project #11-INF1991-03. This work was also carried out as part of the QualIHM project supported by the Rgion Wallonne and its Collective Research Programme funding (convention #1217570).

References

1. Chandler, S.: Social BPM: gateway to enhanced process efficiency, November 2011. http://www.virtusa.com/blog/2011/11/ visited on September 2012
2. Kajan, E., Faci, N., Maamar, Z., Loo, A., Pljaskovic, A., Sheng, Q.Z.: The Network-based business process. IEEE Internet Computing, **18**(2), March/April 2014
3. Maamar, Z., Faci, N., Kouadri Mostéfaoui, S., Kajan, E.: Network-based conflict resolution in business processes. In: Proceedings of the 10th IEEE International Conference on e-Business Engineering (ICEBE 2013), Coventry, UK (2013)

---

[1] sourceforge.net/projects/bpmn.
[2] www.xes-standard.org.
[3] www.promtools.org.
[4] graphml.graphdrawing.org.
[5] A screencast is available at https://www.youtube.com/watch?v=Py5oGPQot64.

TL-VIEWS: A Tool for Temporal Logic Verification of Transactional Behavior of Web Service Compositions

Scott Bourne[✉], Claudia Szabo, and Quan Z. Sheng

School of Computer Science, The University of Adelaide,
Adelaide, SA 5005, Australia
{scott.bourne,claudia.szabo,michael.sheng}@adelaide.edu.au

1 Introduction

The execution of Web service compositions is subject to reliability concerns as component services execute in potentially long-running, distributed, and heterogeneous mediums that cannot guarantee reliable communication. *Transactional behavior* is used to contain, handle, and undo the effects of potential faults, but deriving and ensuring requirements for this behavior from application-specific logic remains a big issue [3]. Transactional requirements can be applied at the component or composition level, but the state-of-the-art methods for specifying and verifying them at design-time is prone to user error and scalability issues [2,3].

This paper presents TL-VIEWS (Temporal Logic VerIfication of transactional bEhavior of Web Service compositions). The contributions of TL-VIEWS are (i) an expressive Web service composition modeling approach based on the separation of functional and transactional perspectives, (ii) design-time verification against pre-defined rules for *well-formed* transactional behavior, and (iii) verification against *application-specific transactional requirements*, which are specified in an easy-to-use manner. In the following sections, we overview the technical design and main features of TL-VIEWS, and sketch the proposed demonstration. A TL-VIEWS video demonstration can be found at https://vimeo.com/100029510.

2 TL-VIEWS Transactional Behavior Verification

TL-VIEWS adapts the statechart-based modeling method proposed in our previous work [2] to separate Web service behaviors. The *control behavior* is an application-independent model that maintains the transactional state of the composition, while the *operational behavior* contains the application-dependent flow of business tasks. Execution and recovery operations are directed by the control behavior, according to events reported from the operational behavior. This modeling approach provides a detailed view of both the functional and transactional behavior of the composition, and allows each perspective to be

© Springer International Publishing Switzerland 2015
F. Toumani et al. (Eds.): ICSOC 2014, LNCS 8954, pp. 418–422, 2015.
DOI: 10.1007/978-3-319-22885-3_39

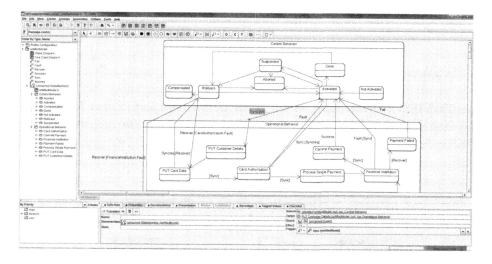

Fig. 1. Specifying a web service composition as control and operational behaviors

designed and modified independently by relevant domain experts. Figure 1 shows an example of this modeling approach using the TL-VIEWS user interface.

The two behavior models communicate using a set of *inter-behavior messages*. These allow the control behavior to direct execution, and the operational behavior to report events and status. Moreover, they permit the definition of conversation rules that describe well-formed transactional behavior. Our supporting work [1] contains a complete list of inter-behavior message types and conversation rules.

TL-VIEWS employs model checking techniques to verify that Web service compositions with transactional behavior satisfy application-*independent* and application-*dependent* correctness properties. The conversation rules ensure correctness properties in inter-behavior conversations, namely, avoiding deadlock, incomplete execution, and inconsistency between the behavior models. Furthermore, TL-VIEWS enables the user to define application-dependent transactional requirements for verification [2]. We propose a set of transactional requirement *templates*, that enable users to formalize common transactional requirements in temporal logic without expert knowledge in the language. Model checking is then used to ensure the design satisfies the transactional requirements of the user [1, 2].

The main features and contributions of TL-VIEWS include:

- A graphical user interface enabling Web service compositions to be modeled as control and operational behavior statecharts, as shown in Fig. 1.
- Automatic formalization of business transactional requirements in temporal logic without requiring expertise in the language.
- Design-time formal verification against (i) pre-defined well-formed transactional behavior, and (ii) user-defined transactional requirements.

– State-space reduction to avoid state explosion during model checking, making the tool more feasible to large and complex designs.

3   Architecture Overview

The TL-VIEWS architecture, shown in Fig. 2, leverages and utilizes ArgoUML[1] and NuSMV[2], for the graphical modeling user interface and model checking functionality respectively. The key modules are discussed below.

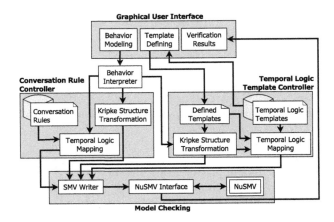

Fig. 2. Architecture of TL-VIEWS

The *Graphical User Interface* adapts ArgoUML to enable composition modeling as interacting control and operational behaviors (Fig. 1), and to define transactional requirements. The *Behavior Interpreter* transforms the control and operational behaviors into an intermediate model for the Conversation Rule Controller and the Temporal Logic Template Controller.

The *Conversation Rule Controller* formalizes the conversation rules into LTL and CTL and reduces the state space of the control and operational behaviors, thus improving the time complexity of the verification process, in particular for large models. The models are reduced to a Kripke structure, which is a finite-state system $\mathcal{K} = \langle \mathcal{S}_k, \mathcal{I}, \mathcal{T}_k, \mathcal{L} \rangle$, where $\mathcal{S}_k$ is a finite set of states, $\mathcal{I} \subseteq \mathcal{S}_k$ is the set of initial states, $\mathcal{T}_k \subseteq \mathcal{S}_k \times \mathcal{S}_k$ is the transition function, and $\mathcal{L}$ is the labelling function that assigns *atomic propositions* to each state, representing the inter-behavior message being used. Our algorithm based on the depth-first traversal of the design constructs this Kripke structure as inter-behavior messages are sent, capturing the inter-behavior conversations and reducing state space.

---

[1] http://argouml.tigris.org/.
[2] http://nusmv.fbk.eu/.

The *Temporal Logic Template Controller:* maps the user's transactional requirements to temporal logic and generates a Kripke structure that reduces the design model. The transactional requirements provided by the user may involve states from both the control and operational behaviors and inter-behavior messages. Therefore, the atomic propositions in this Kripke structure include the control and operational behavior states and inter-behavior messages used in transactional requirement definition. As in the Conversation Rules Controller, a Kripke structure is constructed by a depth-first traversal of the control and operational behaviors, adding Kripke states and transitions to the structure as necessary atomic propositions are encountered. Lastly, the defined requirements are mapped to LTL and CTL according to template specifications [2].

NuSMV is for *Model Checking* used due to its support of LTL and CTL. The Kripke structures and temporal logic properties are transformed into NuSMV's input language, then the model checker is invoked and the results presented. Our Kripke reduction provides a performance benefit during model checking, including the overhead of the algorithm. For example, on an Intel Core i7 3.40 GHz 4 GB RAM system running Windows 7, conversation rule verification time with 100 operational behavior states was reduced from 0.052 to 0.028 s.

4   TL-VIEWS in Action: Scenario

To demonstrate the TL-VIEWS tool, we model and verify an example online payment composition, constructed using the PayLane Web service API[3]. The composition enables a customer to pay using credit card or direct deposit, either by entering payment details or by reusing previous sales data.

Firstly, the designer models the composition as interacting *control* and *operational* behaviors, as shown in Fig. 1. The operational behavior model contains the necessary business operations in the process, such as entering payment details, processing card payments, and handling refund requests. Inter-behavior messages are used to specify transactional behavior.

The control and operational model is then automatically verified according to application-independent conversation rules. These rules ensure that the inter-behavior conversations start correctly, avoid deadlocking scenarios, and terminate in a valid way. In the event that the design violates a rule, a contradicting sequence of states is presented to the user, and can be used to revise the design.

The user can specify application-dependent transactional requirements of the design, by selecting from our provided template set and assigning variables. The design can be automatically verified against the set of transactional requirements specified by the user. This is enabled by mapping the variables entered into concrete properties of temporal logic, and applying model checking. Contradicting stack traces of any violated requirements are presented to the user, in order to provide useful information for design revision.

---

[3] http://devzone.paylane.com.

5   Conclusion

TL-VIEWS can identify and resolve of conformance issues to transactional requirements of Web service compositions at design-time, preventing costly re-development operations, and improving the reliability of the implementation. Web service compositions are modeled using a graphical interface as interacting control and operational behavior statechart models, which are automatically verified against general correctness criteria in the form of conversation rules. A set of temporal logic templates are provided to formalize transactional requirements drawn from business logic in a simple and error-proof way. State space reductions allows TL-VIEWS to verify large and complex designs.

References

1. Bourne, S., Szabo, C., Sheng, Q.Z.: Ensuring well-formed conversations between control and operational behaviors of web services. In: Liu, C., Ludwig, H., Toumani, F., Yu, Q. (eds.) Service Oriented Computing. LNCS, vol. 7636, pp. 507–515. Springer, Heidelberg (2012)
2. Bourne, S., Szabo, C., Sheng, Q.Z.: Verifying transactional requirements of web service compositions using temporal logic templates. In: Proceedings of the 14th International Conference on Web Information Systems Engineering (2013)
3. Cardinale, Y., El Haddad, J., Manouvrier, M., Rukoz, M.: Transactional-aware web service composition: a survey. IGI Global-Advances in Knowledge Management Book Series (2011)

SmartPM: Automated Adaptation of Dynamic Processes

Andrea Marrella[1]([✉]), Massimo Mecella[1], Sebastian Sardina[2],
and Paola Tucceri[1]

[1] Sapienza University of Rome, Rome, Italy
{marrella,mecella}@dis.uniroma1.it, paola.tucceri@gmail.com
[2] RMIT University, Melbourne, Australia
sebastian.sardina@rmit.edu.au

Abstract. In this demonstration paper, we present the first working version of SmartPM, a Process Management System that is able to automatically adapt dynamic processes at run-time when unanticipated exceptions occur, thus requiring no specification of recovery policies at design-time.

Keywords: Process management system · Adaptation · Dynamic scenario

Introduction. Nowadays, the maturity of process management methodologies has led to the application of process-oriented approaches in new challenging domains beyond business computing [2], such as healthcare, emergency management, and domotics. In those *dynamic* settings, process enactment is influenced by user decision making and coupled with contextual data and knowledge production. During process enactment, variations from structured reference models are common due to exceptional circumstances arising (e.g., autonomous user decisions, exogenous events, or contextual changes), thus requiring the ability to properly *adapt* the process behavior. According to [6], *process adaptation* can be seen as the ability of a process to react to *exceptional circumstances* (that may or may not be foreseen) and to modify its structure accordingly. In dynamic scenarios, traditional manual implementation of exception handlers at design time is not feasible for the process designer, who has to anticipate all potential problems and ways to overcome them in advance [5]. Furthermore, many *unanticipated exceptional circumstances* may arise during process execution, and their handling requires a manual intervention of a domain expert at run-time. However, the complexity of the operational context may transform the manual definition of a recovery procedure at run-time in a time-consuming and error-prone task. To tackle the above issues, we present the first working version of SmartPM, a Process Management System (PMS) that is able to *automatically adapt dynamic processes at run-time* when *unanticipated exceptions* occur, thus requiring *no specification of recovery policies at design-time*.

F. Toumani et al. (Eds.): ICSOC 2014, LNCS 8954, pp. 423–427, 2015.
DOI: 10.1007/978-3-319-22885-3_40

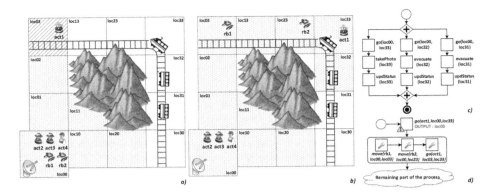

Fig. 1. A train derailment situation; area and context of the intervention.

Demonstration Scenario. We consider the emergency management situation described in Fig. 1(a), in which a train derailment is depicted in a grid-type map. A possible concrete realization of an incident response plan for our scenario is shown in Fig. 1(c), through a BPMN process composed of three parallel branches, with tasks instructing first responders to act for evacuating people from train coaches, taking pictures of the locomotive, and assessing the gravity of the accident. To execute the process, a response team is sent to the derailment scene. The team is composed of four first responders, called *actors*, and two *robots*, initially all located at location cell *loc*00. It is assumed that actors are equipped with mobile devices for picking up and executing tasks, and that each provide specific capabilities. For example, *act*1 is able to extinguish fire and take pictures, while *act*2 and *act*3 can evacuate people from train coaches. The two robots, in turn, are designed to remove debris from specific locations. When the battery of a robot is discharged, *act*4 can charge it. In order to carry on the response plan, all actors and robots ought to be continually inter-connected. The connection between mobile devices is supported by a fixed antenna located at *loc*00, whose range is limited to the dotted squares in Fig. 1(a). Such a coverage can be extended by robots *rb*1 and *rb*2, which have their own independent (from antenna) connectivity to the network and can act as wireless routers to provide network connection in all adjacent locations. Due to the high dynamism of the environment, there is a wide range of exceptions that can ensue. So, suppose for instance that actor *act*1 is sent to the locomotive's location, by assigning to it the task GO(*loc*00, *loc*33) in the first parallel branch. Unfortunately, however, the actor happens to reach location *loc*03 instead. The actor is now located at a different position than the desired one and is out of the network connectivity range (cf. Fig. 1(a)). Therefore, the PMS initially has to find a recovery procedure to bring back full connectivity, and then find a way to re-align the process. To that end, provided robots have enough battery charge, the PMS may first instruct the first robot to move to cell *loc*03 in order to re-establish network connection to actor *act*1, and then instruct the second robot to reach location *loc*23 in order

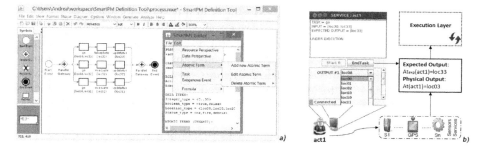

Fig. 2. A screenshot of the SmartPM definition tool (a) and the task handler (b).

to extend the network range to cover the locomotive's location $loc33$. Finally, task GO($loc03, loc33$) is reassigned to actor $act1$ (cf. Fig. 1(b)). The corresponding updated process is shown in Fig. 1(d), with the encircled section being the recovery procedure. We note that the execution of a dynamic process can be also jeopardized by the occurrence of *exogenous events* (e.g., a fire burnt up into a coach) that could change, in asynchronously manner, some contextual properties of the scenario, by possibly requiring the process to be adapted accordingly.

The SmartPM Approach and System. The SmartPM approach builds on the dualism between an *expected reality*, the (idealized) model of reality that is used by the PMS to reason, and a *physical reality*, the real world with the actual values of conditions and outcomes. Process execution steps and exogenous events have an impact on the physical reality and any deviation from the expected reality results in a mismatch to be removed to allow process progression. At this point, an external state-of-the-art planner is invoked to synthesise a recovery procedure that adapts the faulty process instance. The implementation of the SmartPM approach relies on three architectural layers that cover the modeling, execution and monitoring stages of the process life-cycle.

The *Presentation Layer* provides a GUI-based tool called SmartPM Definition Tool[1] (cf. Fig. 2(a)), which assists the process designer in the definition of the process model at design-time. Process knowledge is represented as a *domain theory* that includes all the contextual information of the domain of concern, such as the people/services that may be involved in performing the process, the tasks, the data and so forth. Data are represented through some *atomic terms* that range over a set of *data objects*, which depict entities of interest (e.g., locations, capabilities, services, etc.), while atomic terms can be used to express properties of domain objects (and relations over objects). For example, the term $At[act : Actor] = (loc : Location\_type)$ is used for recording the position of each actor in the area. In addition, the designer can define *complex terms*. They are declared as basic atomic terms, with the additional specification of a well-formed first-order formula that determines the truth value for the complex term. For example, the complex term $Connected[act : Actor]$ can be defined to express that

---

[1] It was developed with the JGraphX graphical library (http://www.jgraph.com/).

an actor is connected to the network if s/he is in a covered location or if s/he is in a location adjacent to a location where a robot is located. *Tasks* are collected in a specific repository and are described in terms of preconditions - defined over atomic and complex terms - and effects, which establish their outcomes. Finally, a process designer can specify which *exogenous events* may be catched at runtime and which atomic terms will be modified after their occurrence. Once a valid domain theory is ready, the process designer uses the BPMN graphical editor provided by the SmartPM Definition Tool to define the process control flow among a set of tasks selected from the tasks repository.

The *Execution Layer* is in charge of managing and coordinating the execution of dynamic processes. First of all, the domain theory specification is translated into situation calculus and IndiGolog [1] readable formats.[2] The situation calculus is a logical language designed for representing and reasoning about dynamic domains. On top of that, we use the IndiGolog high-level agent programming language for the specification of the process control flow. Hence, an executable model is obtained in the form of an IndiGolog program to be executed through an IndiGolog engine. To this end, we customized an existing IndiGolog engine[3] to *(i)* manage the process routing and decide which tasks are enabled for execution; *(ii)* collect exogenous events from the external environment; *(iii)* monitor contextual data to identify changes or events which may affect process execution. Specifically, after each task completion (or exogenous event occurrence), the physical and expected realities are updated to reflect the actual and intended outcome of task performance (or the contextual changes produced by an exogenous event). If the two realities are misaligned, the running process instance needs to be adapted. Process participants interact with the engine through a *Task Handler*, an interactive GUI-based application that supports the visualization of assigned tasks and allows to notify task completion by selecting an appropriate outcome (cf. Fig. 2(b)).

To enable the automated synthesis of a recovery procedure, the *Adaptation Layer* of SmartPM relies on the capabilities provided by a PDDL-based planner component (the LPG-td planner [3]), which assumes the availability of a *planning problem*, i.e., an initial state and a goal to be achieved, and of a *planning domain* definition that includes the actions to be composed to achieve the goal, the domain predicates and data types. Specifically, if process adaptation is required, *(i)* we translate the domain theory defined at design-time into a planning domain, *(ii)* the physical reality into the initial state of the planning problem and *(ii)* the expected reality into the goal state of the planning problem. The planning domain and problem are the input for the planner component. If the planner is able to synthesize a recovery procedure, the plan is converted into an executable IndiGolog process so that it can be enacted by the IndiGolog engine. Otherwise, if no plan exists for the current planning problem, the control passes back to the process designer, who can try to manually adapt the process instance. More information about SmartPM can be found at: http://www.dis. uniroma1.it/~smartpm.

---

[2] The formal model underlying the SmartPM system is described in [4].

[3] http://sourceforge.net/projects/indigolog/.

Acknowledgements. This work has been partly supported by the Sapienza award SPIRITLETS, the project PIA Regione Calabria COSM-FACTORY, and the EU project VOICE.

References

1. De Giacomo, G., Lespérance, Y., Levesque, H., Sardina, S.: Indigolog: a high-level programming language for embedded reasoning agents. In: Seghrouchni, A.E.F., Dix, J., Dastani, M., Bordini, R.H. (eds.) Multi-Agent Programming, pp. 31–72. Springer, US (2009)
2. Di Ciccio, C., Marrella, A., Russo, A.: Knowledge-intensive processes: characteristics, requirements and analysis of contemporary approaches. J. Data Semant. **4**, 29–57 (2014)
3. Gerevini, A., Saetti, A., Serina, I., Toninelli, P.: LPG-TD: a fully automated planner for PDDL2.2 domains. In: ICAPS 2004 (2004)
4. Marrella, A., Mecella, M., Sardina, S.: SmartPM: an adaptive process management system through situation calculus, IndiGolog, and classical planning. In: KR 2014 (2014)
5. Reichert, M., Weber, B.: Enabling Flexibility in Process-Aware Information Systems. Challenges, Methods, Technologies. Springer, Heidelberg (2012)
6. Sadiq, S.W., Sadiq, W., Orlowska, M.E.: Pockets of flexibility in workflow specification. In: ER 2001 (2001)

Author Index

Printed in the United States
By Bookmasters